RISK MANAGEMENT AND INSURANCE

Twelfth Edition

James S. Treischmann
Terry College of Business
University of Georgia

Robert E. Hoyt
Terry College of Business
University of Georgia

David W. Sommer
Terry College of Business
University of Georgia

THOMSON
SOUTH-WESTERN

Australia · Canada · Mexico · Singapore · Spain · United Kingdom · United States

THOMSON
SOUTH-WESTERN

Risk Management and Insurance, 12/e

James S. Trieschmann, Robert E. Hoyt & David W. Sommer

VP/Editorial Director:
Jack W. Calhoun

VP/Editor-in-Chief:
Michael P. Roche

Executive Editor:
Michael R. Reynolds

Senior Developmental Editor:
Susanna C. Smart

Marketing Manager:
Heather MacMaster

Production Editor:
Margaret M. Bril

Technology Project Editor:
John Barans

Sr. Manufacturing Coordinator:
Sandee Milewski

Production House:
Cover to Cover Publishing Inc.

Printer:
Courier
Kendallville, Indiana

Design Project Manager:
Anne Marie Rekow

Internal Designer:
Anne Marie Rekow

Cover Designer:
Anne Marie Rekow

Cover Images:
© Brand X Pictures, Business
Speak—Jon Allen

brief contents

contents

preface

Risk management continues to evolve as an important field of study within the realm of finance. An important development is that many organizations now consider all of the risks that they face in a more integrated manner than in the past. Thus, the concept of *enterprise risk management* is continuing to gain acceptance among organizations.

Risk Management and Insurance, 12th edition, recognizes this developing viewpoint. The text is intended to assist the student in identifying and analyzing all types of risk and in managing it through insurance and alternative tools. The 12th edition blends the concept of enterprise risk management into several different chapters, while still maintaining the features of the book that are important for introductory classes in both insurance and risk management. As in the previous two editions, risk management is the transcending concept within which insurance finds its place.

The overall assumption throughout this edition is that risks can be managed if they are identified prior to a loss, and insurance is an important—but not the only—tool available for that purpose. Thus, the word *insurance* appears only infrequently until Chapter 6. Before insurance is considered at length, the text provides substantial discussion of the myriad of potential losses facing businesses and individuals, together with the general risk management process and the many alternative risk management tools, including loss control, risk retention, and risk transfer. Still, insurance is often an extremely valuable part of the overall risk management plans of individuals and small firms.

With the publication of this 12th edition we are pleased to welcome Dr. David W. Sommer as a new coauthor. Dr. Sommer is a professor in the Terry College of Business at the University of Georgia and is also an officer of the Southern Risk and Insurance Association. He is recognized as an expert in many areas of the risk management and insurance field, including liability risk management and insurance, enterprise risk management, and employee benefits.

TEXT ORGANIZATION

Part 1 begins with an exploration of the nature of risk in **Chapter 1**, leading naturally into a detailed treatment of the risk management process in the remaining seven chapters included in Part 1. **Chapters 2 through 4** present a comprehensive overview of the various exposures to risk that may exist, including some financial risks not previously mentioned in earlier editions. The material on statistical analysis and capital budgeting remains in Part 1 because this placement puts these topics in context with overall risk management decision making. Of course, the important elements of insurance theory still remain. The principles and policy provisions common to many forms of insurance are included in Part 1 as part of the discussion of insurance as a risk management technique. More detailed treatments of specific types of insurance are provided later in the text. The *enterprise-wide approach* to risk management is particularly emphasized in **Chapters 5 and 8**.

Part 2 of the text continues the risk management orientation, with an emphasis on topics important for business entities. The various forms of insurance are presented as major risk treatment possibilities, but topics such as captive insurers, disaster management, and alternative risk financing also have been developed more completely than in prior editions. The terrorist attacks of September 11, 2001, have had far-reaching effects on the risk management and insurance world. Various references to the widespread implications of these attacks are incorporated throughout this edition.

Part 3, Personal Risk Management Applications: Property—Liability, is devoted to risk exposures involving personal automobiles and homeownership. The common insurance policy forms for dealing with these forms of risk are thoroughly discussed, and appropriate updates have been added. The subject of automobile safety, loss control, and trends in automobile safety comprise the subject matter of Chapter 14, illustrating a range of risk management topics in connection with automobile losses.

Part 4, the focus of the discussion in Part 4 shifts from property and liability risks to those dealing with the potential loss of life, health, and/or income. In keeping with the text's risk management orientation, relevant material on Social Security and other government insurance programs is integrated into appropriate chapters, rather than being segregated into a "social insurance" chapter as is often done in textbooks devoted primarily to insurance. The important role of managed health care and efforts to regulate it are discussed. Updated information on qualified retirement plans and newly introduced health savings accounts are included in this part of the text.

Part 5, The Risk Management Environment, includes three chapters on institutional aspects of risk management and insurance. The focus is on the nature of the risk management and insurance industry, as well as on the government regulations that impact it. Increased coverage of international insurance issues is especially evident in Chapter 22, which contains discussion of the effects of globalization on risk management and on the insurance business.

PEDAGOGICAL FEATURES

From a pedagogical perspective, the 12th edition retains the features that were well regarded in the 11th, with increased usage of the popular Netlink first introduced in the 10th edition. Each chapter contains at least one Netlink suggesting a specific site on the World Wide Web (with appropriate address information provided) for students to investigate. These sites were chosen to help make the material in each chapter come alive in a timely, interactive manner. Each chapter also includes two Internet-related questions based on specific Web sites related to the material in that chapter. In most cases, the questions require the student to do some activity at the site rather than merely read additional text. For example, in one question the student obtains an online insurance quote.

The other pedagogical features retained from the 11th edition include learning objectives and an opening vignette at the beginning of each chapter, chapter summaries, and a compilation of Questions for Review and Discussion. Each chapter also contains boxed material taken from current literature to further illustrate concepts discussed within the main body of the chapter. There are three series of boxes, each identified by distinctive icons. The International Perspectives boxes illustrate the application of risk management considerations on a global basis. Ethical Perspectives boxes present ethical dilemmas common in the field of risk management. The Professional Perspectives boxes illustrate practical applications of text material, many of which are based on recent interviews with practicing risk management professionals. Further assistance for the student in identifying risk management concepts throughout the text is provided through the use of a distinctive risk management icon.

The material in the appendices supplements and complements the text material. Present value and annuity tables are included, as are sample policy forms for automobile, homeowners', life insurance, and disability income insurance. The glossary that was expanded and improved in the last edition has been revised and updated in this edition.

SUPPLEMENTS

- An *Instructor's Manual with Test Bank and Transparency Masters* is available to supplement the pedagogical items included within the text itself. The manual contains additional discussion questions and objective questions to provide instructors with more choices in composing tests.

- *ExamView Pro® Computerized Testing Program* contains all of the questions in the printed test bank. This program is an easy-to-use test creation software compatible with Microsoft Windows. Instructors can add or edit questions, instructions, and answers, and select questions by previewing them on the screen, selecting them randomly, or selecting them by number. Instructor's can also easily convert tests into a WebCT or Blackboard uploadable format.

- A Web site at http://trieschmann.swlearning.com contains links to all Internet sites within the text as well as Instructor Resources and Student Resources. Within the instructor resources button, registered instructors can access Word files of the instructor's manual and test bank, and PowerPoint slides are accessible from this site for both students and instructors. The site also includes a sample risk management checklist that can assist in the risk identification phase of the risk management process, with the specific example used being commercial real and personal property.

- PowerPoint slides are available for use by students as an aid to note-taking, and by instructors for enhancing their lectures. Slides include charts and tables from the text as well as lecture outlines.

- TextChoice is the home of Thomson Learning's online digital content. TextChoice provides the fastest, easiest way for you to create your own learning materials. You may select content from hundreds of our best-selling titles, choose material from one of our databases, and add your own material. Contact your South-Western/Thomson Learning sales representative for more information.

- *Effective Use of a Financial Calculator* by Pamela L. Hall is a handbook designed to teach students effective use of a financial calculator and is suitable for use in corporate finance (introductory, intermediate, and advanced), investments, and personal finance courses. Covering key financial concepts, *Effective Use of a Financial Calculator* provides step-by-step, problem-solving examples using three of today's most popular financial calculators: TI BAII PLUS, HP 10B, and HP 17BII.

ACKNOWLEDGMENTS

We would like to thank many individuals for their kind assistance in preparing the 12th edition. Much of the material builds on previous editions, for which University of Georgia Professor Sandra Gustavson was one of the lead authors. We thank Sandra for her contributions and acknowledge our reliance on her past work. In addition, we are especially grateful to the following persons for their reviews and suggested changes:

Julie Cagle, Xavier University
David Cather, University of Pennsylvania
Varadarajan V. Chari, Northwestern University
Thomas Coe, Quinnipiac University
Ann Costello, University of Hartford
Kenneth J. Crepas, Illinois State University
R. B. Drennan, Temple University
Alan Eastman, Indiana University of Pennsylvania
Stephen Elliott, Northwestern State University
Michael Finke, University of Missouri
Louis J. Firenze, Northwood University
Beverly Frickel, University of Central Oklahoma
Deborah S. Gaunt, Georgia State University
Karen L. Hamilton, Columbus State University

Carol A. B. Jordan, Troy State University
Peter Kensicki, Eastern Kentucky University
Kathleen S. McNichol, LaSalle University
Bob Nagy, University of Wisconsin—Green Bay
Nicos Scordis, St. John's University
Roger Severns, Minnesota State University
Thomas G. Smith, Fort Valley State College
Joe Stanford, Bridgewater State College
William J. Warfel, Indiana State University

Finally, we extend our special thanks to University of Georgia graduate students André Liebenberg, Joe Ruhland, and Tera George for their assistance with various manuscript preparation tasks, including their help in identifying many of the Web sites used in the Netlinks.

James S. Trieschmann
Robert E. Hoyt
David W. Sommer

Risk and the Risk Management Process

PART 1

chapter 1

Introduction to Risk

Eastman Enterprises specializes in home renovation, landscape design, and the historic preservation of buildings. It began operations in Pennsylvania and expanded rapidly, and now has branches throughout the midwestern and southeastern regions of the United States.

Because of the firm's phenomenal rate of growth, Eastman's managers have had virtually no time to think about anything other than trying to meet customers' demands. No thought has been given to the potential consequences of events such as employee injuries or actions that might damage customers' property. Even the very basic potential problem of loss due to fire has received only cursory attention from management. The attitude is best characterized by owner Carol Eastman's statement: "Maybe we'll have time to think about those things tomorrow. Nothing really terrible has happened yet, and we've got a business to run!"

As Eastman may soon discover, the time for a business to think about terrible things is before they happen—afterward may be too late. For example, the likelihood that a tornado will hit Eastman's headquarters building may seem remote, but if it does happen, the potential consequences could be disastrous. Eastman could lose not only its main building but also the equipment and inventory stored inside. Vital computer records might be destroyed, key personnel could be injured, and operations could be curtailed for weeks or months. Such damage could also impact business at Eastman's other locations, resulting in a much greater total loss than management ever imagined.

The many uncertainties that may cause losses for businesses and individuals, as well as ways to manage those uncertainties, form the basis of this book. This first chapter explores the nature of uncertainty, also known as risk.

CHAPTER OBJECTIVES

After studying this chapter, you should be able to

1. Explain three ways to categorize risk.
2. List the components of an entity's cost of risk.
3. Give several examples of risks involving property, liability, life, health, loss of income, and financial losses.
4. Distinguish between chance of loss and degree of risk.
5. Give examples of three types of hazards.
6. Identify the difference between hazards and perils.
7. Explain the evolving concept of integrated risk management.
8. Explain the four steps in the risk management process.

Risk, which is often used to mean uncertainty, creates both problems and opportunities for businesses and individuals in nearly every walk of life. Executives, employees, investors, students, householders, travelers, and farmers all confront risk and deal with it in various ways. Sometimes a particular risk is consciously analyzed and managed; other times risk is simply ignored, perhaps out of lack of knowledge of its consequences.

Risk regarding the possibility of loss can be especially problematic. If a loss is certain to occur, it may be planned for in advance and treated as a definite, known expense. It is when there is uncertainty about the occurrence of a loss that risk becomes an important problem. Thus, if a store owner knows for sure that a certain amount of shoplifting will occur, this loss may be recovered by marking up all goods by the necessary percentage. There is little

**netlink**

For links related to news, commercial products, and issues associated with risk management and insurance, visit http://www.riskinfo.com.

or no risk involved unless actual shoplifting is greater than normal. The store is more concerned about the risk of abnormal shoplifting losses than about those viewed as normal or expected.

THE BURDEN OF RISK

The idea of risk bearing can be tantalizing. After all, it is a well-known investment principle that the largest potential returns are associated with the riskiest ventures. There are some risks, however, that involve only the possibility of loss. For example, businesses located near the Mississippi River confront the possibility of periodic flooding. When a flood occurs, loss caused by property damage and lost revenues is likely. On the other hand, no gain is expected merely because in some years a flood does not occur.

The risk surrounding potential losses creates significant economic burdens for businesses, government, and individuals. Billions of dollars are spent each year on strategies for financing potential losses. But when losses are not planned for in advance, they may cost even more. For example, a multimillion dollar adverse liability judgment may reduce a business's profitability, lower its credit ratings, cause a loss of customers, and perhaps result in bankruptcy if the firm has not made adequate plans to pay for the loss.

Risk of loss may also deprive society of services judged to be too risky. A member of the American Medical Association once commented that without malpractice insurance many physicians would refuse to practice medicine. The comment arose from publicity given to reports that many insurers planned to withdraw malpractice coverage from the market because of heavy losses and inadequate rates. Further, physicians in several states in 2003 went on strike as a response to the absence of affordable malpractice insurance. Thus, the inability to transfer risk to others threatened the reduction of vital medical services because physicians feared the risk of loss from legal suits brought by patients. Similarly, businesses of all types may be reluctant to engage in projects that are otherwise strategically attractive if the potential losses appear to be unmanageable.

Businesses, as well as individuals, may try either to avoid risk of loss as much as possible or to reduce its negative consequences. Overall, an entity's **cost of risk** is the sum of: (1) expenses of strategies to finance potential losses, (2) the cost of unreimbursed losses, (3) outlays to reduce risks, and (4) the opportunity cost of activities forgone due to risk considerations. For a particular firm, the first two components of the cost of risk are often the easiest to measure. When insurance costs are rising, as they did dramatically from 2001 to 2003, firms tend to place more emphasis on retaining losses and on efforts to keep losses from happening. In a 2003 survey of corporate insurance buyers 92 percent of buyers reported increasing their deductibles, while 60 percent said they were self-insuring to some extent. Two-thirds of buyers reported that they had increased their loss control and safety efforts to better control their cost of risk.[1] To minimize the cost of risk efficiently, one must study the subject of risk, learn more about the different types of risk, and find ways to deal with risk more effectively.

DEFINITIONS OF RISK

Thus far, the terms risk and uncertainty have been used interchangeably. However, many forms of uncertainty exist and, in a comprehensive study of risk, it is helpful to define the concept more precisely. This book deals primarily with the type of uncertainty in which the possible outcomes are either "loss" or "no loss," rather than with uncertainties that also present the opportunity for profit. It must be noted, however, that organizations increasingly are considering the broader set of risks that they face, regardless of type. This new view reflects the realization that risks from different sources interact to define the overall risk profile of the firm and recognizes the importance of all forms of risk that affect a firm's ability to realize its strategic objectives. Therefore, although much of this book focuses on risk regarding the possibility of loss, the discussion throughout also addresses the most significant elements of the new emerging viewpoint. Three common ways to classify risk are described in this section. As illustrated in Figure 1-1, these groupings are not mutually exclusive. Rather, risks can be categorized simultaneously according to all three types of classifications.

Pure versus Speculative Risk

An important classification of risk involves the concepts of pure risk and speculative risk. **Pure risk** exists when there is uncertainty as to whether loss will occur. No possibility of gain is presented by pure risk—only the potential for loss. Examples of pure risk include the un-

FIGURE 1-1   Types of Risk

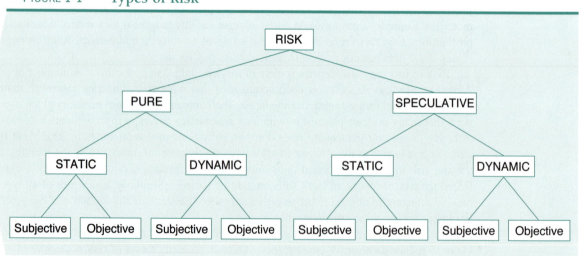

---

1   Sam Friedman, "Buyers Boost Loss Control, Risk Retention," *National Underwriter, Property & Casualty/Risk & Benefits Management Edition*, 107, no. 45, November 10, 2003, 22.

certainty of damage to property by fire or flood or the prospect of premature death caused by accident or illness. In contrast to pure risk, **speculative risk** exists when there is uncertainty about an event that could produce either a profit or a loss. Business ventures and investment decisions are examples of situations involving speculative risk. Gains as well as losses may occur, changing the nature of the uncertainty that is present.

Both pure and speculative risks may be present in some situations. It is important to recognize that many profit-motivated, speculative risk decisions made by individuals and firms can have an impact on pure risk exposures. For example, a firm purchasing land for development is making a decision that entails speculative risk. However, if after the purchase it discovers that the land contains a latent pollution problem, the firm would then face a new pure risk. Another example is the decision that a firm makes to introduce a new product. This decision may represent primarily a speculative risk. But as has been seen for products like asbestos and silicon breast implants, this decision also is accompanied by the pure risk associated with potential product liability. Failure to consider the overlapping effects of these two types of risk can lead to decisions that overstate the potential benefits to the firm.

Static versus Dynamic Risk

Another way of classifying risk involves the extent to which uncertainty changes over time. **Static risks**, which can be either pure or speculative, stem from an unchanging society that is in stable equilibrium. Examples of pure static risks include the uncertainties due to such random events as lightning, windstorms, and death. Business undertakings in a stable economy illustrate the concept of speculative static risk. In contrast, **dynamic risks** are produced because of changes in society. Dynamic risks also can be either pure or speculative. Examples of sources of dynamic risk include urban unrest, increasingly complex technology, and changing attitudes of legislatures and courts about a variety of issues.

Static and dynamic risks are not independent; greater dynamic risks may increase some types of static risks. An example involves uncertainty due to weather-related losses. This risk is usually considered to be static. However, recent evidence suggests that environmental pollution caused by increased industrialization may be affecting global weather patterns and thereby increasing this source of static risk.

Subjective versus Objective Risk

A third way to classify risk is by whether it is objective or subjective. **Subjective risk** refers to the mental state of an individual who experiences doubt or worry as to the outcome of a given event. In addition to being subjective, a particular risk may also be either pure or speculative and either static or dynamic. Subjective risk is essentially the psychological uncertainty that arises from an individual's mental attitude or state of mind. **Objective risk** differs from subjective risk primarily in the sense that it is more precisely observable and therefore measurable. In general, objective risk is the probable variation of actual from expected experience. This term is most often used in connection with pure static risks, although it also can be applied to the other types of uncertainties. Details regarding measurement of objective risk are included later in this chapter.

The concept of subjective risk is especially important because it provides a way to interpret the behavior of individuals faced with seemingly identical situations yet arriving at different decisions. For example, one person may be ultraconservative and tend always to take the "safe way" out, even in cases that may seem quite risk-free to other decision makers. Objective risk may actually be the same in two cases, but may be viewed very differently by those examining this risk from their own perspectives. Thus, it is not enough to know only the degree of objective risk; the attitude toward risk of the person who will act on the basis of this knowledge must also be known.

SOURCES OF RISK

The emphasis of this book is on pure risks. The array of pure risks encountered is vast. Some of these risks are static, while many others are extremely dynamic. This section briefly describes the common sources of pure risks, which include **property risks**; **liability risks**; and **life, health, and loss of income risks**, with some consideration also given to financial risks of a speculative nature. A more extensive discussion of these topics is provided in subsequent chapters.

Property Risks

All businesses and individuals that own, rent, or use property are exposed to the risk that the property may be damaged, destroyed, or stolen. For example, lightning may strike a building, causing a fire that destroys the structure and the inventory, supplies, and equipment inside. Property owned or used outside of the building may also be susceptible to loss. Typical examples include trucks, automobiles, and mobile equipment. To fully analyze property risk exposures, businesses must consider both the types of property susceptible to loss and the potential sources of such risk. Sources include not only fire and lightning but also theft, tornadoes, hurricanes, explosions, riots, collisions, falling objects, floods, earthquakes, and freezing, to name only a few.

If property damage is extensive, a business may be forced to shut down temporarily, thereby incurring a loss of income in addition to the expense of replacing the damaged property. But in some instances involving severe property damage, management may decide that temporarily closing the business is not a viable option. For example, Rocky Mountain Bank likely would never regain its customers if it were to close for several months following a fire and not allow its customers to transact necessary banking business. In this situation, the bank would probably incur the extra expenses necessary to continue operations from a different location while repairs were made to its own premises.

In addition to risks arising out of property they own and/or use, businesses also are exposed to risks associated with property owned or used by other firms. For example, an explosion at ABC Company's clothing factory may interrupt the supply of suits and dresses that QED Department Store usually purchases from ABC. Thus, QED may incur income losses as a result of ABC's property damage. Similarly, if QED Department Store is the primary buyer of clothes manufactured by ABC, then a fire loss that requires QED to close temporarily likely will also have an adverse impact on ABC. Another illustration of losses to one business affecting another business involves companies selling primarily over the Internet. Such firms typically utilize others to make deliveries to their customers and could suffer significant losses if the delivery firms were unable to perform.

Liability Risks

A second major category of risks is liability exposure. U.S. society has become increasingly litigious in recent years, with businesses and individuals often held financially liable for damages resulting from a vast and expanding array of situations. Liability judgments may result in payments made to compensate injured parties as well as to punish those responsible for the injuries, with multimillion dollar awards no longer rare. Even when an individual is eventually absolved of liability, the expenses involved in defending a case often prove to be substantial. Consequently, both individuals and businesses must be careful to identify all sources of liability risk that may affect them and then make suitable arrangements for dealing with such exposures to loss.

As an illustration of some specific sources of liability risk, all entities that own or use real property are susceptible to liability losses if others are injured on their premises. For example, the owner of Bill's Fix-It Shop may be responsible for injuries suffered by a customer

INTERNATIONAL PERSPECTIVES

Olympic Exposures

Over the years, the Olympic Games have presented a host of interesting and challenging exposures to loss. Revenues from the games typically come from the sale of television broadcast rights, ticket sales, and commercial sponsorships. Identifying all of the risks associated with the Olympics is always a major undertaking. In the past, more than 1,000 official vehicles have been required, ranging from vans and buses for shuttling athletes and personnel to the various events, to "stretch" limousines for transporting visiting foreign dignitaries. Thus, the collision peril and its associated losses must be recognized and managed. In planning for the 2000 Summer Games in Sydney, Australia, a total of 10,000 athletes were expected, together with about 5,000 officials, 50,000 volunteer workers, and 9 million spectators.

Sources of risk are carefully analyzed throughout the preparations for each Olympics. Because many of the sports are inherently dangerous, the possibility of personal injury to competitors as well as spectators is always present. And the fact that some of the athletes may be young teenagers only complicates the risk management challenge. Terrorism and computer systems security are also major risks. At the 1996 Games in Atlanta, one person was killed and more than 100 were injured when a pipe bomb exploded at a downtown entertainment area known as Centennial Park. Organizers for the 2004 Games in Athens, Greece, increased their $650 million security budget by over 20 percent following the September 11 terrorist attacks. The computer network for the Athens Games covers 60 venues and links 10,000 PCs and 400 laptops. So securing the network against hackers and assuring its reliability are key challenges.

Some very serious loss exposures may not be obvious. For example, weather-related perils can force the postponement of a ticketed event, such as the opening ceremony. The cancellation of the television coverage contract, often the largest single source of revenue, would be devastating. Such a cancellation actually did occur in 1980, when the United States boycotted the Moscow Olympics to protest the Soviet invasion of Afghanistan.

Source: Kate Tilley, "Risk Management an Olympic Task," *Business Insurance*, June 22, 1998, 27, 30; Ross Bentley, "2004 Olympics Present Mammoth Security and Network Challenge," *Computer Weekly*, October 14, 2003, 22, Kerin Hope, "Greeks Rethink Athens Security Plan," *Europe*, no. 412, January 2002, 35.

who trips and falls over trash stored near the entrance to the building. Another common liability risk arises from automobile use. Drivers involved in accidents may be liable if their actions are judged to be the cause of harm to someone else or to another person's property. Businesses also face other situations that may result in damages payable to others. For example, if customers are injured by a firm's products or through the actions of a company's employees, the business may be held responsible for several million dollars worth of losses. Similarly, actions that pollute the environment or violate the personal rights of employees may also prove to be expensive from a liability perspective. These examples only begin to illustrate some of the situations that may result in severe losses for an individual or a business. Additional details about liability risks are discussed in later chapters.

Life, Health, and Loss of Income Risks

Potential losses associated with the health and well-being of individuals make up the third and final category of sources of risk. The possibility of the untimely death of star salesperson Ann Costello exposes her employer to potential loss if a replacement with the same skills and experience is not readily available. Even if Ann could be easily replaced, in many cases employee deaths are disruptive for other workers and may result in temporarily reduced productivity. This phenomenon is especially true if the death is due to job-related conditions.

Ann's employer may also face risks associated with Ann's potential death through the employee benefits provided to workers. Death benefits typically include a lump sum payment to survivors. Of course, employees also may face additional risks related to their premature death. For instance, the potential death of a parent exposes young children to the risk that their primary source of income may disappear. In addition, death usually results in certain expenses that must be paid before assets can be used for the support of survivors. Examples include funeral and burial costs, existing debts, and possibly estate and inheritance taxes.

Businesses and individuals also face risks associated with health problems. Persons who become ill or who are injured in accidents will incur expenses for medical treatment, and the cost of such treatment is becoming increasingly expensive. Sometimes businesses arrange to pay some or all of such expenses for their employees, regardless of whether a sickness or injury is job related. As medical costs increase, however, more and more individuals (whether employed or not) must pay substantial sums each year for medical care for themselves and their families. In addition to these expenses, there is another potential loss associated with sickness and accidents. If a previously employed individual is severely injured or gravely ill, that person may be unable to work for several months or even years. The resultant loss of income can have serious repercussions on the financial stability of the person and family involved.

Other risks that confront an employed individual are those associated with unemployment and retirement. Both events result in the loss of an income source that previously existed. A significant difference, however, relates to timing. Retirement usually is not a surprise and therefore presents many options for advance planning. In contrast, abrupt layoffs often are not expected and are therefore harder to plan for ahead of time. Through pension and other retirement benefits, as well as unemployment insurance provided in each state, businesses are also affected by these risks that their employees face.

Financial Risk

Although the major emphasis of this book is on pure risks, it is increasingly important that risks from other sources be considered as well. A variety of **financial risks**, which often are speculative in nature, can impact on a firm's earnings. Examples of these financial risks include credit risk, foreign exchange risk, commodity risk, and interest rate risk. Although most of these financial risks tend to have the characteristics of speculative risks, they still present the firm with some of the same problems associated with pure risks. Although the techniques used to manage these risks may be very different from those used to manage pure risks, it remains critical that these risks be identified and assessed in order for the firm to achieve its business goals.

MEASUREMENT OF RISK

Once risk sources have been identified, it is often helpful to measure the extent of the risk that exists. As noted previously, risks that are classified as subjective cannot be precisely measured. In contrast, the amount of objective risk is often more readily observable. Several important concepts related to the measurement of objective risk are discussed in this section.

Chance of Loss

The long-term chance of occurrence, or relative frequency of loss, is defined to be the **chance of loss**. The concept has little meaning if applied to the chance of occurrence of a single event. Rather, it is meaningful primarily when applied to the chance of a loss occurring among a large number of possible events. Thus, chance of loss is expressed as the ratio of the number of losses that are likely to occur compared to the larger number of possible losses in a given group. For example, suppose 1,000 buildings in a particular city are considered to be suscep-tible to the risk of loss due to a tornado. If past experience indicates that 20 of these buildings are likely to be damaged by a tornado during a given time period, then the chance of loss due to a tornado is 2 percent. This number is determined by dividing the probable number of losses (20) by the number of buildings exposed to loss (1,000).

In making chance of loss calculations, it is common practice to perform separate compu-tations for different causes of loss. In this sense, the term **peril** is used to describe a specific contingency that may cause a loss. For example, one of the perils that can cause loss to an au-tomobile is collision. Other perils are illustrated by considering ways in which a building can be damaged; examples include fires, tornadoes, and explosions. Sometimes conditions exist that either increase the chance of loss from particular perils or tend to make the loss more se-vere once the peril has occurred. Such conditions are known as **hazards** and can be classified in the following three ways.

Physical Hazard

A **physical hazard** is a condition stemming from the material characteristics of an object. Consider the peril of collision, which may cause loss to an automobile. A physical condition that makes the occurrence of collision more likely is an icy street. The icy street is the haz-ard, and the collision is the peril. The chance of loss due to collision may be higher in winter than at other times of the year because of the greater incidence of the physical hazard of icy streets.

Physical hazards include such phenomena as the existence of dry forests (a hazard affect-ing the peril of fire), earth faults (a hazard for earthquakes), and the existence of oily rags in a firm's storage closet (a hazard for fire). Such hazards may or may not be within human control. For example, the oily rag hazard can easily be eliminated. Other physical hazards, such as weather conditions, usually cannot be controlled, although their existence often may be observed.

Moral Hazard

The condition known as **moral hazard** stems from an individual's mental attitude. It is associated with intentional actions designed either to cause a loss or to increase its severity. Moral hazards often are typified by individuals with known records of dishonesty. In addition, the existence of insurance may sometimes exacerbate the existence of moral hazard. For ex-ample, managers who purchase fire insurance on a factory full of unprofitable, out-of-date equipment may feel an incentive to "sell the building to the insurance company" by arranging for a fire to destroy the property. Moral hazard also describes the change in attitude that can occur when insurance is available to pay for loss, such as the tendency for individuals to consume more health care if the costs are covered by insurance.

Other examples of moral hazards in-volve accidents and sicknesses, especially where an employer provides generous in-come replacement during the time an em-ployee is unable to work. In these situations, workers who are not pleased with their jobs or who fear being laid off in the future may be inclined to suffer an "accident" or

net*link*

Controlling fraud is a major purpose of the National Insurance Crime Bureau, which was formed in 1992. Visit its Web site at http://www.nicb.com to learn about the methods used to detect and fight fraud. Also, visit the Coalition Against Insurance Fraud's Web site at http://www.insurancefraud.org and read the "Fraud Case of the Month" or browse the "Fraud Hall of Shame."

ETHICAL PERSPECTIVES

Moral Hazard

A top equestrian, George Lindemann, Jr., insured his prize show horse, Charisma, for a quarter of a million dollars. After a series of lackluster performances, however, Charisma died suddenly from what appeared to be colic, a common killer of horses. Ironically, many observers believed that the $250,000 insurance settlement was more than the horse was worth alive, due to its poor showings just prior to its death.

During this time, the FBI was involved in an investigation regarding horse killings and related insurance fraud. They had arrested Tommy Burns, who said he was paid to kill horses so their owners could collect any insurance proceeds. In cooperation with the FBI, Burns gave the names of his clients for the ongoing investigation. Lindemann's name was mentioned, and soon the fact that Charisma had performed poorly prior to its death was seen as more than just a coincidence.

During Lindemann's trial, Burns testified that Charisma had not died of natural causes, but instead died of electrocution, which can easily be disguised as colic. Lindemann was convicted of wire fraud, sentenced to 33 months in jail, and fined $500,000. Further, he was ordered to make restitution of the $250,000 insurance settlement and to pay for the cost of his incarceration. Thus, killing Charisma not only cost Lindemann the competition, but also cost his freedom.

Source: Matt O'Connor, "Equestrian, Trainer Sentenced to Prison in Horse-Killing Scheme," *Chicago Tribune*, January 19, 1996, sec. 2, p. 2.

contract an "illness." Closely related to this are cases where the original accident or illness is indeed legitimate but the recovery period is intentionally extended by the injured or sick person. Reasons for such behavior include the lack of a sufficient financial incentive to return to work and the psychological satisfaction some sick persons experience from the attention and concern given to them by their family and friends.

Morale Hazard

The mental attitude of a careless or accident-prone person is known as **morale hazard**. Sometimes a subconscious desire for a loss may exist, even though the individual is not fully aware of this desire. In other cases, circumstances may cause someone to be indifferent to the possibility of a loss, thus causing that person to behave in a careless manner. For example, suppose the managers of ABC Company believe the federal government will provide disaster assistance that will fully compensate ABC for all earthquake losses it may incur. In making plans for a new building near a major fault line, ABC's management may be tempted to ignore more expensive construction designs and procedures that can lessen damage from earthquakes. In essence, ABC's assumption regarding the potential for federal disaster aid makes its management indifferent to the prospect of loss and, therefore, more prone to make unmindful decisions.

Degree of Risk

The amount of objective risk present in a situation, sometimes referred to as the **degree of risk**, is the relative variation of actual from expected losses. More precisely, the degree of risk is the range of variability around the expected losses, which are calculated using the chance of loss concept by means of the following formula:

$$\text{Objective Risk} = \frac{\text{Probable variation of actual from expected losses}}{\text{Expected losses}}$$

Consider the possibility of fire losses to buildings in Acworth and Branson. There are 100,000 buildings in each city and, on average, each city has 100 fire losses per year. By looking at historical data, statisticians are able to estimate that the actual number of fire losses in Acworth during the next year will very likely range from 95 to 105. In Branson, however, the range probably will be greater, with at least 80 fire losses expected and possibly as many as 120. The degree of risk for each city is computed as follows:

$$\text{Risk}_{\text{Acworth}} = (105 - 95) / 100 = 10 \text{ percent}$$

$$\text{Risk}_{\text{Branson}} = (120 - 80) / 100 = 40 \text{ percent}$$

As shown, the degree of risk for Branson is four times that for Acworth, even though the chances of loss are the same.

A few other observations are important regarding degree of risk and chance of loss. If a loss has already occurred, the probable variation of actual from expected losses in that particular situation is zero and, therefore, the degree of risk is zero. At the opposite extreme, if it is impossible for a loss to occur, the probable variation also is zero and the degree of risk is zero as well. Finally, in measuring the degree of risk, results are meaningful only in terms of a group large enough to analyze statistically. If the numbers involved are very small, then the range of probable variation may be so large as to seem virtually infinite when viewed in a relative sense.

To illustrate this latter point, consider the Online Action Corporation, which is concerned about the possible death of Barbara Thomas, a valuable, highly paid 24-year-old worker in its product development department. Online Action has been informed that Barbara's probability of dying during the next year is 0.3 percent. Or, using the terminology introduced in this chapter, the chance of loss due to the peril of death is 0.003. The degree of risk is not particularly meaningful, however, when applied only to Barbara's life. Either Barbara will die or she will not, making the relative variation of actual from expected losses extremely large:

$$\left(\frac{1-0}{0.003}\right) = 333.33 = 33{,}333 \text{ percent}$$

MANAGEMENT OF RISK

In the previous sections, several types of risk that affect individuals and businesses were introduced, together with ways to measure the amount of objective risk present. After sources of risk are identified and measured, a decision can be made as to how the risk should be handled. A pure risk that is not identified does not disappear; the business or individual merely loses the opportunity to consciously decide on the best technique for dealing with that risk. The process used to systematically manage risk exposures is known as **risk management**.

Some persons use the term risk management only in connection with businesses, and often the term refers only to the management of pure risks. In this sense, the traditional risk management goal has been to minimize the cost of pure risk to the company. But as firms broaden the ways that they view and manage many different types of risk, the need for new terminology has become apparent. The terms **integrated risk management** and **enterprise risk management** reflect the intent to manage all forms of risk, regardless of type.

Many businesses have a special department charged with overseeing the firm's risk management activities; the head of such a department often has the title of **risk manager**. The traditional type of risk manager may be charged with minimizing the adverse impact of losses on the achievement of the company's goals. In implementing the more integrated approach to risk management, however, some firms have formed risk management committees. Some firms also have created a new position of **chief risk officer** (CRO) to coordinate the firm's risk management activities, regardless of the source of the risk. As part of his or her duties, the risk manager and/or CRO is likely to be involved in many aspects of a firm's activities. Examples may include developing employee safety programs, examining planned mergers and acquisitions, analyzing investment opportunities, purchasing insurance to protect against some types of risk, and setting up pension and health plans for employees. The evolution of integrated risk management reflects a realization of the importance of coordinating the many risk management activities of the firm in order to meet its strategic goals.

Whether the concern is with a business or an individual situation, the same general steps can be used to systematically analyze and deal with risk. Known as the **risk management process**, these steps form the basis for the remaining chapters in Part 1 of this book. At this point they can be summarized as follows:

1. *Identify risks*. There are many potential risks that confront individuals and businesses. Therefore, the first step in the risk management process is to identify relevant exposures to risks. This step is important not only for traditional risk management, which focuses on pure risks, but also for enterprise risk management, where much of the focus is on identifying the firm's exposures from a variety of sources, including operational, financial, and strategic activities.

2. *Evaluate risks*. For each source of risk that is identified, an evaluation should be performed. At this stage, pure risks can be categorized as to how often associated losses are likely to occur. In addition to this evaluation of loss **frequency**, an analysis of the size, or **severity**, of the loss is helpful. Consideration should be given both to the most probable size of any losses that may occur and to the maximum possible losses that might happen. As part of the overall risk evaluation, in some situations it may be possible to measure the degree of risk in a meaningful way. In other cases, especially those involving individuals, computation of the degree of risk may not yield helpful information.

3. *Select risk management techniques*. The results of the analyses in step 2 are used as the basis for decisions regarding ways to handle existing risks. In some situations, the best plan may be to do nothing. In other cases, sophisticated ways to finance potential losses may be arranged. The available techniques for managing risks are discussed in the next several chapters, together with consideration of when each technique is appropriate.

4. *Implement and review decisions*. Following a decision about the optimal methods for handling identified risks, the business or individual must implement the techniques selected. However, risk management should be an ongoing process in which prior decisions are reviewed regularly. Sometimes new risk exposures arise or significant changes in expected loss frequency or severity occur. As noted in this chapter, even pure risks are not necessarily static; the dynamic nature of many risks requires a continual scrutiny of past analyses and decisions.

SUMMARY

1. Risk is defined as uncertainty concerning loss.
2. Risk creates an economic burden for society by raising the cost of certain goods and services and eliminating the provision of others.
3. The cost of risk includes outlays to reduce risks, the opportunity cost of activities forgone due to risk considerations, expenses of strategies to finance potential losses, and the cost of unreimbursed losses.
4. Pure risk exists when there is uncertainty as to whether loss will occur. Speculative risk exists when there is uncertainty about an event that could produce either a profit or a loss.
5. Static risks are present in an unchanging, stable society. Dynamic risks are produced by changes in society.
6. Subjective risk refers to the mental state of an individual. Objective risk, which is measurable, is the probable variation of actual from expected experience.
7. There are many sources of risk. One way of classifying them is in relation to property, liability, life, health, loss of income, and financial exposures.
8. Chance of loss is the long-term relative frequency of a loss due to a particular peril, or cause of loss. The degree of risk is the relative variation of actual from expected losses.
9. A hazard is a condition that increases the chance of loss due to a peril. Hazards can arise out of both physical conditions and the mental attitudes of individuals.
10. Risk management is the process used to systematically manage exposures to pure risk. The four steps in the process are (1) identify risks, (2) evaluate risks, (3) select risk management techniques, and (4) implement and review decisions.
11. Integrated or enterprise risk management is an emerging view that recognizes the importance of risk, regardless of its source, in affecting a firm's ability to realize its strategic objectives.

internet*exercises*

1. Changing legislation and court decisions are major sources of dynamic risk. The Law News Network provides information on current court decisions and changes in legislation. Set your browser to http://www.law.com and select a current issue or recent court decision that could change an industry's level of risk. Which industry could this decision affect and how?
2. Simulate your own natural disaster at http://www.wcmsolutions.com. Locate the product "The Storm," which lets you control the weather. What potential losses could occur as the result of your storm?

QUESTIONS FOR REVIEW AND DISCUSSION

1. Define risk. List some ways in which risk creates an economic burden for society.

2. Differentiate between the following types of risk: (a) pure versus speculative, (b) static versus dynamic, and (c) subjective versus objective.

3. Give an example of a risk that is both pure and static.

4. Differentiate between a peril and a hazard and give an example of each.

5. Classify each of the following hazards as physical, morale, or moral.
   a. A careless driver
   b. A person who suffers an exaggerated case of whiplash following an automobile accident
   c. A worker who occasionally leaves a dangerous machine unattended to talk with friends
   d. An employee who occasionally embezzles money
   e. Icy road conditions

6. Define risk management and identify the four steps in the risk management process. How does enterprise risk management differ from the traditional form of risk management?

7. Explain why the degree of risk decreases as the chance of loss increases (assuming a constant number of exposure units).

8. ABC Company owns 10,000 cars and has determined that it is very likely to suffer between 60 and 70 collision losses this year. XYZ Company also owns 10,000 cars and has determined that it is likely to experience 50 to 80 collision losses this year. Compute the degree of risk for each company, assuming that the companies expect to suffer 65 losses each.

9. For each of the following hazards, state the peril to which the hazard relates.
   a. A drunk captain of an oil tanker
   b. A poorly constructed dam
   c. A highly flammable material
   d. A dangerous heart condition
   e. A defective lock on a warehouse

10. You are informed that you have just received an inheritance from a great uncle who was something of an eccentric. You have your choice of (a) taking $10,000 in cash or (b) joining in a game of drawing balls from a bowl containing 90 black balls and 10 white ones. If you draw a black ball, you receive $1,000; if you draw a white ball, you receive $100,000. Which choice would you take and why? Explain how this situation illustrates the economic burden of risk.

11. Company A owns 100 buildings and averages 2 fires per year. Company B owns 1,000 buildings and averages 30 fires per year. Company A never experiences more than 3 fires a year, although in some years there are none. In some years Company B has as many as 36 fires but never has fewer than 24. Who is faced with the greater objective risk? Who has the greater chance of loss? Explain.

12. It has been said that a well-informed buyer experiences less risk than an uninformed buyer. Do you agree? Why? What type of risk is referred to in this statement? Explain.

13. Why is variation used as a measure of the degree of risk instead of another measure such as the expected annual loss? Explain why there is a higher degree of risk if the probability of the occurrence of a loss is 80 percent than if the probability of a loss is 99 percent. At what two probabilities of the occurrence of an event would you expect risk to totally disappear? Explain.

14. If you were hired by a company and asked to accurately estimate the maximum loss potential from property, liability, life, health, and loss-of-income risks, which classification would generally be easiest to estimate? Why? What would make the estimation of the potential losses difficult for the other classifications?

chapter 2

Risk Identification and Evaluation

McCullough and Associates is a management consulting firm headquartered in Boston, with operations throughout the northeastern part of the United States. The company was formed in 2001 by its owner and chief operating officer, Barry McCullough. McCullough currently has about 200 consultants and an additional 150 employees working in supporting roles. The firm has developed a reputation for being especially helpful in solving personnel and financial management problems. As Barry McCullough and his management team plan for the future, they want to be very systematic in identifying key issues, opportunities, and potential problems that may confront the company in the years ahead.

One area that has not received much attention to date is that of pure risk exposures. Thus, Barry McCullough has recently assigned one of his top consultants to take on the responsibility for identifying all of the potential risks confronting his firm. After the exposures have been identified, McCullough wants to know the relative importance of each one. For example, is the risk of loss due to fire potentially more damaging than the risk of adverse liability judgments? What losses are most likely to happen in a given year, and how much would probably be lost in each case? Can consistency be expected from one year to the next? McCullough believes that it is impossible to make good risk management decisions without first having answers to these and similar questions. Such issues form the basis for this chapter.

CHAPTER OBJECTIVES

After studying this chapter, you should be able to

1. Explain several methods for identifying risks.
2. Identify the important elements in risk evaluation.
3. Explain three different measures of central tendency.
4. Explain three different measures of variation.
5. Discuss the concept of a probability distribution and explain the importance to risk managers.
6. Give examples of how risk managers might use the normal, binomial, and Poisson distributions.
7. Explain how the concepts of risk mapping and value at risk are used in an enterprise-wide evaluation of risk.
8. Explain the importance of the law of large numbers for risk management.

The risk management process and its context were introduced at the end of the previous chapter. You'll recall that the risk management process has four sequential steps: risk identification, risk evaluation, selection of appropriate risk management techniques, and implementation and review. The first two steps in the risk management process are discussed in this chapter; subsequent chapters address the remaining steps in the overall process.

RISK IDENTIFICATION

The identification of risks and exposures to loss is perhaps the most important element of the risk management process. Unless the sources of possible losses are recognized, it is impossible to consciously choose appropriate, efficient methods for dealing with those losses should they occur.

A **loss exposure** is a potential loss that may be associated with a specific type of risk. Loss exposures are typically classified in the same way as are pure risks, which were discussed briefly in Chapter 1; that is, loss exposures can be categorized as to whether they result from property, liability, life, health, or loss of income risks.

All of these exposures will be analyzed in greater detail throughout this book. At this point, it is helpful to consider techniques for identifying and evaluating risks present in particular settings. Approaches used by many risk managers involve loss exposure checklists, financial statement analysis, flowcharts, contract analysis, on-site inspections, and statistical analysis of past losses.

Loss Exposure Checklists

One risk identification tool that can be used both by businesses and by individuals is a **loss exposure checklist**, which specifies numerous potential sources of loss from the destruction of assets and from legal liability. For each item on the checklist, the user asks the question, "Is this a potential source of loss to me or my firm?" In this way, the systematic use of loss exposure checklists reduces the likelihood of overlooking important sources of risk.

Some loss exposure checklists are designed for specific industries, such as manufacturers, retail stores, educational institutions, or religious organizations. Such lists tend to be quite lengthy, because they attempt to cover all the exposures that various entities are likely to face. Consideration is given to the cost to repair or replace property, to income losses that may accompany the destruction of assets, and to likely sources of legal liability.

A second type of checklist focuses on a specific category of exposure. The example checklist that is available on the course support Web site at http://trieschmann.swlearning. com deals with potential losses associated with real and personal property. Both the risk of physical damage and the risk of liability arising from the use of property are explored through the questions included in this checklist. Although many items may not be relevant to a particular organization, the questions usually address specific exposures in considerable detail. Thus, these checklists can be helpful not only in risk identification but also in compiling information necessary for an in-depth evaluation of risks that are identified.

Financial Statement Analysis

Another approach that can be used by businesses to identify risks is **financial statement analysis**. Using this method, all items on a firm's balance sheet and income statement are analyzed in regard to risks that may be present. By including budgets, long-range forecasts, and written strategic plans in the analysis, this method can also help identify possible future risks that may not currently exist.

To illustrate this method of risk identification, consider the asset categories included on the balance sheets of business entities. Buildings owned by a firm are usually noted on its balance sheet, and leased buildings may be noted in footnotes to the financial statements. Future building acquisitions may be noted in budgets and strategic plans. Once such present and future buildings are identified, potential losses associated with them can then be considered. The loss exposures associated with building damage may include repair costs, the value of inventories and equipment inside, loss of income while the building cannot be used, and injuries to employees and customers inside the building. If a building is leased, relevant concerns would also include the disposition of the lease if the building is destroyed, including cost estimates of alternative facilities. This example does not begin to exhaust the range of possible losses that might result from damage to a building. It does, however, illustrate the thought process that is essential to the financial statement analysis method of risk identification.

Flowcharts

A third tool—the **flowchart**—is especially useful for businesses in identifying sources of risk in their production processes. The simplified flowchart in Figure 2-1 illustrates how they can pinpoint areas of potential losses. The question may be asked, "What events could disrupt the even and uninterrupted flow of parts to the final assembly floor, on which the whole production process depends?" For example, where are paints and solvents kept for the activities undertaken at Stage 3 in the figure? Are appropriate steps being taken to safeguard these materials from fire? Are floors kept clean and free of grease that might cause spills? Are any particular dangers threatening the storage of finished products that may require special protection? If the finished products are fragile, are appropriate protective measures being taken in loading and unloading?

Only through careful inspection of the entire production process can the full range of loss exposures be identified. And for some firms, even that may not be sufficient. It may be important, for example, to expand the flowchart to include the suppliers of parts and materials, particularly if a firm's production process is dependent on only a few suppliers. Thus, if there is only one possible supplier of a crucial part, a complete risk analysis will include identification of potential losses to that supplier as well as to the firm itself. Similar situations may arise if a firm manufactures products that are purchased by only a few customers. In this case, expansion of the flowchart to include customers will help identify risks that might otherwise be overlooked.

FIGURE 2-1   Flowchart for a Production Process

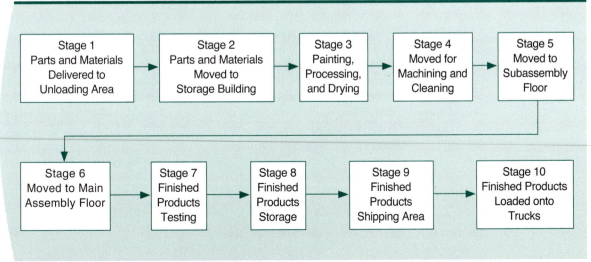

Contract Analysis

The analysis of contracts into which the firm enters is another method for identifying potential exposures to risk. It is not unusual for contracts to state that some losses, if they occur, are to be borne by specific parties. For example, a company may require building contractors that it hires to bear the cost of any liability suits arising out of the builder's construction operations. In this way, the cost of suits that might otherwise be incurred by the hiring firm will be borne by the builder.

This type of **contractual liability** may be found not only in construction contracts but also in sales contracts and lease agreements. For example, a property owner with a superior bargaining position may require her tenants to be responsible for all injuries that occur on the leased premises, even if caused by the property owner's own negligence. In other situations, she might agree to bear the liability arising out of a tenant's negligence. Ideally, the specification of who is to pay for various losses should be a conscious decision that is made as part of the overall contract negotiation process. And this decision should reflect the comparative advantage of each party in managing and bearing the risk. But even where that ideal is not possible, it is important to examine all contracts so that important sources of risk are identified prior to the occurrence of any losses.

On-Site Inspections

Because some risks may exist that are not readily identifiable with the tools discussed thus far, it is important for business risk managers to visit periodically the various locations and departments within the firm. During these visits, it can be especially helpful to talk with department managers and other employees regarding their activities. Through this type of personal interaction, the risk manager can become better informed about current exposures to risk as well as potential future exposures that may arise.

Statistical Analysis of Past Losses

A final risk identification tool that may be helpful for larger firms is that of statistical analysis of past losses. A **risk management information system (RMIS)** is a computer software program that assists in performing this task. Some characteristics of past losses that may prove to be important in this regard include the cause of loss, the particular employees (if any) involved, where the loss occurred, and the total dollar amount of the loss.

To illustrate how these factors can prove important, suppose a trucking company experiences several vehicle accidents involving the same driver. Upon further investigation, the firm may discover that it has several problem drivers because it is not adequately checking the driving records of its employment applicants. Similarly, a restaurant chain that experiences a large number of employee injuries at its Dallas location may have safety hazards present that warrant additional investigation. As risk management information systems become increasingly sophisticated and user-friendly, it is anticipated that more businesses will be able to effectively use statistical analysis in their risk management activities. The trend toward Web-based access to RMIS also has enabled firms to provide systems access to decision makers throughout the firm. This improved access provides decision makers with immediate availability of important risk management information.

RISK EVALUATION

As noted briefly in Chapter 1, once a risk is identified, the next step in the risk management process is to estimate both the frequency and severity of potential losses. In this way, the risk manager obtains information that is helpful in determining the relative importance of identified risks and in selecting particular techniques for managing those risks.

In some cases, no particular problem would arise even if losses were incurred regularly, because the potential size of each loss is small. Thus, the daily occurrence of some inventory breakage may be an expected part of some businesses and would warrant only minimal attention from the risk manager. But other losses that occur infrequently yet are relatively large when they do occur (such as accidental deaths or destruction by a large fire) may be treated entirely differently. Such losses might cause bankruptcy if they were to happen with no means in place to counteract the resulting adverse financial effects for the firm.

One complicating factor in evaluating exposures is that many losses do not result in complete destruction of the asset involved. For example, if Jim Carson's business is struck by lightning, the building will not necessarily burn to the ground. In evaluating the risk of loss from this peril, Jim should consider three things: (1) the frequency with which lightning may strike his building, (2) the **maximum probable loss** that would likely result if lightning did strike, and (3) the **maximum possible loss** if the building were completely destroyed. The difference between these last two factors is that the maximum probable loss is an estimate of the likely severity of losses that occur, whereas the maximum possible loss is an estimate of the catastrophe potential associated with a particular exposure to risk. In other words, what is the worst possible loss that can result from a given occurrence? To assess that potential, Jim needs to consider not only the loss of the building itself but also the destruction of inventory and equipment located inside. Furthermore, if Jim would seek to operate his business from another location in the event of loss, then his estimate of maximum possible loss should also include the cost of such temporary facilities.

The actual estimation of the frequency and severity of losses may be done in various ways. Some risk managers consider these concepts informally in evaluating identified risks. They may broadly classify the frequency of various losses into categories such as "slight," "moderate," and "certain," and may have similarly broad estimates for loss severity. Even this type of informal evaluation is better than none at all. But as risk management becomes increasingly sophisticated, most large firms attempt to be more precise in evaluating risks. It is now common to use probability distributions and statistical techniques in estimating both loss frequency and severity. These topics are considered in the next several sections of this chapter.

Risk Mapping or Profiling

With the evolution of integrated or enterprise risk management, alternative methods of risk identification and assessment have emerged. One such method is **risk mapping**, sometimes referred to as **risk profiling**. Since integrated risk management is based on identifying all the risks facing the firm, it is not unusual for a firm to identify in excess of 100 risks when using this approach. Cataloguing and making sense of so many risks requires a structured process. Risk mapping or profiling involves arraying these risks in a matrix, with one dimension being the frequency of events and the other being the severity. Each risk is then marked to indicate whether it is covered by insurance or not. By considering the likelihood and severity of each of the risks in this matrix, as well as the extent to which insurance protection is already available, it becomes possible for the firm to identify the risks that are most likely to seriously affect the firm's ability to achieve its goals.

Statistical Concepts

Before discussing some techniques for statistically estimating loss frequency and severity, it is useful to review some essential concepts from the field of probability and statistics.

Probability

The **probability** of an event refers to its long-term frequency of occurrence. All events have a probability between 0 (for an event that is certain not to occur) and 1 (for an event that is

PROFESSIONAL PERSPECTIVES

Risk Management Information Systems (RMIS)

Risk management information systems are software tools designed to assist risk managers in their functions. Traditional RMIS software emphasizes claim management, safety monitoring, and financing losses. Other tools available in a RMIS are management of insurance policies, exposure data, and insurance certificates. The following are examples of the successful use of RMIS by risk managers:

1. Reporting: Creation of reports that summarize loss payments and estimates of future losses. Accounting and finance departments use these reports in preparing the organization's financial statements.
2. Examination of the causes of accidents: by identifying the reasons for accidents, risk managers can determine where safety and loss prevention expenditures would be most helpful. A large number of employees or customers slipping and falling in a certain area may warrant a review of cleanup procedures or a study of the costs for installing special carpet.
3. Review of claims adjustment process: risk managers use RMIS to evaluate the performance of claims adjusters by comparing actual results to standards. Typi-

cal evaluation areas are promptness of initial contact, case settlement time, amount paid for type of injury, and accuracy of the adjuster's case value estimate.

The RMIS marketplace is evolving, with new products being introduced regularly. The primary distribution platform for new products is the Internet. The emergence of the Internet as a critical tool for business communication and services has rapidly impacted RMIS, as many vendors have "Web-enabled" new and existing products to take advantage of the Internet's broad availability and low end user maintenance costs. The Internet has also permitted older "legacy" systems to remain viable in the marketplace because end users work with a newer, standard interface even though processing may be occurring on a mainframe or other older computer system.

Software products also have been introduced to serve special application needs, such as catastrophe simulation software to assist in examining the effects of disasters on a group of exposed properties, and hazardous material tracking programs to record the uses and locations of potentially hazardous items.

Source: Ahmed Moinuddin, Vice President–Technical Services, INSUREtrust.com, LLC, Atlanta, Georgia.

certain to occur). To calculate the probability of an event, the number of times a given event occurs is divided by all possible events of that type. For example, if 150 accidents are observed to occur to 1,000 automobiles in operation, it can be said that there is a 0.15 probability of an accident (150 ÷ 1,000). This concept is the same one described in Chapter 1 in defining the term *chance of loss*. A **probability distribution** is a mutually exclusive and collectively exhaustive list of all events that can result from a chance process and contains the probability associated with each event. Thus, a risk manager may monitor the events (losses) that occur to a fleet of automobiles to determine how often losses of a particular size occur. The firm may then use that distribution to predict future losses.

Measures of Central Tendency or Location

When risk managers speak of various **measures of central tendency or location**, they are concerned with measuring the center of a probability distribution. Several types of such measures exist, but the most widely used is the **mean**. Usually signified by the $\bar{x}$, the mean can be defined as the sum of a set of n measurements $x_1, x_2, x_3, \ldots, x_n$ divided by n:

$$\bar{x} = \frac{x_1 + x_2 + x_3 + \ldots + x_n}{n}$$

INTERNATIONAL PERSPECTIVES

Loss Exposures Abroad

The global economy has become a reality for many firms. As international operations expand, it is important for management to recognize that the same risk may result in very different estimates for the maximum probable loss and maximum possible loss in different countries. With differing loss frequency and severity estimates, the most appropriate risk management techniques are also likely to vary from country to country. Several examples illustrate this point.

In the United States, risk managers often concentrate much time and effort in identifying, evaluating, and managing liability exposures. However, the rest of the world is not as litigious, thus making liability losses outside of the United States less problematical. The analysis of potential property losses may also vary. For instance, the proliferation of very old buildings throughout Europe presents unique problems. In Pacific Rim countries, the potential for catastrophic loss due to typhoons or other windstorms is very real. Risk evaluation in countries experiencing frequent currency devaluation (such as Brazil) can also be challenging, because property valuations become obsolete so quickly.

Risks of loss due to crime also vary considerably from one country to the next. For example, in Eastern Europe and the former Soviet Union, deficiencies in the computer infrastructure makes it nearly impossible to track stolen vehicles in the same way that it is possible in most Western countries. And the risk of loss to employees due to kidnapping or other violence is well-known in many Latin American countries. Often, the dynamic risk of political unrest merely exacerbates such problems, making the risk manager's job continually challenging.

Source: Ariel Silva, Vice President, International Department, Marsh of Washington, D.C., Inc.

For example, the mean of the five values 1, 1, 2, 2, and 4 is $(1 + 1 + 2 + 2 + 4) \div 5 = 10 \div 5 = 2$. A related concept is the **expected value**. It is obtained by multiplying each item or event by the probability of its occurrence. For instance, assume the following hypothetical distribution of loss from fire to a group of buildings:

Event	Amount of Loss if Event Occurs ($)		Probability of Loss		
A	$ 1,000	≥	0.40	=	$ 400
B	2,000	≥	0.30	=	600
C	5,000	≥	0.20	=	1,000
D	10,000	≥	0.10	=	1,000
Total	$18,000		1.00	=	$3,000 (Expected value)

To determine the mean or expected value of losses, multiply each loss amount by its probability and then sum. The expected value is $3,000. In effect, the expected value figure is a weighted average and reflects the best estimate of long-term average loss for a given loss distribution.

Another measure of central tendency is the **median**, which is the midpoint in a range of measurements. It is the point such that half of the items are larger and half are smaller than it. For instance, in a series of five losses of $1,000, $3,000, $5,000, $6,000, and $30,000, the median loss would be $5,000. Half of the losses are greater than that value, and half are smaller. (The mean of the series is $9,000.) One of the advantages of the median is that it is not affected greatly by extreme values, as is the mean. In the preceding loss situation, $5,000 does a much better job of describing the average loss than $9,000, because the extreme loss of $30,000 distorts the mean. The loss distribution in this example is said to be positively skewed or skewed to the right. This pattern is typical of loss distributions in practice.

Finally, the **mode** is the value of the variable that occurs most often in a frequency distribution. Thus, if a firm experienced eight losses of $25, $30, $30, $40, $40, $40, $50, and $60, the mode would be $40. As a measure of central tendency for risk managers, the mode is not as widely used as the mean or median.

Measures of Variation or Dispersion

Because risk is synonymous with uncertainty, an extremely important statistical concept is that of variation from what is expected. The **standard deviation**, usually represented by the Greek letter σ, is a number that measures how close a group of individual measurements is to its expected value or mean. For example, assume a manufacturer has 100 employees who are injured during a year. The dollar loss from these injuries ranges from $500 to $25,000, with an expected value of $12,500. The range of the individual losses is rather great, from $500 to $25,000. To say that the average injury loss is $12,500 is not very descriptive of the magnitude of the average loss, especially if one is comparing it with another group of 100 losses that range in severity from $11,000 to $14,000 but also have an average loss of $12,500. It is helpful to state precisely just how the two groups differ. By comparing the standard deviation of two sets of injuries, the precise variation in injuries becomes clear.

To calculate the standard deviation of a group of measures, one must first determine the mean or expected value. Then the mean is subtracted from each individual value, and the resulting figure is squared. The squared differences are added together, with the sum divided by the total number of measurements. The result is the mean of the squared deviation, which is known as the **variance**. The square root of the variance is the standard deviation. An example illustrating these calculations for a set of five losses is provided in Table 2-1.

As an example of how to use the information provided by measures of dispersion, suppose there are two factories with the same average loss. However, the dollar loss of all injuries in one factory falls within one standard deviation of the mean loss, whereas only 10 percent of the injuries in the other factory do so. With such data, there can be a much better understanding of the risk associated with injury loss in these two factories. The dispersion of losses in the first factory is much less than in the second. Thus, the standard deviation is a gauge of the dispersion of values about the mean and, hence, of the risk or uncertainty.

TABLE 2-1   **Calculating the Standard Deviation of Losses**

Losses ($)	Mean Loss* ($)	Deviation from Mean ($)	Squared Deviations ($)
10	30	−20	400
20	30	−10	100
30	30	0	0
40	30	10	100
50	30	20	400
			1,000

Variance = 1,000 ÷ 5 = 200
Standard deviation = $\sqrt{200}$ = $14.14
* Mean loss = ($10 + 20 + 30 + 40 + 50) ÷ 5 = $30

When the standard deviation is expressed as a percentage of the mean, the result is the **coefficient of variation**, which is one way to characterize the concept of mathematical risk to the insurer. It is the method used in Chapter 1 to measure objective risk. If losses from a group of exposure units have a low coefficient of variation, there is less risk (less variation) associated with this group of exposures than with another group with a higher coefficient of variation.

Loss Distributions Used in Risk Management

Probability distributions can be very useful tools for evaluating the expected frequency and/or severity of losses due to identified risks. In risk management, two types of probability distribution are used: empirical and theoretical. To form an **empirical probability distribution**, the risk manager actually observes the events that occur, as explained in the previous section. To create a **theoretical probability distribution**, a mathematical formula is used. To effectively use such distributions, the risk manager must be reasonably confident that the distribution of the firm's losses is similar to the theoretical distribution chosen.

Three theoretical probability distributions that are widely used in risk management are: the binomial, the normal, and the Poisson.

The Binomial Distribution

Suppose the probability that an event will occur at any point in time is p. Then the probability q that the event will not occur can be stated by the equation $q = 1 - p$. One can calculate how often an event will happen by means of the **binomial formula**, which indicates that the probability of r events in n possible times equals:

$$\frac{n!}{r!\,(n-r)!} \geq p^r\, q^{n-r}$$

Note that the expression $n!$ is read "n factorial" and refers to a successive multiplication of the numbers $n, n - 1, n - 2, \ldots, 1$.

Suppose that a risk manager needs to estimate the probability of the number of losses in a particular group. If the firms own a fleet of 10,000 automobiles, the binomial formula may be used to calculate the chance of 10 losses, 100 losses, 200 losses, or any other number of losses, provided that p can be reasonably estimated. Similarly, if there are 100 exposure units, such as separate retail stores, and it is known from past experience that the separate probability of loss of any one store by fire each year is 0.01, reference to a binomial table tells us that the probability is

0.366	that 0 stores will burn
0.370	that 1 store will burn
0.185	that 2 stores will burn
0.061	that 3 stores will burn
0.018	that 4 or more stores will burn
1.000	Total

The Normal Distribution

As the number of observations increases, a mathematical concept called the **central limit theory** states that the expected results for a pool or portfolio of independent observations can be approximated by the **normal distribution**, which is a very useful type of mathematical distribution. Shown graphically in Figure 2-2, it is perfectly bell shaped. When one knows its mean and standard deviation, the distribution is said to be completely defined.

For instance, the loss distribution in Figure 2-2 is a normal distribution of 500 losses with a mean value of $500 and a standard deviation of $150. When risk managers have this

FIGURE 2-2   Normal Probability Distribution of 500 Losses

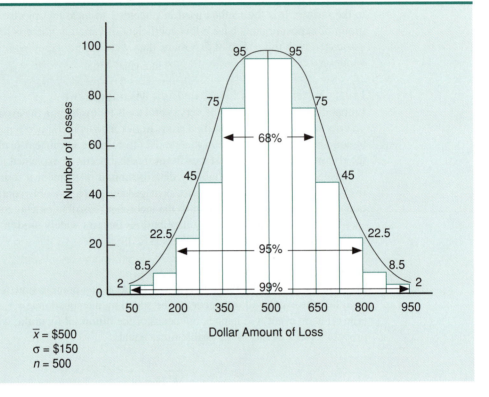

$\bar{x}$ = $500
σ = $150
n = 500

information, they can assume that about 68 percent of all losses will be within 1 standard deviation of the mean. The figure shows that 340 losses (75 + 95 + 95 + 75) are between $350 and $650, which is the range of ±1 standard deviation. Likewise, about 95 percent, or 475, of all losses should occur within two standard deviations of the mean. These losses would be within the $200 to $800 range. About 99 percent of all observations should be within 3 standard deviations of the mean. If risk managers know that their loss distributions are normal, they can assume that these relationships hold, and they can predict the probability of a given loss level occurring or the probability of losses being within a certain range of the mean.

It should be noted that the binomial distribution requires variables to be **discrete** (i.e., there is either a loss or no loss). With the normal distribution, variables may be **continuous**, having a value of any number.

The Poisson Distribution

The **Poisson distribution** is another theoretical probability distribution that is useful in risk management applications. For example, auto accidents, fires, and other losses tend to occur in a way that can be approximated with the Poisson distribution. One determines the probability of an event under the Poisson distribution using the following formula:

$$p = \frac{m^r e^{-m}}{r!}$$

where p = the probability that an event n occurs

r = the number of events for which the probability estimate is needed

m = mean = expected loss frequency

e = a constant, the base of the natural logarithms, equal to 2.71828

The mean m of a Poisson distribution is also its variance. Consequently, its standard deviation σ is equal to $\sqrt{m}$.

To obtain a better understanding of how the Poisson distribution is used to calculate probabilities, consider the following example. Suppose the Ferguson Company owns 10 trucks. In a typical year, a total of one loss occurs, thus allowing p to be estimated to be 0.1. What is the probability of more than two accidents in a year? Or stated another way, what is the probability of three or more accidents? The answer is 8.03 percent, which is calculated in Table 2-2.

Note that the probabilities in Table 2-2 are similar to those calculated previously for the binomial distribution, where the mean loss was also equal to 1. When the probabilities of loss are greater, the difference between the two distributions is greater. However, it should be noted that as the number of exposure units increases and the probability of loss decreases, the binomial distribution becomes more and more like the Poisson distribution.

From a risk management viewpoint, the Poisson distribution is most desirable when more than 50 independent exposure units exist and the probability that any one item will suffer a loss is 0.1 or less. However, when there are fewer than 50 exposures but each one can suffer multiple losses during the year, it can still be used. Given these characteristics, the Poisson distribution can be a very useful probability distribution for risk managers.

Other theoretical distributions used in risk management include the Gamma, the Log Normal, the Negative Binomial, and the Pareto. Comparison to the firm's actual data can confirm whether a particular theoretical distribution is appropriate. These other theoretical distributions are positively skewed, which is a trait often exhibited by data in risk management applications.

TABLE 2-2   **Probability of Losses Using the Poisson Distribution**

Number of exposure units = 10
Probability of loss = p = 0.1
Expected loss frequency = m = 0.1 × 10 = 1.0

Possible Losses	Probability		
0	$\dfrac{(1.0)^0 e^{-1}}{0!*}$ =	$\dfrac{1 \times 0.3679}{1}$	= 0.3679
1	$\dfrac{(1.0)^1 e^{-1}}{1!}$ =	$\dfrac{1 \times 0.3679}{1}$	= 0.3679
2	$\dfrac{(1.0)^2 e^{-1}}{2!}$ =	$\dfrac{1 \times 0.3679}{2 \times 1}$	= 0.1839
3	$\dfrac{(1.0)^3 e^{-1}}{3!}$ =	$\dfrac{1 \times 0.3679}{3 \times 2 \times 1}$	= 0.0613
4	$\dfrac{(1.0)^4 e^{-1}}{4!}$ =	$\dfrac{1 \times 0.3679}{4 \times 3 \times 2 \times 1}$	= 0.0153

*0! = 1
Probability of 3 or more losses = 1 – Probability of 0, 1, or 2 losses
= 1 – (0.3679 + 0.3679 + 0.1839)
= 0.0803

Integrated Risk Measures

The assessment of risk in an integrated risk framework requires additional quantification techniques. One approach being used is **value at risk (VAR)**. Value-at-risk analysis has been used by banks to quantify financial risk, but is increasingly being considered by other types of firms that wish to assess all types of risks in a coordinated framework. VAR analysis constructs probability distributions of the risks alone and in various combinations, to obtain estimates of the risk of loss at various probability levels. This type of analysis yields a numerical statement of the maximum expected loss in a specific time period and at a given probability level. The VAR approach is similar to the concept of maximum probable loss described previously, but it provides the firm with an assessment of the overall impact of risk on the firm. For example, consider the isolated risk that disability payments may have to be paid to injured workers. Suppose the firm estimates that at the 95 percent probability level, total disability payments in one year will be less than $100,000. Thus, the VAR equals $100,000. To obtain a broader estimate of the firm's VAR, probability distributions for a variety of risks facing the firm would be combined.

To find out more about the theoretical probability distributions that can be used in risk management, go to http://mathworld.wolfram.com and browse under "Probability and Statistics." You can also find a wealth of information there on the other concepts presented in this chapter.

One significant advantage of using VAR in enterprise risk management is that it considers correlation between different categories of risk. The relationship among different risks may either increase or decrease the overall effect of the risks facing an organization. For instance, increases in unemployment can lead to increases in criminal activity and workers' compensation claims, and to decreases in a firm's sales. The combined impact of these three risks could be substantially different from what might be estimated by considering each risk alone. Ultimately, it is the net effect of risk that is critical to the ability of a firm to achieve its goals.

Another measure sometimes used in an enterprise-wide assessment of risk is **risk-adjusted return on capital (RAROC)**. This approach attempts to allocate risk costs to the many different activities of the firm, such as products, projects, loans, and so on. In effect, RAROC assesses how much capital would be required by the organization's various activities to keep the probability of bankruptcy below a specified probability level. As a result of RAROC, managers are forced to consider risk levels in evaluating the profitability of their decisions.

ACCURACY OF PREDICTIONS

A question of interest to risk managers is how many individual exposure units are necessary before a given degree of accuracy can be achieved in obtaining an actual loss frequency that is close to the expected loss frequency. As discussed in this section, the number of observed losses for a particular firm must be fairly large to accurately predict future losses. If the number is not sufficiently large, then the firm may still perform risk evaluation by choosing an appropriate theoretical probability distribution similar to the firm's own distribution of losses.

Law of Large Numbers

Objective risk was defined in Chapter 1 to be the ratio of the probable variation of actual from expected losses, divided by expected losses. As noted there, the degree of objective risk is meaningful only when the group is fairly large. In fact, the concept becomes increasingly meaningful (and useful) as the size of the group exposed to the risk expands. The **law of large numbers**, which can be derived and proven mathematically, states that as the number of exposure units (in other words, persons or objects exposed to risk) increases, the more likely it becomes that actual loss experience will equal probable loss experience. Hence, the degree of objective risk diminishes as the number of exposure units increases.

An individual seldom has a sufficient number of items exposed to a particular risk to reduce the degree of risk significantly through the operation of the law of large numbers. Large businesses may be better equipped to do so. For example, suppose RBW Rental Car Company owns a fleet of 10,000 automobiles available for rental. While it is impossible to predict which particular cars will incur physical damage losses in any given year, RBW may be able to predict fairly accurately how many of the cars will be damaged. The accuracy of RBW's prediction is enhanced because of the large number of exposure units (cars) involved.

To illustrate more precisely the effects of the law of large numbers, assume that QQQ Company and RRR Company own 100 and 900 automobiles, respectively. These cars are used by the sales personnel of each firm and are driven in the same general geographical territory. The chance of loss in a given year due to collision is 20 percent. Thus, the expected number of losses is $0.20 \times 100 = 20$ for QQQ and $0.20 \times 900 = 180$ for RRR. Suppose further that statisticians have computed that the likely range in the number of losses in one year is 8 for QQQ and 24 for RRR. As shown, RRR's degree of risk is only one-third that for QQQ:

$$\text{Objective risk }_{QQQ} = \frac{\text{Range}}{\text{Expected}} = \frac{8}{20} = 40\%$$

$$\text{Objective risk }_{RRR} = \frac{\text{Range}}{\text{Expected}} = \frac{24}{180} = 13.3\%$$

In this example, the crucial input values are the likely ranges in actual results. In general, the range of possible results decreases on a relative basis as the number of exposure units increases.

In the previous example it was assumed that the underlying chance of loss was the same for QQQ and RRR. Consider now the effect of changing the long-term chance of loss while maintaining the same number of exposure units. At first glance it appears that the higher the chance of loss, the higher the risk. However, the opposite is actually true. As the chance of loss increases, the variation of actual from expected losses tends to decrease if the exposures remain the same. In less technical language, as a loss becomes more and more certain to happen, there is less and less uncertainty that it will not happen. And if a point is finally reached where an event is sure to happen, then there is no risk at all.

To illustrate, assume that employers A and B, each with 10,000 employees, are concerned about occupational injuries to workers. Employer A is in a "safe" industry, with the chance of loss of a disabling injury in its plant being equal to 0.01. Employer B is in a more dangerous industry, with its chance of loss equal to 0.25. It has been determined that the probable variation in injuries in employer A's plant will be no more than 20, whereas in employer B's plant the probable variation will not exceed 87. Thus, the degrees of objective risk are computed to be

$$\text{Objective risk }_A = \frac{20}{(0.01)(10,000)} = \frac{20}{100} = 20\%$$

$$\text{Objective risk }_B = \frac{87}{(0.25)(10,000)} = \frac{87}{2,500} = 3.5\%$$

Although B's chance of loss is much greater than A's, its degree of risk is only 17.5 percent of A's risk ($3.5 \div 20 = 0.175$). In general, the degree of objective risk will vary inversely with the chance of loss for any constant number of exposure units.

In summary, the two most important applications of the law of large numbers in relation to objective risk are as follows:

1. As the number of exposure units increases, the degree of risk decreases.
2. Given a constant number of exposure units, as the chance of loss increases, the degree of risk decreases.

Number of Exposure Units Required

Given the law of large numbers, risk managers know that as the number of exposure units becomes infinitely large, the actual loss frequency will approach the expected true loss frequency. But it is never possible for a single entity to group together an infinitely large number of exposures. Thus, the question arises as to how much error is introduced when a group is not sufficiently large. More precisely, a risk manager might ask, "How many exposure units must be grouped together in order to be 95 percent sure that the estimate of the maximum probable number of losses differs from expected losses by no more than 5 percent?"

It is assumed that the expected losses for a very large population of exposures either are known, can be estimated from industry-wide data, or can be determined subjectively. Essentially, the risk manager wishes to know how stable the loss experience will be, that is, how much objective risk must be accepted for a given number of exposure units. Certain mathematical and statistical laws help provide an answer to this question. Although the assumptions required by these laws may not always hold in the real world, they enable the risk manager to make an approximation that will be of considerable help in making a sound decision. The required assumption is that the losses occur in the manner assumed by the binomial formula. In other words, each loss occurs independently of each other loss, and the probability of loss is constant from occurrence to occurrence.

netlink

If you enjoy mathematics and statistics, you might want to consider a career as an actuary. Set your browser to the Society of Actuaries' home page (http://www.soa.org) to learn more about the role of actuaries in the insurance industry. Also, read accounts of a day in the life of an actuary at http://www.beanactuary.org.

A simple mathematical formula is available that enables insurers to estimate the number of exposures required for a given degree of accuracy. However, unless mathematical tools—such as the following formula—are used with great caution and are interpreted by experienced persons, erroneous conclusions may be reached; the following formula is included only as an illustration of how such tools can be of help in guiding an insurer to reduce risk. The formula is based on the assumption that losses in an insured population are distributed normally and concerns only the occurrence of a loss and not the evaluation of the size of the loss, which is an entirely different problem and beyond the scope of this book.

This formula is based on the knowledge that the normal distribution is an approximation of the binomial distribution and that known percentages of losses will fall within 1, 2, 3, or more standard deviations from the mean:

$$N = \frac{S^2 \, p(1-p)}{E^2}$$

where p = probability of loss
N = the number of exposure units sufficient for a given degree of accuracy
E = the degree of accuracy required, expressed as a ratio of actual losses to the total number in the sample
S = the number of standard deviations of the distribution

The value of S indicates the level of confidence that can be stated for the results. Thus, if S is 1, it is known with 68 percent confidence that losses will be as predicted; if S is 2, there is 95 percent confidence; and if S is 3, there is 99 percent confidence.[1]

As an example, suppose that in the preceding case the probability of loss is 0.3 (not an unusual probability in certain areas for collision of automobiles) and that it is desired that there be 95 percent confidence that the actual loss ratio (number of losses divided by the total number of exposure units) will not differ from the expected 0.3 by more than 2 percentage points. In other words, the risk manager wants to know how many units there must be in order to be 95 percent confident that the number of losses out of each 100 units will fall in the range from 28 to 32. Substitution in the formula yields

$$N = \frac{S^2 \, p(1-p)}{E^2} = \frac{(2^2)(0.3)(0.7)}{(0.02)^2}$$

or 2,100 exposure units. The value of S is 2 in this case because of the requirement of a 95 percent confidence interval statement. That is, it is known that 95 percent of all losses will fall within a range of 2 standard deviations of the mean.

In the preceding illustration the probability of loss was very large. For many risks, it is somewhat unusual to experience such large probabilities. It is much more common for the probability of loss to be about 5 percent or less. If the probability of loss is only 5 percent, the risk manager will undoubtedly want a higher standard of accuracy than was true in the preceding case. The example in Table 2-3 illustrates that 7,600 exposure units are needed in this situation to have 95 percent confidence that the actual loss ratio will be within 10 percent of the expected.

The example in Table 2-3 illustrates a fundamental truth about risk management: *When the probability of loss is small, a larger number of exposure units is needed for an acceptable degree of risk than is commonly recognized.* Mathematical formulas such as the one used in these examples can assist risk managers considerably in making estimates of the degree of risk assumed with given numbers in an exposure group.

TABLE 2-3	Calculating the Number of Exposure Units Required

Probability of loss $= p = 0.05$
Degree of accuracy $= E = 0.1 \times 0.05 = 0.005$
Degree of confidence $= S = 2$ standard deviations
Exposure units needed $= N$

$$N = \frac{S^2 \, p(1-p)}{E^2} = \frac{(2^2)(0.05)(0.95)}{(0.005)^2} = 7,600$$

---

1   J. T. McClave, P. G. Benson, and T. Sincich, *A First Course in Business Statistics*, 7th ed. (Upper Saddle River, N.J.: Prentice Hall, 1998), 70.

SUMMARY

1. Loss exposure checklists, financial statement analysis, flowcharts, contract analysis, on-site inspections of property, and the statistical analysis of past losses can be helpful in identifying risk.

2. After risks are identified, they should be evaluated regarding their expected frequency of occurrence, the probable severity of associated losses, the maximum probable loss, and the maximum possible loss. Risk mapping is one way to catalogue the wide variety of risks identified.

3. A probability distribution is a mutually exclusive and collectively exhaustive list of all events that result from a chance process. Risk managers use both empirical and theoretical probability distributions of losses in evaluating identified risks.

4. The mean, median, and mode are ways of measuring the center of a probability distribution.

5. The variance, standard deviation, and coefficient of variation are important ways of measuring the variation of actual from expected experience.

6. Three theoretical distributions that are especially useful for risk managers are the normal, binomial, and Poisson distributions.

7. Value-at-risk (VAR) analysis involves the construction of probability distributions of risks alone and in various combinations to obtain estimates of the risk of loss at various probability levels.

8. The law of large numbers indicates that as the number of exposure units increases, the degree of risk decreases. And, given a constant number of exposure units, as the chance of loss increases, the degree of risk decreases.

9. When the probability of loss is very small, a larger number of exposure units is needed to achieve the same degree of risk than when the probability of loss is large.

internet*exercises*

1. Many software products are available to help a business assess its level of risk. Search for a description of a current product on the World Wide Web. (Several products are described at http://www.riskworld.com under the software link.) Read the description of the product you choose. What information do you think risk managers would need to have available for the software to help them in their decision making?

2. Most catastrophe predictions involve the use of past loss data. The Web site located at http://weather.unisys.com displays the patterns traveled by past hurricanes and tropical storms. Look for the hurricane data link and then enter the year of the storm. Use this site to track the 1992 Hurricane Andrew. How could a risk manager for a firm with significant property exposures in Miami, Florida, use this information?

QUESTIONS FOR REVIEW AND DISCUSSION

1. List and briefly describe three methods of identifying risks.
2. Identify the important elements in risk evaluation.
3. Explain why theoretical probability distributions are useful for risk managers.
4. If a peril is expected to result in a loss with an expected annual frequency of 0.02 and an expected severity of $1 million, calculate the expected annual loss. If another peril is expected to result in a loss with an expected annual frequency of 20 and an expected severity of $1,000, calculate the expected annual loss.
5. PTY Company has experienced the following numbers of losses in the past 10 years: 3, 4, 3, 3, 1, 0, 2, 2, 3, 3. Calculate the mean, median, mode, variance, standard deviation, and coefficient of variation for this loss experience.
6. MDC Corporation's losses are assumed to be distributed normally, with a mean of $10,000 and a standard deviation of $2,000. Calculate the probable range of losses, given that the MDC risk manager desires 99 percent confidence in the estimate. How would the range change if only 95 percent confidence was needed?
7. Losses to Callaghan Company are assumed to be distributed normally, with a mean of $75,000 and a standard deviation of $4,000. Calculate the probable range of losses if the risk manager desires 95 percent confidence in the estimate.
8. QAZ Company owns a fleet of 100 automobiles, for which the probability of loss is approximately equal to 0.05. Use the Poisson distribution to estimate the probability that QAZ will suffer two or fewer auto accidents next year.
9. If a corporation doubles the number of exposure units, what may be said to happen to the degree of objective risk? Explain your answer and state the basic principle illustrated.
10. WFS Corporation owns three cars and two buildings. Because these numbers are not very large, what options are available to the WFS risk manager in evaluating possible losses to the cars and the buildings? Explain.
11. A risk manager stated, "If a risk is to be properly controlled, it must be perceived, and it must be appreciated in terms of probable frequency and possible severity." The writer went on to give two examples, as follows:
    a. A company brings together in two airplane flights nearly all of its dealers and distributors from a certain country.
    b. Another company makes a special contract with the government of a foreign country to set up a factory in that country. Special machinery is to be sent by ship, and customs duty is to be waived if the machinery arrives by a certain date. For each of these situations, indicate the potential loss exposure for the company.
12. What data would be most helpful to include in a risk management information system designed particularly for an automobile manufacturer? How might the RMIS requirements for such a firm differ from those of an amusement theme park? Explain.
13. What do you think would be the advantages and disadvantages of the risk-adjusted return on capital (RAROC) concept, as viewed from the standpoint of management of a large multinational corporation? Explain.

chapter 3

Property and Liability Loss Exposures

In this chapter, you will learn about property and liability loss exposures. A risk manager must identify, treat, and review risk management decisions concerning such exposures every day. During this process, the risk manager must also be aware of insurance markets.

Insurance markets are subject to what is often called the **underwriting cycle**; that is, prices, coverages, and deductibles exist in an ever-changing marketplace. This cycle is composed of two distinct parts: hard and soft markets. In a **hard market**, premiums increase at a very rapid rate. For instance, commercial general liability premiums rose 41 percent in 2002. Higher deductibles were also required, and contract provisions were restricted. In some cases, coverage was not available at any price. Thus, in hard markets, a risk manager's options are limited. The property and liability loss exposures can be identified and measured, but the cost and availability of insurance may complicate effective decision making.

The opposite of a hard market is a **soft market**, in which premiums may be gradually increasing or actually declining. For example, after the hard market of 1984–86, total premiums for business liability actually declined from 1988 through 1991. The soft market had arrived. Deductibles were lower, contract terms were more attractive, and higher limits of liability were available. While the soft market began in 1988, it continued into 2000. This time period (1988–2000) is the longest soft market in the history of the commercial property–liability insurance industry. Even the record losses from Hurricane Andrew and the Northridge earthquake did not harden it. A combination of declining investment returns and losses from the terrorist attacks of September 11 brought a return of the hard market in 2001, and it has persisted through 2003.

 In reading the material on loss identification, you should think about the effects that hard and soft markets have on how risk managers treat these loss exposures.

CHAPTER OBJECTIVES

After studying this chapter, you should be able to

1. Identify the kinds of property subject to loss and the types of losses that may occur.
2. Define the basic payments made under liability insurance contracts.
3. Distinguish between criminal law and civil law.
4. Understand what a tort is.
5. Describe negligence and the characteristics of a negligent act.
6. Explain some of the defenses against a claim of negligence.
7. Discuss factors that are causing individuals and businesses to maintain higher standards of care.
8. Identify the basic types of liability exposure and give an explanation of each.

PROPERTY LOSS EXPOSURES

The two major categories of property are real property and personal property. **Real property** has been defined as "land, all structures permanently attached to the land, and whatever is growing on the land." **Personal property** has been defined as "all property other than real property, and therefore its primary characteristic is that it is not permanently attached to real property."[1]

Common examples of real property are buildings and attachments to buildings, land, and crops or other items growing on the land. Personal property is everything else, such as automobiles, money, clothes, radios, furniture, sailboats, jewelry, tickets to a rock concert, textbooks, paintings, personal computers, airplanes, chemicals, and animals.

When property is damaged, there may be both direct and indirect losses. A **direct loss** occurs when there is damage to property, as when a fire damages a home. An **indirect loss** occurs when a direct loss causes expenses to increase or revenues to decline. For example, after a fire, the owner of a home can no longer rent the basement apartment to college students, and the rent is lost. Also, additional funds must be spent by the homeowner for rental of a motel room or an apartment while the home is being repaired.

Because of this dual nature of property losses, many insurance contracts insure both direct and indirect losses in the same contract. For instance, a homeowners' policy insures direct losses to real and personal property as well as indirect losses that result when the insured dwelling is damaged by an insured peril.

When dealing with property insurance, there are usually only two parties to the contract: the insured and the insurer. Payments are made to the insured for covered losses caused by insured perils. If a person purchases fire insurance and a windstorm damages the property, there is no coverage. However, if the insured accidentally starts a fire, it is covered. Property insurance pays the policyholder without regard to fault.

Not all types of property are insurable. Generally, insurance contracts only cover loss to tangible property. Coverage cannot be purchased for loss of goodwill or loss of a copyright. Also, raw land is difficult to insure. Most flood and earthquake insurance contracts exclude damage to land. Individuals and corporate risk managers must take this fact into consideration when evaluating property loss exposures and how to treat them.

Of course, one of the big problems with flood insurance is that people do not purchase it. During the great flood in the summer of 1993, billions of dollars worth of property was damaged in the midwestern United States. However, much of the property was uninsured. About 40 percent of the farmers in the affected areas had flood insurance that covered loss of a crop that was planted but could not be harvested. Another group of farmers lost income because the floods kept them from being able to plant their crops. There is a flood insurance program underwritten by the federal government with a special rider, entitled the Preventive Planting Policy, but very few farmers purchased this endorsement.

Although the 1993 flood was large, the damage it caused ($3 to $5 billion) was not nearly as huge as the devastation that Hurricane Andrew caused. With total losses estimated at $18 billion or greater, Andrew was clearly one of the largest natural disasters ever. Because of its magnitude, insurers had difficulty obtaining reinsurance policies to cover their catastrophic loss exposures. As a consequence, insurance companies had to reduce their number of customers in Florida.

---

1   Jerome Trupin and Arthur L. Flitner, *Commercial Property Risk Management and Insurance*, 7th ed. (Malvern, PA: American Institute for Chartered Property Casualty Underwriters, 2003), 1.6.

PROFESSIONAL PERSPECTIVES

Real Estate Boom

Often when one thinks of large losses from a single event, the picture of an airplane crash or many people killed in a burning building comes to mind. However, the largest losses from single events are usually property losses. For instance, on October 23, 1989, Phillips Petroleum suffered one of the largest land-based property losses ever. The explosion at the Phillips plastics plant located in Pasadena, Texas, registered 3.2 on the Richter scale and was started by the escape of hydrocarbons. At least seven workers were killed, and direct and indirect property losses were expected to exceed $1.1 billion. The direct property losses were estimated to be $700 million and indirect losses, $400 million. Phillips had $1.3 billion in property insurance and suffered a loss of only $70 million, which was its deductible. It took more than two years to rebuild the plant.

Source: Michael Bradford, "Blast Rips Phillips Complex," *Business Insurance*, October 30, 1989, 1, 66.

Sex and Property Loss Exposures

Not all property losses occur to objects. For insurance purposes, animals are considered property. Firms that work with animals must be able to manage loss to or from the animals and learn to manage the animals during the mating season.

> Yes, risk managers even have to manage sex risks. Actually, the management of sex is routine for firms that work with animals. An example is Ringling Bros. and Barnum & Bailey Circus. The company owns many different types of animals, ranging from goat kids to elephants. While the firm's employees are experts at working with animals, they must be aware of the "mating season." A normally quiet and friendly animal may become quite aggressive. For instance, male Asian elephants are more difficult to handle when the females are in heat. Attempting to train a male elephant under such circumstances is not a wise move for any trainer or circus owner. To manage this situation, the circus mainly uses female Asian elephants for performances and males are primarily used for breeding purposes. This procedure protects the firm's property, employees, and the elephants.[2]

LIABILITY EXPOSURES

One of the most serious financial risks that risk managers must deal with is that of loss through legal liability for harm caused to others. Insurance for liability losses is more complex than property insurance, because people other than the insured and the insurer are involved. In addition, liability is usually determined by proving negligence, a concept that is difficult for most people to understand. Negligence as a basis for determining liability for industrial accidents and illness has been supplanted by workers' compensation laws in most cases. Public attention has recently been focused on another area of negligence, that of medical malpractice, and legislative solutions for handling this risk have been proposed.

The following case is illustrative of the sometimes catastrophic losses that occur because of negligence. An 11-year-old boy was hit on the right side of the head in a schoolyard fight. He was taken to the hospital, but X-rays showed no evidence of skull fracture. He was sent home, although he was pale and groggy and perspiring heavily. When he did not improve by

2   Sally Roberts, "Keeping the Circus Safe," *Business Insurance*, May 13, 1966, 15.

that night, his father took him to the hospital, and this time doctors decided to operate. They removed a large blood clot pressing on his brain. It was determined that had the doctors operated immediately the first time, the boy would have made a good recovery; because of the delay, however, permanent brain damage occurred. The boy was left mute and paralyzed from the neck down. The family sued the doctors, the hospital, and the school district for negligence and was awarded damages of $4,025,000.[3] Because of this case, many pediatricians will no longer treat children with head injuries; they refer the patients to neurosurgeons.

As another example, consider two major airline crashes in the United States. In July 1985, an L-1011 jet crashed in Dallas, Texas, and 137 persons were killed. Insurers reserved $125 million for the loss. Also in July, but four years later, a DC-10 crashed in Sioux City, Iowa, and that loss was estimated to be between $110 million and $120 million.

Because the losses occurred in the United States (as opposed to occurring in a foreign country where international agreements would restrict payments to injured airplane passengers), the liability payouts were large.[4] Given such large loss exposures to liability claims, it is little wonder that major airlines carry hundreds of millions of dollars of liability insurance.

The High Cost of Asbestos

In January 2004, U.S. energy firm Halliburton reported a $1.1 billion charge to cover claims from people suffering from asbestos-related diseases. It faces more than 300,000 claims from people who have been affected by asbestos in former Halliburton products. In the past many building materials contained asbestos, which when in dust form is a carcinogen. Although Halliburton has a total of $2 billion due from insurance firms, it has calculated that it faces $4 billion in liabilities.[5] In addition to the costs that will be borne by industry in general, researchers have estimated that asbestos liability could ultimately cost U.S. insurers as much as $65 billion.

Because of the complexity of liability losses and liability insurance, the remainder of this chapter is concerned with liability. Specific types of liability exposures will be discussed later in the chapter. First we will consider the types of liability damages, criminal and civil law, torts, negligence, and changes in tort law that have affected liability.

TYPES OF LIABILITY DAMAGES

Individuals may be sued for numerous types of liability damages. However, insurance contracts are designed to pay only for certain types of losses. Because the primary focus of this text is the use of insurance to handle risk, it is appropriate to identify the damages that insurance contracts will cover early in the chapter so that you will be better able to understand subsequent material in both this and following chapters. In terms of liability, insurance

netlink

Attorneys find the Internet to be a valuable tool for informing potential claimants about liability issues in their localities. Set your browser to http://www.chicagolegalnet.com and sample the legal topics and issues addressed by one such firm.

---

3 "The Patient Becomes the Plaintiff," *Time*, March 24, 1975, 60.
4 "Jury Rules Delta Not Negligent in 1985 Dallas Jetliner Crash," *Business Insurance*, May 8, 1989, 1; Carolyn Aldred and Linda J. Collins, "Crash Won't Hike Rates," *Business Insurance*, July 24, 1989, 1.
5 Heather Tomlinson, "Halliburton Sets Aside $1.1 Billion for Claims," *The Guardian*, January 30, 2004, online edition.

PROFESSIONAL PERSPECTIVES

The Great Chicago Flood

On April 13, 1992, a section of an underground freight tunnel collapsed in Chicago. Ordinarily, such an event would cause little damage; however, this tunnel was beneath the Chicago River. More than 250 million gallons of water flooded the tunnel and caused more than $300 million in losses. Much of the loss was indirect (loss of business income or increase in expenses). Firms lost rents, parking fees, spoiled food, and banquet bookings, and the Chicago Board of Trade had to close. DePaul University's downtown campus had to shut down for a week before new facilities could be made operational. Several major downtown department stores also were forced to close. Adding to the difficulty of determining the nature of the loss was the question of whether it was due to a flood or just water damage; often flood coverage is different from water damage coverage. In December 1995, the Illinois Appellate Court ruled that the state's sovereign immunity law protected the City of Chicago against liability for losses that did not include related property damage. Most firms that suffered loss of income did not have direct property damage. In a related case, the U.S. Supreme Court, in May 1996, ruled that Great Lakes Dredge and Docking Company, the firm that punctured the century-old underground freight tunnel, was protected by federal admiralty law. The firm was ultimately liable for $40 million in damages due to lawsuits.

Sources: Sarah J. Harty and Gavin Souter, "A Flood of Questions," *Business Insurance*, April 20, 1992, 1; Sara Marley and Lori Block "Questions Include How Much Will Insurer's Payout, Who's to Blame," April 27, 1992, 60; Sara Marley, "Flood Waters Subside, but Questions Remain," May 4, 1992, 48; Sara Marley, "Insurers Subrogating Chicago Flood Losses Force Big Obstacles," December 14, 1992, 29.

policies are usually restricted to pay for bodily injury, property damage, personal injury, and legal expenses.

Bodily Injury

Bodily injury liability includes liability for losses a person may incur because his or her body or mind has been harmed. Such losses include payments for medical bills, loss of income, rehabilitation costs, loss of services (household as well as marital), pain and suffering damages, and punitive damages.

Pain and suffering damages are designed to compensate the injured party for the pain endured due to the negligent behavior of the defendant. They are considered noneconomic damages and are often greater than economic losses, such as loss of income and medical expenses.

Punitive damages are assessed when it is deemed that the defendant acted in a grossly negligent manner and deserves to have an example made of his or her behavior so as to discourage others from acting that way. Punitive damages are usually imposed in addition to other damages and can be for very large amounts. In 18 states, including New York and California, insurance policies are not allowed to pay punitive damages. The reasoning is that the defendant is not punished if the insurance company pays the punitive damages.

Property Damage

Liability for damage to real and personal property may arise. There may be a loss from actual damage to the property, as well as loss of use of the property. The loss of use exposure may include both loss of income, because the property cannot be used, and payments for extra expenses, because property must be rented to replace the damaged property.

PROFESSIONAL PERSPECTIVES

Punitive Damages

Punitive damages have become a problem for risk managers. General Motors (GM) lost a lawsuit involving a model of pickup truck that has the gas tank located outside the truck's steel frame. One of these trucks was struck on the side of the gas tank during a crash; it exploded, killing the teenage driver. A jury awarded the parents of the teenager $105 million, of which $101 million was for punitive damages. Between 1973 and 1987, GM built about 4.7 million pickup trucks with side-mounted gas tanks. While the verdict was subsequently thrown out by the Georgia Court of Appeals in 1994, by 2003 it is estimated that GM had paid at least $495 million to settle claims from accidents involving these pickups. In a recent U.S. Supreme Court case, some restriction was placed on

punitive damages. The case involved Dr. Ira Gore and his new BMW. His new vehicle was damaged in shipment, and $600 was spent by BMW to repaint it. Dr. Gore was most upset that this fact was not disclosed to him. He sued and won a judgment for $4,000 in compensatory damages and $4 million for punitive damages. In this case, there was no bodily injury to anyone and actually little harm. In addition, the court noted there was no evidence of bad faith on BMW's part, no adverse effects on car safety, and no deliberately false misstatements made. Yet a $4 million award was given. This amount was deemed to be high as it was 1,000 times the amount of the compensatory award!

Sources: "GM Hit With $10.5 Million Award," *Business Insurance*, February 8, 1993, 2, 22; "Supreme Court Refuses to Hear Redlining Case," *Federal and State Insurance Week*, February 26, 1996; "Court's Decision Not to Hear HUD Case Disappoints Insurer Groups," *The Standard*, March 1, 1996.

Personal Injury

Personal injury liability losses result from libel, slander, invasion of privacy, false arrest, and the like. Typically, **libel** involves written, printed, or pictorial material that damages a person's reputation by defaming or ridiculing the person. **Slander** involves spoken words that are defamatory and/or injurious to a person's reputation.

Legal Expenses

Individuals or organizations being sued must be prepared to retain a lawyer for their defense, as the defense process can be very costly. In some types of loss exposure, such as product liability, the cost of defense may be as great as or greater than damage awards.

CRIMINAL AND CIVIL LAW

People can generally be held accountable under two different types of legal proceeding: criminal and civil. **Criminal law** is directed toward wrongs against society. Examples of such wrongs would be murder, robbery, rape, and assault with a deadly weapon. Charges under criminal law are made by a government body or agent, such as a city, county, state, or federal prosecutor, and the guilty party is subject to fine and/or imprisonment.

Civil law is directed toward wrongs against individuals and organizations. A person may be tried for criminal and civil charges for the same action. For example, if you murder someone, the state will try you for murder, and the heirs of the murdered person may sue you in civil court for damages. Normally, in a civil action the guilty party is only required to pay a fine and/or damages, to perform a certain action, or to refrain from performing an action. Breach of contract and negligent acts are two examples of cases that would go to a civil court.

TORTS

A **tort** is a legal injury or wrong to another that arises out of actions other than breach of contract, in which courts will provide a remedy by allowing recovery in an action for damages. A **legal injury** results when a person's rights are wrongfully invaded. Examples of such rights are the right of personal privacy, the right to enjoy one's property unmolested, and the right to be free from personal injury. Examples of torts are libel, slander, assault, and negligence. We are mainly concerned here with protection against the financial consequences of civil action arising from only one of these torts, negligence, which arises from the omission or commission of an act. Insurance against intentional torts, such as false arrest, libel, slander, trespass, battery, and assault, is also available.

BASIC LAW OF NEGLIGENCE

The basic law of **negligence** has many threads that are sometimes difficult for the layperson to disentangle. To see what this basic law is all about, one needs first to understand what conditions must be met before an act is considered actionable negligence. Next, one must appreciate what defenses are recognized by the courts for the protection of defendants. No matter how wrong a defendant may have been, if a suitable defense that satisfies the law can be raised, the defendant may be shielded from liability. Finally, it is necessary to appreciate how this interaction of negligence and defenses operates in the many different sets of relationships that make up our legal culture—that is, relationships that exist between employer and employee, landlord and tenant, buyer and seller, principal and agent, and driver and pedestrian. Additional standards of conduct are applied in each relationship. The law is extremely complex and is changing constantly; therefore, only a summary of highlights can be given here.

The Negligent Act

Negligence is the failure to exercise the degree of care required by law. What is required by law is understood to be the conduct that a reasonably prudent individual would exercise to prevent harm.

A Negative Act

A negligent act may be the failure to do something (a **negative act**) as much as it may be the doing of something (a **positive act**). It arises from a breach of legal duty to another. One may drive an automobile into the rear of another car. As such, this is a positive act. An example of a negligent act that is a negative act is failing to signal a turn.

Negligence may be the failure to act when there is a duty to act. Thus, a gas company was held liable for a loss when it had agreed to inspect a customer's gas pipe but failed to do so.[6]

A Voluntary Act

A negligent act is one that is done voluntarily—it is a **voluntary act**. If an act is done involuntarily, the act is excusable. If such were the case, the plaintiff could not collect damages. For example, it is easy to see that if one person puts a gun into the hand of another, directs the second person's aim at a target, and helps pull the trigger, the second person is hardly a free agent; and if the shot injures a person, there is doubt that the second person is necessarily negligent.

---

6 *Trimbo v Minnesota Valley Natural Gas Company*, Minnesota Supreme Court, 110 N.W. 2d 168 (1961).

A negligent act is not excused because there was no intention to cause harm. Unintentional injury to another may give rise to both criminal and civil action. Negligent acts are essentially those in which the defendant may try to be excused by saying, "I didn't mean to."

The law does not expect perfection to be the standard by which conduct is judged. The care expected of a trained physician who is a specialist is higher than that expected from an intern. The degree of care expected from a child is different from that expected from an adult.

An Imputed Act

Liability for a negligent act may be imputed from another person. Thus, one is liable not only for one's own acts but also for the negligent acts of servants or agents acting in the course of their employment or agency. Employers may be sued because of the negligent acts of their employees. These **imputed acts** may also create what is called **vicarious liability**. Liability for the negligence of another can rest on a contract to assume that liability. Thus, a baseball club may be held liable for accidents arising out of the use of a ballpark owned by the city and leased from it, simply because the club had assumed such liability under the lease.

Proximate Cause of the Loss

To give rise to action for damages, a negligent act must, of course, be the proximate cause of the loss; there must be an unbroken chain of events leading from the negligent act to the damage sustained. Suppose person A negligently damages person B's car, and this causes B to be late for an important business engagement. B charges that, as a result, a sale was lost that would have netted $50,000. Can B add $50,000 to the claim for damages? Carrying the example further, suppose B claims that not only did he lose the sale but, as a result of losing it, he also lost his job. Further, because of the lost job, his wife had to go to work, necessitating the expense of purchasing a second automobile and of hiring a nanny for the children. May B also add these expenses to his claim? It is clear that the court must draw a line in determining proximate cause, or a host of sources for damage claims would open up.

DEFENSES AGAINST NEGLIGENCE CLAIMS

Even if a person is guilty of a negligent act, certain defenses can be used to bar liability for such negligence. These defenses may be based on contributory negligence, assumed risk, or guest–host statutes.

Contributory Negligence

In **common law**, if both parties are to blame in a given accident, each is guilty of **contributory negligence** and may not collect against the other, even if the defendant was 90 percent to blame and the plaintiff was only 10 percent to blame. One must come into court with "clean hands."

Assumed Risk

Under certain circumstances, a defendant may raise the defense that the plaintiff has no cause for action because the plaintiff assumed the risk of harm from (1) the conduct of the defendant, (2) the condition of the premises, or (3) the defendant's product. Managements of baseball parks are sometimes sued when baseballs hit members of the viewing crowd. Assuming that reasonable care has been exercised to provide appropriate wire screens, courts usually hold that a person who views a ball game is assuming the risks normally attributed to viewers and must accept the consequences as a normal result of a game.

Guest–Host Statutes

An exception to the general trend toward absolute liability in our society has been the passage of what are known as **guest–host statutes**. These laws relate to the standard of care owed by an automobile driver to a passenger. The general effect of the laws is to reduce the standard of care owed to a guest in a car in such a manner that the guest must prove that the driver was guilty of gross negligence or willful injury, such as might be the case if the driver were intoxicated. Under guest–host laws, ordinary negligence will not be sufficient to sustain a case against the driver. In a number of states, guest–host statutes have been declared unconstitutional.

FACTORS LEADING TO HIGHER STANDARDS OF CARE

During the past 20 years, dramatic changes have occurred in tort law. These changes have led to situations in which individuals and corporations are held to a much higher standard of care. The following paragraphs examine the factors that have influenced this trend.

Expanding Application of Liability

Courts tend increasingly to impose liability in new factual settings. For example, traditionally a manufacturer might not often have been held liable for making a faulty product, such as a gas tank that leaked and caused an accident. However, decisions in California held a manufacturer and a dealer liable for loss from what was defined as an unsafe gas tank design. In another case, the owner of a chimpanzee that caused 10 persons to contract hepatitis was held liable. Before this case, most suits involved situations in which an animal caused an injury, not an illness. In still another case, an airline was charged with undue delay in obtaining proper medical treatment for a passenger who suffered a heart attack.

Weakening of Defenses Against Liability

Workers' compensation was the first major example of social insurance in the United States. All states have now passed this type of legislation, which represents an abandonment of the principles of negligence law in determining liability for occupational injury. Before these laws were passed (most were enacted between 1910 and 1920), the principles of negligence governed, and an employee had to seek damages from the employer for occupational injuries. Because this system proved inefficient, time consuming, and generally unsatisfactory, especially for the employee, it was replaced by workers' compensation laws. The employee now receives a payment for on-the-job injuries according to a schedule set up for this purpose, regardless of whom, if anyone, is to blame for the injury.

Similar principles have been applied in the several states that have passed no-fault laws regarding bodily injuries in automobile accidents (see Chapter 14). In some of these laws, the rights of the plaintiff to bring legal action for negligence against other drivers have been restricted.

The defense of contributory negligence likewise has been weakened in various ways. In all but four states and the District of Columbia, a statute has been enacted that replaces this principle with one called **comparative negligence**. Under this doctrine, the liability of the defendant is reduced by the extent to which the plaintiff was contributively negligent. If the plaintiff was 20 percent negligent, the defendant is liable for only 80 percent of the plaintiff's damages. In some states, the plaintiff recovers nothing if he or she is more than 50 percent at fault.

Another way in which the defense of contributory negligence has been weakened is in the **last clear chance rule**. Under this rule, a plaintiff who was contributively negligent may still have a cause of action against the defendant if it can be shown that the defendant had a last clear chance before the accident to avoid injuring the plaintiff but failed to do so. Thus, it is possible that a jaywalker may collect if hit by a motorist who had a chance to swerve but did not.

Res Ipsa Loquitur

Another illustration of the trend toward absolute liability lies in the more frequent use of a rule known as **res ipsa loquitur**—"the thing speaks for itself." Under this rule, a plaintiff may sometimes collect without actually proving negligence on the part of the defendant. It should be noted that under common law, before an action can be sustained against a party, negligence must be shown; that is, it must be shown that there was some failure on the part of the defendant to use the degree of care required of a reasonably prudent person in the same circumstance. Testimony of witnesses and of the injured parties must usually be brought to bear upon the case.

Res ipsa loquitur may be applied to establish a case against the defendant when (1) the defendant is in a position to know the cause of the accident and the plaintiff is not, (2) the defendant had exclusive control of the instrumentality that caused the accident, and (3) the use of the instrumentality would not normally cause injuries without the existence of negligence in its operation. As may be guessed, this doctrine has been used frequently in aircraft and medical malpractice liability cases.

Expansion of Imputed Liability

The passage of vicarious liability laws provide still more evidence of the stricter view of negligence taken by society today. The effect of vicarious liability laws is to place liability on the owner of a car for the negligence of the driver, thereby expanding the common law rule applicable to employers and principals. A number of states have such laws. Thus, in these states, under certain circumstances the owner of a car may be held liable simply because in good faith he or she loaned the car to someone and that person negligently caused harm.

A major problem faced by large corporations is **joint and several liability**. When an accident occurs and several different parties are negligent, the plaintiff may sue and collect from one or more of the negligent parties. Under joint and several liability, the plaintiff can collect the entire judgment from a large corporation that was barely at fault, say 5 or 10 percent. The major **tort feasor** (person or organization liable) in such cases is often an individual or small corporation with little or no insurance.

The federal government established what is called **Superfund legislation** (comprehensive environmental response compensation and liability) to help fund the cleanup cost of major pollution sites. Under this law, persons or firms have joint and several liability. For example, if Don Jordan purchases a site that was previously occupied by a filling station and the government determines that it is a hazardous waste site because oil and gasoline seeped into the ground from leaky underground tanks, the Environmental Protection Agency (EPA) can require Don to pay for the cleanup. He is liable for the entire cost. If he can identify previous owners, then he can collect from them, but at his own cost. This legal doctrine (joint and several liability) places increased burdens on large corporations, for they have the funds to pay for the decontamination and the government does not have to look elsewhere for a responsible party. When the State of Georgia built the Georgia Dome (site of the 2000 Super Bowl), it had to pay $5 million for decontamination costs. One of the previous owners (a paint factory) had caused the pollution, but it was no longer in business. Because the doctrine of joint and several liability is so burdensome, corporations often fight the EPA about being a responsible party. It is estimated that more than 80 percent of the funds spent on the Superfund enforcement is for overhead (legal fees, etc.) and less than 20 percent for cleaning up the environment.

Changing Concepts of Damage

Another factor worth noting in assessing the trend toward absolute liability is the more liberal interpretation of what types of damages may be allowed in negligence actions. Courts generally allow as damages claims for medical bills, loss of income, loss of life, property damage, and other losses for which the proximate cause was negligence. Thus, damages have usually been allowed for such things as pain and suffering and loss of the conjugal relation by a spouse. However, damages have been awarded for such intangible losses as mental anguish, presumably under the theory that pain and suffering need not be physical to establish damages.[7]

Awards can also be used to punish defendants because their actions constituted gross negligence or willful and wanton misconduct. In a famous case in California involving an accident in a Ford Pinto, $100 million in punitive damages were awarded by the jury. On appeal, this amount was substantially reduced.

Every state allows punitive damages except Massachusetts, Nebraska, and Washington. As the idea of punitive damages is to punish the tort feasor, some states do not allow insurance policies to pay punitive damages. However, 32 states have no restrictions on insurance policies paying for punitive damages. In 38 states insurance is allowed to pay punitive damages when vicarious liability or other special circumstances exist.[8]

Increased Damage Awards

Not only have courts tended to widen the types of cases for which damages are awarded, but they have also tended to increase greatly the amounts of these damages. Various reasons have been advanced for this tendency of courts to be more generous than formerly in assessing the awards given in negligence actions. The effect of inflation in reducing the purchasing power of the dollar has undoubtedly had a considerable effect, especially in the 1980s. Perhaps the existence of liability insurance has caused juries to be more generous than they would be if it were known that the plaintiff would have to pay damages personally.

Because of unexpectedly large losses under liability insurance contracts in the mid-1980s, many insurers either began to withdraw from underwriting this coverage or raised insurance premiums to very high levels. In 2002 total U.S. tort system costs amounted to a "litigation tax" of $721 per U.S. citizen. The insurance industry is supporting various types of tort reform to be considered by state legislatures.[9] According to a poll by the American Tort Reform Association, 83 percent of Americans think there are too many lawsuits. These reforms included the following:

1. Imposing restrictions on the right to sue

2. Abolishing punitive damages in civil suits

3. Reducing the standard of care required in making products to that standard existing at the time the product was made instead of at the time the loss occurred

4. Placing a ceiling on noneconomic damages, such as pain and suffering

5. Repealing the **collateral source rule**, under which courts could ignore other sources from which a plaintiff might receive indemnity for loss. Repealing this rule would reduce the amounts awarded to liable insured parties.

---

7   Harold Chase, "Changing Concepts of Legal Liability and Their Effect on Liability Insurance," proceedings (82nd Annual Meeting, Fire Underwriters Association of the Pacific, March 5–6, 1958), 24.

8   "Post-Judgment Interest, Prejudgment Interest, Punitive Damages: United States and Canada," American Re-Insurance, 2002.

9   "U.S. Tort Costs: 2002 Update, Trends and Findings on the Cost of the U.S. Tort System," Tillinghast-Towers Perrin, 2002.

Median liability verdicts for medical malpractice increased from $457,500 to $1,000,000 from 1996 to 2001, an increase of 119 percent (see Table 3-1). Mean awards increased 107 percent. Both award figures increased faster than the rate of inflation. On the product liability side, median awards increased from $700,000 to $1,500,000, or by 114 percent, and mean awards from $2,670,917 to $9,113,218, or by 241 percent. Clearly, mean awards have risen very rapidly and have been trending higher since 1996. Regardless of how one might choose to interpret these data, it is safe to say that awards have been increasing faster than the rate of inflation in these two categories.

 ## TYPES OF LIABILITY EXPOSURES

Risk managers must be concerned with numerous types of liability exposures. These exposures arise out of different functions performed and standards of care required of persons or organizations. The situations or relationships reviewed in the following paragraphs include contractual, employer–employee, and property owner–tenant liabilities; consumption of products; completed operations of a contractor; professional acts; principal–agent liability; and the ownership and operation of automobiles. Insurance to cover these liability exposures is discussed in later chapters.

Contractual Liability

Under the concept of contractual liability, one's liability may be imputed to another by contract. For example, a city may require that a street paving contractor hold the city harmless for all negligence arising out of the operations of the contractor. In this way, suits that might otherwise be directed against the city will be directed against the contractor. Similarly, a railroad may make a contract with a manufacturer that if there is any negligence action arising out of the operation of the railroad's locomotives or trains that have entered the manufacturer's property on a spur track to pick up shipments, the manufacturer will assume the liability. The railroad's liability has thus been transferred by means of a contract. Other common contracts by which liability is transferred are leases, contracts to perform services or to supply goods.

Employer–Employee Liability

Employers are still subject to the law of negligence with respect to employment not covered by workers' compensation laws. In fact, workers' compensation laws do not cover all classes

TABLE 3-1   **Liability Claims**

Year	Medical Malpractice		Product Liability	
	Median	Mean	Median	Mean
1996	$ 457,000	$1,884,633	$ 700,000	$2,670,917
1997	500,000	1,930,540	525,000	3,336,679
1998	700,000	2,920,915	1,002,625	2,691,619
1999	700,000	3,288,228	1,600,000	5,917,968
2000	1,000,000	3,409,684	1,775,000	6,054,674
2001	1,000,000	3,902,058	1,500,000	9,113,218

Source: *2002 Current Award Trends in Personal Injury*, Jury Verdict Series (Horsham, PA: LRP Publications, 2003).

of employees. For example, farm workers and employees of a firm that hires less than a specified number of people are often excluded from coverage. Railroad employees and sailors are also exempt from workers' compensation laws.

The duties owed by an employer to employees, breach of which may give rise to liability, are the following:

1. The employer must provide a safe place to work.
2. The employer must employ individuals reasonably competent to carry out their tasks.
3. The employer must warn of danger.
4. The employer must furnish appropriate and safe tools.
5. The employer must set up and enforce proper rules of conduct of employees, as they relate to safe working procedures.[10]

If a garage provides a jack to raise automobiles but does not take steps to see that it is in good working condition and the employee using the jack is injured because the jack breaks (through no fault of the worker), the employer has probably breached a common law duty to the employee. An employee who disregards danger signals or fails to use the tools provided and is injured as a result is guilty of at least contributory negligence and under common law cannot recover. This would not affect the worker's right to workers' compensation.

The employer may use the common law defenses in suits by employees, providing these defenses have not been lost for one reason or another. If a worker brings an action against an employer for some breach of care, the employer may argue either that the worker was partly to blame (contributory negligence defense) or that the worker should have known that there were certain risks on the job and cannot complain because one of these risks materialized (assumption of risk).

Property Owner–Tenant Liability

In situations that involve the use of real property, the tenant or owner owes a certain degree of care to those who enter the premises. In most states, the degree of care is governed by the status of the person entering. Common law recognizes three classes of individuals who enter premises: invitees, licensees, and trespassers. The degree of care owed to an invitee is highest, and that owed to a trespasser is lowest.

Invitees are individuals who are invited on the premises for their own benefit as well as for that of the landlord or tenant. Typical invitees are customers in a retail store and guests at a hotel or at a public meeting. It is not sufficient merely to warn an invitee of danger; in addition, positive steps must be taken to protect an invitee from a known danger and to discover unknown dangers.

During the years 1980–82, several hotel accidents occurred that involved the property owner–tenant relationship. In each case, the persons injured were invitees. In the MGM Grand hotel fire in Las Vegas, 85 persons were killed, and 268 others were injured. Another fire at the Westchase Hilton in Houston killed 12 persons, and a fire at the Stouffers Inn in White Plains, New York, killed 26 persons. The collapse of the skywalk at the Kansas City Hyatt Regency resulted in 200 injured persons and 114 people killed. These accidents produced liability losses that were in the millions.[11]

Licensees are those who are on the premises for a legitimate purpose with the permission of the occupier. Typical licensees are police officers and fire fighters; others, who may be licensees or invitees, are milk delivery drivers, messengers, and meter readers. The land-

---

10 Thomas Gaskell Shearman and A. A. Redfield, *A Treatise on the Law of Negligence*, 1:438; 2:
441–42.
11 "Despite Disasters, Hotel Coverage Plentiful," *Business Insurance*, May 31, 1982, 3.

lord has the duty to warn the licensee of danger and to refrain from causing deliberate harm, but no other duty.

Trespassers include all those other than invitees and licensees who enter on the premises. No care is owed to a trespasser, but an owner cannot set a trap for or deliberately injure a trespasser. If the trespasser is injured by some unknown, hidden hazard, the landlord or tenant is not liable. In one case, an Iowa farmer set a shotgun trap for a prowler, and the prowler was shot in the leg. The injured man was able to collect damages from the farmer even though he had no right to be on the premises.

To illustrate these concepts, consider the owner of a retail store who has just polished the floors to such a high degree of slickness that they constitute a definite hazard to safe walking. A burglar enters the store at night, slips, and breaks a leg. Clearly, the owner is not required to pay any medical bills or otherwise compensate this trespasser. If a delivery driver had a similar accident, the courts would probably hold the owner innocent of negligence, provided that the owner had taken reasonable steps to warn people that the floors were slick. However, if a customer slipped and broke a leg on the slick floor, the courts would award damages if the store owner could have taken reasonable steps to reduce the hazard.

There is a current trend to abolish the classifications of trespasser, licensee, and invitee and to hold the occupier of the land liable under most circumstances for failure to exercise due care. Another example of landowner responsibility being expanded is the case of *Lee v Chicago Transit Authority (CTA)*.[12] In this case, Mr. Lee, a 46-year-old Korean immigrant who could not read English, walked onto the tracks of the CTA and was killed when he came in contact with the electrified third rail that provides power to operate commuter trains. Mr. Lee bypassed impediments to keep people away from the rail and, because he could not read English, ignored the signs warning of danger. In addition, he had a blood alcohol level of .341, which is more than three times higher than the legal limit for driving an automobile in Illinois. After several appeals, the Illinois Supreme Court found the CTA liable. The U.S. Supreme Court refused the case, so the Illinois court ruling was upheld. The CTA had to pay a judgment of $1.5 million.

Assumption of Liability by Tenant

When an individual leases a building, the question arises as to what extent the landlord is responsible for injuries to tenants. In general, when the landlord releases possession of the building, the tenant takes on whatever duty the landlord owes to members of the public. In some instances, the landlord is liable to a third person because the landlord has retained possession of the area where the third person was injured. For example, in the hallways of an apartment house occupied by several tenants, the owner has been held liable for negligence to tenants and to members of the public. In one case involving a tenant who tripped and fell over a crack in the cement slab leading to her apartment, a substantial judgment was rendered when the tenant's leg had to be amputated.[13] In another case, the landlord was held liable when a tenant was injured by a loose floorboard on the front porch that had been poorly repaired.[14]

In most states it is both common and legal to require, by terms of the lease, that the tenant assume whatever liability the landlord may have had (or to reimburse the owner for

---

12 *Lee v Chicago Transit Authority*, 605 N.E. 2d 493 (Ill. 1992).

13 *Petrillo v Maiuri*, 20 CCH Neg. 572.

14 *Koleshinske v David*, 20 CCH Neg. 264. However, a court refused to charge a railroad with negligence when an 11-year-old boy was injured on an overhead wire as he climbed atop one of the railroad's freight cars. The court said it would be asking too much to require the railroad to make its property "childproof" along its 275 miles of track. *Dugan v Pennsylvania Railroad*, 6 CCH Neg. 32d 443.

ETHICAL PERSPECTIVES

To Be or Not To Be

A pregnant woman took a drug manufactured during the policy period of the manufacturer's liability policy. At a later date that was not within the policy period, her baby was born with birth defects. It was decided that these birth defects were a result of the mother taking the drug. The manufacturer's problem was that of determining when the injury actually took place. The manufacturer made a claim with the liability insurer that was its insurer at the time the fetus would have been originally injured—when the woman took the drug. However, the insurer refused the claim on the basis that the fetus would not be a "person" insured under the contract. The court decided that an un-born fetus later born alive after a liability insurance policy lapsed was a "person" within the meaning of the liability insurance policy under consideration. Birth defects suffered by this person as a result of his mother's ingestion during pregnancy of a drug manufactured by the insured constituted a bodily injury caused by an occurrence within the scope of coverage of the policy. The injury and damage to the fetus were sustained during the gestation period of the mother, and this did occur prior to the lapse of the policy. It was not the actual birth thereafter that gave rise to the injury and damage.

Sources: *Endo Laboratories, Inc., et al. v Hartford Insurance Group et al.*, U.S. Court of Appeals, November 19, 1984; *Insurance Law Reporter* (Riverwoods, IL.: Commerce Clearing House, 1985), 1254–59.

liability) for injuries to members of the public or to employees of the tenant. However, there are some types of owner liability that cannot be shifted in this manner. Examples are liability for the violation of a safety ordinance; failure of a subcontractor to comply with such ordinances; and failure of the contractor to exercise reasonable care in excavations, blasting, or the use of fire.

Attractive Nuisance Doctrine

Under a doctrine that has become known as the **attractive nuisance doctrine**, the liability of the occupier of land may be changed so that a trespassing child is considered, in many jurisdictions, to be an invitee. Because of contractual liability, it is important that risk managers be aware of an organization's contracts and contract negotiations. Various legal fictions have been invented to establish that there had been an implied invitation to children and that there had been an intention to harm because the landlord had placed an allurement of some kind known to attract children, who are incapable of recognizing or appreciating the danger involved. The courts, in utilizing the attractive nuisance doctrine, usually consider the age of the child in rendering judgments.

Consumption or Use of Products

A manufacturer, wholesaler, or retailer is required to exercise reasonable care and to maintain certain standards in the handling and selection of the goods in which it deals. If injury to person or property results from the use of a faulty product, there may be grounds for legal action in the courts. Such actions are generally based on grounds of breach of warranty, strict tort, or negligence.

Breach of Warranty

A warranty may be expressed or implied. Often a seller gives a written or an express warranty on goods or services sold, and it is the breach of this written contract that may give rise to a court action. However, under the Uniform Commercial Code, the seller is held to have made certain unwritten or implied warranties concerning the product. These warranties are that (1) the seller warrants that the goods are reasonably fit for their intended purpose and (2) the seller warrants that when the goods are bought by description instead of by actual inspection, the goods are salable in the hands of the buyer. Breach of implied warranty is most often used as the basis for suits for faulty products. There is an implied warranty that goods are fit for a buyer's particular purpose when the seller knows the buyer's purpose and the buyer relies on the seller's judgment in making the purchase.

Cases of liability of a manufacturer for faulty products may be brought by the injured consumer directly or by a retailer who has paid a judgment as a result of selling a faulty product, particularly in the case of food, medicine, explosives, or weapons. For example, a manufacturer paid a judgment of $111,000 when a fire resulted from the heating of some roofing primer in order to thin it.[15] The manufacturer had provided no warning that the mixture would release explosive gases when heated.

Retailers have paid losses resulting from their handling of products. In one case, a dealer sold floor stain under its own private brand. Due to faulty manufacture, the mixture exploded, causing a loss to the user, but the court held that the dealer was liable because it must answer for a product it has accepted as its own. Breach of the implied warranty of fitness has formed the basis of most suits against restaurants that serve poisoned food and against drugstores that sell faulty medicines or cosmetics.

Strict Tort

Under strict tort liability, the manufacturer or distributor of a defective product is liable to a person who is injured by the product, regardless of whether the person injured is a purchaser, a consumer, or a third person such as a bystander. It must be shown that there was a defect in the product and that the defect caused harm. The manufacturer cannot claim as a defense that no negligence was committed or that the defect was in a component purchased from another manufacturer.

Negligence

Another basis for product liability is negligence. A person injured because of the condition of a product may be entitled to sue for damages sustained on the theory that the defendant was negligent in the preparation or manufacture of the product or failed to provide adequate instructions or warnings. A manufacturer is held to have the knowledge of an expert with respect to the product involved and must, therefore, take reasonable steps to guard against the dangers of inadequacies apparent to an expert.

In a famous early case, it was held that a manufacturer or a vendor had no liability for negligence unless it had a contractual relationship with the injured party.[16] Thus, an injured person could bring action only against a retailer with whom there was a contractual relationship, and not against the manufacturer. Later cases brought about a relaxation of this defense, known as **lack of privity** between the injured party and the manufacturer. A landmark case, *MacPherson v Buick Motor Company*, which concerned the breaking of a defective wheel, established the precedent that, in the court's language, "[i]f the nature of a thing is such that it is reasonably certain to place life and limb in peril when negligently made, it is then a thing of danger."[17] It should be emphasized, however, that a manufacturer or seller does not guarantee the safe use of the product. For example, a court refused to indemnify damage incurred

---

15 *Panther Oil & Grease Mfg. Co. v Segerstrom*, 224 Fed. 2d 216.
16 *Winterbottom v Wright*, 10 M.&W. 109, Eng. Rep. 402 (ex. 1842).
17 *MacPherson v Buick Motor Company*, 217 N.Y. 382.

ETHICAL PERSPECTIVES

The High Cost of Strict Liability

One of the largest aviation-related losses on record was decided on the basis of strict liability. The defendant was Teledye Continental Motor Aircraft, and the plaintiff was the estate of Robert Gross and family. Mr. Gross, his wife, and his two children died in an airplane that caught on fire due to a fuel leak in the plane's engine; the engine was built by Teledye. Mr. Gross had made the company aware of the problem before the accident. The plane developed engine problems while in flight, and when Mr. Gross made an emergency landing, the entire plane caught on fire, and the passengers were killed. Under the doctrine of strict liability, the plaintiff was able to show that Teledye made the engine and that the faulty engine caused the loss. The award was for $107 million, and Teledye had no insurance to cover the loss. On appeal the jury's award was reduced by the court to $1.1 million.

Source: *Business Insurance*, March 1, 1993, 2.

when a sparkler set fire to a child's dress. The court reasoned that there would have been little danger if the article had been used properly.[18]

During the past several years the product liability area has been very explosive as courts have continued to expand manufacturers' liability. Large losses are occurring and are expected to continue to occur to the makers of Agent Orange, diethylstilbestrol (DES), and asbestos. Millions of persons have been exposed to DES and asbestos, so the magnitude of potential losses is gigantic.

Completed Operations of a Contractor

A contractor who carelessly installs a water boiler or an electrical appliance that later explodes or causes a fire, resulting in damage to the property or person of another, may be held liable for negligence arising out of the faulty installation. This is known as **completed operations liability**, under which the damage must occur after the contractor has completed the work and the work has been accepted by the owner or abandoned by the contractor. Examples of completed operations liability include the following cases. A contractor was held liable for extensive property damage when a rubber hose connection broke in an air-conditioning system several months after the installation and admitted many gallons of water into the attic of a building.[19] In another case, a contractor was involved in litigation 17 years after he repaired an iron railing; it was alleged that faulty repair work caused injury to a person leaning on the railing.[20] An electrical contractor paid $12,000 for the death of a 3-year-old child electrocuted by an improperly installed outlet on which the work had been completed 15 months prior to the accident.[21] In May 1979, an oil rig in the Gulf of Mexico collapsed and sank. Eight people were killed, and 20 were injured. Firms involved with building or replacing the oil rig paid losses of more than $10 million. A survivor whose face was badly burned and disfigured received a $4.5 million award.[22]

---

18 Suel O. Arnold, "Products Liability Insurance," *Insurance Law Journal*, October 1957, 618, citing *Beznor v Howell*, 203 Wis. 1, 223 N.W. 788.
19 *Saunders v Walker*, 86 Sou. 2d 89.
20 *Hanna v Fletcher*, 8 CCH Neg. 2d 1017.
21 *Kurdziel v Van Es*, 6 CCH Neg. 2d 1080.
22 "Waker Gets $4.5 Million in Ranger 1 Rig Collapse," *Business Insurance*, June 7, 1982, 2.

Note that if the conduct of a contractor causes injury while the contractor is still in control of the operation, the liability is similar to that of an owner or a tenant of real property. Insurance contracts differentiate between that type and the completed operations types of liability.

Professional Acts

Closely related to product liability is the area of negligence law known as **professional liability**. Just as a manufacturer is required to make a product reasonably fit for its intended purpose, so the seller of services is required to use reasonable care not to injure others in the performance of those services. Physicians, accountants, architects, insurance agents, lawyers, pharmacists, and beauticians are examples of those who have a professional liability exposure.

The standard of care required of professional people is broadly interpreted to mean that these individuals must possess the degree of skill, judgment, and knowledge appropriate to their calling and must conduct themselves according to recognized professional standards. These standards naturally vary from profession to profession and are changing constantly as each particular field develops. Failure to take X-rays of a patient's hip cost one physician a judgment of $38,000. The injury was diagnosed as a bruise instead of a fracture and resulted in severe complications.[23] Before it was considered standard procedure to take X-rays following an accident, the same failure would not have constituted negligence.

Although damage suits for medical malpractice often lead to large settlements, a study released in 1990 showed that actual malpractice is relatively rare. Of hospital cases examined, the incidence of adverse events was only 3.7 percent. Further, even when the defendant wins, defense costs can be high. According to A.M. Best, in 2001 defense costs in medical malpractice cases made up 30 percent of total loss costs.[24]

Malpractice settlements have often been large, and the physician may often be at a procedural disadvantage. For example, in a California case the physician, a specialist in vascular surgery, employed a standard diagnostic procedure to determine the specific nature of the patient's difficulty. This procedure involved the injection of certain drugs, which, for unknown reasons, caused the permanent paralysis of the patient from the waist down. The physician had previously performed 50 such injections with no adverse effects. The doctrine of *res ipsa loquitur* was employed, thus permitting the jury to find for the plaintiff unless the doctor could prove no negligence. An award of $250,000 was handed down, but it was later reduced to $215,000.

Use of the doctrine of *res ipsa loquitur* in medical malpractice cases appears to have had the effect of turning doctors into insurers, which may result in doctors being unwilling to try new procedures and treatments for fear of financial bankruptcy if the treatments should fail.

Insurance agents under general principles of agency law frequently have been held to be liable for negligence. For example, if an agent agrees to obtain insurance for a client and then, through neglect, fails to do so, the agent may be held liable for losses that the client incurs because of lack of appropriate coverage.[25] If the policy was obtained but turns out to be worthless because the insurer was insolvent, the agent can be held liable.[26] Agents have also been held liable in cases where their clients fail to comply with a warranty or condition in the policy and the insurer is thereby relieved from liability.[27] In one case, a client told his regular agent that he was about to lease a building in another state. The agent did not request to

---

23 *Agnew v Larson*, 5 CCH Neg. 2d 33.
24 Insurance Information Institute, "Medical Malpractice," September 2003.
25 *Adkins and Ainley v Busada*, 270 A. 2d 135 (DC App. 1970).
26 Annot., 29 ALR2d 171, 174 (1953).
27 *Ibid.*

see a copy of the lease or make any other inquiry. Later the client was held liable for a $41,000 fire loss to the building because the terms of the lease made the lessee liable. The agent was held liable for the loss for not advising the client of the potential liability in the lease or recommending appropriate insurance.[28] Fire legal liability insurance should have been purchased.

Even attorneys have not escaped malpractice suits for negligence in the conduct of their profession. In one case, an attorney was successfully sued for $100,000 for failing to perform adequate research in a divorce case. The attorney had neglected to claim the husband's military pension as community property in the property settlement and as a result, the wife was unable to share in more than an estimated $322,000 of pension income.

Following the beating of Rodney King in Los Angeles and other cases of alleged use of excessive force by law enforcement, another type of professional liability coverage has drawn attention: police professional liability (PPL). While this policy does not cover criminal penalties, it does cover the damages awarded by a civil court. In the Rodney King case, a PPL would probably have covered the incident because the police were attempting to make an arrest.[29]

Principal–Agent Liability

Under the doctrine of **respondeat superior**, a master is liable for the acts of servants if the servants or agents are acting within the scope of their employment. An employee thus imposes liability on the employer for negligent harm to a third party, even if the employee is acting contrary to instructions, as long as he or she is doing the job. If an employee is told to solicit orders for a product and in so doing carelessly runs into the customer, the employer will probably be required to answer for the agent's act. If the employee is instructed not to call on person X, but does call on and injures X, the employer cannot plead in defense that the agent acted contrary to instructions.

A distinction is made between acting as an agent or a servant and acting as an independent contractor. In the former case, the employer not only controls what is to be done but also directs the manner in which it shall be done. In the latter, the employer pays the contractor for completing a certain job but does not exercise any control over how it is done. It is logical that the employer is not held liable for the carelessness of an independent contractor to as great a degree as for the carelessness of an agent or a servant. However, exceptions to this statement do exist. Examples include hiring contractors to perform inherently dangerous work and landlords fulfilling their duty to maintain safe premises.

Ownership and Operation of Automobiles

Under common law, an automobile owner or operator is required to exercise reasonable care in the handling of the automobile. Three situations may be distinguished in this important area of negligence:

1. Liability of the operator
2. Liability of the owner for the negligence of others operating the car
3. Liability of employers for the negligence of their servants or agents using automobiles in their employer's business, even when the employer is not the owner

Liability of the Operator

The typical damage suit in the field of automobile liability is one that charges the operator with carelessness that is the proximate cause of either bodily injury or property damage to an

---

28 *Hardt v Brink*, 192 F. Supp. 879, 881 (D Wash. 1961). See also Joseph R. O'Conner, *Liability of Insurance Agents and Brokers* (Madison, WI: Defense Research Institute, 1970).

29 "Police Professional Liability Insurance," *The Risk Report*, March 1991, 1–8.

injured third party. As in the other areas of liability, it is impossible to lay down a comprehensive statement of what constitutes negligence in the operation of an automobile. In some states, departures are made from common law by adoption of the principle of comparative negligence and the last clear chance rule. (See previous discussions of these concepts.) In certain cases, guest–host statutes operate to lessen the liability of operators to passengers.

Liability of the Owner-Nonoperator

The question arises, "Under what conditions can an automobile owner be held liable for damages when not personally to blame for the alleged negligence?" If one gives a loaded gun to a child and tells the child to entertain himself or herself and the child accidentally injures or kills someone, then the owner of the gun might well be held guilty of negligence.

Does the same situation hold if one lends one's car to a person without investigating this person's qualifications to handle the car and someone is subsequently injured through the operator's negligence? The courts have generally agreed that the automobile is not a "dangerous instrumentality" in itself and that one is justified in assuming that the borrower of an automobile is competent to handle it unless there is obvious evidence of incapacity or known recklessness. Illustrating this is the case of an employer who successfully defended an action charging negligence in failing to examine a bus driver who, having recently returned to work from an illness, suffered a fatal heart attack and crashed the bus, causing injuries to the plaintiffs.[30]

However, several exceptions exist to the general rule that an owner is not liable for acts of operators of automobiles. In many states, vicarious liability laws have the effect of making the parent of a minor child liable for damage done by negligent operation of the car by a minor. Usually the owner-parent has signed the minor's application for a driver's license, and in so doing is bound to be responsible for the minor's negligence. In a few states, any person furnishing a car to a minor is liable for the minor's negligence. In another set of jurisdictions, the owner is liable for personal injuries or property damage due to the negligence of any driver.

Another application of the agency relationship in establishing liability of an owner for negligence of an operator is the so-called **family-purpose doctrine** recognized in approximately half the states. Under this doctrine, an automobile is looked upon as an instrument to carry out the common purposes of a family. Therefore, the owner ought to be responsible for its use when any member of the family uses it because this member is actually the agent of the family head and is carrying out a family function. Yet the courts have not seen fit to extend this doctrine to any other instrument or possession, such as a bicycle or a boat, in common use by a family. It would appear that the family-purpose doctrine is a legal fiction to establish the liability of the person most likely to be able to respond financially for damages incurred in the use of the automobile. Similar reasoning was applied in an Illinois case. A car owner was even held liable to a third party for the negligent driving of a thief who took a car in which the owner had left ignition keys, in violation of an ordinance to the contrary.[31]

Liability of Employers

Even those who do not own automobiles may be liable for damages through their negligent operation if by some legal construction the nonowner can be shown to be responsible. The legal construction normally employed is *respondeat superior*. The employer is liable for the negligent actions of employees whether their acts are in or out of an automobile. The ownership of the automobile is immaterial in such cases.

---

30 *General Electric Company v Rees*, 5 CCH Auto Cases 2d 330.
31 *Ney v Yellow Cab Company*, 3 CCH Auto Cases 2d. 888.

MISCELLANEOUS LIABILITY

The preceding examples illustrate the major areas of negligence liability. In a similar way, legal decisions form the framework of the common law of negligence of many other types of relationships in modern society. For example, there is a body of decisions (and some statutory enactments) surrounding the areas of the liability of a parent for the negligent acts of children, of the liability of a trustee to beneficiaries for mishandling of trusts, and of the liability of owners of animals for destruction or injuries caused by these animals. Detailed inquiry into the liability law for these and other areas is beyond the scope of this text.

SUMMARY

1. The two major categories of property are real property and personal property. They are subject to direct losses and indirect losses that may or may not be insured. Usually only tangible property is insurable.

2. Negligence is the failure to exercise the degree of care required of a reasonably prudent individual in a given set of circumstances. Negligence that is the proximate cause of injury to the property of another may, in the absence of effective defenses, give rise to substantial court judgments against the responsible party.

3. Common law defenses that bar liability for a negligent act include contributory negligence and assumed risk. Statutory and contractual defenses also are available.

4. Courts are unmistakingly tending to impose liability, and a trend toward "absolute" liability has emerged. Evidence of this trend includes a weakening of the common law defenses and the recognition of new theories of liability.

5. An employer owes employees certain duties, the breach of which may give rise to damage suits against the employer. In most cases, an employer's liability to employees is governed by workers' compensation statutes.

6. The degree of care owed by a landlord or a tenant to members of the public and others who are on private property depends, in common law, on whether the person is said to be an invitee, a licensee, or a trespasser. The highest degree of care is owed to an invitee, and the lowest to a trespasser.

7. The liability of a manufacturer or a vendor for damage caused by faulty products is well-established. Product liability actions are based on some failure on the part of the manufacturer to exercise reasonable care in the manufacture of a product, on the part of the vendor for breach of express or implied warranty concerning the appropriateness of a product for its intended use, or on strict tort liability.

8. Under *respondeat superior*, an employer is liable for the negligent acts of servants or agents performed while the employee is acting within the scope of employment. This holds true even if the employee is acting contrary to instructions. It is under this doctrine that an employer is usually held liable for the negligence of an employee who is driving an automobile while performing the employer's business.

9. An automobile operator is liable for negligence in the operation of his or her car. In many cases the owner of the car, if someone other than the operator, may be held liable as well. The family-purpose, last clear chance, *respondeat superior* doctrines, and vicarious liability laws have operated to extend and to tighten the liability law applicable to owners, nonowners, and operators of automobiles.

10. Professional liability exists for individuals expected to be qualified to render a professional service but who fail to meet the standards of care or practice looked upon as necessary by other members of their profession.

internet*exercises*

1. Go to http://www.sba.gov/ and click on "Disaster Recovery." Explore the relief efforts and programs available to small business owners in the event of natural disaster. Which of these programs would be most helpful to a business in your local area if a tornado strikes?

2. Set your browser to http://www.cafelaw.com, pick a type of injury, and use the link associated with that topic to see the advice given to potential claimants in Florida about this type of liability case. How could a business in Florida use this information to protect itself against possible liability claims?

QUESTIONS FOR REVIEW AND DISCUSSION

1. What are the elements of a negligent act?
2. Identify and explain some of the defenses to the charge of negligence.
3. What types of losses do bodily injury liability and personal injury liability cover?
4. What are the three classes of persons giving rise to liability to a property owner?
5. What is the attractive nuisance doctrine?
6. What is *res ipsa loquitur*, and how does it relate to medical malpractice?
7. Who may be liable for the operation of an automobile?
8. What types of tort reform is the insurance industry supporting?
9. Some courts have held that if the state workers' compensation board issues a safety order to regulate the conduct of employees on the job, and if a member of the public is injured as a result of the violation of this order by an employee, the employer is liable unless it can be proved that the conduct was excusable. Is this an example of the "trend toward absolute liability," or is it a normal consequence of the common law duty of an employer to protect members of the public from harm? Discuss.
10. The owners of a swimming beach were sued by the parents of a boy who drowned when he swam into deep water and the lifeguard failed to reach him in time to save him. The plaintiffs argued that the defendant beach owners should have had more lifeguards. The defendants tried to prove that they had enough guards for normal needs and that the boy was guilty of contributory negligence in swimming out into deep water, which, rather than the absence of a sufficient number of life-

guards, was the cause of his death (*Spiegel v Silver Beach Enterprises*, 6 CCH Neg. 2d 874).
   a. Decide who should win this case. Why?
   b. How does this case illustrate the basic requirements of a negligent act?

11. Tweed, age 59, a casketmaker from California, visited his doctor, a general practitioner, complaining about a pain in his right shoulder. The doctor diagnosed it as arthritis, ignoring a suggestion by a consulting radiologist that "a tumor must also be considered." The pain got worse in spite of 41 costly shots of a steroid drug over a three-month period. Tweed went to an orthopedic surgeon who X-rayed the shoulder and misdiagnosed the problem. Eight months later an associate of the orthopedic surgeon happened to see the X-rays and identified the illness as bone cancer. If the malignancy had been spotted in its early stages, Tweed might have been saved; instead, the illness was classified as terminal. Tweed sued both the original doctor and the surgeon; Tweed's lawyer settled out of court for $300,000.

    Do you think that the elements of negligence existed in the case? Is a doctor liable for failure to cure a patient? Compare this case with one in which a mechanic fails to discover a leaking brake fluid line that later causes an accident.

12. A prominent attorney was asked why medical malpractice suits are becoming more common. The attorney responded, "Because medical malpractice is becoming more common and is increasingly being recognized by the average patient." Do you agree? Suggest other possible reasons.

chapter 4

Life, Health, and Loss of Income Exposures

S teve Cooper, age 27, is being considered for the position of vice-president for marketing at Horizon Securities in Raleigh, North Carolina. Yesterday Steve received a copy of Horizon's employee benefits package in the mail. The benefits seem to be extensive, though the descriptions are too technical to be understood fully with only one reading.

To assess the value of the benefits package to himself and his family, Steve has decided to systematically apply the risk management process. That is, he and his wife plan to list all of their exposures to loss, along with estimates of the likely frequency and severity of each exposure. Then they'll look at their resources and see how the Horizon benefits package may (or may not) complement those resources in their individual situation.

The benefits from Horizon focus primarily on exposures due to accident, sickness, death, and retirement. Thus, Steve will concentrate his initial analysis in those areas. As he begins, his mind quickly boggles at all of the possible ways his death or loss of health could affect others. He and his wife each work full time to maintain their desired standard of living. If they move to Raleigh and buy a new house and then one of them dies, the survivor would definitely face financial difficulties. Steve is also sufficiently confident about his future success with Horizon that he suspects that his death might cause problems for Horizon itself. Similarly, a lengthy illness that kept him out of work for several months (or years) might also cause problems for both Horizon and the Cooper family. And that's ignoring the ever-increasing cost of medical care itself!

As Steve contemplates these issues, his mind drifts many years into the future. It's hard to picture himself retired, but he does hope that he lives that long. Actually, it's easier to imagine being laid off and unemployed than it is to envision retirement. But Steve knows that he really should plan for both possibilities with realistic assessments of these exposures. All of these issues form the basis for this chapter.

CHAPTER OBJECTIVES

After studying this chapter, you should be able to

1. List and describe the types of potential losses associated with the risk of premature death.

2. Discuss the factors influencing the need to partially or fully replace a deceased's income for his or her surviving children and/or spouse.

3. Describe ways a business can lose money when an employee or owner dies prematurely.

4. Explain the nature of a mortality table and give examples of how it can be used for personal risk management.

5. Describe several types of medical expense loss that can be incurred.

6. Distinguish between types of disability loss and explain the nature of the subjective element in disability.

7. Explain the general principles underlying the unemployment insurance that exists in all states.

8. Describe several factors influencing the frequency and severity of income losses due to retirement.

The risk management approach can be applied to all types of risks that face businesses and individuals. Attention is now turned to a more complete analysis of the risk management process as applied to the potential loss of an individual's life, health, or income. The nature of the exposures arising from these risks forms the basis for this chapter, with consideration given not only to the risk identification process but also the likely frequency and severity of the losses considered.

EXPOSURES DUE TO PREMATURE DEATH

Because death is sure to happen to everyone, it can be argued that there really is no risk associated with it—that is, because death is a certainty, the degree of risk associated with its occurrence is zero. Although this argument is true from a long-term perspective, it is not especially helpful. Most people do indeed face a risk associated with death; the risk is one of timing. Death is sure to occur ultimately, but the specific day and time it will strike are generally unknown for most of a person's life. If death occurs suddenly when an individual is performing important and unique functions for an employer, the resultant financial loss to the business can be significant. Similarly, if death occurs during a period when an individual is a major financial provider for young children or other dependents, the effects on the survivors can be devastating. At the other extreme, it can be equally disastrous if death occurs "too late," causing a person to outlive his or her financial resources.

From a risk management perspective, it is common to speak of the risk associated with **premature death**. In this sense, premature does not mean "before an individual is ready" to die. Rather, premature deaths are those that occur before the life stage where death becomes increasingly accepted by society as part of the natural, expected order of life. On average, baby boys born in the United States in 2000 can expect to live for 74.1 years; newborn baby girls can expect to live to be 79.5.[1] Some persons believe that for newly born children, any deaths that occur prior to these ages are premature. Although this type of intuitive definition has psychological appeal, it is not optimal for planning purposes.

In applying risk management principles to analyze a situation involving the death of one or more individuals, it is helpful to classify any death prior to a planned retirement age as premature. Of course, specific retirement ages vary among individuals, according to distinct needs and preferences. But because the financial requirements and resources of survivors are often considerably different before and after a person's retirement, this linking of planned retirement to the definition of premature death is especially useful in the personal risk management process. Many of the financial needs commonly associated with premature death are discussed in the following sections.

Executor Fund

When a person dies, there are some immediate expenses associated with the funeral and burial or other disposition of the body. Table 4-1 lists typical services that can be provided through a funeral home; these services can be paid for on an itemized basis or through package plans and average over $5,000 in addition to the cost of a cemetery plot and headstone. Casket prices range from about $1,000 to many thousands of dollars, and cemetery plots with "perpetual care" arrangements also vary considerably in price, depending on size and location.

Soon after the funeral, arrangements must be made for paying the deceased's outstanding debts and for transferring any remaining assets and personal effects to survivors. Even if

---

1   *National Vital Statistics Report*, 51, no. 3, December 19, 2002.

TABLE 4-1	Services That Can Be Provided or Arranged by Funeral Directors
Body preparation Embalming Temporary refrigerated storage Clothes *Funeral or memorial service* Visitation room rental Chapel rental Clergy Music Flowers	*Transportation of body* Hearse rental Limousine rental Motorcycle escorts Long-distance arrangements *Final disposition of body* Casket Cemetery referrals Cremation Urn for storage of ashes

an individual has a valid will in effect at the time of death, this process of estate settlement is often time consuming and may involve considerable expense. If large sums of money are involved, estate and inheritance taxes may also need to be paid. The term **executor fund** is sometimes used to refer to these expenses because the **executor** of the estate (the person appointed to carry out the terms of the deceased's will) needs funds to pay for the expenses incurred as a result of the death.

Of course, executor fund expenses arise no matter when death occurs; they are not relevant only for premature deaths. In fact, some expenses such as estate taxes may grow more burdensome as a person ages and accumulates large amounts of wealth. In analyzing the potential severity of loss due to the risk of death at any age, personal risk managers should not assume that estate settlement costs will be minimal. Consideration should be given not only to the transfer costs and the amount of estate assets available to pay them but also to the degree of liquidity inherent in the estate. If sufficient cash is not available to pay the executor fund expenses, then other assets will need to be liquidated to pay these costs—a situation that may result in substantial losses due to forced sales of nonliquid assets.

For example, consider the case of 45-year-old Bill Crawford, who owns and operates a medium-sized farm in central Illinois. Bill is a single parent with custody of three children who are dependent on him financially. He owes $35,000 in miscellaneous debts and currently has about $6,000 in cash savings. Bill's major asset is his farm, which—when economic conditions are good—is estimated to be worth about $1 million. If Bill were to die under these circumstances, his intentions are that his children should inherit the farm and use it to provide for their income needs. However, without additional liquid resources, it is very likely that the farm would have to be sold to pay Bill's executor fund needs—the costs of funeral, burial, debt retirement, estate taxes, and attorney fees. If an interested buyer is not readily available, the sale may yield substantially less than the farm's $1 million value. Consequently, Bill's children may lose a valuable, income-producing asset their father intends for them to have, while at the same time not receiving full value for it due to the nature of the forced sale. Of course, this unfortunate result does not have to happen. By carefully identifying the types of needs that would arise with his death, Bill can make suitable arrangements now to provide the necessary liquid resources to better assure that his post-death goals for his children are achieved.

Income Needs of Survivors

In analyzing the risk of premature death, a major concern for many people is the impact their death will have on the financial position of their families. If someone is providing full or partial monetary support for other family members, that individual's death will affect the family financially as well as emotionally. Complicating the analysis, however, is the fact that as a person passes through different stages of life, the degree to which others are financially dependent on him or her changes. The discussion in this section focuses on the potential needs of three different categories of survivors: children, spouses, and others, including elderly parents. No consideration of the many potential resources for meeting identified needs is included at this point, because other chapters later in this text are devoted to a thorough discussion of such available resources.

Surviving Children

Young children usually are totally dependent on their parents for food, clothing, shelter, and other necessities. Consequently, a parent's death has the potential for eliminating a child's primary or sole source of income. As children grow older, most eventually become substantially, if not totally, financially independent of their parents. Thus, the timing of a parent's death will affect children differently, depending on the ages and circumstances of the children when the death occurs.

In evaluating the income needs of surviving children following a parent's death, one item that is often analyzed separately, apart from basic food and shelter items, is that of a college education. Some parents believe they have a responsibility to provide for their children's education beyond the high school level. When considering the possibility of their premature death, such parents include higher education costs in their children's list of income needs. This expense can be quite substantial and likely will continue to increase in the future. For example, the average annual total cost of attendance at a four-year public college is over $11,000, while for private colleges it is about $25,000.[2] If costs increase by 6 percent per year, the total cost of four years of private college attendance for someone born today will be over $300,000! Not all parents feel a sense of responsibility regarding college, however. Many believe that their children should pay for their own educations and thus do not include the costs of college in their personal risk management plans.

Surviving Spouse

Just as the financial dependence of children on parents changes over time, so does that of individuals who are married to each other. During the course of their married lives, there may be many situations in which people shift the degree to which they depend on each other financially. If they are married at a young age, perhaps one person will work full time while the other attends college. Following graduation, roles may reverse. During periods when both people are employed, there may be substantial dependence on both salaries in order to maintain a particular standard of living. For example, families may be able to afford home ownership only when both husband and wife are gainfully employed on a full-time basis.

But the relative degree of financial dependence of each spouse on the other is always subject to change. If both persons are employed, there may be times when one of them is offered a promotion in a different city. At that point, a decision must be made regarding both the promotion and the spouse's job. If the spouse resigns his or her position and moves to the new location, there often will be a period of unemployment while the spouse searches for a new job.

And of course, when children enter the picture, work patterns may also change. Some couples decide that one person will forgo employment for some period of time and stay at home with the children. Clearly, in this situation there is considerable financial dependence on the income of the employed spouse. What may be less obvious is that there is also

---

2 http://www.wiredscholar.com.

dependence on the child care services provided by the person who elects to remain at home. If that person dies prematurely, his or her services will need to be replaced in some manner, particularly if the children are very young. Often, however, it is neither desirable nor financially feasible for either parent to give up employment completely. Sometimes one person may switch from full-time to part-time work while the children are young. Or both parents may make substantial adjustments in work habits to help with child-rearing tasks. The fact that many alternatives exist plus the reality that, in most marriages, the degree of financial dependence on each spouse varies over time combine to make the analysis of potential income needs due to a spouse's premature death a truly dynamic endeavor.

Other Surviving Dependents

During some periods in life, an individual may provide some degree of financial support for persons other than a spouse or children. Often such dependents are related in some manner to the person providing financial assistance, but not always. One example might involve an elderly parent who lives with a grown child. The parent may pay the child for food, clothing, and other such expenses, but the amount paid usually is less than what it would cost if the parent were to move into a retirement or nursing home. Thus, if the child were to die, there likely would be a financial impact on the parent, who would have to make other living arrangements.

Other examples of some financial dependence feasibly might involve grandchildren, grandparents, nieces, nephews, brothers, sisters, close friends, and sometimes roommates. As the variety of different lifestyles abounds, it is increasingly important in personal risk analysis to identify all of the people who might be affected financially due to a person's premature death. When significant financial dependence exists in nontraditional relationships, risk identification is especially important if a person wants to minimize the adverse financial consequences of his or her death. The reason is that some post-death resources that normally might be available from employers or government programs may be unavailable if a dependent does not fit into a traditional relational category such as "spouse," "child," and so on. Thus, the arrangement of a suitable personal risk management plan may be more complicated in such situations.

Business-Related Exposures

If a person is employed or owns a business, additional types of losses may result from premature death. For example, if an employee performs services that would be especially hard to replace, that person may be considered a **key employee**. His or her death may cause plans or projects on which the individual was working and in which the firm had invested money to be abandoned. Alternatively, the business may seek a replacement following the death. Costs involved may include loss of efficiency for a period of time, increased salary to attract someone new, and/or training and development expenses for the replacement. All of these costs may prove to be substantial.

Sometimes it is not just the services performed but the personal relationships that have been established that would be hard to duplicate. Thus, the death of a very well-liked salesperson may cause a firm to lose valuable customers if their loyalty was primarily linked to the person who died. Merely replacing the deceased salesperson will not be sufficient to maintain the customer base. Each firm must make its own best estimates of its exposure due to the premature death of key employees and make appropriate plans to manage that risk.

Another source of business loss due to death involves those persons who have ownership rights in a firm. When a sole proprietor, a partner, or a major stockholder dies, that person's ownership in the business may pass to persons unfriendly to the firm or may even result in liquidation of the firm in order to pay the person's executor fund expenses. Competitors may obtain controlling ownership by purchasing shares from families of deceased stockholders.

PROFESSIONAL PERSPECTIVES

Business Exposures

A 59-year-old Connecticut man owned a construction business in which he was also the most important (key) employee. His family included a wife and six children. Soon after receiving the news that he had developed ALS (amyotrophic lateral sclerosis, known as Lou Gehrig's disease), the man found it difficult to continue operating the business. Cash flow problems developed, banks were unwilling to lend money under the circumstances, and the man began to quickly deplete the emergency cash reserves he had on hand. He and his family faced the possibility of losing everything for which they had worked so hard.

Luckily, the man had previously purchased a substantial amount ($800,000) of life insurance. By making use of a special option offered by the insurer, payment of part of the insurance was able to be made while the man was still alive, thus relieving the cash flow problems for both his business and his family. (See the discussion of accelerated death benefits in Chapter 16.)

Source: Gary Wolff, Wolff-Zackin Insurance, Vernon, Connecticut.

Or those who inherit the deceased's rights may enter the business but, because of inexperience, may cause losses or even bankruptcy. All of these possibilities cause many firms to be concerned about the risk of business continuation in the event of premature death of some or all of the owners. The risk management process is applicable in analyzing and preparing for all of these types of losses.

Likelihood of Premature Death

In analyzing the risk of premature death, consideration must be given not only to the severity of various associated losses but also to the likely occurrence of premature death itself. Aggregate death rates in the United States have been declining for many years due to advances in medical technology and improved economic status. As shown in Table 4-2, diseases primarily affecting aged persons (such as heart disease, cancer, and stroke) now account for over 60 percent of all deaths. Data on causes of death is not especially useful, however, in

TABLE 4-2	Causes of Death in the United States

Cause	Percentage of Deaths
Diseases of the heart	30.3
Cancer	23.0
Stroke	7.0
Pneumonia and influenza	2.7
Chronic lower respiratory diseases	5.5
Accidents	4.1
Alzheimer's disease	1.9
All other	25.5
Total	100.0

Source: *National Vital Statistics Report*, 49, no. 11, October 12, 2001.

calculating the probability of premature death. For that type of computation, mortality tables have been developed.

A **mortality table** expresses the probabilities of living and dying at various ages in a convenient format for a particular assumed population of persons. Table 4-3 illustrates one example, called the 2001 Commissioners Standard Ordinary Mortality Table (the 2001 CSO Table for short). It was constructed by insurance actuaries and is based on the mortality experience of persons with life insurance. For each age from 0 to 120 years, the probability of death is stated in terms of deaths per 1,000 people. In this table, by age 121 death is assumed to be a certainty. Thus, for every 1,000 persons who live to age 120, all 1,000 are expected to die within the year, as indicated by the "Deaths per 1,000" entry for age 120. It is interesting to note that prior to the development of the 2001 CSO Table, the most widely used mortality table was the 1980 CSO Table. The 1980 CSO Table assumed that everyone would die by age 100. The extension of the 2001 CSO Table to age 120 reflects the dramatic increase in U.S. longevity rates in recent decades.

Because the 2001 CSO Table is based on insured lives, the death rates contained in it differ somewhat from rates computed for the general U.S. population. After all, aggregate death statistics include people in

netlink

Set your browser to: http://www.nmfn.com/tn/listpages--calculator_list_pg, scroll down, and play the "Longevity Game" to see the impact of lifestyle and family history on expected life span.

TABLE 4-3   **2001 Commissioners Standard Ordinary (CSO) Mortality Table**

Age	Deaths per 1,000 Male	Deaths per 1,000 Female	Age	Deaths per 1,000 Male	Deaths per 1,000 Female
0	0.97	0.48	19	0.98	0.46
1	0.56	0.35	20	1.00	0.47
2	0.39	0.26	21	1.00	0.48
3	0.27	0.20	22	1.02	0.50
4	0.21	0.19	23	1.03	0.50
5	0.21	0.18	24	1.05	0.52
6	0.22	0.18	25	1.07	0.54
7	0.22	0.21	26	1.12	0.56
8	0.22	0.21	27	1.17	0.60
9	0.23	0.21	28	1.17	0.63
10	0.23	0.22	29	1.15	0.66
11	0.27	0.23	30	1.14	0.68
12	0.33	0.27	31	1.13	0.73
13	0.39	0.30	32	1.13	0.77
14	0.47	0.33	33	1.15	0.82
15	0.61	0.35	34	1.18	0.88
16	0.74	0.39	35	1.21	0.97
17	0.87	0.41	36	1.28	1.03
18	0.94	0.43	37	1.34	1.11

TABLE 4-3   **2001 Commissioners Standard Ordinary (CSO) Mortality Table _(continued)_**

	Deaths per 1,000			Deaths per 1,000	
Age	Male	Female	Age	Male	Female
38	1.44	1.17	80	70.14	43.86
39	1.54	1.23	81	78.19	49.11
40	1.65	1.30	82	86.54	54.95
41	1.79	1.38	83	95.51	60.81
42	1.96	1.48	84	105.43	67.27
43	2.15	1.59	85	116.57	74.45
44	2.39	1.72	86	128.91	80.99
45	2.65	1.87	87	142.35	90.79
46	2.90	2.05	88	156.73	101.07
47	3.17	2.27	89	171.88	112.02
48	3.33	2.50	90	187.66	121.92
49	3.52	2.78	91	202.44	126.85
50	3.76	3.08	92	217.83	136.88
51	4.06	3.41	93	234.04	151.64
52	4.47	3.79	94	251.14	170.31
53	4.93	4.20	95	269.17	193.66
54	5.50	4.63	96	285.64	215.66
55	6.17	5.10	97	303.18	238.48
56	6.88	5.63	98	321.88	242.16
57	7.64	6.19	99	341.85	255.23
58	8.27	6.80	100	363.19	275.73
59	8.99	7.39	101	380.08	297.84
60	9.86	8.01	102	398.06	322.21
61	10.94	8.68	103	417.20	349.06
62	12.25	9.39	104	437.56	378.61
63	13.71	10.14	105	459.21	410.57
64	15.24	10.96	106	482.22	443.33
65	16.85	11.85	107	506.69	476.89
66	18.47	12.82	108	532.69	510.65
67	20.09	13.89	109	560.31	545.81
68	21.85	15.07	110	589.64	581.77
69	23.64	16.36	111	620.79	616.33
70	25.77	17.81	112	653.84	649.85
71	28.15	19.47	113	688.94	680.37
72	31.32	21.30	114	726.18	723.39
73	34.62	23.30	115	765.70	763.41
74	38.08	25.50	116	807.61	804.93
75	41.91	27.90	117	852.07	850.44
76	46.08	30.53	118	899.23	892.44
77	50.92	33.41	119	949.22	935.11
78	56.56	36.58	120	1000.00	1000.00
79	63.06	40.05			

all states of health, whereas insured persons usually have been subjected to some degree of medical screening before being accepted for coverage. Working in the other direction, death rates in insurance mortality tables are purposely overstated to a degree for conservativeness, so as to reflect the possibility of unusual fluctuations in death rates in some years. Still, the 2001 CSO Table can be useful as an estimation of death rates for personal risk management analyses.

Figure 4-1 contains a graph of 2001 CSO death rates on a semilogarithmic scale. Death rates during the first few years of life are higher than they are following ages 9 or 10. After about age 35, death rates increase but are still relatively low. Beginning at about age 60, however, death rates begin to climb significantly. At age 60, the rate is 2.6 times what it was at age 50, and by age 70 the death rate is another 2.6 times the age 60 rate. As noted, the rate at age 120 is assumed to be 100 percent for this mortality table. The figure also demonstrates the fact that at every age, the death rate is higher for males than for females.

Needs versus Human Life Values

As a final note concerning the analysis of the risk of premature death, it is useful to distinguish between two related concepts. The discussion in this chapter has focused on the potential financial needs associated with premature death, with consideration given to both the frequency and severity of associated losses. In subsequent chapters, alternative resources for meeting these needs are discussed. This approach of identifying needs and resources is consistent with the overall risk management process used throughout this text, in which identified risks are analyzed and alternatives are considered and combined into a comprehensive plan for their management.

A concept known as **human life value** also is sometimes mentioned as having relevance. A person's human life value is the sum of money that, when paid in installments of both prin-

FIGURE 4-1   The Motality Rate, 2001 CSO Mortality Table

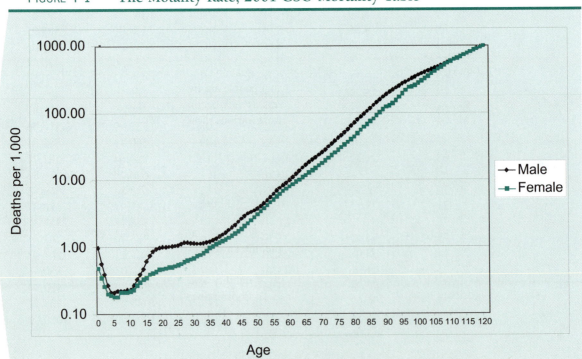

cipal and interest over the individual's remaining working life, will produce the same income as the person would have earned, after deducting assumed amounts for taxes and personal maintenance expenses. For example, Karen is 30 years old and is currently earning $40,000 per year. Suppose that her earnings are expected to increase by 7 percent annually, that she expects to pay approximately 20 percent of her gross salary each year in taxes, and that her own living expenses are expected to be about 30 percent of each year's gross salary. If Karen plans to work until age 65, her human life value under this set of assumptions is $824,849, based on an interest rate of 6 percent. (See Table 4-4 for the details of this computation.) Chapter 21 further discusses the issue of determining the appropriate amount of life insurance to purchase.

EXPOSURES DUE TO LOSS OF HEALTH

The loss exposures associated with the potential loss of health are usually just as important as those that arise due to the risk of premature death. Losses resulting from health problems usually fall into two categories: (1) expenses that must be paid for medical care and (2) income that cannot be earned due to time away from work while health problems persist.

One of the differences in analyzing the risk of premature death versus the loss of health is that if premature death occurs, it is irreversible and permanent. On the other hand, while loss of health can be permanent, it is more often a temporary phenomenon. Throughout their lives, most people become sick on numerous occasions. Often they may consult with a doctor and lose a few days from work before recovering and returning to a normal routine. Of course, some health problems are more permanent in nature, with this possibility increasing as a person ages. But the inherent uncertainty regarding the length of time that most health problems will endure presents some interesting aspects for the analysis of risks in this area.

Medical Care Expenses

Although the majority of medical care expenses are due to either illness or accident, it must be recognized that some such expenses also are of a routine nature and are incurred primarily to prevent future health problems. Expenditures for medical care in the United States have exploded in recent years and now equal about 16.7 percent of disposable personal income.[3] In some ways, the mere fact that people are living longer contributes to the high cost of health care, because health problems usually become more frequent and severe with age. Many people who might have died from various diseases in past years are still alive due to recent medical discoveries, but the longer people live, the more extensive is the medical treatment they are likely to need.

An associated development is the expensive new medical technology and the insatiable demand of patients for state-of-the-art treatment. When new technology becomes available, all hospitals in a city may rush to buy it, even though total expected usage of the new equipment in a particular geographic area may not justify multiple purchases. Hospital administrators often believe that the latest technology will help attract both doctors and patients to their facilities. While this belief may be true, the situation certainly contributes to the continuing escalation of costs.

Increasing frequency and severity of liability awards for medical malpractice also contribute to the cost problem, as doctors and hospitals must pay higher malpractice insurance

---

3   *Source Book of Health Insurance Data—2002* (Washington, D.C.: Health Insurance Association of America, 2002), 65.

TABLE 4-4   **Illustration of Human Life Value Computation**

Age (1)	Gross Salary ($) (2)	Net Earnings After Taxes and Living Expenses ($) (3)	6 Percent Present Value Factor (from Appendix B) (4)	Present Value of Net Earnings ($) (3) × (4)
30	40,000	20,000	1.00000000	20,000
31	42,800	21,400	0.94339623	20,189
32	45,796	22,898	0.88999644	20,379
33	49,002	24,501	0.83961928	20,572
34	52,432	26,216	0.79209366	20,766
35	56,102	28,051	0.74725817	20,961
36	60,029	30,015	0.70496054	21,159
37	64,231	32,116	0.66505711	21,359
38	68,727	34,364	0.62741237	21,560
39	73,538	36,769	0.59189846	21,764
40	78,686	39,343	0.55839478	21,969
41	84,194	42,097	0.52678753	22,176
42	90,088	45,044	0.49696936	22,385
43	96,394	48,197	0.46883902	22,597
44	103,141	51,571	0.44230096	22,810
45	110,361	55,181	0.41726506	23,025
46	118,087	59,044	0.39364628	23,242
47	126,353	63,177	0.37136442	23,462
48	135,197	67,599	0.35034379	23,683
49	144,661	72,331	0.33051301	23,906
50	154,787	77,394	0.31180473	24,132
51	165,622	82,812	0.29415540	24,359
52	177,216	88,608	0.27750510	24,589
53	189,621	94,811	0.26179726	24,821
54	202,895	101,448	0.24697855	25,055
55	217,097	108,549	0.23299863	25,292
56	232,294	116,147	0.21981003	25,530
57	248,555	124,278	0.20736795	25,771
58	265,954	132,977	0.19563014	26,014
59	284,570	142,285	0.18455674	26,260
60	304,490	152,245	0.17411013	26,507
61	325,805	162,903	0.16425484	26,758
62	348,611	174,306	0.15495740	27,010
63	373,014	186,507	0.14618622	27,265
64	399,125	199,563	0.13791153	27,522
			Human Life Value:	$824,849

premiums. In an attempt to avoid litigation, doctors may also engage in **defensive medicine**, in which extra procedures and tests are performed in addition to those that are probably necessary for a given patient. Another relevant factor leading to higher costs for some persons is the phenomenon of **cost shifting**, through which higher hospital charges are assessed to some patients but not to others. Some cost shifting has always taken place, as hospitals tried to cover the cost of care provided free of charge to indigents arriving in their emergency rooms. In recent years, however, cost shifting has accelerated due to the success of some large employer plans in negotiating lower health care prices for their employees. Rather than experience an overall decrease in income, doctors and hospitals have responded by charging higher prices for those with less negotiating power.

As costs continue to escalate, anxiety about the affordability of quality medical care has led to proposals for health care reform. In the following sections, many potential medical expenses are identified and briefly discussed, with some information provided about the frequency and severity of these expenses.[4]

Hospitalization

Approximately 37 percent of personal health care expenditures in the United States is attributable to hospital costs. Persons who are hospitalized can expect to incur expenses for such items as room and board, laboratory tests, supplies (such as bandages or crutches), and prescription drugs, as well as services by physicians, surgeons, nurses, and other professionals. Incidentals such as telephones and televisions generally must be paid for in addition to the cost of the room itself. The disruption to the lives of other members of one's family may also result in increased expenses during a hospital stay. For example, family members' transportation needs and eating several meals away from home may cause added expenses. Similarly, a spouse or parent may take time off from work in order to spend more time at the hospital, thus resulting in reduced income for the family unit.

Both the frequency and severity of losses associated with hospitalization vary considerably by geographic location. It is not surprising that some areas of the United States are more expensive than others with respect to medical care, but geographic differences also exist regarding the average length of hospital stays. For example, someone who is admitted to the hospital can expect to stay 5 days according to the national average. However, in Hawaii and Nebraska, the average stay exceeds 8 days per admission, and in New York the average stay exceeds 9 days. At the other end of the scale, the average hospital stay is less than 4.5 days in Idaho, Oregon, New Mexico, and New Hampshire. Considering all of the expenses associated with hospital care, extra days as an inpatient can quickly result in thousands of dollars in additional charges that might not have been incurred had the patient been discharged sooner.

Physicians' and Surgeons' Services

Almost by definition, hospital stays are not routine, but the same cannot be assumed of services provided by physicians. Many services are the direct result of illness or injury, whereas others are of a routine, preventive nature. Physicians' and surgeons' fees vary according to the geographic area, the medical specialty of the provider, and the type of visit (initial, follow-up, or in the hospital). Specialties that are usually associated with higher fees include neurosurgery, thoracic and orthopedic surgery, and obstetrics and gynecology. Fees for general and family practice and pediatrics tend to be considerably lower, on average.

Dental Care

One type of medical expense that is often considered apart from other expenses is that of dental care, to which about 5 percent of all personal health care expenses is now attributable.

---

4 All statistics cited are from *Source Book of Health Insurance Data—2002*, unless otherwise stated.

Some of the incurred expenses are for major restorative work, but many result from procedures that are preventive in nature. Dental expenses tend to be lower on average and considerably more predictable than the cost of medical care. The emphasis that is traditionally placed on preventive dental care is entirely appropriate because untreated dental problems usually get continually worse, as compared with many types of injuries and illnesses that often heal on their own even if not treated professionally.

Prescription Drugs and Other Expenses

Over 5 percent of U.S. personal health care expense is for prescription drugs. Other expenses include eyeglasses and other miscellaneous medical items. As with dental expenses, the cost for these items tends to be lower and more predictable than for other types of medical services. Not surprisingly, this fact often influences how individuals decide to manage these particular loss exposures.

Mental Health Services

At times during their lives, many persons suffer from some form of mental or emotional problem that may respond to treatment from providers of mental health services. Common problems include depression, anxiety, phobias, and obsessive-compulsive behavior. In addition, substance abuse (which includes both alcohol and drug dependency) is often treated by mental health professionals. In the past, the social stigma associated with these types of problems often kept afflicted persons from seeking professional help. In recent years, however, such stigmas have become less prevalent, and the use of mental health services has increased considerably. The cost of these services has also risen dramatically.

Mental health service providers have a variety of backgrounds, with some being better suited than others to handle certain types of problems. Psychiatrists are medical doctors and can therefore prescribe drugs as well as engage in other forms of therapy. As research into mental illness progresses, one of the interesting discoveries is that many disorders have been traced to chemical imbalances and other physical problems that respond well to drug therapies. Such findings serve to further lessen the stigma previously attached to many mental and emotional problems. In addition to psychiatrists, other professionals who can provide some types of mental health services include psychologists, social workers, and some specially trained clergy.

As a general rule, persons who experience severe mental or emotional difficulties, as well as those who have substance-abuse problems, should consider seeking professional help. Mental and emotional problems are sometimes accompanied by a variety of physical symptoms, including back pain, headaches, hypertension, and ulcers. Treatment of the symptoms rather than the underlying causes may bring only temporary, limited relief. Further, the consequences of some mental illnesses can be especially dangerous. For example, severe clinical depression may lead to suicide if left untreated.

Long-Term Care

The percentage of the population age 65 and older has been increasing in the United States for many years. But the age-85-and-over group has been growing at an even faster rate, and the age-100-and-over group is growing even faster than that. This fact is important because chronic diseases, such as arthritis, Alzheimer's, and osteoporosis, become more prevalent with age. Persons afflicted with these and other ailments are less likely to be able to maintain independent living arrangements as they grow older. While in prior years such persons may often have moved in with their grown children, this solution is expected to be less viable in future years. Reasons include geographic dispersion of families, more childless couples, more life-long singles, and the increased incidence of family arrangements such that no one can be at home throughout the day to care for elderly relatives. For most people in the United States today, the preceding factors combine to increase the probability that they will need some type of assistance in living in the future.

Nursing home care is only one form of **long-term care** that is now available to elderly individuals. There are several varieties of nursing home care, depending on the extent of medical services required. **Skilled nursing home care** involves ongoing medical services, with residents seen regularly by physicians. At the other extreme, **custodial nursing homes** and smaller entities known as **personal care homes** do not involve medical services; they concentrate on providing personal care services such as assistance with bathing, dressing, eating, and other daily activities. Facilities also exist to provide **intermediate nursing home care**. These facilities offer fewer medical services than those with skilled care but more than are available at those with custodial care. For elderly persons who cannot live completely independently but who are unable or unwilling to move to a nursing or personal care home, alternatives such as **home health care** assistance and home delivery of meals might be considered. The availability of these services varies considerably in different geographic locations.

The expense associated with long-term care depends in part on the level of medical services provided. The cost for one year of custodial nursing home care can easily exceed $50,000. This can be especially significant to married couples if one partner enters a nursing home and the other must continue to pay the normal expenses of maintaining a separate household. Sad stories abound in which adequate financial resources are not available to finance necessary long-term care. If suitable arrangements are not made ahead of time, it is not unusual for persons to completely exhaust their entire life savings within a year of entering a long-term care facility. The potential severity of this loss exposure, combined with the increasing frequency of its occurrence, make long-term care especially important from a personal risk management perspective.

Loss of Income

When a person is unable to work because of an illness or an injury, that individual is said to have a **disability loss**. Most disabilities are **temporary disabilities**; the majority of persons eventually recover and return to work. If someone is expected to remain disabled until death, however, then the condition is referred to as **permanent disability**. A further distinction concerning types of disability loss is whether the disability is a **total disability** or a **partial disability**. Someone who is totally disabled is completely incapable of gainful employment during the time of the disability; partial disability results in a decreased ability to earn a living but not a complete cessation of employment possibilities. Temporary and permanent disabilities can each be either total or partial, although in many instances someone who initially is totally disabled may later be more accurately classified as only partially disabled, as his or her recovery progresses.

One of the interesting aspects of disability risk analysis is that in many instances there is a subjective element to the loss. That is, a person's ability or inability to work following an illness or accident is not always easy to assess. Some people have a higher tolerance for pain than do others, and some have a greater intrinsic desire to be in the workplace rather than at home. Thus, the same accidental injury that causes Sam Jones to be disabled for six months may result in only two months of disability for Amelia Lopez. The size of the income loss resulting from the disability may be another strong motivating factor for some people to return to work, especially if alternative income sources are not present. The point is that while events such as premature death are quite easy to define, such is not generally the case with disability. This difference results in many peculiarities involving resources that can be used to manage the disability risk, as discussed in later chapters.

Causes of Disability

Disabilities arise due to both accidents and illnesses, with the latter being the most common cause. Workers in major metropolitan areas of the United States lose an average of about three days per year due to acute illnesses and injuries, and about 15 percent of the population suffers a physical limitation from one or more chronic health conditions. Many major causes of disability are not major causes of death. For example, infection, respiratory illnesses, and injuries often result in disability, but they are relatively minor causes of death.

There also are differences between males and females regarding causes of disability. Males are more likely to suffer disabilities due to accidents, whereas females are considerably more prone to illnesses that result in disability. As is the case with mortality, the risk of disability increases with age. At all ages, females have a higher overall probability than males of becoming disabled, whereas males have a higher probability than females of dying.

Length of Disability

To gauge the likely severity of disability for personal risk management purposes, **continuance tables**, such as that illustrated in Table 4-5, have been developed. Just as the 2001 CSO Mortality Table (Table 4-3) was based on lives insured for life insurance, the information in Table 4-5 is also based on insured lives, this time on the experience with persons who owned insurance to protect against disability.

Table 4-5 provides information regarding the likelihood of initial and continuing disability for 25-year-olds employed in generally nonhazardous occupations. For example, of 100,000 males who fit this description, 5,996 are expected to suffer a disability due to an accident. One month following the accident, 5,151 of them will still be alive and disabled. The others will have either recovered or died. But of these 5,151 disabled for at least a month, only 783 will be disabled for as long as one year. (Again, the remainder will either die or get better and return to work.) For all four categories illustrated in Table 4-5, as well as for similar tables for other ages, it is important to note the rate at which disabled persons recover. Thus, although it is quite likely that

Go to http://www.nmfn.com/tn/ listpages--calculator_list_pg and scroll down to "What are the Odds?" to find an estimate of your probability of becoming disabled for 90 days or more before age 65.

many people will at some point in their lives suffer a disability resulting in time lost from work, the probability that the disability will be permanent is rather low. That unlikely prospect does not eliminate the need to make adequate arrangements in the event that a long-lasting disability does occur, but it may affect the particular risk management techniques that are selected to deal with this risk.

Effects of Disability

The primary loss that results from disability is the loss of the income that would have been earned had the person not become sick or injured. The length of time that the disability persists is the major determining factor in assessing the overall size of the income loss. As discussed under the topic of premature death, income losses can have varying impacts on family members and others, depending on the degree to which other persons rely on that income for their support. It was obviously not important to discuss the effects of income loss on the one who died when analyzing the risk of premature death. However, with disability losses, there is a definite impact on the one who is disabled, regardless of whether there are other persons who are financially dependent on that person.

TABLE 4-5   **Disability Continuance Table for 25-Year-Old Workers in Supervisory, Clerical, and Technical Occupations**

	Disability from Accident		Disability from Sickness*	
	Males	Females	Males	Females
Number of workers exposed to disablement	100,000	100,000	100,000	100,000
Number of persons initially disabled	5,996	3,505	4,661	8,097
Number still disabled after:				
1 month	5,151	3,083	3,844	6,885
2 months	4,549	2,731	3,162	5,693
3 months	4,123	2,468	2,784	4,991
4 months	2,903	1,721	1,881	3,336
5 months	2,178	1,275	1,378	2,409
6 months	1,712	988	1,076	1,855
7 months	1,413	796	886	1,491
8 months	1,205	665	756	1,244
9 months	1,060	574	669	1,083
10 months	953	508	607	969
11 months	863	453	557	877
1 year	783	407	514	801
2 years	408	207	267	408
3 years	295	158	193	312
4 years	244	137	160	270
5 years	216	126	142	249
10 years	171	108	112	214
To age 65	167	107	109	210

*Only sicknesses that persist for more than seven days are included in this table.

Source: Derived from "Report of the Committee to Recommend New Disability Tables for Valuation," *Transactions of the Society of Actuaries* 35, 1985, 449–601.

Further, in contrast to the situation with death, no significant decrease in living expenses is expected when a person is disabled. The sick or injured person still must eat and have shelter, whereas such expenses are eliminated when a person dies. Far from decreasing, monthly living expenses may indeed increase if the disabled person requires special nursing care or other assistance with daily activities. Periodic medical expenses also are expected when a person is disabled. Thus, the drain on individual or family financial resources caused by long-lasting disabilities is potentially worse than that due to death because expenses may increase at the same time that income decreases.

OTHER INCOME LOSS EXPOSURES

In addition to death or disability, income can be lost through unemployment and retirement. This section briefly considers the nature of these two exposures to risk.

ETHICAL PERSPECTIVES

Sudden Deaths Among Athletes

On March 4, 1990, the hometown crowd roared its approval as Loyola Marymount's 23-year-old, 6-foot 7-inch senior basketball player, Hank Gathers, leaped for another successful slam dunk. The crowd quickly grew solemn, however, as the muscular star fell to the floor and began convulsing. Within moments, Hank Gathers was dead. In the years since this tragedy, all too many other athletes have died suddenly and unexpectedly, including NBA star Reggie Lewis in 1993, Olympic gold medalist Sergei Grinkov in 1995, triple gold medallist Florence Griffith Joyner in 1998, and in 2001 alone, Minnesota Vikings offensive lineman Korey Stringer, University of Florida freshman Eraste Autin, and Northwestern defensive back Rashidi Wheeler. In all of these cases, the deaths were especially shocking, given the athletic prowess of the individuals involved. A closer look at Hank Gathers' situation reveals additional distressing insights.

As a junior, Hank Gathers led the nation in both scoring and rebounding and was almost certain to be selected in the first round of the National Basketball Association's college draft. Earlier in the season, Gathers had collapsed while standing at the free-throw line and was subsequently diagnosed as having cardiac arrhythmia (irregular heartbeat). The tragedy of his death was made worse by the fact that Gathers feasibly could have retired comfortably before the fateful game. This diagnosis could have triggered Gathers's reported decision to acquire a $1 million disability income insurance policy.

It is not uncommon among Division I college athletes with significant draft potential to purchase insurance protecting themselves against the tremendous loss of income that might result from a career-threatening injury or illness. In general, athletes have a greater disability exposure compared with other professionals. Before they will be seriously considered for multimillion dollar salaries, they must be judged to be in top physical health. Consequently, there may be temptations to disguise or downplay the risk associated with some health problems. Cardiac conditions can end an athlete's career while not presenting any major hazard with respect to most other occupations.

Unemployment

During peacetime years in recent decades, the U.S. unemployment rate has typically ranged between 4 and 7 percent. Some unemployment is generally thought to be a necessary component of a free-enterprise system, but that is small comfort to persons who are unemployed against their will. As with disability, the major loss is the income that would have been earned had the person not lost his or her job, with the associated consequences for any persons dependent on the unemployed one for financial support.

netlink

Learn more about unemployment policies as they relate to the insurance industry by visiting http://www.secure.law.cornell. edu/topics/unemployment_ compensation.html.

In analyzing their exposure to income loss due to unemployment, individuals should be aware that government unemployment insurance programs are in effect in all states. Unemployment insurance is designed primarily to alleviate the effects of short-term, involuntary unemployment. It also offers only a floor of protection, leaving the remaining loss to be handled by private solutions. To offer full wage restoration might tend to reduce initiative to work, remove incentive for personal saving, cause unwarranted work stoppages, and discourage efforts on the part of private industry to stabilize employment.

The unemployment insurance laws of all states must conform to minimum federal requirements, with the programs financed primarily through employer-paid payroll taxes. The effective tax paid by employers depends critically on the employer's record of employment stability, under a system termed **experience rating**. Most states have a standard tax rate of a percentage of payroll, but employers with favorable benefit cost experience will pay less, while some other employers will pay more.

To be eligible to collect unemployment insurance benefits, an unemployed worker usually must either have worked for some minimum period during the previous 12 months or have earned some minimum amount of wages. Most states require a one-week waiting period before benefit payments begin. Claimants also must be able to work if work is offered. Thus, physical illness usually would cause a worker to be ineligible for benefits. In most cases, a worker can satisfy the ability-to-work requirement by registering for work at a public employment office.

States also have provisions under which a worker may be disqualified from receiving benefits. Having been disqualified, the worker loses the benefits for some specified number of weeks (often three to eight) or for the duration of the unemployment, or else suffers a reduction in benefit, depending on the nature of the disqualification. Major reasons for disqualification are voluntarily quitting a job without good cause; discharge for misconduct connected with the work; refusal, without good cause, to apply for or accept suitable work; and unemployment due to a labor dispute. If a worker refuses a job offer because the wages, hours, or other conditions of work are substantially less favorable than those prevailing for similar work in the locality, there would be no general disqualification. Other factors considered are distance from the worker's home; the worker's experience and training; and the extent of hazards in the new job affecting the claimant's health, safety, and morals. Claimants are also disqualified for fraudulent misrepresentations in order to obtain benefits and, furthermore, must repay the amounts paid to them as a result of such misrepresentations. The enforcement of all these conditions varies among states, not only because of legal provisions but also because the administrative agency may choose to enforce them differently.

The various states have developed somewhat complicated and diverse formulas for defining the benefits under their unemployment insurance acts. There is general agreement on the main features, but it is necessary to examine the laws of individual states to determine the specific rights of an insured worker. The benefit amount is some fraction of the wages earned during a base period preceding the unemployment. Once a claim is filed and the weekly income payments begin, a benefit year commences, and payments typically continue for a period of up to 26 weeks. Some states have extended this period to as many as 39 weeks, and benefits beyond these limits are sometimes authorized under federal legislation. The benefit formula is so arranged that if a worker has been fully employed during the base period, the worker may, subject to a minimum and maximum amount, expect to receive benefits equal to about one-half of the normal wage. In many states the worker may receive between 50 and 70 percent of the average weekly covered wage within the state.

State laws usually permit some unemployment benefits if the worker is not totally unemployed but is able to earn some small amount of money—say, through odd jobs—that is less than the worker's usual wage. In most states the amount of the benefit is the regular benefit less actual earnings or other payments. If actual earnings are less than some allowances, for example, one-half or one-third of the weekly benefit, there is no reduction in payment. These provisions reduce the temptation for a worker to cease all attempts at earning something for fear of losing the unemployment check.

Retirement

It is certain that a young person will either cease working and retire or die prior to retirement. There is a high probability that most young people will indeed live to the traditional retirement age of 65. Often, however, the transition to full retirement is not an event that happens on a particular date; instead, retirement transitions are frequently processes that take place over several months or years. A person may retire from full-time employment and immediately begin part-time work elsewhere, thus not completely leaving the workforce for many years. Married couples also may have different work patterns, with one partner remaining fully employed while the other moves into part-time work. Or perhaps one partner retires completely and the other continues working. At what point is the couple said to be "retired"?

The answer is primarily important from the perspective of the individuals themselves and the plans they have made for dealing with their eventual loss of earned income. Sources of income for elderly persons may consist of payments from employee retirement plans, federal Social Security benefits, part-time earnings, investment income from financial assets, or public assistance. Unfortunately, statistics indicate that as people age, many of them have very limited amounts of guaranteed income and few financial or property assets.

Many experts believe that between 70 and 80 percent of preretirement income is needed for a retired, married couple to maintain the same standard of living that was enjoyed prior to retirement. Complete replacement of all preretirement income usually is not necessary, due to the lower expenditures for clothing, transportation, entertainment, education, savings, and food that often accompany retirement. Furthermore, housing expenses will decline when a mortgage is completely paid off. But the size of these decreases is not significant over time for many people. Consequently, retirement may involve a reduced living standard unless suitable arrangements have been made to provide sufficient retirement income sources.

A complicating factor in analyzing the risk associated with retirement is that few people know exactly how long they will live. Thus, persons who regularly make withdrawals from their savings for the payment of retirement living expenses may outlive their resources. Even those persons who are assured of receiving a monthly pension for as long as they live may have problems in this regard if their pensions are not adjusted for increases in the cost of living. Furthermore, the two people in a marriage usually do not die simultaneously, and one cannot be assured as to which partner will live longer. If some sources of income will end with a particular person's death, his or her spouse faces the possibility of a significant income loss if the "wrong" partner dies first.

Finally, it must be recognized that many of the loss exposures discussed previously in this chapter are also relevant for retired persons. The executor fund needs to exist whether death occurs before or after retirement. For wealthy retirees, the estate tax and other estate distribution costs can be significant expenses, and much effort often is devoted to minimizing those components of the executor fund. Medical expenses also continue following retirement and often become more frequent and severe as persons age. As noted, the prospect of paying for long-term care is becoming an increasing reality as average life spans increase. All of these potential losses, as well as any financial dependencies that exist, must be considered in a thorough analysis of the risks associated with retirement.

SUMMARY

1. The executor fund needs associated with death include funeral and burial costs, estate and inheritance taxes, estate distribution costs, and outstanding debts of the deceased.

2. The income needs of survivors following a premature death depend on the type of survivor. After a parent's premature death, children's income needs vary according to the ages and individual circumstances of the children. In a marriage, the degree of financial dependence on one person or the other often varies over time, thus complicating the analysis of potential income needs due to a spouse's premature death. Elderly parents or other dependent survivors may also have income needs.

3. Premature death can result in losses for businesses, especially if the deceased was a key employee, a partner, a sole proprietor, or a major stockholder. A key employee's death may result in the abandonment of projects on which the key person was working as well as extra training costs for a replacement. Loss of someone with an ownership interest can result in losses if that interest is sold to pay executor fund expenses.

4. Aggregate death rates in the United States have been declining due to advances in medical technology and improved economic status. In assessing the possibility of an individual person's premature death, standard mortality tables can be useful.

5. Needs arising from death must be distinguished from a person's human life value, which is the sum of money that will produce the same income as would have been earned during the person's remaining working life, after deducting taxes and personal maintenance expenses.

6. Loss exposures related to the risk of health problems include medical expenses that may be incurred and income that may not be earned due to an inability to work while health problems persist.

7. The percentage of U.S. disposable personal income spent on medical care has increased in recent years, with a little less than half of all personal health care expenditures now attributable to hospital costs.

8. Use of both mental health services and long-term care arrangements for elderly persons is increasing as the need for such services becomes better recognized and more socially acceptable.

9. Disability losses can be either permanent or temporary. In addition, they can be either total or partial with respect to a person's ability to be gainfully employed. Many disability losses are partially subjective in nature. Continuance tables can be constructed to assess the likely length of time that a disability will last.

10. Unemployment insurance is financed through employer-paid payroll taxes and is designed to alleviate the effects of short-term, involuntary unemployment. Claimants must be willing and able to work if work is offered.

11. Retirement transitions often take place over a period of time. Factors complicating retirement risk analysis include uncertainty about individual life spans, frequently inadequate income sources, and the increased probability that health problems will occur as a person ages.

internetexercises

1. Consider the financial impact of being disabled. Use the disability calculator at the following Web site to estimate the income need that would result if someone is unable to work: http://www.life-line.org/disability/index.html. How might the inputs for most people (and the resultant income needs) change for someone at age 25 versus age 50? Explain.

2. The World Health Organization collects health-related data for countries all over the world. Set your browser to http://www.who.int and look in the Countries section. Pick five different countries at random and compare life expectancies across the countries. Does the extent of variation surprise you? Also look at the total health expenditures per capita. How highly correlated do life expectancies and health expenditures appear to be?

QUESTIONS FOR REVIEW AND DISCUSSION

1. List several types of expense for which the executor fund is designed to pay.
2. Give two examples of business-related premature death exposures.
3. Survivors' income needs tend to change over time. For each of the following classes of survivor, describe a scenario in which the income need of a survivor will likely change over time.
   a. Surviving children
   b. Surviving spouse
   c. Surviving parents
4. Refer to Table 4-3 to answer the following:
   a. At what age is the probability of death lowest?
   b. From a group of 10,000 females aged 30, how many are expected to die this year?
   c. What is the probability that a 20-year-old female will live to at least the age of 25?
5. Referring to Table 4-4, what would Karen's human life value be if she planned to quit working at age 60 instead of age 65?
6. List the five major categories of medical care expenses. Which of these types of expenses accounts for the largest percentage of health care expenditures? Explain.
7. Distinguish between skilled nursing home care, custodial nursing home care, and intermediate nursing home care.
8. Contrast the loss exposures of a worker becoming disabled to those occurring at the worker's death.
9. Suggest possible reasons for the increase in the proportion of disposable income spent for medical care in the United States.
10. Explain two methods of distinguishing between disability losses and explain the subjective element to a disability loss.
11. What are the main requirements that must be met before unemployment insurance benefits are payable to a particular individual?
12. Why is the degree of risk associated with the occurrence of death zero? List as many financial risks associated with premature death as you can. Are there also financial risks associated with living longer than expected? If so, give some examples.
13. Referring to Figure 4-1, what are some reasons that you believe explain the "hump" in the slopes of death rates for people aged 15 to 30? What do you think the reasons for the larger hump in the death rates for males could be?
14. How does the term human life value differ from the amount of financial need that will be experienced after a person's death? Why is human life value not the best measure of the severity of a loss for computing loss exposure resulting from premature death? Why do you think that human life value is the measure of loss severity typically used to compute damages on wrongful death claims if it is not the best measure for loss exposure from premature death?
15. It has been said that an average businessperson would not think of leaving a factory uninsured but neglects to insure the lives of key executives who may be more valuable than the building. Do you agree? In what way might a key executive be more valuable to a company than a building?
16. It is said that the decrease in death rates brings about an increase in disability rates. How might this statement be true? What other factors might explain an increase in disability rates?

chapter 5

Mary Boose owns and manages Boose Dynamics, which specializes in the design and manufacture of new forms of exercise equipment. Located in Jasper, Indiana, Boose sells its equipment to health and fitness clubs nationwide. The nature of Boose's products exposes the firm to a variety of risks. Some examples include the possibility that someone might be injured on a piece of Boose equipment and claim that it was improperly made. Another person might have a heart attack and die while working out, with the surviving family members claiming that the Boose equipment was to blame.

Boose has been conscientious about identifying and analyzing the sources of risk to which it is exposed. Now the company must consider alternative ways to deal with those risks. It's possible that there may be some forms of equipment that Boose will decide not to manufacture at all because of the high probability of serious losses. However, Boose is generally committed to this industry and in most cases wants to explore risk management alternatives that are compatible with continuing to produce a wide variety of new products. If Boose can determine ways to produce safer products that have a reduced likelihood of causing losses, the firm will examine the economic feasibility of alternative manufacturing/inspection processes. Similarly, Boose is interested in exploring ways to make the health and fitness clubs bear more responsibility for losses, even when they involve Boose equipment. These approaches to solving risk management problems form the basis of this chapter.

Risk Management Techniques: Noninsurance Methods

CHAPTER OBJECTIVES

After studying this chapter, you should be able to

1. Give examples of the use of risk avoidance and explain when it is an appropriate risk management technique.

2. Differentiate between frequency reduction and severity reduction and give examples of each.

3. Explain three different forms of loss control, differentiated on the basis of timing issues, and provide examples of each.

4. List several potential costs and benefits associated with loss control measures.

5. List four forms of funded risk retention.

6. Explain the essential elements of self-insurance and describe the financial as well as nonfinancial factors that affect a firm's ability to engage in funded risk retention.

7. Describe the nature of risk transfer as a risk management tool and list five forms of risk transfer.

8. Explain how risk management adds value to a corporation.

After identifying and evaluating exposures to risk in the previous two chapters, systematic consideration can be given to alternative methods for managing each exposure. The four basic methods available for handling risks are risk avoidance, loss control, risk retention, and risk transfer.

RISK AVOIDANCE

Risk avoidance is a conscious decision not to expose oneself or one's firm to a particular risk of loss. In this way, risk avoidance can be said to decrease one's chance of loss to zero. For example, the eccentric chief executive of a multibillion dollar firm may decide not to fly to avoid the risk of dying in an airplane crash. Dr. Gary Liebenburg may decide to leave the practice of medicine rather than contend with the risk of malpractice liability losses. Similarly, firms may decide not to enter the pharmaceutical line of business to avoid costly product liability suits. Yet another example of risk avoidance is to delay taking responsibility for goods during transportation. A customer presented with a choice of terms of sale may have the seller assume all risks of loss until the goods arrive at the buyer's warehouse. In this way the buyer avoids the risk of loss to the property until delivery has actually occurred.

Risk avoidance is common, particularly among those with a strong aversion to risk. However, avoidance is not always feasible and may not be desirable even when it is possible. Risk managers must always weigh the relative costs and benefits associated with activities that give rise to risks. When a risk is avoided, the potential benefits, as well as costs, are given up. For example, the doctor who quits practicing medicine avoids future liability risks but also forfeits the income and other forms of satisfaction that may be associated with a career in medicine. The firm that avoids manufacturing pharmaceuticals relinquishes potential profits as well as liability risks. And if a business is to operate at all, certain risks are nearly impossible to avoid. An example is the liability risk of owning or leasing premises from which the business is conducted.

LOSS CONTROL

When particular risks cannot be avoided, actions may often be taken to reduce the losses associated with them. This method of dealing with risk is known as **loss control**. It is different than risk avoidance, because the firm or individual is still engaging in operations that give rise to particular risks. Rather than abandoning specific activities, loss control involves making conscious decisions regarding the manner in which those activities will be conducted. Common goals are either to reduce the probability of losses or to decrease the cost of losses that do occur.

Types of Loss Control

Effective loss control sometimes requires technical knowledge of the exposure itself, as is the case with safety engineering in many manufacturing processes. In other instances, loss control measures may be quite simple and straightforward. Two methods of classifying loss control involve focus and timing.

Focus of Loss Control

Some loss control measures are designed primarily to reduce loss frequency. Thus, when Epermanis Corporation cleans up its storage

netlink

Many college students turn to 24-hour retailing jobs to earn extra cash. These jobs offer flexible working hours, but pose an above-average risk for workplace violence. Check out OSHA's guidelines for reducing risk at around-the-clock retail establishments at http://www.osha.gov/SLTC/workplaceviolence/latenight/.

areas and discards the oily rags previously stored there, it is practicing loss control designed to lessen the chance that the firm will suffer a fire. This form of loss control is referred to as **frequency reduction**. Some firms expend considerable funds in an effort to reduce the frequency of injuries to its workers. In this regard, it is useful to consider the classic **domino theory** originally stated by H.W. Heinrich.[1] According to this theory, which is illustrated in Figure 5-1, employee accidents can be viewed in light of the following five steps:

1. Heredity and social environment, which cause persons to act in a particular way
2. Personal fault, which is the failure of individuals to respond appropriately in a given situation
3. An unsafe act or the existence of a physical hazard
4. Accident
5. Injury

Each of the five steps can be thought of as a domino that falls and in turn causes the next domino to fall; if any of the dominos prior to the final one are removed, then the injury will not occur. On the basis of this theory, it is often argued that the emphasis of loss control should be on the third domino, or step. Thus, by removing physical hazards and eliminating unsafe actions by employees, the frequency of injuries to workers can be reduced.

In contrast to frequency reduction, consider an auto manufacturer having air bags installed in the company fleet of automobiles. This firm is engaging in **severity reduction**. The air bags will not prevent accidents from occurring, but they will reduce the probable injuries that employees will suffer if an accident does happen. Two special forms of severity reduction are separation and duplication. **Separation** involves the reduction of the maximum probable loss associated with some kinds of risks. For example, a firm may disperse work operations in such a way that an explosion or other catastrophe will not injure more than a limited number of persons. Through such separation, the firm is reducing the likely severity of overall firm losses by reducing the size of the exposure in any one location. **Duplication** is a very similar technique, in which spare parts or supplies are maintained to replace immediately

FIGURE 5-1   Heinrich's Domino Theory

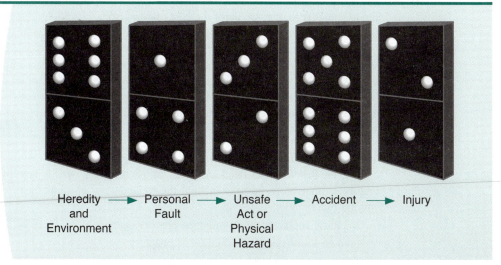

Heredity and Environment → Personal Fault → Unsafe Act or Physical Hazard → Accident → Injury

1 H. W. Heinrich, *Industrial Accident Prevention*, 4th ed. (New York: McGraw-Hill Book Co., 1959), 14–16.

damaged equipment and/or inventories. This type of loss control also helps to reduce the severity of losses that do occur.

Of course, some activities serve to reduce both the frequency and the severity of losses due to particular risks. If obstetrician Dr. John Smith is careful to learn the latest developments in his specialty area of medicine, he may lessen the likelihood of malpractice liability losses (frequency reduction) and decrease the size of any adverse judgments for cases brought against him (severity reduction).

Timing of Loss Control

Some loss control methods are implemented before any losses occur. All measures with a frequency-reduction focus, as well as some based on severity reduction, are of this type; they are called **pre-loss activities**. One example is employee safety education programs, which are designed to reduce both the frequency and severity of injuries to workers. Although some firms may not realize the need for such programs until after a significant loss, the effectiveness of safety programs is meaningful only for prospective future losses.

The second timing classification for loss control measures is that of activities that take place concurrently with losses. The activation of building sprinkler systems illustrates this concept of **concurrent loss control**. Such systems are triggered only after a fire begins and are designed to extinguish the fire quickly and thereby decrease the severity of the resultant loss. Of course, a firm's installation of a sprinkler system must take place prior to the loss, but the actual sprinkler activity should take place only at the same time as fire losses. If activated at any other time—either before or after a fire—the result will be water damage caused by the sprinkler, rather than a reduction in fire damages.

The third timing category is that of **post-loss activities**. As with concurrent loss control, post-loss activities always have a severity-reduction focus. One example is trying to salvage damaged property rather than discard it. Thus, the partial restoration of a wrecked automobile and subsequent sale of the car to an automobile wholesaler can reduce the overall severity of a loss due to an automobile accident.

Decisions Regarding Loss Control

A major issue for risk managers is the decision about how much money to spend on the various forms of loss control. In some cases it may be possible to reduce significantly the exposure to some types of risks, but if the cost of doing so is very high relative to the firm's financial situation, then the loss control investment may not be money well spent.

The general rule is that to justify the expenditure, the expected gains from an investment in loss control should be at least equal to the expected costs. This comparison of costs and benefits, which is similar to the financial decision making used for other capital budgeting issues, is discussed in Chapter 8. Before such methods can be used effectively, however, the risk manager must have a clear understanding of all of the costs and benefits associated with a particular form of loss control.

Potential Benefits of Loss Control

Many of the benefits associated with loss control are either readily quantifiable or can be reasonably estimated. These may include the reduction or elimination of expenses associated with the following:

- Repair or replacement of damaged property
- Income losses due to destruction of property
- Extra costs to maintain operations following a loss
- Adverse liability judgments
- Medical costs to treat injuries
- Income losses due to deaths or disabilities

ETHICAL PERSPECTIVES

Cost versus Safety

Corporations are sometimes faced with the need to make important decisions that are later subjected to intense scrutiny. One example involves decisions made by Ford Motor Co. in the manufacture of some of its automobiles during the 1970s and early 1980s. During this time, Ford's Pinto and Mustang models were particularly criticized as being unsafe, with a tendency to burst into flames following rear-end collisions. Several such accidents occurred, sometimes resulting in the tragic loss of life. General Motors also has had similar allegations made against it with respect to some of its pickup trucks and other vehicles manufactured between 1973 and 1987. The complaints against GM alleged that the trucks' side-mounted fuel tanks increased the likelihood that the trucks would catch fire following a side collision.

In addition to several liability suits arising out of these problems, a 1978 accident involving a Pinto led to a criminal case in which Ford itself was charged with three counts of reckless homicide. The basic allegation was that Ford knew that problems existed with the Pinto's design, but the firm had decided that it would be more expensive to fix the cars than merely to settle any civil liability suits that might arise. Many in the legal community characterized the situation as one in which Ford allegedly sacrificed safety in favor of profits.

During the trial, the prosecution argued that Ford's internal records indicated that the safety problems could be corrected by spending an additional $11 per vehicle. With 11 million cars and 1.5 million light trucks sold, the total cost to fix the alleged defect would have been about $137 million. But by correcting the problem, it was estimated that Ford would have prevented about 180 burn deaths, 180 serious burn injuries, and 2,100 burned vehicles. The associated liability settlements that would have been saved from the prevention of these accidents were valued at a total of $49.5 million. Thus, the prosecution contended that Ford compared the $137 million cost to the potential savings of only $49.5 million and decided that safety would not be cost effective. Ford vigorously denied all allegations that it consciously and deliberately manufactured unsafe automobiles. In the end, Ford was exonerated from the criminal charges, although it did pay adverse liability judgments arising out of some of the accidents.

In the case of GM, the company also continuously insisted that its vehicles were safe. However, a crash-safety report written by a low-level engineer at GM in 1973 estimated that 500 people died annually in GM vehicles "where bodies were burnt" and that GM could prevent such fires and the resulting deaths by spending $2.40 per vehicle in safety improvements. GM settled a post-collision fuel tank fire case in September 1999, to avoid having the memo entered into evidence. At that time, GM faced about 100 fuel system fire suits. In the cases of both Ford and GM, important questions are raised. For example, how should a firm value human life in making its internal loss control decisions? And when does safety cost "too much"?

Sources: Francis T. Cullen, William J. Maakestad, and Gray Cavender, *Corporate Crime Under Attack: The Ford Pinto Case and Beyond* (Cincinnati, OH: Anderson Publishing Co., 1987); Milo Geyelin, "How an Internal Memo Written 26 Years Ago Is Costing GM Dearly," *The Wall Street Journal*, September 29, 1999, A1.

Another potential quantifiable benefit of loss control is a reduction in the cost of other risk management techniques used in conjunction with the loss control. An example is the decrease in insurance premiums (discussed in Chapters 6 and 7) that often accompanies a loss control investment. Effort should also be made to estimate the tax savings, if any, that may result. Such savings will ensue if the loss control expenditures are tax deductible, either all at once or over time through depreciation.

There may also be loss control benefits for which a dollar value cannot be easily estimated. Examples include the reduction in subjective risk that may accompany lower expected loss frequency and severity, as well as improved public and employee relations associated with fewer and less severe losses.

Potential Costs of Loss Control

Compared to estimating the benefits of a proposed investment in loss control, it is usually easier to estimate the potential costs. Two obvious cost components are installation and maintenance expenses. For example, a sprinkler system will have an initial cost to install it and also will have ongoing expenses necessary to maintain it in proper working order.

The challenge in cost estimation is often in identifying all of the ongoing expenses. For example, if a security guard is hired, the cost will include not only the guard's salary but also employee benefits and any other variable expenses associated with employees. To further complicate the process, some of the ongoing costs of loss control may merely be increases in other expenses. For example, utility bills may increase if a loss control measure draws on significant amounts of power to function. In spite of these complicating features, however, it is only through a careful estimation of all potential costs and benefits that appropriate risk management decisions can be made regarding loss control.

RISK RETENTION

A third technique for managing risk, known as **risk retention**, involves the assumption of risk. That is, if a loss occurs, an individual or firm will pay for it out of whatever funds are available at the time. Retention can be planned or unplanned, and losses that occur can either be funded or unfunded in advance.

Planned versus Unplanned Retention

Planned retention involves a conscious and deliberate assumption of recognized risk. Sometimes planned retention occurs because it is the most convenient risk treatment technique or because there are simply no alternatives available short of ceasing operations. At other times, a risk manager has thoroughly analyzed all of the alternative methods of treating an existing risk and has decided that retention is the most appropriate technique. Ways to compare alternative risk treatment methods are the subject of Chapter 8.

When a firm or individual does not recognize that a risk exists and unwittingly believes that no loss could occur, risk retention also is under way—albeit **unplanned retention**. Sometimes unplanned retention occurs even when the existence of a risk is acknowledged. This result can ensue if the maximum possible loss associated with a recognized risk is significantly underestimated. For example, a manufacturer of kitchen appliances may recognize the potential for product liability suits. But the potential size of adverse liability judgments may be much greater than the manufacturer anticipates. Thus, even though the exposure is recognized, if the firm elects to purchase insurance based on its estimate of the maximum possible loss, it is engaging in unplanned retention of losses that exceed that estimate.

Funded versus Unfunded Retention

Many risk retention strategies involve the intention to pay for losses as they occur, without making any funding arrangements in advance of a loss. If a loss happens, it is paid for from the firm's current revenues. For example, a convenience food store may decide to absorb the expense of shoplifting losses as they occur, rather than making any special advance arrangements to pay for them. This **unfunded retention** makes sense in this situation, because some level of shoplifting losses is often viewed as part of the overall cost of doing business. Glass breakage is another exposure that many firms manage using unfunded retention. In general, unfunded retention should be used with caution, because financial difficulties may arise if the actual total losses are considerably greater than what was expected. In contrast to unfunded retention, a firm or individual may decide to practice **funded retention** by making various preloss arrangements to ensure that money is readily available to pay for losses that occur.

PROFESSIONAL PERSPECTIVES

Investing in Safety

As of 1993, Louisville-based KFC had not invested in safety measures in any logical or meaningful way. Frequency and severity of losses were climbing, particularly in the slips and falls category (over 50 percent of all accidents), and these injuries were adversely affecting profitability. It was up to the Risk Management Department to convince senior management that investment in safety was a legitimate way to increase profits.

A proposal was made and approved to set aside $1 million to invest in safety on a one-year trial basis, with Risk Management required to show the return on investment to obtain future funding. One of the main features that sold the program to senior management was that each of the six geographic operating divisions (each with about 300 stores) was to develop its own list of stores to invest in, coached by Risk Management, choosing from a pre-approved list of slip and fall investment options. This was a major departure from the traditional centralized risk management decision-making structure of the past, but one that was clearly consistent with KFC's decentralized approach to profit and safety accountability. This approach generated considerable operational buy-in and ownership, while leveraging the centralized purchasing and project management assets of the Risk Management Department.

The result? The first year the initial investment of $1 million was "paid back" within six months through a tremendous 54 percent reduction in slips and falls. That resulted in corresponding reductions in payments for employee and customer injuries. Senior management could clearly see the value of investments in safety and, as a result, the program was renewed and eventually named the Safety Annual Operating Plan. By mid-1996, KFC had treated over 1,500 of its 2,000 stores with a variety of slip-reducing techniques. Combined with other cost-saving initiatives, KFC has seen its cost per store for employee injuries cut in half during this time period. Total savings across all these initiatives are over $5 million per year during the program's existence. It is not surprising that this overall investment program is now an ongoing part of KFC's planning and financial allocation process, and an accepted part of doing business.

Source: Chris Duncan, Senior Director, Loss Prevention, KFC USA Inc.

Credit

The use of credit may provide some limited opportunities to fund losses that result from retained risks. It is usually not a viable source of funds for the payment of large losses, however. Further, unless the risk manager has already established a line of credit prior to the loss, the very fact that the loss has occurred may make it impossible to obtain credit when needed. For example, creditors may be unwilling to loan money to replace destroyed assets if those are the very assets that normally would have been used as collateral for the loan. For these reasons, credit tends not to be a major source of financial resources for most firms' funded retention programs, except in cases where prior credit commitments have been arranged.

Reserve Funds

Sometimes a reserve fund is established to pay for losses arising out of risks a firm has decided to retain. If the maximum possible loss due to a particular risk is relatively small, the existence of a reserve fund may be an efficient means of managing risk. For example, a firm may set aside $5,000 in liquid assets to pay for periodic repair or replacement of office equipment. Thus, when a fax machine or computer breaks down, the firm has funds readily available for the repair bill, which likely will be considerably less than the total reserve fund.

When the maximum possible loss is quite large, however, a reserve fund may not be appropriate. If a small employer plans for a $50,000 reserve fund to pay for any hospital costs its employees incur, it has no way of knowing whether this fund is adequate. A single period of hospitalization could easily exhaust the savings, and a second period of hospitalization might occur before the fund could be restored. For this type of exposure, alternative risk management techniques probably would be more appropriate than risk retention, especially for a small firm.

Self-Insurance

If a firm has a group of exposure units large enough to reduce risk and thereby predict losses, the establishment of a fund to pay for those losses is a special form of planned, funded retention known as **self-insurance**. Some people object to this particular term, because the word insurance usually implies that a risk is transferred to another party, as discussed in the next chapter. Obviously, self-insurance will not involve a transfer of risk in this sense. In spite of such objections, the term self-insurance continues to be used to describe some special situations in which risk retention has been consciously selected as an appropriate risk management technique. The mere establishment of a reserve fund is not self-insurance, as the term is used in this book. There are two necessary elements of self-insurance: (1) existence of a group of exposure units that is sufficiently large to enable accurate loss prediction and (2) prefunding of expected losses through a fund specifically designed for that purpose.

Captive Insurers

One final form of funded risk retention is the establishment of a **captive insurer**, which combines the techniques of risk retention and risk transfer. Captive insurers are discussed in Chapter 12.

Decisions Regarding Retention

In any given situation, there are several factors to consider in assessing retention as a potential risk management technique. These factors include financial resources, ability to predict losses, and feasibility of establishing retention programs.

Financial Resources

A large business can often use risk retention to a greater extent than can a small firm or an individual, in part because of the large firm's greater financial resources. Thus, losses due to many risks may merely be absorbed by such a firm as the losses occur, without much advance planning. Some risks are recognized and their retention is planned, but in many cases no attempt is made to prefund those losses because their potential size would not cause undue financial hardship. Examples for some businesses might include pilferage of office supplies, breakage of windows, and burglary of vending machines.

In the case of funded retention, large firms also are often better able to utilize the retention technique than are small firms. For a given size, firms that are financially healthy will be better able to retain risk than those that are not. The following elements from a firm's financial statements should be considered when choosing possible retention levels:

1. Total assets
2. Total revenues
3. Asset liquidity
4. Cash flows
5. Working capital (current assets – current liabilities)
6. Ratio of revenues to net worth
7. Retained earnings
8. Ratio of total debt to net worth

For all of these items except the last one, the greater the number, the greater is the firm's ability to retain risk. In the case of the ratio of total debt to net worth, firms with lower ratios are in a better position to fund risk retention than are those with higher ratios.

Ability to Predict Losses

Another important consideration in evaluating the desirability of risk retention is the degree to which losses may or may not be predictable. Although a firm may be able to retain the maximum probable loss associated with a particular risk, problems may result if there is considerable variability in the range of possible losses. As noted in Chapter 2, the ability to predict losses is enhanced when a firm has a large enough group of items exposed to the same risk to enable it to accurately predict loss experience.

Thus, if SCH Company employs 30,000 workers nationwide, it should be able to accurately predict its likely costs associated with work-related injuries. It can then make careful estimates of the funds needed to meet these losses and decide if it wants to pay for them as they are incurred or set aside money ahead of time. In the latter case, SCH probably can set up a fund with relative certainty that, within some margin for error, the fund will actually equal the losses incurred.

Feasibility of the Retention Program

If the decision to retain losses involves advance funding, administrative issues may need to be considered. Similarly, if the risk is likely to result in several losses over time, there will be administrative expenses associated with investigating and paying for those losses. An example is a decision by ASH Corporation to retain expenses arising from injuries to its employees. Because many relatively small losses can be expected over time, ASH must prepare for the administrative issues that will arise in its retention program. Administrative issues are of particular concern when a firm decides to set up a self-insurance or captive insurer arrangement. This topic is discussed in greater detail in Chapter 8, following consideration of the remaining risk management techniques.

RISK TRANSFER

The final risk management tool is **risk transfer**, which involves payment by one party (the **transferor**) to another (the **transferee**, or risk bearer). The transferee agrees to assume a risk that the transferor desires to escape. Sometimes the degree of risk is reduced through the transfer process, because the transferee may be in a better position to use the law of large numbers to predict losses. In other cases the degree of risk remains the same and is merely shifted from the transferor to the transferee for a price. Five forms of risk transfer are hold-harmless agreements, incorporation, diversification, hedging, and insurance.

Hold-Harmless Agreements

Provisions inserted into many different kinds of contracts can transfer responsibility for some types of losses to a party different than the one that would otherwise bear it. Such provisions are called **hold-harmless agreements**, or sometimes **indemnity agreements**. The intent of these contractual clauses is to specify the party that will be responsible for paying for various losses. Usually, no dollar limit is stated. Thus, the transferee must pay for all losses covered by the agreement, regardless of size.

An example of a hold-harmless agreement is that of a landlord who includes a clause in his apartment leases making tenants responsible for all injuries that guests may suffer while on the leased premises. This transfer entails a shift in responsibility for paying for losses, but there is no actual reduction in the original risk because the tenants' ability to predict losses is no greater than that of the landlord.

Forms of Hold-Harmless Agreements

Hold-harmless agreements differ in the extent to which risk is transferred. The **limited form** merely clarifies that all parties are responsible for liabilities arising from their own actions. For example, AAA Construction Company is building an office complex for Orion, Inc. AAA engages EEE Contractors to do the electrical wiring in the buildings. The limited-form hold-harmless agreement between AAA and EEE specifies that EEE is responsible for any liability losses arising from faulty wiring. AAA is responsible for any other types of problems. In the absence of this agreement, it is possible that AAA could be held responsible for faulty wiring losses, because AAA is the general contractor for the project.

A second type of hold-harmless agreement is the **intermediate form**, in which the transferee agrees to pay for any losses in which both the transferee and transferor are jointly liable. In the preceding example, suppose EEE is concerned that AAA does not always adhere to building codes in its construction projects. Further, EEE's services are in considerable demand. Thus, before EEE agrees to do the electrical wiring for AAA, it insists that AAA sign an intermediate-form hold-harmless agreement, in which AAA is the transferee and EEE is the transferor. Not only will AAA have to pay for losses for which it is solely responsible, but it will also have to pay for any losses for which EEE and AAA are judged to have both been at fault. Note, however, that EEE will only be successful in transferring its liability risk if AAA has sufficient financial resources available to pay for resultant losses. The agreement between EEE and AAA does not eliminate EEE's ultimate responsibility to third parties (such as Orion, Inc., the owner of the office complex) if AAA is financially unable to pay for losses it has promised to bear. Consequently, EEE must be concerned about AAA's financial resources before relying on the hold-harmless agreement as a complete method of managing a particular type of risk.

The **broad form** is the third type of hold-harmless agreement. It requires the transferee to be responsible for all losses arising out of particular situations, regardless of fault. As noted in the next section, the broad form is not always legally valid.

Enforcement of Hold-Harmless Agreements

Hold-harmless agreements are not always legally enforceable. If the transferor is in a superior position to the transferee with respect to either bargaining power or knowledge of the factual situation, an attempt to transfer risk through a hold-harmless agreement may not be upheld by the courts. This result is particularly true of broad-form hold-harmless agreements.

For example, contracts between a candy manufacturer and its distributors may state that each distributor must assume the burden of paying for all losses to consumers caused by problems with the candy. This clause constitutes a broad-form hold-harmless agreement through which the candy manufacturer (transferor) attempts to transfer all risks associated with its product to the distributors (transferees). But what if the distributors are high school student groups selling the candy to make money for field trips? What if a defective ingredient causes hundreds of students to become ill after eating the candy? The inequality in knowledge and bargaining power between the manufacturer and the students likely will make the manufacturer's attempt to transfer such losses to the student groups invalid.

Incorporation

Another way for a business to transfer risk is to incorporate. In this way, the most that an incorporated firm can ever lose is the total amount of its assets. Personal assets of the owners cannot be attached to help pay for business losses, as can be the case with sole proprietorships and partnerships. Through this act of incorporation, a firm transfers to its creditors the risk that it might not have sufficient assets to pay for losses and other debts.

Diversification

While risk management might not be the primary motivation, many of the production decisions that a firm makes can serve to transfer risk. **Diversification** across various businesses or geographic locations, while frequently justified by business synergies or economies of scale, also results in the transfer of risk across business units. Additionally, this combining of businesses or geographic locations in one firm can even result in a reduction in total risk through the portfolio effect of pooling individual risks that have different correlations. For example, a firm with two production facilities may sustain windstorm damages to its facility in Nebraska resulting from a tornado. However, it is unlikely that the same storm would cause damage to its facility in Georgia.

Hedging

Hedging involves the transfer of a speculative risk. It is a business transaction in which the risk of price fluctuations is transferred to a third party, which can be either a **speculator** or another **hedger**. For example, an airline faces significant price risk from fluctuation in the price of the jet fuel that it buys. The airline sells airline tickets well in advance of the date on which it promises to transport its passengers. The price that the airline pays for jet fuel on the day that it transports its passengers may either increase or decrease relative to the price on the date that it set its ticket prices, causing either profit or loss. The airline prefers to avoid the price risk and concentrate on its main business operation: transporting goods and passengers. Therefore, on the basis of the quantity of jet fuel it expects to buy, the airline enters into an equal and opposite transaction in the oil futures market whereby a speculator, in effect, assumes the price risk. The speculator agrees to take the price risk in the hope of making a profit on the total transaction. In other words, the speculator hopes to make the right guesses about price trends more often than not. The speculator is the risk transferee, and the transferor is usually a businessperson wishing to pass on a price risk to someone who is more willing and able to bear it. Alternatively, the third party opposite the transaction made by the airline may itself be a hedger. For example, because an oil company benefits from increases in the price of oil, its risk exposure with respect to oil prices is the mirror image of an airline's exposure to oil price risk. That means the oil company could hedge its exposure to oil price risk by taking a position in the futures market exactly opposite to that of the airline. In this case, both the oil company and the airline reduce their risk by investing on opposite sides of this futures market transaction. In addition to futures contracts, forwards, swaps, and options are other commonly used tools for hedging speculative risk.

Insurance

The most widely used form of risk transfer is insurance, which is discussed in Chapters 6 and 7.

THE VALUE OF RISK MANAGEMENT

Some elements of risk management, such as loss control decisions, can be viewed as positive net present value projects. As discussed previously, if the expected gains from an investment in loss control exceed the expected costs associated with that investment, the project should increase the value of the firm.

However, shareholders in a publicly traded corporation can eliminate firm-specific risk by holding a diversified portfolio of different company stocks. As a result, the shareholder would appear to care little about the management of nonsystematic or firm-specific risk, risk that the shareholder can eliminate through portfolio diversification. This would appear to make many risk management activities, such as various forms of risk transfer, negative net present value projects. Nevertheless, corporations do engage in a number of activities directed at managing firm-specific risk, including the use of risk transfer. Why is this economically justified?

David Mayers and Clifford W. Smith Jr., in the April 1982 issue of the *Journal of Business*, suggest five reasons for the transfer of risk by the corporation. First, insurance contracts and other forms of risk transfer can allocate risk to those of the firms' claimholders who have a comparative advantage in riskbearing. Although shareholders can achieve risk reduction through portfolio diversification, employees, managers, customers, and suppliers are more limited in their ability to diversify away firm-specific risk. Second, risk transfer can provide benefits by lowering the expected costs of bankruptcy. Third, risk transfer increases the likelihood that the firm will meet its obligations to its debtholders and assures that funds will be available for future investment in valuable projects. Fourth, the comparative advantage of insurers in providing services related to risks, also known as real services, such as claims handling or loss prevention, can be an advantage of risk transfer through insurance. Fifth, when the tax system is progressive the additional tax from increases in earnings is greater than the reduction in taxes associated with decreases in earnings. Hence, risk transfer, by reducing the volatility of reported earnings, can reduce the firm's expected taxes.

When evaluating risk management from the perspective of its impact on the value of the corporation, the source of the risk is less important than its effect on volatility. Regardless of whether the reduction in earnings comes from fire damage to the corporation's property, or from an increase in commodity prices, the financial impact on the shareholders is the same. This broader view of risk underpins the movement toward **enterprise risk management**. Additionally, this holistic view reflects the realization that appropriate risk management must consider the fact that the corporation faces a portfolio of risks. And just as investment theory suggests that diversification can reduce the risk associated with a portfolio of securities, diversification within the portfolio of risks facing the corporation can alter the firm's risk profile. Ignoring these diversification effects by managing the firm's many risks independently can lead to inefficient use of the corporation's resources. Some of the tools of integrated risk management are discussed in Chapter 8.

Integrated Risk Management

The enterprise or holistic view of risk management encompasses building a structure and a systematic process for managing all of a corporation's risks, such as damage to property and injury to employees. Enterprise risk management considers financial, commodity, credit, legal, environmental, reputational, and other intangible exposures that could adversely impact the value of the corporation. The formation by some firms of the new position of chief risk officer (CRO) reflects a realization of the importance of identifying all risks that could negatively impact the firm. A 2001 survey by the Center for Strategic Risk Management at the University of Georgia suggests that the responsibilities of the CRO include: implementation of a consistent risk management framework across the organization's business areas; implementation and management of an integrated risk management program, with particular emphasis on operational risk; communication of risk and the integrated risk management program to stakeholders; and mitigation and financing of risks. This broader perspective of risk has some important implications for the selection of risk management techniques. These implications are discussed in Chapter 8.

SUMMARY

1. Risk avoidance is a conscious decision not to be exposed to a particular risk of loss. It is not always feasible, and even when it is, it is often not desirable.

2. Loss control involves actions to reduce the losses associated with particular risks. Some forms of loss control concentrate on reducing the frequency of losses, whereas others focus on reducing loss severity. Two special forms of severity reduction are separation and duplication.

3. Heinrich's domino theory states that employee injuries take the final place in the following sequence: heredity and social environment, personal fault, an unsafe act or physical hazard, an accident, and the resultant injury.

4. Another way of classifying loss control is whether it involves actions prior to a loss, concurrent with a loss, or after a loss occurs.

5. Expected gains from an investment in loss control should at least equal the expected costs in order to justify the expenditure. But it is not necessarily easy to identify and quantify all potential costs and benefits.

6. Risk transfer involves payment by the transferor to the transferee, who agrees to assume a risk that the transferor desires to escape. Risk retention involves the assumption of risk, and can be planned or unplanned. It can also be either funded or unfunded prior to a loss.

7. Four types of funded retention possibilities are the use of credit, the establishment of a reserve fund, self-insurance, and captive insurers.

8. Self-insurance involves prefunding of expected losses and a sufficiently large group of exposure units to enable accurate loss prediction.

9. Large businesses can often use risk retention to a greater extent than can small firms, partly because of their more extensive financial resources. Other factors to consider are the ability to predict losses and the overall feasibility of the retention program.

10. All else being the same, the greater the following, the greater is a firm's ability to use risk retention: assets, revenues, liquidity, revenues/net worth, and retained earnings. All else being the same, firms with lower debt-to-equity ratios are better able to use risk retention.

11. Four types of noninsurance risk transfer methods are hold-harmless agreements, incorporation, diversification, and hedging.

12. Three types of hold-harmless agreements are limited form, intermediate form, and broad form. Hold-harmless agreements may not be legally enforceable if the transferor is in a superior position to the transferee with respect to either bargaining power or knowledge of the factual situation.

13. Risk management activities such as risk transfer add value to a publicly traded firm by efficiently allocating risk among the firm's claimholders, reducing bankruptcy costs, increasing the likelihood that obligations to debtholders are met, providing access to the real services of insurers, and reducing expected tax liabilities.

internetexercises

1. Red Cross disaster planning guidelines can be found on the World Wide Web at http://www.redcross.org under Disaster Services. Which disasters are most likely to affect your area? Is your home prepared to deal with these potential crises? What steps can you take to implement more thorough loss control?

2. A variety of derivative securities have been developed that serve to mitigate risk associated with the weather. Any company whose revenue is affected by weather has a potential need for weather risk management products. For more details on the types of firms that may have a need for weather risk management products and to see what types of weather that a firm can protect itself from visit http://www.weatherderivs.com. What other common risks could be reduced using derivative securities?

QUESTIONS FOR REVIEW AND DISCUSSION

1. Explain the concept of risk avoidance. When is it an appropriate risk management technique?

2. Suppose that XYZ Corporation owns 25 warehouses. Explain how XYZ can use frequency-reduction and severity-reduction techniques to control fire losses with respect to its warehouses.

3. Give an example of the use of separation as a loss control technique. When might duplication be used instead?

4. What are the general categories of costs and benefits that firms might consider in analyzing potential investments in loss control?

5. Define risk retention and explain why a large corporation may be able to use this technique more effectively than an individual or a small company.

6. Differentiate between planned and unplanned retention, as well as between funded and unfunded retention. Are all of these forms of retention appropriate risk management techniques? Explain.

7. Explain the viability of credit as a source of funding for risk retention.

8. List the two necessary elements of self-insurance and explain the difference between self-insurance and the establishment of a reserve fund by a business.

9. What specific financial factors are important when considering the appropriate level of risk retention for a firm? Explain how these factors are relevant.

10. What are the roles of the transferor and the transferee in risk transfer?

11. Explain the differences among the three types of hold-harmless agreements.

12. Explain why a hold-harmless agreement may not be legally enforceable. Give an example of a situation in which the agreement likely would not be upheld by the courts.

13. How is incorporation a form of risk transfer? Who is the transferor and who is the transferee when incorporation is used?

14. How is diversification a form of risk transfer? In what way does it result in risk reduction?

15. The purchase of required textbooks can represent a significant investment for college students. Identify several risks to your textbooks and explain some possible techniques for managing these risks. Discuss the risk management techniques that you have chosen and the reasons for your choices.

16. A common mistake made by people unfamiliar with risk management is to think of self-insurance as being synonymous with risk retention. Discuss the differences between these concepts and the relationship between them.

17. Illuminating Concepts sells lighting fixtures on both a retail and wholesale basis. It also provides installation services for its products, at an additional cost. With respect to the risk of adverse liability judgments arising out of its products and installation services, what are some suggested loss control activities that should be considered? Classify each suggestion as to whether it emphasizes frequency or severity reduction, as well as whether it involves preloss activities, concurrent loss control, or post-loss activities.

18. In the situation described in the previous question, what are the likely costs and benefits associated with each suggested loss control measure? For which forms of loss control do you believe the benefits will outweigh the costs? Explain.

19. The Great Lakes Recreational Area encompasses several waterfront activities, including swimming, boating, and fishing. It has a history of numerous injuries to its employees as well as to its patrons. Explain how the Heinrich domino theory can be used to analyze potential loss control measures that might be useful for Great Lakes to consider.

20. One aspect of the value of risk management to a corporation is the fact that managing risk can increase the likelihood that the firm will meet its obligations to its debtholders. Can you think of examples of lenders requiring individuals who buy a home or car to engage in some form of risk management? Explain.

chapter 6

Insurance as a Risk Management Technique: Principles

Larry Cox is starting a custom construction business that will specialize in kitchen interiors. Larry has done this type of work in the past for other firms, but he is tired of working for others and now wants to control his own destiny. He has hired three workers that he knows well from prior jobs and is now acquiring office, display, and machine shop space. Larry hopes to begin operations within a month or so.

One of the issues in getting started is that of identifying and managing some of the pure risks that will be associated with the new business. Larry is familiar with the risk management process and has identified numerous risks with which he will be faced, but he's not sure of the best alternatives for dealing with all of them. Because his business is just getting started, Larry has very little extra capital to cushion any losses; thus, he suspects that he will need to utilize insurance to a greater extent than might a larger, more established firm.

As Larry thinks about this issue, he realizes that he has never given the concept of insurance a great deal of thought. He has always taken for granted that it could be obtained to cover anything, but now Larry wonders if that is true. Are there some risks for which insurance is not available? Then there are various legal questions that Larry is also pondering. Can he buy insurance now to cover a business that is not yet operational? Does it matter whether he deals with an insurance agent or an insurance broker in arranging the coverage? If Larry accidentally buys more insurance than he really needs, how will that affect his recovery for a loss? And given all the uncertainties in his life now, what if Larry unwittingly provides a wrong answer or two on the application for insurance? Will all of his insurance be void? These and other similar issues are discussed in this chapter.

CHAPTER OBJECTIVES

After studying this chapter, you should be able to

1. Define *insurance* and explain how it differs from other methods of risk transfer.
2. Identify situations that give rise to insurable interest and explain how this principle supports the principle of indemnity.
3. State how the subrogation process works and how it is useful.
4. Determine what makes a risk insurable.
5. List the legal requirements of a contract and describe the distinguishing legal characteristics of insurance contracts.
6. Differentiate between insurance agents and brokers and describe the sources for their authority.
7. Define *social insurance* and explain the basic principles underlying most social insurance programs.
8. Describe the central costs and values of insurance to society.

The general concept of transfer as a risk management technique was discussed in Chapter 5. Insurance is a special form of this technique and may be defined in two major contexts: as an economic or social institution designed to perform certain functions and as a legal contract between two parties, the **insured** (transferor) and the **insurer** (transferee).

THE NATURE OF INSURANCE

As an economic institution, **insurance** involves not only risk transfer but also pooling and risk reduction. **Pooling** is the sharing of total losses among a group. Pooling within a large group facilitates **risk reduction**, which is a decrease in the total amount of uncertainty present in a particular situation. Insurance accomplishes risk reduction by combining under one management a group of objects situated so that the aggregate losses to which the insureds are subject become predictable within narrow limits. Thus, overall risk for the group is reduced, and losses that result are pooled, usually through the payment of an insurance **premium**. Thus, through the insurance mechanism, insureds transfer various risks to the group and exchange a potentially large, uncertain loss for a relatively smaller certain payment (the premium).

Insurance is sometimes likened to gambling, because it is possible for one party to receive a great deal more than is given in the transaction—just as is possible in gambling. But from an economic standpoint, gambling and insurance are exact opposites. Gambling creates a new risk where none existed before, whereas insurance is a method of eliminating or greatly reducing an already existing risk.

Insurance is usually implemented through legal contracts, or **policies**, in which the insurer promises to reimburse the insured for losses suffered during the term of the agreement. Implicit in insurance transfers is the assumption that the insurer will indeed be able to pay whatever losses may occur. Sometimes, however, insurers become insolvent and are unable to keep their promises to pay insured losses. In such cases, insureds may have to bear the cost of losses that they had assumed had been adequately transferred through the purchase of insurance policies. Thus, when using insurance as a risk management technique, it is important to consider the financial condition of the insurer and the probability that it will be able to pay for all insured losses that may occur. Some of the factors to consider in this regard are discussed in Chapter 24.

There are some situations in which the purchase of insurance is the best way to manage a particular risk, due to the insurer's ability to handle risk efficiently through the law of large numbers. But it must be stressed that insurance should never be automatically assumed to be the only way to deal with a given risk. Rather, it should be considered as one of many potential techniques available through the risk management process. In fact, many risk managers consider insurance as a method of last resort, to be used only when other risk management techniques are not sufficient by themselves. In the sections that follow, many of the important principles underlying the insurance mechanism are discussed.

PRINCIPLE OF INDEMNITY

The **principle of indemnity** is one of the most important precepts for many types of insurance—particularly for property insurance. According to this principle, the insured may not collect more than the actual loss in the event of damage caused by an insured peril. This principle serves to control moral hazards that might otherwise exist. Because insurance is designed to merely **indemnify**, or restore insureds to the situations that existed prior to a loss, the likelihood of intentional losses is greatly reduced because payment for losses will not exceed the value of the property destroyed—regardless of the amount of insurance that may have been purchased.

Another important result of the principle of indemnity is the typical inclusion in property insurance contracts of clauses regarding the existence of other insurance. The purpose of such clauses is to prevent the insured from taking out duplicate policies with different insurers in the expectation of recovering more than the actual loss. Typically, such clauses provide that all policies covering the same loss will share losses that occur. Different ways in which this sharing may occur are discussed in Chapter 7.

There are some exceptions to the application of the principle of indemnity in property insurance. One issue involves the appropriate way to measure losses. For example, suppose Alliance Corporation has 10-year-old office furniture that is destroyed in a fire. Should this loss be valued at what it would cost to replace the furniture with new furniture or with comparable 10-year-old furniture (if such could be found)? Although replacement with new furniture would technically violate the principle of indemnity, such is done in many property policies. This valuation issue is discussed in more detail in Chapter 7. Another exception to the indemnity principle arises from the **valued policy laws** that some states have enacted, whereby the insurer must pay the entire face amount of a fire insurance policy in the event of total loss of the insured object. Some transportation policies also are written on a valued basis, and it is assumed that the insured will take out insurance equal to the full value of the object. Finally, the principle of indemnity is not usually applicable in the field of life insurance. When the insured dies, no attempt is made to measure the amount of the loss. Instead, the full amount of the life insurance policy is paid upon the death of the insured.

PRINCIPLE OF INSURABLE INTEREST

A fundamental legal principle that strongly supports the principle of indemnity is that of **insurable interest**, which holds that an insured must demonstrate a personal loss or else be unable to collect amounts due when a loss caused by an insured peril occurs. If insureds could collect without having an insurable interest, a moral hazard would exist, and the contract would be deemed contrary to public policy. The doctrine of insurable interest is also necessary to prevent insurance from becoming a gambling contract. An important reason for requiring insurable interest in life insurance is to remove a possible incentive for murder.

What Constitutes Insurable Interest

One important issue is determining which persons or organizations can have insurable interests. The legal owner of property having its value diminished by loss resulting from an insured peril has an insurable interest and can collect if he or she is able to demonstrate that a financial loss has occurred. But ownership is not the only evidence of insurable interest. For example, XMA Corporation leases a building under a long-term lease whereby the lease may be cancelled if a fire destroys a certain percentage of the value of the building. XMA has an insurable interest in the building because of the lease.

There also are other rights that are sufficient to establish an insurable interest in a property. Thus, the holder of a contract to receive oil royalties has an insurable interest in the oil property so that in the event of an insured loss, indemnity can be collected, the amount of the indemnity being measured by the reduction in royalty resulting from the insured loss. Likewise, legal liability resulting from contracts establishes insurable interest in property. For example, garage operators have an insurable interest in the stored automobiles for which they have assumed liability. Secured creditors, such as mortgagees, have an insurable interest in the property on which they have lent money. Building contractors have an insurable interest in property on which they have worked because they have a mechanic's lien. In each of these latter two cases, loss of the building would endanger the ability to collect amounts due. However, general creditors—ones without specific liens on the property—are not regarded as having a sufficiently great property right to give them an insurable interest. In most states, however, a general contractor who reduces a debt to a judgment then has an insurable interest in the debtor's property. A businessperson has an insurable interest in the profits expected from the use of property and in the expenses incurred in managing that property.

An insurable interest always is presumed to exist in life insurance for persons who voluntarily insure their own lives. An individual may procure life insurance and make anyone the **beneficiary** (the one who receives the insurance proceeds when death occurs), regardless of whether the beneficiary has an insurable interest. But one who purchases life insurance on another's life must have an insurable interest in that person's life. Thus, a business firm may insure the life of a key employee because that person's death would cause financial loss to the firm. A wife may insure the life of her husband because his continued existence is valuable to her and she would suffer a financial loss upon his death. Likewise, a husband may insure the life of his wife because her continued existence is valuable to him and he could suffer a financial loss upon her death. The same statement may apply to almost anyone who is dependent on an individual. A father may insure the life of a minor child, but a brother may not ordinarily insure the life of his sister. In the latter case there would not usually be a financial loss to the brother upon the death of his sister, but in the former case the father would suffer financial loss upon the death of his child. A creditor has an insurable interest in the life of a debtor because the death of the debtor would subject the creditor to possible loss.

Of course, there are practical limits as to the amount of life insurance an individual may obtain. Sometimes parties will attempt to avoid the insurable interest requirements in life insurance and use the contract as a wagering agreement. Courts will usually set aside such contracts. For example, two individuals met in a bar and after a short acquaintance, one agreed to insure his life and then assign the policy to the other if reimbursed for the premium. The insured person died, and the insurer refused to pay when the facts surrounding the application became known. The court upheld the insurer's refusal to pay on the grounds that the transaction was conceived to use the life insurance policy as a means of effecting a wager. The intention was to avoid the requirements of insurable interest by having the person whose life was insured take out the policy with the sole purpose of transferring it to another who had no insurable interest.

When the Insurable Interest Must Exist

In property and liability insurance, it is possible to effect coverage on property in which the insured does not have an insurable interest at the time the policy is written but in which such an interest is expected in the future. For example, in transportation insurance a shipper often obtains coverage on the cargo it has not yet purchased in anticipation of buying cargo for the return trip. As a result, the courts generally hold that in property insurance, insurable interest need exist only at the time of the loss and not at the inception of the policy. However, if at the time of the loss the insured no longer has an interest in the property, there is no liability under the policy. For example, suppose that X Company owns and insures an automobile. Later X sells the car to Y Company, and shortly thereafter the auto is destroyed. X, which has no further financial interest in the car, cannot collect under the policy. Further, Y has no protection under the policy because insurance is said to follow the person and not the property. In other words, the policy purchased by X Company does not transfer to Y when the car is sold. Y would have to obtain its own coverage to be able to collect when the loss occurs.

In life insurance, the general rule is that insurable interest must exist at the inception of the policy, but it is not necessary at the time of the loss. The courts view life insurance as an investment contract. To illustrate, assume that a wife who owns a life insurance policy on her husband later obtains a divorce. If she continues to maintain the insurance by paying the premiums, she may collect on the subsequent death of her former husband even though she is remarried and suffers no particular financial loss upon his death. It is sufficient that she had an insurable interest when the policy was first issued. In a similar way, a corporation may retain in full force a life insurance policy on an employee who is no longer with the firm. A creditor may retain the policy on the life of a debtor who has repaid his or her obligation. In other words, in life insurance the general rule is that a continuing insurable interest is not necessary.

PRINCIPLE OF SUBROGATION

The principle of **subrogation** grows out of the principle of indemnity. Under the principle of subrogation, one who has indemnified another's loss is entitled to recovery from any liable third parties who are responsible. Thus, if Dave negligently causes damage to Ed's property, Ed's insurance company will indemnify Ed to the extent of its liability for Ed's loss and then have the right to proceed against Dave for any amounts it has paid out under Ed's policy.

Reasons for Subrogation

One of the important reasons for subrogation is to reinforce the principle of indemnity—that is, to prevent the insured from collecting more than the actual amount of the loss. If Ed's insurer did not have the right of subrogation, it would be possible for Ed to recover from the policy and then recover again in a legal action against Dave. In this way Ed would collect twice. It would also be possible for Ed to arrange an accident with Dave, collect twice, and split the profit with Dave. A moral hazard would exist, and the contract would tend to become an instrument of fraud.

Another reason for subrogation is that it keeps insurance premiums below what they would otherwise be. In some lines of insurance, particularly liability, recoveries from negligent parties through subrogation are substantial. Although no specific provision for subrogation recoveries is made in the rate structure other than through those provisions relating to salvage, the rates would tend to be higher if such recoveries were not permitted. A final reason for subrogation is that the burden of loss is more nearly placed on the shoulders of those responsible. That is, the party that caused the loss is held financially accountable for its actions. Negligent parties should not escape penalty because of the insurance mechanism.

Exceptions to the Principle of Subrogation

Subrogation normally does not exist in such lines as life insurance and most types of health insurance. Also, subrogation does not give the insurer the right to collect against the insured, even if the insured is negligent. Thus, a homeowner who negligently, but accidentally, burns down the house while thawing a frozen water pipe with a blowtorch can collect under a fire policy, but the insurer cannot proceed against the owner of the policy for compensation. Otherwise, there would be little value in having insurance.

It is not uncommon for an insurer to waive rights of subrogation under certain circumstances where, by so doing, there is no violation of the principle of indemnity. Suppose that a manufacturer has agreed to hold a railroad harmless for losses arising out of the maintenance of a spur track that the railroad has placed on the manufacturer's property. In effect, the manufacturer has assumed legal liability that would otherwise be the responsibility of the railroad. Now assume that a spark from one of the railroad's engines sets fire to the manufacturer's building and the railroad is found negligent, and hence legally liable for the ensuing damage. The insurer will pay the loss, but under its right of subrogation could proceed against the railroad. However, the manufacturer has previously agreed to assume all losses arising out of the existence of the spur track. Thus, any amount collected from the railroad becomes the ultimate liability of the manufacturer because of the hold-harmless agreement. Therefore, the insurer will waive the subrogation clause in the manufacturer's insurance policy because to enforce it would mean that the insured would not be compensated for its loss. This waiver can be performed by inserting a waiver-of-subrogation clause in the manufacturer's insurance policy. Such clauses are common.

An insured who acts in such a way as to destroy or reduce the value of the insurer's right of subrogation violates the provisions of most subrogation clauses and forfeits all rights under the policy. For instance, suppose Fred collides with Gladys in an automobile accident. Fred writes Gladys a letter of apology and implies that he is to blame. It is later determined that Gladys is probably negligent and, had it not been for Fred's statement, his insurer would have been able to subrogate against Gladys for the amount paid to Fred. Consequently, the insurer may deny liability to Fred. The insurer's subrogation rights also cannot be avoided by a settlement between the primary parties after the insurer has paid under the policy. In such a case, the insurer is entitled to reimbursement from the insured who has received any payment from the negligent party.

Finally, note that the insurer is entitled to subrogation only after the insured has been fully indemnified. If the insured has borne part of the loss (perhaps due to inadequate coverage), the insurer may claim recovery only after these costs have been repaid. The only exception to this rule is that the insurer is entitled to legal expenses incurred in pursuing the subrogation process against a negligent third party. For example, assume that Query Company's building, valued at $200,000 and insured for $160,000, is totally destroyed through the negligence of contractor James Forehand. Query's insurer subrogates against Forehand and collects $100,000 and has legal expenses of $25,000. The insurer receives $25,000 for legal expenses, Query receives the $40,000 by which he was underinsured, and the insurer receives the remaining $35,000.

PRINCIPLE OF UTMOST GOOD FAITH

Insurance is said to be a contract of **utmost good faith**, in which a higher standard of honesty is imposed on parties to an insurance agreement than is imposed through ordinary commercial contracts. The principle of utmost good faith has greatly affected insurance practices and casts a very different light on the interpretation of insurance agreements than many persons often suppose. The application of this principle may best be explained in a discussion of representations, warranties, concealments, and mistakes.

Representations

A **representation** is a statement made by an applicant for insurance before the policy is issued. Although the representation need not be in writing, it is usually embodied in a written application. An example of a representation in life insurance would be answering yes or no to a question as to whether the applicant had been treated for any physical condition or illness by a doctor within the previous five years. If a representation is relied on by the insurer in entering into the contract and if it proves to have been false at the time it was made or becomes false before the contract is signed, there exist legal grounds for the insurer to avoid the contract.

Avoiding the contract does not follow unless the misrepresentation is **material** to the risk—that is, if the truth had been known, the contract either would not have been issued or would have been issued on different terms. If the misrepresentation is inconsequential, its falsity will not affect the contract. However, a misrepresentation of a material fact may make the contract voidable, at the option of the insurer. The insurer may decide to affirm the contract or to avoid it. Failure to cancel a contract after first learning about the falsity of a material misrepresentation may operate to defeat the insurer's rights to cancel at a later time.

Generally, even an innocent misrepresentation of a material fact is no defense for the insured if the insurer elects to avoid the contract. Applicants for insurance speak at their own

ETHICAL PERSPECTIVES

Subrogation

The interaction between the subrogation clause and the need to waive subrogation rights can raise interesting ethical issues for insurers and insureds, even when no specific waiver-of-subrogation clause exists in an insurance policy. Consider the case of an insured who owned property, of which a portion was leased to another individual, named Polk. As part of the lease agreement, there was a waiver excusing Polk from liability for destruction of the property by fire.

On a date within the insured's policy period, the property was destroyed by a fire. The insured made a claim for recovery of the damages from the insurer. After an investigation of the blaze, the insurer determined that the damages were caused as a direct result of Polk's negligence.

Thus, the insurer paid the amount of the damages to the insured and then started proceedings against Polk to recover (subrogate) for the damages because of Polk's alleged negligence. Polk defended on the grounds that the contract between Polk and the insurer constituted a waiver-of-subrogation clause.

Polk won. The court held that the owner's fire insurer was not entitled to subrogation against Polk for the fire loss paid to the owner. The insurer's right to subrogation could not extend beyond the insured's own rights, and the lease agreement limited the ability to subrogate for fire losses. Thus, because the owner had no rights to collect from Polk, the insurer had no subrogation rights against him either.

Sources: *Continental Casualty Company, et al. v Polk Brothers, Inc.*, Illinois Appellate Court (November 21, 1983); *Insurance Law Reporter* (Riverwoods, IL: Commerce Clearing House, 1985), 980–86.

risk, and if they make an innocent mistake about a fact they believe to be true, they are held accountable for their carelessness. Thus, suppose Cassandra Cole applies for insurance on her automobile and states that there is no driver under age 25 in her family. However, it turns out that her 16-year-old son has been driving the family car without his mother's knowledge. Lack of this knowledge is no defense when the insurance company refuses to pay a subsequent claim on the grounds of material misrepresentation. It is not necessary for the insurer to demonstrate that a loss occurred arising out of the misrepresentation in order to exert its right to avoid the contract. Thus, in the preceding case, assume Cassandra has an accident and it is then learned for the first time that she has a 16-year-old son driving. Since this situation is contrary to that which Cassandra had previously stated, the insurer may usually legally refuse payment.

If the court holds that a statement given in the application was one of opinion, rather than fact, and it turns out that the opinion was wrong, it is necessary for the insurer to demonstrate bad faith or fraudulent intent on the part of the insured in order to avoid the contract. For example, Jeff Meyers is applying for health insurance. He is asked on the application form, "Have you ever had cancer?" and he answers no. Later he discovers that he actually had cancer. The court might well find that the insured was not told the true state of his health and thought that he had some other ailment. If the question had been phrased, "Have you ever been told you had cancer?" a yes or no answer would clearly be one of fact, not opinion. An honest opinion should not be grounds for rescinding an insurance policy.

Warranties

A **warranty** is a clause in an insurance contract stating that before the insurer is liable, a certain fact, condition, or circumstance affecting the risk must exist. For example, an insurance policy covering a ship may state "warranted free of capture or seizure." This statement means that if the ship is involved in a war skirmish, the insurance is void. Or a bank may be insured on condition that a certain burglar alarm system be installed and maintained. Such a clause is a condition of coverage and acts as a warranty. A warranty creates a condition of the contract, and any breach of warranty, *even if immaterial*, will void the contract. This is the central distinction between a warranty and a representation. A misrepresentation does not void the insurance unless it is material to the risk, whereas under common law any breach of warranty, even if deemed to be minor, voids the contract. The courts have been somewhat reluctant to enforce this rule, and in many jurisdictions the rule has been relaxed either by statute or by court decision.

Warranties may be either express or implied. **Express warranties** are those stated in the contract, whereas **implied warranties** are not found in the contract but are assumed by the parties to the contract. Implied warranties are found in policies covering ocean vessels. For example, a shipper purchases insurance under the implied condition that the ship is seaworthy, that the voyage is legal, and that there shall be no deviation from the intended course. Unless these conditions have been waived by the insurer (legality cannot be waived), they are binding on the shipper. A warranty also may be either promissory or affirmative. A **promissory warranty** describes a condition, fact, or circumstance to which the insured agrees to be held during the life of the contract. An **affirmative warranty** is one that must exist only at the time the contract is first put into effect. For example, an insured may warrant that a certain ship left port under convoy (affirmative warranty), and the insured may warrant that the ship will continue to sail under convoy (promissory warranty).

Concealments

A **concealment** is defined as silence when obligated to speak. A concealment has approximately the same legal effect as a misrepresentation of a material fact. It is the failure of an applicant to reveal a fact that is material to the risk. Because insurance is a contract of utmost good faith, it is not enough that the applicant answer truthfully all questions asked by the insurer before the contract is effected. The applicant must also *volunteer* material facts, even if disclosure of such facts might result in rejection of the application or the payment of a higher premium.

The applicant is often in a position to know material facts about the risk that the insurer does not. To allow these facts to be concealed would be unfair to the insurer. After all, the insurer does not ask questions such as "Is your building now on fire?" or "Is your car now wrecked?" The most relentless opponent of an insurer's defense suit would not argue that an insured who obtained coverage under such circumstances would be exercising even elementary fairness.

The important, often crucial, question about concealments lies in whether the applicant knew the fact withheld to be material. The tests of a concealment are as follows:

1. Did the insured know of a certain fact?
2. Was this fact material?
3. Was the insurer ignorant of the fact?
4. Did the insured know the insurer was ignorant of the fact?

The test of materiality is especially difficult because often the applicant is not an insurance expert and is not expected to know the full significance of every fact that might be of vital concern to the insurer. The final determination of materiality is the same as it is in the law of representation, namely, would the contract be issued on the same terms if the concealed fact had been known? There are two rules determining the standard of care required of the applicant. The stricter rule, which usually applies only to ocean vessels and their cargoes, holds that intentional concealment as well as innocent concealment can void the contract. In this case, the fourth test for concealment is irrelevant. For most other risks, however, the rule is that a policy cannot be avoided unless there is fraudulent intent to conceal material facts.

Thus, the intentional withholding of material facts with intent to deceive constitutes fraud. In determining which facts must be disclosed if known, it has been held that facts of general knowledge or facts known by the insurer need not be disclosed. There is also the inference from past cases, though not a final determination, that the insurer cannot void a contract on the grounds of concealment of those facts that are embarrassing or self-disgracing to the applicant.

Mistakes

When an honest mistake is made in a written contract of insurance, steps can be taken to correct it after the policy is issued. Generally, a policy can be reformed if there is proof of a mutual mistake or a mistake on one side that is known to be a mistake by the other party, where no mention was made of it at the time the agreement was made. A *mistake* in the sense used here does not mean an error in judgment by one party but refers to a situation where it can be shown that the actual agreement made was not the one stated in the contract.

As an illustration of this, consider an insurer that issued a $10,000 life insurance policy and, by an error of one of its clerks, included an option at the end of 20 years to receive income payments of $1,051 per year, rather than $105.10 per year. The mistake was discovered 18 years later. When the insurer tried to correct the error, the insured refused to accept payment of the smaller amount. In a legal decision, the court held that the mistake was a mutual one that should be corrected. The error of the insurer was in misplacing a decimal point, whereas the error of the insured was either in not noticing the error or, if noticed, in failing to say anything. Thus, the correct, smaller payment was substituted for the larger, incorrect one stated in the policy.[1]

In contrast to the previous example, suppose Adam believes himself to be the owner of certain property and insures it. He cannot later demand all of the premium back solely because he discovers that, in fact, he was not the owner of the property. This was a mistake in judgment or an erroneous supposition, and the courts will not relieve that kind of mistake.

REQUISITES OF INSURABLE RISKS

In spite of the usefulness of insurance in many contexts, not all risks are commercially insurable. The characteristics of risks that make it feasible for private insurers to offer insurance for them are called the **requisites of insurable risks**. These requirements should not be considered as absolute, iron rules but rather as guides or ideal standards that are not always completely attained in practice. Even when their absence makes it impossible for insurance to be offered by private insurers, however, government agencies may offer some protection. The principles of this "social insurance" are discussed later in this chapter.

Large Number of Similar Objects

One of the most important requirements from the standpoint of the insurer is that the probable loss must be subject to advance estimation, which means that the number of insured objects must be sufficiently large and that the objects themselves must be similar enough to allow the law of large numbers to operate.

If only a few objects are insured, the insurer is subject to the same uncertainties as the insured. The field of life insurance is one in which this requisite works particularly well. Life insurers have gathered reliable statistics over many years and have developed tables of mortality that have proved to be very accurate as estimates of probable loss. Furthermore, life

---

1   *Metropolitan Life Insurance Co. v Henriksen*, 126 N.E. (2d) 736 (Illinois Appellate Court, 1955).

insurance is well accepted; it is relatively easy for the insurer to obtain a large group of exposure units. Here the law of large numbers works so well that for all practical purposes the life insurer is able to eliminate its risk. On the other hand, insurers may not be able to predict losses nearly so well in areas such as nuclear energy liability and physical loss to ocean-based drilling platforms, where adequate numbers of exposures may be lacking.

In addition to having a sufficiently large number of insured objects, the nature of the objects must be enough alike so that reliable statistics on loss can be formulated. It would be improper, for example, to group commercial buildings with private residences for purposes of fire insurance, because the hazards facing these classes of buildings are entirely different. Furthermore, the physical and social environment of all objects in the group should be roughly similar so that no unusual factors are present that would cause losses to one part of the group and not to the other part. Thus, buildings located in a hurricane zone must not be grouped with buildings a thousand miles from the coast.

It should also be noted that sometimes insurers act as risk transferees even when it is impossible to obtain a sufficiently large number of exposure units to allow the law of large numbers to operate. In these situations, risk is not reduced as part of the transfer, and the insurer should be thought of merely as a transferee for such transactions.

Accidental and Unintentional Loss

There must be some uncertainty surrounding the loss. Otherwise, there would be no risk. If the risk or uncertainty already has been eliminated, insurance serves no purpose; the main function of insurance is to reduce risk. Thus, if a key employee is dying from an incurable disease that will cause death within a given time, there is little uncertainty or risk concerning the payment of loss. Thus, insurance is not feasible. Theoretically, the insurer could issue a policy, but the premium would have to be large enough to cover both the expected loss and the insurer's cost of doing business. The cost of such a policy would probably be too high for the prospective insured.

Because of the requirement that the loss be accidental, insurers normally exclude in all policies any loss caused intentionally by the insured. If the insured knew that the insurer would pay for intentional losses, a moral hazard would be introduced, causing both losses and premiums to rise. If premiums become exceedingly high, few would purchase insurance, and the insurer would no longer have a sufficiently large number of exposure units to be able to obtain a reliable estimate of future losses. Thus the first requirement of an insurable risk would not be met.

Such a scenario is similar to the phenomenon of **adverse selection**, which is the tendency of insureds who know that they have a greater than average chance of loss to seek to purchase more than an average amount of insurance. When an insured possesses knowledge about likely losses that is unavailable to insurers, the insured is said to have **asymmetric information**. The existence of asymmetric information is one cause of adverse selection. In general, insurers try to control adverse selection by investigating potential insureds and then providing coverage only to those who meet specified standards. This process of selecting and classifying insureds from among the many applicants is called **underwriting** and is discussed in Chapter 23.

To illustrate the unfortunate effects that adverse selection would cause if insurers did not practice underwriting, consider the example of crime insurance. Businesses operating in high-crime areas are the ones most likely to want to buy crime insurance, even at a premium that is too high to be attractive to firms in safer locations. If an insurer does not engage in some degree of underwriting, it may find itself selling primarily to very high-risk firms. Subsequent loss payments will be more than expected, and premiums will have to be increased. As premiums increase, fewer businesses will be interested in the insurance, and the only ones who will ultimately find the protection economically attractive will be those with a very high chance of loss. At this point, the insurance arrangement may be said to have entered a "death spiral," in which it will eventually fail due to the lack of several of the necessary requisites.

Determinable and Measurable Loss

The loss must be definite in time and place. It may seem unnecessary to add this requirement because most losses are easily recognized and can be measured with reasonable accuracy. It is a real problem to insurers, however, to be able even to recognize certain losses, let alone measure them. For example, an insurer may agree to pay the insured a monthly income if the individual should become so totally disabled as to be unable to perform the duties of his or her occupation. The question arises, however, as to who will determine whether the insured meets this condition. Often it is necessary to take the insured's word. Thus, it may be possible for a dishonest person to feign illness in order to recover under the policy. If this happens, the second requirement, that the loss is not intentional, is not met.

Even if it is clear that a loss has occurred, it may not be easy to measure it. For example, what is the loss from "pain and suffering" of an auto accident victim? Often only a jury can decide. What is the loss of a cargo on a sunken ship? It often takes a staff of adjusters many months or even years to decide. Thus, before the burden of risk can be safely assumed, the insurer must set up procedures to determine whether loss has actually occurred and, if so, its size.

Loss Not Subject to Catastrophic Hazard

Conditions should not be such that all or most of the objects in the insured group might suffer loss at the same time and possibly from the same peril. Such simultaneous disaster to insured objects can be illustrated by reference to large fires, floods, earthquakes, and hurricanes that have disrupted major geographical areas in the past. In 1992, insurers doing business in south Florida were reminded of this possibility when Hurricane Andrew struck, resulting in widespread damage for hundreds of thousands of insureds across the state. The history of fire insurance reveals that very few major U.S. cities have escaped suffering a catastrophic fire at some time in their history. One example from the early 1900s is San Francisco, which was nearly destroyed by an earthquake and the fires that resulted. If an insurer is unlucky enough to have on its books a great deal of property situated in areas such as these when catastrophe occurs, it obviously suffers a loss that was not contemplated when the premiums were formulated. Most insurers reduce this possibility by ample dispersion of insured objects. It is also possible for insurers themselves to purchase insurance against the possibility of excessive losses. This insurance for insurers is called **reinsurance** and is discussed in greater detail in Chapter 23. Following the September 11 terrorist attacks many firms had difficulty obtaining insurance for so-called trophy properties due to the recognition by insurers of the catastrophic loss potential associated with these buildings. This situation was made worse by the lack of reinsurance for such properties.

This requisite concerning the absence of a catastrophic hazard also effectively eliminates many speculative risks from the possibility of being insured. For example, consider the uncertainty that a retailer faces in connection with the price at which inventories can be sold. Suppose it wishes to insure that the price of its product will not fall more than 10 percent during the year. Such a risk is subject to catastrophic loss because simultaneous loss from this source is possible to all products. Further, the losses are not subject to advance calculation because, in an ever-changing, competitive market, past experience is an inadequate guide to the future. Hence, the insurer would have no realistic basis for computing a premium. Furthermore, in times of rising prices, few would be interested in the coverage, and in times of falling prices, no insurer could afford to take on the risk. The insurer could get no "spread of risks" over which to average out good years with bad years.

PROFESSIONAL PERSPECTIVES

Rain Insurance

Is rainy weather insurable? How about late-blooming cherry blossoms? To what extent do these exposures meet the requisites of an insurable risk? Insurers are always on the watch for new opportunities to meet the risk management needs of businesses and individuals.

In 2003 with the spring leisure season nearing in Japan, Japanese nonlife insurance companies were beefing up their weather derivative products that offer compensation for declines in sales caused by unusual weather patterns. Tokio Marine and Fire Insurance Co. in spring 2002 launched a new insurance product named "Sakura Zensen" that targeted falling sales in the event of late appearing cherry blossoms. But due to unusually warm weather that year, cherry blossoms started blooming in the Tokyo metropolitan area on March 16, the earliest in history announced by the Meteorological Agency, se-

verely hitting unprepared travel agencies, hotels, and restaurants.

Drawing a lesson from this, Tokio Marine and Fire launched a separate product in 2003 that offered compensation for damages caused by an early flowering of cherry blossoms. An official at Tokio Marine and Fire said the new product was drawing steady demand as businesses recall the previous year's nightmare. Among other insurers, Mitsui Sumitomo Insurance Co. began selling a new product that compensates for losses in sales caused by prolonged spring rains. The product is designed to compensate policyholders if the number of rainy days exceeds a certain level during the spring leisure season between mid-March and late May. Sompo Japan Insurance Co., meanwhile, was trying to attract clients with a new product that compensates for rainy weekends.

Source: Anonymous, "Cherry Blossom, Spring Rain Insurance Flowering in Japan," *Jiji Press English News Service*, February 4, 2003, 1.

Large Loss

Although an insurer theoretically might be willing to provide insurance regardless of the potential size of a particular loss, a requisite from the standpoint of the insured is that the maximum possible loss must be relatively large. The **large-loss principle** states that businesses and individuals should insure potentially serious losses before relatively minor losses. To do otherwise is uneconomical because small losses tend to occur frequently and are very costly to recover through insurance. If one can pay for a loss from savings or current income, it is probably too small a loss to give insurance high priority as a method of risk treatment.

As an example, suppose there is a 2 percent probability that a collision will completely destroy a $20,000 car owned by QPC Corporation. QPC may realize that the expected value of such a loss is $0.02 \times \$20,000$, or $400. Yet collision insurance might cost $750 because the insurer must charge enough to pay for all expected losses plus the cost of doing business. Should QPC buy the insurance? If a $20,000 automobile represents a large portion of QPC's total assets, insurance may be purchased. But if the car is one of a large fleet and represents only a small fraction of total assets, the purchase of insurance is unlikely.

Probability of Loss Must Not Be Too High

The final requisite of an insurable risk is that the probability of loss must be reasonable, or else the cost of risk transfer will be excessive. This requisite is of concern primarily for the potential insured, rather than the insurer. Due to the element of risk,

For information on legal issues
concerning insurance and
recent lawsuits filed, visit
http://www.insure.com/lawsuits/.

insureds are often willing to pay more to avoid a loss than the true expected value of that loss. In fact, if it were not for this phenomenon, insurance could not exist, for insurers must always charge more for their service than the expected value of a loss. But the more probable the loss, the greater the premium will be. And a point ultimately is reached when the loss becomes so likely that when the insurer's expenses are added on, the cost of the premium becomes approaches or even exceeds the full value of the item insured. At this point, insurance is no longer feasible because the insured will not be willing to pay the necessary premium. Three illustrations of the application of this requisite are included in Table 6-1, which also summarizes the extent to which other requisites are present for the three risks illustrated.

REQUIREMENTS OF AN INSURANCE CONTRACT

A **contract** is an agreement embodying a set of promises that are legally enforceable. These promises must have been made under certain conditions before they can be enforced by law. Insurance policies are contracts and, as such, must comply with the elements required of all valid contracts.

Requirements of All Valid Contracts

In general, there are four requirements that are common to all valid contracts:

1. *Agreement must be for a legal purpose.* For insurance policies, this requirement means that the contract must neither violate the requirement of insurable interest nor protect or encourage illegal ventures.

2. *Parties must have legal capacity to contract.* Parties who have no legal capacity to contract include insane persons who cannot understand the nature of the agreement; intoxicated persons; corporations acting outside the scope of their charters, bylaws, or articles of incorporation; and minors. Some states make exceptions for the last category, under which minors who have reached a certain age (for example, $14\frac{1}{2}$ years) are granted the power to make binding contracts of insurance.

3. *There must be a valid offer and acceptance.* The general rule in insurance is that it is the *applicant* for insurance, not the agent, who makes the offer. The agent merely solicits an offer. When the contract goes into effect depends on the authority of the agent to act for the insurer in a given case.[2] In property and liability insurance, it is the custom to give

TABLE 6-1	Examples of Requisites of Insurable Risks: Do these risks meet the requisites of insurability?		
Requisite	Risk of Flood	Risk of Tornado	Risk of Disability
Large number of similar objects	Yes	Yes	Yes
Accidental and unintentional	Yes	Yes	Maybe
Determinable and measurable	Yes	Yes	Maybe
Not subject to catastrophic hazard	No	Maybe	Yes
Large loss	Yes	Yes	Maybe
Probability of loss not too high	Maybe	Yes	Maybe

2 Powers of insurance agents are discussed in greater detail later in this chapter.

local agents authority to accept offers of many lines of insurance on the spot. In such cases, it is said that the agent will **bind** the insurer. If the insurer wishes to escape from its agreement, it may usually cancel the policy upon prescribed notice. In life insurance, the agent generally does not have authority to accept the applicant's offer for insurance. The insurer reserves this right, and the policy is not bound until the insurer has accepted the application. If the insurer wishes to alter the terms of the proposed contract, it may do so, and this is construed as making a counteroffer to the applicant, who may then accept or reject it.

A legal offer by an applicant for life insurance must be supported by a tender of the first premium. Usually, the agent gives the insured a **conditional receipt** that provides that acceptance takes place when the insurability of the applicant has been determined. Let us say that Todd Ichihara applies for life insurance, tenders an annual premium with the application, receives a conditional receipt, passes the medical examination, and then is run over and killed by a truck, all before the insurer is even aware that an application has been made for insurance. Todd's beneficiaries may collect under the policy if it is determined that Todd was actually insurable at the time of the application and had made no false statements in the application. An applicant for life insurance who does not pay the first annual premium in advance has not made a valid offer. In this case, the insurer's agent transmits the application to the home office, where it is processed and questions of insurability are determined. The insurer sends the policy back to the agent for delivery, and the agent is instructed to deliver (offer) the policy only if the insured is still in good health. The offer can be accepted by paying the annual premium at the time of delivery.

4. *Promises must be supported by the exchange of consideration.* A **consideration** is the value given to each contracting party. The insured's consideration is made up of the monetary amount paid in premiums, plus an agreement to abide by the conditions of the insurance contract. The insurer's consideration is its promise to indemnify upon the occurrence of loss due to certain perils, to defend the insured in legal actions, or to perform other activities such as inspection or collection services, as the contract may specify.

DISTINGUISHING CHARACTERISTICS OF INSURANCE CONTRACTS

In addition to the general requirements for all valid contracts, insurance contracts and their issuing parties have several characteristics that distinguish them from other contracts and contracting parties.

Aleatory Contract

Insurance is classified as an **aleatory contract**, in which the values exchanged by the contracting parties are not necessarily equal. This characteristic is due to the fact that the outcome of the contract depends on the risk of whether a loss will occur. If a loss does take place during the policy period, then the amount paid by the insurer usually will exceed the premium paid by the insured. If no loss occurs, then the premium exceeds the amount paid by the insurer. But even though the insurance policy itself is aleatory, the entire book of business written by the insurer is anything but aleatory, because premiums are calculated to be sufficient to pay all expected claims.

Conditional Contract

Insurance is classified as a **conditional contract** because insureds must perform certain acts if recovery is to be made. If the insured does not adhere to the conditions of the contract, payment is not made even though an insured peril causes a loss. Typical conditions include payment of premium, providing adequate proof of loss, and giving immediate notice to the insurer of a loss. Thus, the conditions are a part of the bargain.

Contract of Adhesion

The insurance contract is said to be a **contract of adhesion**, meaning that any ambiguities or uncertainties in the wording of the agreement will be construed against the drafter—the insurer. This principle is due to the fact that the insurer had the advantage of writing the terms of the contract to suit its particular purposes. And in general, the insured has no opportunity to bargain over conditions, stipulations, exclusions, and the like. Therefore, the courts place the insurer under a legal duty to be explicit and to make its meaning absolutely clear to all parties. In interpreting the agreement, the courts will generally consider the entire contract as a whole, rather than just one part of it. In the absence of doubt as to meaning, the courts will enforce the contract as it is written. It is no excuse that the insured does not understand or has not read the policy.

An extension of the concept of adhesion is the doctrine of **reasonable expectations**, which goes further than just saying that ambiguities should be decided in favor of the insured. The doctrine provides that coverage should be interpreted to be what the insured can reasonably expect. Limitations and exclusions must be clear and conspicuous. An example of this doctrine is illustrated by the case of an insured's policy that provided for burglary protection only when the building was open. But the literature used to sell the insurance referred to all-risk or comprehensive crime protection and included a picture representing a burglary after a building was closed. The insured's claim resulted from a burglary loss after the building was closed and was denied by the insurer. But the courts ruled that the insured had a reasonable expectation for coverage to apply and required the insurer to pay for the loss.

Unilateral Contract

Finally, an insurance policy is a **unilateral contract**, because only one of the parties makes promises that are legally enforceable. Insureds cannot be forced to pay premiums or adhere to conditions. Of course, if they do not do so, the conditional nature of the contract keeps them from being able to collect for insured losses. But if the insured does what has been promised, then the insurer is legally obligated to perform in the event of a covered loss.

ROLE OF AGENTS AND BROKERS

An agent is a person given power to act for a principal, who is legally bound by the acts of its authorized agents. The law recognizes two major classes of agents: general and special. A **general agent** is a person authorized to conduct all of the principal's business of a given kind in a particular place. In contrast, a **special agent** is authorized to perform only a specific act or function. If anything occurs that is outside the scope of this authority, the agent must obtain special power to handle it. Thus, in a legal sense, insurance agents do not necessarily have to serve in the channel of distribution for insurance, although that is the most common use of the term *insurance agent*.

An insurance agent should be assumed to be the legal agent of the insurer, unless information to the contrary is known. In contrast, an insurance **broker** is the legal agent of the prospective insured and is engaged to arrange insurance coverage on the best possible terms. The broker has contacts with many insurers but may not have an agency agreement with them. Thus, a broker is free to deal with any insurer that will accept the business. The broker cannot bind any insurer orally to a risk unless the broker has an agency agreement with the insurer. Thus, in dealing with a broker, one should not assume coverage the moment the insurance is ordered. One is covered only when the broker contacts an insurer that agrees to accept the risk. The distinction between an agent and a broker is not always clear, because in some situations a person may simultaneously be both an agent and a broker. Typically, courts will construe the evidence in the light most favorable to the insured.

ETHICAL PERSPECTIVES

Who Belongs to a "Household"?

How far can an insurer go in denying coverage based on the definitions within an insurance policy? Is it necessary to define every word in the policy, even if some are commonly interpreted in a particular manner? Can insureds be sure that coverage really exists if every term is not carefully defined?

An interesting case involved the definition of the word "household." Mary Maccia owned a home in Bloomfield, New Jersey, and lived in it for nearly 30 years. One day Mary fell, was injured, and then moved in with her daughter in another town for what she hoped would be a short time during her recuperation. Because Mary intended to return to her own home, she maintained her homeowners coverage on it. However, as time passed and she was unable to return home, Mary grew worried about vandalism and burglary at her home. So she asked her grandson Donald and his wife Marcella to move into her vacant home. They did so and paid many of the bills associated with the home. Mary continued to insure the property under the same homeowners policy.

A year later, Marcella's dog knocked down and seriously injured a woman, who in turn sued Marcella. Although a homeowners policy typically defends against such suits (see Chapter 15), the insurer in this situation refused to do so, arguing that Marcella was not covered by Mary's policy. Marcella was eventually found liable for damages of $230,000. In denying coverage, the insurer pointed out that the definition of who was insured in the policy was "any relative if a resident of your household." No definition of this term was included in the policy, but the insurer argued that household means "living together." Since Mary and Marcella never lived under the same roof, the insurer concluded that Marcella was not part of Mary's household and therefore was not entitled to insurance protection. Thus, the relevant question became one of defining the term "household."

The Supreme Court of New Jersey found that the term "household" was ambiguous. The term could mean either "living in the same house" (in which case Marcella would not be covered) or "living at the insured premises" (allowing Marcella to be covered by the insurance). Because the insurer had the opportunity to narrowly define the term and did not do so when it wrote the policy, the court ruled that the resultant ambiguity must be resolved in favor of the insured. Therefore, the insurer could not legitimately deny coverage in this situation.

Source: 1999 N.J. LEXIS 834 (S.Ct.N.J. 1999).

Authority of Agents and Brokers

The basic source of authority for all insurance agents (using the word *agent* in its broad sense) comes from stockholders or policyowners and is formulated by the charter, bylaws, and custom of a given insurer. For agents and brokers in the insurance distribution channel, there are two distinct sources of authority: the agency agreement and ratification. The **agency agreement** sets forth the specific duties, rights, and obligations of both the insurer and the agent. Unfortunately, the agreement is often inadequate as a complete instrument; hence, the agent may do something that the principal did not intend. This situation gives rise to the other method by which an agent may receive authority from the principal, known as **ratification**. If an agent performs some act outside the scope of the agency agreement to which the insurer later assents, then the agent has achieved additional authority through ratification. For example, suppose Marsha Richmond sells an insurance policy covering a particular building against loss by fire. Marsha is not authorized to do this, but she later persuades insurer PGH to accept this risk. She thus becomes PGH's agent by ratification.

Two other principles are important in understanding the law of agency. One of these is the concept of **waiver**, which is the intentional relinquishing of a known right. In contrast,

estoppel operates when there has been no intentional relinquishing of a known right. Estoppel operates to defeat a "right" that a party technically possesses. Waiver is based on consent, whereas estoppel is an imposed liability. Often these two doctrines are not clearly distinguished even in court actions, and sometimes they are used interchangeably. They are of interest primarily in understanding how the acts of insurance agents may or may not be binding on insurers.

Waiver and estoppel situations often arise when the insurance policy is first put into force. Suppose an agent writes a fire insurance policy with the full knowledge that some condition in the policy is breached at the time it is issued. For example, the insured might be engaged in a type of business that the insurer has instructed its agents not to cover and has excluded in the policy. The agent issues the policy anyway, and there is a loss before the insurer has had an opportunity to cancel the contract. Most courts would say that the action by the agent constituted an acceptance of the breached condition, and the insurer would be estopped from denying payment of the claim.

PRINCIPLES OF SOCIAL INSURANCE

Social insurance is offered through some form of government, usually on a compulsory basis. It is designed to benefit persons whose incomes are interrupted by an economic or social condition that society as a whole finds undesirable and for which a solution is generally beyond the control of the individual. Social insurance plans are usually introduced when a social problem exists that requires government action for solution and where the insurance method is deemed most appropriate. Examples are the problems of crime, poverty, unemployment, mental disease, ill health, dependency of children or aged persons, drug addiction, industrial accidents, divorce, and economic privation of a certain class, such as agricultural workers. Insurance is not an appropriate method of solution for many of these problems because the peril is not accidental, fortuitous, or predictable. In other instances insurance is perhaps feasible, but due to the catastrophic nature of the event (as in unemployment), private insurers cannot undertake the underwriting task because of lack of financial capacity. This means that if the insurance method is to be used as a solution to certain problems, government agencies must either administer or finance the insurance plan. Following the September 11 attacks firms could not secure terrorism insurance in the private insurance market, leading to calls for a government role in providing such coverage. Subsequently the federal government did become involved in providing a backstop for insurers offering terrorism coverage. Although the specific details of various social insurance programs are discussed in later chapters of this text, an understanding of social insurance can be facilitated by an appreciation of the basic differences between these and privately sponsored insurance devices.

netlink

The National Academy of Social Insurance offers internships and other monetary awards to students interested in the field of social insurance. Details are described at http://www.nasi.org. Click on "About the Academy" to find information on these internships.

Compulsion

Most social insurance plans are characterized by an element of compulsion. Because social insurance plans are designed to solve some social problem, it is necessary that everyone involved cooperate. This principle is in sharp contrast to private insurance, which has very few compulsory features.

Set Level of Benefits

In social insurance plans, little if any choice is usually given as to what level of benefits is provided. Further, all persons covered under the plan are subject to the same benefit schedules, which may vary according to the amount of average wage, length of service, or job status. In private, individual insurance, of course, one may usually buy any amount of coverage desired.

Floor of Protection

A basic principle of social insurance in a system of private enterprise is that it aims to provide a minimum level of economic security against perils that may interrupt income. This principle, known as the **floor-of-protection concept**, is not always strictly observed, but it is still a fundamental theme of most social insurance coverage in the United States. The purpose of social insurance plans is to give all qualified persons a certain minimum protection, with the idea that more adequate protection can and should be provided through individual initiative. The incentive to help oneself, a vital element of the free-enterprise system, is thus preserved.

Subsidy

All insurance devices have an element of subsidy in that the losses of the unfortunate few are shared with the fortunate many who escape loss. In social insurance it is anticipated that an insured group may not pay its own way but will be subsidized either by other insured groups or by taxpayers. Some social insurance plans have access to general tax revenues if the contributions from covered workers are inadequate.

Unpredictability of Loss

For several reasons, the cost of benefits under social insurance cannot usually be predicted with great accuracy. Therefore, the cost of some types of social insurance is unstable. For example, in a general depression, unemployment may rise to unusual heights, causing tremendous outlays in benefits that may threaten the solvency of the unemployment compensation fund.

Conditional Benefits

In social insurance programs, benefits are often conditional. For example, if one earns more than a specified amount, various social insurance benefits may be lost. One might argue that it is wrong to attach conditions to recovery in social insurance, under the theory that one should receive benefits as a matter of right. However, an insured worker has no particular inalienable right, except the right given by the social insurance law under which the worker is protected. The employee's right can and probably should be conditional. To have it otherwise would mean that some would be receiving payments not really needed, and either the costs would rise or others would be deprived of income that is their sole source of support. One of the basic advantages of social insurance is this very flexibility, which permits those most in need to receive a greater relative share of income payments than others whose economic status is such that they do not require as much.

Contributions Required

In order to qualify as social insurance, a public program should require a contribution, directly or indirectly, from the person covered, the employer, or both. Thus, social insurance does not include public assistance programs wherein the needy person receives outright gifts and must generally prove inability to pay for the costs involved. This does not mean that the beneficiary in social insurance must pay *all* of the costs, but the beneficiary must make some contribution or else the program is not really an insurance program but rather a form of public charity. For example, welfare payments to dependent children are not a form of social insurance, as the term is normally understood, although such payments are undoubtedly made to solve a social problem that could have been met by insurance.

Attachment to the Labor Force

Although it is not a necessary principle of social insurance, most social insurance plans cover only groups that are or have been attached to the labor force. The basic reason for this is that nearly all such plans are directed at those perils that interrupt income. Private insurance contracts, of course, are issued to individuals regardless of employment status. The requirement of attachment to the labor force has been a subject of frequent criticism by those who want a greater expansion of social insurance.

Minimal Advance Funding

In contrast to many forms of private insurance, social insurance usually does not provide large accumulations for advance funding. This means that if, for example, a future retirement benefit is promised, the full cost of paying for this benefit is not set aside in the year in which the promise is made. Instead, the benefit is paid from future revenues at the time the benefits must be paid out to the retiring worker. Full advance funding in social insurance programs is not necessary, and in fact is undesirable from an economic standpoint. To collect enough money currently to pay all the future benefits that are promised would require a huge increase in social insurance taxes, an action that could well produce a business depression. Advance funding is not necessary because social insurance programs are backed by the taxing power of government. Social insurance programs and the revenues to support them are expected to continue indefinitely and require no advance funding. In private insurance, on the other hand, advance funding is needed to guarantee future benefits to the insured. Private organizations have no guaranteed source of future revenues, and in fact may go completely out of business, leaving would-be beneficiaries stranded without effective recourse against the insurer.

SOCIAL AND ECONOMIC VALUES AND COSTS OF INSURANCE

It has been implied in the foregoing discussion that to distinguish between insurable and uninsurable risks serves a useful purpose. Insurance has peculiar advantages as a device to handle risk and so ought to be used to bring about the greatest economic advantage to society. To establish the validity of this point, some of the social and economic values and costs of insurance are contrasted in this section.

Social and Economic Values

Reduced Reserve Requirements

Perhaps the greatest social value—indeed, the central economic function—of insurance is to obtain the advantages that flow from the reduction of risk. One of the chief economic burdens of risk is the necessity of accumulating funds to meet possible losses, and one of the great advantages of the insurance mechanism is that it greatly reduces the total of such reserves necessary for a given economy. Because the insurer can predict losses in advance, it needs to keep readily available only enough funds to meet those losses and to cover expenses. If each insured had to set aside such funds, there would be need for a far greater amount. For example, in many localities, a $100,000 building can be insured against fire and other physical perils for about $500 a year. If insurance were not available, the insured would probably feel a need to set aside funds at a much higher rate than $500 a year.

Capital Freed for Investment

Another aspect of the advantage just described is the fact that the cash reserves that insurers accumulate are made available for investment. Insurers as a group, and life insurance firms in particular, are among the largest and most important institutions collecting and distributing the nation's savings. From the viewpoint of the individual, the insurance mechanism enables renting an insurer's assets to cover uncertain losses rather than providing this capital internally, much like renting a building instead of owning one. Capital that is thereby released frees funds for investment purposes. Thus, the insurance mechanism encourages new investment. For example, if an individual knows that his or her family will be protected by life insurance in the event of premature death, the insured may be more willing to invest savings in a long-desired project, such as a business venture, without feeling that the family is being robbed of its basic income security. In this way a better allocation of economic resources is achieved.

Reduced Cost of Capital

Because the supply of investable funds is greater than it would be without insurance, capital is available at a lower cost than would otherwise be possible. This result brings about a higher standard of living because increased investment itself will raise production and cause lower prices than would otherwise be the case. Also, because insurance is an efficient device to reduce risk, investors may be willing to enter fields they would otherwise reject as too risky. Thus, society benefits from increased services and new products, the hallmarks of increased living standards.

Reduced Credit Risk

Another advantage of insurance lies in its importance to credit. Insurance has been called the basis of the nation's credit system. It follows logically that if insurance reduces the risk of loss from certain sources, it should mean that an entrepreneur is a better credit risk if adequate insurance is carried. Today it would be nearly impossible to borrow money for many business purposes without insurance protection that meets the requirements of the lender.

Loss Control Activities

Another social and economic value of insurance lies in its loss control or loss prevention activities. Although the main function of insurance is not to reduce loss but merely to spread losses among members of the insured group, insurers are nevertheless vitally interested in keeping losses at a minimum. Insurers know that if no effort is made in this regard, losses and premiums would have a tendency to rise. It is human nature to relax vigilance when it is known that the loss will be fully paid by the insurer. Furthermore, in any given year, a rise in loss payments reduces the profit to the insurer, and so loss prevention provides a direct avenue of increased profit.

A few illustrations of loss prevention and control in the field of property and liability insurance include (1) investigation of fraudulent insurance claims, (2) research into the causes of susceptibility to loss on highways, (3) recovery of stolen vehicles and other auto theft prevention work, (4) development of fire safety standards and public educational programs, (5) provision of leadership in the field of general safety, (6) provision of fire protection and engineering counsel for oil producers, and (7) investigation and testing of building materials to see that fire prevention standards are being met. In the life and health insurance industry, continuous support is given by private insurers to programs aimed at reducing loss by premature death, sickness, and accidents.

Business and Social Stability

Finally, the existence and availability of insurance can lead to increased business and social stability. Several illustrations may be helpful in envisioning this point. For example, if adequately protected, a business need not face the grim prospect of liquidation following a loss. Similarly, a family need not break up following the death or permanent disability of one or more income producers. A business venture can be continued without interruption even though a key person or the sole proprietor dies. A family need not lose its life savings following a bank failure. Old-age dependency can be avoided. Loss of a firm's assets by theft can be reimbursed. Whole cities ruined by a hurricane can be rebuilt from the proceeds of insurance.

Social Costs of Insurance

No institution can operate without certain costs. The costs for an insurance institution include the operation of the insurance business, losses that are caused intentionally, and losses that are exaggerated.

Operating the Insurance Business

The main social cost of insurance lies in the use of economic resources, mainly labor, to operate the business. The average annual overhead of property insurers accounts for about 27 percent of their earned premiums but ranges widely, depending on the type of insurance. In life insurance an average of 17 percent of the premium dollar is absorbed in expenses. In other words, the advantages of insurance should be weighed against the cost of obtaining the service.

Losses That Are Intentionally Caused

A second social cost of insurance is attributed to the fact that if it were not for insurance, certain losses would not occur—losses that are caused intentionally by people in order to collect on their policies. Insurers are well aware of this danger, however, and take numerous steps to keep it to a minimum.

Losses That Are Exaggerated

Related to the cost of intentional losses is the tendency of some insureds to exaggerate the extent of damage that results from purely unintentional losses. For example, Company RRR has an old photocopy machine that does not work well. When a small fire in RRR's building causes some smoke damage throughout the building, RRR may be tempted to claim that its fire insurance should pay for a new photocopy machine. The old machine likely has been affected by smoke, but in reality the machine did not work well before the fire and probably would have been replaced soon anyway. The existence of insurance tempts RRR to exaggerate its loss in this situation. Similarly, health expenses for families that have health insurance may be higher than the expenses for uninsured families. Once an accident or sickness has occurred, an individual may decide to undergo more expensive medical treatment, or the physician may prescribe it if it is known that an insurer will bear most or all of the cost.

SUMMARY

1. Insurance reduces risk by combining under one management a group of objects situated so that the aggregate losses to which the insureds are subject become predictable within narrow limits. Losses that result are shared among the insureds, usually through the payment of an insurance premium.

2. The principle of insurable interest is necessary for an insurance contract to be valid. The principles of indemnity and subrogation reinforce the principle of insurable interest.

3. Because insurance is a contract of utmost good faith, breach of warranty or a material misrepresentation on the part of the insured can void the coverage. A concealment has the same legal effect as a material misrepresentation.

4. An insurance contract must not be against public policy, must be enacted by parties with legal capacity to contract, must be effected through a valid offer and acceptance, and must be supported by a monetary consideration. Insurance is a contract of adhesion, and any ambiguities are construed against the insurer. Insurance policies are also aleatory, conditional, and unilateral.

5. Insurance is effected through agents who have varying degrees of authority, depending on the custom in different lines of insurance and on the doctrines of waiver and estoppel. Brokers are agents of the insured.

6. From the standpoint of the insurer, there are four requisites of insurable risk: (a) there must be a sufficient number of similar insured objects to allow a reasonably close calculation of probable future losses, (b) the loss must be accidental and unintentional in nature, (c) the loss must be capable of being determined and measured, and (d) the exposure units must not be subject to simultaneous destruction.

7. From the viewpoint of the insured, there are two main requirements of insurability: (a) the loss must be severe enough to warrant protection and (b) the probability of loss should not be so high as to command a prohibitive premium when compared with the possible size of the loss.

8. In contrast to private insurance, social insurance (a) is compulsory, (b) does not allow individual choice in selecting the amount of benefit, (c) provides only a minimum level of benefit, (d) is subsidized by groups other than the insured group, (e) has a total cost that is often unpredictable, (f) covers only individuals who have been attached to the labor force and who meet certain minimum requirements, and (g) offers conditional benefits.

9. There are many social and economic values of insurance, but perhaps the greatest value lies in the reduction of risk in society. The benefits of insurance are achieved at certain social costs, the chief of which is the cost of the economic resources used to operate the insurance business.

internetexercises

1. Did you know that you can purchase insurance to protect yourself in the event that you are abducted by aliens? To see a description of such a policy, set your browser to http://www.sirhuckleberry.com/ng/home-h-e.html and look under "Policies." Explain how alien abduction meets (or does not meet) each of the requisites of an insurable risk.

2. Because of governmental involvement, most social insurance programs are subject to continual change. Set your browser to http://www.nasi.org to explore the current social insurance issues. Which of these issues do you consider to be the most important? Why? Do any of the current proposals violate the principles of social insurance? Explain.

QUESTIONS FOR REVIEW AND DISCUSSION

1. Explain the effect of an honest mistake in an insurance contract.
2. Under what conditions, if any, is it necessary to prove insurable interest on the part of a beneficiary in life insurance? Explain.
3. Distinguish between the doctrine of insurable interest and the principle of indemnity.
4. D has a house valued at $150,000. D takes out insurance in two companies, each policy in the amount of $100,000. If the house is totally destroyed, can D collect in full from both companies? Why or why not?
5. In an application for life insurance, Oki Yasunari stated that she had no illness, that she went to a physician only twice a year for a checkup, and that she had no application for insurance pending with any other company. Shortly after the policy was issued, Oki died. The company denied liability when it was discovered that Oki had seen a doctor 6 times within 10 weeks preceding her application. Furthermore, the insured had applied to another insurance company for $100,000 of life insurance at the same time.
   a. May the insurer properly deny liability?
   b. What legal doctrine of insurance is involved in this case?
6. What is the difference between an express warranty and an implied warranty?
7. Can one have an insurable interest in property and still not own the property? Explain.
8. Distinguish a warranty from a representation.
9. Name and explain the requirements of a contract and what additional features underlie contracts of insurance.
10. Explain the principle of adhesion.
11. Name the requisites of insurable risk from the standpoint of (a) the insurer and (b) the insured.
12. Distinguish between waiver and estoppel.
13. What is adverse selection? Why is underwriting necessary to control adverse selection?
14. What are the social values of insurance? What are the social costs? Explain.
15. A writer on the subject of insurance states, "An adequate explanation of insurance must include either the building up of a fund or the transfer of risk, but not both." Is this statement in conflict with the position taken in this text? Explain.
16. Virginia expresses disappointment that a whole year has passed and, due to no accidents, she has been unable to collect anything from her car insurance policy, for which she had paid $700 in premiums. Is Virginia's disappointment based on sound insurance principles? Explain.
17. A firm warrants that certain parts in its used automobiles are in good running order and will function properly for a period of one year. If the parts fail, the warranty pays for the replacement. The state insurance department attempted to impose its regulations on this firm because "the company is warranting the mechanical reliability of the mechanical features of the auto, and this amounts to insuring the buyer against any defects in those parts." The firm's representatives claimed, on the other hand, that it was warranting only the fact that its inspectors had inspected a particular auto. How would you decide whether this is a proper example of insurance or not? What is your decision? Explain.
18. It has been suggested that the following risks are uninsurable. For each risk, indicate whether you agree or disagree and why.
   a. Risk of punitive damages awarded to punish and to deter the wrongdoer from repeating actions that cause a loss.
   b. Risk of loss through an economic depression.
   c. Risk that trade secrets of a firm might be stolen, thus causing the firm the loss of potential profits there from.
   d. Risk from loss of a market that is captured by a competitor with a better product.
   e. Risk that a rezoning or a shift of population will reduce the value of a location owned by a firm for marketing purposes.
19. A motorist was involved in a minor accident. A shop gave her a repair estimate of $200. When the shop owner heard that the loss would be paid by insurance, however, the estimate was increased to $500. In explanation, the shop owner stated that the higher estimate involved the replacement of a bumper, rather than its repair. Should the extra cost be allowed by the insurer? If so, is anyone the loser in this case other than the insurer? Discuss.
20. Which of the three social costs of insurance do you believe is most important? Why?

chapter 7

Insurance as a Risk Management Technique: Policy Provisions

M ax Lankau owns a chain of Fast Mart convenience stores, located throughout Miami and south Florida. Many of his stores were completely destroyed when a hurricane unleashed its violence in that area. Even several years later, south Florida—including Fast Mart and its customers—was still recovering from the aftermath.

As an entrepreneur, Max had purchased property insurance for the Fast Mart stores that covered him in the event of hurricane damage. But he had never paid a great deal of attention to the specifics of his insurance policies. During the months following the hurricane, Max was forced to learn much more about the policies than he had ever thought he wanted to know. Not only were the deductibles and limits important, but clauses with names such as "coinsurance" caused Max considerable surprise in some instances by severely limiting his recovery below what had been lost. Further, Max discovered that in some cases the revenues he lost due to his stores being shut down cost him much more than the actual physical damage. Unfortunately, that loss was not covered by the type of insurance Max had purchased for Fast Mart.

As Max repairs his damage and rebuilds his business, he has resolved to become thoroughly familiar with all of the many provisions in his insurance policies. When he finds an exclusion that seems to eliminate coverage that he thinks he needs, Max asks his agent about the possibility of paying additional premium dollars to remove the exclusion. And when he does not understand a particular policy condition, Max is relentless in making his agent explain it to him. In this way, Max hopes to avoid many of the pitfalls that he discovered the hard way after the hurricane disaster. The types of issues that Max is now dealing with form the basis for this chapter.

CHAPTER OBJECTIVES

After studying this chapter, you should be able to

1. Identify and understand the basic parts of an insurance policy.
2. Explain the difference between named-perils and open-perils property insurance coverage.
3. Explain why exclusions are used in insurance contracts and identify the major types of exclusions.
4. Describe how the interests of mortgagees are protected in insurance policies and why the mortgagee clause gives the best protection to the mortgagee.
5. Distinguish between the actual cash value basis of recovery and replacement cost.
6. Describe the different types of deductibles and explain why deductibles are used in insurance policies.
7. Indicate why insurance companies use insurance to value provisions and explain how the coinsurance clause operates.
8. Explain what apportionment clauses are and how the pro-rata clause operates.

There are many similarities in insurance contracts that are best studied and analyzed at one time. For example, most contracts contain certain exclusions and conditions that must be met. An understanding of these common elements greatly facilitates the understanding of insurance contracts, and thus their usefulness as a risk management tool. Although in some cases, a given policy may use a different name for a certain type of provision or condition, in general major parts of a policy are (1) the declarations, (2) the insuring agreement, (3) the exclusions, and (4) the conditions. Other important aspects of a policy include its definitions, the basis of recovery, and clauses limiting the amount of recovery.

This chapter covers primarily conceptual aspects of policies. In the sections that follow, some of the concepts described are especially applicable to certain types of insurance; specific details concerning these types are discussed in later chapters.

DECLARATIONS

In the **declarations** section of the policy, which is usually on the first page, the policy number is given, as well as the address of the insured or the insured property. The insured's name, the agent's name, and the premium are also given. For property insurance in which a creditor has an interest in the property, the name of the creditor may also be included in the declarations. In addition, some underwriting information may be stated on the declarations page, such as the type of building or, in the case of automobile insurance, a description of the automobile. In policies under which an insured has options for coverage, those options that have been chosen by the insured will be shown on the declarations page.

THE INSURING AGREEMENT

One of the first elements of any contract is a statement of the essence of what is agreed on between the parties. In insurance this is found in the insuring clause, or **insuring agreement**, which normally states what the insurer agrees to do and the major conditions under which it so agrees. If a loss due to an insured peril occurs, the insurer promises to compensate the insured if the insured meets the conditions of the contract. If the conditions are not met, the insurer has no obligation to pay. The full body of the policy follows the insuring agreement.

The insured promises only to pay the premium and to conform to the conditions of the policy. Conforming to the conditions is a part of the consideration, so technically the insured just agrees to provide consideration. The most crucial part of the agreement is the statement of what the insurer promises. Within or right after the insuring agreement, one may also find a list of the perils insured against and the definition of the insured.

Named-Perils versus Open-Perils Agreements

There are two general approaches used in writing insuring agreements in property insurance. The traditional one is the named-perils approach. The other, which is now being used more extensively, is the open-perils approach. The **named-perils agreement**, as the name suggests, lists the perils that are covered. Such perils often include, but are not limited to, fire, lightning, explosion, riot, smoke, theft, falling objects, and collapse. Perils not named are, of course, not covered. The **open-perils agreement** states that it is the insurer's intention to cover risks of accidental loss to the described property except those perils specifically excluded. The insurance industry once used the term all-risk instead of open-perils to describe this type of agreement, but this phrase proved confusing for insureds. Since such policies do have numerous excluded perils and do not really protect against all possible risks, the all-risk terminology was considered by many to be misleading. Further, in some court cases the all-risk terminology resulted in findings of coverage for insureds where none was intended by the insurer.

Defining the Insured

All policies of insurance name at least one person or organization that is to receive the benefit of the coverage provided. That person is referred to as the **named insured**; in life insurance, that person may also be called the **policyholder**. In addition, many contracts cover other individuals' insurable interests in the described property or cover them against losses outlined in the policy. These individuals are often called **additional insureds**, and they normally receive coverage somewhat less complete than that of the named insured.

For example, automobile policies usually cover not only the person designated on the policy as the named insured but also the insured's spouse if he or she is a resident of the same household. The policy also covers any other persons who are driving with the permission of either the named insured or the spouse, provided they are not driving the automobile in connection with any automobile business such as a service station, a garage, or a parking lot.

Likewise, insurance for homeowners usually covers not only the named insured but also his or her legal representatives. Thus, if the named insured dies, the policy, by virtue of this provision, is effective in covering the estate for a limited period of time. Liability policies usually protect the insured, the spouse, and the relatives of either if they are living in the same household.

EXCLUSIONS

Exclusions are used to help define and limit the coverage provided by an insurer. Policies often have very broad insuring agreements, with the coverage subsequently narrowed by the use of exclusions. Risk managers must pay particular attention to the exclusions in their insurance contracts. Typically, exclusions are used to restrict coverage of given perils, losses, property, and locations.

Excluded Perils

Practically all insurance policies exclude from coverage certain perils among those factors that can cause losses. Normally, a separate section of the contract lists and describes all the excluded perils. It is vital that the exclusions be noted and understood. Providing for exclusions is the drafter's way of describing and limiting the insuring agreement to make it definite and unambiguous.

One complicating factor in the analysis of many insurance contracts is the fact that policies may define and limit the peril in such a way that it is partially covered, but not completely so. Thus, fire from specific causes may be excluded, such as fire caused by order of civil authority. Sometimes even the question of what constitutes fire may arise. A **fire** may be defined as combustion in which oxidation takes place so rapidly that a flame or glow is produced. Rust is a form of oxidation but, of course, is not fire. Scorching or heat is not fire. Furthermore, the fire must be a **hostile fire**; that is, it must be of such a character that it is outside its normal confines. Fires intentionally kindled in a stove are not usually covered, and neither are articles accidentally thrown into the stove. Such a fire is said to be a **friendly fire**. However, once the fire escapes its confines it becomes hostile, and all losses resulting from it are usually covered. For instance, scorching caused by a lighted cigarette falling onto a rug generally would be considered as having been caused by a hostile fire. A lighted cigarette may be considered as friendly while in an ashtray, but it is outside its intended place (and therefore hostile) when it reaches a rug.

Additional examples of partially covered perils may be helpful. For instance, explosions are often covered in property policies, unless they result from the bursting of steam boilers, steam pipes, steam turbines, or other parts of rotating machinery owned or controlled by the insured. In life insurance, death from war may not be covered. Some accidental death policies pay only for travel accidents or nonoccupational accidents. In general, perils may be excluded or limited in various ways for at least three different reasons: because they are basically uninsurable, are covered elsewhere, or will be covered under a separate endorsement.

Perils That Are Basically Uninsurable

In all types of insurance it is very common to exclude loss arising out of war, warlike action, insurrection, and rebellion because losses from such sources cannot be predicted with any degree of reliability and are often catastrophic in nature. Likewise, perils such as wear and tear, gradual deterioration, and damage by moth and vermin are excluded in most property policies because losses from these sources are not accidental; they are in the nature of certainties and, hence, uninsurable (except at very high premium rates). For a similar reason, losses to property resulting from deliberate action by the insured, such as arson, faulty construction, or voluntary increase of the hazard, are excluded. In life insurance, suicide within two years of the application (one year in some policies) is an excluded peril for the same reason.

Perils to Be Covered Elsewhere

Some perils can be more easily covered in contracts that are specially designed for them. Thus, personal automobile policies exclude losses arising out of business uses of trucks, and commercial automobile coverage excludes, under well-defined conditions, personal uses of the vehicle. The problems of insuring business risks and personal risks are entirely different, and policies are designed for each purpose. These exclusions serve the purpose of eliminating duplicate coverage. Another example of this type of exclusion is in the exclusion of certain water damage and flood losses from homeowners policies. Such perils present special problems and must be insured separately.

Perils Covered Under Endorsement at Extra Premium

Still other perils are excluded because the insurer intends to charge extra for their coverage through an **endorsement** that may be added to the policy at the option of the insured. The exclusion of earthquake damage in property insurance is an example of this type of exclusion, because in most cases earthquake coverage can be added with an earthquake endorsement for an additional premium.

Excluded Losses

Most insurance contracts contain provisions excluding certain types of losses, even though the policy may cover the peril that causes these losses. For example, commercial property policies usually cover any **direct loss** for which covered perils are the **proximate cause**. According to the doctrine of proximate cause, a peril may be said to cause a loss if there is an unbroken chain of events leading from the peril to the ultimate loss. In property insurance, direct losses are the costs to repair or replace the property itself. For fire losses, the direct loss also includes such losses as damage from water or chemicals used to fight the fire and broken windows or holes chopped in the roof by firefighters, because these losses are often an inevitable result of the fire itself.

In policies covering only direct losses, any resultant loss of income resulting from the interruption of business operations is considered an **indirect loss** and would be excluded. Separate insurance is necessary for protection against indirect losses. Similarly, most property policies do not automatically cover losses caused by the application of building codes (or similar laws) requiring that a more expensive type of construction be used in replacing a building destroyed by fire.

The same distinction between direct and indirect losses can be made regarding health problems. If a health insurance policy is designed to cover medical expenses due to accident or illness (a direct loss), it generally will not cover the lost wages that result when the injured or sick person cannot go to work (an indirect loss). The indirect loss must be covered under a separate contract often known as disability insurance.

Excluded Property

A property insurance policy may be written to cover certain perils and resultant losses, but it will be limited to certain types of property. For example, a common exclusion is loss to money, deeds, bills, bullion, and manuscripts. Unless it is written to cover the contents, a policy on a building includes only the integral parts of the building itself and excludes all contents. Automobile policies give little or no protection to personal property transported in the vehicle. And liability policies usually exclude the property of others in the care, custody, or control of the insured.

Why are certain types of property excluded from insurance coverage? There are a variety of reasons, many of which are interrelated. First, it may be the intent of the insurer to cover certain types of property under separate contracts. A good example is the general pattern of excluding property relating to a business from policies designed primarily to insure property for personal uses. Thus, automobiles used as taxis are excluded from coverage under personal automobile policies. Second, the property involved might be subjected to unusually severe physical or moral hazards or be especially susceptible to loss. The exclusion of bullion and manuscripts, for example, is made at least in part for this reason. Finally, property might be excluded because of difficulties in obtaining accurate estimates of its value at the time of loss. Special treatment of items such as works of art is often necessary, as is the insurance of intangible property, such as accounts receivable.

Excluded Locations

The insuring agreement for property policies makes it clear that the coverage applies only while the insured property is at a location specified in the declarations. Relatively few property insurance contracts give complete worldwide protection. Coverage is often restricted to property in set locations, with only a small part of the insurance applicable when some of the property is located somewhere other than on the described premises of the insured. The rationale for this limitation is that property risks vary greatly depending on the location of the property, and insurers wish to restrict their coverage to areas that they have had an opportunity to inspect and approve. Similarly, automobile insurance is usually limited to cover the auto while it is in the United States, its possessions, or Canada. If the car is in Europe or Mexico, for example, coverage is not applicable.

An exception to the location limitations in property policies becomes effective if a loss threatens and the property is moved to a safe place for the sake of preserving it from destruction. Permission is usually granted to remove the goods to another place for a limited time, such as 30 days, for safety. This coverage for removal usually is very broad with few limitations. If property is damaged while being transported to a new location, the insurer pays. If the insured drops an item while carrying it from the endangered location and it breaks, coverage exists. Courts have even held that theft resulting from the removal process is covered, even though theft may be specifically excluded from the policy itself.

COMMON POLICY CONDITIONS

In addition to exclusions, risk managers must be careful concerning the **conditions** included in their insurance policies. All insurance contracts are written subject to certain conditions, breach of which is usually grounds for refusal to pay in the event of loss. Therefore, the conditions should be read with care, even though in some cases the insurer does not insist on exact compliance. Most of the conditions have to do with such matters as loss settlements, actions required at the time of loss, valuation of property, cancellation of coverage, and suits against the insurer.

Fraud

Many contracts state that misrepresentation of a material fact, concealment, or fraud will void the contract. This condition may be inserted in the contract as much to serve as a warning to the insured as it is to state a condition that would be enforced by the courts even if the policy said nothing about it. As an example, suppose Jason moves into a new community and requests an agent to issue insurance on his new home. Because Jason has had some questionable insurance dealings in the past, he gives his son's name as the prospective insured, instead of his own. During the term of the **binder** (a temporary insurance contract that becomes effective immediately), a fire loss occurs. Investigation after the loss shows that Jason has 20 unsatisfied claims against him. If the insurer had known this fact, no insurance binder would have been given.

Protection for Mortgagees

In property insurance, the **mortgagee** (the person or organization holding the mortgage) requires some kind of protection by the insurance policy because, if the property were to be destroyed, it is much less likely that the debt would ever be paid. A mortgagee can protect its interest in insured property in at least four ways.

Separate Insurance for the Mortgagee's Interest

The mortgagee can purchase separate insurance covering its interest. This plan has the disadvantage, however, that both the mortgagee and the mortgagor will be obtaining insurance on the same values. For example, if a building is valued at $120,000 and has a $90,000 mortgage, the interest of the mortgagee is $90,000 and the interest of the owner is $120,000. If each purchased separate coverage, there would be a total of $210,000 of insurance on the building, which is far more than is necessary to protect the value exposed.

Assignment by the Insured

The mortgagee can also be protected through an **assignment**, which is the transfer of rights from one party to another. The insured could simply take out a policy and then assign its benefits to the mortgagee after obtaining the permission of the insurer. The difficulty with this method is that if the owner defaults on the premium or otherwise violates a policy provision, the coverage may be cancelled and with it the protection of the mortgagee. In other words, the mortgagee receives no better protection under an assignment than is secured by the person making the assignment.

Loss Payable Clause

A third way for the mortgagee to be protected is through a **loss payable clause**. Such a clause simply states that the benefits, if any, shall be payable to the person named. However, if the insured were to violate the policy, such as by defaulting on the premium, no loss would be payable, and the mortgagee would receive no payment. Most jurisdictions treat the loss payable clause as an assignment of any rights to payment belonging to the insured. Thus, if the insured has no rights to collect, neither does the mortgagee in these jurisdictions.

Mortgagee Clause

Finally, the mortgagee may be protected by the **mortgagee clause**, which overcomes the limitations of the other methods and is now in almost universal use. Under a standard mortgagee clause, the mortgagee has the following rights:

1. To receive any loss or damage payments as its interest may appear, regardless of any default of the property owner under the insurance contract, and regardless of any change of ownership or increase of the hazard.

2. To receive 10 days' notice of cancellation.

3. To sue under the policy in its own name.

In exchange for these rights, the mortgagee has the following obligations under the standard mortgagee clause:

1. To notify the insurer of any change of ownership or occupancy or increase of the hazard that shall come to the knowledge of the mortgagee.

2. To pay the premium if the owner or mortgagor fails to pay it. In most jurisdictions, this has been interpreted to mean that the mortgagee must pay the premium only if it wishes to enjoy the protection under the policy.

3. To render proof of loss to the insurer in case the owner or mortgagor fails to do so.

4. To surrender to the insurer any claims it has against the mortgagor to the extent that it receives payment from the insurer.

Regarding point 4, under some conditions the insurer may deny liability to the property owner (mortgagor) and therefore retain, through subrogation, all rights that the mortgagee may have had against the mortgagor. To illustrate, assume that a mortgagee, protected under the standard mortgagee clause, has a $200,000 mortgage on a $250,000 building and that a $50,000 fire loss is deliberately caused by the insured. The insurer denies liability to the insured but must pay the mortgagee $50,000. The mortgagee must now surrender to the insurer $50,000 of its claim against the mortgagor. Alternatively, the insurer has the right to pay the mortgagee the entire $200,000 debt, obtain an assignment of the mortgage, and collect in full against the mortgagor. In this way, the mortgagor does not obtain any of the benefits of the insurer's payment to the mortgagee through a reduction of debt. Instead of owing the mortgagee, the mortgagor now owes the insurance company $200,000.

Notice of Loss

Most contracts of insurance require the insured to give immediate written notice of any loss, if practicable. If it is not practicable to do so, the loss must be reported within a reasonable length of time. For example, if a forest fire destroys Allan's summer cabin that is situated in a remote area, he may not be able to reach outside communications for several days. If Allan made an attempt to notify the insurer as soon as reasonably possible, he would still be able to collect on the insurance policy. The purpose of this provision is to give the insurer a reasonable opportunity to inspect the loss before important evidence needed to support the claim and establish the actual amount of damage is dissipated. As another example, a person injured in an accident may be unable to give immediate notice of loss. However, failure to notify the insurer promptly would not violate the notice of loss provision in the health insurance policy.

Proof of Loss

After a property loss occurs, the insured has a certain period, usually 60 to 90 days, to give the insurer formal proof of the loss and its amount. It is not enough that the insurer be notified of the loss; it is necessary for the insured to prove the amount of the loss before being able to collect. Usually an insurance adjuster or agent aids the insured in preparing the proof, but the burden is on the insured to accomplish the task. In this connection, the insured must submit to examination under oath as to the accuracy of proof; produce all books of account, bills, invoices, and so on that might help in establishing the loss; and cooperate in any reasonable way to assist the insurer in verifying the proof.

In some cases, establishing the proof of loss is an extremely specialized and expensive task. In insurance for ocean vessels and cargoes, for example, specialists known as **average adjusters** must spend years collecting all the proofs of loss that result from a sunken ship and that involve hundreds of cargo owners, in order that a final settlement can be made and the loss apportioned among the various insurers that are liable. In large fire losses, adjusters from

ETHICAL PERSPECTIVES

Notice of Losses

Texas Eastern Transmission Corporation used a lubricant containing polychlorinated biphenyls (PCBs), which caused significant pollution to the environment. The company began negotiations with the Environmental Protection Agency (EPA) regarding financial responsibility for the pollution damage. The eventual negotiated settlement for the cleanup was set at $750 million.

Texas Eastern had insurance that might have paid some or all of this amount if the policy conditions had been properly observed. However, Texas Eastern did not notify its insurer of the pending loss until many years after it began talks with EPA. When the insurer denied the claim due to the lack of immediate notice, Texas Eastern sued for recovery, which was denied. The courts stated that the "delay in providing notice to the carriers was unreasonable and prejudicial. . . . Texas Eastern never wanted carriers to interfere with what was a carefully negotiated settlement with EPA and waited until the settlement was substantially agreed upon before providing any notice to the carriers." As a result, the insured also forfeited its right to collect on its insurance.

Source: Margo D. Beller, "Court Lets Insurers Off the Hook in Texas Eastern Pipeline Cleanup," *Journal of Commerce*, June 7, 1993, 11A.

all over the nation may spend months in the destroyed area reconciling all conflicts over claims for losses.

Once the proof of loss is agreed on by all parties, payment is due within 60 days. This period gives the insurer time to investigate further, if it wishes, or to liquidate securities in the event the loss is extremely large. Finally, the policy provides that any legal suit must be commenced within 12 months of the loss. This provision places a sort of statute of limitations on all disputes and prevents indefinite prolongation of uncertainty about them.

Appraisal

Most contracts of property insurance provide that if the two parties cannot agree on a loss settlement, each may select a competent and disinterested appraiser to determine the loss. An impartial umpire, selected and paid by each party, settles any remaining differences. Although insurers and insureds do not often resort to this somewhat expensive procedure, it must be complied with in many states before suit can be brought for recovery under the policy where the cause of the suit is failure to agree on the value of the loss.

During the settlement process, the insurer reserves the right to (1) take over the damaged property and to pay the insured its sound value, (2) to repair or rebuild it, or (3) to make a cash settlement for the amount of the loss. Normally the last method is used. These are insurer options—not those of the insured. The insured may not elect to abandon the property that has been partially or totally destroyed and demand payment there for.

Preservation of the Property

Most property insurance contracts contain provisions requiring the insured to do everything possible to minimize losses to insured property from the insured peril. For example, after a fire, the insured must protect the property from further damage. Thus, the insured must take all reasonable steps to cover property that has been removed from the building so as to protect it from rain or exposure. If the insured fails to do so, the insurer may be relieved from any further liability for loss.

An interesting variation on this provision, called the **sue-and-labor clause**, is found in many policies covering property in transit. The clause requires the insured to "sue, labor, and travel for, in, and about the defense, safeguard, and recovery of the property insured hereunder." This means that the insured is required to hire a salvage company to protect a stranded ship from further loss, to hire guards to watch over a wrecked truck and its cargo, and to bring suit against any party liable for loss. The insurer agrees to be responsible for these expenses, in addition to paying the full limits of liability under the policy for loss. Thus, if the insured pays a salvage company $50,000 to save a stranded ship, but the effort fails and the ship becomes a total loss, the insurer will indemnify the insured for the value of the ship plus the $50,000 fee for salvage.

Cancellation

All insurance contracts specify the conditions under which the policy may or may not be terminated. In general, life insurance and some health insurance contracts may be terminated by the insured, but not by the insurer, after an initial one- or two-year period. Details for these policies are discussed in Chapters 16 and 17.

For property and liability insurance, contracts may usually be cancelled by either party on specific notice. The policies usually state that the insurer may elect to end its liability for losses after 5, 10, or 30 days' notice. This period gives the insured time to obtain coverage elsewhere and prevent any lapse of protection. In such cases, the insurer is obligated to return any unearned premium on a pro-rata basis. Thus, if the premium has been paid in advance for one year and the insurer cancels after one month has expired, eleven-twelfths of the premium must be returned to the insured. If the insured is the one that cancels the coverage, however, the policy usually provides for a premium refund that is less than the pro-rata amount. The methods of refunding premiums are different because if the insured cancels before the end of the full term, the insurer is entitled to some compensation for the extra cost involved in short-term policies. Furthermore, if there were no penalty involved in such cancellations, there might be a tendency for better risks to drop out, resulting in adverse selection. If the insurer cancels, however, the insured is not penalized for the short-term coverage.

Assignment

As mentioned previously, an assignment is the transfer of the rights of one party to another, usually by means of a written document. In insurance, it is common to allow the insured to assign personal rights under the contract to another person. Usually such permission must be specifically granted. The party granting the right is called the **assignor**, and the party to whom the right is granted is called the **assignee**. In life insurance, the policy provides that if another person is to be given any rights under the contract, such as the right to receive death proceeds to the extent of a debt that existed between the assignor and the assignee, the insurance company must be notified. In the event of the death of the insured, such an assignment must be honored before any named beneficiary receives payment. This scenario is very common when a lender requires protection before granting a loan to a borrower.

When property is sold, the existing property insurance policy may be transferred to the new owner. But because the insurer wishes to reserve the right to choose the ones with whom it will deal, contracts provide that assignment of the policy rights will not be valid without the written consent of the insurer. The personal element in insurance is an important underwriting characteristic; without this provision, the original insured might assign the policy to someone who is a poor moral risk. If allowed, a policy assignment eliminates the necessity of cancelling the old policy, taking a less than pro-rata return of premium, and placing a new policy in force.

PROFESSIONAL PERSPECTIVES

Y2K Litigation

Businesses and organizations around the world spent billions of dollars preparing for the turn of the century and the uncertainty concerning the world's computers when the year 2000 (Y2K) became a reality. Some large technology firms used an interesting strategy to try to recoup some of those expenditures.

These firms (GTE, Unisys, and Xerox) filed suit in 1999 to try to force their property insurers to pay for the expenses they were incurring to correct Y2K problems. Their arguments revolved around the sue-and-labor clause contained in these firms' property insurance policies. The firms, which are all heavily involved in the technology industry, alleged that the approach of year 2000 threatened them in numerous ways. Therefore, the firms took steps to protect themselves against the perceived threat of loss and they wanted their insurers to provide reimbursement for the protective measures.

The applicability of the sue-and-labor clause is complicated by the fact that many companies realized their potential Y2K problems as many as 15 or 20 years in advance. In comparison, the sue-and-labor clause has traditionally been applied to situations involving imminent danger. Although by late 2003 some suits were still pending, a growing number of court decisions had gone in favor of the insurers finding that the year 2000 problem was not covered under commercial property insurance policies.

Source: Ronald S. Gass, "A Test of Seaworthiness," *Best's Review*, January 2000.

DEFINITIONS

Many insurance policies have a section in which key terms are defined. However, other words may be defined in other parts of the policy, and in some cases words used in one part of the policy may be redefined or limited in a later section of the contract. For example, in automobile policies there are different definitions of *covered person* in various sections of the policy.

BASIS OF RECOVERY

Primarily in property insurance, there are substantial differences among policies in the way losses are valued. Property insurance contracts generally use one of two basic methods as the basis for recovery: actual cash value or replacement cost.

Actual Cash Value

The insuring agreement of many property policies states that only the actual cash value of the property at the time of loss will be reimbursed, not to exceed the amount that it would cost to repair or to replace the property with material of like kind and quality. Some insureds might interpret this clause to mean that the insurer will restore all damaged property with material of like kind and quality. However, the insurer sets the actual cash value as a maximum reimbursement. **Actual cash value (ACV)** is interpreted as replacement cost at the time of loss less any depreciation. Depreciation here refers to actual economic depreciation as opposed to accounting or tax depreciation. Thus, if it costs $5,000 to rebuild a 20-year-old roof that is almost worn out, the insurer normally will not rebuild the roof but will make a cash settlement of an amount far less than $5,000 to allow for depreciation. As a contract of indemnity, property insurance is intended to put the insured in the same financial position with respect to damaged property after a loss as before the loss. Thus, deduction for depreciation can be justified. In the case of buildings, factors such as obsolescence and a deteriorated neighborhood may also be considered in arriving at the property's actual cash value.

As discussed in Chapter 6, the actual cash value basis for settling losses may not be used if the state in which the loss occurs has a valued policy law. Valued policy laws generally apply only to real property that is totally destroyed, not to partial losses.

Replacement Cost

Often the basic actual cash value coverage is modified through an endorsement to provide coverage on a **replacement cost** basis, which allows for recovery with no deduction for depreciation. However, the total reimbursement figure is limited to the cost of repairing, replacing, or rebuilding with similar materials and labor. Thus, the insured cannot replace a wood frame building with a reinforced concrete one and expect the insurer to pay the additional cost. The insurer's liability is limited to the replacement cost of a wood frame building or the policy limit, whichever is less. Replacement cost insurance may be purchased on both real and personal property. However, to collect on a replacement cost basis, the property must actually be replaced; the insured may not use insurance proceeds for other purposes.

CLAUSES LIMITING AMOUNTS PAYABLE

In defining the coverage of an insurance contract, there are many ways for the insurer to limit the dollar amounts of recovery. Virtually all policies have some such limits stating the maximum possible payment for losses. In addition, provisions such as deductibles, coinsurance, time limitations, and apportionment clauses may also limit the amount of recovery. Not all of these clauses are used in all types of insurance, although some policies use all of them concurrently.

In general, these types of provisions are used to reduce the costs of offering the insurance service; to limit the number of small, expensive-to-administer claims; to achieve a greater degree of fairness in the rate structure; and to place an upper limit on the insurer's obligation on any one policy. In these ways, the insuring agreement is transformed from a vague promise to indemnify into a definite, measurable contract that meets the requirements of insurable risks.

Dollar Limits

Most insurance contracts provide for maximum dollar limits on recovery for given types of losses. In addition to the limits imposed by the face amount of the policy, there are two general types: specific limits and aggregate limits. **Specific dollar limits** restrict payments to a maximum amount on any one type of loss, which may be a specific type of property or one resulting from a specified peril. **Aggregate dollar limits** restrict payments on any one group of property items or group of losses from the same peril to some overall maximum. Thus, policies for homeowners often have a specific limit of $500 on liability for any one loss to a plant, shrub, or tree. In addition, there may be an aggregate limit that provides that no more than 5 percent of the amount of insurance may apply to plants, trees, and shrubs in any one loss.

As it is used in liability insurance, an aggregate limit means the policy will not pay more than the dollar amount stated during the policy year. If a firm had a $1 million limit per occurrence and a $3 million aggregate limit, the policy would never pay more than $3 million during the policy year, regardless of the number of losses. Another example of dollar limits is found in the manner in which insurers restrict their liability for losses resulting from bodily injury liability. Usually there is a specific limit of liability for damage to any one person, and there is an aggregate limit of liability applicable to loss in any one accident. Thus, if the limits for bodily injury liability are expressed as "$100,000/$300,000," it means that the company will be liable for no more than $100,000 to any one person in a given accident and in no case for more than $300,000 per accident in the event that more than one person files a claim for which the insured is liable.

Deductibles

It is common in many lines of insurance to stipulate that a definite dollar amount, known as a **deductible**, will be borne by the insured before the insurer becomes liable for payment under the terms of the contract. One reason for deductibles is to eliminate small claims. Small losses are expensive to pay, sometimes causing more administrative expense than the actual amount of the payment. Thus, it is to the insured's advantage that deductibles are available, for often the insured is able to save considerable sums in the insurance cost through their use. Similarly, risk managers are able to use very large deductibles as a way to combine insurance and risk retention as tools for managing risks. A second reason for deductibles is to reduce the moral and morale hazards that might otherwise be present. If a business or individual knows that it will have to pay part of a loss, more care may be exercised in preventing or reducing the severity of losses. Further, any incentives to intentionally cause or increase the severity of losses are reduced.

There are many different types of deductibles, some of which accomplish the two purposes for deductibles better than others. The most common forms of deductibles are described in the following paragraphs.

Straight Deductible

The **straight deductible** is one of the simplest and yet most effective deductibles in use. It applies to each loss and is subtracted before any loss payment is made. An example is a $500 deductible for automobile collision losses. If Kathy Wilson has a minor accident with her brand new car, resulting in $300 of damage, a $500 straight deductible will eliminate any recovery from her insurance. But if the loss results in a $1,200 repair bill, the insurance will pay only $700, which is the difference between the $1,200 loss and the $500 deductible. Thus, not only does the straight deductible eliminate the expense of processing all losses that are less than the deductible, but it also makes the insured absorb part of every claim that is paid. In this way, the goals of reducing moral and morale hazards are addressed.

Aggregate and Calendar-Year Deductibles

Another type of deductible is the **aggregate deductible**, which applies for an entire year. With an aggregate deductible, the insured absorbs all losses until the deductible level is reached. At that point, the insurer pays for all losses over the specified amount. Sometimes, the aggregate and straight deductibles are used together. For example, a firm's property insurance policy may have a $1,000 straight deductible, subject to an aggregate deductible of $20,000. With this combination, the firm would never pay more than $1,000 on any one loss and would not absorb more than $20,000 in total property losses during the

netlink

Set your browser to http://farmersinsurance.com to see one insurer's recommendation about the size of your automobile insurance deductible, based on factors such as income, expenses, accumulated savings, and value of car. You'll find the calculator under "Tools/Calculators," then click on "Auto Calculator."

year. If only a straight deductible of $1,000 were used, the firm would have a potential liability much greater than $20,000 if numerous losses less than $1,000 occur and total more than $20,000.

Aggregate deductibles also are used in health expense insurance, although they are generally called **calendar-year deductibles**. A $200 to $400 calendar-year deductible is common in health insurance, as discussed in greater detail in Chapter 17. Compared with the straight deductible, aggregate and calendar-year deductibles are not as successful in eliminating the cost of processing small claims, because all losses will likely be reported to the insurer for credit toward meeting the deductible.

Disappearing Deductible

When a **disappearing deductible** is used, the size of the deductible decreases as the size of the loss increases. Finally, at a given level of loss, the deductible completely disappears. The reduction in the deductible results from the fact that losses are adjusted according to a formula such as

$$P = (L - D) \times (1 + R)$$

where P = payment by insurer
L = loss
D = deductible
R = recapture factor

For example, consider a policy with a $1,000 deductible and a recapture factor of 4 percent. All losses under $1,000 are absorbed by the insured. For a loss of $9,000, the insurer would pay [($9,000 − $1,000) × (1 + 0.04)] = $8,320. In essence, the deductible has been reduced from $1,000 to only $680, which is $9,000 − $8,320. For this set of factors, the deductible will disappear completely for losses of $26,000 or more. If the insured desired the deductible to disappear at $10,000 rather than $26,000, then the recapture factor would change from 4 percent to 11 percent, and the associated premium would be higher.

Franchise Deductible

A **franchise deductible** is expressed either as a percentage of value or as a dollar amount. Under a franchise deductible, there is no liability on the part of the insurer unless the loss exceeds the amount stated. Once the loss exceeds this amount, however, the insurer must pay the entire claim. In insurance for ships and their cargoes, it is common to use a franchise deductible expressed as a percentage of the amount insured. Thus, the policy might provide that there shall be no loss payable unless the loss equals or exceeds 3 percent of the total value. But once the loss reaches the 3 percent level, the insurer is responsible for 100 percent of the claim.

Coinsurance

The term **coinsurance** has different meanings in various types of insurance. In health insurance, the coinsurance clause functions much like a straight deductible, expressed as a percentage. For this reason the clause is often referred to in health insurance as the copayment. Its purpose in health insurance is to make the insured bear a given portion, say 20 percent, of every loss because it has been found through experience that without such a control the charges for doctors and other medical services tend to be greatly enlarged, thus increasing the premium to a prohibitive level. The insured who must personally bear a substantial share of the loss is less inclined to be extravagant in this regard. The use of coinsurance for health insurance is discussed in Chapter 17.

In property insurance, the coinsurance clause is a device to make the insured bear a portion of every loss *only when underinsured*. Underinsurance is looked on as undesirable for

ETHICAL PERSPECTIVES

Potential for Fraud

The use of a franchise deductible can be justified if the sole purpose is to eliminate small claims. However, the "all or nothing" nature of recoveries with franchise deductibles can also encourage moral hazard. For example, consider Parker Corporation, which is shipping $50,000 worth of inventory from New York to Europe. The cargo is insured for its full value, using a $2,000 franchise deductible. If insured losses appear to cause $1,995 of damage, Parker will collect nothing. But if Parker can "arrange" for only another $5 in damage, then the full $2,000 can be recovered from the insurer.

two reasons. First, insurers are supposed to restore their insureds to the positions or situations they had before the loss. They obviously cannot accomplish this objective unless the insured is willing to protect the whole value of the property. Second, it costs relatively more to insure the businesses of those who are underinsured than it does to handle the businesses of those who purchase insurance equal to the full value of the object. The reason for this phenomenon is that most losses are partial and, hence, the probability of partial losses is higher than the probability of total losses. Rates depend on the probability of loss. Consequently, it follows that the rate charged for partial losses should be higher than the rate charged for total losses. No one knows whether a loss will be total or partial. Yet there is a tendency for the average insured to assume that loss will be partial and therefore underinsure in order to save premium dollars. A more detailed explanation of the rationale for the coinsurance clause is discussed at the end of this section, following the discussion of how the clause operates.

Operation of the Coinsurance Clause

The typical coinsurance clause prorates partial losses between the insurer and the insured in the proportion that the actual insurance carried bears to the amount required under the clause. Usually 80 or 90 percent of the value of the property is the amount required. Thus, if a building with a value of $100,000 has a policy with a 90 percent coinsurance clause, $90,000 of insurance is required. The insured who carries at least this amount collects in full for any partial loss. But the insured who carries half of this amount, or $45,000, collects only half of any partial loss. The insured who carries $60,000 collects two-thirds of any partial loss. The amount collected in any case may be determined by the following formula:

$$\frac{\text{Insurance carried}}{\text{Insurance required}} \times \text{Loss} = \text{Recovery}$$

If the loss equals or exceeds the amount required under the clause (if the loss is nearly total), there is no penalty invoked by the coinsurance clause. Thus, if in the preceding case the loss were $90,000 at a time when the insured is carrying only $60,000 of insurance, substitution in the formula yields

$$\frac{\$60,000}{\$90,000} \times \$90,000 = \$60,000$$

The recovery is $60,000, the amount of insurance carried, and there is no penalty other than the fact that the insured did not carry sufficient insurance to cover the entire loss. But if the loss were $15,000, the recovery would be only ($60,000 ÷ $90,000) × $15,000 = $10,000.

Thus, the coinsurance clause places the burden on the insured to keep the amount of insurance equal to or above the amount required by the clause. Failing this, the insured becomes a coinsurer and must bear part of any partial loss. Other examples illustrating the operation of the coinsurance clause are included in Table 7-1.

Dangers of Coinsurance

There are several factors that, by increasing the value of exposed property without corresponding adjustments in the amount of insurance coverage, might unintentionally cause an insured to become a coinsurer. If inflation increases the replacement cost of the insured's property, the insured is required to increase the amount of coverage or suffer coinsurance penalties. Other factors include unexpected or temporary increases in inventory, increases in supplier prices for replacement goods, and increased investment within the plant or store that modifies or improves the building or its equipment.

In one case, a dealer in farm machinery had decided to take on a new line of vehicles and, on the morning of an explosion that destroyed the store, had received a large shipment of parts for the new line. The dealer suffered severe coinsurance penalties in the loss settlement. In another case, a manufacturer had spent $20,000 per machine to modify them to produce at closer tolerances than had been the case when the machines were purchased for $40,000 each. This increased investment subjected the owner to sharp reductions in the effective insurance coverage through coinsurance penalties.

One solution to such problems is to maintain an appraisal program under which periodic reviews are undertaken by qualified appraisers. Such personnel may be indispensable in proving the amount of the loss, in representing the insured in negotiations with loss adjusters, and in alerting the insured to needed changes in insurance coverage.

Coinsurance Credits

In return for accepting a coinsurance clause in the contract, the insured is offered certain credits in premium rates. For example, a typical reduction in the building and/or content premium is 5 percent when one moves from an 80 percent coinsurance clause to a 90 percent require-

---

TABLE 7-1   Illustrations of the Operation of the Coinsurance Clause

A. Building value = $500,000
Coinsurance requirements = 80%
Insurance carried = $300,000
Loss = $100,000

$$\text{Recovery from insurance} = \frac{\$300,000}{0.80 \times \$500,000} \times \$100,000 = \$75,000$$

B. Building value = $700,000
Coinsurance requirement = 80%
Insurance carried = $600,000
Loss = $100,000
Insurance required = 0.80 × $700,000 = $560,000

Because $600,000 > $560,000, the coinsurance requirement is met, and there is no coinsurance penalty in the recovery of the $100,000 loss.

ment. When an insured chooses a 100 percent coinsurance clause, the rate is reduced 10 percent from that charged when an 80 percent clause is used. By accepting the coinsurance clause, obtaining the lower rate, and buying the minimum amounts of coverage required, the insured can obtain greater insurance coverage for the same total premium compared with what would be paid for a smaller amount of coverage written without the coinsurance clause attached. However, in many jurisdictions, the insured is not given the opportunity to purchase coverage without the coinsurance clause attached.

Coinsurance Rationale

The higher rates necessitated by underinsurance and the rationale of the coinsurance clause in property insurance policies may be illustrated by four simple hypothetical cases.

Case 1: Full Coverage. An insurer is attempting to calculate a pure premium for 10,000 uniform buildings, each valued at $10,000. (The pure premium is that number of dollars that will pay for losses only; it is not adjusted for the cost of doing business.) It is assumed that 99 percent of the buildings have no losses. Of the remaining 100 buildings, 50 suffer a 10 percent loss during the year, 40 suffer a 50 percent loss, and 10 suffer a total loss. It is also assumed that each building's owner purchases insurance equal to 100 percent of its value, or $10,000. The pure premium calculation is as follows:

Insurance in Force ($)	Losses (%)	Fire Losses Payable ($)
99,000,000	0	0
500,000	10	50,000
400,000	50	200,000
100,000	100	100,000
$100,000,000		$350,000

$$\text{Pure premium} = \frac{\$350,000}{\$100,000,000} = 0.0035$$

$$= \$0.35 \text{ per } \$100 \text{ of value, or } \$35 \text{ per building}$$

Case 2: 50 Percent Coverage. Assume that all facts are the same as in Case 1 except that each insured decides to buy insurance equal to only 50 percent of the total value of each building:

(1) Exposed Value ($)	(2) Insurance in Force: 50% of (1) ($)	(3) Losses (%)	(4) Fire Losses Payable (Column 1 × Column 3) ($)
99,000,000	49,500,000	0	0
500,000	250,000	10	50,000
400,000	200,000	50	200,000
100,000	50,000	100	50,000*
Total $100,000,000	$50,000,000		$300,000

*Limited by the face amount of the policy to 50% coverage.

In this case, the insurer must pay out $300,000 in losses. However, if the insurer charges the $0.35 rate, as developed in Case 1, it will collect only $175,000 from policy-holders ($50,000,000 × 0.0035). It will therefore suffer a net deficit of $125,000 due to underinsurance.

Case 3: Charging a Higher Rate. Assume that all facts are the same as for Case 2, except that the insurer decides to charge a higher rate in order to prevent the deficit. Because the total losses payable in Case 2 are $300,000 and there is $50 million of insurance in force, the pure premium must equal ($300,000 ÷ $50,000,000) = 0.006, or $0.60 per $100. This result con-trasts with the situation in Case 1, where a rate of only $0.35 per $100 is needed. But rather than charge a higher rate for coverage, the insurer may utilize the coinsurance clause, which reduces loss payments to the individual insured.

Case 4: Use of Coinsurance Clause. Assume the same facts as in Case 2, except that the insurer attaches a 100 percent coinsurance clause to each policy. The rate charged is $0.35 per $100 of value, which, as shown in Case 3, produces a net deficit without the use of coinsurance.

(1) Insurance in Force ($)	(2) Insurance Required (100%) ($)	(3) Recovery (%)	(4) Fire Losses Incurred ($)	(5) Amount Payable by Insurer (Column 3 × Column 4)
49,500,000	99,000,000	50	0	0
250,000	500,000	50	50,000	25,000
200,000	400,000	50	200,000	100,000
50,000	100,000	50	100,000	50,000
$50,000,000	$100,000,000		$350,000	$175,000

Premiums (0.0035 × $50,000,000) = $175,000
Deficit = 0

In this case, the insurer eliminates what would be a net deficit by reducing loss recoveries by means of the coinsurance clause. Insureds suffer $175,000 of losses through coinsurance penalties. Presumably, it is immaterial to the insurer whether a $0.60 rate is charged (as in Case 3) or whether the coinsurance clause is used to effect "equity" in the rate structure. The insurer might offer the insured a choice: pay the higher rate ($0.60 in the example) or allow attachment of a coinsurance clause and pay the lower rate ($0.35). However, for most prop-erty owners the maximum probable loss is the full value of the property and insuring to value is in their best interest.

Time Limitations

As noted periodically in this chapter, time is of the essence in many insurance policies. There are specified limits of time set forth, for example, during which the loss must be suffered, the insurer is to be notified in the event of loss, the proof of loss is to be submitted, and claims are to be paid.

Some states require that property policies become effective at noon; in the absence of that requirement, policies usually start at midnight. Besides giving the inception and expiration point, the policy term provision states that standard time at the location of the property gov-erns the time. Consider a policy written in New York for a client living in Texas, covering property located in Oregon. In this case, 12 a.m. Pacific Standard (Oregon) Time is the determining point. If a fire begins at 11:55 p.m. on the day the policy expires and most of the loss occurs after 12 a.m., the policy still pays the whole claim.

There are also time limits that affect the dollar amount of coverage. To illustrate, in nearly all contracts guaranteeing the payment of an income or periodic indemnification for loss (such as disability insurance contracts) there are often waiting periods before recovery begins. There are also time limitations that restrict the maximum period for which payments may be made. Thus, in a policy that pays an income to the insured who becomes permanently disabled, it is very common to provide that no income shall be payable during the first 30 to 90 days of disability. Such a provision has the same purpose as a straight deductible, namely, to eliminate small claims and to reduce moral and morale hazard. In addition, the policy may provide that the income shall continue for 1 year, 2 years, 10 years, or life, as the case may be. The insurer always specifies what time limit, if any, shall be imposed. This is necessary to meet the requirement that an insurable risk must be definite and measurable. The provisions of disability income policies are discussed in more detail in Chapter 17.

Other types of time limitations also are found in insurance contracts. In business interruption insurance, for example, the insurer promises to pay both for net profits lost and for necessary continuing expenses that are the result of an interruption of normal business operations due to a named peril. The payment necessarily depends primarily on the length of time the business was shut down as a result of the named peril. In life insurance, the contract is often settled with the beneficiary by paying the proceeds in the form of an income stream, rather than in a lump sum. When this is done, the length of time the income is to continue is spelled out in the policy.

Other Insurance Clauses

Practically all contracts of indemnity, and many valued contracts, contain **other insurance clauses** that limit the insurer's liability in case additional insurance contracts also cover the loss. For example, a contract may agree to pay the insured a certain income on a valued basis if the insured becomes permanently and totally disabled. It might stipulate, however, that in case the insured is collecting under other disability contracts as well, the indemnity will be reduced to the point that the insured will be prevented from collecting more than, say, three-fourths of the income received prior to the disability.

In general, the purpose of other insurance clauses is to establish the procedure by which each insurer's liability may be determined when more than one policy covers the same loss. These clauses uphold the principle of indemnity in insurance. In the absence of such clauses, the insured might collect more than the loss itself, thereby creating a moral hazard. Other insurance clauses may also be called **apportionment clauses** (in property insurance) or **coordination of benefits provisions** (in health insurance). Life insurance policies do not contain such clauses, because life insurance is not a contract of indemnity. Thus, an insured may have several life insurance policies that all will pay the full face amount at death. Several common other insurance provisions are discussed in the following paragraphs.

Pro-Rata Clause

The **pro-rata clause** is a type of apportionment clause found in many property insurance contracts. It typically states that if more than one policy is in force on a given piece of property, each policy will pay in the ratio of the face value of each policy divided by the total amount of insurance in force on the property. For example, if there were four policies in force on a country club for $100,000, $200,000, $300,000, and $400,000, then they would pay 10, 20, 30, and 40 percent of each loss. On a $100,000 loss, the policies would pay $10,000, $20,000, $30,000, and $40,000, respectively. If the pro-rata clause did not exist, the insured would collect $400,000 on a $100,000 loss, greatly increasing the moral hazard.

A problem arises with the pro-rata clause when one of the insurers goes bankrupt or for some other reason refuses to contribute. The clause actually says the proration takes place whether all the insurance is collectible or not. Consequently, in the preceding case, if the insurer providing $400,000 in coverage went into receivership and could not pay on the loss, the other firms would still contribute only $10,000, $20,000, and $30,000 to the loss. The insured would have to absorb the $40,000 or collect from a guaranty fund of the state. Under the pro-rata clause, the risk of insurer insolvency is not transferred to the other insurers, but is assumed by the insured.

It is worth noting that the pro-rata clause applies only to policies that cover the same legal interest. If there is more than one interest involved, such as in the case of a lessee and an owner, and there are two policies on the property, each insurer must pay to the fullest extent of its liability, and the payment will not be reduced by action of the pro-rata clause. Thus, suppose a lessee spends $50,000 improving a property and insures this value. Because the value of all permanent improvements to real estate reverts to the landlord upon expiration of the lease, the landlord also has an interest in the improvements and may insure them. Because there are two interests, there may be two policies of $50,000 each. In the event that a fire destroys the entire property, both insurers would have to pay to the fullest extent of the insurable interest of each insured.

Another special case can arise when not all policies are identical. For example, suppose AAA Company has a building valued at $100,000. AAA has fire policies with two insurers, X and Y, in the amount of $50,000 each. The policy with insurer X is written to cover windstorm losses, but the policy with insurer Y covers primarily fire and does not cover windstorm. X's policy contains a pro-rata liability clause. In the case of a windstorm loss of $10,000, X pays only the proportion that its policy bears to all fire insurance on the property, or one-half. Thus, AAA Company collects $5,000 from X and nothing from Y because Y's policy did not insure against windstorms. The only solution to this problem is to make sure that all policies insuring the property are identical in their coverage.

Equal Shares

An alternative to the pro-rata approach to apportionment is the **equal shares** method, often used in liability insurance. With this method, insurers covering the same loss share the loss equally, up to their respective limits of liability. For example, suppose Keane Sporting Club is covered by the following three liability policies: $100,000 with insurer A, $500,000 with insurer B, and $500,000 with insurer C. If Keane suffers an adverse liability judgment of $90,000, it will be equally divided among the insurers, with each of the three policies contributing $30,000.

Now suppose the adverse liability judgment is $450,000, which is also covered by all three policies. If this loss were divided equally among the three insurers, each would pay $150,000. However, because that amount exceeds insurer A's policy limit, insurer A will only pay its limit of $100,000. The remaining $350,000 loss can be equally shared by the other insurers. Thus, the total loss is paid in the following manner: $100,000 by insurer A, $175,000 by insurer B, and $175,000 by insurer C.

Other Insurance Prohibited

In some property policies, the other insurance clause specifically prohibits the purchase of other insurance on the covered property. The insurance protection purchased by many homeowners has this type of other insurance clause.

Excess and Primary Coverage

The final approach to stating other insurance clauses is to specify that a particular policy is to always pay either first or last. If the policy pays last, then the policy is said to be **excess**. In this case, the insurance applies to losses only after the limits of liability of all applicable insurance contracts have been exhausted. The converse of excess coverage is **primary** coverage, in which a particular policy will pay up to its limits before any other coverage becomes payable. Clearly, all else being the same, the premium for primary coverage will exceed that for excess protection.

Many liability insurance policies are set up on an excess basis. For example, suppose Klepzig Tire Manufacturing Co. has $500,000 in liability insurance from insurer X, with a $1 million excess liability policy from insurer Y. If Klepzig incurs a $750,000 adverse liability judgment, insurer X will pay up to its limit of $500,000. Then the excess insurance provided by insurer Y becomes payable, up to either its limit or the amount necessary to cover the remaining loss. In this case, insurer Y will pay $750,000 – $500,000, or $250,000.

SUMMARY

1. There are two general types of insurance agreements: named perils and open perils.
2. It is common to cover more than one individual as the insureds under most insurance policies. These secondary interests normally do not receive as broad coverage as is given to the named insured.
3. All contracts of insurance contain exclusions. There may be excluded causes of loss or excluded perils such as war, wear and tear, and intentional damage. There are often excluded losses and excluded property, so that even if a loss due to an insured peril occurs, not all of the loss may be covered. Most policies exclude or limit losses caused in certain locations, such as while the goods are away from a named location or while they are abroad.
4. The practice of limiting amounts payable is common to insurance contracts. Thus, there are various kinds of dollar limits, deductibles, coinsurance arrangements, time limitations, and other insurance clauses. These clauses may encourage the insured to take out complete insurance to value, or they may discourage this course of action. They also serve to control moral or morale hazards.

internetexercises

1. Travelers Group provides a cost estimator for small business owners on its Web site at http://www.travelers.com/smallbusiness. Select an industry and then choose "Insurance Advisor" and complete a few questions to receive a customized insurance profile. What are some insurance policy provisions that will be important for a firm in the industry that you chose?

2. Set your browser to http://www.thefederation.org and select the "Hot Cases" link. Find a recent case involving a dispute over exclusions in an insurance policy. Summarize the facts of the case and explain why you agree or disagree with the court's decision.

QUESTIONS FOR REVIEW AND DISCUSSION

1. Distinguish between a straight and a franchise deductible. Which one will save the insured the most money?
2. Differentiate between excluded perils and excluded losses, giving examples of each type of exclusion.
3. A property insurance policy is written with a 90 percent coinsurance clause and a policy limit of $45,000. The actual replacement cost of the structure, less depreciation, is found to be $100,000.
   a. What amount may be collected under this policy in the event of the following losses: (1) $1,000, (2) $5,000, (3) $50,000, (4) $80,000, or (5) $90,000? Explain.
   b. Does the clause reduce recovery below the amount insured in all of the previous cases? Why?
4. Answer question 3a assuming that the amount of the insurance is $60,000 instead of $45,000.
5. Explain the reasoning underlying the use of the coinsurance clause in property insurance. Is there any way to accomplish the purpose other than through the use of coinsurance? Explain.
6. The mortgagee clause protects the lender's interest. Describe three ways the mortgagee clause aids the mortgagee.
7. An insured has the following four liability insurance policies: $300,000 with insurer A, $300,000 with insurer B, $700,000 with insurer C, and $900,000 with insurer D. Each policy apportions losses using the equal shares method.

   a. How much will each policy pay for a $200,000 loss?
   b. How much will each policy pay for a $2 million loss?
8. An insured's building is covered by the following three property insurance policies: $100,000 with insurer A, $300,000 with insurer B, and $600,000 with insurer C. Using the pro-rata method of apportionment, how much would each policy pay for a $100,000 loss? (Assume there are no applicable coinsurance or deductible clauses.)
9. Describe the limitations that likely will be placed on Pam Quaker when she wants to receive replacement cost coverage on her home that has been damaged by fire.
10. Explain the major reasons for excluding certain perils from insurance contracts. Do you believe these reasons are sufficiently compelling to justify most such exclusions? Explain.
11. Why are life insurance policies not cancellable by the insurer, although property insurance policies are?
12. Y's house and its contents become a total fire loss, but Y has only a vague idea of what property actually was destroyed because there was no inventory of the household goods.
    a. How might Y go about establishing the value of the loss?
    b. Is it likely that Y will be able to collect full indemnity, assuming that Y was fully insured? Why or why not? Discuss.

chapter 8

Selecting and Implementing Risk Management Techniques

Bryan Kehoe has just been hired as the first risk manager for a women's clothing chain, Edna's Alternative Fashions (EAF). With more than 50 locations in Florida, EAF recently opened several stores in California, where its unique styles are particularly appealing. EAF is privately owned and operated by a chief executive who took early retirement from another clothing retailer. The owner tends to disregard and/or underestimate important risks, which is one of the reasons Bryan was hired.

Since beginning work, Bryan has been compiling immense amounts of data concerning potential risks and their expected frequency and severity. He is now attempting to make sense of the data and formulate a complete risk management plan for EAF. Some of the immediate issues to be considered are the following: (1) Because the shoplifting risk happens so regularly, should that risk be treated differently than other risks confronting EAF? (2) The California stores could suffer a total loss if an earthquake occurs, yet earthquake insurance seems almost too expensive to be cost-effective. For whatever insurance is purchased for this and other risks, what deductible levels would be best? (3) What about the possibility of building up a self-insurance fund to avoid paying operating expenses and profits of insurers? Even if self-insurance is feasible for EAF, should Bryan recommend it, given senior management's attitude toward subjective risk? These and other issues are addressed in this chapter.

CHAPTER OBJECTIVES

After studying this chapter, you should be able to

1. Give examples of when risk avoidance might be a wise risk management decision.
2. Describe how loss control is used as a complement to risk retention and risk transfer.
3. Explain the concept of present value and its relevance for risk management decision making.
4. Explain the relationship of expected loss frequency and severity to the optimal use of risk retention.
5. Discuss the use of statistical analysis in the selection of deductible levels.
6. Describe several characteristics of firms that may find self-insurance to be a feasible risk management alternative.
7. Explain the major considerations in implementing risk management decisions.
8. Describe the concept of enterprise risk management and some of the alternative risk transfer tools that firms use in this framework.

The selection of appropriate risk management techniques is a dynamic problem. The best method for handling a particular exposure today may not be the best method a year from now because so many relevant factors change regularly. For example, the nature of an exposure may shift over time, as discussed in Chapter 1. Or the expected frequency and severity of losses may vary, causing estimates for the maximum possible loss and maximum probable loss to fluctuate. Finally, the cost and availability of different risk management tools cannot be assumed to remain constant. Thus a risk management plan that seems to be both effective and efficient one year may not make as much sense in the next.

All of these factors make it clear that the risk management process should be an ongoing one rather than an exercise that is performed once and then forgotten. As exposures to risk are identified and analyzed, available risk management tools and techniques must be considered. The steps for selecting among available risk management techniques for a given situation may be summarized as follows:

1. Avoid risks if possible.
2. Implement appropriate loss control measures.
3. Select the optimal mix of risk retention and risk transfer.

AVOID RISKS IF POSSIBLE

Risks that can be eliminated without an adverse effect on the goals of an individual or business probably should be avoided. Without a systematic identification of pure risk exposures, however, some risks that easily could be avoided may inadvertently be retained.

Consider the plight of the not-for-profit organization, Hunger No More, which operates several shelters to feed and house homeless persons. A wealthy patron dies, leaving the entire estate to Hunger No More. Included in the estate are an apartment complex in Florida and some undeveloped land near a hazardous waste site in New York. Both properties present substantial risks, whether Hunger No More is aware of them or not. But the organization likely will not be interested in keeping these properties and actively managing the risks inherent in them. After carefully considering its goals and priorities, as well as the possible and probable losses associated with the properties, Hunger No More may decide that the best solution is to sell the real estate and use the cash to finance its other activities. By doing so, the organization will avoid several risks present in the acquired properties.

IMPLEMENT APPROPRIATE LOSS CONTROL MEASURES

For risks that a business or individual cannot or does not wish to avoid, consideration should be given to available loss control measures. In analyzing the likely costs and benefits of loss control alternatives, it should be recognized that loss control will always be used in conjunction with either risk retention or risk transfer. That is, even if substantial funds are spent to reduce loss frequency and severity, some risk will still be present. In fact, as discussed in Chapter 1, objective risk may actually increase when actions are taken that decrease the chance of loss. Thus, either the remaining risk will be retained or it will be transferred to another party. This phenomenon is true whether it is specifically planned or happens by default.

Therefore, part of the cost/benefit analysis regarding potential loss control is recognition of the likely effects on the transfer or retention of the risk existing after loss control measures are implemented. For example, AKF Store is concerned about burglars breaking into its building, because it is located in a high-crime neighborhood. To help protect itself, AKF is considering installing a high-power security and alarm system. In analyzing this situation, AKF should think about both the effect on the chance of loss due to burglary and the fact that the cost of its crime insurance may be lowered if it installs a reliable system.

PROFESSIONAL PERSPECTIVES

Leveraging New Data to Answer Old Questions

Through a variety of efforts and focused attention, KFC USA has had considerable success in reducing employee accidents and thereby lowering its workers' compensation costs. For example, in 1991, KFC owned 1,400 stores with workers' compensation costs of $18 million annually. In 1996, KFC owned 2,000 stores, and its cost was only $13 million—a $5 million savings annually, and a per-store reduction of 50 percent. These impressive results came from a variety of traditional tactics, such as expanded use of light-duty work for injured workers, tighter control of medical costs, better training, and significant investment in safety programs and processes. While KFC was proud of these results, additional improvements were harder to come by, and future breakthrough improvements seemed unlikely without a major change in direction.

KFC started with the hypothesis that the Pareto Principle (80/20 rule) might be applicable. That is: a small number of stores may account for a disproportionate amount of losses. What they found when analyzing the data is that 20 percent of its stores (400 of 2,000) accounted for 78 percent of all incurred workers' compensation losses each year from 1994 to 1996. Further, KFC had a significant number of stores that had never had an accident. The next step was to identify what was unique about the "high-risk" stores compared to the "low-risk" stores.

KFC gathered data from multiple sources, not limited to just traditional risk management information, to answer the question "what's different?" Examples included facility size, location, customer demographics, management tenure, turnover, hourly turnover and training levels, overall operations effectiveness scores, sales, profits, and customer feedback information. The data were compiled for all 2,000 stores, and then comparisons for high risk, low risk, and totals were developed across each category of data, and across categories.

What KFC found was that high-risk stores are generally different in the following ways: (1) High-risk stores had less tenured (less experienced) managers, and those managers had less experience in that particular store. (2) High-risk stores generally were more complex operationally (included delivery, buffet, etc.) and had higher sales volume. (3) High-risk stores did worse on operational effectiveness scores, as well as on training hourly workers. (4) High-risk stores had high -employee turnover. (5) High-risk stores delivered substantially less profit per sales dollar than comparable volume stores.

These data clearly showed the importance of operational, recruiting, and training excellence in making a store a safe store, and the importance of effective human resources in managing risk. Given this information, KFC can now develop tactics and strategies to focus on the "80/20" stores to leverage its limited resources on the stores and areas with the greatest return potential.

Source: Chris Duncan, Senior Director, Loss Prevention, KFC USA, Inc., Louisville, Kentucky.

The selection between risk retention and risk transfer as the optimal risk management technique may change after loss control expenditures are made. As an example, consider Bill, who has received several traffic citations for unsafe driving. Until Bill attends traffic safety classes, he may be unable to purchase automobile insurance and may be forced to retain all risks associated with his bad driving habits. Or consider once again the example of AKF Store. Because of the potential severity of many crime-related losses, AKF has considerable crime insurance. After installing its special security and alarm system, as well as employing security guards to patrol the area regularly, AKF may decide that the potential frequency and severity of crime losses has been reduced to a level where risk retention is now possible. Hence, AKF may purchase less insurance and engage in relatively more risk retention following the loss control measures.

Analyzing Loss Control Decisions

Fortunately, the techniques used in making capital budgeting decisions in finance and accounting can be applied to risk management decisions regarding loss control. Consider Cole Department Store, which has been experiencing both substantial shoplifting losses as well as occasional vandalism to its building. Cole is considering hiring 24-hour security guards in an attempt to decrease both the frequency and severity of these losses. The estimated annual cost of this 24-hour protection is $60,000, which will cover salaries and employee benefits for the guards. By analyzing the pattern of past losses, Cole estimates that the presence of security guards will decrease shoplifting losses by $30,000 and vandalism losses by $20,000. In addition, Cole's property insurance premiums are expected to decrease by $5,000. Should the guards be hired?

An answer based only on these financial considerations can be obtained by comparing the size of the savings with the amount of cash outlay required to hire the guards. The estimated savings are:

$30,000	Decreased shoplifting losses
20,000	Decreased vandalism losses
5,000	Lower insurance premium
$55,000	Estimated savings from hiring guards

Because the $55,000 in savings is less than the $60,000 cost of hiring the guards, Cole may conclude that the potential savings do not justify the loss control expense. Before making a final decision, however, Cole should review both the estimated costs and savings. Cole should also consider whether there are any additional relevant factors that may have been overlooked. For example, would the presence of a security guard make employees feel safer? Would this intangible consideration make it possible to hire better employees? What about customer relations? Would they be enhanced by the presence of a guard? The financial calculations provide a good starting point for decision making, but the final decision often will be made in light of additional, less quantifiable considerations.

In the previous example, all costs and benefits from the proposed investment in loss control were to occur in the same year. When a longer period of time is involved, the calculation becomes more complicated. Before looking at another example involving a period longer than a year, it is useful to review some basic financial concepts.

Present Value Analysis

Consider first of all the role of interest. If $1 is invested at an annual interest rate of i, then the interest earned during the first year is $i \times 1 = i$, and the total in the fund at the end of the year is $1 + i$, which is the original $1 plus the i in interest earnings. If no payments are made from the fund during the second year, the total amount in the fund after two years will be

$$\text{Principal} + \text{Interest} = (1 + i) \times i(1 + i) = (1 + i)^2$$

In general, the relationship is such that an original sum of P invested at an annual interest rate of i for N years will accumulate to a value of Q as follows:

$$P(1 + i)^N = Q$$

To illustrate this concept, suppose that CVB Company puts $100,000 into an interest-bearing account, to eventually be used to improve its loss control program. If the fund earns interest of 7 percent per year, then after three years the fund will have grown to $122,504:

$$\$100,000 \times (1.07)^3 = \$122,504$$

A slightly different way of thinking about the role of interest in these types of situations is to ask the question "How much money must be invested now at interest rate i so that it accumulates to a value of $\$Q$ after N years?" By rearranging the terms in the previous general formula, P is:

$$\frac{Q}{(1 + i)^N} = P$$

This result is referred to as the **present value** of $\$Q$ for N years at interest rate i. Suppose JKL Company wants to have $500,000 available in five years to spend on upgrading the earthquake resistance of its California buildings. If JKL can earn an 8 percent return on its money, it would need to invest only $340,292 now in order to have $500,000 available five years from now:

$$\frac{\$500,000}{(1.08)^5} = \frac{\$500,000}{1.469328} = \$340,292$$

Tables are available based on many different values of i and N so that present value computations can be done quickly by simply multiplying $\$P$ by a factor shown in the table. (Several examples of such tables are included in Appendix A.) Financial calculators and spreadsheet packages also provide an easy way to perform present value computations.

An Example

Now consider the example of whether Factory Company should install a sprinkler system to protect its plant in case of a fire. It is estimated that the system will cost $600,000 and have a useful life of 15 years, with no salvage value. The firm's insurer has stated that installation of the sprinkler system will reduce Factory's insurance premiums by $63,000 a year. Factory's risk manager estimates that uninsured losses to property, as well as those involving injuries to employees, will be reduced $80,000 a year. It is also estimated that maintenance and repair costs to the sprinkler system would be $3,000 a year. When borrowing funds, Factory must pay interest at approximately a 10 percent rate, and its tax rate is 40 percent.

To solve this problem systematically, Factory Company should compare the present value of the after-tax cash flows from the installation of the system with the present value of the cash outlay and maintenance cost that the system would require. The cost of the sprinkler system represents a cash outlay of $600,000 for the firm. The insurance premium savings and loss reduction represent a cash inflow of $143,000 a year ($63,000 + $80,000). The maintenance cost will be a $3,000 cash outflow each year. If the **net present value** (present value of the cash inflow minus the present value of the cash outflow) is positive, the system should probably be purchased. But if the net present value is negative, it probably should not be purchased unless there are other less quantifiable factors to be considered.

From Table 8-1, it can be seen that there is a cash outflow of $600,000 in year 0 and a net after-tax cash inflow of $100,000 in years 1 through 15. The cash inflow consists of $143,000 of savings minus $3,000 for maintenance and $40,000 a year in income taxes. Because depreciation is a noncash expense, it is deducted to determine the firm's tax liability but is added back to the firm's cash flow in order to determine the cash inflow of the project. Consequently, the $100,000 of cash flow represents $60,000 of after-tax cash savings and $40,000 of depreciation.

In this example, the cash flows are the same for each of the 15 years. So one can multiply the $100,000 by the present value of $1 per year for 15 years at the firm's 10 percent cost of capital (7.6060, from Table A-4). This figure represents the present value of a dollar received at the end of each year for 15 years. By multiplying 7.6060 by $100,000, one determines the present value of the cash inflows, which is $760,600. When $600,000 (the cost of

TABLE 8-1	Net Present Value Analysis of Installation of Sprinkler Systems

Year	0	1 . . . 15
Installation costs	$600,000	
Loss reduction		$ 80,000
Premium savings		63,000
Maintenance		−3,000
Before-tax-cash flow		$140,000
Depreciation		−40,000
Taxable savings		$100,000
Taxes (0.4 × $100,000)		−40,000
Income after taxes		$ 60,000
Depreciation		40,000
After-tax cash flow		$100,000

Present value of the cash flow = $100,000 × 7.6060 = $760,600

Net present value (NPV) of the investment = $760,600 − $600,000 = $160,600

Decision: Because the NPV is positive, make the investment.

installation) is subtracted from $760,600, a net present value of $160,600 is obtained. From this analysis, Factory Company's risk manager can state that the installation of the sprinkler system is desirable.

SELECT THE OPTIMAL MIX OF RISK RETENTION AND RISK TRANSFER

As previously stated, loss control decisions should be made as part of an overall risk management plan that also considers the techniques of risk retention and risk transfer. To further complicate the decision-making process, risk retention and risk transfer often will both be used, with the relevant question being, "What is the appropriate mix between these two techniques?"

General Guidelines

As a rule, risk retention is optimal for losses that have a low expected severity, with the rule becoming especially appropriate when expected frequency is high. Physical damage losses to the cars within a large fleet driven by thousands of salespersons working for the same firm may fall into this category. Thus, no attempt may be made to transfer this risk to a third party; rather, the risk is retained, and an extra

netlink

Fire sprinkler systems are perhaps the most commonly cited example of loss control, but most people know little about them and, thankfully, have never seen one in action. For extensive information on fire sprinkler systems, including facts and myths about sprinklers and the history of fire sprinkler system, see http://www.rollinsfire.com.

amount is added to the price of the product being sold to pay for expected losses due to collision and other damages to the cars. Of course, loss control measures such as safety instruction may be implemented as well. But due to the nature of the risk, retention likely will make sense. At some point, however, the company also may want insurance to protect against the possibility that the total of the losses could be greater than expected. Management must decide how to distinguish between losses that are to be retained and those that are to be transferred to a third party.

Another general guideline applies to risks that have a low expected frequency but a high potential severity. In this situation, risk transfer often is the optimal choice. Small business owner Michael is concerned about possible tornado losses. He knows that it is quite possible his firm will never be damaged by a tornado. If he does have such a loss, though, Michael also knows that his building and all its contents could be completely destroyed. Because his firm would not be able to pay for such a large loss from either current income or accumulated savings, the appropriate decision for Michael is to transfer this risk to a third party, probably an insurance company. As part of this decision, Michael may decide to retain part of the exposure and only buy insurance for losses that exceed a specified level.

Finally, when losses have both high expected severity and high expected frequency, it is likely that risk transfer, risk retention, and loss control all will need to be used in varying degrees. Such a situation is, of course, not a desirable one to be in and should probably be accompanied by a reexamination of overall goals and priorities. Thus, some doctors in medical specialties that are frequent targets of large malpractice suits have decided either to change specialties or to leave the practice of medicine altogether. In the latter case, risk avoidance is seen as a rational response to potential losses that have high frequency as well as high potential severity.

What constitutes "high" and "low" loss frequency and severity in applying the preceding guidelines must be established on an individual basis. What is low loss severity for a multimillion dollar company may be quite high for a "Mom and Pop" firm or an individual. In this regard, concepts such as total assets, net worth, and expected future income all are relevant. Subjective risk considerations such as those discussed in Chapter 1 also are important, as persons with a different tolerance for risk will often classify situations differently. A summary of the guidelines discussed in this section is provided in Table 8-2.

Selecting Retention Amounts

Because in many situations both risk retention and risk transfer will be used in varying degrees, it is important to determine the appropriate mix of these two risk management techniques. Both capital budgeting methods and statistical procedures may be used in selecting an appropriate retention level, with insurance purchased for losses in excess of that level.

TABLE 8-2   **Guidelines for Using Different Risk Management Techniques**

Expected Frequency	Expected Severity	Technique*
Low	Low	Retention
High	Low	Retention
Low	High	Transfer
High	High	Avoidance

*Loss control also should be considered in conjunction with each technique.

But because the price of insurance does not necessarily vary proportionately with different levels of retention, the appropriate mix between retention and transfer is not an exact science. In general, decision makers try to minimize their total costs, considering not only the losses that are retained but also the premiums that must be paid for insurance that is purchased. Only at the end of the year (or other relevant time period) will it be known what the optimal decision at the beginning of the year would have been.

The Deductible Decision

Selecting a particular deductible level is one way of mixing risk retention and risk transfer. Deductibles help lower the cost of insurance as well as increase its availability. They also may make management more loss conscious, because a firm must absorb losses within the deductible level. However, as a general rule, risk managers do not accept a deductible unless (1) the firm can afford the associated losses and (2) sufficient premium savings will result.

For example, the risk manager of Alliance Corporation is faced with the following choices in purchasing automobile insurance for the company-owned cars used by the Alliance sales force:

Deductible per Car ($)	Annual Premium per Car ($)
100	2,000
250	1,700
500	1,500
1,000	1,400

As the deductible increases, the premium decreases. But the amount of premium savings is not in direct proportion to the size of the deductible. Thus, $300 in premium savings results by increasing the deductible from $100 to $250. But only $100 in savings results from increasing the deductible from $500 to $1,000. The risk manager may decide that the additional premium savings from a $1,000 deductible does not sufficiently justify the associated increase in risk retention.

A more complex example is that of Hall Shoe Corporation, which operates 100 shoe stores in 100 cities. All stores are located in suburban shopping centers, have similar construction characteristics, and have the same fire rating. Each store has a value of $150,000. Table 8-3 shows the firm's losses for the past 12 months, which are typical of its loss experience during the past several years. From the table, Hall Shoe's risk manager can determine that the mean loss was $8,000 ($40,000 ÷ 5) and that the median loss was $2,500. The standard

TABLE 8-3   Hall Shoe Corporation's Fire Losses

200X	Amount ($)
January 30	2,000
March 17	30,000
May 30	1,000
July 4	2,500
October 12	4,500
	$40,000

deviation is about $11,000, and the loss frequency is five fires per year per 100 stores. The firm is willing to retain no more than $10,000 in fire losses during the year. In effect, it wants to have an aggregate deductible equal to $10,000. The risk manager must determine the size of the per-occurrence deductible that should be selected in order to absorb no more than $10,000 in losses during the year.

This problem can be solved by employing some of the statistical techniques discussed in Chapter 2. The firm has more than 50 loss exposures, and the probability of loss is less than 10 percent (5 ÷ 100 = 5 percent). These two characteristics indicate that the Poisson distribution may be suitable to use in simulating losses. Because the mean is distorted by the $30,000 loss, the median is a better measure of central tendency in this case. In other words, the loss distribution is skewed.

Using the Poisson distribution and an average loss frequency of five per year, the probability of losses can be computed as shown in Table 8-4. For example, using the formula

$$p = \frac{(m^r e^{-m})}{r!}$$

the probability of no losses at all would be

$$\frac{(5^0 e^{-5})}{1} = 0.0067$$

Therefore, the probability of one or more losses is 1 − 0.0067, or 0.9933.

Table 8-4 may be interpreted as follows. There is a 0.0318 chance that 10 or more losses will occur when only 5 losses are "expected" on the average; there is a 0.0681 chance that 9 or more will occur, and so on. Thus, if Hall Shoe chooses a deductible of $1,000 per occurrence, there is a 0.0318 chance that its losses will equal or be greater than $10,000 (10 × $1,000), a 0.0681 chance that the losses will equal or be greater than $9,000 (9 × $1,000), and so on.

If the firm raises the deductible to $2,000, an aggregate loss of $10,000 could be exceeded after five losses. The table shows that the probability of five or more losses is 0.5595. If this frequency is unacceptable due to management's subjective risk level, then the deductible level should be reduced. By continuing this process, some number may be chosen that represents the maximum acceptable deductible.

TABLE 8-4   **Probability of Losses Using a Poisson Distribution with $m = 5$**

Number of Losses	Probability of Losses
0 or more	1.0000
1 or more	0.9933
2 or more	0.9596
3 or more	0.8753
4 or more	0.7350
5 or more	0.5595
6 or more	0.3840
7 or more	0.2378
8 or more	0.1334
9 or more	0.0681
10 or more	0.0318

Once an appropriate maximum per-occurrence deductible is selected, the risk manager should then compare premium savings available for deductibles less than the maximum. In the Hall Shoe example, suppose the firm can save $500 by taking a $1,000 deductible (versus no deductible at all) and can save $450 by taking a $500 deductible. The $500 deductible may be selected even though prior analysis indicates that a $1,000 deductible would be acceptable. This result may occur because Hall Shoe may reason that a savings of only $50 does not justify an extra $500 loss retention per-occurrence. Table 8-4 shows about a 56 percent probability of having five or more losses. Thus, there is a 56 percent chance that losses would aggregate to $2,500 or more by accepting an extra $500 deductible. The $50 saving would be viewed as the price of a risk where the average expected loss is $1,400 ($0.56 \times \$2,500$), a rather unfavorable trade-off. The chances are that Hall Shoe would view the gain of $50 as being too small to offset a possible loss of $2,500 whose probability is 0.56.

The Self-Insurance Decision

The possibility of self-insurance is another way of mixing risk retention and risk transfer. For example, suppose past loss data for a large fleet of automobiles owned by BNM Corporation indicate a 95 percent probability that total annual collision losses for BNM will be less than $50,000. BNM may then decide to self-insure losses up to this level and purchase insurance that will pay only if total losses for the year exceed $50,000. In this way, BNM realizes some of the advantages of self-insurance while still maintaining adequate protection if losses are greater than expected. The most important element in the previous example, of course, is the specific dollar amount of losses that should be retained. The same statistical techniques used to select deductibles can be used in choosing a retention level for a self-insurance program.

The cash flow advantage of funds set aside in a reserve fund is an additional factor that must be considered in assessing the value of self-insurance as a way of handling risk. Because losses are not always paid out in the year in which the event producing them occurs, a company has the use of self-insurance funds for varying periods and may earn interest on them until such time as the losses are actually paid. The concept of present value that was discussed previously in this chapter can be helpful in analyzing self-insurance funding decisions.

For example, consider a self-insurance fund set up by ABC Company to pay the medical expenses of employees who are injured on the job. From past experience, ABC estimates that, on average, employees who hurt their backs incur 40 percent of their total medical costs immediately following the injury. During each of the next two years, 30 percent of the total expenses are incurred. If total expenses are expected to be $100,000 for an employee injured today, only $40,000 will be paid from the self-insurance fund initially. The present value tables in Appendix A are used to find the amounts needed for the next two years. If the fund is earning annual interest of 8 percent, then only $0.92592593 \times \$30,000 = \$27,778$ must be in the fund today to pay the second year's $30,000 costs. Even less ($0.85733882 \times \$30,000 = \$25,720$) is needed now for the final expected payment of $30,000 two years in the future. As summarized in Table 8-5, the total present value of the expected medical claims is $93,498.

The $6,502 in interest earnings represents one advantage of the self-insurance program to ABC for this one loss. Funds released because they will be made up by this interest may be invested or used to reduce other borrowing needs of the firm. Other cash flow advantages also may exist if ABC's actual expenses of administration are less than would be charged by third parties if ABC did not have a self-insurance program.

In assessing the financial aspects of a self-insurance program, the value of operating funds to the firm must also be considered. If the monies in the reserve fund are invested in a liquid form that can be readily converted to cash, the firm may experience some loss because the funds might have been more profitably used in the business as working capital. Suppose that funds invested in XYZ Corporation are worth 15 percent but that monies placed in a liquid account earn only 8 percent. The difference, 7 percent, is the **opportunity cost** of funds

TABLE 8-5   Present Value of Self-Insured Expenses

(1) Year	(2) Expenses Paid ($)	(3) Present Value Factor for $1 at 8 Percent Interest	(4) Present Value of Expenses
0 (Now)	40,000	1.00000000	$40,000
1	30,000	0.92592593	27,778
2	30,000	0.85733882	25,720
			$93,498

set aside in the self-insurance program. If XYZ believes that $100,000 should be set aside now to guarantee the availability of cash at the time of a loss, then the opportunity cost of the plan is 7 percent of $100,000, or $7,000. That amount must be compared with the cost of alternative risk management techniques before deciding to continue with a self-insurance arrangement.

Even though it may be clear that a firm can save money in the long run with self-insurance, management may prefer stable, predictable insurance premiums each year. Further, some companies prefer to avoid the details of managing self-insurance programs and instead to concentrate on their main operations. The following conditions are suggestive of the types of situations where self-insurance by a business is both possible and feasible:

1. The firm should have a sufficient number of objects so situated that they are not subject to simultaneous destruction. The objects also should be reasonably similar in nature and value so that calculations of probable losses will be accurate within a narrow range.

2. The firm must have accurate records or have access to satisfactory statistics to enable it to make good estimates of expected losses. To increase the accuracy of the calculations, it may be wise to use data that cover a long period of time. If outside data are used, caution must be employed to assure that the data are applicable to the firm's own experience.

3. The firm must make arrangements for administering the plan and managing the self-insurance fund. Someone must pay claims, inspect exposures, implement appropriate loss control measures, keep necessary records, and take care of the many administrative details. If the necessary specialized executive talent is not available within the firm, it may be possible to contract for these services to be done by an independent **third-party administrator (TPA)**. However, if management does not appreciate the necessity of paying continuing attention to numerous details in some manner, then the self-insurance arrangement will not be a satisfactory risk management solution.

4. The general financial condition of the firm should be satisfactory, and the firm's management must be willing and able to deal with large and unusual losses. If management is unwilling to set up adequate reserves for funding the optimal retention level, then insurance may be used to a greater extent than might be indicated by mathematical analyses.

IMPLEMENTING DECISIONS

After the decision has been made regarding the appropriate mix of various risk management techniques, the decision must be implemented. This step in the risk management process may involve considerable interaction among risk managers, insurance agents, brokers, and insurance carriers. Several of the considerations involved in this process are discussed in this section.

Risk Manager versus Insurance Agent

Students sometimes wonder why an employee in a business firm is needed to handle loss exposures when similar services are offered by a commercial insurance agent or broker. Is it not a waste to have two separate persons with identical or overlapping duties and responsibilities? Because the agent has to be paid the same commission whether a risk manager is dealt with, is not the cost of maintaining a risk management function in the enterprise an unnecessary outlay? Several answers to these questions are briefly presented here.

First, the risk manager and the insurance agent or broker do *not* perform identical functions; the job of the risk manager is considerably broader in scope than merely buying insurance. Second, firms have often found from experience that it is difficult to coordinate insurance programs without having someone from inside the firm primarily responsible—an outside broker cannot have the degree of familiarity with internal business affairs necessary to best perform the insurance-buying function. Third, the firm needs someone with primary concern for the needs of the firm. A broker receives compensation only if the firm purchases insurance or pays for a service provided by a broker. With a risk manager making the decisions, the firm's interest comes first. Fourth, the responsibility for the protection of corporate property is often considered too important to place in the hands of an outsider. One of the basic duties of a corporate director is to exercise due care in protecting corporate assets against impairment. To expose these assets to loss through failure to supervise effectively their proper insurance might expose the directors to legal liability to the stockholders. If corporate officers do not directly supervise the insurance, they must delegate the authority to another—and this person is increasingly being recognized as a full-time employee, the risk manager of the company.

In summary, risk management supplements and complements, but does not necessarily duplicate or replace, the functions performed by insurance agents and brokers. Both functions are needed, especially in large firms where risk management is a vital and complex function.

Organization for Risk Management

Figure 8-1 depicts an organizational chart for the risk management function in a large firm. Note that in this firm the risk manager supervises a variety of activities including all kinds of insurance, self-insurance programs, foreign risks, and safety administration. Claims and loss records are also under the risk manager's control. The risk manager is only two levels beneath the president of the firm and may have 5 to 10 professional employees to assist in administering risk management. The duties and responsibilities of the risk manager tend to increase with the size of the firm. As illustrated in Table 8-6, a risk manager's compensation also tends to increase with the size of the firm.

Commercial Risk Management

One of the first actions a risk manager should take when developing a program is to develop a risk management policy statement to guide the decision-making efforts of the risk management department; this statement is normally expressed in general terms. The firm will also have numerous minor policies that are quite specific to certain tasks, such as "It will be the policy of the firm to have at least a $50,000 deductible on all insurance contracts."

A **risk management policy** is a plan, procedure, or rule of action followed for the purpose of securing consistent action over a period of time. The advantage of having definite policies to guide risk managers is that, once the rule is adopted, executives do not have to restudy recurring problems before making decisions.

FIGURE 8-1   Organization for Risk Management

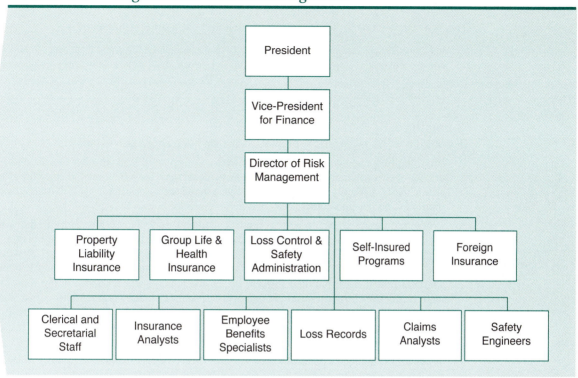

Segments from a statement of risk management policy for a large regional bank are as follows:

It is the objective of the bank to manage, control, and minimize the risk that must be met, to the end that the financial condition of the bank and assets entrusted to it be not seriously jeopardized, that its material resources be conserved to the maximum extent possible and practicable, and that its personnel be protected from hazards . . .

It shall be the policy of the bank to purchase insurance coverage when the risk is of catastrophic nature or beyond the capacity of the company to absorb from current funds, when the ex-

TABLE 8-6   Average 2002 Compensation of Risk Managers

Company Size (sales)	Compensation (salary + bonus)
Greater than $15 billion	$234,011
$7 billion to $15 billion	$198,258
$4 billion to $7 billion	$173,227
$2 billion to $4 billion	$144,330
$1 billion to $2 billion	$126,477
$501 million to $1 billion	$109,903
$201 million to $500 million	$96,399
Less than $200 million	$81,423

Source: Sam Friedman, "Risk Manager Salaries Rise, But So Do Employer Demands," *National Underwriter* (Property & Casualty/Risk & Benefits Management ed.) 7, no. 14, April 7, 2003, 10.

penditure for premiums is justified by services incidental to the insurance contract or other expected benefits; or when required by law.

This is a statement of insurance management policy for a drug manufacturer:

> It is our policy to assume the risks of property damage, legal liability, and dishonesty in all cases where the exposure is so small or dispersed that a loss would not significantly affect our operations or financial position, and to insure these risks as far as practicable whenever the occurrence of a loss would be significant.

Managing a Risk Management Program

In managing a risk management program, a person has many duties to perform:

1. First, the loss exposures must be identified and measured with respect to size and frequency. Then an analysis must be made to determine how to treat the loss exposure: retain, avoid, prevent, or transfer. Once these items are determined, the risk management plan must be put into action.

2. When putting the plan into action, the risk manager must decide who is to do the work. That is, will in-house staff be employed, or will the work be given to people outside the firm (outsourcing)? Prior to the 1990s, much of the work was done in-house. However, with the downsizing of corporate staffs in the 1990s, much more of the work is outsourced. Often, large national brokers or service vendors are retained by the risk manager. It is not uncommon for a risk manager to use an insurance company for a firm's risk management information system (RMIS) and a broker for loss prevention services. Both these functions can be performed by persons other than employees of the firm. For example, electric utility companies often use a combination of such services.

3. When a risk manager is building the insurance side of a risk management program, specifications for coverages must be developed, and several brokers will bid for the account. During this process, the risk manager is not only creating the insurance program but also choosing a broker. Most risk managers take their program to the market at least once every three to five years. The broker may not change that often, but the insurers can. The broker plays a role as advisor as well as the person who provides access to insurance markets.

4. In addition to managing risk, the risk manager must manage a department within a firm. Reports have to be written for management and information provided to the operating units so that they will know their cost of risk as well as information on losses—how to reduce them, and procedures to follow after they have occurred. Most large corporations have a detailed plan for situations when a major loss occurs. For instance, when North Carolina periodically is hit by hurricanes and tornados, employers once again discover how difficult it is for employees to get to work when the roads are blocked. On such occasions, one firm employs a tree service firm from Atlanta to go to North Carolina and clean up employees' yards so the employees are more able to come to work.

5. Another important task for the risk manager is to negotiate and settle claims with insurers and/or claimants. When major losses create claims of millions of dollars, much attention must be given to the process of proving the claims. Risk managers may retain persons who are experts in handling certain claims, such as business income losses. Of course, when the firm is being sued, the risk manager must work with the legal department to ensure that the claim is handled in the correct manner and that the interests of the firm are protected. One large manufacturer was engaged in so much litigation that it actually built an information system on many of the courts in which it had suits. The system contained information on awards, judge's personality, the attitude of juries, and other pertinent information with regard to having a trial in that jurisdiction.

6. With the development of relatively low-cost local area networks (LAN) and secure Web access, risk managers need to be able to develop risk management information systems (RMIS). The information contained in these systems should be organized in such a manner that timely and accurate reports can be made for management, insurers, outside

vendors, and others in the firm who need information. By developing an RMIS, a risk manager can reduce the department's dependence on the firm's data processing department and design a system that is tailored for the needs of a risk management department.

SUBJECTIVE RISK MANAGEMENT

This chapter has dealt mainly with selecting and implementing techniques for managing objective risk. Because objective and subjective risks are often both present in the same situation, some consideration must also be given to managing subjective risk. In one sense, the techniques applied to objective risk also should affect subjective risk. If risks have been systematically identified and analyzed, and if decisions have been made regarding the appropriate methods for dealing with those risks, then in most cases subjective risk can be expected to decrease. In addition, two other specific ways to deal with the existence of subjective risk are obtaining more information and group discussion.

Obtaining More Information

Perhaps the best way of handling subjective risk is by adding knowledge through research, training, or education. A risk averter may be more willing to accept risk once there is a better understanding of the uncertainties. With better knowledge, one is likely to perceive less risk in a given situation. Similarly, a risk taker may be willing to assume even greater risks as knowledge increases.

Group Discussion

It has been demonstrated that perceived subjective risk declines after group discussion of the problem. This fact suggests that an effective way to reduce subjective risk is to set up discussion groups, committees, or seminars before decisions are made. In this way, bolder and quicker action may result, and indecision may be reduced.

ENTERPRISE RISK MANAGEMENT AND ALTERNATIVE RISK TRANSFER

As described at the end of Chapter 5, firms increasingly are broadening their perspective of risk. Enterprise risk management, rather than focusing solely on pure or hazard risks, seeks to consider all exposures that could negatively affect the firm's ability to achieve its strategic goals. Russ Banham, in the April 1999, issue of *CFO Magazine*, states that the goal of enterprise risk management is to identify, analyze, quantify, and compare all of a firm's exposures stemming from operational, financial, and strategic activities. The exposures in this enterprise-wide view of risk include traditional insurable risks such as liability, as well as financial, commodity, legal, environmental, and other less-tangible exposures such as reputational effects and reduction in brand image.

Traditionally, the risk management tools described in this chapter—avoidance, loss control, risk retention, and risk transfer—have been applied primarily to the pure or hazard risks facing a firm. Further, even when similar risk management techniques have been applied to other categories of risk, the risk management activities of the firm have remained compartmentalized and relatively uncoordinated. Evan R. Busman, in the January 1998, issue of *Risk Management*, observes that risk management for many firms has been performed by different individuals with narrowly defined specialties. The traditional risk manager handles pure or hazard risk; the treasurer focuses on credit and monetary risk; strategic business units develop controls for operational and commodity risk; and marketing and public relations staff focus on reputational risk.

In addition to the organizational segmentation of risk management within the firm, risk management tools used to manage risks in these separate categories often differ. The techniques of insurance and self-insurance are commonly limited to the treatment of pure risks, such as fire, product liability, and workers' compensation. However, futures, options, swaps, and other derivatives contracts are typically applied to the management of financial risks, such as foreign exchange, commodity price, and interest rate risk.

The traditional method of assigning the risk management process to different functional areas, using what has been called a "silo" approach, can lead to less efficient management of risk for the firm as a whole. Many types of risks may be relatively uncorrelated with each other. As a result, combining these risks produces a form of "natural" hedging. As an example, earthquake damage to a multinational firm's property in one part of the world would be unlikely to have any correlation with its exposure to foreign exchange risk in another part of the world. The combination of these risks within the same firm reduces the level of risk. The traditional silo approach could actually reduce the overall efficiency of the firm's risk management activities by destroying the natural hedging that exists at the enterprise-wide level.

As the enterprise-wide view of risk management has progressed, the role of the traditional risk manager and risk management tools also have been evolving. Indicative of their changing role, traditional risk managers are increasingly being called on to become involved in the management of various non-hazard or financial risks facing their firms. Based on a survey of risk managers, Table 8-7 reports the percentage of risk managers involved in the management of various financial risks.

Alternative Risk Transfer Tools

A growing array of alternative risk transfer tools have been introduced since the mid-1990s ("alternative" here means an option to traditional insurance). Although the market shares of some of the alternative risk transfer tools are relatively small, the pace of innovation and new product development has been very brisk. A sampling of alternative risk transfer tools includes:

Captives: an insurer owned by a non-insurance firm or organization for the purpose of accepting the risks of the parent firm. Although captives were originally conceived as an alternative to traditional insurance, they provide firms with a potentially effective vehicle for assuming the broader risks involved in enterprise risk management. Given their popularity, captives are discussed in greater detail in Chapter 12.

Finite risk or financial insurance: risk transfer contracts that are based on the concept of spreading risk over time, as opposed to across a pool of similar exposures. Generally, these contracts involve a limit on the extent of risk ultimately transferred by the insured.

TABLE 8-7   **Financial Risks Managed by the Risk Management Department**

Non-operational (Financial) Risk	Percentage of Respondents
Political risk	36.4
Interest rate risk	23.7
Exchange rate risk	22.4
Counterparty credit risk	12.4
Asset price risk	9.0

Source: L. Lee Colquitt, Robert E. Hoyt, and Ryan B. Lee, "Integrated Risk Management and the Role of the Risk Manager," *Risk Management and Insurance Review*, Fall 1999, 43–61.

PROFESSIONAL PERSPECTIVES

The Scope of Enterprise Risk Management

Enterprise risk management covers all sorts of risks, from pedestrian to exotic. Here are 10:

1. Adverse commodity price fluctuations
2. Failure of a company's electronic data processing system
3. Lapses in communications links with customer markets and suppliers
4. Disruptions caused by political upheaval
5. Obstacles to timely strategic planning
6. Regulatory changes that disrupt the business environment
7. Changes in technology that hamper strategic goals
8. Lapses in due diligence relating to mergers and acquisitions
9. Counterparty reliability in financial hedges
10. Spoilage or crop disease causing damage to the quantity, quality, or marketability of grain supplies

Source: Willis Group.

The primary focus is on smoothing losses during the period of the contract, usually 5 to 10 years. Further, these contracts usually involve a sharing of the investment returns between the insurer and the insured.

Multiline/multiyear insurance: insurance contracts that combine a broad array of risks (multiline) into a contract with a policy period that extends over multiple years (multiyear). The combination of risks might be limited to pure risks, such as a blending of liability, workers' compensation, auto, and property risks into one policy with common limits and deductibles. Alternatively, the contract might involve a blending of insurance risks with financial risks such as commodity, credit, or currency risks.

Multiple-trigger policies: these contracts reflect the notion that to the shareholders of the firm, the source of the risk is not as important as the impact of the risk on the earnings of the firm. These contracts pool risks that in combination could have a very serious impact on the value of the firm. Most of the multiple-trigger policies issued thus far have combined a pure risk with a financial risk. The policy is "triggered," and payment is made, only upon the occurrence of an adverse event in each risk category. For example, a power company might buy a policy that is triggered if it experiences an unscheduled outage at one of its power plants, the first risk, during a period of extreme price volatility for electricity, the second risk.

Securitization: the creation of securities such as bonds or derivatives contracts, options, swaps, futures, that have a payout or price movement that is linked to an insurance risk. Examples include catastrophe options, earthquake bonds, catastrophe bonds, and catastrophe equity puts (CatEPuts). The driving motivation behind many of the securitized contracts is the interest in tapping the extensive risk transfer potential available in the capital markets. USAA and Tokyo Fire and Marine are two insurers that have used such tools to transfer hurricane and earthquake risks, respectively. Additionally, Tokyo Disneyland was purported to be the first noninsurer to use earthquake bonds to transfer risk to the capital markets, without the involvement of any insurer.

Table 8-8 reports the extent of use by risk managers of these alternative risk transfer tools. The table also reports their expectation regarding the use of the tools within the next five years. Significant increases are anticipated in the use of most of these tools. The risk managers forecast an almost fourfold increase in their use of the vehicles that involve the highest degree of risk integration, hazard and financial risk integrated contracts and securitization.

TABLE 8-8   Use of Alternative Risk Management Methods

Method	Percentage of Respondents	
	Current	Next 5 Years
Multiyear contracts	70.4	71.5
Captives	38.3	50.9*
Finite risk/financial reinsurance	26.6	52.8*
Blended risks (hazard only)	25.6	34.8*
Blended risks (hazard and financial risks)	7.1	29.3*
Securitization techniques	4.2	17.9*

*Differences in proportion (significant at 0.01 level)

Source: L. Lee Colquitt, Robert E. Hoyt, and Ryan B. Lee, "Integrated Risk Management and the Role of the Risk Manager," *Risk Management and Insurance Review*, Fall 1999, 43–61.

SUMMARY

1. Because of the dynamic nature of risks and the techniques for managing them, risk management decisions must be reviewed regularly.

2. The steps for selecting among risk management techniques are (a) avoid risks if possible, (b) implement appropriate loss control measures, and (c) select the optimal mix of risk retention and risk transfer.

3. Present value analysis can be useful in deciding how much money to spend on loss control. If the net present value of the cash flows is positive, expenditures are justified.

4. "High" versus "low" loss frequency and severity classifications are useful in deciding on an appropriate mix of risk retention and risk transfer. Risk retention tends to be optimal when expected severity is low, especially if expected frequency is high.

5. Risk transfer is appropriate when expected frequency is low but there is high potential severity. If losses have both high expected frequency and severity, a variety of risk transfer, risk retention, risk avoidance, and loss control may be necessary.

6. Both capital budgeting and statistical analysis can be used to select the best mix of risk retention and risk transfer. This mix may be accomplished through the selection of a deductible and/or the establishment of a self-insurance fund.

7. Self-insurance may provide some financial advantages to a firm because interest can be earned on funds that are not currently needed to pay for losses.

8. Businesses considering self-insurance should analyze their ability to predict probable losses, maintain accurate loss records, administer the many details of the arrangement, and deal with large and unusual losses.

9. Risk managers in businesses must learn how to work with a variety of persons, both inside and outside of their firms, in implementing appropriate risk management decisions.

10. In addition to avoidance, control, retention, and transfer, two methods for reducing subjective risk are obtaining more information and group discussion.

11. Enterprise risk management is changing the way firms approach the management of risk. The integration of risk management strategies across all categories of risk facing the firm is causing firms to utilize alternative risk transfer tools, such as blended risk contracts, multiple-trigger insurance policies, and securitization of risk.

internetexercises

1. An example of a technical tool that a risk manager can use to estimate probability and severity of future losses is a fire simulation model. Try one at http://dimacs.rutgers.edu/~biehl/fire.html. This simulation models the spread of fire as a function of the probability that a burning tree will set its neighbor afire, and can include factors of wind and obstacles. Describe a situation in which this simulation might be important to a risk manager.

2. College students are often required to perform risk management activities on behalf of organizations to which they belong. Triangle Fraternity offers a risk management manual for its chapters at http://www.triangle.org/docs/riskmgmt.pdf. Do you notice a pattern in which risks are insured and for which risk management procedures are designated? Why is insurance not offered for all risks?

QUESTIONS FOR REVIEW AND DISCUSSION

1. Why must risk management decisions be reviewed regularly?
2. What are the three steps for selecting among available risk management techniques?
3. Explain how an investment in loss control may change the optimal mix between risk retention and risk transfer in a given situation.
4. If a firm wants to have $1 million in cash available in three years, how much must it invest now at an 8 percent interest rate?
5. What are the potential cash inflows and cash outflows to be considered in a net present value analysis of a loss control decision?
6. Explain the relationships of expected loss frequency and severity in the use of risk retention and risk transfer.
7. In selecting a deductible, how does the risk manager balance considerations of potential premium savings and the firm's ability to pay losses?
8. Explain the concept of the opportunity cost of funds and how it relates to self-insurance.
9. Identify four considerations that should be analyzed by a business before it decides to use self-insurance.
10. Identify and describe two specific methods of reducing subjective risk.
11. A firm earns 25 percent interest on its invested capital. Interest available on assets that have a low degree of risk and are highly liquid is 10 percent. The firm is considering retaining a certain risk, but top managers believe that a loss reserve fund of $100,000 is necessary. Insurance against the risk is available for an annual premium of $10,000. On the basis of only these facts, do you believe that the firm should retain this risk, or do you believe that commercial insurance should be purchased? What other information would you like to have before you make a decision? Explain.
12. The future value $Q of an amount $P invested today at an annual interest rate i for a period of N years can be calculated using the following formula: $P(1 + i)^N = Q$. Explain in your own words how this formula works. Compare this formula with the formula used to compute the amount needed to be invested today at an annual interest rate i so that it accumulates to a value of $Q after N years: $Q \div (1 + i)^N = P$. Discuss the mathematical relationship between these two formulas and explain in your own words why it exists.
13. WPR Corporation owns 5,000 hotels and motels throughout the world. If you were the WPR risk manager, what risks might you suggest should be treated through the risk avoidance technique? Why?
14. Discuss the pros and cons of using statistical analysis to select an appropriate retention level for a self-insurance program.
15. Airlines face significant risk from increases in the price of jet fuel. The failure of their computerized reservation systems also can have a materially adverse effect on their operations. How could an airline use the concepts of enterprise risk management and alternative risk transfer tools to manage these risks?

Commercial Risk Management Applications: Property–Liability

PART 2

chapter 9

Risk Management and Commercial Property— Part I

Corporations face ever-changing property loss exposures. Creative risk managers must be able to design risk management programs that are cost-effective while also covering severe losses. During the recent past, firms in the United States suffered some of the largest catastrophes ever. Hurricane Andrew caused destruction with losses of more than $20 billion. For the risk manager, losses of this size determine whether the firm's risk management plan is working. If it does not work, the risk manager may be unemployed.

When disasters like hurricanes and earthquakes occur, risk managers learn valuable lessons. For one, how do you start getting things back to normal? After Hurricane Andrew, employees returning to work found the devastation so great that most of the structures in the area no longer existed or were not functional. Public utilities were not operational, and years after the storm, the community struggled to recover. Many businesses never recovered.

In January 1994, an earthquake struck California. Insured damages were more than $15 billion, and a major aftershock in March caused damage to some of the repairs that had been made after the original earthquake.[1]

According to the Insurance Information Institute, the terrorist attack of September 11, 2001, was the most expensive loss in the history of the insurance industry. Over 100 insurers around the globe are expected to pay an estimated $40.2 billion in claims. Of this total, an estimated $20.5 billion represents direct property damage to the World Trade Center and other property, as well as business income losses.

In reading this chapter on commercial property, you should keep in mind these questions: How can this peril cause a catastrophic loss? Will destruction of a type of property cause a catastrophic loss to the firm? What preloss activities can a risk manager take to lessen the impact of the peril or destruction of the property?

CHAPTER OBJECTIVES

After studying this chapter, you should be able to

1. Explain how the Simplified Commercial Lines Portfolio policy meets property loss exposures.
2. Identify property and perils covered by boiler and machinery insurance.
3. Describe how insurance contracts can be designed to insure property that fluctuates in value.
4. List the different types of consequential loss exposures and types of insurance coverage available for such loss exposures.

---

1   Judy Greenwald, "Insured Losses Expected to Hit at Least $3 Billion," *Business Insurance*, January 31, 1994, 1, 21.

In this and the next chapter, our emphasis will be on the property insurance needs of business organizations. We shall examine the types of property loss exposure that business firms typically face, and the types of insurance coverage available to insure them. Let us begin by examining several of the property insurance contracts that businesspersons use to protect their property:

1. The Commercial Package Policy (CPP)
    a. Building and personal property coverage form (BPP)
    b. Boiler and machinery
    c. Liability (see Chapter 11)
    d. Crime (see Chapter 10)
2. The business owners program
3. Difference in Conditions Insurance (DIC) and builders' risk
4. Reporting forms
5. Consequential loss exposures and insurance policies.

THE COMMERCIAL PACKAGE POLICY (CPP)

In January 1986, a new, simplified approach to commercial insurance coverage was introduced by the insurance industry. Under the Commercial Package Policy (CPP), the insured can obtain almost all types of insurance coverage. Not only is a wide variety of coverage available, but also broader contract provisions are included in the CPP. The CPP has seven separate sets of coverage: commercial property, liability, crime, boiler and machinery, commercial auto, inland marine, and farm. Commercial auto coverage will be discussed in Chapter 11.

It is important to realize that an insured can pick and choose coverages in the CPP. That is, property insurance can be purchased in the CPP, and liability insurance can be purchased elsewhere. However, the CPP allows many insureds to use one policy to meet most of their insurance needs. (Workers' compensation and ocean marine insurance must be purchased separately.) Also, the CPP has many options available. One can buy basic property insurance for completed buildings and add coverage for buildings under construction. Loss of business income coverage also can be added. Thus, basic coverage might be just for direct loss to completed buildings and their contents. But by endorsement, buildings under construction could be added, as well as loss of business income coverage.

In the newer versions of the CPP, a broad exclusion is made with respect to the actions of any insured, even if a given insured is innocent of any wrongdoing. In one case involving State Farm, a grandson occupied a house owned by his grandmother, but she lived elsewhere. She was declined the right of recovery because (without her knowledge) he allegedly set fire to the property and made misrepresentations on loss claims. Because he was an insured under the policy, she had to accept responsibility for his actions. Likewise, cases exist where an innocent spouse is denied coverage when a husband sets fire to their property. However, there have been cases where an innocent insured was allowed recovery. Such cases usually involve no family relationships.

Building and Personal Property Coverage Form (BPP)

Basic protection for buildings and personal property in the CPP is provided under the **building and personal property coverage form (BPP)**. In this form, the definitions of all insured property are given, as well as any limitations or extensions of coverage. Property coverage is divided into three major categories: buildings, your business personal property, and the personal property of others.

Buildings

The buildings category includes the building(s) described on the declarations page; any additions, extensions, fixtures, and machinery and equipment constituting a permanent part of the described building(s); and service equipment. In rental properties, appliances provided by the owner are considered part of the building. These inclusions are important to the insured because the building rate is normally less than the contents rate. Thus, any item declared as part of the building saves money for the insured.

Your Business Personal Property

This category includes business personal property owned by the insured and usual to the occupancy of the insured. Of course, limitations and exclusions exist, such as those found in the homeowners policy. For instance, motor vehicles, aircraft, and watercraft are subject to such limitations or exclusions.

Because of the definitions of building and business personal property, it is possible for a piece of property, such as a refrigerated locker, to be covered under both definitions. When this occurs, the insured can choose the broadest coverage that might apply to the property.

Personal Property of Others

The third type of property insured, personal property of others, consists of two parts: (1) improvements and betterments and (2) personal property of others in the insured's control. Improvements and betterments represent alterations made to a leased building by the insured that the insured cannot legally remove when the lease is terminated. Examples include modification of a storefront, decorations, partitions, paneling, and wall-to-wall carpeting. The personal property of others exposure develops in situations where the insured repairs the property of others. Radio, shoe, auto, boat, and watch repair businesses all have this exposure.

Extensions of Coverage

In addition to the basic coverage that exists when the premium is paid, the BPP has extensions of coverage that expand protection to six other categories of property. These extensions are meant to supplement the basic coverage. If major exposures exist in any of the six areas, the insured needs to purchase additional insurance. The six extensions are as follows:

1. *Newly acquired or constructed property:* subject to a maximum of $250,000 per building. The insured must report additions or newly acquired buildings within 30 days.

2. *Your business personal property at newly acquired premises:* subject to $100,000 maximum per building. Coverage expires 30 days after acquiring the property.

3. *Personal effects and property of others:* $2,500 of coverage for the personal effects of the named insured, officers, and employees and for the personal property of others in the insured's care, custody, or control.

4. *Valuable papers and records—cost of research:* $2,500 limit, covering the cost of researching, replacing, or restoring the lost information on lost or damaged valuable papers and records (other than electronic data).

5. *Property off-premises:* $10,000 limit, covering property while it is temporarily at a location the insured does not own, lease, or operate. Only insured perils are covered, and property in a vehicle is excluded.

6. *Outdoor property:* $1,000 limit, but not more than $250 per tree, shrub, or plant. Coverage applies to outdoor fences, radio and television antennas (including satellite dishes), signs, trees, shrubs, and plants. Perils insured against are limited to fire, lightning, explosion, riot or civil commotion, and aircraft. Stock of outdoor trees, shrubs, and plants is treated like any other type of stock and is not subject to the limitations on this extension of coverage.

All of these extensions of coverage are an additional amount of insurance, and they apply only if the policy has an 80 percent or higher coinsurance clause.

Specific versus Blanket Coverage

Under the general form, coverage may be on one of two bases: specific or blanket. Under **specific coverage**, property at one or more locations is listed and specifically insured. Under **blanket coverage**, property at several locations may be insured under a single item. For example, the policy could provide $1 million of insurance on all contents at plants in five different cities, or classes of property usually insured separately might be lumped together and insured as a single item, such as $100,000 on stock, furniture, fixtures, and machinery.

Common Clauses in the BPP

Some of the common clauses found in the BPP involve coinsurance, subrogation, electrical apparatus, power failure, operation of building laws, and alterations and repairs. The power failure clause reads that spoilage due to power failure from an insured peril is not covered unless the loss of power is from an on-premises insured peril. If a windstorm blows down a transmission line next door, no coverage is available. The alteration and repair provision allows the insured to make this type of modification without its being considered an increase in hazard, which would cause the coverage to be suspended. The building law clause reads that no loss will be paid that results from the operation of building codes. The electrical apparatus clause states that no loss to electrical items will be covered if caused by artificially generated electrical currents, unless fire ensues, and then loss is covered only for the fire damage.

In addition to these common clauses, two important exclusions were added to property policies in 2002. Mold claims have skyrocketed in a few states in the early 2000s. Many common building products like drywall, lumber, paneling, and insulation are susceptible to damage from mold if adequate moisture is present. Prior to 2002, mold was listed in the so-called "wear and tear" exclusion. However, in spite of this the findings of coverage as a result of court decisions in several states led to a new exclusion of "fungus, wet rot, dry rot, and bacteria." Limited coverage for these exposures can be added back by endorsement. Following the terrorist attacks of September 11, many insurers faced exclusions in their reinsurance coverage for terrorism. As a result, insurers began excluding terrorism from their policies. The Terrorism Risk Insurance Act (TRIA) was enacted in November 2002, by the federal government to provide a backstop for insurers that could not get reinsurance coverage for terrorism. With the enactment of the law, several endorsements were developed to allow the insurance buyers to obtain coverage for terrorism in commercial property policies.

Insured Perils

Three options are present in the BPP with respect to insured perils: basic, broad, and special cause of loss forms.

The basic form covers fire, lightning, explosions, windstorm and hail, smoke, riot or civil commotion, vandalism, sprinkler linkage, sinkhole collapse, and volcanic action. If an insured does not have automatic sprinklers, no charge is made for that peril.

The broad form includes the basic perils plus falling objects (exterior damage must occur before interior damage is covered); the weight of ice, sleet, and snow; and accidental discharge of water or steam from a system or appliance containing steam or water other than an automatic sprinkler system. Table 9-1 provides the name and a brief description of the various basic and broad form perils, as well as the special form.

The special cause of loss form covers all direct physical losses except those that are excluded. Examples of excluded perils are earth movement, flood, war, enforcement of building

TABLE 9-1	Commercial Property Forms—Peril Analysis

Causes of Loss—Basic Form

1. Fire—hostile fire—outside intended container or receptacle.
2. Lightning—undefined and unmodified in the policy.
3. Explosion—does not include damage caused by water rupture in pipes.
4. Windstorm or hail—includes hurricanes, tornadoes, and hail.
5. Smoke—causing sudden and accidental loss; no coverage for gradual loss.
6. Aircraft and vehicles—damage caused by vehicle owned by the insured not covered.
7. Riot or civil commotion—covers looting at the time and place of the riot.
8. Vandalism—no coverage for glass (other than glass building blocks); no coverage for loss resulting from theft.
9. Sprinkler leakage—leakage or discharge from a sprinkler system.
10. Sinkhole collapse—does not cover cost of filling sinkholes or coal mine collapse.
11. Volcanic action—does not cover earthquake; does cover airborne shock or blast, ash, dust, and lava flow.

Causes of Loss—Broad Form
Basic perils plus:

1. Falling objects—personal property in open not covered; must have exterior damage to structure before coverage for interior personal property.
2. Weight of snow, ice, or sleet—no coverage of personal property outside of structure and gutters and downspouts.
3. Water damage—accidental discharge or leakage of water or steam as the direct result of the breaking or cracking of any part of a system or appliance containing water or steam other than an automatic sprinkler system. Must maintain heat in structure to have coverage for freezing losses.

Causes of Loss—Special Form

1. All direct physical loss unless excluded.
2. Earthquake, flood, mudslide, war, nuclear reaction or contamination, and boiler explosion are among perils excluded.

ordinance, smog, insect damage, and wear and tear. The old name for this type of coverage was "all risk." The new name is "open perils."

Debris Removal

The BPP form includes coverage for debris removal; however, if the loss is greater than or equal to the policy, then there is additional debris coverage up to $10,000. Within the form, a sublimit exists on debris removal equal to 25 percent of the covered physical loss. If debris removal costs exceed 25 percent of the covered physical loss, then the extra $10,000 of coverage also applies.

Besides debris removal coverage, the BPP provides coverage for costs of pollutant cleanup and removal from land or water at the described premises. However, protection is limited to $10,000, and the loss must be reported to the insurer in writing within 180 days. It is not the purpose of this clause to provide environmental impairment insurance.

Subrogation

Practically all contracts of property insurance are subject to the right of subrogation by the insurer against any liable third party. This right is very important. It may turn out, for example, that while the insured's property insurance provides coverage for a loss, someone else has agreed to assume this liability by contract or is held liable because of its negligence in causing the damages. If the insurer pays the claim, it has a right to any such claims that the insured may have had against others. Such recoveries assign responsibility to the party that is responsible for the damages, holding that party accountable for its actions.

The following case is an example of this concept. On April 20, 1992, a freight tunnel beneath the Chicago River collapsed. More than 250 million gallons of water poured into a series of tunnels, causing $300 million in insured losses. After the insurers paid their policyholders, they filed suits against (subrogated) responsible parties. In one such case, Hartford Group, Inc., filed suit for $3.4 million against Great Lakes Dredge and Dock Company, the firm that allegedly caused the hole in the tunnel.[2]

Endorsements Used with the BPP

Numerous endorsements are available for an insured to use with the BBP. An insured can add earthquake and radioactive contamination to the list of insured perils. The limits of recovery on such property as outdoor signs, trees, shrubs, plants, and radio and television antennas may be increased. Special market value endorsements are available for distilled spirits and wines.

Two endorsements that modify the BPP include replacement cost and ordinance coverage. The replacement cost endorsement is like that found in the homeowners policy and changes the basis of recovery from actual cash value to replacement cost. The ordinance and law endorsement is used when an older building must be repaired according to a more stringent building code. This endorsement normally is used only when replacement cost coverage exists.

Boiler and Machinery Insurance (Equipment Breakdown Coverage)

Explosions caused by steam boilers, compressors, engines, electrical equipment, flywheels, air tanks, and furnaces constitute a serious source of loss that the layperson often does not recognize.

Special Characteristics

Boiler and machinery insurance has been developed along somewhat different lines from the usual insurance contract. Recognizing that prevention of losses is even more important than indemnification of loss, insurers have taken on the service of inspection and servicing of boiler operations and technical machinery. The insurer typically sends an inspector to the insured plant two or more times each year, depending on the size of the firm. In many states, these inspections substitute for an inspection required by law. Technical specialists examine boilers and pressure vessels both internally and externally, using special equipment to detect minute cracks, crystallization, deterioration of insulation, vibration, and general wear. Failure of a vessel to pass an inspection may mean imminent danger to continued operations. As a result, the insurer reserves the right to suspend coverage immediately if recommended repairs or replacements are not made.

---

2 Sara Marley, "Insurers Subrogating Chicago Flood Losses Face Big Obstacles," *Business Insurance*, December 14, 1992, 1, 29.

The form provides coverage for direct damage to property owned by the insured and property in the insured's care, custody, or control and for which the insured is liable. The insuring clause excludes loss when the proximate cause is fire, because fire losses are paid under the BPP. Besides the basic coverage, four extensions exist: expediting expense, defense, supplementary payments, and **automatic coverage**.

Insuring Agreements

The following comments describe the basic coverages commonly found in boiler and machinery policies and in the endorsements that may be added.

Loss to Property. Perhaps the chief reason for the purchase of boiler and machinery insurance is either to replace damaged property belonging to the insured in the event of sudden or accidental loss or to prevent the occurrence of such a loss. As previously noted, the insuring clause excludes loss when the proximate cause is fire, because fire losses are paid under the BPP. Indirect losses are excluded but may be insured separately by endorsement. The insurer reserves the right to replace or repair the property or to indemnify for its actual cash value. Unlike most property contracts, property in the insured's care, custody, and control also is covered.

Expediting Expenses. The insurer agrees to pay for the **expediting expenses**, or the reasonable extra cost of expediting repair of the machinery, including overtime costs and the extra costs of express or other rapid means of transportation. Payments under this section may not exceed $5,000 or the amount payable under the section for loss of property of the insured, whichever is less.

Optional Endorsements

Many optional endorsements are available to the boiler and machinery coverage in the CPP policy. Three of them are discussed here.

Business Income Insurance. One of the important types of loss stemming from the failure of a steam boiler or other vital machinery is the shutdown of an entire plant. Thus, business income insurance, often called **use and occupancy** in this line of insurance, is commonly added by endorsement to the boiler and machinery contract. It is similar to business income insurance as written in connection with the BPP and is available on the valued form or on a replacement cost basis. On the valued form, a daily indemnity is stated (e.g., $1,000 per day) with an aggregate limit (e.g., $50,000). This amount is paid without proof of loss in case the plant is totally shut down. Proportionate parts of this amount are paid for partial shutdowns.

netlink

The loss control services offered by boiler and machinery insurers can be very valuable. Explore the following site to see what one insurer is doing in this regard and to read about risk management/loss control for equipment breakdown and recent claims for different types of businesses: http://www.hsb.com/hsbiq/.

Extra Expense. A need for extra expense coverage could arise from the failure of a heating plant boiler, forcing a business to install temporary alternative methods of heating at considerable expense. A power plant failure may force the firm to purchase standby power from another source at extra cost. Extra expense insurance is especially appropriate for office or apartment buildings, schools, and stores, where failure of an insured object would not usually stop operations but would cause considerable extra cost to keep everything running in its absence.

Consequential Damage. The **consequential damage endorsement** provides protection when an interruption of power is due to failure of an insured object on the insured's own premises. For example, if the insured has a cold-storage warehouse filled with perishable foodstuffs and the refrigeration system is inoperative due to failure of the compressor system within the insured's plant, indemnity would be payable under a consequential damage endorsement. Firms such as cold-storage warehouses, breweries, creameries, florists, ice plants, and hothouses are among the more likely candidates for consequential damage and **power interruption coverage**.

BUSINESS OWNERS POLICY

The business owners program is designed for certain small- to medium-sized businesses. It is a stand-alone policy and cannot be added to the CPP. The underwriting manual defines *small-to medium-sized* to mean (1) apartments and (2) office buildings of less than six stories and with a total area of less than 100,000 square feet. Other types of occupancies may have up to 25,000 square feet per building. Besides these size guidelines, a list of noneligible occupancies is also given, including certain contractors, bars, places of amusement, lending institutions, manufacturers, and automobile businesses.

Property Forms Used

Only two property forms are used: *standard* and *special*. Options are limited, but coverage is quite broad. Mandatory coverage exists for both direct and indirect loss to property, liability (bodily injury, property damage, and personal injury), and medical payments. Options include outdoor signs ($1,000), money and securities, employee dishonesty, and mechanical breakdown. In addition, several endorsements are available. Examples of these endorsements are earthquake, spoilage, utility services, and computer coverage.

Recovery Basis

Prior to 1996, the business owners program assumed the insured would insure 100 percent to value but did not have a coinsurance requirement. Many "old line" underwriters questioned the lack of a coinsurance clause, but it was still written without coinsurance. However, after a decade of use, practical experience has shown the need for an insurance-to-value requirement, because many insureds underreported their property values. The current policy form does not have a coinsurance requirement. However, it does have an insurance-to-value requirement. For full replacement cost coverage to apply the amount of insurance at the time of the loss must be at least 80 percent of the full replacement cost. Otherwise, settlement is at actual cash value or the amount adjusted as if an 80 percent coinsurance requirement applied.

OTHER COMMERCIAL PROPERTY FORMS

Two additional commercial property programs and forms exist with which you should be familiar: the difference in conditions and the builders' risk. The difference in conditions form is used to give all-risk coverage, and the builders' risk form insures buildings under construction.

Difference in Conditions Insurance

Difference in Conditions Insurance (DIC) is written with the insured's basic contract because DIC excludes the basic cause of loss perils. However, it can be written to insure almost any other peril, including earthquake and flood. It has no coinsurance or pro-rata clause but usually has a sizable deductible. As a general rule, only large firms purchase the coverage, but its use is becoming more popular, and smaller businesses are starting to use it. DIC coverage is like a donut (see Figure 9-1). The donut hole is the basic cause of loss perils, which are excluded in the DIC, and the donut—what the DIC covers—can include flood, earthquake, boiler and machinery, and open perils. Firms will often use the combination of the basic cause of loss form and the DIC to give much broader coverage than the special form provides. This contract is usually purchased by larger businesses, and its limit is in the millions.

Builders' Risk

The builders' risk form is used to insure buildings under construction. The usual approach is to use a completed value form that requires the insured to purchase an amount of insurance equal to the finished value of the building. However, because the exposure is equal to that value only when the structure is finished, the rate charge is usually 55 percent of the standard rate. Using this approach, the insured has full coverage during the construction period and does not have to be concerned with filing reporting forms and updates with the insurer. The policy may be written so that the insurable interests of the building owner, the general contractor, and the subcontractor are covered. The BPP has several builders' risk forms available for insureds to use.

FIGURE 9-1   The Donut of Difference in Conditions Insurance

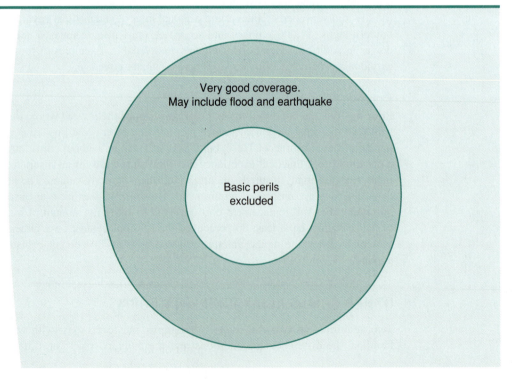

REPORTING FORMS

Reporting forms are available in the CPP policy. They are designed to adjust insurable coverage on contents to changing property values at one location or in different locations. Reporting forms have several advantages: (1) the amount of insurance protection is automatically adjusted to changes in values of property at different locations; (2) new locations are automatically covered; (3) the insured does not have to pay premiums on limits of liability in the policy but rather pays premiums according to the actual values at risk; (4) the possibility of having gaps in coverage or duplication of insurance is virtually eliminated; and (5) the insured avoids being short-rated when coverage is reduced.

An important purpose of reporting forms is to adjust insurance protection for business firms that have many plants located in different geographical areas or that wish protection to be adjusted automatically to constantly changing values at these plants. It would be cumbersome, indeed, if a business enterprise carrying on a nationwide operation involving 10 manufacturing or processing plants and 20 warehouses and other distribution centers had to purchase a separate policy for each location. For example, undoubtedly much duplication of coverage would occur when goods were shipped from one location to another (being insured by both the sender and the receiver), and likely many instances of omission would occur of insurance protection altogether (each party believing the other to have taken care of the insurance).

The insured purchases an insurance policy with a stated maximum as its limit. This figure is the most the insurer will ever pay. However, the insured is only charged for the exposure that exists and may receive a refund at the end of the policy period. Each period, usually monthly, the insured is required to report to the company what the actual values were at each location on a specific date. If the insured understates the actual value and later suffers a loss, there is a penalty in the recovery, and only that portion of the loss that the amount reported bears to the actual values at risk can be recovered (this provision acts like a 100 percent insurance-to-value clause). Thus, if the insured reported $50,000 of inventory at Location C and it was determined that the true value was $60,000, only five-sixths of any subsequent partial loss can be recovered. Also, if the insured fails to make a report on the required date, recovery is limited to the values reported on the last date a report was made. Thus, the insured is denied automatic protection when values rise between reporting dates. For example, if on January 1 the insured reports correctly $10,000 of values at Location D, with a stated maximum of $64,000 on the policy, and on January 15 there is a loss of $30,000 (made possible because incoming shipments of goods raised the values exposed), the entire loss is paid. However, if the loss occurs on February 15 and no report was made on February 1, when it was due, the limit of liability is $10,000.

CONSEQUENTIAL LOSS COVERAGE

The nature of **consequential losses** can best be understood through an example. Suppose a small manufacturer suffers a serious fire that shuts down its plant for two months while repairs are being made. The manufacturer is fully insured against direct loss by fire but carries no consequential loss coverage. The fire policy pays for the cost of lost raw materials, goods in process, and finished goods, as well as repairs to machinery and buildings. However, the manufacturer finds that it is necessary to keep certain key employees, such as plant managers and salespeople, on the payroll to help with the reorganization and to render service to customers. In addition, expenses are incurred, such as taxes, insurance premiums, interest, heat, light, power, and depreciation, regardless of the volume of operation. Finally, the manufacturer has not been able to earn any profit on the unsold finished goods or on the volume of goods that normally would have been produced during this period. The sum of such losses may be so severe that the manufacturer is unable to continue in business. Consequential damage contracts have been devised to indemnify for this type of loss.

Business income coverage is usually written as an endorsement to the BPP or is listed on the form. The insured perils usually include the basic cause of loss perils in the BPP. Also, the indirect loss situation may be insured under an all-risk endorsement. Thus, if an interruption of business income or other consequential loss results from damage to property by any of the perils in the contracts, the insured is indemnified. Consequential loss contracts may be divided into time-element contracts and contracts without a time element. Both are discussed in the following sections.

Time-Element Contracts

Businesses face indirect losses of a much greater magnitude than do individuals. This statement is true not only because businesses handle larger amounts of money but also because the restoration can take much longer. It may take one or two years to rebuild a factory, whereas most houses can be rebuilt within three to six months. **Time-element contracts** measure the indirect loss in terms of x dollars per unit of time that passes until the subject matter can be restored.

In this section, we shall examine the following types of time-element business consequential losses: business income, extra expense, and leasehold interest.

Business Income Insurance

Business income insurance undertakes to reimburse the insured for profits and fixed expenses lost as a result of damage to the property from an insured peril. Thus, one of the important problems in this line of insurance is to acquire a firm understanding of methods of determining losses, which, by their very nature, depend on future events. Because the future is an unknown quantity, this problem is sometimes complicated.

Basic Characteristics. The business income contract has certain fundamental provisions that are frequently a source of misunderstanding. The policy will indemnify the insured subject given the following conditions:

1. Physical damage to property by a fire or other insured peril must be present.
2. A reduction in business must occur, and this reduction must result from the physical damage caused by the named peril and not from some other cause such as a strike or a shortage of supplies.
3. During the period of restoration, it must be established that the business would have continued to operate had it not been for the occurrence of loss from the insured peril.
4. The loss must occur during the policy term at the described location.
5. If the insured loss had not occurred, the business would have earned a profit or a portion of fixed costs.

If the business had only been breaking even at the time of the occurrence of the insured loss, a question would be raised as to whether any profits would have been earned. If it were found that no profits would have been made even if the business had not been shut down, no real loss from this source would have occurred, and hence no indemnity for lost profits would be paid. Of course, if the business had been earning enough money to cover its fixed expenses, these costs would be reimbursed. Thus, even though a business is losing money, an insurable value can exist to the extent that it was earning its fixed expenses. As might be surmised, a considerable source of conflict can occur to resolve the question as to what profits might be in the future.

Business Income Loss. The value of the possible loss may be measured by different methods, but the central idea is to examine the income statement of the firm and derive from this statement the various items of income and expense that are to be insured. An example of such a technique is as follows:

Total gross sales from all sources derived from the use and occupancy of the described building	$400,000
Less:	
Cost of materials consumed in the manufacturing process, or the cost of goods sold in a mercantile business	$200,000
Cost of supplies	40,000
Sales taxes	20,000
Bad debts	4,000
Total	$264,000
Remainder—Profits and all other continuing expenses	$136,000

In other words, the process of isolating the insurable value is to deduct from total gross sales the expenses and costs that are variable—that is, those that may be discontinued if a fire or other peril were to cause a shutdown of the business. The amount so obtained is the **insurable value** and forms the basis of the loss settlement. The BPP gives it the name *business income*. The insurer will pay for pretax net income plus continuing expenses.

Coinsurance. The importance of determining business income value becomes even more evident when it is realized that most business income forms contain a coinsurance clause. Coinsurance requirements vary from 50 percent upward, depending on the amount of coverage desired. If the business concern elects to take the 50 percent form, it is required to carry at least 50 percent of its profits plus operating expenses. Failing to carry this amount, it becomes a coinsurer.

To illustrate, assume that the sum of the annual fixed costs and profits during the prior year was $160,000. When the policy was originally issued, the insurable value was $250,000; the firm now carries $100,000 of business income insurance. In the event of a shutdown for three months, and assuming an even rate of operations and earnings, the firm will have lost three-twelfths of its year's profits and fixed costs, or $40,000. Does the firm collect this amount? No, because it has not been carrying the amount of insurance required by the coinsurance clause. It carries $100,000 and is required to carry $125,000 (one-half of its annual insurable value of $250,000). Thus, it collects only 80 percent of the loss, or $32,000. Methods that may be employed to avoid the coinsurance penalty are discussed next.

How Much Insurance to Carry? The question frequently arises, "How much business income insurance should be carried?" The answer depends on what the firm believes the maximum loss might be. Coinsurance forms are available that allow the insured to carry as little as one-half of its annual insurable value. However, if the firm has reason to believe it might take as much as a year to restore the business to regular operations, it should, of course, carry insurance equal to its full insurable value.

It should be remembered that some firms operate on a seasonal basis, and a few months' operations might account for an entire year's profits. If the loss occurs just before an operating season that lasts only three months, a whole year's profits might be lost, and probably a good part of the year's expenditures for fixed costs would not be earned. Such a situation would, of course, justify carrying insurance on the profits and fixed expenses of a whole year. The policy does not require that the lost profits or expenses be incurred in any particular time period, as long as they do not exceed the time that it reasonably takes to restore the building and to resume operations.

On the other hand, the loss may be only partial; that is, if the business is only partially shut down, indemnity can be collected for the partial loss. If it takes an entire year to make repairs and to restore normal operations, and the firm is forced to reduce operations by one-fourth of its normal level, the indemnity would be one-fourth of the annual insurable value, assuming the operations to be level throughout the year.

An endorsement is available to alter some of the basic requirements. Under the terms of the **extended-period-of-indemnity endorsement**, the period of loss is defined to mean that period necessary to return to normal business operations, not just the period necessary to re-open the business physically. For example, a small manufacturing company may suffer a fire that stops physical operations for three months. At the restarting of business, however, its chief customers have found new suppliers, and it may take several more months to obtain new customers and to achieve the same level of operation it enjoyed prior to the fire. The business income coverage form includes coverage for up to 30 days. The extended-period endorsement is then offered in units of 30 days, so the previous manufacturer could purchase two additional units of coverage or as much as needed. If the manufacturer is able to resume normal operations in less than 90 days, it can recover only for the shorter period, because the contract is on an indemnity basis.

Insurance-to-Value Requirements. In the commercial property form, the insured can choose coverage with or without an insurance-to-value requirement. The basic business income coverage has a minimum 50 percent coinsurance clause. However, by endorsement an insured can choose one of three alternatives to coinsurance including a maximum period of indemnity, a monthly amount of indemnity, or an agreed amount. A fourth option is no coinsurance.

In the standard approach, the insurance-to-value requirement is based on the estimated business income that is expected during the 12 months following the date of purchase of the insurance policy. If the policy is purchased on March 15, 2006, then the 12-month period would end on March 14, 2007. This approach is a decided improvement over older forms that used the 12-month period immediately following the loss. The new approach reduces some of the uncertainty associated with estimating the required amount of insurance, as the insured knows exactly which 12 months will be used in making the calculation. Usually a 50 percent minimum coinsurance clause is present in the business income form. For businesses with a restoration period (the reasonable time necessary to repair or rebuild the damaged property) greater than six months, this requirement does not pose a problem. But because a 50 percent coinsurance clause implicitly assumes a six-month restoration period, those firms with a maximum restoration period of less than six months may have to purchase more insurance than they can collect. To address this problem, the BPP has two optional coverages from which to choose: maximum period of indemnity and monthly limit of indemnity.

Maximum Period of Indemnity. This option replaces the insurance-to-value requirement with a maximum restoration period of 120 days. If the maximum restoration period for an insured is less than 120 days, this is an excellent option. However, if the insured underestimates the restoration period and it goes beyond 120 days, the insurance will not pay beyond the loss of the first 120 days.

Monthly Limit of Indemnity. This approach is designed for small businesses and does not have a coinsurance clause. The rate is higher under this form than for the business income form, and recoveries are limited to 16.66 percent or 33.33 percent of the total amount of coverage in any one month.

To assure full recovery for any loss, the insured must carry sufficient limits so that the selected limit will cover the total earnings for any one month. As an example, suppose a retail store obtains one-fourth of its year's earnings in the month of December, which is not an uncommon occurrence. To recover in full for a shutdown during the month of December, the firm must carry policy limits equal to four times its December earnings. This limit is not cumulative but applies monthly. No prorating of coverage occurs for loss periods of less than one month. Suppose the firm has $20,000 of coverage with a 25 percent monthly limitation and is shut down for 40 days. It is established that the loss during the first 30 days is $6,000 and the loss for the remaining 10 days is $2,000. The recovery is limited to $5,000 for the first 30 days (one-fourth of $20,000), plus $2,000 for the remaining 10 days. Thus, if the firm believes that the maximum period of shutdown is four months and that the maximum loss in any one month is $6,000, it should take $24,000 of coverage with a one-third monthly limitation.

Agreed Amount Clause. The agreed amount clause substitutes an agreed amount of coverage for the coinsurance clause. However, the insured must complete and sign a business income worksheet when the endorsement is purchased. If that statement underestimates income, then a penalty will be applied if a loss occurs. This is a good endorsement to use to manage coinsurance requirements.

Contingent Business Income. It sometimes happens that a firm is forced to shut down, not because an exposure to a peril occurred and damaged its plant, but because an insured peril forced the shutdown of a plant belonging to a supplier or to an important customer on whom the firm depends. Thus, a manufacturer of air conditioners may find that its plant is shut down because the supplier of compressors has suffered a fire. The consequential loss is just as severe, perhaps, as if the fire had occurred at the firm's own plant, because it may require several months to obtain another supplier. Similarly, a firm may find that its chief customer has cancelled orders because of a fire or other disaster at its plant.

To meet such situations, **contingent business income insurance** has been devised. The regular business income policy will not cover the losses previously described because the insured peril did not cause any damage at the firm's own property. Insurable value for contingent business income insurance is calculated in the same manner as it is for business income insurance. The coverage form is called *business income from dependent properties*.

Extra Expense Insurance

Certain types of business firms do not find it possible or expedient to close down following the destruction of their physical plants. Firms such as laundries, newspapers, dairies, public utilities, banks, and oil dealers will often continue their businesses using alternative facilities. The closing of these firms would deprive the public of a vital service or would involve a complete loss of goodwill or of business to competitors.

Because these firms will continue to operate if a loss occurs, business income insurance is not attractive. If business income insurance were purchased, they could not collect it or could collect only a very small part of it because they would be maintaining full or partial operations. Such firms need **extra expense insurance** that covers expenses beyond the normal cost of conducting business. Examples of extra expenditures include rental of quarters, purchase of extra transportation facilities, leasing of substitute equipment, overtime payments to employees, the cost of moving to temporary facilities, and the cost of additional advertising to inform the public the firm is still operational.

It should be mentioned that the business income form contains both business income and extra expense coverage. However, for insureds who must maintain operations, the extra expense only option is more economical because under the business income form they would have to pay for business income protection on which they would never collect.

Leasehold Interest Insurance

A **leasehold** may be defined as an interest in real property that is created by an agreement (a lease) that gives the lessee (the tenant) the right of enjoyment and use of the property for a period of time. A leasehold may become very valuable to the lessee because changing

PROFESSIONAL PERSPECTIVES

Losses to You from Someone You Depend On

How much of your company's operations rely on another entity? How disruptive would a long-term computer outage be to your company's ability to maintain normal business operations? What if you lost a key source of raw material or component parts from a supplier? What if the financial markets were interrupted again or a transportation disruption occurred in the United States? The events of September 11, 2001, highlighted the importance of some of these dependencies.

Today's risk manager is faced with many of these questions and will often look to contingent business interruption (CBI) insurance to soften the financial impact of these events. What is CBI insurance? Contingent business interruption insurance and contingent extra expense coverage is an extension to other insurance that reimburses lost profits and extra expenses resulting from an interruption of business at the premises of a customer or supplier. The contingent property may be specifically named, or the coverage may blanket all customers and suppliers. CBI insurance is also known as *contingent business income insurance* or *dependent properties insurance*. Coverage is usually triggered by physical damage to customers' or suppliers' property or to property on which the insured company depends to attract customers. The type of physical damage must be the same as insured under the controlling policy. Four situations exist in which this coverage is widely used:

- When the insured depends on a single supplier or a few suppliers for materials.
- When the insured depends on one or a few manufacturers or suppliers for most of its merchandise.
- When the insured depends on one or a few recipient businesses to purchase the bulk of the insured's products.
- When the insured counts on a neighboring business to help attract customers, known as a *leader property*.
- Contingent claims from September 11 include damage at an attraction property (World Trade Center) and damage to a variety of businesses and industries that collectively include both suppliers and customers.

Source: Daniel T. Torpey, "Contingent Business Interruption: Getting All the Facts," http://www.irmi.com, May 2003.

business conditions, improvements in the property, and good management may increase the rental value of real estate considerably above the rental due under the lease. For example, Y Department Store may negotiate a 20-year lease on its store building, calling for a rental payment of $12,000 per year. Due to a growing business community, comparable property might rent for $15,000 within five years after the lease has been signed. This increase in value creates what is known as *leasehold interest*, or *leasehold value*.

Given the situation previously described, what insurance problems are raised? If the lease is lost because of the occurrence of a fire or other physical damage to the building, Y Department Store might be forced to sign a new lease calling for an increased rental of $15,000. It is very common in leases to provide that the agreement is void or voidable if the premises are destroyed by fire, if a certain percentage of the sound value of the premises is destroyed by fire, or if the premises are so damaged that they cannot be restored within a given number of days. It is this source of loss that is insurable under a form of coverage known as **leasehold interest insurance**.

Contracts Without a Time Element

Contracts with out a time element are used to insure losses that result from fire but where the loss cannot be measured either by direct damage by fire or in terms of elapsed time.

Manufacturers Selling Price

The BPP covers goods and finished stock that are sold but not delivered at selling price. This endorsement applies this approach to finished stock regardless of whether it has been delivered. It differs from business income insurance in that the latter covers profits that would have been earned in the future had the fire or other insured peril not damaged the firm's plant. The **manufacturers selling price** endorsement covers the loss of the profit element in goods already manufactured but destroyed before they could be sold. Suppose that a plant is manufacturing refrigerators and is disabled by fire. Among the lost property, stored in a warehouse are finished refrigerators with a sales value of $10,000. This figure includes an expected profit of $2,000. The BPP indemnifies the insured only for the replacement cost, which would be $8,000. The business income policy would not cover the $2,000 loss of expected profit because the policy applies only to refrigerators that would have been produced during the period of interruption by fire and not to those already produced. To receive full indemnity for its $2,000 loss, the manufacturer would have to be covered by the manufacturers selling price endorsement.

Accounts Receivable Insurance

Accounts receivable insurance attempts to indemnify an insured for the loss brought about because of the inability to collect from open account (unsecured) debtors after a fire destroys accounts receivable records. If a catastrophe such as fire makes it impossible to prove the existence of a debt because there are no records of the transaction, some debtors may refuse to honor their obligations. Most debtors are honest and will pay, but a loss from unscrupulous debtors may result as a consequential loss from fire or other peril.

The accounts receivable insurance is written on a special-form basis, with various exclusions including bookkeeping, accounting, or billing errors and omissions. The coverage applies only while the accounts receivable records are on the premises, but for an additional premium the records may be covered while at another temporary location. It may be required that the records be stored in a vault or a safe when the business is closed.

Rain or Event Insurance

Rain, as such, seldom causes any direct damage to property. The accumulation of water due to extended rainfall, of course, does cause much loss to property in the form of flood or rising water, but such coverage is generally not available from private insurers. Rain itself, however, may be a source of considerable indirect loss because its occurrence may greatly reduce the expected profits of promoters of an outdoor or public event. Anyone having a financial interest in an event that is dependent on good weather for its success can purchase **rain insurance** to cover the loss of profits and fixed expenses or extra expenses due to rain, hail, snow, or sleet.

The advisability of purchasing rain insurance depends on the promoter's estimate of the actual effect of rainfall on anticipated attendance and the resulting profit. In some areas rain is so common that it does not discourage attendance substantially, whereas in other locations even a light rainfall will ruin attendance. If an event is very popular and is sold out by advance ticket sales that are nonrefundable, the profit is assured in advance, and there is no reason for rain insurance. Among the possible users of rain insurance are sponsors of auction sales, sporting events, boat excursions, carnivals, fairs, conventions, and dances.

Hospital Disaster Risk Management

When one thinks of hurricanes, usually catastrophic property damage, loss of income, and increased expenses come to mind, not liability losses. However, many businesses such as utilities and hospitals may have liability suits arise from their alleged negligence in preparing for a major storm.

INTERNATIONAL PERSPECTIVES

Event Coverage for the Olympics

The 1992 Summer Olympics in Barcelona, Spain, were insured for bad weather. During the two summers before the Olympics, torrential rain fell during the time period in which the Olympics were to be held, and so $150 million of insurance for TV rights was purchased. The actual insurable loss amount was $500 million, but no one felt a total loss could occur. The $150 million represented the minimum probable loss; the $500 million represented the maximum possible loss.

Source: Maria Kielmas, "Cover in Place; Let the Games Begin," *Business Insurance*, July 20, 1992, 3,18.

In September 1999, Hurricane Floyd struck the east coast from Florida to Maine. While the wind damage was less than expected, large amounts of flooding took place.

Many power lines were blown down and electrical service was interrupted. Hospital risk managers plan for such emergencies, and they have emergency electrical generators on the premises. When utility service is interrupted, the emergency power is supposed to operate. Risk managers will frequently test to see if the generators are operational and that an adequate fuel supply is on hand. However, sometimes, even these plans do not work.

After the remains of Floyd hit Providence, Rhode Island, one of the hospitals lost electrical power due to a large surge of electricity throughout the system. When hospital administrators turned on the emergency generators, the generators did not work. It seems the same power surge that caused loss of service had damaged the electrical equipment in the hospital. Several patients were on ventilators and other life support systems in Intensive Care Units (ICUs), and there was no electricity.

Staff quickly went to the various rooms and operated the equipment manually until the fire trucks arrived. Why did the hospital need fire trucks? As a backup to the unit's generator failure, the hospital had arranged for the fire department to bring its fire trucks, which had electrical generators, to the hospital. Electrical connections were made to the generators and wiring was run up 5 to 10 stories to the critical areas. All of these events took place within two to three hours.

The liability from the event will come from any patient who suffered any harm or died during this period. What compounds the problem for the hospital is that the people in ICUs and on life support were in critical condition in the beginning. It does not take much of a power interruption in these cases to cause serious injury or death.

Certainly, the hospital may be sued, but it is also possible that the manufacturer of the electrical equipment, the engineer who designed and chose the equipment, and even the utility company also may be sued. Eventually, one or all may end up paying bodily injury losses.

SUMMARY

1. The building and personal property coverage form (BPP) provides coverage for buildings, your business personal property, and personal property of others.

2. Coverage under the BPP may be specified (in which the property insured is specifically listed) or blanket (in which multiple properties are insured under a single item).

3. Boiler and machinery insurance exists because of the severe and crippling losses that can stem from an exploding boiler or broken machinery. Not only direct losses but also many types of indirect losses are so caused. Inspection of boilers and other insured machinery is an important feature of the boiler contract and accounts for a substantial element of cost in the premium.

4. Reporting forms are used to insure property that fluctuates in value from one period to the next.

5. Consequential losses are often greater than the loss of property destroyed directly by fire or some other peril, yet they are often overlooked in an otherwise complete insurance program.

6. The major contracts of insurance covering indirect or consequential losses are classified under two headings: time-element contracts and contracts without a time element. Time-element policies measure the loss in terms of given time periods, whereas those without a time element have some other basis for measuring loss.

7. The most important type of time-element contract is called business income insurance and is designed to indemnify the insured for loss of profits and fixed expenses that are occasioned by stoppage of business due to some named peril.

8. Other time-element contracts of insurance are (a) contingent business income insurance, which indemnifies for losses due to interruption of the business of a major supplier or customer, and (b) extra expense insurance, which indemnifies for the extra cost caused when a named peril, while not causing a business shutdown, necessitates a higher cost of operation than normal.

9. Examples of contracts of insurance without a time element are (a) manufacturers selling price insurance which indemnifies the insured for loss of profits expected from the sale of finished goods; (b) accounts receivable insurance, which indemnifies for accounts rendered uncollectible because a fire or other named peril destroys the records that give evidence of the debts; and (c) rain insurance, which indemnifies for the loss of profits and for expenses incurred when rain or another type of precipitation decreases expected attendance at some public event.

internet*exercises*

1. Assume you are the owner of a dry cleaning business and that a power surge disables your equipment for two weeks. As a result you need new equipment and cannot generate income for two weeks. Further, it takes another month before business returns to its past level. Visit the following site and select the appropriate industry: http://sb.thehartford.com. Then explore the site to determine which coverages would apply. Would your BOP policy pay for your losses?

2. Sometimes firms attempt to exaggerate their business income claims following a loss. This problem has led to the development of such specialties as "forensic accounting." Visit the following site and describe which aspects of forensic accounting firms' services can save insurers money: http://www.fasna.org/.

QUESTIONS FOR REVIEW AND DISCUSSION

1. Bond Company takes out $100,000 of business income insurance with 50 percent coinsurance. It is estimated that business income is $200,000. Perez Company also estimates business income at $200,000, but it takes out $150,000 coverage on the business income form with 50 percent coinsurance. In each case, actual business income turns out to be $400,000.
   a. Contrast the coverage coinsurance effects.
   b. If Perez's business income had increased to $500,000, would it have been subject to coinsurance penalties? Why or why not?
   c. Could Perez have collected as much as $150,000 if its business income had been $250,000? Why or why not?

2. What are the extensions of coverage in the building and personal property form? Why are they included in the contract?

3. How does the building and personal property form provide coverage for insured perils? Explain the different options available for insured perils.

4. Why do insureds need reporting forms?

5. What are some of the problems associated with business income insurance policies?

6. Under accounts receivable insurance, what three indemnities are made by the insurer?

7. What is a leasehold interest?

8. What coverages are provided by the boiler and machinery insurance policy?

9. In a sense, life insurance may be properly termed a consequential loss contract. Explain.

10. Distinguish between time-element contracts and contracts without a time element.

11. If business improves considerably during the year, the individual purchaser of business income insurance may fail to collect in full for partial loss under the policy. How is this possible? Explain.

12. How should a firm go about determining how much business income insurance to carry? Discuss.

13. A dairy asks its agent to look into a business income insurance policy, but the agent, upon inquiry, states that this type of insurance would not be suitable for the dairy. The agent recommends another policy. Why might business income insurance not be appropriate for the dairy, and what other policy might the agent recommend?

chapter 10

Risk Management and Commercial Property—Part II

Often, risk managers require insurance policies that are flexible with respect to the perils and locations that are covered as well as the amount of coverage. For example, satellite insurance must provide coverage for the satellite while it is on earth, while it is in transit from earth to outerspace, and while it is in orbit; the insured perils in such policies normally include damage to the satellite and loss of business income. It is not unusual for a satellite to be insured for $100 million—a great deal of money for what could quickly become a giant firecracker!

Insuring airplanes is a constant loss exposure for the airline industry. Each airplane can be worth as much as $40 million. Coverage must be tailored for the geographic area in which the airline operates, and total limits must be high enough so that an entire fleet of planes is insured. Another complication is that aviation rates frequently vary a great deal from year to year. USAirways experienced a rate increase of more than 100 percent for its 1993 coverage, which was placed on the London market; its premiums increased from $31.5 million to $70 million.

Back on the ground, risk managers often find themselves needing to insure heavy construction equipment such as power cranes, bulldozers, and front-end loaders, all of which are used at construction sites as well as on roads being built or maintained. This equipment is exposed to transportation perils while in transit and is subject to other losses at construction sites or on the premises of the insured. Of course, dealers in this type of equipment also need protection, and they require higher limits because of concentration values. Those on or near interstate highways face an increased risk of theft because criminals know that they will have a quick getaway. Add to all this the fact that these dealers' inventories include tractors, which seem to be especially attractive to thieves, and you get an idea of how complex such coverage can be.

From satellites to tractors, risk managers need insurance policies to provide coverage. While reading this chapter, you should reflect on how the policies described in this chapter compare with those in Chapter 9 with respect to the perils, locations, and types of property that are covered.

CHAPTER OBJECTIVES

After studying this chapter, you should be able to

1. Identify the perils of transportation and the carrier's liability on the land and on the sea.
2. List the major types of property insurance available for ocean and inland marine loss exposures.
3. Describe expressed and implied warranties as they are used in ocean marine insurance.
4. Explain how floater insurance policies help meet the insurance needs of businesses whose property is moved from one location to another.
5. Explain the need for and use of title insurance.
6. Explain the differences between insurance and bonding.
7. Identify the differences among burglary, robbery, and theft.

In this chapter on business property insurance, various types of policies that are used to insure personal property are studied, including the following:

1. Transportation policies that include ships and their cargo, as well as personal property carried by trains and trucks. Such policies include coverages for items that may be transported by land, air, or sea.

2. Floaters that concern property that will be or is capable of being moved from one place to another.

3. Several miscellaneous coverages: credit, title, and glass insurance.

TRANSPORTATION INSURANCE

Insurance on the risks of transportation of goods is one of the oldest and most vital forms of insurance. All types of trade depend heavily on the availability of insurance for successful and expeditious handling. If it were not possible to trade with others, it would not be feasible to manufacture goods on a mass-production basis; without mass production, life would be entirely different and probably not as comfortable and easy.

Insurance played a vital part in stimulating early commerce. In Roman times (and earlier), **bottomry contracts** and **respondentia contracts** governed the terms under which money was borrowed to finance ocean commerce. Under these contracts, the lender of money took as security for a loan either the ship itself, in the case of bottomry bonds, or the cargo, in the case of respondentia bonds. However, if the ship or cargo was lost as a result of ocean perils, the loan was cancelled. If the voyage was successful, the loan was repaid and substantial interest was charged mainly because the interest included an allowance for the possibility of loss of the security; this extra charge was essentially an insurance premium.

The Perils of Transportation

The perils that may cause a loss to goods being transported may be appreciated by realizing the inability to control adequately or completely the forces of nature or to prevent human failure as it affects the safe movement of goods. For example, in spite of the gyroscope, the compass, radar, sonar, and all the other modern safety devices, ocean tragedies still occur. Storms can capsize even the largest ocean vessels. Huge waves driven by hurricane winds often dump tons of sea water onto a vessel and damage cargo stowed inside. Engine failure may subject a ship to the mercy of a storm, driving the ship aground, where it quickly breaks up due to the pressure of waves grinding it against rocks and sand. Poor visibility still causes collisions, and fires occur frequently. Goods are sometimes lost as a result of basic dishonesty, negligence, or incompetence of the crew handling them or through faults in the management of the vessel. Likewise, loss of goods shipped on land comes from sources such as overturn of the vehicle, collision, fire, theft, flood, rough or careless handling, and unusual delays that result in spoilage.

The Liability of the Carrier

The question arises, "Is not the carrier of the goods responsible for their safe movement?" The answer is yes, to some extent. The common law liability of the carrier differs depending on the country in which the transportation conveyances are chartered, the applicable statutes, custom, the type of shipping, and other factors.

The Carrier's Liability in Ocean Transportation

In the field of ocean shipping, the carrier, or shipowner, is responsible only for failure to exercise due diligence. The responsibility of the carrier, which is spelled out by the Carriage of Goods by Sea Act, passed in the United States in 1936, is to make the ship seaworthy, to

PROFESSIONAL PERSPECTIVES

You Win Some and You Lose Some

On March 24, 1989, the ship *Exxon Valdez* ran aground and spilled 11 million gallons of heavy crude oil into Prince William Sound in Alaska. Exxon stated that it paid $3.2 billion in cleanup costs and voluntary compensation agreements to those damaged by the oil spill.

On June 10, 1996, a Houston jury decided Exxon was covered by its excess global cargo policies for the accident, and those insurers should pay $250 million to Exxon. Chalk up $250 million for Exxon.

On June 11, 1996, a federal judge voided an agreement that Exxon had with seven Seattle-based seafood processors that required them to return $750 million to Exxon. These firms were scheduled to receive 15 percent of the $5 billion punitive damages assessed against Exxon (0.15 × $5 billion = $750 million) and had agreed to return these funds to Exxon. The $5 billion judgment for punitive damages was declared in 1994. The net effect of the two decisions is Exxon was down $500 million.

As the 15th anniversary of the spill approached, the legal battles raged on. In January 2004, a federal judge in Anchorage ruled that ExxonMobil should pay $4.5 billion in punitive damages to individuals harmed by the oil spill. ExxonMobil promised further appeals arguing that in light of U.S. Supreme Court rulings regarding guidelines for punitive damages that a figure of $25 million would be appropriate.

Sources: D. Lenckus, "Exxon Decisions Will Be Appealed: Oil Grants Fortunes Mixed in Outcomes of Two Cases," *Business Insurance*, June 17, 1996, 1, 33; R. Holland, "ExxonMobil: Pay Up," *Bond Buyer*, January 30, 2004, 37.

---

employ proper crew, to equip and supply the ship, and to make all holds and other carrying compartments safe and fit for the goods stored there. In addition, the carrier must exercise due care in loading, handling, and stowing cargoes.

The act lists specific causes for which the carrier is definitely not liable. For example, the carrier is not liable for loss resulting from

1. Errors in navigation or management of the vessel.
2. Strikes or lockouts.
3. Acts of God.
4. Acts of war or public enemies.
5. Seizure of the goods under legal process.
6. Quarantine.
7. Inherent vice of the goods.
8. Failure of the shipper to exercise due care in the handling or packing of the goods.
9. Fire.
10. Perils of the seas.
11. Latent defects in the hull or machinery.
12. Other losses where the carrier is not at fault.

Even though the carrier must prove that it was not to blame, the shipper of the goods has little claim against the carrier for loss of goods by some force outside the control of the carrier, such as windstorm or other perils of the sea.

The Carrier's Liability in Land Transportation

The common law liability of the land carrier is considerably greater than that of the ocean carrier, but it is still not absolute. In addition to being responsible for failure to exercise due

INTERNATIONAL PERSPECTIVES

Fire in the Eurotunnel

Eurotunnel, the tunnel connecting France and England, suffered a fire loss in late 1996. Although no lives were lost, eight persons were treated for smoke inhalation. Property damage included 15 trucks on board the train. In addition, damage occurred to rail wagons, part of the track, power cables, and tunnel walls. It is estimated that $1.7 million in revenue was lost for each day the tunnel was closed. Eurotunnel P.L.C. was insured for $450 million. It was estimated the tunnel would be fully operational in 3 to 4 weeks. While the tunnel has had an outstanding safety record, this accident raised several questions:

1. Why did the tunnel ventilation system not blow the smoke away from the train as it was designed to do?
2. Are open-sided rail wagons safe to operate in this tunnel? When such wagons are used, they cannot contain the fire since they are open sided.
3. Why did it take the Kent Fire Brigade over an hour to respond to the fire? (It has a fire station at the Dover entrance, and French firemen were at the scene in less than 20 minutes.)

Source: E. Elsworth and G. Souter, "Eurotunnel Fire Insured," *Business Insurance*, November 25, 1996, 1, 39.

diligence, the land carrier is responsible for all loss to the goods *except* for acts of God, acts of public enemies or public authority, acts or negligence of the shipper, or inherent vice or quality of the goods.

Acts of God have been interpreted to mean perils such as earthquakes, storms, and floods that could not have been reasonably guarded against. Fire is not an act of God, and hence the carrier is liable for damage caused by this peril to goods in its custody.

The term *public enemy* has been interpreted to mean the action by forces at war with a domestic government, not acts of gangsters, mobs, or rioters. Thus, the carrier is liable for losses of goods by organized criminals as well as by a single thief. However, the carrier is not liable for loss when the goods are taken by legal process against the owner, such as confiscation of contraband.

Under the heading **acts of negligence of the shipper** come such causes of loss as improper loading or packing and instances where the nature of the goods is concealed. Thus, if packages contain glassware but are not clearly marked "fragile," the carrier may be excused from loss due to breakage. Loss from poor packing that was visible to the carrier when the goods were accepted for shipment falls on the carrier.

A loss from the **inherent nature of the goods** may be illustrated by losses due to decay, heat, rust, drying, or fermentation. In one case, the shipper sent a train car of Christmas trees from Vermont to Florida. When the trees arrived, it was found that they had sustained damage by mold and rot. Investigation revealed that the trees had been shipped with excessive moisture and were locked in a steel car. As the train proceeded south, temperatures rose and the heat ruined the shipment. The carrier was held not liable because the loss stemmed from the inherent nature of the goods.[1]

---

1   *Austin v Seaboard Air Line Railway Co.*, 188 Fed. (2d) 239 (1951).

Need for Transportation Insurance

The preceding discussion reveals that many types of transportation losses fall outside the responsibility of the common carrier. Furthermore, common carriers have been slow to settle losses for which they are legally liable. In land transportation, the shipper usually sends goods under what is known as a **released bill of lading**. The effect of shipping goods under a released bill of lading is to limit the dollar liability of the carrier for any loss to the goods. In return, the shipper obtains a lower freight rate. In effect, the difference in freight rates is intended to compensate the shipper for the added risk of loss that must be assumed. Thus, a shipper may use outside insurance in order to achieve a prudent level of security and safety.

OCEAN TRANSPORTATION INSURANCE

Modern commerce has caused insurance to develop and attain the high degree of refinement it has today. As world trade grew and values at risk became larger, the need for coverage became more apparent. Larger ships and more advanced instruments of navigation made long voyages possible, and with these changes came the realization that insurance protection was almost a necessity. The major source of underwriting capacity was England, probably because that country was among the first to develop a complex system of admiralty law, a very necessary adjunct to successful insurance underwriting.

The data in Table 10-1 show that the U.S. market for ocean marine insurance increased almost 126 percent from 1980 to 2002. Lloyd's of London is the major market for ocean marine insurance, and the relatively low U.S. numbers reflect that situation.

Major Types of Coverage

The four chief interests to be insured in an ocean voyage are

1. The vessel, or the hull.
2. The cargo.
3. The shipping revenue or freight received by the shipowners.
4. Legal liability for proved negligence.

If a peril of the sea causes the sinking of a ship in deep water, one or more of these losses can result. However, each of these potential losses can be covered under various insurance policies.

TABLE 10-1 | **United States Ocean Marine Insurance Premiums**

Year	($ billions)
1980	$1.065
1985	1.176
1990	1.178
1995	1.946
2000	1.716
2002	2.411

Source: The Fact Book, *Insurance Information Institute*, New York, 2004, 77.

INTERNATIONAL PERSPECTIVES

Covering the War

Although the standard Lloyd's contract on ocean marine insurance excludes war coverage, such coverage can be purchased through special markets at Lloyd's. In fact, during the war in the Persian Gulf, Lloyd's opened on Sunday for the first time in its 303-year history. This action was necessary because the coverage had to be written within 24 hours of departure. Because of the hostile action taking place in the Persian Gulf, rates were as high as 3.5 to 5 percent of the value of the property for a single trip. That is, if a ship was worth $25 million, the premiums would be $875,000 to $1,250,000.

A typical trip is for seven days. Brokers were quoting $50 million of protection and indemnity liability coverage on an excess basis for a premium of more than $150,000 for six days of coverage. With respect to airplanes, war risk premiums were 0.075 percent to 2.5 percent per flight. On a per-passenger basis, these charges could run as high as $100 per passenger per flight.

Thus, although war risk coverage was available during the height of the war, it was expensive. It was so expensive, in fact, that the government of Israel entered the insurance market and offered marine hull and war risk coverage. After the Israeli action, war risk coverage for its ports dropped by as much as 80 percent.

Sources: S. Shapiro and G. Souther, "Underwriters Adjust to Persian Gulf War," *Business Insurance*, January 28, 1991, 1, 87; S. Shapiro, "Weekend Opening a First for Lloyd's," *Business Insurance*, January 28, 1991, 87.

Hull Policies

Policies covering the vessel itself, or **hull insurance**, are written in several different ways. The policy may cover the ship only during a given period of time, usually not to exceed one year. The insurance is commonly subject to geographical limits. If the ship is laid up in port for an extended period of time, the contract may be written at a reduced premium under the condition that the ship remain in port. The contract may cover a builder's risk while the vessel is constructed.

Cargo Policies

Contracts insuring cargo against various types of loss may be written to cover such losses only during a specified voyage, as in the case of a hull contract, or on an open basis. The latter is probably the most common type of contract. Under an **open contract**, no termination date is set, but either party may cancel upon giving notice, usually 30 days. All shipments, both incoming and outgoing, are automatically covered. The shipper reports to the insurer at regular intervals as to the values shipped or received during the previous period. The shipper declares the classes of goods and the ports between which these goods move. Usually a limit is placed on the values that may be insured on a single vessel and a limit on the goods stowed on deck.

Freight Coverage

The money paid for the transportation of the goods, or **freight**, is an insurable interest because in the event that freight charges are not paid, the carrier has lost income with which to reimburse expenses incurred in preparation for a voyage. Under the laws of the United States, the earning of freight by the hull owner is dependent on the delivery of cargo, unless this relationship is altered by contractual arrangements between the parties. If a ship sinks, the freight is lost, and the vessel owner loses the expenses incurred plus the expected profit on the ven-

PROFESSIONAL PERSPECTIVES

Risk Management and the Riverboat Gambler

Many more states are passing laws that allow gambling, and often the laws specify that casinos must be located on a body of water. Thus, about 90 such gambling boats are in operation. They range in use from vessels that can actually operate as riverboats to barges sitting in a few feet of water. Regardless of the type of boat, substantial risk of windstorm and flood losses exists. Vessels operating along the Gulf of Mexico are exposed to hurricanes. The boats need to be designed to withstand category 4 and 5 storms or be capable of being moved to safety. Even if plans exist for moving them, detailed plans must be prepared for the moves.

For instance, in Biloxi, Mississippi, 14 local casino boats would need to be moved if a major storm occurs. The problem is that not enough tugboat operators are available to move them at the same time, and nobody wants to be the last boat out with a category 5 hurricane coming to town.

Besides wind, flooding creates special problems. When major waterways are at flood stage, riverboats are not accessible from their docks. Gamblers cannot come on board, and revenue is lost. Even if customers can board, rapidly flowing rivers make navigation dangerous and subject the boat, crew, and customers to increased risk.

Source: D. McLeod, "Gaming Not the Only Risk Aboard Casino Boats," *Business Insurance*, May 13, 1996, 16.

---

ture. The carrier's right to earn freight may be defeated by the occurrence of losses due to perils ordinarily insured against in an ocean marine insurance policy. The hull may be damaged so that it is uneconomical to complete the voyage, or the cargo may be destroyed, in which case, of course, it cannot be delivered. Also, the owner of cargo has an interest in freight arising from the obligation to pay transportation charges. Freight insurance is normally made a part of the regular hull or cargo coverage instead of being written as a separate contract.

Legal Liability for Proved Negligence

In the **running down clause (RDC)** in ocean marine insurance policies covering the hull, the hull owner is protected against third-party liability claims that arise from collisions. Collision loss to the hull itself is included in the perils clause as one of the perils of the sea. The RDC is intended to give protection in case the shipowner is held liable for negligent operation of the vessel that is the proximate cause of damage to certain property of others. The vessel owner or agent of that owner who fails to exercise the proper degree of care in the operation of the ship may be legally liable for damage to the other ship and for loss of freight revenues. The RDC normally excludes liability for damage to cargo, harbors, wharves, or piers and for loss of life or personal injuries.

To provide liability coverage for personal injuries, loss of life, or damage to property other than vessels, the **protection and indemnity (P&I) clause** is usually added to the hull policy. This clause is intended to provide liability insurance for all events not covered by the more limited RDC, except liability assumed under contract. Similarly, the policy may be extended to insure the shipowner's liability under the Federal Longshoremen's and Harbor Worker's Compensation Act.

Perils Clause

In 1779, Lloyd's of London developed a more-or-less standard ocean marine policy containing an insuring clause, the wording of which has been retained almost in its original form in policies issued today. This clause, which has been the subject of repeated court decisions interpreting almost every phrase, is as follows:

> Touching the adventures and perils which we the assurers are contented to bear and to take upon us in this voyage; they are of the seas, men of war, fire, enemies, pirates, rovers, thieves, jettisons, letters of mart and countermart, surprises, takings at sea, arrests, restraints, and detainments of all kings, princes, and people, of what nation, condition, or quality soever, barratry of the master and the mariners, and of all other perils, losses, and misfortunes, that have or shall come to the hurt, detriment, or damage of the said goods and merchandise, and ship, etc., of any part thereof.

This clause might be interpreted as an all-risk contract because it refers to certain named perils "and all other perils, losses, and misfortunes." However, the courts have interpreted the quoted phrase to mean "all other *like* perils." Hence, it cannot be said that the policy is an all-risk contract, although it is very broad in its coverage. Essentially, the insuring clause covers perils *of* the sea and not all perils. Perils *on* the sea, that is, those not finding their inherent cause arising from the sea, are not insured unless they are specifically mentioned. Fire, for example, is a peril on the sea and is insured by specific mention. Examples of perils of the sea are the action of wind and waves, stranding, and sinking. Gradual wear and tear caused by the ocean is not considered a covered peril.

The insuring clause does not specifically exclude the perils of war. However, most modern policies contain a **free-of-capture-and-seizure (FC&S) clause** that excludes all loss arising out of war. In 1982 a normal war risk premium for a ship was 2 cents per $100. In the area around Lebanon, it was 25 cents per $100. In the Iraq and Iran area, rates were $1.25 per $100, or five times higher.[2] In the ocean marine policy, losses from pirates, assailing thieves, or overtly dishonest actions by the ship's master or crew (*barratry*) are considered similar to burglary and robbery protection on land and are not losses from war. Typically, pilferage is not covered, but it may be added by endorsement.

Deductibles

Ocean marine insurance policies have two chief types of deductible clause: memorandum and free of particular average. Attached to cargo policies, the **memorandum clause** lists various types of goods with varying percentages of deductibles that apply on a franchise basis. Thus, the memorandum clause may specify that no loss payment will occur for loss to tobacco under 20 percent and neither to sugar under 7 percent nor to any partial loss to cheese or certain other perishables.

Some policies covering the cargo and the hull may have a type of deductible known as the **free-of-particular-average (FPA) clause**. In ocean marine insurance terminology, the word *average*, stemming from the French word *avarie*, means loss or damage to a ship or a cargo. *Particular average* means a partial loss to an interest that must be borne entirely by that interest. Particular average is contrasted to general average, which will be explained shortly. The free-of-particular-average clause usually provides that no partial loss will be paid to a single cargo interest unless the loss is caused by certain perils, such as stranding, sinking, burning, or collision. Often the FPA clause is limited to those losses under a certain percentage, such as 3 percent.

General Average Clause

The **general average clause** refers to losses that must be partly borne by someone other than the owner of the goods that were damaged or lost. General average losses may be total or partial, whereas particular average losses, by definition, are always partial. To illustrate, suppose

---

2   Stacy Shapiro, "Insurers Face Aircraft Loss in Lebanon," *Business Insurance*, July 19, 1982, 2, 46.

that a certain cargo of lumber, wrapped in a large bundle, is stored on deck. To lighten the ship during a heavy storm that is threatening the safety of the voyage, the captain orders the lumber, worth $5,000, to be jettisoned. The action of the captain is successful in saving the ship and all the other interests. Such a sacrifice is termed a *general average*, and the interests that were saved would be required to share a pro-rata part of the loss. Thus, if the ship and freight interests were valued at $100,000 and the other cargo interests at $95,000, the shipowner would have to pay one-half (100/200) of the value of the lumber. The other cargo interests would share 95/200 of the loss, and the owner of the lumber would bear 5/200 of the loss. All ocean marine policies provide coverage for general average claims that may be made against the insured.

Sue-and-Labor Clause

Of basic importance to the ocean marine insurance policy is the **sue-and-labor clause**, under which the insured is required to do everything possible to save and preserve the goods in case of loss. The insured who fails to do this has violated a policy condition and loses the rights of recovery. This means that the insured must incur reasonable expenses such as salvage, attorney, or storage fees, which may be reimbursed by the insurer even if such expenses fail to recover the goods. It is possible to recover for a total loss plus sue-and-labor charges even if the face amount of the policy proceeds is exhausted.

Abandonment

In ocean marine insurance, two types of total loss are recognized: actual and constructive. **Actual total loss** occurs when the property is completely destroyed. **Constructive total loss** occurs when, even though the ship or other subject matter of insurance is not totally destroyed, it would cost more to restore it than it is worth. Under U.S. law, before constructive total loss is said to have occurred, the damage must equal 50 percent or more of the ship's value in an undamaged condition; under British law, damages must exceed 100 percent of the ship's sound value. In most hull policies, the British rule is stated as a policy provision to the effect that if it costs more to repair the ship than its agreed-on value as stated in the policy, the ship may be abandoned to the insurer and the insured collects the full amount of the policy. The salvage then belongs to the insurer, who is usually in a better position to dispose of it than the insured because the insurer deals with salvage companies all over the world and is experienced in such matters.

Warehouse-to-Warehouse Clause

Under the terms of the **warehouse-to-warehouse clause**, such protection as is afforded under the insuring agreement extends from the time the goods leave the warehouse of the shipper, even if it is located far inland, until they reach the warehouse of the consignee.

Coinsurance

Although there is no coinsurance clause as such in the ocean marine policy, losses are settled as though each contract contained a 100 percent coinsurance clause. Ocean marine contracts are usually valued. Total losses result in an enforceable claim for the entire limit of liability as stated in the policy, and partial losses are determined, insofar as possible, by sale of the damaged article or by independent appraisal.

Warranties in Ocean Marine Insurance

Two types of warranty exist in marine insurance: express and implied. **Express warranties** are written into the contract and become a condition of the coverage relating to potential causes of an insured event. **Implied warranties** are important, too. However, they are not written into the policy but become a part of it by custom. Breach of warranty in marine insurance voids the coverage, even if the breach is immaterial to the risk.

Express Warranties

Express warranties are often used to effect certain exclusions. The following discussion reviews several of these warranties.

FC&S Warranty. Under the FC&S (free of capture and seizure) warranty, both parties agree that there shall be no coverage in the case of loss from such perils as capture, seizure, confiscation, weapons of war, revolution, insurrection, civil war, or piracy.

SR&CC Warranty. Under the SR&CC (strike, riot, and civil commotion) warranty, it is agreed that the insurer will pay no loss due to strikes, lockouts, riots, or other labor disturbances. An endorsement is available to add coverage for these exposures.

Delay Warranty. Under the delay warranty, the insurer excludes loss traceable to delay of the voyage for any reason, unless such liability is assumed in writing.

Trading Warranty. A class of express warranty known as trading warranties is important in ocean marine insurance. Examples of trading warranties are those restricting the operation of the ship to a given area, such as a certain coastal route; those specifying that the insurance issued represents the true value of the ship or other interests; and those restricting the time during which the ship may operate, such as only during the open season on the Great Lakes.

Implied Warranties

Three types of implied warranty exist in marine insurance. These relate to seaworthiness, deviation, and legality.

Seaworthiness. If a ship leaves port without being in safe condition, the implied warranty as to seaworthiness has been breached, and the entire coverage is immediately void. If the ship was seaworthy when it left port but became unseaworthy later on, the warranty is not breached. Seaworthiness involves such factors as having a sound hull, engines in good running order, a qualified captain and crew, proper supplies for the voyage to be undertaken, and sufficient fuel.

Deviation. The warranty as to deviation is breached when a vessel, without good and sufficient reason, departs from the prescribed course of the voyage but without the intention of abandoning the voyage originally contemplated. The liability of the insurer ceases the moment that the ship departs from its course, but mere intention to deviate, not accompanied by an actual change of course, does not relieve the insurer of liability. Undue delay may constitute a deviation. The deviation or delay does not have to increase the hazard of the voyage in order to release the insurer because any breach of warranty, regardless of whether the warranty was material to the risk, voids the contract. Even if the ship later resumes course and then suffers a loss, no coverage is available unless later negotiations with the insurer have restored the insurance.

There are certain causes that will excuse a deviation that has not been authorized by contract. These fall into two main groups: unavoidable necessity and aiding in saving human life. Unavoidable necessity may be proved when a ship is blown off course, puts into a port of distress, deviates to escape capture, is taken over by mutineers, or is carried off course by a warship. Aiding in saving human life is illustrated by a ship's deviating to help a vessel in distress. It is to be noted, however, that deviation to save property only is not permitted.

Legality. The implied warranty of legality is one that is never waived. If the voyage is illegal under the laws of the country under whose dominion the ship operates, the insurance is void. Under the laws of the United States, for example, insurance on a ship engaged in running marijuana would be void, but such a purpose might not be illegal under the laws of another country, and in that country the insurance contract would be enforceable. To provide insurance for illegal enterprise is obviously against public policy, and this accounts for the fact that the warranty of legality cannot be waived.

LAND TRANSPORTATION INSURANCE

In the early period of industrial development, buyers of goods generally took delivery at an ocean port and conducted most of their business from that port. With the growth of inland centers of commerce, shipments of ocean cargo by way of railroad or canal became common, and pressure grew for an extension of the ocean marine contract to cover the perils of land transportation. The warehouse-to-warehouse clause was developed to meet this need. But the ocean marine contract was not suited to the needs of land transportation insurance, and so there developed a branch of insurance known as inland marine.

The Marine Definition

Inland marine insurance is defined by criteria known as the *nationwide marine definition of the National Association of Insurance Commissioners*. This definition, first formulated in 1933 and revised in 1953 and 1976, serves as a guide for regulatory authorities in governing rating procedures, underwriting methods, contract provisions, and other matters. The five subjects of insurance that are recognized include contracts covering imports, exports, domestic shipments, instrumentalities of transportation and communication, and floaters.

The nationwide marine definition does not distinguish between inland or ocean marine insurance. It permits insurance on certain classes of goods and contains a section of prohibited risks. In general, mobility is the basis for differentiating between permitted risks and prohibited risks.

Inland Transit Policy

A basic contract covering domestic shipments that are shipped primarily by land transportation systems is known as the **inland transit policy**. Sometimes called the *annual transit floater*, this form of insurance is designed for manufacturers, retailers, wholesalers, and others who ship or receive a substantial volume of goods. The contract usually covers shipments by rail and railway express and by public truckers; it also may cover coastal shipments by ship between ports on the eastern coast of the United States and the Gulf of Mexico. It covers goods that are in the hands of other transportation agencies in connection with rail, railway express, or steamer shipments. Shipments by mail or by aircraft are not usually covered unless they are specifically named in the policy.

Trip Transit Insurance

For the individual or business firm that makes only an occasional shipment, the trip transit policy is especially applicable. This policy covers on a named-perils basis and is written for a specific shipment of goods between named locations. The type of conveyance may be either a common carrier or a private carrier of some type, such as on a truck or other vehicle. It is common to insure household furniture, merchandise, machinery, or livestock under trip transit insurance contracts. The insured perils, conditions, and exclusions are similar to the inland transit contract. For example, leaking, marring, scratching, and breaking are excluded unless caused by certain named perils. This limitation is of special interest to shippers of household goods that are susceptible to damage by freight car movement.

FLOATER CONTRACTS

The practice of insuring property at a fixed location or while it is being transported by a common carrier is well established. The need for coverage is universally recognized, and owners of such goods rely on fairly standard contracts to protect them. A more difficult insurance problem is the risk of loss associated with property that is either not at a fixed location or not being transported by a common carrier.

For example, Contractor Brown owns $1 million worth of equipment that is used in building bridges and roads. This equipment includes such items as cranes, tractors, diggers, winches, hoists, small tools, cement mixers, and cable. The equipment is being moved constantly from job to job and is exposed to losses from many types of perils, including landslide, theft, flood, fire, windstorm, collision, explosion, and vandalism. The equipment is seldom located at any one place very long, so coverage under traditional property insurance forms is not suitable. Also, the equipment is neither being moved by nor in the custody of common carriers, so that usual transportation insurance forms are not applicable. Clearly, specialized attention is needed for Brown's problem. The answer is found in a floater policy—to be precise, in the contractors' equipment floater.

The term **floater policy** has never been satisfactorily defined, but it is generally understood to be a contract of property insurance that satisfies three requirements:

1. Under its terms, the property may be moved at any time.
2. The property is subject to being moved; that is, the property is not at some location where it is expected to remain permanently.
3. The contract insures the goods while they are being moved from one location to another, that is, while they are in transit, as well as insuring them at a fixed location.

Bailed Property

A **bailment** exists when one has entrusted personal property to another, such as in the case of laundries, repair establishments, and garages. Special forms of insurance (such as the BPP) are available to some bailees, the owners of such establishments, to cover loss to bailed goods for which they might be liable. Homeowners forms also cover such losses, but only with respect to the bailor's (the individual's) interest. Other bailees use floater policies to cover losses to bailed property.

Business Floater Policies

The nature of business property necessitates complex types of floaters, including block policies, scheduled property floaters, and miscellaneous business floaters.

Block Policies

The term *block* in insurance language, while having no precise meaning, connotes the general idea of a contract that is somewhat broader than the traditional forms of inland marine or fire insurance. A **block policy** covers *en bloc*, on an all-risk basis, the stock in trade or the equipment belonging to a business firm, no matter where the property happens to be located. Block policies exist for jewelers, furriers, camera and musical instrument dealers, and agriculture and construction equipment dealers.

Jewelers' Block Policy. One of the oldest and broadest of all block contracts, the **jewelers' block policy** is written to insure all the stock in the trade of a typical jeweler on an all-risk basis. Such property as jewels, watches, precious metals, glassware, and gift items are covered whether they belong to the jeweler or to a customer. Also, these items are covered if they belong to another firm and are in the store on consignment so that the jeweler is legally liable for their safety or has a financial interest in them.

The jewelers' block policy covers not only property belonging to the jeweler as an owner but also property of the customer bailor. Thus, the jewelers' block policy is an example of bailee liability insurance. Its coverage may be extended to insure property anywhere in the world and while in transit to or from the jeweler's place of business, such as while the property is in the hands of messengers, salespersons, customers (on approval), common carriers, other jewelers, repairers, the post office, or an express agency.

Scheduled Property Floater Risks

Many types of movable business property are insurable under a form known as the **scheduled property floater**, a general or skeleton form to which is attached an endorsement describing specific types of property and the conditions under which they are insured.

Included among the various types of property insured under the scheduled property floater are contractors' equipment, computer equipment, mobile agricultural equipment, office machinery, salespersons' samples, theatrical equipment, railroad rolling stock, oil-well drilling equipment, patterns and dies, goods on exhibition, neon and mechanical electric signs, radium, livestock, and instrumentalities of transportation and communication. Because the inland marine floater forms covering these types of property are similar in nature, only two commonly used floaters—the contractors' equipment floater and the EDP floater—will be discussed here.

Contractors' Equipment Floater. One of the most important classes of property insured under the scheduled property floater form is contractors' equipment. The **contractors' equipment floater** is typical of most floaters on scheduled property. Contractors' have a special need for protection against the many perils that can cause loss to movable equipment. Large sums are often invested in a single piece of equipment that is used under basically dangerous conditions.

The contractors' equipment floater insures such items as tractors, steam shovels, cement mixers, scaffolding, pumps, engines, generators, hoists, drilling machinery, hand tools, cable, winches, and wagons.

Electronic Data Processing (EDP) Floater. Most firms today depend heavily on computer equipment. Although such equipment is covered as unscheduled property in the BPP, **electronic data processing (EDP) floaters** can cover special perils not addressed in the BPP, and they can cover property in transit. As computer equipment becomes more portable, this property is often utilized by firms' employees away from the insured premises. EDP floaters also can provide coverage for data and media and for business income and extra expense associated with loss of use of EDP equipment. Valuation under EDP floaters also can be on an upgraded value basis, which allows for replacement with the latest state-of-the-art equipment. This can be very important given the rapid pace of technological advancement in EDP equipment.

CREDIT INSURANCE

The use of credit in modern economic societies is universally recognized as a key factor in facilitating growth.[3] Without credit, it is doubtful that the modern industrial economy could have developed at all. However, the use of credit has created many complex problems, not the least of which is the risk that debts will not be paid because of the occurrence of some peril that is often outside the control of the debtor.

---

3 One of the earliest works on credit insurance was published in 1848 by Robert Watt and was entitled *Principles of Insurance Applied to Mercantile Debt.*

PROFESSIONAL PERSPECTIVES

Art Appreciation

During the 1980s, the price of fine art increased dramatically. For example, a single painting by Vincent Van Gogh sold for more than $80 million. With such high values placed on art, loss prevention and insurance must be a concern.

The emphasis in most national art museums is on loss prevention; the national treasury stands as the ultimate bearer of the loss. Loss prevention measures include smoke detectors; trained guards in each room of the museum or one guard for each two rooms; and controlling humidity, temperature, and lighting in the building. Some museums even have individual paintings monitored by electronic devices, so if the painting even barely moves, a signal is sent to museum personnel. However, losses still may occur. In 1991, armed thieves broke into the Van Gogh

Museum in Amsterdam and stole 20 paintings; they were all recovered within the day. Unfortunately, museums are not always so lucky, and on at least two occasions in 1990, works were stolen from Dutch museums and not recovered.

When art is placed on tour, the exposure is much greater. The lending institution can no longer depend on complete control. Thus, while loss prevention is still emphasized, insurance also is purchased when the art tours a country or the world. For instance, in 1990 the Van Gogh Museum had a centenary exhibit that went on tour and was insured for $2.7 billion. The museum paid a $1 million premium. This coverage is an example of a very sophisticated floater policy and was written in Lloyd's market.

Source: M. Kielmas, "Van Goghs Uninsured for Damage by Thieves," *Business Insurance*, April 22, 1991, 37, 43.

Types of Credit Insurance

Many types of **credit insurance** exist. Several of the major types offered by private insurers and through government programs are discussed in the following sections.

Insurance of Bonds

A development related to loan insurance is the practice of issuing insurance against the default of credit instruments, such as municipal bonds, in order to improve the instruments' investment quality and reduce interest costs. The insurance guarantee may reduce the risk enough to enable the sale of bonds by small municipalities that might not otherwise be able to issue their bonds at reasonable cost.

Credit Life and Credit Accident/Sickness

Insurance against failure to pay a debt because of death of the borrower is known as **credit life insurance**. This contract is basically the same as any contract of life insurance except for the manner in which it is arranged and marketed. Suffice it to say that credit life insurance should not be confused with other forms of credit insurance. A similar comment applies to credit accident and sickness insurance that is arranged to liquidate payments on an installment debt during the time the debtor is disabled because of accident or sickness.

Domestic Merchandise Credit Insurance

In the United States, Canada, Mexico, and most European countries, sellers may obtain insurance, called **domestic merchandise credit insurance**, against the insolvency of domestic debtors on credits arising out of the sale of merchandise on an unsecured basis. Such coverage has been sold in the United States since 1890. Insurance against failure to repay a cash loan is generally not available in the United States, except as it is applied for through a government agency.

Government Credit Insurance

Several types of government credit insurance exist. Probably the most well known is the **deposit insurance program**. The Federal Deposit Insurance Corporation (FDIC) insures accounts held in insured institutions. The maximum amount of liability per account is $100,000.

Another federal program is **cash loan credit insurance**. Government agencies (the Department of Veterans Affairs, or VA, and Small Business Administration) sponsor programs to insure cash loans made by banks to individuals and certain business enterprises that cannot obtain credit from other sources.

A very popular government credit program is the one that insures long-term loans made to property owners. The Federal Housing Administration and the VA are the two best-known agencies in this area of credit insurance.

TITLE INSURANCE

Title insurance is a device by which the purchaser of real estate may be protected against losses in case it develops that the title obtained is not legitimate or can be made legitimate only after certain payments are made. Defects in titles may stem from sources such as forgery of public records, forgery of titles, invalid or undiscovered wills, defective probate procedures, and faulty real estate transfers. Thus, a person may occupy real property for years only to find that the one who conveyed title was not the rightful owner. True ownership may lie in the possession of another, for example, a former spouse who had been wrongfully deprived of property rights.

Usually all rights in real property, such as encumbrances, liens, and easements, must be duly recorded in the courthouse of the county or parish in which the property lies. Before title insurance became common, the real property buyer usually retained an attorney to search these records and render an opinion on the validity of the title. The attorney based this opinion in large part on an **abstract**, which is a brief history of title to the land. The purpose of the abstract is to reveal the nature of any legal obstacle that may cloud the title or leave a way open for someone else to make a legal claim against the land.

After examining the abstract and perhaps other matters that may not appear as a matter of public record, the attorney rendered an opinion. The attorney, however, could be held liable only for negligence in the title search. If it turned out that there was some unusual defect in title not discoverable by a reasonable and diligent search, no remedy was available for the unfortunate "owner" of the land. Thus, the need for a formal guarantee of the completeness and accuracy of the title search arose. Note that if the title is defective, title insurance does not guarantee possession of the property.

The Title Insurance Contract

No standard title insurance contract exists, but the general form of the insuring clause is fairly uniform. The insurer agrees to indemnify the owner against any loss suffered "by reason of unmarketability of the title of the insured to or in said premises, or . . . from all loss and damage by reason of liens, encumbrances, defects, objections, estates, and interests, except those listed in Schedule B." Schedule B is a separate endorsement on which is listed all title defects or rights in the property found during the title search.

Defense

Under the typical policy, the insurer agrees to defend the insured in any legal proceedings brought against the insured concerning the title, assuming that the action involves a source of loss not excluded under the contract. The insured is required to notify the insurer of any such proceedings and to cooperate in any legal action by the insurer.

Premium

The premium in title insurance is paid only once, and it keeps the policy in force for the named insured for an indefinite period. If the property is transferred, a new premium must be paid for the protection of the new purchaser. The old policy is not assignable to the new buyer. Usually no reduction in premium occurs, even if the property is transferred a short time after the prior purchase. Thus, if a residence is built in one year and is resold five times in the next five years, a title insurance premium might be charged five times.

GLASS COVERAGE FORM

Plate glass has assumed great significance in modern architecture, not only as physical protection against the elements but also because of its advertising value. Use of plate glass in show windows is of great importance in successful merchandising, which explains the importance of **glass insurance**. The BPP with the special causes of loss form does provide coverage for glass, as does the BOP. However, all three causes of loss forms in the BPP have limitations that may make separate glass coverage necessary.

A comprehensive glass policy provides a place in the declarations for a detailed description of each plate of glass, the value of lettering and ornamentation, the position of the plate in the building, and its size. The insuring clause indicates that the insurer agrees to the following:

1. To pay for damage to the glass and its lettering or ornamentation by breakage of the glass or by chemicals accidentally or maliciously applied[4]
2. To pay for the repair or replacement of frames when necessary
3. To pay for the installation of temporary plates or the boarding up of windows when necessary
4. To pay for the removal or replacement of any obstructions made necessary in replacing the glass

No dollar amount of liability is stated. Unlike fire insurance loss settlement procedures, it is the practice of insurers to replace the glass insured under the policy and to do so immediately after the loss. Insurance on the replacement glass continues as before without extra premium.

CRIME

Crime against property in the United States is one of the most serious and most underinsured perils. It is estimated that less than 10 percent of loss to property from ordinary crime is insured. In addition, although statistics on losses are not available, facts suggest that loss from organized crime is tremendous. The problem has become so serious in recent years that the federal government has entered the field of burglary and robbery insurance.

Crime Insurance and Bonds

Two basic types of financial protection exist against the catastrophic losses that can be caused by crime: (1) surety bonds and fidelity bonds and (2) burglary, robbery, and theft insurance.

---

4 Scratching or defacing is not the same as breakage and is not insured.

Surety bonds and fidelity bonds provide guarantees against loss through the dishonesty or incapacity of individuals who are trusted with money or other property and who violate this trust. **Theft insurance**, on the other hand, provides coverage against loss through stealing by individuals who are not in a position of trust.

Insurance versus Bonding

A **bond** is a legal instrument whereby one party (the **surety**) agrees to reimburse another party (the **obligee**) should this person suffer loss because of some failure by the person bonded (the **principal** or **obligor**). Thus, if a contractor furnishes a bond to the owner of a building, the surety will reimburse the owner if the contractor fails to perform as agreed and thereby causes a loss to the owner.

A bond may appear to be a contract of insurance, but some important differences should be considered:

1. In bonding, the surety sees as its basic function the lending of its credit for a premium. It expects no losses and reserves the legal right to collect from the defaulting principal. The insurance contract is set up with the presumption that there will be losses and is viewed by its managers as a device to spread these losses among the insured group.

2. The nature of the risk is different. Usually a bond guarantees the honesty of an individual and the capacity and ability of that individual to perform. These are matters within the control of the individual. The insurance contract, ideally, covers losses outside the control of the individual.

3. In bonding, if the principal defaults and the surety makes good to the obligee, the surety enjoys the legal right to attempt to collect for its loss from the principal. In insurance, the insurer does not have the right to recover losses from the insured; this would defeat the purpose of the contract.

4. The bonding contract involves three primary parties, whereas the insurance contract normally involves only two.

5. Finally, in insurance, the contract is usually cancellable by either party, and nonpayment of premium or breach of warranty by the insured is usually a good defense on the part of the insurer to obviate its liability. In bonding, the surety is often liable on the bond to the beneficiary regardless of breach of warranty or fraud on the part of the principal. In addition, the bond often cannot be cancelled until it has been determined that all the obligations of the principal have been fulfilled.

Fidelity and Surety Bonds

Strictly speaking, all bonds are surety bonds, but it is convenient to classify them as fidelity bonds and surety bonds.

Fidelity bonds indemnify an employer for any loss suffered at the hands of dishonest employees. As such, the bonds are hardly distinguishable from insurance as far as the employer is concerned. Although technically there are three parties to a fidelity bond—the employer (obligee), the employee (obligor), and the insurer (surety)—in practice the main parties are only two, the employer and the surety.

Surety bonds, sometimes known as *financial guaranty bonds*, are contracts among three parties: the principal (obligor), the person protected (obligee), and the insurer (surety). Under the contract, the surety agrees to make good any default on the part of the principal in the principal's duties toward the obligee. For example, the principal might be a contractor who has agreed with the obligee for a given consideration to construct a building meeting certain specifications. The owner-obligee requires the contractor to post a bond to the effect that this contract will be faithfully performed. If the contractor fails in some way, the surety must "make good" to the owner and then has the right to recover any losses from the contractor.

ETHICAL PERSPECTIVES

Who Watches the Watcher?

A former bank risk management officer was convicted by a federal jury of four felonies for embezzling $25 million worth of securities from his bank. He had taken five $5 million bearer securities from a bank vault and delivered them to a stockbroker, claiming he had received them from three owners in Spain and Brazil. He instructed the broker to sell the securities and wire the proceeds to a Bermuda bank account, prosecutors said. The risk manager faced up to 50 years in prison and $1.75 million in fines.

Source: "Risk Manager Convicted in Theft," *Business Insurance*, May 7, 1990, 70.

Types of Fidelity Bonds

Fidelity bonds may be classified into two groups: (1) bonds in which an individual is specifically bonded, either by name or by position held in the firm and (2) bonds that cover all employees of a given class, called **blanket bonds**. Blanket bonds also may cover perils other than infidelity.

Bonds in Which an Individual Is Specifically Bonded. These bonds are of two types. An **individual bond** names a certain person for coverage. If the employer suffers any loss through any dishonest or criminal act of the employee, either alone or in collusion with others, while the employee holds a position with the employer, the surety will be good for the loss up to the limit of liability, called the **penalty** of the bond. **Schedule bonds** may list many employees by name and bond them for specified amounts, in which case the bonds are known as *name schedule bonds*. Additional names may be added or old names deleted on written notice to the surety.

Blanket Bonds. Blanket bonds have several advantages over individual or schedule bonds, making the use of blanket bonds heavily favored among most business firms:

1. Automatic coverage of a uniform amount is given on all employees, thus eliminating the possibility that the employer may select the wrong employee for bonding.
2. New employees are automatically covered without need of notifying the surety.
3. If a loss occurs, it is not necessary to identify the employees who are involved in the conspiracy in order to collect, as is required on individual or schedule bonds. It need only be shown that the loss was due to employee infidelity.
4. Because blanket bonds are subject to rate credits for large accounts, the cost may be no more than that of schedule bonds.

Two major types of blanket bonds exist: the blanket position bond and the commercial blanket bond. These two bonds, whose terms are standardized by the Surety Association of America, differ primarily in the manner in which the penalty of the bond is stated. The **blanket position bond** has a penalty, ranging from $2,500 to $100,000, that applies to each employee. The **commercial blanket bond** has a penalty, ranging upward from $10,000, that applies to any one loss.

Types of Surety Bonds

Surety bonds may be classified into three categories: construction bonds, court bonds, and miscellaneous surety bonds. A brief description of each type follows.

Construction Bonds. A commonly used surety bond is the construction bond. Construction bonds are further subdivided into contract, **owners' protective**, bid, and **completion bonds**.

Contract Construction Bond. From the standpoint of premium volume, probably the most important type of surety bond is the **contract construction bond** (sometimes called a *final* or *performance bond*). The contract construction bond guarantees that the principals (contractors) involved in construction activities will complete their work in accordance with the terms of the construction contracts and will deliver the work to the owner free of any liens or other debts or encumbrances. To the owner, particularly in the case of corporate or municipal owners that let contracts for large projects go to the lowest bidder, the construction bond is an indispensable financial security mechanism. Only through use of a third-party guarantee, namely the guarantee of the surety company, can the owner realistically give a contract to the lowest bidder.

Bid Bond. A **bid bond**, in contrast to a contract construction bond, guarantees that if the bidder is awarded the contract at the bid price and under the terms outlined, the bidder will sign the contract and post a construction bond. The bid bond thus involves the same risk as the contract construction bond.

Burglary, Robbery, and Theft Insurance

As used in insurance contracts, the meanings of the terms *burglary*, *robbery*, and *theft* are important in explaining the extent of coverage. These terms always refer to crimes by persons other than the insured, officers or directors of the insured, or employees of the insured, coverage on which is provided by fidelity bonds.

Burglary is defined somewhat narrowly to mean the unlawful taking of property from within premises closed for business, entry to which has been obtained by force. Visible marks of the forcible entry must be present. Thus, if a customer hides in a store until after closing hours or enters by an unlocked door, steals some goods, and leaves without having to force a door or a window, the definition of burglary is not met under a burglary policy.

Robbery is defined to mean the unlawful taking of property from another person by force, by threat of force, or by violence. Personal contact is the key to understanding the basic characteristic of the robbery peril. If a burglar enters a premises and steals the wallet of a sleeping night guard, this crime is not one of robbery because no violence or threat thereof existed. The person robbed must be cognizant of the act. On the other hand, if the thief knocks out or kills the guard and then robs the guard or the owner, the crime would be classified as robbery. Robbery thus means the forcible taking of property from a messenger or a custodian.

Theft is a broad term that includes all crimes of stealing, robbery, or burglary. Theft is a catch-all term and is usually not distinguished from **larceny**. Thus, any stealing crime not meeting the definition of burglary or robbery is theft. Confidence games or other forms of swindles are thefts, not robberies or burglaries.

Forgery losses involving the passing of bad checks are among the most common types of dishonesty losses and yet are among the easiest to prevent. Most such losses are caused by amateurs; it is estimated that only one-third of all check losses are caused by professionals. Forgery most commonly involves the issuance of entirely fictitious checks, although alteration of, and false signatures upon, legitimate checks are frequent.

Business Coverages

A variety of coverages are available to insure against crime losses. Several of the crime coverages available in the CPP are outlined in Table 10-2. The table also indicates to which types of property the coverages apply. A firm can pick and choose from these options based on the specific crime exposures that it faces. Also, the insuring agreements can be combined to form a stand-alone policy.

TABLE 10-2   Basic Crime Coverages under the CPP

Peril	Property Covered
1. Employee theft	M&S and BPP
2. Forgery or alteration	Checks, drafts, and notes
3. Inside the premises—Theft of money and securities	M&S
4. Inside the premises—Robbery or safe burglary of other property	Property other than M&S
5. Outside the premises	M&S and BPP
6. Computer fraud	M&S and BPP
7. Fund transfer fraud	M&S
8. Money orders and counterfeit paper currency	Money orders and counterfeit paper currency

M&S = money & securities; BPP = business personal property

Federal Crime Insurance

Because of difficulties in securing private insurance, particularly in some large city areas, the federal government began to offer crime insurance to the public in 1971 in certain states on a subsidized basis. Coverages are noncancellable and include burglary, robbery, and theft. Premiums are quoted so that the cost of crime coverage appears affordable to the average buyer.

To be eligible for federal crime insurance, the insured must (1) live in a state deemed eligible for the crime coverage; (2) meet certain protective device standards; (3) agree to permit inspections of the premises at reasonable times; (4) agree to report to the insurer all crime losses, whether a claim is filed; and (5) accept the form of coverage prescribed by the Federal Insurance Administration (FIA).

Risk Management of the Crime Peril

Management may attempt to handle the crime risk through several methods, including assumption, loss control, and insurance. Each of these methods is deficient in some respect. The method of assumption may invite ruin. Loss control efforts tend to be haphazard and are often ineffective. Insurance methods suffer from adverse selection, high costs, and gaps in protection because of narrow definitions of perils.

Assumption

Many firms retain the crime risk, as many losses are small and expensive to insure. For instance, individual shoplifting losses are usually small but may be frequent. The combination of high frequency and low severity makes the crime risk very suitable to a frequency of loss retention and control. If insurance is used to handle such a risk, the premium will be prohibitive because the insurer would have to collect enough premiums to pay for the losses and cover administrative expenses.

Insurance

Even with rapid detection of crime, effective systems of court action, and rehabilitation efforts applied to the criminal, it appears that crime is a problem that will always characterize society. Insurance remains as a potentially effective device to spread the inevitable crime losses among insureds.

Unfortunately, insurance as a way of handling the crime risk suffers from serious weaknesses. Crime insurance is used sparingly and, as previously noted, covers less than 10 percent of the total crime loss in the United States. Adverse selection is present due to the tendency of those applicants who are most likely to suffer loss (such as pawnshops and jewelry and liquor stores) to apply for the most coverage. A moral hazard exists in the temptation of those who are insured to take advantage of opportunities to arrange a robbery or burglary with an accomplice in order to collect illegally from the insurance company. Also, it is often difficult to establish the amount of the loss when it occurs because of inadequate inventory control methods or lack of adequate records. For example, a burglary of a retailer might occur, evidence of which is obvious. But the insured may try to include in the loss claim some shortages of inventory that are in reality due to shoplifting or employee theft. It may be difficult for the claims adjuster to prove otherwise.

Even though insurance is not a total solution to the problem of managing the crime risk, it is one of the most immediately practical methods by which the business firm may obtain financial protection against crime.

DISASTER RISK MANAGEMENT: A CASE STUDY

It was a typical August day in Georgia: the temperature was in the 90s and so was the humidity! A roofing contractor had been working on TCB Company's copper roof for the last several weeks and was ready to begin installation of the new roof.

In the early afternoon, a roofing company employee took a propane torch and began to work on a vent in the roof. Although he was trying to be careful, the heat created by the torch passed through the copper and started a fire inside the building's fifth floor. The worker became aware of the situation because he could see and smell the smoke. However, he was on the roof outside the building, and the fire was on the inside of the fifth floor. By the time he reached the inside with a fire extinguisher, the smoke was so thick that he could not enter the space where the fire was located. He could not contain the fire. Meanwhile, the fire alarm had been activated, and the building was evacuated. All roofing company workers and TCB employees were unharmed, but the fire was out of control and spreading.

Set your browser to http://www. ogara-hess.com and examine some of the sophisticated security measures and equipment available to protect corporations' employees while traveling.

The fire station was less than a mile away, and firefighters were quickly on the scene. However, much of the fifth floor had been subdivided into small rooms, and it was difficult to reach the actual position of the fire. In addition, the building had asbestos sprayed on it and the ceiling tile had asbestos in it. Firefighters had to be concerned about asbestos fibers in the air. The surrounding buildings also made it difficult to drive the fire engines close to the building, and the use of an aerial ladder truck was delayed because trees had to be cut to make a path for the truck.

What started out as a fire located in a small portion of the building led to one that took eight hours and more than a million gallons of water to extinguish. The entire fifth floor of the building was destroyed, and smoke and water damage occurred throughout the entire building. In addition, the asbestos ceiling tiles collapsed under the weight of the water that came from the firefighters' hoses. Thus, there was asbestos contamination throughout the building, and after the fire the building was considered a regulated building. That is, it could not be used until the asbestos was removed. Clearly, the firm needed to activate its disaster plan.

Early the next morning, the firm's president called a meeting to inform everyone that the building restoration was the firm's number one priority, and temporary space would be rented while restoration took place. Once the fire inspector had conducted his analysis, the building was entered by men in moon suits to recover the computer equipment. Asbestos particles had to be removed, and any residue left by smoke or water cleared from the equipment. The building contained more than $2 million in computer equipment. Since the firm did not have the expertise to recover their equipment, it retained an outside expert—the same company that decontaminated Union Bank Tower in Los Angeles as well as One Market Plaza in San Francisco. Within two weeks, all equipment had been cleaned or sent to the junk room. Meanwhile, it was determined that part of the building could be put back into production within four weeks. However, it would take more than 18 months to replace the fifth floor and repair the rest of the building.

It was clear that several departments would not be able to return to the building for 9 months (later it was determined to be 18 months); space was rented, and those departments' computer equipment was installed at the temporary location. Rental furniture was obtained and placed in those departments where the fire and/or water had destroyed the furniture, and the telephone company installed new phones. Because of the asbestos contamination, all furniture that contained fabric was declared a constructive total loss (it would cost more to clean it than it would be worth).

While it took four weeks to repair the usable part of the building and to prepare rental space, the firm lost little business, because it was the slow time of the year and short-term (four weeks) emergency space was found. Employees who were needed at the office to conduct business reported to work daily, while others worked at home.

Because the firm's president provided excellent leadership and made events happen, TCB Company was able to maintain operations and meet its business goals. Because of his leadership, activities that often took a month were done in a week or less. Adequate direct and indirect property insurance was available, plus the roofer's liability insurance. The firm had comprehensive property insurance for damage to property on a replacement cost basis (real and personal property), loss of business income, and extra expense insurance. In addition, the policy had coverage for increased cost of construction due to the enforcement of building laws and demolition insurance. Because there was little question as to whose negligence caused the loss, the roofer's liability carrier was involved from day one. While it took 10 months to actually receive a check, TCB knew that the roofer's carrier would pay. The total cost of the fire was close to $10 million.

Referring to the facts in this case, discuss the following:

1. What factors occurred that contributed to the delay in extinguishing the fire?
2. Describe how the existence of commercial insurance made the recovery easier.
3. Explain the importance of executive leadership in disaster recovery plans.

SUMMARY

1. The major types of policies in ocean marine insurance are contracts covering the hull, the cargo, the freight, and the legal liability of the carrier for proved negligence. The coverage is broad, but it is still on a named-perils basis.
2. Warranties in ocean marine insurance are of extreme importance, and any breach, no matter how slight, voids the contract. Express warranties are typified by trading warranties of various kinds. The implied warranties are those of seaworthiness, deviation, and legality.
3. Insurance on the perils of land transportation grew out of contracts of ocean marine insurance. The marine definition delineates five types of insurance to be allowed as marine insurance, with no distinction now being made between ocean and inland marine. The five types are contracts covering imports, exports, domestic shipments, instrumentalities of communication and transportation, and floater risks. The one element common to all these contracts is that the subject of insurance is essentially mobile, either actually or constructively.

4. The inland policy and the trip transit policy are basic contracts covering the perils of land transportation. In general, it is cheaper and better to use these policies than to rely on insurance covering the interest of the common carrier or on the common law liability of the common carrier for safe carriage of the goods.

5. Block policies, issued on an all-risk basis to specific types of retail and wholesale concerns by inland marine insurers, are significant because they have tended to set the pattern for all-risk insurance on floating business property, issued under the CPP. Common block policies are the jewelers', the camera and musical instrument dealers', and the equipment dealers'.

6. In contrast to block forms, scheduled property floaters, generally issued on a named-perils basis, cover an extremely wide variety of floating business property. Examples of the different needs met by these forms are the contractors' equipment floater and the EDP floater.

7. Credit insurance seems useful when a firm has a few large accounts, the failure of any one of which would cause a severe and crippling loss, or when it is desired to use the credit and collection services of the insurer. A careful analysis must be made of the firm's exposure to loss, and the policy must be tailored to fit these specific needs.

8. Title insurance is purchased largely for the title investigation that accompanies it. Also important, of course, is the protection it gives against losses caused by discovery of defects that impair the marketability of the insured title.

9. Crime statistics show that the perils of dishonesty and human failure cause more total losses than other major perils. Yet the crime peril is greatly underinsured. Prominent among the reasons for this fact are the tendency for business firms to refuse to recognize that trusted employees can and do steal and the lack of publicity that attends these crimes.

10. The two major types of crime protection are (a) bonds and (b) burglary, robbery, and theft insurance. Bonds give protection against losses due to embezzlement or other stealing by persons in a position of trust, whereas theft insurance gives protection against crimes of so-called outsiders.

11. Some important differences exist between bonds and insurance. Basically, bonds provide the surety's financial guarantee of the principal's honesty and ability, with the understanding that the surety can attempt to recover from the principal. In an insurance contract, the insurer pays on behalf of the insured and has no recourse against the insured.

internet*exercises*

1. Set your browser to http://www.rma.usda.gov and examine the nature of the products offered by the USDA-FCIC's Risk Management Agency. What attributes of the agricultural industry make it a candidate for government-sponsored insurance programs such as these? How do such programs compare to those offered by private industry?

2. Passing counterfeit money is a form of theft. The United States Secret Service offers tips on identifying and reporting counterfeit currency. Go to http://www.treas.gov/usss/ and use the links under the topic "Know Your Money" to learn how to detect counterfeit currency and what to do when you detect it. Examine some currency in your possession to see if you are confident that it is genuine.

QUESTIONS FOR REVIEW AND DISCUSSION

1. Why is glass insurance needed?
2. What perils are insured against in an ocean marine insurance policy?
3. Identify and explain the major ocean marine coverages available.
4. How does the liability of the carrier differ between land and ocean transportation?
5. With respect to ownership, what types of property are covered under a jewelers' block policy?

6. A writer stated that credit risk cannot be transferred entirely to an external agency; some residual risk must always rest on the shoulders of the independent businessperson as a necessary consequence of engaging in business. Explain why this is true or untrue.

7. In *Bolta Rubber Company v Lowell Trucking Corporation*, 37 N.E. 2d 873, a trucking company was insured under a motor cargo policy to protect its legal liability as a common carrier. The policy contained a warranty that each insured truck would be equipped with a burglar alarm in good working order. A truck was held up. It was determined that the burglar alarm system had been turned off at the time of the holdup. The trucker was held liable for $1,000. Discuss the liability and rights of the insurer and the trucker.

8. The antiquated wording in the 1779 Lloyd's ocean perils clause is retained in its essential outline in modern-day policies. Suggest reasons for this.

9. The *SS Victory* runs aground as it enters the harbor at Honolulu. Due to various contingencies, it is impossible to refloat the vessel before a storm strikes. Considerable damage is done to the vessel and the cargo, especially to the Number 3 hold, in which Smith Company's merchandise (pens and pencils) is packed. The pens and pencils are so badly battered that in order to save the shipment from being a total loss, it is necessary that $2,000 be spent on reconditioning them. Smith Company seeks recovery from the insurer for the entire $5,000 for which the shipment is insured, on the grounds that there is actually a total loss. Do you agree? Why or why not?
   a. Explain in your own words the meaning of *general average*.
   b. Why should the various interests be required to pay such claims?

10. Discuss the various attributes of a floater policy.

11. Of what benefit is title insurance if the insurer excludes all title defects occurring after the policy is issued and, in addition, all defects known to exist before the policy is issued? Explain.

12. a. It is claimed that the premium for title insurance is unfairly high when the property is transferred frequently. Do you agree?
    b. What justification could the title insurer have for not reducing the premium when the property is transferred frequently?

chapter 11

The U.S. legal system is an outgrowth of English Common Law that has been modified by statute and by case law. The system in the United States is designed so that every person can have his or her day in court. Lawyers take many cases on a contingency fee basis; if the case is lost, the attorney receives little or nothing. If the case is won, the attorney receives from one-third to one-half of the award. This type of legal environment gives rise to much litigation and increased standards of care.

The increasingly litigious nature of our society has made liability risk a major concern for individuals and businesses in the U.S. Aside from the numerous actions people and businesses take to reduce the likelihood of having lawsuits filed against them, they also spend billions of dollars each year to purchase liability insurance to protect them if they get sued. The insurance industry is therefore also deeply concerned with managing liability risk. Lloyd's of London was placed in dire financial condition because it failed to price its products properly and the legal environment changed much more rapidly than it expected. In reading this chapter, you should reflect on the issues of an expanding theory of legal liability, increases in standards of care required of people, and who should pay for the losses.

Risk Management and Commercial Liability Risk

CHAPTER OBJECTIVES

After studying this chapter, you should be able to

1. Describe the content of insuring clauses in commercial general liability policies and the supplementary benefits of such policies.
2. Explain how limits of liability are determined in commercial liability policies.
3. Differentiate between claims-made coverage and occurrence coverage.
4. Identify the different parts of the commercial general liability policy, the policy's exclusions, and several endorsements that can be used with it.
5. State the difference between professional liability insurance and regular liability insurance.
6. Indicate how businesses use commercial umbrella policies.

Liability insurance is an outgrowth—in fact, an inevitable result—of the legal relationships in society that can produce successful lawsuits against individuals for negligence. This is a key factor in understanding the scope of and the reasons for the liability contracts discussed in this chapter.

As it became recognized that negligence could form the basis for a damage suit, a demand arose for protection against the financial consequences of such suits. At first, the courts frowned on liability insurance in the belief that contracts of this nature would tend to encourage reckless conduct and thus result in more injuries to persons and property. Later, it was recognized that a true need existed for financial protection and that the existence of properly designed insurance did not cause an unwarranted degree of irresponsible conduct. Today, the law takes the attitude that failure to obtain liability insurance against the consequences of negligence in itself constitutes irresponsible financial behavior. The prime example is that all states have enacted legislation imposing penalties for failure to provide some sort of financial protection against negligence in the operation of automobiles.

COMMON LIABILITY CONTRACT PROVISIONS

No matter what type of liability a policy insures against, certain provisions appear in virtually all liability insurance contracts. They include the insuring clause, supplementary payments, definition of the insured, exclusions, limits of liability, specification of claims-made or occurrence coverage, and notice.

The Insuring Clause

As described in Chapter 7, a key part of any insurance contract is the insuring agreement. Although insuring agreements vary by policy, a typical insuring agreement in a liability policy might read like the following:

> We will pay those sums that the insured becomes legally obligated to pay as damages because of bodily injury or property damage to which this insurance applies. We will have the right and duty to defend the insured against any suit seeking those damages.

The following points apply to the interpretation of this typical agreement:

1. The liability insurance policy almost invariably states that the insurer is bound to pay only the sums that the insured is legally obligated to pay. Unless specifically insured, voluntary payments are not covered, even if made in good faith out of what is felt to be a moral obligation to the injured party. This, of course, does not mean that every case must be brought into court to determine legal obligation—it is estimated that more than 95 percent of all cases are settled out of court.

2. The policy also states that the insurer has the right and duty to defend the insured against any suit seeking damages for bodily injury or property damage to which the insurance applies. The fact that the insurer agrees to defend any suit, even if it is groundless, false, or fraudulent, relieves the insured of the worry and expense of defending against both valid as well as nuisance cases. Even a groundless claim can be expensive to defend against. The insurer already has an experienced legal staff, the cost of which is distributed over many claims in a given year, and can thus handle each case efficiently. Without insurance, a business might need to retain counsel for every suit against it, even if the amount involved is small. Liability insurance can transfer much of that burden to the insurer. It should be noted that the term *any suit* does not mean that the insurer will defend a court action falling outside the scope of the insurance coverage. For example, a particular liability policy may specifically exclude coverage for liability related to automobiles. Therefore, the insurer would have no duty to defend an insured against a lawsuit arising out of an auto accident.

3. Generally, the act causing the injury must be accidental for insurance to apply. It will be recalled that a basic requirement of an insurable peril is that it be fortuitous. In spite of this, most liability policies now appear without the "caused by accident" clause. Instead, wording is substituted under which the insurer is liable for any "occurrence" giving rise to legal liability. Even though these policies declare that injuries caused intentionally by the insured are excluded, there is the probability that the use of "occurrence" gives more coverage than the "caused by accident" wording. The word *accident* suggests a sudden, unexpected, abnormal event, whereas the word *occurrence*, when modified to exclude intentional acts, connotes unexpected and abnormal but not necessarily sudden events. For example, suppose a contractor is blasting an excavation for a new building and, although no immediate damage is observable to neighboring properties, over a period of days the earth is so shaken that the foundations of nearby buildings are damaged. Under the "caused by accident" wording, some doubt may exist that this injury is covered because the contractor should know the probable consequences of his actions and no sudden damage is caused due to the blasting. Under the "occurrence" wording, unless it is demonstrated that the contractor deliberately continued actions known to be destructive, the liability for the damage would be recovered.

Supplementary Payments

Supplementary payments are an important part of any liability insurance contract. These payments are made in addition to any benefits supplied by the basic liability policy. The insurance company promises to provide coverage for bodily injury and property damage liability and also supplementary benefits. Typically, the insurer (referred to as *we* in the following list) states that it will pay

1. All expenses we incur.
2. Up to $250 for cost of bail bonds required because of accidents or traffic law violations arising out of the use of any vehicle to which the bodily injury liability coverage applies. We do not have to furnish these bonds.
3. The cost of bonds to release attachments, but only for bond amounts within the applicable limit of insurance. We do not have to furnish these bonds.
4. All reasonable expenses incurred by the insured at our request to assist us in the investigation or defense of the claim or "suit," including actual loss of earnings up to $250 per day because of time off from work.
5. All costs taxed against the insured in the "suit."
6. Prejudgment interest awarded against the insured on that part of the judgment we pay. If we make an offer to pay the applicable limit of insurance, we will not pay any prejudgment interest based on that period of time after the offer.
7. All interest on the full amount of any judgment that accrues after entry of the judgment and before we have paid, offered to pay, or deposited in court the part of the judgment that is within the applicable limit of insurance.

Liability insurance has sometimes been termed *defense insurance* because in a majority of cases liability suits are settled out of court by negotiation between attorneys. The insured knows that the worry and care of negotiations are assumed by the insurer. The following points concerning the supplementary payments provisions are worth noting:

1. The first supplementary payment, all expenses we incur, would include all the defense costs incurred by the insurer in defending the insured against covered lawsuits. These defense costs can be a substantial portion of the total cost of liability claims. In analyzing a liability insurance policy, it is critical to verify whether the policy covers defense costs. Most policies do, but some do not. In addition, it is important to determine whether the defense costs are included within the policy limits, or are in addition to the limits. Obviously, it is better for the insured if defense costs are in addition to the limits, so the full amount of the limits is available to pay damages. If defense costs are within the limits,

as they are in some policies, the insured will have to consider whether higher policy limits are needed to assure adequate coverage.

2. Sometimes courts require that the alleged wrongdoer post a bond to guarantee that, pending the outcome of a negligence action, he or she will not dispose of property subject to confiscation if the case is lost. For cases in which a decision has been lost in the lower court and is appealed to a higher court, a bond must be posted to guarantee that if the defendant loses in the higher court, the judgment will be paid. The insurer agrees to pay the premium on these bonds, plus any accrued interest after the date of the judgment.

3. Under the other terms of the liability policy, the insurer has the right to require the insured to appear in court personally in legal actions arising under the policy, and otherwise cooperate in the defense of such cases. The insurer agrees to pay the insured's reasonable expenses arising from this assistance.

Definition of the Insured

All contracts of liability insurance specifically set forth the party who is to be considered an insured. The concept of who is an insured in liability policies is generally very broad, and the wording differs for each type of policy. In the case of a business firm, the intent is to include all partners, officers, directors, and proprietors in their capacities as representatives of the particular business. Employees are also generally insureds while performing duties related to the business. It is not uncommon to write liability contracts, for payment of an extra premium, naming other parties as additional insureds.

Exclusions

Among the various liability insurance contracts, certain exclusions appear almost universally. Among these are the following:

1. In the case of business policies, all nonbusiness activities giving rise to damage suits are excluded. In personal contracts, all business pursuits giving rise to damage suits are excluded.

2. An attempt is made in each policy to exclude all sources of liability intended to be covered in other contracts or intended to be covered by a special provision for an extra premium. Thus, in the commercial general liability (CGL) policy, most liability from pollution is excluded.

   The primary type of pollution coverage present in commercial general liability policies pertains to a situation that occurs at a location not owned, rented, or occupied by the insured. The substance causing the loss must not have been brought to the site by the insured. For instance, if an insured contractor is digging at the worksite of a client and punctures an underground gas pipe, and escaping gas sickens some people nearby, the resulting liability should be covered. Clearly, this coverage is extremely limited. For insureds with minor pollution exposure, the pollution liability coverage endorsement is available. For those with significant pollution exposure, a separate pollution liability policy should be purchased.

3. Nearly all liability contracts exclude damage to property belonging or rented to the insured or to property in the care, custody, or control of the insured, under the general theory that a person cannot be liable to oneself for one's own negligence. The insured is expected to obtain physical damage insurance, such as the coverages discussed in the last two chapters, to cover the accidental loss of property that he or she owns or uses for which he or she is otherwise legally liable.

The question sometimes arises as to the conditions under which property is in the care, custody, or control of the insured. For example, suppose a mechanic is working on the fan belt of an engine in a customer's car and the fan blade accidentally breaks off and punctures the radiator. Is the damage covered under the garage liability policy? Or is it excluded under the argument that the car is in the care and custody of the insured and hence damage to any part of the car is excluded? A liberal policy interpretation would hold that the damage is covered and that only damage to property actually being worked on is excluded. In one case a contractor installed a heat exchange unit. While it was being tested, but before the job was abandoned, damage resulted. The court held that the damage was covered.[1] In another case, however, the court held that damage to a concrete retaining wall by a bulldozer was excluded because the wall was "in the care, custody, and control" of the contractor at the time of the damage.[2] No general rule seems to be applicable to such cases, except the general rule that always applies: ambiguities in contractual language will be construed against the insurer.

Some insurers offer broadened policies, under which the "care, custody, and control" exclusion is liberalized. Of special interest to contractors, the **broad form property damage liability program**, as it is called, spells out in considerable detail just what property is covered and under what terms.

Limits of Liability

Under all liability insurance policies, various types of limits of liability exist. For example, in the Business Auto Policy contract, the limits might be $250,000 for bodily injury liability for any one person and $500,000 for each accident. For property damage liability, a limit may be set of $100,000 for each accident. This restriction means that if three or more of the insured's customers are injured in a single accident, an overall limit of $500,000 is in effect for that accident, with no more than $250,000 paid to any individual customer. If more than one insured is named in the policy, the question arises: "Are these limits of liability applicable to each insured, thus doubling or tripling the stated limits?" The answer is no.

In some policies, such as the comprehensive personal liability (CPL) policy, only a single limit of liability exists. Both bodily injury and property damage liability are insured under this limit. Because no per-person restrictions are in place with respect to bodily injury, the entire policy limit may be paid to one person.

Aggregate limits also are used in liability policies. Under the aggregate limit approach, the policy limit is placed on an annual basis rather than on an occurrence basis. If the aggregate limit is set at $2 million, regardless of the number of claims or their severity, the insurance company would only pay up to $2 million on the insured's behalf during the year. Under a $2 million occurrence limit and no aggregate limit, it is possible that an insurer could pay several $2 million claims during the contract year.

Another important aspect of the policy limit is the time period covered. The policy obviously has inception and termination dates, but does it cover a loss when a person is exposed (**exposure doctrine**) to a product or a dangerous substance, or should coverage apply only when the claimant's disease or injury is discovered (**manifestation doctrine**)? Still a third approach is to say that all policies in force during the exposure and manifestation period apply. This last approach is called the **triple-trigger approach** and provides the greatest amount of coverage for the insured. These doctrines were very important in the DES drug trial (*Eli Lilly v Home Insurance Company*, 764 F. 2d 876) and in asbestos-related trials.[3]

In October 1981, the District of Columbia Court of Appeals ruled in a case that the triple-trigger rule was more appropriate, and in March 1982, the Supreme Court of the United States declined to review the case when it was appealed.

Although the triple-trigger approach is very attractive to insureds, it causes problems for insurers. For instance, a firm could self-insure for three years and then purchase insurance for

---

1 *Boswell v Travelers Indemnity Company*, 8 CCH Fire and Casualty Cases 936.

2 *Jarrell Construction Company v Columbia Casualty Company*, 8 CCH Fire and Casualty Cases 642.

3 Rhonda L. Rundle, "Keene Jackpot: $300 Million in Coverage," *Business Insurance*, October 26, 1981, 1, 47.

a large amount in the fourth year. Because either the exposure or the manifestation approach would apply, the insurance would cover the three years when the insured did not purchase insurance. This entire area of policy limits is very complex, particularly in the product liability line.

To address some of the problems presented by the courts' liberal interpretation of policy limits, insurance companies have established a new set of limits in the Commercial Package Policy (CPP). The liability coverage in the CPP policy is called the *commercial general liability form*. In our discussions, *CGL* means commercial general liability.

The CPP has separate limits of liability for general liability, product and completed operations liability, personal and advertising liability, medical payments, and damage to premises rented to you. In addition, an annual aggregate limit of liability applies to all claims for general liability, personal and advertising injury, medical payments, and damage to premises rented to you. Once the total amount claimed from these exposures exceeds the annual aggregate, the insurance company will not pay any more claims under that policy. The aggregate limit means that the policy will pay only up to a predetermined amount per year, regardless of the number of claims. The product and completed operations liability limit is separate from the overall aggregate liability limit. However, it also has an aggregate limit that represents the maximum amount that the insurer will pay in one year for products and completed operations claims.

Claims-Made versus Occurrence Coverage

Due to the tremendously high dollar amount of claims and awards associated with asbestos and other "long tail" liability exposures, the insurance industry is attempting to reduce its uncertainty concerning the payment of future claims. A liability line is said to have a long tail when that line will take a long time (e.g., 4 to 10 years) to develop claims from a given event. Product liability and professional liability are examples of long tail liability lines.

Under the traditional **occurrence policy**, any event in 2004 that led to a claim in 2004 or any future year would be covered by the 2004 policy. Thus, if a member of the public was exposed to a harmful substance in 2004 and it took 10 years for the injury to manifest itself, the 2004 insurer is expected to defend and settle the claim in 2014 and beyond. This approach gives the insured great certainty, but leaves the insurer in a situation where it does not know the cost of its product (2004 losses) for 5, 10, or 15 years.

Prior to the 1970s, the occurrence approach worked in a reasonable manner. However, the combination of changing legal standards and rapid economic inflation led to a situation where insurers felt they could no longer accurately price their products under an occurrence policy. As a result, the **claims-made policy** was developed.

Under the original claims-made policy, a 2004 policy pays only for those claims that are made during 2004. The event that caused the claim to be made can occur in 2004 or any prior year. Once the year 2004 is over, the insurer can determine the total amount of claims paid and of claims outstanding and can have more current data to price its product for the following year. The only major uncertainty to the insurer for the 2004 policy year is whether the loss reserve on reported claims is accurate. However, the certainty gained by the insurer is offset by greater uncertainty on the part of the insured.

Under the claims-made approach, the insured has protection for 2004 events only if insurance is purchased every year after 2004. If for some reason insurance is not purchased in 2006 (for example, coverage is not available or is priced too high), and a claim from a 2004 event is filed in 2006, the insured does not have any protection. See Table 11-1 for examples illustrating the operation of claims-made and occurrence policies.

Compared to occurrence form polices, claims-made policies increase the chance of an insured having a gap in coverage. Suppose a new business is formed in year x and purchases a claims-made liability policy beginning that year. Now suppose that after year $x + 5$ the

TABLE 11-1   **Explanation of Claims-Made and Occurrence Policy**

	Occurrence Policy		Claims-Made Policy*			
Policy 2003 No Insurance	A 2004	B 2005 Event A Event B	C 2006	D 2007	E 2008	F 2009
Event D						
	Event E					

*The retroactive date is January 1, 2006.
Event A occurs and is reported in 2005. Policy B pays.
Event B occurs in 2005 and is reported in 2008. Policy B pays.
Event C occurs in 2007 and is reported in 2009. Policy F pays.
Event D occurs in 2003 and is reported in 2007. No coverage because loss occurred before the
   retroactive date.
Event E occurs in 2004 and is reported in 2009. Policy A pays.

insurer does not renew the policy because of poor loss experience, and the insured must find another insurer. The new insurer will most likely choose a retroactive date of January 1 of year $x + 6$. The retroactive date determines the time after which events must have occurred in order to have coverage for claims made in year $x + 6$. In the present case, it is possible the insurer would allow the retroactive date to be year x, but most likely it would be the beginning of year $x + 6$. Any claim in year $x + 6$ for events that occurred from year x to year $x + 5$ will not be paid by the new policy. Plus, because the claims were made after year $x + 5$, the old expired policy will not cover the claims either. Thus, the insured is left without any coverage for such claims.

To ease the burden placed on the insured by the claims-made policy, the insurance industry has instituted the following special provisions for such policies.

Basic Extended Reporting Period

The basic **extended reporting period** provision is usually automatically provided and has two parts. The first gives the insured an extra 60 days for a claim to be made for an event (unknown to the insured) that occurred before the policy expired. For example, on a policy expiring December 31 of year x, an event could have happened on December 24, year x, and a claim not made until February 15, year $x + 1$. The policy would still cover the loss, even though the policy has expired. If the claim had been made on March 15, year $x + 1$, no coverage would be available on the policy.

The second provision provides an **extended period of indemnity** of five years for known events for which claims were not filed during the policy year. Again, assume a loss on December 24, year x, that is known to the insured and the insurer. In year $x + 4$, a claim resulting from that event is filed. In this situation, the claims-made policy covering year x will pay the claim. However, if the claim is made in year $x + 7$, the policy will not pay because the claim is made after five years have elapsed.

These two provisions provide some added protection for the insured, but even when combined, they are not as good as the traditional occurrence policy. To match the coverage of the traditional occurrence coverage, the insured must purchase the **supplemental tail**.

Supplemental Tail

This endorsement must be requested in writing within 60 days of the end of the policy term; if the policy ends on December 31, the endorsement must be requested by March 1. The supplemental tail has its own aggregate limit equal to the original policy's limit, and the insurer cannot charge more than 200 percent of the original policy's premium for the endorsement. This premium is paid only once, and the insured then has coverage forever for events that occurred between the claims-made policy's retroactive date and date of expiration. Although the supplement can be expensive, it does offer an alternative for an insured with a severe long tail liability loss exposure.

Notice

Like all insurance policies, liability contracts require immediate notice of accident and claim or suit. It is especially important that this condition be complied with; otherwise, available witnesses may be dispersed and evidence dissipated so as to make it difficult or impossible to determine later what actually happened. Such information is vital to the successful defense of the insured, and without prompt notice the insurer is greatly handicapped.

COMMERCIAL LIABILITY INSURANCE

Various types of business liability policies are available for business concerns. Our investigation will focus on the commercial general liability, employment practice liability, business auto, professional liability, and commercial umbrella policies.

Commercial General Liability

The **commercial general liability (CGL)** policy is designed to give the insured considerable flexibility. It covers, on an occurrence or a claims-made basis, a variety of liability losses, including bodily injury and property damage liability losses resulting from conditions of the premises, business operations, products, and completed operations. It also provides coverage for liability arising out of various intentional torts.

Losses arising from the conditions of the premises include situations in which a customer slips on a wet spot on the floor, falls down unsafe stairs, or is exposed to caustic chemicals on the insured's premises. Business operations liability losses could result from performing activities at a customer's home. For example, while installing drapes, the insured's employee could damage property at the customer's home, or a furniture store's delivery people could drop a piece of furniture on a customer's foot.

In order to be considered product liability, bodily injury or property damage must result from a business's product, and the loss must occur away from the business's premises and after the business has relinquished control of the product.

Completed operations losses are most often associated with contractors or maintenance people. These losses are said to occur after a person has finished the job and given control of it to the customer. (If the loss occurs while the contractor is working on the item, the loss is considered a business operations loss.) Examples of completed operations losses are as follows: (1) A steel bin built by a contractor collapsed; after the collapse, it was found that certain welds were not made. Extensive damage to buildings and machinery occurred, and one person was killed. The court awarded a judgment of $199,650.[4] (2) A plumbing firm was held liable for $5,000 of water damage to a home when a pipe connected to a washbowl became

---

4   *F.C. & S. Bulletins*, Sales Section, Losses, Pro-3 (Cincinnati, OH: The National Underwriter Company, 1986).

disconnected. The court ruled that the plumber had been negligent in installing the pipe.[5] (3) A thermostatic fan system was installed by a furnace company and was not operating properly. The furnace company was called several times to fix it but before the firm did so, the system caused $5,500 of damage for which the furnace company was held responsible.[6]

The CGL also covers liability losses from certain intentional torts such as libel and slander, false arrest, and invasion of privacy. For example, if in an advertisement, Firm A unknowingly makes a false statement about the quality of Firm B's product, and Firm B sues them for libel, Firm A's CGL would cover this lawsuit.

Newly acquired organizations are covered for 90 days under the CGL policy. Newly acquired premises are automatically covered for the duration of the policy. After the policy's term expires, the insurer will audit the exposure and collect an additional premium if any new premises have been acquired or if unforeseen exposures have developed. Likewise, it would refund some premium if the deposit premium had been in excess.

Exclusions in the CGL

Although the CGL provides broad coverage, it also contains numerous exclusions. The bodily injury and property damage liability coverage section lists 15 separate exclusions. Although all 15 exclusions are important, we will briefly look at four of them.

Automobile. Virtually all liability related to automobiles, including liability from incidents occurring during the loading and unloading of automobiles, is excluded under the CGL. One exception is for liability arising out of the parking of nonowned automobiles on the premises. This exception is beneficial to restaurants and hotels whose employees park their customers' automobiles. Businesses needing more significant coverage for auto liability should purchase separate business auto coverage, as described in a later section.

Product Recall. The act of recalling (withdrawing) defective products from the marketplace is excluded in the CGL; this is known as the **sistership exclusion**. A manufacturer can purchase recall insurance to cover this exposure. Protection is available in nonstandard markets under specialty forms that contain detailed provisions requiring the insured (1) to take all reasonable steps to prevent further loss once a defective product is identified and (2) to repair faulty work.

Liquor Liability. Liability arising from the responsibility imposed by a liquor law is excluded. Known as the **dramshop exclusion**, this provision appears in most liability contracts because in some states the dramshop laws make the seller or distributor of alcoholic beverages liable for losses that can be traced to the use of alcohol sold or distributed by him or her. Thus, an intoxicated person may leave an establishment that dispenses liquor and injure someone or destroy property. Under a state's dramshop law, the liability might be traced back to the insured establishment. The CGL liquor liability exclusion only applies to insureds who are in the business of manufacturing, distributing, or selling alcoholic beverages. Other businesses, such as a bank hosting a holiday office party where liquor is served, have liquor liability coverage under the CGL. For those in the alcoholic beverage business, this liability may be covered by purchasing liquor liability coverage for an additional premium.

Pollution. In the commercial general liability policy, liability for pollution loss is excluded, with only minor exceptions. In the old comprehensive general liability policy, accidental pol-

---

5 *Rinkle v Lees Plumbing and Heating Co.*, 10 CCH (Negligence 2d) 347.
6 *Handy v Holland Furnace Co.*, H CCH (Negligence 2d) 988.

PROFESSIONAL PERSPECTIVES

The Tort System is Expensive

According to a report by Tillinghast-Towers Perrin, the cost of the U.S. tort system (insured and uninsured) has increased an average of 9.8 percent per year over the period 1951–2002. In 2002 alone, the cost of the tort system rose 13.3 percent to $233 billion. Tort costs in 2002 were $809 per man, woman, and child citizen of the United States, and are equivalent to a 5 percent tax on wages. Less than half of the tort costs actually went to the injured parties, with the remainder consumed by claimants' attorney fees, defense costs, and other administrative costs. Of the amounts actually paid to injured parties, less than half was to compensate for actual economic loss, with the rest paid for noneconomic losses such as pain and suffering. The report attributes the rapidly rising tort costs to increases in class-action lawsuits and large claim awards, record jury awards in medical malpractice cases, an increase in shareholder lawsuits against corporate boards of directors, and an increase in medical inflation, which increases bodily injury claim costs.

Source: *U.S. Tort Costs: 2003 Update: Trends and Findings on the Costs of the U.S. Tort System*, Tillinghast-Towers Perrin.

lution was covered, but courts were so liberal in their interpretation of an accident that insurers felt that they had to exclude the pollution peril nearly completely. Businesses with significant pollution exposures should look into purchasing specialized pollution policies.

Endorsements

Fewer endorsements are needed today than in the past because the commercial general liability form is designed to give coverage for medical payments, advertising and personal liability (e.g., libel and slander), contractual and host liquor liability (for those not in the alcoholic beverage business), limited worldwide coverage, and limited nonowned watercraft coverage and coverage for damage to premises rented to the insured. However, for an additional premium, insurance companies are willing to add endorsements that give even broader coverage. Examples of such endorsements are product recall insurance, pollution insurance, and full worldwide coverage. Two additional endorsements are described below.

Exclusion of Specific Accident(s), Products, Work, or Location(s). This endorsement to the CGL gives the insurance company the ability to exclude losses from a specific product or accident, a batch of a product, or a given location or locations of the insured. Through the use of this endorsement, the insured may be able to obtain an earlier retroactive date in a claims-made policy than if the specific items were not excluded. Also, the endorsement can be used when the insured wants to self-insure some products or locations but buy insurance on the others.

Vendor's Endorsement. Because of the importance of the product liability hazard, many retailers refuse to handle the goods of a manufacturer or a wholesaler unless they are provided with evidence that the distributor has protected them with product liability insurance. This is usually accomplished by naming the retailer in a **vendor's endorsement** as an additional insured on the wholesaler's or manufacturer's product liability policy. This endorsement covers not only claims based on breach of the manufacturer's warranty but also those claims based on the retailer's negligence or on the retailer's own warranty of the goods.

PROFESSIONAL PERSPECTIVES

Superfund

One of the reasons that the pollution exclusion is so stringent is the possible liability that exists for a business to become a potentially responsible party (PRP) under the 1980 Superfund law. Anyone who has contributed waste to a Superfund site is a PRP. Under this law, PRPs can be held liable for actions that were perfectly legal at the time. In addition, PRP's can be held liable for actions performed by others on a strict liability basis; that is, the owner of land can be held liable for the actions of the previous owner without regard to fault. Finally, the law imposes joint and several liability, meaning that a party contributing only a small portion of waste to a Superfund site may have to pay for the entire cost of cleaning up the site. Because this legislation is so powerful, it has led to a torrent of litigation in which different contributors to waste sites have sued each other, each trying to reduce their own share of cleanup costs. Litigation expenses have been enormous. Modest Superfund reform was passed in 2002, providing some protection for small businesses and developers of abandoned urban sites, but controversy over the law continues. The Superfund taxes imposed on industry expired after 1995, and the program is facing severe funding challenges, even as the number of contaminated Superfund sites continues to grow.

Source: Steven Brostoff, "Superfund Off Legislative Radar Screen," *National Underwriter, Property & Casualty/Risk and Benefits Management Edition*, March 25, 2002, 12–14.

Employment Practices Liability

Employment practices liability (EPL) is a recent development in terms of insurance coverage and is an issue that risk managers must be especially concerned about. Prior to the 1990s, little need existed for this coverage. However, with changes in employment law and the corporate restructuring that has occurred in recent years, EPL has become more important. This coverage protects businesses against lawsuits alleging sexual harassment, wrongful termination, and discrimination.

Examination of Table 11-2 reveals how the size of awards has changed. The median jury award for employment practices liability cases increased by more than 56 percent from 1996 to 2002. Clearly, this loss exposure is significant, and proper management procedures must be put in place to minimize losses. For example, in the case of sexual harassment, the worst action a supervisor can take is to ignore an employee's complaint about sexual harassment in the workplace. All parties' rights should be protected, but action should be taken.

To get an idea of the resources available to help insurers, attorneys, and others in evaluating the likely cost of a lawsuit, visit http://www.juryverdictresearch.com and view a sample report from the Case Evaluation Service.

Business Auto Coverage

If a company ever uses motor vehicles in the course of business, it needs separate business auto coverage. This protection is obtained through the use of the **Business Automobile Policy (BAP)**. Under the terms of this policy, coverage is provided for liability resulting from the use of automobiles as well as physical damage that occurs to a firm's automobiles. The term

TABLE 11-2	Employment Practices Liability Awards

Year	Award Median
1996	$128,000
1997	$140,858
1998	$150,845
1999	$146,550
2000	$182,500
2001	$175,000
2002	$200,000

Source: *Employment Practices Liability: Jury Award Trends and Statistics–2003 Edition*, Jury Verdict Research Series, Horsham, PA: LRP Publications, 2003.

automobile in the policy means a land motor vehicle, trailer, or semitrailer designed for travel on public roads. The definition does not include mobile equipment, which is insured under the CGL for liability exposures. Therefore, most business motor vehicles can be insured under a BAP. For instance, motorcycles, dump trucks, tractor-trailers, and buses may be insured. Insureds can choose from a variety of coverages that are indicated by a series of symbols, numbered from 1 to 9:

1. Any auto
2. Owned autos only
3. Owned private passenger autos only
4. Owned autos other than private passenger autos only
5. Owned autos subject to no-fault insurance
6. Owned autos subject to compulsory uninsured motorist laws
7. Specifically listed autos
8. Hired autos only
9. Nonowned autos only

By choosing only those coverages needed, an insured can minimize the firm's automobile insurance costs. For instance, a firm may cover private passenger autos under symbol 1 for liability but use symbol 4 for collision and loss other than collision. Such a firm would be fully covered for liability, but would be a self-insurer with respect to physical damage to a private passenger auto. High-cost vehicles such as dump trucks and tractor-trailers would be insured for physical damage.

Assume an insured desired to have liability coverage to apply to any vehicle that was driven by any employee or other persons acting on behalf of the corporation. Uninsured motorist protection and personal injury protection (PIP) were desired, as well as physical damage on owned private passenger cars. Given these requirements, the BAP's declarations page would be completed as shown in Figure 11-1.

By reading the symbols shown on the declarations page, one would know that the insured had bodily injury and property damage liability protection while driving any vehicle. However, physical damage (property insurance) would apply only to owned private passenger cars. If the insured desired to insure owned trucks as well as passenger vehicles, symbol 2 would be used for physical damage. With respect to no-fault coverage (PIP), protection is provided for all owned autos subject to the no-fault law. Uninsured motorist protection would apply

Figure 11-1   Use of Symbols in BAP Policy

NAMED INSURED ___Insurance, Inc.___ POLICY NO. ___1___

FORM OF BUSINESS:
☑ CORPORATION   ☐ INDIVIDUAL
☐ PARTNERSHIP   ☐ OTHER _____

ITEM TWO
SCHEDULE OF COVERAGES AND COVERED AUTOS

This policy provides only those coverages where a charge is shown in the premium column below. Each of these coverages will apply only to those "autos" shown as covered "autos." "Autos" are shown as covered "autos" for a particular coverage by the entry of one or more of the symbols from the COVERED AUTO Section of the Business Auto Coverage Form next to the name of the coverage.

COVERAGES	COVERED AUTOS (Entry of one or more of the symbols from the COVERED AUTOS Section of the Business Auto Coverage Form shows which autos are covered autos)	LIMIT THE MOST WE WILL PAY FOR ANY ONE ACCIDENT OR LOSS	PREMIUM
LIABILITY	1	$	
PERSONAL INJURY PROTECTION (or equivalent No-fault Coverage)	5	SEPARATELY STATED IN EACH PIP ENDORSEMENT MINUS $ Ded	
ADDED PERSONAL INJURY PROTECTION (or equivalent added No-fault Coverage)		SEPARATELY STATED IN EACH ADDED PIP ENDORSEMENT	
PROPERTY PROTECTION INSURANCE (Michigan only)		SEPARATELY STATED IN THE P.P.I. ENDORSEMENT MINUS $ Ded FOR EACH ACCIDENT	
AUTO MEDICAL PAYMENTS		$	
UNINSURED MOTORISTS	2	$	
UNDERINSURED MOTORISTS (When not included in Uninsured Motorists Coverage)		$	
PHYSICAL DAMAGE COMPREHENSIVE COVERAGE	3	ACTUAL CASH VALUE OR COST OF REPAIR, WHICHEVER IS LESS MINUS $ Ded. FOR EACH COVERED AUTO BUT NO DEDUCTIBLE APPLIES TO LOSS CAUSED BY FIRE OR LIGHTNING. See ITEM FOUR for hired or borrowed "autos."	
PHYSICAL DAMAGE SPECIFIED CAUSES OF LOSS COVERAGE		ACTUAL CASH VALUE OR COST OF REPAIR, WHICHEVER IS LESS MINUS $25 Ded. FOR EACH COVERED AUTO FOR LOSS CAUSED BY MISCHIEF OR VANDALISM. See ITEM FOUR for hired or borrowed "autos."	
PHYSICAL DAMAGE COLLISION COVERAGE	3	ACTUAL CASH VALUE OR COST OF REPAIR, WHICHEVER IS LESS MINUS $ Ded. FOR EACH COVERED AUTO. See ITEM FOUR for hired or borrowed "autos."	
PHYSICAL DAMAGE TOWING AND LABOR (Not available in California)		$ for each disablement of a private passenger "auto."	
		PREMIUM FOR ENDORSEMENTS	
		ESTIMATED TOTAL PREMIUM	

only to autos owned by the insured. As with physical damage, the insurer expects others to insure their own cars for this protection.

Risk Management Tips—Commercial Auto

The standard BAP gives only basic coverage. To provide broader coverage for employees, risk managers may want to consider three endorsements and/or adjustments:

1. *Employees as Insureds.* The standard BAP does not cover employees while driving their own cars on company business. Employees have to look to their own insurance for coverage. By adding the employees-as-insureds endorsement, employees driving their own cars for business purposes will be covered by the BAP.

2. *Delete the Fellow-Employee Exclusion.* Fellow-employee lawsuits are not covered by the BAP. By deleting the exclusion, employers are giving their employees better protection while driving vehicles on the company's behalf.

3. *Drive Other Car Coverage.* This provides broader coverage for employees who are assigned corporate cars. For instance, it would cover the employee while driving a friend's car on personal business.

Professional Liability Insurance

Because general liability policies usually contain exclusions for all claims arising out of error or mistake of a professional person in the performance of the duties of the profession, separate **professional liability** policies covering this important form of legal liability have been developed. These contracts are sometimes referred to as **malpractice policies** and **errors-and-omissions policies**, depending on the type of professional person utilizing them. General characteristics of professional liability contracts are analyzed first, and then some specific examples of these policies are discussed.

Professional versus Other Liability Contracts

Important differences between professional liability and other liability insurance contracts are as follows:

1. In professional liability insurance, the insurer often needs the permission of the insured to settle claims out of court by tendering sums in return for releases of liability by the plaintiff. The practice of out-of-court settlement is very common in other liability claims, but it is easy to see that to allow this in the case of professional liability would tend to damage the reputation of, for example, a doctor who appears to admit malpractice by settling claims in this manner. Therefore, even though it might be less expensive for the insurer to pay a claim regardless of its validity, the professional person has the right to insist that the insurer defend him or her in the courts.

2. The professional liability policy is usually written with only one major insuring clause, with no distinction made between bodily injury or property damage liability, and with no limit *per occurrence*. Usually a limit of liability *per claim* is stated. Thus, if the policy has a $500,000 limit of liability per claim and a $2 million aggregate limit and two damage suits arise out of a single error—for example, one by the patient and another by the patient's spouse—the limits of liability would be $1 million ($500,000 per claim). Other liability policies, on the other hand, invariably state the limits of liability in terms of an amount per accident or per occurrence.

3. The professional liability policy does not restrict its coverage to events that are "caused by accident" because usually the act that gives rise to a claim is deliberate. The event has an unintended result, but may not always be described as accidental. For example, a druggist may sell a medicine for the relief of itching. If this medicine causes a severe allergic reaction in the customer, certainly the result is unintended, but the act of selling the drug was deliberate. Medical malpractice insurance covers such a loss.

4. The professional liability policy usually does not exclude damage to property in the care, custody, or control of the insured, as do general liability contracts. Normally this type of loss will be at a minimum because, for the most part, the contracts cover personal injuries.

5. Product liability policies insure against claims arising out of a breach of warranty of the vendor regarding the goods. If a retailer says a product is good for a certain purpose and it turns out to be definitely wrong for this purpose, "an action lies" for which the policy must respond. In the professional liability policy, however, generally an exclusion exists for any agreement guaranteeing the results of any treatment. A suit by a patient, irritated because the treatment failed when the doctor promised it would succeed, is thus not covered. The policy responds to suits based on the physician's error, mistake, or malpractice in rendering the service, but not to any warranty for successful results; these cannot be guaranteed. Similar clauses are found in other types of professional liability contracts.

Medical Malpractice Insurance

One of the major professional liability contracts is the physicians', surgeons', and dentists' liability policy, commonly known as *medical malpractice insurance*. Such policies typically contain two insuring agreements, one providing coverage to the individual insured for their professional liability, and one providing coverage for the insured's association, corporation, or partnership. For example, if an insured physician's patient feels he has been injured due to the physician's negligence, the patient might sue both the physician as well as the professional corporation or partnership with which the physician is associated. Between the two insuring agreements, the entire lawsuit would be covered.

In addition to covering the insured for his or her own actions, the insuring agreement covers the insured's liability for the act of a nurse, assistant, technician, and so on, but does not cover the personal liability that might attach to such a person. The nurse, assistant, or technician is expected to provide professional coverage separately for their own liability. Often the insurer permits this coverage to be endorsed on the employer's policy.

One important aspect of the insuring agreement of this and most types of professional liability insurance is that it limits coverage to professional liability. General liability losses such as those covered by the CGL are not covered by medical malpractice insurance. If a patient slips on a wet doormat while entering the premises, the malpractice policy would not cover any damages because this is not part of a professional service. The professional thus needs general liability insurance as well as professional liability coverage.

In addition to limiting coverage to professional liability, physicians' professional liability insurance policies contain a number of exclusions. Common exclusions include liability arising out of criminal acts, discrimination, and pollution.

The medical malpractice area has had great volatility, occasionally reaching the crisis state. In the crisis years, rates increase at a very high rate. Then, after insurers and the medical community adjust to new court decisions and/or the higher rates, or state legislatures intervene with malpractice reform legislation, the market stabilizes. In Table 11-3, the mean and median medical malpractice awards are given for the years 1996, 1997, 1999, and 2001.

The data indicate that the magnitude of medical malpractice awards continues to increase dramatically faster than the rate of inflation. The median award rose 119 percent and the mean award 107 percent from 1996 to 2001. During the same period, the consumer price index increased only 11.4 percent.

Set your browser to http://www. schinnerer.com and then select the link for the industry of your choice to view a specialized professional liability insurance program available to that industry.

ETHICAL PERSPECTIVES

Protesting Medical Malpractice Premiums

Medical malpractice liability is one of the most contentious areas in the tort reform debate. Premiums for medical malpractice insurance have been rising at very rapid rates. Dr. Gregory Saracco, a general surgeon in West Virginia, borrowed money in 2002 to pay $73,000 in malpractice insurance premiums, and those premiums were going to rise to $100,000 in 2003. Dr. Saracco was one of a number of West Virginia surgeons who participated in a walkout to protest high medical malpractice insurance premiums. Almost all surgeries were cancelled during the walkout. At least one patient was transferred 90 miles away for an operation. Similar walkouts have occurred or were narrowly avoided in other states as well, including Pennsylvania, Mississippi, and New Jersey. Physicians in some states have threatened to move to other states where liability costs are lower. Efforts have been made at the federal level to limit noneconomic damages in malpractice cases to $250,000 in order to lower insurance costs, but so far no such legislation has made it through Congress. In the meantime, some states have passed their own reforms.

Source: Gavin McCormick, "West Virginia Doctors Protest Insurance Costs," *Sioux City Journal Online Edition*, January 3, 2003.

Insurance Agents' and Brokers' Errors-and-Omissions Liability

The agents' and brokers' errors-and-omissions policy insures the agent against all losses that the agent must pay because of negligent acts, errors, or omissions of employees in dealing with clientele. Although these contracts are not standardized, most insurers give the agent the option of protection against similar claims from the insurance companies represented. The policy pays only if legal liability on the part of the agent can be proved and does not respond to payments made to customers voluntarily in order to preserve goodwill. Like other professional liability contracts, errors-and-omissions insurance covers only professional mistakes.

To collect, the agent generally need only show that the claim was brought during the policy term, regardless of when the professional mistake occurred. However, for the protection of the agent, the contract typically requires that if the insurer refuses to renew, the coverage is extended for one year against claims arising from mistakes occurring during the policy term. It might happen, for example, that an agent realized on December 28 that an error was committed for which the agent is liable, there having occurred a loss left uninsured because of the agent's mistake. The professional liability insurer, learning of this, might refuse to

TABLE 11-3	Medical Malpractice Awards	
Year	Mean ($)	Median ($)
1996	1,884,633	457,500
1997	1,930,540	500,000
1999	3,288,228	700,000
2001	3,902,058	1,000,000

Source: *2002 Current Award Trends in Personal Injury*, Jury Verdict Research Series, Horsham, PA: LRP Publications, 2002.

renew the errors-and-omissions policy in the knowledge that a claim would not be submitted before the expiration of the policy on December 31. The provision granting the extension of coverage on such claims thus protects the agent from being unjustly denied recovery on the errors-and-omissions contract.

Other Professional Liability Insurance

In addition to doctors and insurance agents and brokers, a number of other professionals can obtain insurance protection for their professional liability exposures. Just a few will be mentioned here. Lawyers, for example, purchase attorneys' professional liability insurance to cover lawsuits alleging negligent provision of services. Professional liability policies exist for architects and engineers as well. If an architect negligently designs a building, and the building collapses after being built, the architect's professional liability policy would cover claims for the resulting bodily injuries and property damage. Accountants' professional liability insurance would protect accountants from suits by clients or others alleging financial loss due an accountant's negligent audit, tax, or other professional services.

Commercial Umbrella

To purchase liability limits large enough to pay for catastrophic losses, companies purchase **commercial umbrella** policies. These policies, or combinations of them, are used to give limits of liability of $100 million or more. Commercial umbrella liability policies are not uniform, and a good deal of variation of policy wording among insurers exists. Thus the following discussion provides only an overview of the topic.

The commercial umbrella insurer will require primary insurance in the form of a general liability policy (probably the CGL), a business auto policy, workers' compensation and employer's liability, and insurance for any owned watercraft. Often the commercial umbrella will not cover owned aircraft liability even if there is primary insurance. For the most part, the insured must have $500,000 to $1 million limits of primary coverage.

Coverage under the umbrella is quite broad. Property in the insured's care, custody, and control may be covered; worldwide products coverage is available; and employer's liability and liquor liability are insured. In fact, umbrellas are frequently written with few exclusions, and endorsements are used to limit coverage. This approach is the opposite of the one used in primary insurance policies, where endorsements usually broaden coverage.

To obtain high limits of liability coverage, insureds can also buy excess umbrella policies. These policies pay only after the underlying umbrella pays, and the excess umbrella policy usually "follows form"; that is, it provides coverage on conditions identical to those of the underlying layers of coverage.

A Profile of a Catastrophic Liability Program

In this example, illustrated in Figure 11-2, the insured has $1 million of primary coverage in the form of a CGL with a $1 million per-occurrence limit. After that policy, an umbrella policy is in effect that will pay an additional $9 million. Note that the umbrella not only increases the amount of coverage but also expands coverage. The two areas at the bottom of Figure 11-2 denoting $50,000 represent the broader coverage of the umbrella, which will provide coverage for losses not covered by the CGL. Such losses are subject to a $50,000 deductible.

On top of the umbrella are excess umbrellas of $20 million, $30 million, and $50 million. These policies often state they will follow the form of the primary umbrella. Whatever the primary umbrella covers, they will also cover. In this case, the excess umbrellas provide $100 million of additional coverage. The insured has $110 million of protection. It is not unusual for a large corporation to have multiple layers of coverage.

FIGURE 11-2   Structure of Layered Liability Program

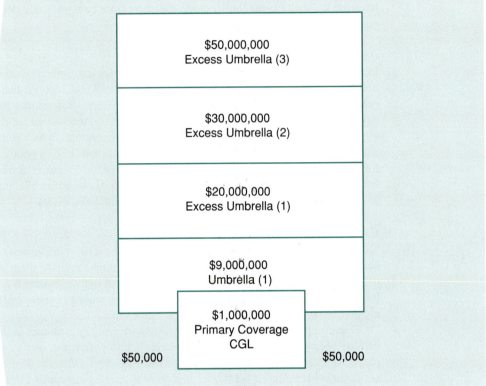

$50,000,000
Excess Umbrella (3)

$30,000,000
Excess Umbrella (2)

$20,000,000
Excess Umbrella (1)

$9,000,000
Umbrella (1)

$1,000,000
Primary Coverage
CGL

$50,000 $50,000

SUMMARY

1. All liability contracts have certain elements in common. The insuring agreements are fairly well standardized. The insurer has the right and duty to defend covered claims and pay resulting judgments. Liability contracts vary in the definition of who is insured. Most liability contracts guarantee that the insurer will bear the cost of defense in addition to paying any judgments up to the limits of liability.

2. Common exclusions peculiar to liability contracts include (a) nonbusiness activities, in the case of business liability policies, and business activities, in the case of nonbusiness liability contracts; and (b) damage to property in the care, custody, and control of the insured. Because of its inherent ambiguity, the latter exclusion has resulted in much litigation.

3. Most business liability insurance is now written on the commercial general liability (CGL) form. One can insure general, products, and completed operations liability; personal injury; advertising liability; medical payments; and liability for dam-

age to premises rented to the insured in this contract. The form has two options for events that "trigger" coverage: claims-made and occurrence. Claims-made coverage is generally not as desirable as occurrence coverage for the insured.

4. Products and completed operations liability insurance, which may be written with the CGL, is distinguished from general liability insurance in several ways, the major distinctions being that the occurrence giving rise to the claim must take place away from the main premises of the business and must arise out of a faulty product sold or a service rendered by the insured after the insured has completed work. Products liability coverage never covers loss to the product itself, but only damage caused by the faulty product.

5. Professional liability (malpractice) insurance covering liability for claims arising from professional errors is distinguished from other liability contracts in a number of ways. Generally, professional liability contracts do not permit out-of-court settlements without the permission of the

insured. They can be issued on a per-claim basis instead of a per-accident basis, and they do not restrict their coverage to accidental occurrences. Professional liability policies will neither cover dishonest or criminal acts nor insure any claim arising out of any guarantee that professional services rendered will accomplish a specified result.

internet*exercises*

1. Visit http://www.iii.org/individuals/ business/optional/professionalliability/ and read about why someone might need professional liability insurance. After reading, list five professions other than those discussed in this chapter who you feel might need professional liability insurance.

2. Set your browser to http://www.coverex.com/ business_liability.asp and look at the questions a business must answer to receive a business liability insurance proposal from this company. For each question, why do you think the information is being requested? Are there any questions you feel are irrelevant? What questions would you add?

QUESTIONS FOR REVIEW AND DISCUSSION

1. Define *legal liability insurance*.
2. Identify the exclusions that are almost universal to liability insurance contracts.
3. Explain the difference between claims-made and occurrence coverage.
4. What are the coverages provided by the commercial general liability policy?
5. What are the differences between professional liability insurance and other liability insurance policies?
6. Why do businesses purchase commercial umbrella policies, and what are the general characteristics of such policies?
7. Do you feel that the claims-made policy with the supplemental tail endorsement is as good as the occurrence policy? Explain your answer.
8. What effect, if any, do you think aggregate limits in the CGL have on the level of liability limits purchased by risk managers? Explain your answer.
9. Mr. Wood purchases a furnace to install in a mobile home that he sells to Ms. Hampson. Mr. Wood is in the business of selling mobile homes. If the furnace explodes and Ms. Hampson brings suit against Mr. Wood, how would his CGL respond, considering that he did not manufacture the furnace?
10. A department store has a CGL policy with product liability coverage. A woman came into the store to look at an automatic washer. After she purchased the washer, she asked to see once again how the bleach dispenser operated. During the demonstration of the machine, a metal strap snapped out and bruised her hand. Medical attention was necessary, and a claim for damages resulted.
   a. Under which portion, if any, of the CGL policy would this claim be paid if negligence is found?
   b. How, if at all, would your answer change if the accident occurred after the washer had been delivered to the home of the buyer?
11. In *Meiser v Aetna Casualty & Surety Co.*, 98 N.W. (2d) 919, the insured, a plastering subcontractor, spilled plaster on some expensive windows. In attempting to remove the plaster at the request of the owner, the windows were damaged. The plasterer was sued by the owner of the windows, and the liability insurer under the CGL denied liability on the grounds that the windows were "in his care, custody, and control" and were therefore excluded from coverage. Decide this case, stating your reasons.
12. In *Marks v Minnesota Mining and Manufacturing Co.*, San Francisco, County Superior Court #78976, November 1983, a 34-year-old housewife underwent insertion of silicone breast implants manufactured by the defendant, a division of 3M Corporation. On three occasions, the implants spontaneously ruptured. The defendant disclaimed liability.
   a. Do you think the defendant should be liable? Explain your answer.
   b. What type of business liability coverage would the defendant need for insurance protection? Explain.

chapter 12

For many risk managers the single largest expense is the cost of injuries to employees. These injuries must be compensated because of state and federal laws requiring employers to pay for work-related injuries. These laws are generally called workers' compensation laws.

In terms of total dollars (premiums and self-retained losses) managed by risk managers, workers' compensation is the largest loss exposure. On an annual basis, more than $60 billion is spent on workers' compensation. This loss exposure is characterized by fairly high frequency but less severity. Also, for larger firms, there are many separate loss exposures (their employees). Given this environment, workers' compensation losses present an excellent example of an exposure that can be managed with other techniques than just insurance. Risk managers can use a combination of loss assumption, prevention, avoidance, and transfer to manage this exposure.

Unlike many lines of insurance, workers' compensation is experience rated, and higher losses mean automatic rate increases. Thus, the risk manager has much greater incentive to manage losses. Workers must be protected from accidents, and when accidents do occur, steps must be taken to provide good treatment in a timely manner.

Workers' Compensation and Alternative Risk Financing

CHAPTER OBJECTIVES

After studying this chapter, you should be able to

1. State the different alternatives available to fund workers' compensation losses and the relative importance of each alternative.
2. Describe how workers' compensation insurance developed and identify recent trends in the field.
3. List coverages provided in a workers' compensation policy.
4. Calculate retrospective insurance premiums.
5. Understand how a retrospective insurance plan can be used as an alternative to self-insuring workers' compensation.
6. Determine the cash flow benefits of self-insuring workers' compensation.
7. Identify all the functions a self-insurer must perform.
8. Understand captive insurance companies and how risk managers can use them.

WORKERS' COMPENSATION INSURANCE

Workers' compensation insurance covers the loss of income and the medical and rehabilitation expenses that result from work-related accidents and occupational disease. It is the single largest line of commercial insurance, with premium volume of $29 billion in 2002 according to the Insurance Information Institute. During the 1970s, workers' compensation premium growth was very high, but it slowed during the 1980s. Part of this reduction was due to the deep recession in 1982 that reduced the number of persons employed and led to intense price competition among insurers. However, the growth increased for the rest of the 1980s. In the early 1990s, this line suffered significant losses. By the mid-1990s high investment returns had returned this line to profitability and intense price competition returned. However, declining investment returns and skyrocketing loss costs resulted in deteriorating profits. Investment returns in 2002 were only 12 percent of premiums compared to 20 percent in 1997. Several years of increased pricing resulted in some improvement in profitability in 2002.

Workers' compensation developed in the latter half of the 1800s in Europe and in the early 1900s in the United States because of hardships placed on workers by common law. Under common law it was difficult for workers to collect from employers for job-related injuries. Under workers' compensation, a worker receives a guarantee of compensation, and the employer is protected from employees seeking damages for work-related injuries.

MAJOR REFORM

Because of various weaknesses observed in workers' compensation, The National Commission on State Workmen's Compensation Laws was created under the authority of the Occupational Safety and Health Act of 1970 to determine the extent to which state laws provided adequate, prompt, and equitable compensation to injured workers. About 40 studies were commissioned and later published in three volumes.[1] In general, the studies raised doubts about the effectiveness of workers' compensation as it operated in the United States at the time the studies were made.

Since the studies were published and the 1972 final report of the commission rendered, state legislatures have passed numerous reforms to comply with some 19 of its "essential" recommendations. These recommendations include objectives calling for (1) full coverage for medical care and rehabilitation, (2) adequate income replacement, (3) coverage of all workers, (4) cost-of-living adjustments, and (5) improved data systems.[2] Because of the commission's recommendations, tremendous change has occurred. By 1979 all states had unlimited medical care, and coverage was mandatory in 50 jurisdictions.

Insurance Methods

There are three methods by which an employer can provide employees with the coverage required by law:

1. Purchase a workers' compensation and employers' liability policy from a private commercial insurer.
2. Purchase insurance through a state fund or a federal agency set up for this purpose.
3. Self-insure.

All states require selection of one of these methods by employers subject to the law.

---

1 *National Commission of State Workmen's Compensation Laws*: vol. I, *Principles of Workmen's Compensation*; vol. II, *Income Maintenance Objective*; vol. III, *The Safety Objective* (Washington, D.C.: U.S. Government Printing Office, 1973).
2 *Ibid.*

PROFESSIONAL PERSPECTIVES

Police Protection

A Berkeley, California, police officer found that he was not entitled to workers' compensation benefits for an injury arising out of an off-duty basketball game, even though he was required by the department to keep himself in good physical condition.

The officer injured his knee while playing basketball during his lunch break. He argued that not only was he supposed to be in top condition but, because he was a member of a hostage negotiating team, he also was supposed to keep himself in even better shape than other able-bodied police officers.

However, a California appellate court ruled that in a case such as this, where the employer expects employees to be in top physical condition, it was reasonable to allow the employer to limit its liability for workers' compensation to injuries sustained in designated and preapproved athletic activities. To hold otherwise would render the employer liable for any injury received in any recreational or athletic activity.

Source: *Taylor v WCAB*, California Court of Appeals, quoted in Anonymous, "Legal Briefs: Recreational Injury Not Compensable," *Business Insurance*, May 22, 1989, 50.

Private Insurance

The standard workers' compensation and employers' liability policy has two major insuring agreements: (1) Coverage A, to pay all claims required under the workers' compensation law in the state where the injury occurred, including occupational disease benefits, penalties assessable to the employer under law, and other obligations; and (2) Coverage B, to defend all employee suits against the employer and pay any judgment resulting from these suits. Coverage B is separate and distinct from Coverage A. Although it was not anticipated that there would be many employee suits, such claims are surprisingly frequent because methods are constantly being found to bring an action against the employer in spite of the intention of the statutes to discourage such suits. Under Coverage B, there is a separate limit for bodily injury by accident or by disease. Coverage B is similar to that given in general liability policies. There is no specific limitation for Coverage A; any limits are outlined by the state compensation law.

While the private insurance method involves a contract between the employer and the insurer, the insurer deals directly with the employee and is primarily responsible to the employee for benefits. Thus, even if the employer should go out of business, the injured employee's security is not jeopardized.

State Funds and Federal Agencies

In 20 states, an employer has the choice of using a private insurer or a state fund as the insurer of workers' compensation.[3] In 5 states, the employer does not have this choice but must insure in an exclusive state fund or, in 3 of those states, may self-insure.[4] Five of the compul-

---

3 Arizona, California, Colorado, Idaho, Kentucky, Louisiana, Maine, Maryland, Minnesota, Missouri, Montana, Nevada, New Mexico, New York, Oklahoma, Oregon, Pennsylvania, Rhode Island, Texas, and Utah. South Carolina maintains a competitive state fund for counties and municipalities.

4 North Dakota, Ohio, Washington, West Virginia, and Wyoming. In Ohio, Washington, and West Virginia, qualifying employers can elect to self-insure.

PROFESSIONAL PERSPECTIVES

Having Your Cake and Eating It, Too

An alternative to self-insurance that is becoming more popular is the large deductible plan. When this approach is used, the insured can receive all the benefits of insurance: (1) the insurer is licensed in each state in which the insured operates, (2) the premium paid to the insurer is tax deductible, (3) administrative functions are performed by the insurer, and (4) the insured is protected against catastrophic loss. On the other hand, many of the benefits of self-insurance are obtained. The insurance premium is substantially reduced because deductibles of $1 million are not uncommon. This lower premium means premium taxes are reduced, as are residual market assessments. The strong incentive for loss prevention still exists because much of the loss exposure—and much of the cash flow benefits of self-insurance—are retained.

sory state funds were established during the period 1913–1915, when compensation laws were new and the success of private insurers in handling the business was uncertain. Most of the Canadian provinces established exclusive state funds.

In addition to state funds, federal agencies provide for workers' compensation coverage. In 1969, the federal government created an agency to provide coverage for coal miners afflicted with black lung disease. Since 1908 the federal government has operated a workers' compensation system for its civilian employees.

Self-Insurance

In most states, under specified conditions, an employer is permitted to self-insure the workers' compensation coverage.[5] Self-insurance is generally not permitted in Canada. Self-insurers are generally large concerns with adequate diversification of risks and financial resources that enable them to qualify under the law. The use of self-insurance and large loss retention plans has been rising for many years.

Evaluation of Insurance Methods

Data from the National Academy of Social Insurance show that private insurers incurred 55 percent, self-insurers 23 percent, and federal and state funds 22 percent of the cost of workers' compensation in 2001. It seems clear that private insurers are preferred by most employers in states where they are permitted to operate. Some of the major reasons for this are as follows:

1. Private insurers offer the employer an opportunity to insure in one contract all the liability likely for damages arising from work-connected injuries, whether these damages stem from employee suits, statutory benefit requirements, or other sources.

2. Private insurers offer more certainty in handling out-of-state risks. Most compensation laws are extraterritorial, and there are many complexities to consider in making sure of coverage if the employer has widespread interests. Most state funds do not automatically cover such risks.

3. While the expenses of state funds—at least exclusive state funds—are somewhat lower than those of private insurers, this difference is not as great as rough comparisons often lead one to believe. After adjustment for differences in the quantity and the quality of

---

5   Self-insurers usually must post a financial bond.

ETHICAL PERSPECTIVES

Today's Hazardous Duty

An outside sales representative for a gas company was shot to death in the driveway of a vacant home during regular working hours and within the service jurisdiction of his company. The body was found a short distance from the company car, and inches from his body were tools and documents used by the worker in his employment. His widow and minor dependents were awarded workers' compensation benefits; the employer appealed.

The appellate court agreed with the lower court that, under these circumstances, a presumption was raised that the salesman's death arose out of and in the course of his employment.

Source: *Suburban Propane Gas Co. v Deschamps*, Court of Appeals of South Carolina, 1989, described in Anonymous, "Legal Briefs: S. C. Court Finds Homicide Compensable," *Business Insurance*, April 16, 1990, 25.

services rendered, many would argue that the supposed cost advantage of exclusive state funds is of insufficient size to warrant giving up the convenience and certainty involved in the private contract, including the ready availability of agents who provide services not usually supplied by the state fund.

4. Self-insurance has the handicap that it is necessary for the insured to enter into the insurance business, which is essentially unrelated to the insured's main operations. Also, contributions to a self-insurance fund are often not tax deductible, a factor that may add materially to the cost and risk involved in self-insurance.

5. Experience rating and retrospective rate plans (discussed later in this chapter) enable the large firm to use a private insurer's facilities in transferring as much or as little of the risk as is desired at a very modest cost.

Major Features of State Laws

The provisions of workers' compensation laws are subject to constant change, but a pattern exists even though details of the provisions may vary with each meeting of the state legislature. The features necessary for a general understanding of the coverage provided by these laws are described in the following paragraphs.

Employment Covered

Compensation laws do not cover all workers. For example, domestic labor and farm labor are often excluded. Employers with only a few employees are excluded under compulsory laws. Because of various exclusions, about 9 out of 10 workers are covered. One result of this condition is that liability suits are necessary if an excluded worker is to recover anything, even though a basic purpose of compensation legislation was to eliminate this condition as a prerequisite for employee recoveries. It is the small employer who is excluded from compensation laws and who is most likely to be the object of such suits. This smallness often means that either (1) a successful suit will bankrupt the employer or (2) if the employer is more or less judgment-proof, the injured worker will recover nothing.

Income Provisions

Compensation laws recognize four types of disability for which income benefits may be paid. These are permanent and temporary total disability and permanent and temporary partial disability. The laws generally limit payments by specifying the maximum duration of benefits and the maximum weekly and aggregate amounts payable.

PROFESSIONAL PERSPECTIVES

Horseplay at Work

A Brattleboro, Vermont, Rentavision manager sustained an eye injury after he and another co-worker began to shoot staples at one another during a lull between customers.

The manager argued that such horseplay was to be anticipated by employers and that workers' compensation benefits should be paid. The Commissioner agreed and awarded benefits.

However, the Supreme Court of Vermont ruled that the accident was unrelated to any legitimate use of the staplers at the time, indicating there was no commingling of the horseplay and work duties. Thus, the court ruled that the accident occurred during a substantial deviation from work duties. The compensation award was reversed.

Source: *Clodgo v Rentavision Inc.*, Supreme Court of Vermont, 1997, quoted in Stiegler, Mayo H., "Stapler-Shooter's Injury Not Compensable: Court," *Business Insurance*, April 20, 1998, 28.

For permanent total disability benefits, most states permit lifetime payments to the injured worker who is unable to perform the duties of any suitable occupation. In the remaining states, a typical limitation is between 400 and 500 weeks of payments, and there is often a limitation on the aggregate amount payable.

There is a common limitation that income benefits cannot exceed about two-thirds of the worker's average weekly wage or some dollar amount. A few states make extra allowances for dependents. Because average weekly wages have risen faster than legislative adjustments, the limiting factor is usually the dollar maximum.

Weekly benefits for temporary total disability are usually the same as for permanent total disability, except that often there is a lower maximum aggregate limitation and a shorter time duration for such payments.

In addition to income benefits, most workers' compensation laws specify that lump sums may be paid to a worker as **liquidating damages** for a disability, such as the loss of a leg or an eye, that is permanent but does not totally incapacitate the worker. The worker may usually draw income benefits during the time that the permanent partial disability prevents the worker from doing anything, and then the worker may receive a lump sum that varies with the seriousness of the injury.

Survivor Benefits

In the case of fatal injuries, the widow or widower and children of the worker are entitled to funeral and income benefits, subject to various limitations. The maximum benefits to the widow or widower alone are generally less than they would have been to the disabled worker, but if the survivor has children, these benefits are comparable to what the worker would have received for permanent total disability. Based on data from the Insurance Information Institute, fatalities in workers' compensation have been relatively stable at around 6,000 deaths per year for the past 10 years. However, in 2001 workers' compensation fatalities were 8,786. Of this total, 2,886 fatalities resulted from the terrorist attacks of September 11. Highway crashes represent the single largest cause of workplace deaths accounting for one-fourth of all fatalities in workers' compensation.

Medical Benefits

Most workers' compensation laws provide relatively complete medical services to an injured worker, including allowances for certain occupational diseases. In all jurisdictions unlimited medical care is provided for accidental work injuries, and broad coverage for occupational disease is provided.

Rehabilitation Benefits

Benefits for rehabilitation, both physical and occupational, are provided by most states, but it is generally recognized that the quantity and quality of these services are subject to wide variation. Over the years insurers and other service providers have become leaders in developing and implementing rehabilitation programs, both physical and vocational, for injured workers. Part of these efforts may include light-duty or modified-duty programs that are intended to reintroduce the worker to the workplace following an industrial injury. Also, the Federal Vocational Rehabilitation Act includes federal funds to aid states in vocational rehabilitation of individuals who are injured in the workplace.

netlink

To learn more about workers' compensation, visit the Insurance Information Institute's site at http://www.iii.org/media/ hottopics/. Scroll down and click on "Workers' Compensation."

Benefits

In terms of benefits, there is great variability between the states. From Table 12-1, one can see that Georgia has low weekly benefits, $400, and Iowa has the highest among all states, at $1,133. For states that schedule benefits for permanent partial losses, Pennsylvania offers the highest award for a loss of a hand ($204,685 plus temporary disability benefits), Alabama the lowest ($37,400). Among the states only New Jersey and Texas have elective laws. Because of this variability of benefits, the cost per worker varies greatly and some states are at a competitive cost disadvantage if their benefits are significantly greater than other states.

Besides the various state plans, a Federal Employees Compensation plan covers federal employees. It has the highest benefit of any plan. The maximum weekly benefit is $1,596, and payment for a loss of a hand is $364,672.

Experience Rating

Experience rating plans are widely used in workers' compensation insurance. The general theory is that an employer has some control over the loss ratio and is entitled to a credit for a good loss record, or should pay a higher rate if the loss record is poorer than average.

In the experience rating plan adopted by private insurers and administered by the National Council on Compensation Insurance, a national rate-making agency, each employer must have some minimum premium, such as $5,000, that would be payable if standard manual rates were charged. The details of the plan are very complex, but the general procedure is to determine, for each occupational class, some expected loss ratio against which the insured's actual loss ratio is compared. If the actual loss ratio is 90 percent of the expected loss ratio, the insured's rate for the coming year is 90 percent of the manual rate. If the actual loss ratio is 130 percent of the expected loss ratio, the insured must pay 130 percent of the manual rate during the coming year.

Under experience rating plans, not all losses suffered by an insured are counted. The plan uses a stabilizing factor so that unusually large losses cannot operate to increase the small employer's rate unreasonably. However, for the large employer, the employer's loss experience becomes more important as its expected losses become greater.

Medium-sized and small employers receive a smaller credit than they would receive if they were self-rated in years in which losses are low. In those years following a period of high losses, the medium-sized and small employers pay a penalty that is not as large as it would

TABLE 12-1   State Workers' Compensation Provisions

State	Compulsory Law?	Maximum Weekly Benefits ($)	Self-Insurance Allowed?	Loss of a Hand ($)	Medical Care
Alabama	Yes	569	Yes	37,400	UL
California	Yes	602	Yes	64,056	UL
Connecticut	Yes	911	Yes	115,416	UL
Florida	Yes	608	Yes	No Schedule **	UL
Georgia	Yes	400	Yes	64,000	UL
Illinois	Yes	1,012	Yes	190,838	UL
Indiana	Yes	588	Yes	62,500 *	UL
Iowa	Yes	1,133	Yes	192,660	UL
Michigan	Yes	653	Yes	140,395 **	UL
New Jersey	Elective	638	Yes	92,365	UL
New York	Yes	400	Yes	97,600 *	UL
North Carolina	Yes	674	Yes	134,800	UL
Ohio	Yes	644	Yes	112,700	UL
Pennsylvania	Yes	675	Yes	204,685 *	UL
Texas	Elective	537	Yes	No Schedule	UL
Virginia	Yes	691	Yes	102,150	UL
Washington	Yes	711	Yes	80,523	UL
Wisconsin	Yes	669	Yes	88,800	UL
Federal Employees	Yes	1,596	N/A	364,672	UL Subject to fee schedule

UL = Unlimited

* In addition to temporary disability payments.

** Temporary disability payments are deducted from the scheduled amount.

Source: *2003 Analysis of Workers' Compensation Laws*, U.S. Chamber of Commerce, Washington, D.C.: Charts I, VI, and VII. (The 2003 Analysis of Workers' Compensation Laws contains 2002 information, but is updated with changes listed on the Chamber's Web site in 2003.)

be if they were self-rated. Over a period of years, if the loss experience in a given category of industry is consistently bad, the manual rate and expected losses for that class will be adjusted so that in any given period a certain rating class of risks will tend to bear its total loss burden. But experience rating deals with rate adjustments for individual insureds within a given class on a year-to-year basis.

Experience rating in workers' compensation gives employers an incentive to do whatever is within their control to prevent accidents, a very desirable objective of any rating system. It rewards the safety efforts of employers by the test of "What effect did it have?" and not "What effect should it have had?" as is the practice in fire insurance. Employers may spend a great deal of money on safety efforts, but if these efforts fail, no rate credit will be forthcoming.

ETHICAL PERSPECTIVES

The Perils of Not Following Directions

Brian Andrews was employed as a plumber's helper and was told not to engage in heavy lifting after he disclosed a previous back injury. However, Andrews injured his back while trying to carry a 200-pound espresso machine. He filed for workers' compensation. A referee awarded him benefits, but the Compensation Board reversed, finding the injury outside the scope of employment.

The Supreme Court of Oregon reversed the Compensation Board saying that denying compensation for injuries sustained as a result of a worker's failure to follow directions is not compatible with the Workers' Compensation Act. The court argued that the deciding issue was whether the activity was within the boundaries of his ultimate work.

Source: *Andrew v Tektronix Inc.*, Supreme Court of Oregon, 1996, quoted in Stiegler, Mayo H., "Heavy Lifting Against Orders Does Not Preclude Comp," *Business Insurance*, April 7, 1997, 19.

Retrospective Rating

In workers' compensation insurance, experience rating is applied automatically, but **retrospective rating** is entirely a voluntary agreement between the insured and the insurer. If the employer's payroll is such that a standard premium of $1,000 or more is incurred, it is considered that the firm is large enough to develop experience that is partially credible. (A **standard premium** is defined as what the employer would have paid at manual rates after adjustment for experience rating but before any adjustment for retrospective rating.) In practice, an employer likely to use retrospective rating is generally considerably larger than this. Even one accident could easily cause a loss in excess of $1,000. This might cause a substantial increase in the employer's retrospective premium, depending on the nature of the plan selected.

There are various plans of retrospective rating, and the employer must choose one. Assuming that the employer is large enough and that both parties are agreeable to retrospective rating, which plan should the employer use? Essentially, this question reduces to one of how much risk the employer is willing to assume, that is, how great a loss the employer is willing to accept if the experience turns out to be bad, in return for a reduced premium if the experience is good.

The basic **retrospective rating formula** is given by the expression

$$R = [BP + (L)(LCF)]TM$$

where R = retrospective premium payable for the year in question

BP = a **basic premium** (in dollars) designed to cover fixed costs of the insurer in handling the business

L = losses (in dollars) actually suffered by the employer

LCF = **loss conversion factor**, a multiplying factor designed to cover the variable costs of the insurer (such as claim adjustment expenses)

TM = **tax multiplier**, a factor designed to reflect the premium tax levied by the state on the insurer's business[6]

---

6   There are other elements in retrospective rating formulas, such as adjustments for individual loss limitations, but for simplicity they will be ignored in the present discussion.

The basic premium declines as the size of the employer increases, and it differs with the type of plan used. The loss conversion factor is a constant percentage, as is the tax multiplier, regardless of the size of the employer. The formula is subject to the operation of certain minimums and maximums, both of which decline as the size of the employer increases, except for the plan in which the maximum amount paid by the employer is the standard premium.

The operation of the formula is such that the larger the employer, the less risk is associated with the use of retrospective rating. (The maximum and minimum premiums decline.) Yet a relatively small employer who is accepted for retrospective rating has an opportunity to lower the premium if the losses can be kept within bounds and still obtain protection against paying more than would be the case in the absence of the retrospective plan.

RISK MANAGEMENT AND WORKERS' COMPENSATION

Workers' compensation is one of the most frequently self-insured coverages in the risk management area. It is characterized by relatively high-frequency and low-severity losses. In recent years, the motivation to self-insure a portion or all of this exposure has increased because of rapidly rising premium levels. When premiums are high, the cash flow benefits of self-insurance are greater, and self-insurance becomes more attractive.

Factors Favoring Self-Insurance

The basic factors that lead a firm to self-insure revolve around lower costs. These cost savings take the form of lower administrative expenses, cash flow benefits, and a more claims-conscious management.

Lower Administrative Expenses

When a firm establishes a self-insured workers' compensation program, it eliminates most of the premium paid to an insurer. (Some premium is still paid to purchase excess insurance.) In the standard premium, there is a loading (charge) for acquisition costs. These costs include the agent's commission, as well as the cost of inspection and underwriting. In addition, there is the insurer's profit. However, in recent years workers' compensation has been generating underwriting losses.

Cash Flow Benefits

Besides cost savings, the self-insurer also receives substantial cash flow benefits. Actually, the cash flow benefits are probably greater than the cost savings aspect of self-insuring workers' compensation.

Under a traditional insured plan, the insured pays the premium, and at some later date the insurer pays all the claims. In the aggregate, this arrangement provides the insurance company with a large amount of money that can be invested in income-producing securities until the claims are paid. As the insured pays a premium each year, the insurer can always have funds invested in income-producing securities. When a firm self-insures, it holds the money until the claims are paid. As it takes several years (five or more) to pay all the claims from a given year's loss experience, the self-insurer has the use of some of the funds for a fairly long time. Of course, the process is repeated from one year to the next, so there is a perpetual sum of money available for investment in securities or in the self-insured's own operations. The cash flow benefits can be a significant portion of the original premium. If a firm held an amount equal to half a given year's premium for three years at 12 percent interest, it would earn an amount equal to 20 percent of the original premium:

$$0.5p \times [(1.12)^3 - 1] = 0.20p \quad (p = \text{premium})$$

Claims-Conscious Management

Another benefit of self-insurance is that management often becomes more claims conscious when it is paying directly for workers' compensation losses. When insurers are paying the claims, only an indirect effect is seen by operating managers. They pay their insurance premiums, losses occur, and in two or three years premiums may be increased. When firms self-insure, they pay the claims as they occur. There is little or no delay in increased costs when accident rates start to increase. Managers tend to react to these increased costs and become more loss conscious. As a consequence, workers' compensation losses often decline when a firm initiates a self-insurance program.

Factors against Self-Insurance

Self-insurance is not desirable for many firms. Factors that can influence the self-insurance decision include the size of the firm, stability of the workforce, tax consequences, availability of services, and rate of benefit increases.

Size of Firm

A company must be financially capable of retaining self-insured losses. If it cannot absorb those losses, it should not self-insure. Also, it must have a large enough exposure so that it can predict much of its losses. Unless it has numerous losses, it will have a difficult time predicting future experience.

Generally, a firm with an annual premium of less than $250,000 will not self-insure. However, because benefit levels and insurance market conditions vary among the states, a firm might self-insure in one state when its premium volume is $300,000 and purchase insurance in another state when its premium volume is $400,000.

Stability of Workforce

When one considers the stability of a firm's workforce, one is really considering how much turnover the firm has and how rapidly it is expanding. Newly employed people, as well as younger employees, have higher accident rates than more mature workers, and new plants tend to have higher accident rates than established ones. If a firm is planning to open a new manufacturing plant, it may wish to postpone starting a self-insurance program until the new workers are trained and have become accustomed to their new work environment. This adjustment period is often 12 to 24 months.

Likewise, if major plant closings are to occur, self-insurance may be avoided. Often when a firm closes a plant, a much greater number of employees file claims. When one General Motors plant was closed, more than 50 percent of the employees filed workers' compensation claims.

Tax Consequences

An often-stated advantage of an insured workers' compensation program is that premiums are tax deductible when paid. Under a self-insured program, one cannot take a tax deduction until the funds are actually paid. For instance, a worker may become disabled, and the self-insurer knows it has a liability over the expected life of the employee of $700,000. However, no tax deduction is allowed for this liability. Only as dollars are paid to the employee can deductions be made. This rule discourages self-insurers from establishing loss reserves because any reserve would have to be funded with after-tax dollars.

Availability of Services

When a firm decides to self-insure, it must provide or purchase services that were formerly provided by the insurance company. These services include loss control activities, claims adjusting, data processing, and program administration. Today, a firm can usually buy these services from companies that specialize in such activities. Even insurance companies will provide these services on an "unbundled" basis. That is, as a service separate from the insurance coverage. However, the purchase of these services adds to the cost of self-insurance and may lead to a greater administrative burden on the risk manager than if the insurance coverage were purchased. Further, the firm has to monitor the quality of services provided by the third-party vendor, which adds to the cost of this option. In addition to the administrative burden, the desired services may not be available or may be available only at an unattractive price. In such a case, insurance may be the only solution.

Excess Insurance

Most firms do not completely self-insure the workers' compensation exposure because of the catastrophic nature of certain types of workers' compensation losses. Such claims as long-term disability or death may add up to hundreds of thousands of dollars. For instance, if a 25-year-old worker in Iowa were disabled for 40 years, this payment could total $2,294,240. Such a loss truly is catastrophic, and most businesses would not desire to retain it. To prevent such circumstances, self-insurers purchase **excess insurance**.

There are two basic types of excess insurance: specific and aggregate. Under specific excess insurance, the self-insurer absorbs the first x dollars on any loss. This is similar to the flat deductible found in homeowners' insurance, except the size of the deductible is much greater ($50,000 to $100,000). If a firm had a policy with a specific excess limit of $100,000 and all per-accident losses for the year were below $100,000, the specific excess insurance would not pay, even if the sum of all such losses was $400,000.

Under aggregate excess, the policy operates like an aggregate deductible. Typically, the aggregate limit is at least the level of what the workers' compensation premiums would have been if insurance had been purchased. If the premium was $200,000, then the excess insurer would not pay for any claims until $200,000 of losses and associated expenses had been retained by the self-insurer.

Unlike workers' compensation policies, excess policies have dollar limits. So even when a self-insurer purchases excess insurance, it still has some exposure to catastrophic losses.

Risk Management Application:
Retrospective Insurance Plan

In situations where a risk manager does not believe it is in the best interest of the firm to self-insure, or form a captive insurance company (discussed later in this chapter), a retrospective rating approach may be used to try to obtain some of the best aspects of both worlds: good cash flow and less administrative detail.

Under a retrospective plan, the firm is purchasing insurance and receives all the benefits of being insured: approval to operate in all states in which the firm has operations, loss prevention and protection services, claims administration, and a claims information system. Of course, the insurer must load the premium to pay appropriate taxes and assessments.

For the purposes of our discussion, we will assume that the risk manager's firm operates in all 50 states and does not have a large concentration of employment in any one state, conditions that favor a retrospective rating, or retro, plan. We will also assume that the plan meets the IRS's definition of insurance; there must be some possibility of the insurance company paying out more than it receives. If this requirement is not met, there is no loss transfer and the premiums would not be tax deductible when paid.

Details of a Retro Plan

Remember, under a retro plan a firm pays what is called a *standard* premium (manual premium times experience modification factor). The *experience modification factor* is the means by which the ratings adjustment takes into consideration the actual loss experience of the firm. If losses are higher than expected, then rates will go up and vice versa. No volume discounts are given under the retro plan, as there are in a guaranteed cost plan. The standard premium is like an initial premium. It may be adjusted up or down based on the firm's loss experience. Because it is insurance, a minimum premium as well as a maximum premium may be charged; in addition, the premium is tax deductible. The annual premium is often paid over a 12-month period, which provides added cash flow benefits.

At the end of the policy year, the earned premium is determined by the insurance company, and adjustments are made. (The earned premium is a function of payroll, and the exact payroll is not known until the end of the policy year.) After about 9 months, a retro adjustment is made to the first-year premium. This adjustment is a function of reported losses and usually results in a substantial portion of the first-year premium being returned to the insured (positive cash flow). After this adjustment, there is an adjustment every 12 months, which usually results in the insured paying money to the insurer because more losses have developed. If there are no losses in a year (which is not very likely), the insurance company still earns the minimum premium. If the losses are unusually large for a given year, the premium is subject to the maximum premium limitation, and the insurance company pays for all losses above the maximum. It is not uncommon for a retrospective policy to remain in force for 10 years. Each year, an adjustment is made; of course, each year a new retrospective plan is initiated. Thus, over a 10- to 20-year period, a risk manager could have 20 retro plans active. Tracking the progress of these plans on a computer spreadsheet is not difficult, but it does require some effort on the part of the risk manager.

As shown in Table 12-2, the insured's standard premium was $1 million, but the insurer's earned premium was $833,425 (shown in Table 12-3). The insured keeps the difference. If losses continued and/or had been greater, the insured would continue to pay until an earned premium of $1,500,000 was obtained. As $1,500,000 is the maximum premium, the insurer pays the losses after it is reached. The actual calculations for these figures is given in Table 12-4.

Problems with Retros

We have seen the benefits of retro plans, but they have negative aspects as well. Because the standard premium is a function of the manual premium, various loadings are added to the premium; these include assigned risk assessments that can amount to 20 percent or higher. (This means the expected loss ratio can be as low as 40 percent; i.e., a 60 percent expense loading, which makes the retro standard premium very expensive.) Also, premium taxes must be paid, as well as marketing and administrative costs of the insurer and the insurer's loading

TABLE 12-2	Program Parameters	
Maximum premium		$1,500,000
Minimum premium		350,000
Standard premium		1,000,000
Basic premium		100,000
(administrative charge)		
included in minimum premium calculation		
Loss conversion factors (LCF)		1.10
10% charge to adjust claims		
Premium tax factor (PTF)		$1.05
5% premium tax		

TABLE 12-3   Summary of Program's Cash Payments

	Insurer's Earned Premium ($)	Cash Flow ($)	
Year 1	388,750	−1,000,000	Year 1
Year 2	231,000	+611,250	Year 2
Year 3	115,500	−231,000	Year 3
Year 4	57,750	−115,500	Year 4
Year 5	28,875	−57,750	Year 5
Year 6	11,550	−28,875	Year 6
Total	833,425	−11,550	Year 7
		−833,425	Total

TABLE 12-4   Program Cash Flow

	Year 1	Year 2	Year 3	Year 4	Year 5	Year 6	Year 7
1/1/Year 1 Pay standard premium:	−$1,000,000						
9/30/Year 2 Determine earned premium for Year 1: Year 1 losses × LCF × PTF 250,000 × 1.1 × 1.05 + basic premium = 393,750 Make retro adjustment 1,000,000 − 388,750		+$611,250					
9/30/Year 3 Year 2 losses × LCF × PTF 200,000 × 1.1 × 1.05			−$231,000				
9/30/Year 4 Year 3 losses × LCF × PTF 100,000 × 1.1 × 1.05				−115,500			
9/30/Year 5 Year 4 losses × LCF × PTF 50,000 × 1.1 × 1.05					−$57,750		
9/30/Year 6 Year 5 losses × LCF × PTF 25,000 × 1.1 × 1.05						−$28,875	
9/30/Year 7 Year 6 losses × LCF × PTF 10,000 × 1.1 × 1.05							−$11,550

for taking the risk, and the cash flow benefits are usually not as good as in a self-insured plan. Moreover, the IRS has tightened its rules about what constitutes an acceptable retro plan for the purposes of allowing a tax deduction for the payment of the premium.

Several years ago, risk managers and insurers became very aggressive in designing retros. They wanted to keep the deduction benefits of an insurance plan and to duplicate the cash flow benefits of a self-insurance plan. In essence, the result was a self-insured insurance plan. The IRS no longer recognizes these plans as insurance and denies the tax deductibility of the so-called insurance premiums.

A Creative Alternative

A large deductible plan can be used with a retro plan. The insured pays the losses that are within the deductible and takes the tax deduction as the benefits are paid. When losses become greater than the deductible, the insurance company pays the loss. Much of the assigned risk assessments and premium taxes are avoided, because the deductible is so large that the actual premium is rather small; deductibles of $500,000 to $1 million are not uncommon. The large deductible plan can be fitted into a retro so that the insured receives the benefits of a retro, avoids regulatory assessments, and has many of the cash flow benefits of self-insurance. Of course, only large insureds qualify for such plans.

Although these plans aid risk managers and their firms' workers' compensation costs, they have a negative impact on state revenues (reduced premium taxes) and create smaller bases with which to assess assigned risk plan losses, which makes everybody else's assessment higher. (Under an assigned risk plan, an insured is rejected by the regular market and is placed in a special plan for such risks—hence the name "assigned risk.") The hard insurance market of the early 2000s has contributed to continued interest in large deductible plans.

Risk Management Application:
Self-Insuring Workers' Compensation

The student should remember that workers' compensation is a no-fault type of coverage. When a worker is injured at the site of or during the course of employment, then he or she is entitled to medical care, rehabilitation treatment, a weekly payment of wages, and possibly an award for permanent injury; any dependents receive weekly payments if the employee is killed on the job. The weekly payment is supposed to replace the income lost as a result of the injury.

In return for this guaranteed treatment and partial income replacement, the worker gives up his or her right to sue. That is, the employee cannot sue the employer under a tort action. The employee may be able to sue others, but the employer is shielded.

Payment Pattern

In 2002 over 50 percent of the payments made under workers' compensation were for medical benefits, up from 40 percent in 1982. This percentage has been rising steadily as the cost of medical care in workers' compensation has risen faster than the overall rate of inflation in medical care. Also, managed care has become very popular, and it has reduced medical cost for those who use it. Workers' compensation medical care is one of the few medical services that is not subject to managed care review. Some people, (mainly employers) believe that this factor contributes to the increased medical costs for workers' compensation. It is argued that because there is no party trying to control the costs, the medical community can charge more and order more treatment than occurs under managed care and/or that patients do not return to work as quickly as they otherwise would because their medical expenses are paid and they are receiving weekly paychecks. Of course, these types of actions, if they do occur, increase the amount of money paid out under workers' compensation.

In terms of the payout period, most of the medical care occurs in the first two years. These payments are for hospital, medical doctor, prescription drug, and physical therapy charges.

The other major component of workers' compensation losses is for the employee's loss of income. This figure can be a weekly payment while the employee is recovering from his or her injury and/or a payment for some type of partial permanent injury. A *partial permanent injury* occurs when some part of the body receives a permanent injury, but the worker can still return to work; often this involves some type of back injury. The employee is awarded so many extra weeks of compensation for the injury, and these begin after the employee returns to work. Thus, the payout for lost wages is over time. In fact, it can be over 5 to 10 years, or even a lifetime. A characteristic of workers' compensation losses is that their frequency is high and their severity is low (relative to other liability lines). This characteristic means losses are fairly predictable and highly suited for retention.

Cash Flow Model

In modeling the cash flows of a self-insured workers' compensation program, we will use a six-year payout period. A longer one could be used, because in some cases payments continue until the employee dies, but this example is far more typical:

Year	1	2	3	4	5	6
Percentage paid out	30	25	20	15	6	4

If $1,000 in payments were to be made to an employee, the following payout pattern would result:

Year	1	2	3	4	5	6
Payment ($)	300	250	200	150	60	40

If this pattern continued for six years and we assume a similar claim occurs each year, the cash outflow would be shown in the following cumulative payment schedule:

Cumulative Payment Schedule

	Year 1 ($)	Year 2 ($)	Year 3 ($)	Year 4 ($)	Year 5 ($)	Year 6 ($)
Year 1	300	250	200	150	60	40
Year 2		300	250	200	150	60
Year 3			300	250	200	150
Year 4				300	250	200
Year 5					300	250
Year 6						300
TOTAL	300	550	750	900	960	1,000
Float	700	1,150	1,400	1,500	1,540	1,540

(Float = Accrued − Paid)

Each year, additional cash flow accrues to the firm. The first year, it is $700; the second year, $450; the third year, $250; and so on. At the end of the fifth year, the firm will have had a positive cash flow of $1,540 ($5,000 − $3,460 = $1,540). By the sixth year, the cash flows are in equilibrium: the outflows equal the inflows. This will continue as long as the claims pattern and level of employment are stable. In many self-insured plans, employment and losses increase, which means the positive cash flow continues and the float (the difference between accrued and paid) increases. During periods of decline or downsizing, the opposite occurs. The cash flow aspects of self-insuring can be a two-edged sword.

An important factor to consider when deciding whether to self-insure is the rate of return assumed in discounting the payments that will be made in the future. Because insurance premiums represent current dollars, the cash flow of a self-insured plan must be compared with the insurance plan. If the firm can obtain higher returns by investing the funds externally or by utilizing them in its own operations, then self-insurance will be attractive. Holding all factors constant except the discount rate, the higher the discount, the more attractive self-insurance will look.

When a firm decides to self-insure, there are certain operating factors that must be considered. The self-insurer must perform all the functions that had been performed by the insurance company and its agent. In some cases, this reduces costs; in other cases, costs may increase.

A self-insurer does not have to pay marketing expenses, which include costs incurred by the insurer, such as advertising and the support of a marketing department. No commissions have to be paid to insurance agents, and no premium taxes have to be paid to state governments. However, excess-of-loss coverage must be purchased, so there are commissions that will be paid to a broker, but they are less than the commissions that would have been paid on workers' compensation. Also, the self-insurer does not have to pay any assigned risk and/or guaranty fund assessments. The total of these three governmental assessments (premium taxes, assigned risk, and guaranty fund assessments) can run as high as 30 percent of the standard premium.

Because there is no insurer, the self-insurer must create its own accounting system to bill its operating units, a risk management information system must be utilized so losses can be reported on a timely and accurate basis, and loss prevention and protection services must be provided by the risk management department or purchased from an outside vendor. The firm must meet certain qualifications in each state where it is self-insured, and allocations made to a self-insured fund are not tax deductible until payment is made to or on behalf of the employee. Insurance premiums are tax deductible.

Potential Problems

Although self-insurance has many advantages, the risk manager must be willing to address several potential problems. These problems include, but are not limited to, financial ability to retain losses, a large enough exposure base to be able to predict losses accurately, actual management of the plan, establishment of a loss prevention and protection program, maintenance of a risk management information system, availability of excess-of-loss insurance, and top management commitment to the plan.

1. In order to self-insure, the firm must have the liquidity to make payments to employees and to pay their medical bills in a timely fashion. The firm should have the ability to pay large, unexpected losses. Losses do not always occur in a predictable pattern, and the firm must be able to pay large losses, whether they are expected or not.

2. Related to the large, unexpected loss is the need for the self-insurer to have enough of a base to be able to accurately predict losses. If the exposure base is too small, the self-insurer will expose itself to a large variation in losses, and if the large losses occur first, the plan will cause a hardship for the firm. To combat this problem, most self-insurers buy excess-of-loss insurance. Under this insurance plan, the insurance company will pay for any single loss that is greater than a certain dollar amount, such as $100,000 or $250,000. The insured pays the first $100,000 or $250,000, and the insurer pays the loss in excess of this amount, up to the policy limit. The self-insurer is responsible for losses above the policy limit. Under workers' compensation insurance, no policy limit exists, and the insurer is responsible for all losses.

3. A self-insured plan will require the risk manager to be actively involved in managing the workers' compensation program. No insurance company personnel is available to do so.

The risk manager must be willing and able to make this time commitment. The management of the plan will require the risk manager to file proper regulatory reports with the state insurance department and provide the required bonds in each state where the firm is self-insured. Each state usually has different rules and regulations. The risk manager will have to manage insurance programs for the firm in any states in which it isn't (or can't) be self-insured.

4. A loss prevention and protection program must be established. If a firm does not have a good loss control program, it should not self-insure. Self-insurers pay for their own losses, and they pay for them as soon as they occur. There is no sharing of losses with others. Thus, if losses get out of hand, the firm pays for this lack of control, and the risk manager may lose his or her job.

5. A risk management information system (RMIS) must be maintained. In order to have a good loss control system, the risk manager must have accurate and timely information on losses. With this information, the firm's loss control efforts can be directed to where they will be most effective in controlling losses.

6. Excess-of-loss insurance must be purchased. In soft and normal markets, this purchase is easy to make. However, when markets harden, the coverage can be quite expensive, and the availability of higher limits may disappear. The self-insurance program must be flexible enough to work in all types of markets.

7. General management has to realize that once the firm decides to self-insure, it is difficult to return to the world of insurance. The reason for this difficulty is not legal but financial. When a firm switches back to insurance, it must not only pay its insurance premium but also the runoff of self-insured claims, which will take several years. Thus the firm may see a doubling of workers' compensation payments right after the conversion, with the resultant drain on cash flow.

The risk manager must gain general management's active support for the decision to self-insure. Management must be made aware of potential problems of a self-insured program and must show support for it. This is especially true with respect to loss control efforts. Operating managers have to believe that loss control is important to their superiors if such a program is to be successful. A self-insurance program will fail if loss control is not a well-established priority.

Alternative Workers' Compensation Risk Financing Strategies

Various financing plans for workers' compensation programs (retros, large deductibles) often used a letter of credit issued by a financial institution on behalf of the insured. By using this approach, an insured obtains maximum cash flow and tax benefits. However, there are caveats that need to be considered. Each year a new letter of credit must be issued. Thus, the letters of credit add up in value. Assuming a $2 million letter is needed each year, after 10 years a firm could have $20 million in such letters outstanding. The firm's overall debt limit could be adversely affected. Also, letters of credit cost money, and they are more expensive than they used to be as banks have been raising their rates for such letters. In addition, the IRS is taking a tougher position on plans where an insured tries to take a tax deduction for the full premium but pays only a small part in cash (the letter of credit represents the rest of the premium).

Alternative financing strategies do exist and include such programs as investment credit and compensating balance. These programs require one to pay the full premium in cash at the beginning of the year, but give the insured investment earnings from the premiums (investment credit) or reduce the firm's obligations to banks that lend money to the insured (compensating balance). The cash flow benefits of such plans are not as attractive as paid loss retros on large deductible plans. However, with proper minimum and maximum premiums, letters of credit are eliminated, and the tax deductibility of the premium is less likely to be challenged by the IRS.[7]

CAPTIVE INSURANCE COMPANIES

General, auto, and product liability cases can give rise to large awards. For example, Domino's Pizza, Inc., lost a lawsuit concerning an auto accident in which one of its delivery persons ran a red light and injured a woman. Part of the evidence presented to the jury involved Domino's promise to deliver pizza in 30 minutes and that drivers were not driving in a reasonable manner. The jury returned a verdict for $78 million, and Domino's ceased advertising that it would deliver within 30 minutes. Clearly, Domino's could not predict a $78 million verdict, nor could it afford to self-insure such a loss. However, a captive insurance arrangement would have been useful in financing the loss.

Special Tax Status of Insurance Companies

Insurance companies have a special status in the tax code of the United States. They are the only type of company that can establish a loss reserve and take a tax deduction for the loss's accrual. Other corporations can take tax deductions for a loss only after the loss has been paid. Insurance companies can prefund losses with pretax dollars. A manufacturer must use after-tax dollars. If a risk manager could create an insurance company or an organization that would pass the IRS definition of an insurance company, pretax dollars could be used to fund self-insured losses of his or her firm.

Operation of a Captive

A **captive insurer** is really nothing other than a subsidiary formed by a company that, in our discussion, will be called the *parent*. It is a captive of the parent because the parent controls it. Captive insurance companies became very popular in the 1960s and 1970s. During that time, it was possible to create a captive insurance company and take a tax deduction for payments to it, which was like having your cake and eating it, too. The arrangement went like this: A firm paid a premium to its subsidiary and took the deduction. The captive recorded the premium as revenue and increased its loss reserve by almost an equal amount, so the captive did not show a profit. The bottom line was a 100 percent tax deduction for the parent, and the captive held the funds; it did not earn a profit, so it did not pay any income taxes. The organization took the tax deduction and kept the funds in the organization.

Needless to say, the IRS was not excited about this arrangement and began to challenge it in the courts. After many years and many court cases, the rule slowly evolved that a parent could not take the deduction unless the subsidiary had a significant amount of nonrelated risks. That is, the rule required a significant number of exposures that were not a part of the parent organization. For example, Allstate was a captive insurance company owned by Sears. Sears insured loss exposures with Allstate. The IRS challenged the tax deduction taken by Sears and lost the case, because Allstate had a significant amount of unrelated business (about 97 percent). Clearly, a captive does not have to have 97 percent of unrelated business in order for the parent firm to take a tax deduction; the figure is closer to 20 to 35 percent of outside business.

It should be noted that almost all of the payments made to a captive are for expected losses. Only a small loading exists for expenses. Underwriting, loss control, and other administrative expenses are usually paid as they are incurred. Little or no prefunding is needed for

---

7   Eric P. Hein and Michael J. O'Malley, "Two Birds with One Stone: How to Reduce Dependence on Letters of Credit and Accelerate Tax Deductibility," *Risk Management*, April 1, 1996, 59–72.

such expenses, and thus an expense reserve is not needed. The functions associated with these expenses may be performed by the parent's risk management department, its broker, or under an administrative services contract with another party.

Onshore versus Offshore Captives

Creating a captive insurance company in the United States is not a difficult task, but it is relatively expensive. Most states have minimum capital requirements that can run as high as several million dollars. Also, an onshore captive (one domiciled in the United States) is subject to the state laws in which it is incorporated. These laws restrict investment policy insurance contract provisions and may expose the captive to various residual market assessments.

When a captive is created offshore (for example, in Bermuda), the regulatory laws are not nearly as restrictive. Greater freedom is allowed in investment policy and insurance contract provisions, and there are no residual market assessments. Minimum capital requirements are much lower, and some captives have been incorporated with only a small amount of cash and a letter of credit to meet capital requirements. Little upfront money is needed to start such captives. Also, offshore captives can have very favorable income tax laws: low or no income taxes on underwriting and/or investment income.

The IRS has never been a fan of captives, for obvious reasons. Thus, over time it has persuaded Congress to tighten the tax laws regarding captives and to make it easier for the IRS to tax them. Favorable tax advantages still exist, but risk managers must be more careful, and increased legal and operating costs are incurred. However, several states have made the formation of a captive in their state more attractive. For example, Vermont, Hawaii, and South Carolina are three states that have enacted very favorable laws to encourage the formation of captives in their states.

Other Attributes of Captives

In addition to the possibility of using pretax dollars to fund self-insured loss reserves, captives have other attributes that are very valuable.

When a firm writes its insurance in a captive, it can write the policy exactly the way it wishes. After all, it is negotiating with itself. Often, the risk manager of the parent firm is the CEO of the captive, so the parent can make the insurance policy as liberal as it desires.

For some firms that have sought to manage risk on a broader, enterprise-wide basis, captives have offered a useful tool for financing risks that have not traditionally been addressed in the insurance market. Such risks include reputation risk, brand risk, residual value risk on vehicle leases, and weather risk, just to mention a few. Also, based on rulings by the Department of Labor in 2003 some firms began to fund employee benefits through their captives.

Regulatory restraints on investments are less; the captive can invest its funds almost any way it wishes. In some cases, the captive can invest most or all of its funds with other subsidiaries of the parent. Few restrictions are present on the ratio of equity investment to surplus.

Captive insurance companies can have direct contact with reinsurers. Customary practice in the world of insurance has restricted contact between reinsurers and risk managers. However, if the risk manager is also the CEO of a captive insurance company, then the reinsurers are more willing to discuss business with the risk manager in his or her capacity as the CEO of an insurance company that needs to buy reinsurance.

It is through reinsurance that captives can serve as a funding vehicle for self-insured plans and reduce the probability of catastrophic losses. For example, a captive might retain the first $100,000 of a product liability claim and then reinsure all losses above $100,000. The captive is acting as a funding mechanism for the firm's deductible program. Everything else is insured through reinsurance. As the parent's management becomes more comfortable with the plan, the retention level can be raised to $500,000 or even higher. In such an arrangement, the investment income can become quite significant.

Potential Problems of Captives

Captives, like self-insurance, demand the time and energy of the risk manager. They also require the parent to incorporate the captive either on- or offshore, which takes time and money. A firm must have enough of a loss exposure to warrant these expenses. This requirement is one reason companies often group together to form association or industry captives. (*Association captives* are operated by a group of companies that belong to the same trade association, like the American Bankers' Association, or by an association of professionals, like the American Institute of Certified Public Accountants. An *industry captive* is composed of firms from the same industry.) Of course, this spreads the expense, but it also spreads the control. The captive will look more like a regular insurance company and will have management of its own or management representing various ownership interests. When a single-owner captive is used, the parent does not have to share the management or the business of the captive with anyone.

However, if the parent creates a single-owner captive, the tax deductibility of payments will be more problematic. The IRS may require a substantial amount of unrelated business. However, the captive should be very careful with insuring unrelated business, or it could lose a substantial amount of money. In several situations, a captive pursued unrelated business too aggressively, millions of dollars were lost, and the captive went bankrupt. One advantage of the association or industry captive is that it has diverse ownership and insures a significant amount of unrelated business (all the owners place business in the captive, not just a few).

Hard reinsurance markets may make it difficult for the captive to reinsure its business. Without reinsurance, the captive can be a very dangerous undertaking. It is likely that a captive will not be a big player in reinsurance markets. In times of hard markets, it may not have the market muscle to obtain the needed coverage. Large insurance companies with more market power and a greater spread of risk will have an advantage.

Sometimes it is difficult for the risk manager to justify the continued use of a captive in extremely soft markets. The temptation may arise to shut down the captive because insurance is so cheap. The risk manager's superiors may require or strongly encourage the switch. It is important for the risk manager to have continuity in his or her risk management program, and changing from insurance to a captive and then back to insurance can break the continuity of the plan and cost more money.

Financial officers often dislike captives because once money is placed or funds accumulate in a captive, it is difficult to obtain the money except for risk management purposes. Most financial vice presidents desire flexibility and the ability to move money from one area of the corporation to another.

As shown in Table 12-5, Bermuda is the largest market for captive insurance companies with 1,313 in 2002, and has more than twice the number of captives in second-ranking Cayman Islands. Throughout the world, the total number of captives has grown each year to 4,526 in 2002.

In the United States, Vermont is by far the most popular captive company state with 438. It is followed by Hawaii with 101. Even through the extended soft insurance market of the 1990s the number of captives has continued to grow. This growth in an extremely "soft market" provides strong evidence of the valuable role that a captive insurer plays in the risk manager's "tool kit."

CONCLUSIONS

The risk management techniques presented here are only some of the many ways to finance losses. However, like any risk management program, each must be accompanied by a strong loss prevention and protection program to make it successful.

TABLE 12-5   **Most Popular Locations for Captive Insurance Companies, 2002**

Location	Number of Captives
Bermuda	1,313
Cayman Islands	600
Vermont	438
Guernsey	371
Luxembourg	268

Source: A.M. Best Company, Inc.

SUMMARY

1. The basic purpose of workers' compensation insurance is to replace the negligence system as a method of meeting the costs of occupational injuries. All states now have workers' compensation laws, under which benefits include lifetime payments, if necessary, for permanent disabilities; income benefits for dependents; death benefits; lump-sum benefits for permanent partial disabilities; and medical and rehabilitation benefits.

2. Experience rating affects the individual rate an insured must pay after an actual loss experience in a given period has been analyzed. The revisions, if any, affect the future premium rate. Retrospective rating allows the insured to determine the premium, in whole or in part, for the period under consideration; in other words, the final premium for a period is determined by the loss.

3. A retrospective rating plan with a sizable deductible is much like an insured self-insured plan. It has most of the benefits of a self-insured plan and all the benefits of an insurance policy purchased from an insurance company.

4. Self-insuring workers' compensation provides added cash flow for the firm, as well as reduced operating costs. However, it does increase the firm's exposure to catastrophic losses and requires more time for management.

5. The use of captive insurers is an innovative way to retain some of the firm's loss exposures. However, it requires time and money to establish, and premium payments to the captive may or may not be tax deductible. Careful study needs to be undertaken before a captive is created.

internetexercises

1. You may not plan to become a bounty hunter or a circus acrobat, but your job may still be dangerous in comparison to others. Set your browser to http://www.osha.gov/oshstats/work.html and find out how many injuries and fatalities have occurred in your desired line of work. How could you use this information if you were the risk manager of a large conglomerate?

2. Workers' compensation fraud can be a problem. Explore the following site to help form an opinion about whether employers should use surveillance and background checks before hiring new employees: http://www.inu.net/towman/workers_comp.html. Explain your opinion in this regard.

3. Set your browser to http://www.captive.com. Look for the link labeled "Domicile Showcase" and use it to compare and contrast two domiciles for captive insurers. Describe a company that might prefer one domicile to another. Why might it choose the one you specified?

QUESTIONS FOR REVIEW AND DISCUSSION

1. Under what circumstances would a retro workers' compensation plan be better than a self-insured one? When might self-insurance be better?
2. When one self-insures, what costs are reduced?
3. What factors besides the insured's loss and loss adjustment expenses affect the cost of an insured's workers' compensation insurance?
4. What is the basic distinction between experience rating and retrospective rating? What is the basic similarity?
5. It has been argued that retrospective rating eliminates the need for self-insurance in the lines of insurance where it is used. Do you agree? Why or why not?
6. Discuss the factors that favor self-insuring workers' compensation.
7. Why shouldn't everyone self-insure workers' compensation loss?
8. Discuss whether you believe large deductible retrospective workers' compensation plans should be allowed.
9. What effect on workers' compensation insurance would a national health care plan have?
10. Discuss whether workers' compensation insurance should be nationalized.
11. Because workers' compensation is generally required of employers by law, do you feel it should be sold only by the government? Explain your answer.
12. Describe the possible tax advantages of operating a captive insurance company. What conditions must exist to gain all the advantages of a captive insurance company?

Personal Risk Management Applications: Property–Liability

PART 3

T he single largest line of property and liability insurance in the United States is automobile insurance. Americans love their autos. However, with that love affair comes the responsibility of paying for injuries and property damage to others arising out of auto accidents and repairing one's own automobile after accidents.

In recent years, the number and severity of automobile accidents have been declining due to new cars sporting such features as air bags and antilock brakes and to stricter enforcement of traffic laws to reduce the number of drunk drivers. However, problems still exist in the automobile marketplace, some of which are caused by the ever-increasing cost of medical care. In reading this chapter, you should consider how automobile insurance is affected by medical care.

The fact that automobiles are cheap enough for nearly everyone to own has led to constantly increasing losses from liability claims, collisions, and bodily injuries and deaths due to accidents. Insurance premiums have grown from an insignificant amount to one of the largest costs of owning and operating a car. Measured by premium volume, automobile insurance is by far the largest single segment of all property and liability insurance business—almost as large as all other lines combined.

Risk Management for Auto Owners—Part I

CHAPTER OBJECTIVES

After studying this chapter, you should be able to

1. Define the key terms in the Personal Automobile Policy.
2. Identify the major parts of the Personal Automobile Policy.
3. State four major exclusions of the Personal Automobile Policy.
4. Distinguish between collision and loss other than collision.
5. State limitations on the insurance company's right to cancel an auto insurance policy.
6. Describe the various approaches to dealing with the problem of uninsured drivers.
7. Describe the key factors that determine variation in auto insurance premiums across individuals.

THE HIGH COST OF AUTOMOBILE LOSSES

Automobile losses represent exposures to risk that nearly all individuals and risk managers must consider. Of the $377 billion spent by individuals and businesses on property-casualty insurance premiums in 2002, about $164 billion, or over 43 percent, was for auto insurance.[1]

In addition to economic costs, the human toll of auto losses is also very high. Over 40,000 Americans die every year in auto accidents. Death rates per 10,000 persons have remained fairly constant since 1925, ranging between 2.0 and 3.5 per 10,000 persons. Although the number of automobile-related deaths is high, substantial progress has been made over the years in improving the situation. Death rates per 10,000 registered vehicles have declined steadily ever since automobiles came into widespread use, and the decline is continuing. In 1984, the rate was 2.69; it had declined to 2.13 by 1993 and to 1.90 by 2001. Information on fatality rates for recent years is contained in Table 13-1.

A disproportionate number of automobile accidents involve young drivers. For example, in 2002, although only 13.6 percent of drivers were under age 25, they accounted for 20.9 percent of all drivers in auto accidents and 22.8 percent of drivers in fatal accidents. Looking only at drivers under 20, they accounted for 4.9 percent of all drivers, but 11.5 percent of all accidents and 11.6 percent of all fatal accidents. Accident rates stabilize by age 30, and remain relatively stable until about age 70, when they begin rising again.

During the past several years, falling accident rates indicate a significant improvement in driving records. Part of this decrease may be explained by society's greater emphasis on loss prevention and safer cars. Another contributing factor is the reduction (as a percentage of the whole) in the number of youthful drivers. In 1986, youthful drivers (persons under age 25) accounted for 19.7 percent of all drivers. In 1991, that figure was 15.6 percent and in 2002, 13.6 percent. This change represents a decline of over 30 percent between 1986 and 2002. But over the next several years, the relative proportion of youthful drivers will increase.

INSURANCE CLAIMS

Insurers have been faced with rising claims for most types of automobile insurance protection. Statistics illustrating the level to which claims have risen are given in Table 13-2.

TABLE 13-1   **Death Rate per 10,000 Cars**

Year	Rate	Number of Fatalities
1993	2.13	40,150
1995	2.12	40,716
1997	2.06	42,013
1999	1.96	41,717
2001	1.90	42,196

Source: *The Fact Book 2004* (New York: Insurance Information Institute, 2004), 99.

---

1   Unless otherwise stated, the statistics in this chapter come from *The Fact Book 2004* (New York: Insurance Information Institute, 2004).

TABLE 13-2	Average Insurance Claims			
Year	Collision ($)	Bodily Injury Liability ($)	Property Damage Liability ($)	Consumer Price Index
1992	2,266	11,184	1,732	140.3
1997	2,760	9,530	2,167	160.5
1999	3,017	9,524	2,298	166.6
2002	3,400	10,138	2,564	179.9
Change, 1992–2002 (%)	50.04	−9.35	48.04	28.23

Source: *The Fact Book 1996* and *2004* (New York: Insurance Information Institute).

Reviewing Table 13-2, one can see that average property-related losses have risen steadily over the years, while average bodily injury losses have fluctuated both up and down. In fact, average bodily injury liability losses fell every year between 1992 and 1997, then stayed flat for a couple of years, before starting to rise again in 2000. As compared with inflation, as measured by the Consumer Price Index, average collision and property damage liability claims rose dramatically faster than inflation over the period 1992–2002, while average bodily injury liability losses actually fell slightly over this period, although it has risen in the past few years.

The federal government has adopted some minimum vehicle safety and antipollution standards aimed at improving the environment in which automobiles operate. For example, in 1979, bumpers were required to protect new autos from damage when they collide with concrete barriers at 5 miles per hour. In 1980 the rule stated that only minimal damage could occur to the bumper or its fasteners. However, in 1982, the National Highway Traffic Safety Administration reduced bumper standards from a 5-mph no-damage standard to a 2.5-mph standard that allows unlimited bumper damage but no damage to the body of the vehicle.

Table 13-3 lists some 2000–2002 passenger autos with respect to injury claims frequency. It should be noted that these claims frequencies do not reflect only the actual safety of the vehicles. They also reflect who is driving the vehicles. For example, it is quite likely that many of the cars with low injury claims frequency rates are less likely to be driven by teenagers than many of the cars with high claims frequency rates, for reasons that have nothing to do with safety.

Table 13-4 focuses not on injury claims frequency, but on the relative average collision loss payment per insured vehicle. As with injury claims frequency, this number varies widely across different vehicles.

THE NEED FOR INSURANCE

In the face of the high cost of automobile accidents and the substantial probability of being involved in one, what should the average driver do to protect against the financial consequences of this risk? Risk managers of large organizations that own many automobiles often retain the risk of physical damage to the vehicles. But for nearly all individuals, the answer has been insurance, in spite of its high cost. Auto liability insurance is a legal requirement in many states and is far superior to running the economic risk of driving without protection (that is, risk retention). Few individuals own more than two or three automobiles, so an insuf-

TABLE 13-3

Relative Injury Claims Frequency per Insured Vehicle for 2000–02 Passenger Automobiles

Model	Class of Vehicle	Injury Index*
Suzuki Esteem	Small 4-door	239
Kia Rio	Small 4-door	206
Mitsubishi Montero	Midsize 4WD Utility Vehicle	132
Ford Mustang	Midsize Sports Car	120
Acura 3.2 CL	Midsize 2-door	98
Mercedes-Benz C-Class	Midsize Luxury	80
Volvo S60	Midsize 4-door	64
Chevrolet Yukon	Large 4WD Utility Vehicle	32
Chevrolet Silverado 2500	Very Large 2WD Pickup Truck	19
GMC Sierra 2500	Very Large 2WD Pickup Truck	13

*Index = 100 for the average vehicle. Injury index is based on the relative frequencies of injury claims per insured vehicle year.
Source: Highway Loss Data Institute, *Injury, Collision & Theft Losses By Make and Model*, September 2003.

ficient exposure exists to allow self-insurance. Because of the personal catastrophic loss hazard involved in the liability risk, insurance is generally the only feasible solution.

PERSONAL AUTOMOBILE POLICY

As part of the consumer movement designed to produce easier-to-read insurance policies, the **Personal Automobile Policy (PAP)** was introduced in 1977 and revised a number of times

TABLE 13-4

Relative Average Collision Loss Payments per Insured Vehicle for 2000–02 Passenger Automobiles

Model	Class of Vehicle	Collision Index*
Subaru Impreza 4WD	Small 4-door	278
Lexus IS 300	Midsize Luxury	237
Acura RSX	Small 2-door	211
Land Rover Discovery Series II	Midsize 4WD Utility Vehicle	174
Ford Focus	Small 4-door	122
Honda Accord	Midsize 2-door	119
BMW 3-series	Midsize Luxury	113
GMC Yukon XL 1500	Large 4WD Utility Vehicle	52
GMC Sierra 2500	Very Large 2WD Pickup Truck	48
GMC Safari	Minivan	47

*Index = 100 for the average vehicle. Collision index is based on the relative average collision loss payments per insured vehicle year.
Source: Highway Loss Data Institute, *Injury, Collision & Theft Losses By Make and Model*, September 2003.

since. This policy replaced the more difficult to read Family Automobile Policy. Not every insurer uses the PAP form that will be described here. Most auto policies sold are very similar to the PAP, but you should read your own policy if you have questions about your coverage.

Eligibility

To be eligible for the PAP, a car must be owned or leased by an individual or jointly owned by a husband and wife. It is primarily designed for private passenger cars used for pleasure or business, but a pickup truck or van used in farming may be insured, as may a pickup truck or van that is used to deliver or transport goods.

Definitions

Within a PAP, *you* and *your* are used to refer to the named insured and spouse, if a resident of the same household. *We, us,* and *our* refer to the insurance company.

No-fault, as used in this chapter and Chapter 14, means that the insured does not have to prove another person negligent before compensation can be received from an insurer. A person whose car collides with a telephone pole is entitled to bodily injury benefits under no-fault, even though the accident was the driver's fault. On a tort or liability basis, the driver could not receive compensation. (On a liability basis, one must prove another person negligent before compensation may be received.)

The term covered auto includes four categories of vehicles:

1. Any vehicle shown on the declarations page of the policy.

2. Any of the following types of vehicles that you acquire ownership of during the policy period: (a) a private passenger auto (PPA) and (b) a pickup truck or a van meeting certain requirements. For any coverage except coverage for damage to your auto, the newly acquired auto will have the broadest coverage the insured has on any vehicle. If the newly acquired vehicle replaces one shown in the declarations, coverage is provided without having to ask the insurer. If the newly acquired vehicle is an additional vehicle, you must ask the insurer to insure the additional vehicle within 14 days for the coverage to begin on the date you become the owner. For coverage for damage to your auto, you must ask the insurer to insure a newly acquired vehicle within 14 days if you have such coverage for any auto. If you do not have coverage for damage to your auto for any auto, you must ask the insurer to insure the newly acquired vehicle within 4 days if you wish to have coverage for damage to your auto for the new vehicle from the date you become the owner.

3. Any trailer you own.

4. Any auto or trailer you do not own, while used as a temporary substitute for any other vehicle described in this definition that is out of normal use because of its breakdown, repair, servicing, loss, or destruction. This category does not apply to coverage for damage to your auto.

Note that with respect to replacement vehicles, one must only notify the insurer in order to obtain coverage for physical damage to the auto. Liability protection is automatically provided for the policy term. The insurer must be notified to obtain physical damage coverage because there is a high probability that a greater exposure exists. The old auto might be a 1990 Ford and the replacement vehicle a 2004 Mercedes. Obviously, the insurer has a much greater exposure on the Mercedes and needs to decide whether to accept the risk.

A trailer is defined as "a vehicle designed to be pulled by a private passenger-type auto, pickup or panel truck, or van." It also includes a farm wagon or farm implement towed by one of these vehicles.

A family member is defined by the PAP as "a person related to you by blood, marriage, or adoption who is a resident of your household. This includes a ward or foster child." Thus, for example, a visiting aunt is not a family member.

Occupying is defined as "in, upon, getting in, on, out, or off." By using such a definition, the insurer provides protection for more situations than just when the insured is inside the vehicle.

Recent versions have added and clarified some additional definitions, such as bodily injury, business, and property damage. By defining these terms in the policy, the insurance industry is trying to guide the courts to a tighter definition of the terms.

In the PAP, *bodily injury* means bodily harm, sickness, or disease, including any death that results. *Business* means trade, profession, or occupation. *Property damage* is defined as physical injury to, destruction of or loss of use of tangible property.

PERSONAL AUTO POLICY COMPONENTS

The PAP has six major components: (1) liability, (2) medical payments, (3) uninsured motorist, (4) physical damage to your auto, (5) duties after an accident or loss, and (6) general provisions. The first four sections provide four different coverages, and the definitions of terms may vary between sections. For example, the term *insured* is defined differently in each of the first three sections. This illustrates what should be obvious by now: that insurance policies must be read very carefully in order to be properly understood.

Liability

Under liability coverage, the insurer promises to pay bodily injury and property damage claims for which any insured becomes legally responsible due to an auto accident. In addition, the insuring agreement states that the insurer will either settle or defend, at its own discretion, any covered claim or suit. In other words, not only does the insurer have the duty to pay damages, but it also has the duty to provide a legal defense against lawsuits, and it has the authority to decide whether to settle a suit against the insured out of court. The insurer agrees to pay for all defense costs, and these are paid in addition to the policy limits. The insuring agreement also states that there is no duty to defend the insured in situations where the coverage is excluded or after the limits of liability for direct damages have been reached. Many courts have held that an insurance company's duty to defend is greater than the duty to pay damages. By making statements about their duty to defend, insurance companies are trying to narrow the difference between the duty to defend and the duty to pay claims.

With respect to the liability section, the policy defines the insured as follows:

1. For the ownership, maintenance, or use of any auto or trailer, you or any family member.

2. Any person using your covered auto.

3. For your covered auto, any person or organization, but only with respect to legal responsibility for acts or omissions of a person for whom coverage is afforded under liability coverage.

4. For any auto or trailer, other than your covered auto, any person or organization, but only with respect to legal responsibility for acts or omissions of you or any family member for whom coverage is afforded under liability coverage. This provision applies only if the person or organization does not own or hire the auto or trailer.

Items 3 and 4 in this list are best illustrated by example. Item 3 would apply when a fellow employee drives your car on company business, in which case your employer is covered under your policy if an accident occurs and your employer is sued. Item 4 would apply when you drive a fellow employee's car and have an accident; again, the employer is covered under your policy if a lawsuit results. Of course, employment situations are not the only ones covered by these two provisions. Activities involving an individual's church, fraternity, or sorority would also be included.

Supplementary Benefits

Standard supplementary benefits are provided by the PAP. These benefits are in addition to the policy limits. Bail bonds up to $250 are covered for an accident resulting in bodily injury (BI) or property damage (PD). Because of the BI or PD requirement, a bail bond posted for a speeding violation or driving while intoxicated (DWI) is not covered unless either BI or PD occurs. Besides bail bond costs, premiums on appeal bonds and bonds to release attachments are insured. Interest that accrues after a judgment and reasonable expenses incurred at the insurer's request also are included. Up to $200 per day is available for loss of earnings resulting from attending trials or hearings at the insurer's request. No emergency first aid benefits are available, as are contained in many other liability insurance contracts.

Limit of Liability

The limit of liability for this section of the policy is defined using the "split limits" approach. Under this approach, the limit is described by three numbers, such as $100,000/$300,000/$50,000. The first number is the maximum limit of liability for all damages arising out of bodily injury to any one person, while the second number is the maximum limit for all damages for bodily injury resulting from any one accident, regardless of the number of persons involved. Finally, the third number is the limit of liability for all property damage resulting from any one accident. So with these limits, if an accident results in a liability loss of $130,000 per person for three persons and $20,000 of property damage, the policy would pay a total of $320,000 (3 × 100,000 = $300,000 for bodily injury and $20,000 for property damage). Policies also can be sold with a single limit that applies to both bodily injury and property damage, with no per-person bodily injury coverage limitation. If a single limit policy for $350,000 was in place instead of the split limits policy when the accident occurred, it would pay its full limit of $350,000. Whether split limits or a single limit is used, the applicable limit is the most the insurer will pay regardless of the number of insureds. By endorsement, one can choose per-person limits.

Exclusions

The PAP liability section contains 13 exclusions, which we shall briefly examine. No coverage exists for persons who intentionally cause a loss. Damage to property owned or being transported by an insured is excluded, as is property rented to, used by, or in the care of an insured, except for damage to a residence or private garage. Thus, if you drive your neighbor's auto and cause damage to it, no property damage liability coverage is available because that auto was in your care. However, if you have purchased physical damage coverage in the PAP, coverage does exist on borrowed cars for such loss, over and above any collision insurance carried by the car's owner.

Vehicles operated as a public or livery conveyance are not covered. However, share-the-expense car pools are not affected by this exclusion. Courts have generally held that coverage exists in this area if the car is not held out indiscriminately to the general public for the carrying of passengers for hire.

Several exclusions pertain to business use of automobiles. If an employee of the insured is injured, the insured's PAP does not provide liability coverage, unless the injury is to a domestic employee for whom workers' compensation is not required. This provision eliminates business-related accidents but protects the insured's personal exposure.

No protection is given to someone in the automobile business (i.e., the business of selling, repairing, servicing, storing, or parking autos) unless the insured's covered auto is being driven by (1) the insured; (2) a family member; (3) any partner, agent, or employee of the insured or any family member. This exclusion eliminates coverage for a service station mechanic who drives your car and has an accident. As the insured, you are protected by your policy in this case, but the service station is not. The service station needs its own insurance to protect against suits arising out of such accidents.

For those in any other type of business, liability coverage is provided for the business use of private passenger cars and pickup trucks and vans. Thus, students who drive their cars to deliver pizza are covered. No liability coverage is provided for commercial vehicles and large trucks.

No requirement is made in the PAP that the insured have permission to operate the vehicle involved in an accident. However, the policy excludes liability coverage for anyone using a vehicle without reasonable belief that he or she is entitled to do so. An exception to this exclusion applies for family members using the insured's owned covered auto.

Another exclusion, rarely used, excludes coverage for injury or damage for which the insured has coverage under a nuclear energy liability policy.

The final four exclusions describe categories of vehicles for which liability coverage is excluded. First, no coverage is provided for the use of any vehicle with fewer than four wheels. Therefore, motorcycles are not covered. Another exclusion that is important to many people is the one that excludes an auto (other than the covered auto) that is owned by you or furnished or made available for your regular use. For example, if an employer provides you with an automobile, your PAP will not cover it. You need an extended liability endorsement to give protection for such an exposure. This exclusion prevents an insured from obtaining double protection from a single premium; the PAP will not cover both the employee's personal automobile and the vehicle furnished by the employer, when a premium has only been paid for the personal auto.

Not all situations are as clear-cut as an employer-furnished car. Courts are not always consistent in applying the terms *furnished* and *available*. In at least two cases, insureds used another car three to nine times and had to ask permission to obtain the keys, and the courts said coverage existed. The fact that permission had to be obtained to get the keys seemed to be a critical point.[2]

Related to the preceding exclusion is the one that excludes any vehicle, other than the covered vehicle, that is owned by, furnished to, or available for the regular use of any family member. An exception to this exclusion exists when such a vehicle is driven by the named insured or spouse. For example, if Mr. Lilly used his son's car (a car owned by his son, who lives at home and insures his auto separately from Mr. Lilly's), Mr. Lilly is covered on an excess basis by his own PAP. Of course, when his son is driving his own separately insured car, the son is not covered by Mr. Lilly's PAP.

Finally, liability coverage is excluded for any vehicle participating in an organized racing or speed contest while located inside a racing facility.

Other Liability Conditions

Another provision in the PAP is out-of-state coverage, including coverage in a Canadian province. This clause states that if you have an accident in a state having higher required liability limits than your state, the policy will pay up to the higher limits. For instance, if you live in Illinois, the required minimum limits of liability are $20,000/$40,000/$15,000. In Minnesota they are $30,000/$60,000/$10,000. When you are driving in Minnesota, your policy will pay on the basis of $30,000/$60,000/$15,000 if you have an accident in that state. Another issue dealt with in the policy is the determination of when your PAP liability coverage is primary and when it is excess. The general rule is that when your owned auto is involved,

---

2 *Hughes v State Farm*, 1976 CCH (Automobile) 9020; *Waggoner v Wilson*, 1973 CCH (Automobile) 7695.

your policy is primary. When your policy applies to a nonowned vehicle, it is excess. If two policies are applicable to the same owned auto, the PAP will pay its pro-rata share of the loss.

Medical Payments

The PAP will make **medical payments** on a no-fault basis for reasonable and necessary medical expenses caused by an auto accident and sustained by an insured. Such expenses must be incurred and paid within three years of the accident. If more treatment is needed but has not yet been paid, the policy will not cover it. Consequently, one father whose 9-year-old child was injured in a car accident prepaid the medical expenses. The services involved dental work that, because of the child's age, could not be done for several years. The court allowed him to recover his expenses because they met the time limitations and were a direct result of a covered accident.[3] In 1994 the policy was rewritten to pay only for services rendered. Thus the preceding case would no longer be covered.

For medical payments, insured means (1) you or any family member when occupying, or as a pedestrian when struck by, a motor vehicle designed for use mainly on public roads or by a trailer of any type and (2) any other person while occupying your covered auto. If you are struck by a bulldozer, coverage will not exist because such a vehicle is not designed for use on public roads. When you are driving a nonowned motor vehicle, your medical payments will protect you but will not protect any passengers in the vehicle. (To be covered yourself, you must have a reasonable belief that you are entitled to operate the automobile.) Passengers would have to turn to their own medical payments coverage or to that of the owner of the vehicle.

Exclusions

The medical payments coverage does not apply to an injury sustained while riding a motorcycle, but if a motorcycle collides with you or your vehicle, you are insured. No protection is available while your vehicle is used to carry people or property for a fee. As in liability insurance, share-the-expense car pools are exempted from this restriction. Any bodily injury received while occupying a vehicle located for use as a residence or premises also is excluded. This clause eliminates medical payments for losses associated with a mobile home.

No coverage is available for injuries occurring in the course of employment if workers' compensation is supposed to provide benefits. As with liability coverage, no protection exists while occupying an owned auto (other than your covered auto) or one furnished or available for your regular use. Also like the liability section, no coverage exists while occupying a vehicle without a reasonable belief that you are entitled to do so (again, an exception exists for family members using your owned auto). Also, injury sustained while occupying a vehicle while it is being used for business is excluded unless the vehicle is (1) a private passenger auto, (2) an owned pickup or panel truck or van; or (3) a trailer used with a vehicle described in items 1 or 2. Other exclusions are losses due to war, radiation, and racing.

The Insurance Institute for Highway Safety tests and rates vehicles as to how well they protect their occupants in a crash. Look up the ratings of the vehicle you drive most often at http://www.hwysafety.org/, following the links for "vehicle ratings."

---

3 *Maryland Casualty Company v Thomas*, 289 S.W. (2d) 652 (1958).

Other Conditions

The medical payments limits are on a per-person basis, such as $2,000 per person. If six people were in a covered auto at the time of the accident, each of the six could collect $2,000. The PAP specifically states that the maximum amount receivable is the per-person limit stated on the declarations page. This limit is the maximum, regardless of the number of autos insured. For example, if Ms. Epstein had three autos insured with medical payment coverage of $2,000, she could collect only $2,000 for medical payments from an accident. She could not stack the individual limits ($2,000 + $2,000 + $2,000) to obtain $6,000 of protection. Also, the policy states that no one can collect under the medical payments portion of the policy as well as under the liability or uninsured motorists portion. For example, injured passengers in your auto cannot collect twice from your policy, once under liability and once under medical payments. The PAP pays on a pro-rata basis in cases where other insurance applies on an equal basis. However, with respect to nonowned automobiles, it is always excess.

Uninsured Motorist

Uninsured motorist insurance pays for your bodily injuries that result from an accident with another vehicle if the other driver is negligent and does not have any insurance (or has insurance less than that required by law). Punitive damages are not covered—only compensatory damages. Insured persons include the named insured and family members, any person occupying your covered auto, and other persons who are entitled to recovery because of injury in the first two categories. For example, a man could be injured in an accident, and his wife might seek to recover for loss of consortium in addition to any claims her spouse made. In some states, such as Georgia, uninsured motorist insurance also covers vehicle damage. A mandatory deductible is often associated with this vehicle coverage.

Insureds purchase uninsured motorist insurance to protect themselves against other drivers who are uninsured. While many states require or strongly encourage liability insurance, many people do not purchase it, and the difference among the states is great. Table 13-5 gives the uninsured motorist rates for the nine highest-rate states. The national average for uninsured motorists is 14 percent.

From Table 13-5, you can see that the uninsured motorist problem occurs from the east coast to the west coast, from Alaska to Washington, D.C. The only areas not represented in the top nine states are the Midwest and New England.

TABLE 13-5   **State Uninsured Motorist Rates (in Percent)**

Colorado	36
Mississippi	29
Alabama	28
New Mexico	27
California	26
South Carolina	22
Alaska	22
Washington, D.C.	22
Texas	21

Source: Meg Green, "Research Council Study Finds 14% of Drivers are Uninsured" *P/C Best Week*, September 7, 1999, 3.

Uninsured Motor Vehicles

The policy defines an **uninsured motor vehicle** as a land motor vehicle or trailer of any type with the following specifications:

1. One to which no bodily injury liability bond or policy applies at the time of the accident

2. One to which a bodily injury liability bond or policy applies at the time of the accident, but with a limit for liability less than the minimum limit specified by the financial responsibility law of the state in which your covered auto is principally garaged

3. One that is a hit-and-run vehicle whose operator or owner cannot be identified and that hits you or any family member, a vehicle occupied by you or any family member, or your covered auto

4. One to which a bodily injury liability bond or policy applies at the time of the accident but that is covered by a bonding or insuring company that denies coverage or becomes insolvent

However, none of the following is considered an uninsured motor vehicle:

1. One owned by, furnished to, or available for the regular use of you or any family member

2. One owned or operated by a self-insurer under any applicable motor vehicle law unless the self-insurer becomes insolvent

3. One owned by any government unit or agency

4. One operated on rails or crawler treads

5. One designed mainly for use off public roads while not on public roads

6. One located for use as a residence or premises

Exclusions

In addition to the exclusions under the definition of an uninsured motor vehicle, the uninsured motorist coverage has five exclusions for bodily injury:

1. If the injury is sustained while occupying, or when struck by, any motor vehicle or trailer of any type owned by you or any family member that is not insured for this coverage

2. If the claim is settled by the insured or the insured's legal representative without consent of the insurer

3. If the injury is sustained while occupying your covered auto when it is being used to carry people or property for a fee (does not apply to a share-the-expense car pool)

4. If the injury is sustained while using a vehicle without reasonable belief that you are entitled to do so

5. If the coverage directly or indirectly benefits any insurer or self-insurer under any workers' compensation, disability benefits, or similar law. This exclusion is designed to prevent a workers' compensation insurer or a self-insured employer from collecting funds from the uninsured motorist coverage of the insurance company. Uninsured motorist insurance is not intended to pay for workers' compensation claims.

Other Conditions

The maximum limit of liability is the amount shown on the declarations page. As with liability coverage, split limits are used. The number of persons or vehicles insured does not affect this limit. As described earlier for medical payments, no stacking is allowed. Coverage is excess on nonowned vehicles. When a dispute develops between the insured and the insurer on a claim, the policy gives either party the right to ask for binding arbitration. Arbitration takes place in the county in which the insured lives, and local rules of law as to procedure and evidence apply.

Physical Damage to Autos

The next section of the policy is called coverage for damage to your auto. In this section, the insurer provides protection for direct accidental loss to the covered auto or to a nonowned auto. A **nonowned auto** is defined as any private passenger auto, pickup truck, van, or trailer not owned by or furnished for the regular use of you or any family member while in the custody of or being operated by you or any family member, as well as any auto or trailer while used as a temporary substitute for your covered auto while it is out of normal use. Coverage for a nonowned auto is equal to the broadest protection provided for any covered auto.

Coverage is separated into two sections: collision and other than collision. **Collision** is defined as upset of your covered auto or nonowned auto or its impact with another vehicle or object. This definition is new to the PAP, and it clarifies what some persons thought was awkward in the old definition, which used the word *collide* to define the term *collision*. The following losses are considered **other than collision**: losses to an auto caused by missiles, falling objects, fire, theft or larceny, explosion, earthquake, windstorm, hail, water, flood, malicious mischief or vandalism, riot or civil commotion, contact with a bird or other animal, or breakage of glass. If breakage of glass is caused by a collision, you may elect to have it considered a loss caused by collision. (This qualification about damage to glass is made so only one deductible is applied. A car could collide with a telephone pole and have glass damage. Without this alternative approach on glass, a deductible could be required for the collision loss and another deductible, on other than collision, for the glass.) The advantage to the insured for not having the preceding perils considered collisions is that coverage for other than collision usually has a lower deductible than collision coverage. In addition, other-than-collision claims often will not raise an insured's rates, whereas collision claims generally will.

Much discussion has occurred over whether certain accidents were other-than-collision or collision claims. The insured usually desires the claim to be considered as the former. The following examples provide a series of interesting cases on the subject:

1. A moving car caught fire and subsequently wrecked. The court called it an other than collision loss.[4]

2. A bulldozer struck a valve of a liquid propane pipeline. No damage on striking occurred, but gas escaped and froze when exposed to the air. It also froze the bulldozer. The court called it collision.[5] The insured had only collision coverage.

3. A truck backed close to the edge of an excavation site; the dirt gave way, and the truck fell in. The court called it other than collision, and the insurer paid for damage and the cost of pulling out the truck.[6]

4. The insured parked a car in a carport. He said the wind blew the car down the driveway. The insured did not carry collision coverage. The court ruled it was collision because the wind on the day of the accident was only 18 to 25 mph.[7]

5. In the area of water damage, flood losses are usually considered to be losses other than collision. However, when a car plunges off a bridge or highway into a river, lake, or ocean, the resulting loss is considered to be due to collision.[8]

6. In an old case, but one that may occur more often today (especially in Florida), the court held that when a car sank in a roadbed (sinkhole effect), its damage was considered other than collision. No "collision" occurred with an object because the car never moved.[9]

---

4 *American Indemnity Company v Haley*, 25 S.W. (2d) 911 (1930).
5 *New Hampshire Insurance Co. v Frisby*, 522 S.W. (2d) 418 (1975).
6 *City Coal and Supply Co. v American Automobile Insurance Company*, 133 N.E. (2d) 415 (1954).
7 *McClelland v Northwestern Fire and Marine Insurance Co.*, 86 S.E. (2d) 729 (1955).
8 *Triten v First Georgia Insurance Company*, 160 S.E. (2d) 903 (1968).
9 *Aetna Casualty and Surety Company v Cartmel*, 100 Sou. 802 (1924).

Exclusions

The physical damage section excludes loss resulting from the operation of a vehicle used to carry persons or property for a fee (share-the-expense car pools are excepted). Damage resulting from war, radioactive contamination, and discharge of any nuclear weapon is excluded.

The PAP physical damage section has a series of exclusions pertaining to auto accessories. All of the following items are excluded:

1. Loss to equipment designed for the reproduction of sound, unless the equipment is permanently installed in or designed to be solely powered by the electrical system of your covered auto. The question frequently arises as to what constitutes permanent installation. The New York State Supreme Court has ruled that an item is permanently installed if it is bolted to brackets that in turn are bolted to the underside of the insured's vehicle.[10]

2. Loss to any of the following or their accessories: (a) citizens-band radio, (b) two-way mobile radio, (c) telephone, (d) scanning monitor receiver, (e) television monitor receivers, (f) video cassette recorders, (g) audio cassette recorders, and (h) personal computers. This exclusion does not apply to equipment that is necessary for the normal operation of the auto or to a permanently installed telephone designed to be operated by the use of the power from the auto's electrical system.

3. Loss to tapes, records, discs or other media used with the equipment described in 1 or 2.

4. Loss to laser or radar detection equipment.

5. Loss to a camper body, trailer, or motor home not shown in the declarations, as well as associated equipment. This exclusion does not apply to a nonowned trailer or to a camper body or trailer of which you acquire ownership during the policy period if you ask the company to insure it within 14 days after you become the owner.

6. Loss to custom furnishings or equipment in or upon a pickup or van. Custom furnishings or equipment include but are not limited to special carpeting and insulation, furniture, bars, height-extending roofs, and custom murals, paintings, or other decals or graphics. If coverage for such custom items is desired, it may be added by endorsement.

No coverage is given for a nonowned or temporary substitute vehicle used by you or a family member without a reasonable belief that the person is entitled to do so. For example, if you steal a car and wreck it, you have no coverage on that auto. Also, rental car companies are not covered for coverage on a car you rent from them unless you can be held liable under the rental agreement or a state statute.

Finally, the policy excludes damage from wear and tear, freezing, mechanical or electrical breakdown or failures, and road damage to tires. The PAP does not pay for flat tires or worn out engine parts. If you fail to put enough antifreeze in your car in the winter and the engine block freezes and cracks, no coverage applies. However, if someone steals the car and the engine block freezes before it is recovered, coverage is provided because the proximate cause of the loss is presumed to be theft.

Transportation and Towing

The PAP will pay up to $20 per day (up to a maximum of $600) for temporary transportation expenses incurred by you in the event of a covered loss to your auto. In the case of theft, you must wait 48 hours in order to recover. The transportation expenses incurred may be for car rental, bus fare, a taxi, or other transportation. However, such expenses must be used to provide substitute transportation for the covered automobile.

For an additional premium, towing and labor cost coverage may be added. The insurer's limit of liability is generally about $50, and all labor must be performed at the site of the disablement. If you go on a picnic and your car will not start, this coverage will pay up to the

---

10 *Troncillito v Farm Family Mutual Insurance Co.*, 406 N.Y. (2d) 143.

limit to have someone tow your vehicle to a garage or a service station. Given the roadside assistance plans that accompany many car purchases, and number of people with auto club memberships, most persons probably do not need this coverage, but because the premium is so low, many purchase it.

Other Provisions

The insurer limits its liability to the actual cash value of the loss or the amount necessary to repair or replace the property, whichever is less. The policy states that the term *actual cash value (ACV)* includes an adjustment for depreciation and the physical condition of the auto. By making this statement, insurers are trying both to avoid having to pay for the replacement cost of the auto and to reduce misunderstandings about the basis of recovery to which the insured is entitled. In the case of antique or customized automobiles, a stated-amount endorsement may be used. This endorsement sets a specific policy limit, such as $5,000. The stated amount is the maximum the insurer will pay.

The insurer reserves the right to pay for the loss in money, repair, or replacement of the damaged or stolen property. If the car is stolen, the insurer will pay for the cost of returning the vehicle to the owner. If the cost of repair or replacement is greater than the value of the property, the insurer may declare the loss a total loss and pay the ACV of the vehicle. Sometimes it may cost $3,000 to repair a vehicle worth $1,500. In such situations, the insurer will generally pay only $1,500 (less the deductible, if any). New wording in the policy states that if the repair or replacement results in betterment of the property, the insurer will not pay for the amount of the betterment.

The betterment provision of the personal auto policy and the use of "after market" parts has caused significant concern to consumers and insurance companies. Insurers have argued that "after market" parts are just as good as those made by the auto manufacturer and that they cost less so everyone wins because of lower premiums to insureds and lower costs to insurers.

However, an important court decision in Illinois against State Farm Insurance shed a little different light on the situation. That court ruled in a class-action suit that the parts were not the same and awarded the plaintiffs damages in excess of $1 billion! Needless to say, insurers are examining their policy on "after market" parts.[11]

Another policy provision states that the insurance shall not directly or indirectly benefit any carrier or bailee. Such persons include a railroad or shipping line that transports your vehicle as well as a parking lot operation. This provision allows the insurer to subrogate against the bailee when the bailee is negligent in damaging your auto.

Finally, all coverage for nonowned autos is excess over any other collectible insurance.

Duties after an Accident or Loss

When an accident or loss occurs, the insured must promptly notify the insurance company of how, when, and where the accident or loss occurred. Typically, reporting such information to your agent is considered reporting it to the company.

In addition to this requirement, any person seeking coverage under the PAP must be willing to do the following:

1. Cooperate with the company in the investigation, settlement, or defense of any claim or suit

2. Promptly send the company copies of any notices or legal papers received in connection with the accident or loss

---

11 *Snider and Avery v State Farm Mutual Automobile Insurance Co.*, 1st Circuit Court, IL, 1999.

3. Submit, at the company's expense and as often as reasonably required, to physical examinations by physicians selected by the company and to examination under oath

4. Authorize the company to obtain medical reports and other pertinent records

5. Submit a proof of loss when required by the company

A person seeking uninsured motorist coverage also must be willing (1) to notify the police promptly if a hit-and-run driver is involved and (2) to send copies of the legal papers to the company if a suit is brought. The requirement under uninsured motorist coverage with respect to hit-and-run accidents is introduced so that insureds will be discouraged from making a claim that a hit-and-run driver caused damage that was actually caused by the insured. Insurers believe that the requirement to notify the police promptly will reduce the moral hazard.

When a claim is made under the coverage for damage to your auto, you must

1. Take reasonable steps after a loss, at company expense, to protect your covered auto and its equipment from further damage.

2. Notify the police promptly if your covered auto is stolen.

3. Permit the company to inspect and appraise the damaged property before its repair or disposal.

If you have an accident, the insurer will pay towing expenses. If the disabled vehicle is left at the scene of the accident, a chance exists that someone will strip it of its salable parts. Promptly notifying the police when theft occurs increases the probability of recovery. It also reduces the moral hazard of an insured's selling or hiding the vehicle and then reporting it as stolen to the insurer. The third item allows the insurer to make its own claims adjustment if it so desires. In some locations, insureds and repair mechanics have filed inflated claims in order to collect excess monies. This provision helps the insurer prevent such activities.

General Provisions

The policy states that its territorial limits are the United States, its territories or possessions, and Canada. Transportation of the auto between any of these points also is covered. Technically, Puerto Rico, a commonwealth, is also within the territorial limits. It should be noted that Mexico is not a covered territory.

Other conditions include a policy change provision stating that all policy modifications must be in writing. When a policy is changed to give greater coverage without additional charge, the insured's policy is automatically modified. The insured cannot start legal proceedings until full compliance with all policy terms has been met. The policy cannot be assigned without the written permission of the insurer. Bankruptcy of the insured does not relieve the insurer of its obligations.

Policy Cancellation Provisions

The PAP policy has a rather lengthy termination (cancellation) provision. The insured can cancel at any time by returning the policy or giving written notice of the time when the insured intends to cancel. Termination by the company is more complex.

During the first 60 days of the policy, the insurer may cancel for any reason, and it may cancel for nonpayment of premium at any time. The insurer has 60 days to investigate the insured and make its underwriting decision. During the first 60 days, the insurer must give 10 days' notice before cancelling. After the policy has been in effect for 60 days, the insurer can cancel only (1) for nonpayment of premium; (2) if the insured or a resident of the household, or someone who regularly uses the auto, has his or her license suspended or revoked; or (3) if the policy was obtained through material misrepresentation. When cancellation is made after the first 60 days, 20 days' notice must be given. If the insurer decides not to renew the policy at the end of the policy period, it must give 20 days' notice.

For example, if you purchase a six-month insurance policy on February 1, 2007, pay your premium, and do not have your license revoked, after 60 days the insurer cannot cancel your policy. Thus, after April 1, 2007, the insurer must wait until policy renewal time to take action. On or before July 11, 2007 (20 days before the policy expires), the insurer would have to decide not to renew your policy. The effect of this cancellation clause is to give insureds some assurance that coverage will be provided until the policy's expiration date.

If your state requires longer notice than the PAP gives, then your state law will determine the notification period. The insurance company is obligated to give you a refund of the premium if one is due. However, it is not required to tender the refund when it cancels. You may have to ask for it.

Endorsements to the PAP

The PAP may be endorsed to give physical damage coverage to owned trailers. This endorsement is made on a schedule basis. When nonowned autos are furnished for your regular use, the extended nonowned liability endorsement is needed, which gives coverage for nonowned autos furnished for your regular use, for commercial vehicles (trucks) for business use (except auto business), and for the operation of a vehicle to carry persons for a fee.

In the case of a custom van, the insured needs to add a covered property endorsement. If this action is not taken, all custom work on the van will be excluded.

The **underinsured motorists endorsement** is a recent development. It provides the insured protection when another person who is inadequately insured causes the insured to be injured. For example, the negligent third party might carry limits of $50,000, but the insured suffered injuries of $150,000. Uninsured motorist protection will not pay because the $50,000 coverage meets the financial responsibility law. However, if underinsured motorist protection of $100,000 had been purchased, the insured could collect $50,000 from the negligent third party and $100,000 from their own insurance company. In some states this coverage may act as a difference in limits basis. In this example, the insured carried $100,000 underinsured coverage, and the negligent party carried $50,000 of liability limits. Thus, the insured is paid $50,000 by his carrier, the difference in limits ($100,000 − $50,000 = $50,000).

In some states, such as Georgia, underinsured motorist insurance is included in uninsured motorist coverage. Remember, these provisions only apply if the other driver is at fault.

Motorcycles and Other Vehicles

Because of changing lifestyles and the fact that people own more than just one type of motor vehicle, insurance companies have developed coverages to meet the needs of the public. Through the use of the "Miscellaneous Type Vehicle Endorsement," under the PAP a person can insure motorcycles, motor homes, golf carts, or other similar types of vehicles. In addition, a private passenger auto owned jointly by two or more resident relatives other than a husband and wife may be insured—for example, a father and his daughter. Through this endorsement, almost any vehicle may be insured. Coverages available include liability, medical payments, uninsured motorists, collision, and loss other than collision.

When this endorsement is used, the definition of your covered auto is modified to fit the description of the miscellaneous vehicle. All the provisions of the PAP are retained and apply to that vehicle.

Although very similar in coverage to the PAP, this endorsement creates three changes:

1. Newly acquired miscellaneous vehicles are covered if they are like the insured vehicle. Thus, if a motorcycle is insured, then an additional motorcycle would be covered, but a motor home would not.
2. Temporary substitute autos of any kind are covered. However, other than for a temporary substitute auto. No coverage is available for nonowned vehicles.
3. Exclusion with respect to vehicles with fewer than four wheels is changed when a motorcycle is insured.

Snowmobiles

Snowmobiles may be insured by endorsement to the PAP. This approach has advantages over purchasing snowmobile insurance through the homeowners program. When the PAP is used, one can purchase uninsured motorist and physical damage insurance in addition to liability insurance, snowmobiles subject to motor vehicle registrations can be covered, and the named insured and family members may be covered under medical payments.

Auto Loan/Lease Coverage

This endorsement is also known as "gap" insurance. It provides protection to the insured and/or the lending institution for the difference between the actual cash value of a car and the outstanding debt or residual value on a lease.

Today, many car buyers are able to finance new cars with a minimum down payment and low introductory interest rates or low lease payments. In the early years of a car loan, the outstanding balance on the loan often declines less quickly than the actual cash value of the vehicle. If the car is totaled in an accident, the maximum the insurer will pay is the actual cash value, which may be less than what the insured owes.

For example, assume Tommy Stith purchases an $18,000 car with no down payment and low monthly payments spread over a number of years. At the end of three years, the actual cash value of the car may be $12,000, and the insured still owes $15,000 on the loan. If the car is totaled, the insurer will pay $12,000 minus the deductible, and the insured is responsible for the deficiency. With the auto loan/lease coverage endorsement, the insured only pays the deductible. This endorsement may be of benefit to recent college graduates who have limited current resources.

AUTOMOBILE INSURANCE AND THE LAW

What happens if you are seriously injured in an auto accident caused by another driver, but the at-fault driver has no assets and no insurance? Unfortunately, many people have been faced with this situation. In every U.S. state and in all the provinces of Canada, legislatures have passed some form of automobile insurance law designed to deal with the problem of the uncompensated victim of financially irresponsible automobile drivers. In other words, the law has stepped in because without some system of financial guarantees, motorists are forced into retaining risk whether they are financially able or not. (Most often, they are not.) Accordingly, legislatures have attempted various methods to cope with the problem. Laws have taken the following forms:

1. Financial responsibility laws
2. Compulsory liability insurance laws
3. Unsatisfied judgment funds
4. Uninsured/underinsured motorist coverage
5. No-fault laws

The first four methods are discussed in the following sections; no-fault insurance is considered in Chapter 14. Table 13-6 summarizes the required limits of liability for each state and the District of Columbia.

Financial Responsibility Laws

Financial responsibility laws represent a common approach to the general problem of the uncompensated victim of the financially irresponsible motorist. Most such laws have two basic requirements:

1. Motorists without liability insurance who are involved in an automobile accident must obtain and maintain liability insurance or other proof of financial responsibility (for example, a surety bond) of a specified character for a given period, usually three years, as a condition of continued licensing of the operator and registration of the vehicle.

TABLE 13-6   **Automobile Insurance Liability Requirements**

State	Required Limits (thousands of $)	State	Required Limits (thousands of $)
Alabama	20/40/10	Montana	25/50/10
Alaska	50/100/25	Nebraska	25/50/25
Arizona	15/30/10	Nevada	15/30/10
Arkansas	25/50/25	New Hampshire	25/50/25
California	15/30/5	New Jersey	15/30/5
Colorado	25/50/15	New Mexico	25/50/10
Connecticut	20/40/10	New York	25/50/10
Delaware	15/30/5	North Carolina	30/60/25
D.C.	25/50/10	North Dakota	25/50/25
Florida	10/20/10	Ohio	12.5/25/7.5
Georgia	25/50/25	Oklahoma	10/20/10
Hawaii	20/40/10	Oregon	25/50/10
Idaho	25/50/15	Pennsylvania	15/30/5
Illinois	20/40/15	Rhode Island	25/50/25
Indiana	25/50/10	South Carolina	15/30/10
Iowa	20/40/15	South Dakota	25/50/25
Kansas	25/50/10	Tennessee	25/50/10
Kentucky	25/50/10	Texas	20/40/15
Louisiana	10/20/10	Utah	25/50/15
Maine	50/100/25	Vermont	25/50/10
Maryland	20/40/15	Virginia	25/50/20
Massachusetts	20/40/5	Washington	25/50/10
Michigan	20/40/10	West Virginia	20/40/10
Minnesota	30/60/10	Wisconsin	25/50/10
Mississippi	10/20/5	Wyoming	25/50/20
Missouri	25/50/10		

Source: *The Fact Book 2004* (New York: Insurance Information Institute, 2004), 47.

2.   Motorists without liability insurance who are involved in an automobile accident must pay for the damages they have caused, or give evidence that they were not to blame, as a condition for the continued operation of their vehicle.

In their early development, financial responsibility laws often contained only the first requirement, but gradually the second requirement, called **security provisions**, was added. Financial responsibility laws have no penalty other than the suspension of driving privileges and hence are not guarantees that the uncompensated victim will actually be paid. The effectiveness of the laws in this regard rests on the hope that most drivers will be led to purchase insurance rather than face possible loss of their driving privileges.

Although financial responsibility laws are better than nothing, they have serious drawbacks as solutions to the problem of compensating victims of uninsured or financially irresponsible motorists. Major weaknesses include the following:

1.   No assurance is made that all drivers will have liability insurance. The laws aim only at assuring financial responsibility for the irresponsible motorist's second and subsequent victims, not the first victim.

2.   The penalty for not complying with the law is weak; the motorist is subject only to the loss of driving privileges.

3. No protection is given against hit-and-run drivers, people driving stolen cars, or motorists driving illegally. Enforcement procedures against these drivers are difficult and relatively unsuccessful.

Compulsory Insurance Laws

Because of the inherent weaknesses of financial responsibility laws, most states have implemented **compulsory insurance laws**. The laws require that auto liability insurance with at least specified minimum limits be purchased before a vehicle can be licensed or registered. Unfortunately, these laws have not solved the problem. Even in states with compulsory insurance, still a large number of drivers are uninsured. For this reason, alternate mechanisms have been set up to compensate victims of uninsured drivers, as the following describes.

Unsatisfied Judgment Fund

A small handful of states have established **unsatisfied judgment funds (UJF)**. The unsatisfied judgment fund is set up by a state to pay automobile accident settlements that cannot be collected by other means. If the negligent motorist is insolvent, does not carry liability insurance, or has voided insurance through violation of a policy provision, or if the insurer is insolvent, the innocent victim may collect from the UJF after every other means of collection is exhausted. The UJF is actually broader than compulsory insurance, because it covers cases in which insurance was carried but the damages are still uncollectible. The UJF is based on the principle of negligence; hence, if no legal liability exists, no payment can be made from the fund. Furthermore, the UJF has the right of subrogation; that is, it must be paid back by the negligent motorist if he or she obtains property on which liens may be obtained. In any case, the negligent motorist loses driving privileges until the fund is repaid.

Uninsured/Underinsured Motorist Coverage

The solution to the problem of the uncompensated victim of the uninsured motorist that has been proposed and supported by private insurance companies is uninsured/underinsured motorist coverage, which was discussed earlier in this chapter. Under the terms of this coverage, which usually applies only to bodily injury claims (property damage is covered in some states), if it is determined that an insured driver is injured by a driver who is uninsured (or who has insurance with limits inadequate to cover the damages), the injured driver can collect from his or her own insurance company any damages that the negligent uninsured motorist would be legally obligated to pay, up to the insured's own uninsured/underinsured motorist coverage limit. The insurer naturally has the right to collect from the negligent uninsured motorist for any damages paid to the insured motorist, in the unlikely case the that the uninsured driver has the assets to pay. As mentioned in the discussion of the PAP earlier in the chapter, this coverage also applies if the insured is injured by a hit-and-run driver or a driver who is insured but whose insurance company is insolvent.

In some ways, uninsured motorist coverage is a less than satisfying way to deal with the problem of uninsured drivers, since it requires responsible drivers to pay for the irresponsibility of other drivers. However, the approach does overcome an important weakness in the typical financial responsibility law. For a charge, an individual can be certain they have protection against bodily injury damage caused by uninsured motorists. Financial responsibility laws and compulsory insurance laws provide no such assurance. The cost of this coverage is relatively low, and many insureds would be wise to buy limits of $50,000 or more.

 ## RISK MANAGEMENT AND PERSONAL AUTOMOBILE RATING

Before an informed risk management decision concerning personal automobile insurance can be made, an understanding of automobile insurance rating is needed. The average expenditure for auto insurance in the United States in 2001 was $718, making insurance a significant factor in the cost of owning or operating automobiles. For some insureds, the cost is dramatically higher than the average, while for others, it is lower. Given the high cost level and variability of costs across individuals, it is important to understand the key factors influencing the cost of auto insurance.

Rating Factors

As most college students know, two of the key determinants of auto insurance premiums are the age and sex of the driver. **Youthful drivers**, and especially youthful male drivers, tend to pay significantly more for auto insurance than older drivers. Generally, a person is considered a youthful driver until age 25 if female and until age 30 if male. The reason youthful drivers are charged more for auto insurance, of course, is that on average they have higher claims. Recall from earlier in the chapter that young drivers are involved in a disproportionate number of auto accidents. The difference in premiums between males and females is driven by multiple factors. First, males tend to drive more than females, which naturally leads to more accidents. Males account for about 62 percent of total miles driven each year. In addition, males are involved in more fatal accidents per mile driven than females. In 2002, the rate of male drivers in fatal crashes per 1 billion miles driven was 22, while for females it was only 13.

Marital status also affects insurance premiums. Young married drivers pay lower auto insurance premiums than young unmarried drivers. Again, the reason is that statistics show that young married drivers (males in particular) have fewer accidents than young unmarried drivers.

Territory is also a major rating factor. This is obvious by looking at the variation of auto insurance premiums across states. In 2001, the lowest average expenditure on auto insurance, $510, was in South Dakota, while the highest average expenditure, more than double that of South Dakota at $1128, was in New Jersey. Even within a state, premiums vary dramatically by territory. For example, premiums in urban areas tend to be higher due to higher accident rates in cities compared to rural areas.

The principal use of the car is also a rating factor. Rates vary depending on whether the auto is used to drive to and from work, and if so, how far each day. Rates also vary depending on whether the auto is generally used for business or farm purposes.

Most of the previous factors are difficult or impossible for a person to control in order to reduce his or her auto insurance premiums. (While certainly possible, it is very unwise to get married just to reduce your insurance premiums!) However, some of the factors affecting the cost of auto insurance are within the control of the individual. For example, the type of auto driven can significantly influence insurance premiums. Sports cars are more costly to insure for liability than sedans, for example. For physical damage coverages, the value of the auto and its damage resistance are clearly critical factors. Good students also can obtain discounts on their auto insurance, as can youthful drivers who complete a driver education course. Insuring multiple vehicles under one policy can yield a multi-car discount, and purchasing auto and homeowners insurance from the same insurer can yield a multi-policy discount.

Probably the most important thing a person can do to control the cost of his or her auto insurance in the long run is to drive carefully. The insured's driving record has a major influence on premiums. Auto accidents, speeding tickets and other moving violations, and convictions for driving while intoxicated all lead to higher premiums, sometimes dramatically higher.

Another rating factor used by some insurers is credit history. Statistics show that people with poor credit tend to have higher auto insurance claims. Not surprisingly, use of credit history in auto insurance rating has been very controversial. Many insurers feel that it is an entirely appropriate rating factor because of the statistical relationship between poor credit and

ETHICAL PERSPECTIVES

It's a Gray Area

Much has been written on the driving record of persons under the age of 25. However, with the graying of America, more attention is now being paid to the driving records of older Americans. This group (75 and older) has the worst driving record after youthful drivers. Beginning at age 55, driving skills may begin to decline. By age 75, most drivers' skills drop off dramatically. Major problems develop with respect to vision (especially at night), hearing, reaction time, and agility. Medication also may affect older drivers, and some have difficulty seeing over the steering wheel. However, the ability to drive and have a license means independence, and the elderly are often reluctant to give up their licenses. How can concerns for safety be reconciled with individual rights? Some states have begun requiring driving tests of older drivers, while other require vision tests or medical tests. The goal is to allow competent senior citizens to continue to drive and force the others to surrender their licenses.

claims. Critics argue that using credit history is unfair to lower-income insureds who may be more likely to have had credit problems.

Deductibles for Damage to Your Auto

In the PAP, deductibles exist for collision and for loss other than collision (comprehensive). Higher deductibles reduce premiums. The schedules in Table 13-7 provide illustrative examples of the premium discount one can possibly receive for accepting a higher deductible. Choosing a high deductible may not make much of a difference in absolute dollars for a middle-age driver of a safe car in a rural area with no history of accidents or traffic violations. However, for a young, single male with a DWI conviction who drives a sports car, the choice of a $1,000 deductible instead of a $200 deductible can save a significant amount of money.

The Youthful Drive Dilemma

Insurance companies are more sensitive to claims in the automobile line than they are in most other lines. It may not take more than one claim to cause an insured's costs to increase significantly. This statement is especially true with respect to male drivers under 25 and females under 21. Given this sensitivity to losses for youthful drivers, the smart move for many young drivers may be not to purchase collision coverage.

TABLE 13-7 | **Examples of Credits for Collision and Comprehensive Deductibles**

Deductible ($)	Collision	Deductible ($)	Comprehensive
250	95% of $200 deductible rate	200	90% of $100 deductible rate
500	80% of $200 deductible rate	250	85% of $100 deductible rate
1,000	55% of $200 deductible rate	1,000	55% of $100 deductible rate

Source: Southern Mutual Insurance Company.

The rationale follows these lines: (1) Any claim for which the insured is responsible, liability or collision, will cause rates to be increased; (2) it usually takes at least three years of claim-free driving before rates will be lowered; (3) it is often difficult to obtain coverage, even when paying higher rates; (4) given factors 1, 2, and 3, the insured should not make any kind of collision claim, so it is not wise to purchase insurance that will not be used.

This strategy works best when the car involved is worth only a few thousand dollars and there is no outstanding loan on the car. If the insured drives a 2007 BMW, the best strategy would be to purchase collision with a high deductible and to avoid accidents at all costs.

Selection of Liability Limits

When people are choosing their liability limits, if they have any meaningful amount of assets to protect, they should think big. Each year awards increase as both economic inflation and social inflation occur. If liability rate schedules are examined, it can be shown that on a relative basis, higher liability limits are not overly expensive. Table 13-8 shows a typical schedule.

From the table, it can been seen that liability limits can be raised from $40,000 to $500,000 for only a 45 percent increase in premium and can go from limits of $500,000 to $1,000,000 for an additional 10 percent increase in premiums (160 ÷ 145). Such a rating schedule makes higher liability limits an attractive purchase.

TABLE 13-8   **Liability Rate Factor for Personal Auto Policy**

Limit ($)	Factor
40,000	1.00
500,000	1.45
1,000,000	1.60

Source: Southern Mutual Insurance Company.

SUMMARY

1. The cost of automobile accidents is very high in the United States, posing a serious problem as to the most efficient and equitable manner in which the economic burden can be borne. Cars have become safer over the years, and the fatality rate has fallen, but costs are still high.
2. Because a single automobile accident may be catastrophically expensive to the victim, and because of the relatively high probability of loss, insurance is the only feasible method to protect against the risk involved for most people.
3. The provisions of the personal automobile policy (PAP) are representative of those found in most contracts covering the use of automobiles. The PAP is one of the most comprehensive contracts,

insuring against losses due to legal liability for negligence, medical payments, and physical damage to the vehicle. Under the terms of the PAP, the words *insured* and *automobile* are defined broadly to protect the typical car owner and to give nearly the same protection to anyone else driving the automobile with the owner's permission.
4. Liability coverage under the PAP applies to loss due to legal liability for damage to the person or property of others arising out of the ownership, maintenance, and use of the automobile. Medical payments coverage insures the loss due to accidental bodily injuries of occupants of a vehicle regardless of negligence of the insured driver. Physical damage insurance reimburses the owner for

physical loss of a vehicle from almost any peril, whether the insured caused the accident. Uninsured motorist coverage protects insureds when they have an accident with a negligent uninsured motorist.

5. Because the definitions, exclusions, and conditions are as important as they are basic to an understanding of the PAP, they must be studied carefully to ascertain the scope of coverage. In general, coverage granted by the insured's policy when the insured is driving nonowned cars is less comprehensive than when the insured is driving his or her own car.

6. Among the approaches that have been tried to deal with the problem of uninsured drivers are financial responsibility laws, compulsory liability insurance, unsatisfied judgment funds, uninsured/underinsured motorist coverage, and no-fault insurance laws.

7. Auto insurance rates are determined by a number of factors, some of which are under an individual insured's control and some of which are not. The bottom line is that auto insurance premiums can vary dramatically from person to person.

internet*exercises*

1. Set your Web browser to http://www. insweb.com. Choose two drivers and two automobiles with which you are familiar (your own, a friend's, a relative's). The drivers and the automobiles should be substantially different from one another. Obtain a quote for each automobile and each driver. What are the differences in premiums? Considering the questions asked for rating purposes, what do you think caused the differences in the premiums?

2. Set your Web browser to http://www.iii.org and click on the Hot Topics and Issues button. Scroll down to the Insurance Issues section and click on Auto Theft. What is being done to reduce the problem of motor vehicle theft? What is the trend in the number of vehicles stolen each year?

QUESTIONS FOR REVIEW AND DISCUSSION

1. Because Y's car is broken down, Y borrows his son's car to run an errand. The son, who lives with Y in the same household, does not have his car insured. If Y had an accident, would his PAP cover him? Explain why or why not.

2. G's daughter gives permission for a neighbor to borrow her father's car, thinking it will be all right because the neighbor is a good friend of her family. Under the terms of the PAP, will the neighbor be covered while driving G's car? Why or why not?

3. S pulls a large house trailer behind his vehicle each year on a winter vacation that lasts four months.
   a. Assuming limits of $10,000 property damage, what coverage is granted to S under the PAP if the trailer sideswipes another car, causing a $1,000 loss to the trailer and a $2,000 loss to the other car?
   b. Would your answer be different if the trailer had been a small two-wheel camping trailer with sleeping accommodations for two? Why or why not?

4. Josephine has a $100 deductible for collision on her car, whereas Ellen carries a $200 deductible. If Josephine borrows Ellen's car and has a collision in which $200 damage is done, which policy must respond and in what amount? Why?

5. In the case of *Farm Bureau Mutual Automobile Insurance Company v Boecher* (48 N.E. 2d 895), the insured was involved in an accident while driving a car made available to employees by his employer, an auto dealer. The insured, who had

never driven this particular vehicle before, applied for coverage under his private automobile policy and was denied protection on the grounds that the policy excluded coverage on nonowned cars. With reference to the provisions of the PAP, discuss the correctness or incorrectness of the position taken by the insurer.

6. How may motorcycles be insured under the PAP?

7. Under automobile rating methods, what factors reduce a person's rates and what factors contribute to rate increases?

8. If you are riding in a school bus and there is an accident, how will the medical payments section of your PAP respond with respect to your injuries and the injuries of others on the bus? Explain.

9. "About one in four drivers is expected to have an accident in a typical driving year, but some drivers have a much higher probability of loss than others." Explain.

10. Suggest possible reasons why auto manufacturers do not make cars safer than they do, thus reducing insurance costs of operating them.

11. Discuss the basic reason for the exclusion in the PAP of injury to employees of the insured.

12. An insured's son, after becoming intoxicated, broke into the insured's locked vehicle and, while driving it at high speed, wrecked the vehicle. If the insured had loss-other-than-collision insurance but not collision insurance, what line of reasoning might lead to the conclusion that the damage was covered under the PAP? Discuss.

chapter 14

In this chapter, we will examine where the auto insurance premium goes, and what factors influence the cost of auto insurance. Many people assume that much of what is paid as auto insurance premiums simply goes into the profits of the insurance companies. As we will see, this is not generally true.

We will also look at how much of the premium dollar is spent on paying to fix cars, how much is spent on compensating injured people, and how much is spent on lawyers. Once we understand how insurance premiums are spent, we will discuss ways in which auto insurance costs can be brought down, including an alternative to the traditional tort system called *no-fault*. The reason automobile insurance deserves such attention is that nearly half of all property-liability insurance premiums are for either personal or commercial auto insurance. Most states require every driver to have insurance. Auto insurance is an issue that almost everyone must deal with throughout their lives.

Risk Management for Auto Owners—Part II

CHAPTER OBJECTIVES

After studying this chapter, you should be able to

1. Describe how the average automobile insurance dollar is used.
2. Identify and describe some of the key factors that drive automobile insurance costs.
3. Describe actions that individuals, governments, and insurers could take to reduce auto insurance costs.
4. Explain how no-fault auto insurance operates and how it might reduce auto insurance premiums.
5. Discuss the trade-offs among benefit levels, the right to sue, and automobile insurance costs.
6. Review attempts to reduce the problem of drinking and driving.
7. Explain some of the advancements made in auto safety during the past 20 years.
8. Discuss trade-offs among automobile safety, better mileage, and the cost of autos.

WHERE DOES THE AUTO INSURANCE PREMIUM GO?

The one thing most people agree about when it comes to auto insurance is that it is expensive. People often assume that because it is expensive, insurers must make massive profits on each policy sold. It is interesting to look at where the actual premium dollar goes. Table 14-1 provides detailed information on that topic. In 2002, for every $100 in auto insurance premiums collected by insurers, $80 was spent on claims ($33 for payments to injured persons and associated legal costs, $47 for payments for damage to cars), and $24 was spent on expenses (sales commissions, company operations, premium taxes, etc.).[1] In other words, for every $100 received in premiums, $104 was paid out in losses and expenses. Does that mean the insurance industry lost money in auto insurance in 2002? Actually, considering investment gains, insurers made $1 in after-tax profit for every $100 of premiums collected.

TABLE 14-1   U.S. Premium Dollar Expenditures, 2002

	Dollars
Premiums earned	100
Categories of Expenditures	
Payments to Injured Persons	
Medical	10
Wage loss and other economic payments	2
Pain/Suffering/Other noneconomic awards	6
Lawyers' fees	13
Other costs of settling claims	2
Subtotal	33
Payments for Damage to Cars	
Property damage liability	19
Collision claims	18
Comprehensive claims	8
Other costs of settling claims	2
Subtotal	47
Total Claims	**80**
Expenses	
Commissions and other selling expenses	16
General expenses	5
State premium taxes, licenses, and fees	2
Dividends to policyholders	1
Total Expenses	**24**
Claims and Expenses Total	**104**

Source: *The Fact Book 2004* (New York: Insurance Information Institute, 2004), 38.

---

1 Unless otherwise stated, all statistics in this chapter are from *The Fact Book 2004* (New York: Insurance Information Institute, 2004).

Of the $80 of each $100 of premiums that is spent on claims, the majority ($47) is spent on payments for damage to cars. Most of that is either for property damage liability claims or for collision claims. Comprehensive (loss other than collision) claims account for a much small proportion of losses.

The fact that most auto claims expenses are for repairing damage to autos is a key reason why there has been so much controversy over the use of aftermarket parts in auto repair. Aftermarket parts are often dramatically less expensive than original equipment manufacturer (OEM) parts. It is obvious why insurers might be interested in using aftermarket parts in repairing insured vehicles. Some insureds would be happy with this as well, since it would lead to lower premiums. However, some people argue that aftermarket parts are of lesser quality than OEM parts and that insurers must use OEM parts to fulfill their obligation to provide an insurance payment in an amount "necessary to repair or replace the property with other property of like kind and quality." (This quote is from the PAP discussed in Chapter 13.) Insurers have faced numerous lawsuits over this issue.

State legislatures and the industry have responded in a variety of ways to the controversy over aftermarket parts. For example, most states have passed legislation requiring insurers to notify insureds when aftermarket parts are being used. Other states have gone further. In Massachusetts, for example, all vehicles with fewer than 15,000 miles of use must be repaired with OEM parts. Other states have laws that encourage the use of aftermarket parts when they are available. The insurance industry's approach to the issue has been equally varied. Some insurers state that they always use OEM parts. Others generally use aftermarket parts unless the insured has purchased an endorsement that provides for use of only OEM parts. The controversy over OEM versus aftermarket parts is sure to continue.

AUTO DEATH RATES

In any given year, millions of automobile accidents occur resulting in approximately 42,000 auto-related deaths in the United States. Automobile accidents are the leading cause of death for people under the age of 25.

Table 14-2 provides the annual number of deaths from vehicle accidents in recent years, as well as the death rate per 100 million miles driven. The total number of fatalities has stayed relatively stable. The good news is that the death rate per 100 million miles driven has consistently declined over time. In just the 10 years from 1993 to 2002, this rate declined almost 14 percent.

TABLE 14-2   Traffic Deaths, Selected Years

Year	# of Fatalities	Death Rate per 100 Million Miles
1993	40,150	1.75
1995	41,817	1.73
1997	42,013	1.64
1999	41,717	1.55
2001	42,196	1.52
2002	42,815	1.51

Source: *The Fact Book 2004* (New York: Insurance Information Institute, 2004), 99.

The death rate is not equal across the 50 states. As shown in Table 14-3, in 2002 Montana had a death rate of 2.6 per 100 million miles driven, and Mississippi had a rate of 2.4. By contrast, Vermont's rate was 0.8 per 100 million miles, and Massachusetts had a rate of 0.9. In general, southern and western states have the highest rates, and New England has the lowest. In the absolute number of deaths, California and Texas led the way due to their large populations, with 3,926 and 3,727 deaths, respectively. However, their rates per 100 million miles were only 1.3 and 1.7, respectively.

Table 14-3 also reveals that low death rates do not always lead to low average premiums in a state. In fact, some of the states with the lowest death rates have some of the highest average expenditures on auto insurance. Massachusetts, Rhode Island, and Connecticut are prime examples. Congestion seems to be a much bigger factor than the death rate. This is probably not surprising since, as discussed earlier, most claims dollars are spent on auto repair, and congested areas often have large numbers of nonfatal accidents that still cause expensive physical damage. Differing regulatory environments also contribute to the variation in premiums across states. Table 14-4 provides average auto insurance expenditures for additional states.

CAR THEFT

A significant portion of the cost of automobile insurance is due to the theft of cars. Approximately 1.2 million motor vehicles are stolen each year in the United States, with a value of over $8 billion. On average, a car is stolen every 25 seconds. The odds of any particular vehicle being stolen in 2001 was 1 in 194.

An interesting observation is that American thieves tend to prefer stealing foreign cars. Of the 25 most frequently stolen vehicles in 2002, only 4 were domestic. The top domestic vehicle on the list is the 1994 Chevrolet C1500 4 × 2 at number 6. Fifteen of the top twenty-five were Hondas and five were Toyotas, including the top three (the 1989 Toyota Camry, the 1991 Toyota Camry, and the 1990 Toyota Camry).

TABLE 14-3   **2002 Death Rates and 2001 Average Premium Outlay for Selected States**

State	Death Rate per 100 Million Miles	Average Premium Expenditure
Montana	2.6	$572
Mississippi	2.4	637
West Virginia	2.2	707
South Carolina	2.2	617
Louisiana	2.1	839
Arizona	2.1	822
Arkansas	2.1	621
Connecticut	1.0	912
New Hampshire	1.0	686
Rhode Island	1.0	880
Massachusetts	0.9	936
Vermont	0.8	603

Source: *The Fact Book 2004* (New York: Insurance Information Institute, 2004), 40–41, 100.

TABLE 14-4	2002 Average Auto Insurance Expenditures for Selected States	
State	Premium	National Ranking
Alabama	$ 605	39
California	689	23
Connecticut	912	5
Washington, D.C.	1,012	3
Florida	788	13
Georgia	703	22
Illinois	683	25
Indiana	615	35
Iowa	513	49
Louisiana	839	9
Michigan	735	18
New Jersey	1,028	1
New York	1,015	2
North Carolina	565	43
North Dakota	498	51
Ohio	614	36
Pennsylvania	726	19
Texas	735	16
Virginia	610	38
Washington	750	15
Wisconsin	573	41
USA	718	—

Source: *The Fact Book 2004* (New York: Insurance Information Institute, 2004), 40–41.

As might be expected, urban areas tend to have higher theft rates. In 2002, Phoenix-Mesa, Arizona; Fresno, California; and Modesto, California led the nation. Unfortunately, the recovery rate on stolen vehicles is low. One of the reasons is the use of "chop shops." A stolen vehicle is taken to a garage (chop shop) where in minutes the more valuable parts of the vehicle are removed. It is very difficult to prove to which cars all the separate parts belong, and they can be sold without the need to identify the cars from which they came. In addition, more than 200,000 stolen vehicles are illegally exported out of the United States each year. Nine of the ten metropolitan areas with the highest vehicle theft rate in 2002 are in or near port or border communities.

COST CONTAINMENT

Risk managers realize that insurance should be considered within the context of all available risk management tools. For example, several ways exist to lower losses from automobile accidents: (1) reduce the frequency and severity of accidents, (2) restrict payments, and (3) redistribute expenses and losses.

Loss Control and Prevention

If fewer accidents occur, costs should be lower, or at least should not increase as quickly. Accidents can be reduced by building better highways and safer cars and perhaps by lowering speed limits, to name a few options. Expanding the interstate highway system is one way to make highways safer, as are breakaway light posts and guardrails and impact barriers. Although insurers can lobby for such road improvements, they are not in a position to require them or pay for them. Various government units have great demands on their financial resources, and safe roads are only one such demand. Even to the extent to which legislators wish to spend taxpayer money on transportation needs, frequent debates still occur over the proper balance of spending between highways and mass transit. With growing concerns over pollution and congestion, mass transit may get a larger slice of the pie in the years ahead.

For the past 30 years, the federal government and the insurance industry have been encouraging the automobile industry to build safer cars that will not be severely damaged in minor auto accidents. The 5 miles per hour bumper standard has been lowered to 2.5 miles per hour—that is, auto manufacturers have to build cars with bumpers that prevent any damage to the body of the vehicle in accidents occurring at 2.5 miles per hour. Modern bumpers provide little, if any, damage protection in most accidents.

Airbags represent a significant example of automobile safety improvements. As is often the case with new safety innovations, the auto industry did not rush to embrace airbags, since they increase the cost of automobiles. In fact, many safety features in autos have been mandated by the federal government, not promoted by the auto industry.

Many authorities believe that lowering speed limits reduces the number of accidents and certainly has a favorable effect on reducing fatalities. When the speed limit on interstate highways was lowered to 55 miles per hour, the number of auto-related deaths declined. Also, less damage and fewer injuries occurred when accidents did happen. The insurance industry has been a big supporter of lower speed limits. However, many people don't want to drive long distances at 55 miles per hour, especially when the highways are built for speeds up to 85 miles per hour. Thus, by popular demand, speed limits on many highways have been raised.

Vehicle size is an important factor in accident severity. The death rate in the smallest cars on the road is significantly higher than that in the largest cars because small cars offer passengers less protection. Beginning in the 1970s as a result of soaring gasoline prices, a significant trend emerged toward purchasing small cars with excellent gas mileage. In the past decade, the trend has instead been toward larger trucks and sport utility vehicles. SUVs are interesting in that while they are larger and thus provide more passenger protection in accidents, they also tend to have higher rates of rollover. Obviously, while safety is certainly often a factor in people's choice of automobiles, other factors often dominate.

Restriction of Payments

Restricting payments can help hold down the cost of auto insurance. One way insurers can restrict payments is by fighting fraudulent claims. However, insurers must not be so aggressive in their investigations that they deny legitimate claims. Insurers never want to pay fraudulent claims, but being overly aggressive can result in antagonizing honest policyholders, or even lead to bad faith legal claims against the insurer. The goal is to pay every legitimate claim, but *only* legitimate claims. This is a difficult balance with which insurers constantly struggle.

Another way insurers can restrict payments to reduce auto insurance premiums is to encourage the use of larger deductibles by giving attractive rate credits for them. In many cases, persons do not choose the $1,000 deductible option simply because the rate credits do not make it appealing to do so. Consumers may have the financial resources to assume the larger deductible but believe that the $1,000 deductible is a poor buy. Through the use of more attractive pricing of higher deductibles, insurers would reduce overhead and claims adjustment expenses be reducing the number of small physical damage claims.

Redistribution of Losses and Expenses

Most auto liability insurance claims are adjusted according to driver negligence. One party is determined to be at fault, and the guilty party pays for the loss. This process is based on tort law and is adversarial in nature. Those who desire reform, such as insurance companies and some consumer groups, describe the system as wasteful because lawyers' fees and other adjustment expenses consume too much of the premium dollar (see Table 14-1 earlier in this chapter). They say that small claims are frequently overpaid in order to get injured parties to settle quickly and that severely injured persons often do not receive enough payment and do not receive it for a lengthy period of time. They further claim that the contingency fee system encourages too much litigation. People can sue with almost no upfront costs and perhaps obtain a settlement; in essence, they have nothing to lose by suing. Of course, this litigation costs insurers money and helps drive up the cost of auto liability insurance for everyone.

netlink

Visit the "Auto Insurance Forum" at http://www.insure.com/auto/forum/ to see numerous automobile insurance questions submitted by drivers across the country, together with answers provided by insure.com.

Plaintiff lawyers and other consumer groups argue that the present system is satisfactory. They feel it gives the ordinary person his or her day in court and allows access to the legal system for everyone. They believe the costs are worth the benefits. Of course, plaintiffs' lawyers have a great deal to lose if the present system is changed to no-fault, as they receive much of their compensation from lawsuits.

NO-FAULT

Exactly what is a **no-fault** auto insurance system? Under a *pure* no-fault system (which no state has enacted), insureds would purchase auto insurance that would work similarly to property insurance. No person would be held liable for an accident, and the tort system would be eliminated. Each person's auto insurance would pay for damage to his or her car and for injuries to the insured and his or her family while riding in automobiles. No litigation would be necessary about fault, because the insurance policy would pay without regard to fault. The level of benefits would be determined by the consumer when the insurance policy was purchased. Under this system, the injured parties would be sure to receive payment for real economic losses (wages and/or salary) and medical expenses. However, no opportunity would exist to sue and collect for noneconomic losses, such as pain and suffering. Because no liability lawsuits would occur, there would be less need for the involvement of lawyers. Fewer insurance adjusters would be needed because fault would not have to be determined. The money saved through less fault determination could be used to provide consumers more benefits than at present. Thus, a redistribution of benefits would occur from lawyers and adjusters to insureds.

What is the potential sum of money to be gained from the no-fault process? As indicated in the earlier Table 14-1, the Insurance Information Institute has estimated that in 2002 $19 of every $33 paid for bodily injury liability payments goes toward legal fees and noneconomic losses. Not all of this money would be saved if universal no-fault insurance were adopted, but it does indicate the maximum. This $19 represents 57.6 percent of all payments for injuries. On the surface, then, it would seem possible to double payments for real economic losses and medical payments without raising rates. This doubling of payments could occur because the $19 for noneconomic losses and lawyers' fees would be spent on medical expenses, wage losses, and other economic payments. Because of this great potential either

ETHICAL PERSPECTIVES

Sunken Treasure

The Dallas police once found several late-model automobiles in a local swimming hole. It seems the owners had dumped their cars and reported them stolen to collect under their insurance policies. This is only one example of the increasing occurrence of insurance fraud.

On a national basis, fraud in the property-liability insurance industry cost insurers $31 billion in 2002. Insurance fraud is sometimes classified as either "hard" or "soft." Hard fraud involves fabrication of losses, such as

the cars in the swimming hole. Soft fraud is harder to fight. It involves such things as padding claims to cover deductibles and underreporting miles driven to lower premiums. Many people see nothing wrong with such practices, but they add significantly to the cost of automobile insurance each year. The National Insurance Crime Bureau estimates that fraud adds $200 to $300 per year to the average household's insurance premiums.

Source: *The Fact Book 2004* (New York: Insurance Information Institute, 2004), 120.

to save money and reduce rates or to significantly increase benefits, some insurers and consumer groups are strong supporters of no-fault.

Modified No-Fault

Because many Americans do not want to give up their right to bring a tort action and because of strong lobbying efforts by trial lawyers, no pure no-fault plans are in operation in the United States. Instead, various modified no-fault plans have been enacted or proposed by several states. Under these laws, the right to sue is restricted but not eliminated. One set of states uses a dollar threshold system. Once damages from an injury are greater than some dollar amount, called a **dollar threshold**, the insured may bring a tort action. These dollar thresholds vary across states; in Kentucky the threshold is only $1,000, and in Hawaii it is $5,000. Usually, the higher the threshold, the more effective the no-fault law, because litigation is reduced.

Instead of a dollar threshold, some states' laws specify a **verbal threshold**. In these states (Florida, Michigan, New Jersey, New York, and Pennsylvania) a verbal definition is used to determine the threshold. For instance, the Michigan law states that lawsuits may be allowed when fatal injury, serious disfigurement, or serious injury occurs. Most people agree that of the no-fault laws that restrict the consumer's right to sue, Michigan's law is said to be best; it is often given as the standard to compare all other laws or proposed laws.

Add-On States

Yet another approach, called an **add-on plan**, is used by 10 states. With this system, injured parties can collect from their own insurers, just as in a pure no-fault system. The difference is that with the add-on plan, no restrictions are placed on the ability to sue. Hence, the name *add-on*. The first-party benefits are purely an add-on with nothing being taken away in exchange.

Choice No-Fault

Finally, three states (Kentucky, New Jersey, and Pennsylvania) have enacted what are called **choice no-fault systems**. In choice no-fault states, people can choose to pay lower premiums to purchase no-fault coverage that restricts the right to sue, or they can pay higher premiums to retain their ability to sue.

Evaluation of No-Fault

No-fault has strong proponents and equally strong opponents. Since no state has enacted a pure no-fault system, and because states differ along so many dimensions when it comes to auto insurance issues, it is difficult to definitively state what the full implications of no-fault are. However, some studies have attempted to analyze actual and proposed no-fault systems. In a study by the Rand Corporation, various alternative no-fault plans were examined.[2] The study simulated 15 different plans for various tort-liability states and showed the results of choosing a given no-fault plan. The study made it clear that the specifics of the no-fault plan had a tremendous impact on cost implications of the system. For instance, it states, "No-fault can either increase or reduce total costs. In general, total costs:

1. Decline as the tort threshold increases,
2. Increase as the PIP benefit level increases,
3. Are reduced by a PIP deductible,
4. Are reduced if health insurance payments are offset."

In Table 14-5, several no-fault alternatives analyzed in the study are shown that confirm these observations. Even with a strong verbal threshold, if personal injury protection (PIP) benefits are as high as $250,000, no-fault may actually increase rates or at least increase insurer costs. However, a combination of a strong verbal threshold, $15,000 PIP benefits, and a $500 de-ductible in PIP cases leads to a reduction of insurer costs as high as 25 percent. Subsequent studies by Rand studied the choice no-fault approach, and concluded that such a system could reduce total auto insurance costs by about 30 percent.[3]

No-fault automobile insurance will continue to be an issue in the future, as the nation continues to grapple with the high cost of auto insurance. In the continuing debate on no-fault, society will have to decide what it desires: high benefits, the unrestricted right to sue and high costs, or some trade-off among benefits, the ability to sue, and costs. As is usually the case, it seems impossible to have it all.

TABLE 14-5	Potential Savings for Alternative No-Fault Approaches	
Plan	State	Percentage Change in Total Cost to Insurers
Verbal threshold,	California	+7
$250,000 benefit limit	Illinois	+10
	Ohio	+14
Verbal threshold,	California	−25
$15,000 benefit limit,	Illinois	−20
$500 deductible	Ohio	−21

Source: Stephen J. Carroll, James S. Kahalik, and Nick Pace, "The Effects of Alternative No-Fault Approaches to Compensating Auto Accident Victims," Rand Corporation, October 1990, Tables E 1.2, E 1.3, E 1.5, v, vi.

---

2   Stephen J. Carroll, James S. Kahalik, and Nick Pace, *The Effects of Alternative No-Fault Approaches to Compensating Accident Victims*, Rand Corporation, October 1990.
3   Rand Institute for Civil Justice Research Brief, 1995, http://www.rand.org/publications/RB/RB9024/RB9024.html.

ALCOHOL AND DRIVING

Driving automobiles while under the influence of alcoholic beverages is one of the most serious problems confronting society with respect to automobile-related deaths. Out of the 40,000+ such deaths in the United States each year, about 40 percent involve persons who have alcohol in their blood when the accident occurs.[4] In addition to deaths, about 258,000 people were injured in 2002 in alcohol-related auto accidents. These statistics includes both drivers and pedestrians. Over the past 20 years, **driving while intoxicated (DWI)** deaths have declined significantly, but they have actually increased in the past few years.

Part of the cause of the long-term reduction in alcohol-related deaths is due to the continuing efforts to reduce the incidence of drinking and driving and to study what factors are most important in discouraging such behavior. For instance, in the early 1970s many people thought that severe penalties would cause a sharp drop in drunk driving. However, some studies showed that these laws were not very effective. Recent studies have shown that swift action is more important than severe action. If drivers are to be convinced not to drink and drive, they must perceive that there is a high probability that they will be immediately caught and punished. For example, although some question the constitutionality of police roadblocks to check for drunk drivers, such procedures are now used in most states and are reasonably effective in convincing drivers that they will be caught if they drink and drive.

The organization Mothers Against Drunk Driving (MADD) has been very effective in bringing attention to the DWI problem and was a strong force in getting the legal drinking age raised to 21 years. By 1989, all states had done so. Although persons under the age of 21 are still involved in a large number of alcohol-related auto accidents, the raising of the legal drinking age tends to make it more difficult for drivers under the age of 21 to obtain alcoholic beverages. Another potential partial solution to the problem of underage drinking and driving may be some type of curfew for teenagers. Presently, certain communities are passing curfews to help reduce crime and drug problems related to teenagers. However, a side benefit may be a reduction in teenage auto accidents and in the deaths that result from such accidents, especially late-night accidents.

New Laws

In the fight against drunk driving, states are continuing to pass stricter laws, sometimes with the prodding of the federal government. Under a 2001 federal law, states that do not reduce the blood alcohol content (BAC) that defines drunk driving to 0.08 will lose some federal highway construction funds. By the end of 2003, all but three stated had a BAC limit of 0.08. In all states, drivers under the age of 21 have lower allowable BAC, usually between 0.00 and 0.02.

How much does one have to drink to obtain a BAC of 0.08? The Department of Transportation estimates if a 170-pound man drinks five cans of beer or glasses of wine in two hours, he will have a BAC of 0.08. For women, the amount is even less, because their bodies absorb the alcohol faster and often they weigh less than 170 pounds.

Most states have enacted laws imposing 90-day driver's license suspensions of first-time drunk driving offenders. Perhaps the toughest and most controversial law is that of New York City. In 1999, the city started seizing on the spot vehicles of anyone arrested for drunk driving. If the driver is convicted, the vehicle becomes the property of the city. About 30 states also have laws allowing for confiscation of vehicles for drunk driving, but they usually only apply to repeat offenders or underage drinkers. Harsher penalties for repeat drunk drivers make sense, since many drunk driving arrests involve repeat offenders.

---

4 Statistics in this section are from Insurance Information Institute, *Hot Topics and Insurance Issues: Drunk Driving*, http://www.iii.org/media/hottopics/insurance/drunk/, October 2003.

ADVANCES IN DRIVER AND AUTO SAFETY

Risk managers must be concerned about a variety of automobile safety issues. During the past 30 years, significant progress has been made in making driving safer. The number of fatal accidents per mile driven has been declining. In this section, we will examine several of the factors contributing to this improvement.

One of the reasons that the fatality rate has declined is the better emergency room care available today. Before 1970 there were few, if any, board-certified emergency care physicians. Often young doctors worked in emergency rooms on a part-time basis or on weekends. Today, many emergency rooms are staffed with doctors who have been trained for this type of care and who have completed a residency in it. Also, states have developed emergency care centers, and helicopters are available to deliver critically injured persons to them. These advances have allowed injured persons to be cared for more quickly and skillfully. Thus the severity of the loss is reduced, and lives are saved.

Automobile safety features have also helped reduce fatalities and severe injuries in accidents. Early emphasis on car safety was directed toward the exterior of the car and its ability to protect the occupants in a crash. More recent research has shown that the inside of the auto can be dangerous and that modifications were needed. As a result of this research, much of the interior of autos is now padded. For instance, dashboards are softer today than they used to be, providing better head protection in the event of an accident. Similarly, the windshield has been modified so it does not act as an ax when one's head hits it in an accident. In fact, the modern windshield acts like a net and gives with the occupant upon contact. This change has reduced the severity of neck and head injuries. Instrument panels have been redesigned so that they do not protrude and injure occupants when there is a crash, and headrests have been improved.

During the past several years, research also has indicated that small children and babies are highly susceptible to injury when riding in autos. This high injury rate occurred because the child was often in an adult's lap and was not restrained by a seat belt. Today, most state laws require a child to be restrained. The best way to protect a small child or baby is to use a specially designed car seat that is strapped into the back seat of the car. As more and more parents use this new technology, the number of injuries to young children is declining and should continue to decline.

Other safety features introduced in the past 20 years have been center-mounted brake lights, anti-lock brakes and traction control. Unlike the previously described measures, all of which are designed to lessen the severity of accidents once they occur, these features are designed to prevent accidents from happening in the first place. Center-mounted brake lights are an interesting case in auto safety developments. Starting in 1986, these lights became mandatory equipment on all new cars. One of the key factors that led to the enactment of this law was a study of New York City cab drivers that showed that the introduction of the center-mounted brake light was very effective in reducing rear-end collisions.

A continuing problem in auto safety is the human factor. Cars can be made only so crashworthy, and highways can be made only so safe. At some point, individuals have to take responsibility and change their behavior. For instance, everyone knows that wearing seat belts is one of the most cost-efficient actions in reducing occupant injury, but not everyone chooses to wear a seat belt. The trend, however, is encouraging. Seat belt usage hit an all-time high of 79 percent in 2003. Studies show that radio and television advertising has little or no effect on long-term seat belt usage. Like the DWI problem, it seems that drivers must believe that they will be punished before they will use seat belts. Seat belt use tends to be higher in states with primary seat belt enforcement laws, which allow police to stop a car solely because of violation of the state's seat belt law. High-speed driving is a similar problem. When the speed limit was raised to 65 miles per hour on rural interstates, drivers increased their speed on other roads as well, even those that still had the 55 miles per hour speed limit. Driving issues asso-

INTERNATIONAL PERSPECTIVES

Watch for the Horses!

As the 19th century came to a close, automobiles were just coming into use. Of course, they did come to dominate transportation in the 20th century. However, in Great Britain the use of horse-drawn vehicles has increased significantly. In fact, the increased use has led the British government to develop a Code of Practice for Horse Drawn Vehicles.

The code stresses driver and passenger safety. Vehicles are supposed to pass a safety inspection, and horses are to be at least six years old. The code was developed by the Department of Transport, the British Horse Society, and other organizations. Ample protection and care has been given in the code for the horses. Horse-drawn vehicles are rarely used in the United States, but when driving in England, not only should you drive on the left-hand side of the road, but you also should be on the lookout for horse-drawn vehicles.

Source: U.K. Department of the Transport, Code of Practice for Horse Drawn Vehicles, http://www.dft.gov.uk/stellent/groups/dft_roads/documents/page/dft_roads_506863.hcsp.

ciated with sport utility vehicles (SUVs) also can be problematical. SUV safety has improved in recent years, but great controversy still exists regarding the safety of these vehicles, especially in terms of rollovers. The National Highway Traffic Safety Administration regularly crash-tests SUVs to determine the likelihood of injury in various SUV models, as they do with other vehicles.

Although our society often feels that one way to solve a problem is to offer better education for the persons involved with it, this is not always the case with automobile accidents. Research has shown that the greater the percentage of teenagers who take driver education courses in a community, the greater the percentage of accidents involving teenagers. The increase in the accidents is not because driver education courses make teenagers worse drivers but because teenagers drive more after taking the course than before taking it. The greater number of teenagers not only driving but driving more often led to more accidents—the opposite of what was desired.

netlink

Check SUV crash-test results at http://www.nhtsa.org/cars/testing/ncap.

What does the future hold for auto safety? No one really knows, but if the price of oil should rise, great pressure would be placed on auto manufacturers to make smaller, lighter cars. This usually means that those cars will be more easily damaged and less likely to protect occupants in accidents. Reduction of auto fatalities may become secondary in importance as increased auto mileage becomes primary. In the end, technology may help reduce the tension between safety and gas mileage. New hybrid vehicle technology may allow for vehicles large enough to provide for good safety while still being highly fuel-efficient.

AIRBAGS, AUTO PROPERTY DAMAGE, AND TEENAGE DRIVERS

Earlier in this chapter, it was shown that for every dollar of premium collected, 47 cents went to pay for damage to autos. A multitude of reasons exists for the high cost of auto property damage, but ironically one of the reasons has to do with one of the most significant safety developments of the past 20 years: airbags.

During the 1990s, airbags for the driver and front seat passenger became standard equipment on most automobiles. When the car hits an object, the airbags deploy. Thus, the driver and passenger are protected, even if they are not wearing seat belts. After the accident, the airbags must be replaced. Although the damage to the car may be minor, the airbags are a total loss! It can cost in excess of $2,500 to replace the airbags, and their replacement is considered property damage. Hence, the cost of repairing vehicles increases.

On a more positive side, airbags have saved many lives, especially among drivers who have a lower usage rate of seat belts. Typically, seat belt usage is less common among youthful male drivers than any other age group. One would expect the increased installation of airbags to help reduce deaths among teenage male drivers. Since 1990, while the number of teenagers aged 16 to 19 years has increased, the number of teenage males killed in motor vehicle accidents has actually decreased from 4,420 in 1990 to 3,923 in 2002.[5] One cannot give airbags all the credit for this trend, but they have certainly helped. Many drivers are alive and well today because of airbags. The cost of replacing these airbags seems a small price to pay for having saved these lives and for the reduction of serious bodily injury to others.

SUMMARY

1. About 80 percent of auto insurance premiums are used to pay claims. More than half of this 80 percent goes for payments for damage to cars. A significant portion goes to lawyers' fees.
2. Auto death rates and insurance premiums vary widely across states.
3. Urban states with large concentrated populations tend to have the highest auto insurance premiums.
4. Drivers, governments, and insurers can all do things to reduce the cost of auto insurance.
5. Although no-fault insurance may or may not lower rates, it does provide for more money to be paid directly to insureds.
6. Significant progress has been made during the past two decades in reducing drunk driving fatalities and in making automobile driving safer.

internetexercises

1. The LoJack™ stolen vehicle recovery system is a recent innovation in car theft protection. Visit the LoJack Web site at http://www.lojack.com/ and learn how the system works. Where would you expect LoJacks to be most commonly found (that is, type of car and geographic location)? How does LoJack affect automobile insurance premiums?

2. Go to the following Web site and select the state in which you live: http://www.insure.com/states/index.html. What are the major automobile issues in your state today?

---

5   Institute of Highway Safety, *Fatality Facts: Teenagers 2002*, http://www.hwysafety.org.

QUESTIONS FOR REVIEW AND DISCUSSION

1. Explain why insureds often choose $500 deductibles rather than $1,000 deductibles, even when they are willing and able to accept $1,000 losses.

2. How can no-fault insurance reduce automobile insurance rates?

3. What are the advantages of a verbal threshold rather than a dollar threshold under no-fault insurance?

4. Identify some of the possible reasons for the decline in the number of auto deaths related to DWI.

5. Identify five advances in auto safety that have helped reduce auto accidents or have reduced the severity of injuries.

6. How will the existence of many insurance companies (versus only a few companies) help keep automobile insurance rates lower?

7. Explain the effect of higher oil prices on automobile insurance rates.

8. Consider the following statement: "It will be easy to reduce insurance rates 20 percent without reducing benefits." Do you agree or disagree? Defend your answer.

9. Assume you are asked to develop a law that would reform automobile insurance. Explain some of the key provisions in your law.

chapter 15

Risk Management for Homeowners

Joseph and Angela Jamison are newlyweds. They currently live with Angela's parents in Miami, but are planning to purchase their first home soon. They have been told that they will need to get homeowners' insurance, but they are wondering what type of protection this will give them. They want to make sure that if something happens to their new house, they have insurance to pay for it. Living in Florida, they are particularly worried about hurricane risk. They also wonder whether the policy will protect all of their personal property, including Angela's prized possession, her $4,000 wedding ring.

The Jamisons know that homeowners' insurance provides some sort of liability protection, but are unsure of the details. Will it cover them for things they do away from their home? They are planning to get a dog as soon as they move into their house. If the dog bites someone and they get sued, will they be protected? Angela hopes to start up a home-based business in a year or two. What homeowners' insurance implications does that have? These and similar questions will be addressed in this chapter.

CHAPTER OBJECTIVES

After studying this chapter, you should be able to

1. List the basic coverages in a homeowners' policy and the limits of liability for each.
2. Identify property that is excluded from the homeowners' policy and the special dollar limits for certain types of property.
3. Describe how additional living expense losses are determined and how the loss settlement clause in the homeowners' policy operates.
4. Explain the doctrine of concurrent causation and its role in property insurance policies.
5. Identify the perils insured in homeowners' policies.
6. Identify and explain optional endorsements to the homeowners' policy.
7. List the coverages in the comprehensive personal liability (CPL) section of the homeowners' policy and identify the major exclusions in the CPL.
8. Determine appropriate insurance coverages for a personal risk management program.

Traditionally, homeowners' insurance has been a very stable branch of the insurance industry. Premiums tend to increase each year at a moderate rate. This line of insurance is not as sensitive to losses as personal auto; that is, if you have a loss or two, you do not face watching your rates go up dramatically or being placed in a nonstandard company. Occasionally, however, an event occurs that dramatically impacts homeowners' insurance. The biggest of these events was in 1992, and it forever changed the world of homeowners' insurance. In that year, over $19 billion in losses occurred when Hurricane Andrew hit southern Florida, the biggest insured disaster in the history of the world (prior to September 11, 2001). That disaster was quickly followed by Hurricane Iniki. In addition, a hailstorm in Texas and Oklahoma caused $450 million worth of damage, and a riot in Los Angeles resulted in $500 million worth of damage. The combination of losses from these catastrophes and normal losses pushed the combined ratio [(losses plus expenses)/premiums] from an average of 111 for 1988 through 1991 to 156 in 1992. Dozens of insurers went bankrupt as a result of these tremendous losses.

Although the years following 1992 have not been as bad, it is arguable that the homeowners' sector still has not fully recovered from this setback. This situation is important to consumers because, for all practical purposes, homeowners' insurance is a necessity. In order to obtain a mortgage to purchase a home, a consumer must prove that he or she has a valid homeowners' policy and must maintain that policy or a similar one. Homeowners in southern Florida and Hawaii have had availability problems; the situation was so bad in Florida that new laws had to be passed to make insurance available in coastal areas. Some other coastal states have followed suit.

Catastrophic losses concern all risk managers and are often associated with homeowners' insurance. Major hurricanes, earthquakes, floods, and fires can destroy a great deal of property and cause billions of dollars in losses. These types of loss affect the availability of insurance as well as contract provisions. For instance, windstorm coverage will be more available and cheaper in Ohio than Florida. People living along rivers have a much more difficult time with the flood exposure than those living inland. Table 15-1 gives the 10 most costly catastrophes from insured losses in U.S. history. These losses are all quite recent (people did not

TABLE 15-1   **Ten Most Costly United States Catastrophes**

Month and Year	Event	Insured Losses in 2002 Dollars (in millions)
September 2001	World Trade Center/Pentagon terrorist attacks	20,620.9
August 1992	Hurricane Andrew	19,874.9
January 1994	Northridge, CA earthquake	15,173.8
September 1989	Hurricane Hugo	6,086.1
September 1998	Hurricane Georges	3,200.7
June 2001	Tropical Storm Allison	2,539.5
October 1995	Hurricane Opal	2,478.9
September 1999	Hurricane Floyd	2,116.5
March 1993	20-state winter storm	2,178.7
October 1991	Oakland, CA fire	2,245.4

Source: *The Fact Book 2004* (New York: Insurance Information Institute, 2004), 84.

buy very much homeowners' insurance prior to the 1940s), and 6 of them are wind related. All except the terrorist attacks of September 11, 2001, are primarily losses to residential property and thus paid mostly by homeowners' insurance.

In the following material, we will examine the building and personal property loss exposures of individuals. Special attention will be paid to the homeowners' policy.

HOMEOWNERS' PROGRAM: DEVELOPMENT

The most comprehensive protection for owner-occupied, one- to four-family residences is found in the homeowners' program, which is an outgrowth of several attempts by the insurance industry to develop a policy that could provide a more balanced and adequate program of insurance for the average homeowner at a lower cost than would be available if the coverages were purchased separately. The homeowners' policy was developed in 1958 by the Multi-Peril Insurance Conference, an advisory and rating organization for insurance companies. Several major revisions have occurred since then, the most recent being in 2000. Today's homeowners' policy (1) is written in easy-to-understand English, (2) is multiple-line (property and liability exposures are covered), (3) requires a minimum amount of coverage to be purchased, and (4) costs less than if coverages are purchased separately.

Concise Language
The current version of the homeowners' policy is much easier to read than earlier versions. For instance, its insuring agreement states, "We will provide the insurance described in this policy in return for the premium and compliance with all applicable provisions of the policy." The former policy said, "In consideration of the Provisions and Stipulations Herein or Added Hereto and the Premium Above Specified, this Company, for the term shown above at noon (Standard Time) to expiration date shown above at noon (Standard Time) at location of property involved, to an amount not exceeding the limit of liability above specified, does insure the Insured named in the Declarations. . . ." As you can see, today's version is 40 percent shorter and much easier to understand. Even the size of the print has been increased 25 percent so that it is easier to read. All of these changes, resulting from the consumer movement, make for a more desirable contract.

Multiple-Line
A basic objective of the homeowners' program is to provide an opportunity for the homeowner to purchase in one policy any of the many variations of coverage. Coverage is provided for both the home and personal property, broad named-perils or open-perils protection is offered, plus such coverages as personal liability and medical payments to other persons are included.

Minimum Amount of Coverage
A distinguishing feature of this type of policy is that it provides a definite minimum amount of coverage acceptable to the insurer. Consequently, a single indivisible premium is charged, and the insured cannot pick and choose among specific coverages.

Lower Cost
Because the insured is buying a package of coverages, costs are lower. This savings results from a broader range of perils being insured, which gives the insurer a better spread of loss exposures and lower administrative expenses. This arrangement allows insurers to charge substantially less for the total package than if the coverages were purchased separately.

OUTLINE OF HOMEOWNERS' COVERAGES

Although certain coverages are mandatory in the homeowners' program, sufficient flexibility still exists in the amounts required so that the form can fit the needs of most people. The basic coverages of the homeowners' program are:

Coverage		Amount
A	Dwelling	Minimum varies by insurer
B	Other structures	10% of A
C	Unscheduled personal property	50–70% of A
D	Additional living expense	20% of A
E	Comprehensive personal liability	$100,000
F	Medical payments to others	$1,000 per person

Table 15-2 summarizes the coverage offered by most of the primary homeowners' forms, designated HO-2, HO-3, HO-4, HO-5, HO-6, and HO-8. Note that a dwelling must be owner-occupied to qualify for dwelling coverage in this program, and minimum dwelling coverage as specified by the insurer must be purchased. As used in the table, the term **limited named perils** means fire, lightning, windstorm, hail, explosion, riot, civil commotion, aircraft, vehicles, smoke, vandalism and malicious mischief, theft, and volcanic eruption. The **broad named perils** as defined by the forms listed in Table 15-2 are discussed later in this chapter.

The term *open perils* is the new name for what used to be called *all-risk coverage*. The term all-risk coverage seems to imply that all perils are insured against. In reality, coverage is for any direct loss to property except for certain losses specifically excluded in the policy. For instance, no protection is given for loss to property caused by wear and tear or by animals owned or kept by the insured.

The HO-2, HO-3, and HO-5 forms are all for owner-occupants and differ primarily in terms of the perils they cover. The HO-4 form is distinct from all these in that it is not for homeowners at all, but rather for tenants. It is commonly called *renters' insurance*. The key difference between this form and the others, of course, is that no dwelling coverage exists in the renters' policy. The HO-6 is designed for condominium unit owners.

The HO-8 form was developed to meet a special situation in urban areas. Today many persons are moving back into older neighborhoods and renovating the homes there. The market value of the home might be $100,000, but its replacement cost could be $200,000. A standard homeowners' policy would encourage the policyholder to insure to at least 80 percent of replacement value, or $160,000 (0.80 × $200,000 = $160,000). However, insurance companies were reluctant to insure a $100,000 home for $160,000 because of the potential moral hazard. This led to coverage being unavailable for such older dwellings. To meet the needs of the insured and to reduce the moral hazard involved with other forms, HO-8 was developed.

Under the HO-8 form, insureds cannot collect on a replacement cost basis, but they may instead collect on a **cost-to-repair basis**, which is different from actual cash value in two ways: no deduction is made for depreciation, and repairs may not be made with like labor and material. For instance, if a slate roof is destroyed, modern roofing materials, such as asphalt shingles with fiberglass backing, might be used rather than slate. In addition to this restriction, only $1,000 of theft coverage is offered, and a $250 deductible usually applies to theft losses. Unscheduled personal property (Coverage C) is restricted to the premises rather than being worldwide. However, 10 percent of the Coverage C limit or $1,000, whichever is greater, may be used to cover personal property away from the premises. Also, policy limits do not increase for debris removal, and recovery on plants, trees, and shrubs is limited to $250 per item. The perils insured against are the limited named perils discussed previously.

TABLE 15-2   Basic Coverages of Homeowners' Program

Provision	HO-2: Broad	HO-3: Special	HO-4: Tenants	HO-5: Comprehensive	HO-6: Unit Owners	HO-8: Modified
Owner-occupied, 1- or 2-family	Yes	Yes	—	Yes	—	Yes
Minimum limits (with exceptions)	$15,000	$20,000	$6,000 personal property	$20,000	$6,000 personal property	$15,000
Perils insured against	Broad named perils	Open perils for dwelling, broad named perils for personal property	Broad named perils for personal property	Open perils for dwelling and personal property	Broad named perils (except glass)	Limited named perils
A—Dwelling	Amount purchased	Amount purchased	—	Amount purchased	—	Amount purchased
B—Other structures	10% of A	10% of A	Not insured	10% of A	Not insured	10% of A
C—Unscheduled personal property	50–70% of A	50–70% of A	Amount purchased	50-70% of A	Amount purchased	50–70% of A
Unscheduled personal property at secondary residence	10% of C or $1,000, whichever greater	10% of C or $1,000, whichever greater	10% of C or $1,000, whichever greater	10% of C or $1,000, whichever greater	10% of C or $1,000, whichever greater	10% of C or $1,000, whichever greater
D—Additional living expenses	30% of A	30% of A	30% of C	30% of A	50% of C	10% of A
E—Comprehensive personal liability	$100,000	$100,000	$100,000	$100,000	$100,000	$100,000
F—Medical payments to others	$1,000 per person	$1,000 per person	$1,000 per person	$1,000 per person	$1,000 per person	$1,000 per person

Finally, the rates for the HO-8 are high compared to the other forms. Consequently, the insured must pay more for less coverage, but at least homeowners' insurance is now available where previously it was not.

ANALYSIS OF HOMEOWNERS' POLICY

Up to this point, we have outlined the coverages available in the homeowners' program. The following discussion analyzes the property coverage (Section I of the policy) of one of the most popular forms, HO-3. Liability coverage (Section II of the policy) is analyzed later in this chapter.

HO-3 Coverage A—Dwelling

Coverage A is for the **dwelling** on what the policy calls the *residence premises*. **Residence premises** is defined as the one- to four-family dwelling where you reside, other structures and grounds of that location, or that part of any other building where you reside and that is shown as the residence premises in the declarations.

The policy states that Coverage A covers the dwelling on the residence premises shown in the declarations, including structures attached to the dwelling. Examples of a structure attached to the dwelling include a patio roof, a carport, or even an attached greenhouse. If a structure is connected to the dwelling by only a fence or utility line, it is protected by Coverage B. In addition to the preceding items, the dwelling coverage also involves materials and supplies located on or next to the residence premises for use in the construction, alteration, or repair of the dwelling or of other structures on the residence premises. This protection means that a dwelling under construction or one being repaired can be protected by a homeowners' policy. A separate builders' risk policy is not needed by the homeowner. (The builders' risk form was discussed in Chapter 9.)

If you purchase a $200,000 homeowners' policy, Coverage A is for $200,000; the other property limits are a set percentage of that $200,000 and are additional amounts of insurance. A $200,000 homeowners' policy actually provides $360,000 of property-related insurance ($200,000 on the dwelling, $20,000 on other structures, $100,000 on unscheduled personal property, and $40,000 for additional living expenses).

HO-3 Coverage B—Other Structures

Other structures are defined as those separated from the dwelling by clear space or connected by only a fence or utility line. A garage that is not attached to the dwelling is an example of such a structure, as is a greenhouse or a toolshed. If both the dwelling and the other structure are damaged, it is usually to the insured's advantage to have a building considered an other structure because broader limits apply (1.1 × limit of A, versus just the limit of A). However, if only the other structure is damaged, the insured may wish it had been considered part of the dwelling, because the dwelling coverage is 10 times greater.

Coverage B is designed for structures for personal use. Other structures used for business purposes or held for rental are not protected. For example, a lawyer's office in a separate structure on the residence premises would not be covered by the homeowners' policy.

HO-3 Coverage C—Unscheduled Personal Property

Coverage C, for **unscheduled personal property**, is the most complex property insurance in the policy. It covers personal property owned or used by an insured while anywhere in the world, subject to the exclusions discussed in the following section. Types of property protected include such items as jewelry, kitchen appliances, furniture, clothes, stereos, videocassette recorders, televisions, currency, guns, and bicycles. Besides the insured's property, property of others while on the residence premises is protected, if the insured requests it.

Property usually located at an insured's residence other than the residence premises is covered for $1,000 or 10 percent of the amount of Coverage C, whichever is greater. A vacation home is an example of such a residence. Property that is kept year-round at the secondary residence is subject to this restriction. However, personal property (such as a camera, a stereo, or clothes) that is taken to the secondary residence while the insured is temporarily residing there is insured for the full limit of Coverage C.

For most families, Coverage C does not have to be modified when one or more children go to college. Each child's property would be covered for 10 percent of the Coverage C amount. The exception would be if multiple children of the insured all roomed together. In that case, only one limit, 10 percent of C, would apply to the property of all the children living there.

Although Coverage C provides coverage for most types of personal property, certain types of personal property are excluded, and others have dollar limitations. These dollar limitations lower the amount of protection.

HO-3—Property Excluded

Certain categories or types of property are specifically excluded from Coverage C. They include:

1. Articles separately described and specially insured in this or any other insurance, such as an expensive camera, a watch, or a diamond ring.

2. Animals, including birds and fish.

3. Motorized land vehicles, except those not licensed for road use that are used to service an insured's residence or assist the handicapped; thus, coverage for automobiles, motorcycles, golf carts, and snowmobiles is eliminated, but riding mowers used to cut the lawn and motorized wheelchairs are protected.

4. Sound equipment while in an automobile; no coverage exists for citizens' band radios, tape decks, and their accessories or antennas while in an automobile. These items can be insured in an auto policy.

5. Aircraft and hovercraft and their parts. Model airplanes are covered.

6. Property of roomers, boarders, and other tenants, except those related to an insured.

7. Property contained in an apartment regularly rented or held for rental to others by any insured.

8. Property rented or held for rental to others away from the residence premises.

9. Books of account, drawings, or other paper records; or electronic data processing tapes, wires, records, discs, or other software media containing business data. However, the costs of blank or unexposed records and media are covered.

HO-3—Special Dollar Limits

Certain types of property have special dollar limits placed on them that restrict an insured's recovery. If a person needs higher limits for the restricted items, additional coverage can be purchased through an endorsement to the policy and the payment of an additional premium. The following restrictions apply:

1. $200 limit on money, bank notes, bullion, gold other than goldware, silver other than silverware, platinum, coins, and medals

2. $1,500 on securities, deeds, manuscripts, passports, tickets, and stamps

3. $1,500 on watercraft, including their trailer furnishings, equipment, and outboard motors

4. $1,500 on trailers not used with watercraft

5. $1,500 for loss by *theft* of jewelry, watches, furs, and precious and semiprecious stones

6. $2,500 for loss by *theft* of silverware, silver-plated items, goldware, gold-plated items, and pewter

7. $2,500 for loss by *theft* of guns

8. $2,500 on property on the residence premises, used primarily for business purposes

9. $500 on property away from the residence premises, used primarily for business purposes

10. $1,500 for loss to electronic apparatus, while in or upon a motor vehicle, if the electronic apparatus is equipped to be operated by power from the electrical system of the vehicle while retaining its capability of being operated by other sources of power

11. $1,500 for loss to electronic apparatus, while not in or upon a motor vehicle, if the electronic apparatus:

    a. Is equipped to be operated by power from the electrical system of the vehicle or conveyance while retaining its capability of being operated by other sources of power

    b. Is away from the residence premises

    c. Is used primarily for business

If an insured desires, coverage on currency can be raised, but good risk control prohibits keeping substantial amounts of cash in the house anyway. If a person has a coin collection, additional insurance is most likely needed. For instance, the cost of a 1914-D Lincoln-head penny in uncirculated condition will easily exceed the $200 limit that the homeowners' policy will pay. The insured must purchase specific insurance on the collection and must remember that homeowners' insurance will then no longer apply to the collection because it excludes coverage when items are specifically insured.

The limitation of $1,500 on securities, manuscripts, stamps, and so on is important for stamp collectors and persons who invest in stocks and bonds. Stamp collectors need to take the same precaution as coin collectors. Investors should keep their securities in safe deposit boxes or with their brokers. The $1,500 coverage on watercraft applies to all types of watercraft and not just canoes and rowboats. A bass boat or a speedboat will require a separate policy, because these watercraft are often worth many thousands of dollars.

The potential loss of personal property due to theft is usually small when compared with the value of a dwelling. Nevertheless, the theft coverage in the homeowners' policy is often a concern to an insured. A $1,500 limit is placed on theft of jewelry, watches, and furs; a $2,500 limit on theft of silverware; and a $2,500 limit on theft of firearms. Coverage on these items may be increased through an increase-in-special-limits endorsement. However, when insureds have collector items or highly valuable jewelry, guns, or silverware, they should insure those specifically with the purchase of a personal articles floater. (This policy, which can provide high limits of coverage for specified items on an open-perils basis, is discussed later in this chapter.)

The inclusion of $2,500 of on-premises coverage and $500 of off-premises coverage for business property gives insureds limited protection for such property. However, the business property must be in the nature of personal property, insured in the homeowners' policy, and damaged by an insured peril. The electronic apparatus limitations apply to such items as portable televisions and cellular phones.

HO-3 Coverage D—Additional Living Expenses

Coverage D is for **additional living expenses**. It covers the increased cost of living that results from an insured peril damaging the residence premises and making them uninhabitable. The insured is allowed to maintain his or her normal standard of living. If people live in a $150,000 home, they do not have to move to a motel at a $15-per-night room charge. However, if they live in a $35,000 home, they most likely cannot move to a hotel with a $110-per-night room charge. Also, only the increased cost of living is covered. Thus, if it normally costs $250 a month to feed a family and fire damage forces them to eat out, only the cost in excess of $250 per month is paid by the insurance company. See Table 15-3 for a loss example.

In addition to the increase in living expenses, this provision pays for loss of rental income (less rental expenses). This lost income would arise from a situation in which the insured rented a basement room to someone and a fire made it uninhabitable. If the rent and utilities cost $150 per month, of which the electric bill was $20, then the insurance would pay $130 per month until repairs had been completed. The repair time is limited to the shortest reasonable time required to repair the damage.

For many homeowners in south Florida, Coverage D limits were exhausted after Hurricane Andrew. Little rental property was available, and what could be found was expensive. In addition, repair time was much longer than normal because the demand for repair was much greater than the supply of contractors. The repair time was longer under Hurricane Andrew than Hurricane Hugo because the devastation was much greater and was concentrated in south Florida. Hugo hit both North Carolina and South Carolina.

TABLE 15-3   **Additional Living Expense Example**

Loss	Normal Expenses ($)	Covered ($)
Rent an apartment at $600 per month (Insured must continue to pay mortgage if it remains outstanding.)	0	600 per month
Meals at $1,350 per month	600	750 per month
Dry cleaning and laundry at $300 per month	100	200 per month
Utilities at $175 per month	275	−100 per month
Travel at $400 per month	225	175 per month
Property storage at $275 per month	0	275 per month
School supplies at $75 per month	75	0
Net recovery per month		1,900

HO-3 Additional Coverages
Section I of the HO-3 policy has 12 additional coverages, which are described in the following paragraphs.

Debris Removal
The cost of removing debris caused by an insured peril is covered by the policy and is included in the limit of liability. However, when the limit of liability has been exhausted, an additional 5 percent may be used to pay for debris removal. Hence, if Coverage B is for $6,000 (10 percent of $60,000) and it costs $6,000 to repair a garage, then up to $300 in addition to the $6,000 may be spent to remove debris from the premises.

Debris removal of fallen trees is covered up to $1,000 if felled by windstorm, hail, or weight of ice and snow, although no more than $500 will be paid for the removal of any one tree. The peril of weight of ice and snow is a major source of losses in the south. During ice storms and snowstorms, pine trees accumulate a lot of snow and ice, causing them to break.

Reasonable Repairs
Repairs made by the insured to protect the property from further loss, after loss from an insured peril has occurred, are covered by the policy. However, this provision does not in any way increase the insured's limit. If Coverage B is for $6,000, the repairs to protect against further damage and to fix the structure must not exceed $6,000.

Trees, Shrubs, and Other Plants
Up to 5 percent of the Coverage A limit can be used to pay for loss to trees, shrubs, and other plants, subject to a limit of $500 for any one item. This coverage is additional insurance. The perils insured against are limited. The policy specifies that only loss due to fire, lightning, explosion, riot or civil commotion, aircraft, vehicles not owned or not operated by a resident of the residence premises, vandalism, malicious mischief, and theft are covered. Under the vehicle coverage, if the insured drives a vehicle into some shrubs on the premises and $200 worth of damage is done, no coverage exists. However, if the insured's neighbor drives the neighbor's car into the same shrubs, protection is provided.

Fire Department Service Charge

In situations where the insured lives in a rural area and a city fire department makes a charge for responding to a call, the policy will pay up to $500 for such charges. The charge must result from an insured peril, and no deductible applies to this coverage.

Removed Property

If property must be removed from the premises due to an insured peril, the removed property provision gives all-risk coverage during removal and 30 days thereafter. This coverage for removal is very broad with few limitations. If property is damaged while being transported to a new location, the insurer pays. If the insured drops an item while carrying it from the endangered location and it breaks, coverage exists.

Credit Card, Electronic Fund Transfer Card, Forgery and Counterfeit Money

Although federal law limits a person's liability to $50 per lost credit card, a missing or stolen wallet full of cards can lead to a loss of several hundred dollars. Therefore, the $500 coverage for unauthorized use of credit cards is useful. However, if the unauthorized user is a member of the insured's household, no coverage exists. Thus, if a teenage son or daughter charges (without permission) a $500 stereo to his or her father, the father will have to pay.

Coverage also exists for forged or altered checks, fund-transfer cards, and counterfeit money accepted in good faith. The forged check exposure can arise when a checkbook is lost or stolen and someone writes checks on it. When the government finds counterfeit money, it retains the money and does not reimburse the citizen.

No deductible applies to any of these items, and the insurer will pay defense costs for court suits brought against the insured under the credit card or forgery coverage. But because the amount of protection under this coverage is only $500, it is doubtful that the insurer would spend much on defense costs.

Collapse

Coverage is restricted to collapse due to a peril named in the policy. Namely, collapse is covered if resulting from (1) the perils insured against in Coverage C, personal property; (2) hidden decay and hidden insect or vermin damage; (3) the weight of contents, equipment, animals, or people; (4) the weight of rain that collects on the roof; and (5) the use of defective materials or methods in construction or remodeling, if the collapse occurs during remodeling. The restrictive definition of collapse applies both to the dwelling and to its contents. It is intended that collapse caused by earthquake, mudslide, or flood not be covered.

Glass or Safety Glazing Material Replacement

The policy provides coverage for breakage of glass or safety glazing material (safety glass) of a covered building, storm door, or storm window. Coverage also is provided for property damaged by such broken glass.

Landlord's Furnishings

If the insured rents out part of the residence premises as an apartment, the insured's appliances, carpeting, and other furnishings in the apartment are covered for the Coverage C perils, except theft. The limit of coverage is $2,500, and it does not increase the overall limit.

Loss Assessment

This provision provides the insured $1,000 of coverage if he or she is assessed for damage to property that is owned by an association of property owners of which the insured is a member. The damaged property must be collectively owned by all members of the owners' association, and the peril causing the loss must be covered under Coverage A for a dwelling.

Ordinance or Law

Up to 10 percent of the limit for Coverage A is provided as additional insurance for increased costs resulting from an ordinance or law relating to repair of a covered structure damaged by a covered peril. For example, if current building codes require an old damaged structure to be repaired with materials that are more expensive than the original materials, the policy would pay the increased costs, subject to the 10 percent limit.

Grave Markers

The policy will pay up to $5,000 for loss to grave markers on or away from the residence premises, as long as the loss is caused by a Coverage C peril. Therefore, theft or vandalism of a grave marker would be covered.

Special Conditions in Homeowners' Property Coverages

The property section of the homeowners' policy contains typical conditions pertaining to insurable interest and duties of the insured after a loss occurs. Also included are an appraisal clause, a provision as to other insurance, a mortgagee clause, and other normal property insurance conditions. However, two areas of the conditions section deserve special attention and will be discussed in some detail.

Loss Settlement Clause

The **loss settlement clause** determines how items will be valued for adjustment purposes. The homeowners' policy provides replacement cost coverage on the dwelling and actual cash value (ACV) coverage for personal property (within dollar limitations). The loss settlement clause helps classify certain items as to whether recovery is on an ACV basis (replacement cost minus depreciation) or on a replacement cost basis. It states that personal property and structures that are not buildings shall be covered on an ACV basis. In addition, it specifies certain other items as covered only on an ACV basis. All carpeting (whether wall-to-wall or not), household appliances, awnings, outdoor antennas, and outdoor equipment are covered on an ACV basis.

When a loss occurs to a building or other structure under Coverage A or B, the insured can make a claim on either an ACV or replacement cost basis. The reason it may sometimes be to the insured's advantage to collect on an ACV basis is because of the policy's coinsurance clause. (See Chapter 7 for a full explanation of the operation of a coinsurance clause.) If a claim is filed on a replacement cost basis, then an 80 percent coinsurance requirement applies. In determining the value of the dwelling for purposes of the coinsurance clause, one does not include the cost of the land, excavations, or foundations. If an insured's home has a replacement cost of $200,000, the insured needs at least $160,000 in dwelling coverage in order to receive full payment for a Coverage A or B loss on a replacement cost basis ($200,000 × 0.8 = $160,000).

The insured can choose the basis of the claim after the loss occurs. Assume the insured with a home having a replacement cost of $200,000 has only purchased $60,000 of dwelling coverage, and then has a loss that is $20,000 on an ACV basis and $40,000 on a replacement cost basis. In this case, the insured should file the

Visit the "Home Insurance Forum" at http://www.insure.com/ home/forum/ to see numerous homeowners' insurance questions submitted by persons across the country, together with answers provided by insure.com.

claim on an ACV basis. An ACV claim will pay $20,000, while a replacement cost claim will pay only $15,000 ($60,000/$160,000 × $40,000). However, if the insured had purchased at least $160,000 of coverage, the full $40,000 replacement cost of the damage would have been payable.

Pair-and-Set Clause

When part of a set or one of a pair is lost, the **pair-and-set clause** is used to determine the loss payment. The insurance company will pay only for the difference between the ACV of the item before and after the loss. This means that the loss of one of a pair of items, such as diamond earrings, is not a total loss. Only the difference in value of the earrings before and after the loss is paid. However, in many cases an insurance company will take possession of the remaining item and pay a total loss or replace the item. Given insurers' familiarity with wholesale jewelers, the replacement option is often exercised.

PERILS COVERED IN HOMEOWNERS' INSURANCE

In the homeowners' program, the various forms offer different insured perils. These differences were shown previously in Table 15-2. The following discussion focuses on HO-3, which gives (1) open-perils coverage on the dwelling and other structures and (2) broad named-perils coverage on unscheduled personal property.

Open-Perils Dwelling Exclusions

As mentioned previously, open-perils coverage includes all physical losses *except* certain specifically excluded losses. Thus, to determine what is insured, you must investigate the exclusions. Homeowners' policies with open-perils coverage (such as HO-3 Coverage A and B) contain a number of such exclusions. These exclusions pertain to (1) freezing; (2) fences, pavement, patios (except roofs), swimming pools, foundations, and so on; (3) buildings under construction; (4) vacancy; (5) mold, fungus, or wet rot; and (6) general open-perils exclusions.

Freezing

Loss caused by freezing of plumbing, heating, or air-conditioning systems is excluded while the dwelling is vacant, unoccupied, or under construction unless heat is maintained or the water system is shut off and the water pipes are drained. When people go on a vacation in December, they must maintain the heat in their home or drain the water pipes, or else their insurance will not pay for losses due to freezing. Leaving the heat on with the thermostat at its lowest setting usually meets this requirement.

Fences, Pavement, Patios, and Similar Structures

When fences, pavement, patios, swimming pools, foundations, retaining walls, bulkheads, piers, wharves, or docks are damaged by freezing, thawing, or the weight of ice or snow, no coverage exists. Given the heavy snowfall in the northern section of the United States, this exclusion can be quite important.

Buildings under Construction

While a dwelling is under construction, no theft coverage exists for materials and supplies used in such activity. Coverage begins when the dwelling is completed and occupied. Notice that both conditions must be met: completion and occupancy.

Vacancy beyond 60 Days

When a building is vacant for more than 60 days, coverage for vandalism, malicious mischief, breakage of glass, and safety glazing materials is suspended. When the building is no longer vacant, coverage is restored. For the purposes of this coverage, a dwelling under construction is not considered vacant.

Mold, Fungus, or Wet Rot

Mold, fungus, and wet rot are generally excluded. However, an exception to the exclusion provides coverage for mold, fungus, or wet rot that is hidden within the walls, floors, or ceilings of a structure if the loss results from water or steam from a plumbing, heating, or air conditioning system, or a household appliance.

General Open-Perils Exclusion

Open-perils contracts have one exclusion provision that is almost universal to such coverage. Excluded by this clause are such things as (1) wear and tear; (2) inherent vice (natural or characteristic defect or blemish); (3) latent defect; (4) mechanical breakdown; (5) rust, mold, and wet or dry rot; (6) contamination; (7) smog; (8) smoke from agricultural smudging or industrial operation; (9) settling, cracking, shrinking, bulging, or expansion of pavements, patios, foundations, walls, floors, roofs, or ceilings; and (10) loss due to birds, vermin, rodents, insects, or domestic animals. If your pet Saint Bernard knocks down a door or causes other damage to the dwelling, the loss is excluded. Likewise, termite damage is excluded.

All-Property Exclusions

In addition to the exclusions that pertain specifically to Coverages A and B, several general exclusions apply to all property. These exclusions include (1) earth movement (not limited to earthquake), (2) flood and several other types of water damage, (3) war, (4) intentional loss, (5) neglect by the insured to protect the insured property from loss at and after the time of loss, and (6) spoilage. The last item needs some explanation.

Spoilage resulting from the interruption of electrical power or other utility service (usually natural gas) caused by an off-premises event is not covered. However, if lightning strikes the power line pole on the premises and causes power interruption, then the policy will pay for the ensuing loss. Usually, such losses are related to frozen and refrigerated foods. However, if electric power is lost in winter, the heater fan cannot operate, and even with natural gas heat freezing damage could occur unless the insured drained the dwelling's water system. If the insured were away on vacation, this action would not be taken, and loss to the dwelling would occur.

Concurrent Causation

During 1982 and 1983, court case law in California developed a legal doctrine called **concurrent causation**. This doctrine greatly expanded coverage under open-perils insurance policies so that if a peril is not excluded, it is covered. Thus, the courts held that even if an excluded peril such as flood, earthquake, or contamination occurred, coverage would exist if a concurrent event occurred and the concurrent event (peril) was not excluded.

In the California cases, the concurrent event was the improper actions of third parties. To be specific, a flood caused loss to property in the Palm Desert area of California; although the flood caused the damage to the dwelling, improper maintenance of flood structures (dikes) allowed the flood to occur.[1] The improper maintenance was deemed to be the concurrent event, and it was not excluded from the policy. Thus, the damage by the flood was deemed covered by the open-perils policy. On appeal by the insurance company, the Ninth Circuit Court of Appeals ruled for the insured and required the insurance company to pay the loss.

---

1 *SafeCo Insurance Company of America v Guyton*, 692 Fed. (2d) 551 (1982).

Because of the court decision on concurrent causation and a similar decision on the collapse peril, today's insurance policies have a rather lengthy exclusion with respect to events that might result from concurrent causation. The collapse peril has been redefined to cover only collapse losses resulting from certain named perils.

Named-Perils Protection

The HO-3 policy includes named-perils protection for personal property. The 16 different perils listed in the policy are (1) fire and lightning; (2) windstorm and hail; (3) explosion; (4) riot and civil commotion; (5) aircraft; (6) vehicles; (7) smoke; (8) vandalism and malicious mischief; (9) theft; (10) falling objects; (11) weight of ice, snow, or sleet; (12) accidental discharge or overflow of water or steam; (13) sudden and accidental tearing apart, cracking, burning, or bulging; (14) freezing; (15) damage from artificially generated electrical current; and (16) volcanic eruption. The following discussion examines the meaning of these perils.

Fire and Lightning

In the named-perils tradition, *fire* means hostile fire. *Lightning* is self-explanatory. Sometimes the question is raised as to what constitutes a fire. A fire may be defined as combustion in which oxidation takes place so rapidly that a flame or glow is produced. Rust is a form of oxidation but, of course, is not a fire. Scorching or heat is not fire. Furthermore, the fire must be a hostile fire, that is, it must be of such a character that it is outside normal confines. Fires intentionally kindled in a stove are not covered in the policy, and neither are articles accidentally thrown into the stove. Such a fire is said to be a *friendly fire*. However, once the fire escapes its confines, it becomes hostile, and all loss resulting from it is covered. (See Chapter 7 for a more detailed explanation.)

Direct loss caused by fire also includes such losses as damage from water or chemicals used to fight the fire and broken windows or holes chopped into the roof by firefighters, because these are often an inevitable result of the fire itself.

Windstorm and Hail

Windstorm coverage is somewhat restricted because certain types of property are excluded. Watercraft and their trailers, furnishings, equipment, and outboard motors are excluded, except when inside a fully enclosed building. Obviously, this coverage does the insured no good when the watercraft is on a lake or river. Rain driven by wind through an open window that damages furniture is not covered. However, if a closed window is blown out or part of the roof is blown away and the furniture is damaged by wind-driven rain (or sleet, sand, or dust), coverage would exist.

The magnitude of damage that can occur from a windstorm was redefined by hurricanes Hugo, Andrew, and Iniki. These storms caused billions of dollars of destruction on a scale not seen for many years. Andrew and Iniki caused loss ratios in Florida and Hawaii to rise to well over 900; that is, for every $1 collected by the insurer, over $9 was paid in losses.

In the face of such storms, insureds may seem helpless. Clearly, people cannot prevent a hurricane, but they can contribute to minimizing losses. First, as citizens, they can require strong enforcement of building codes. Much of the damage from Andrew could have been prevented if existing building codes had been enforced. For instance, a major problem existed with respect to roof construction. Roofs were not properly attached to homes, and staple guns had been used to attach roof decking. When Andrew moved onshore, these roofs were blown off or apart, and the rain poured into the homes. All the drywalls were soaked and fell apart. The contents of the homes were exposed to the rain and wind and were severely damaged. Even if quick repair of the roofs could have limited the damage, there was no way to do so. The streets were blocked by debris, and the devastation was so great that not enough contractors were available to do the repairs.

PROFESSIONAL PERSPECTIVES

Way Up in Smoke

Fires in the United States have caused billions of dollars of damage. Six of the largest fires (in terms of cost) in U.S. history are listed below. The earliest among those listed was in Chicago in 1871; the most recent was in New York in 2001. Note that the figure given for the World Trade Center loss differs markedly from the one given in Table 15-1. These two numbers were drawn from different sources, and the reality is that right now the ultimate cost of the 9/11 attacks is highly uncertain. Any stated number for total losses from the events of that day is only an estimate at this point.

Location	Year	Loss ($ billions; in 2002 dollars)
1. World Trade Center terrorist attacks	2001	33.93
2. San Francisco earthquake and fire	1906	6.98
3. Great Chicago fire	1871	2.51
4. Oakland fire storm	1991	1.98
5. Great Boston fire	1872	1.12
6. Phillips Petroleum Plant, Texas	1989	1.09

Source: *The Fact Book 2004* (New York: Insurance Information Institute, 2004).

Insurance companies sent an army of adjusters to the area, but it was difficult to get there and just as difficult to find insureds. Their homes were no longer standing, and no street signs were in place! When owners of property could be identified, insurers often tendered the entire value of the insurance policy. The damage was so great that it equaled or exceeded the policy limits.

Explosion

The term *explosion* is undefined in the policy and thus is broadly interpreted by the courts. It would include a natural gas explosion as well as a sonic boom.

Riot and Civil Commotion, Aircraft, and Vehicles

These terms are also undefined in the HO-3 form. Damage to trees, shrubs, and plants by a vehicle driven or owned by a resident of the residence premises is excluded. *Aircraft* include self-propelled missiles and spacecraft.

An interesting loss concerning the vehicle coverage occurred a number of years ago. The term *vehicle* used in the HO-3 policy is unmodified. The policy just states that it excludes damage to personal property caused by vehicles. *Vehicle* has been defined as any means of carrying persons or goods; it is not limited to motorcraft. An insured was on an ocean cruise, the ship hit an iceberg, and damage occurred to the insureds' personal property on board the ship. The ship was deemed a vehicle, and because Coverage C is on a worldwide basis, the loss was paid.

Smoke

This peril only includes sudden and accidental damage from smoke. Loss caused by smoke from agricultural smudging or industrial operations is excluded.

Vandalism or Malicious Mischief

Typically, this peril involves the concept of willful intent to damage the property. However, the HO-3 form does not mention this limitation, so a liberal definition of the term can be assumed.

Theft

The policy states that the theft peril "includes attempted theft and loss of property from a known location when it is likely that the property has been stolen." In case of loss, the police must be notified if the insured expects to collect under the policy. This coverage is rather broad, and the insured is required only to show that theft of the item is a reasonable explanation of the loss. However, it is not the intent of the insurer to pay for property that the insured simply loses, and no coverage exists if any insured steals the property. Because sons, daughters, and spouses are insureds, any property stolen by them from the named or other insured is not covered. Two special situations exist concerning the theft peril coverage: limitations on the premises and limitations off the premises.

Limitations on the Premises. Any materials or supplies used in the construction of a dwelling are not covered for theft until the building is completed and occupied. Although this is the same exclusion that existed for the dwelling itself, it is also necessary in this section because supplies and materials, before they are attached to the dwelling, are personal property. In addition to this limitation on the premises, no coverage is available for any property in that part of the residence premises rented by the insured to another. If you rent a room to a son or daughter or other relative (presumably an adult), coverage exists. However, if others (except a person under 21 in your care) occupy that space, no theft coverage exists in the area they rent.

Off-Premises Limitations. Four off-premises restrictions exist, involving (1) trailers and campers, (2) watercraft, (3) secondary residence, and (4) student property.

No trailers or campers are insured for theft away from the premises. Watercraft and their furnishings, equipment, and outboard motors also are excluded. The third exclusion concerns property at another residence owned, rented, or occupied by any insured. No theft coverage exists on property at that type of residence unless an insured is temporarily residing there. If the insured has a summer home, no theft coverage exists on property left there except when the insured is residing in it. Therefore, during the winter months personal property at an unoccupied summer home has no theft protection.

One important exception to this exclusion does exist, which creates the fourth limitation. It involves property of a student while at a residence away from home. If the student has been at the "away-from-home residence" any time during the 60 days immediately before the loss, coverage exists. When a student goes home for Christmas and leaves a television at school, coverage does exist for the set if it is stolen, even though the student was not residing there at the time of the loss. However, coverage does not exist for personal property that a student leaves at school during the summer months and subsequently finds missing in the fall. No coverage exists after the student has been away for more than 60 days.

It should be noted that homeowners' policies issued during or after 1984 provide theft coverage for property left in an automobile on or off the premises, whether the automobile is locked or unlocked at the time of the theft. In prior policies, the insured had to purchase an extended theft endorsement to obtain this coverage. Thus, the new homeowners' policy gives broader coverage and eliminates a temptation for the insured to break his or her own car window and claim that a thief broke into the car and stole some property therein.

Falling Objects

The falling object does not pertain to property inside the building unless the roof or an exterior wall is first damaged by the falling object. Damage to the falling object itself is not covered. For instance, if a tree falls on the house, the tree is not covered by the falling object peril, but the house and any contents inside that are damaged by the tree are covered. This exclusion on the fallen object also excludes coverage for china that is dropped and broken or a picture that falls from the wall and is broken.

Weight of Ice, Snow, or Sleet

In the HO-3 policy, this coverage applies only to contents inside the dwelling, which is itself covered on an open-perils basis. Thus, the roof would have to collapse from the weight of ice and snow, and then the contents would have to be damaged, for coverage to exist.

Accidental Discharge or Overflow of Water or Steam

The overflow or accident must come from within a plumbing, heating, or air-conditioning system or from within a household appliance. Coverage exists neither for the appliance from which the steam or water escaped nor for loss due to freezing, overflow, or discharge that occurs off the residence premises. In communities with little space between dwellings, it is possible for the overflow on one premises to flow to another. One usually thinks of this peril as resulting from situations such as an accidental discharge from a washing machine or a child forgetting to turn off the bath water. Sumps, sump pumps, and any related equipment are not considered part of a plumbing system.

Sudden and Accidental Tearing Apart, Cracking, Burning, or Bulging of a Steam, Hot Water, or Air-Conditioning System or an Appliance for Heating Water

The obvious example of this peril is a water heater that explodes. No coverage for freezing is provided under this peril.

Freezing

This peril covers freezing of a plumbing, heating, or air-conditioning system or a household appliance. No coverage exists when the dwelling is unoccupied, unless the insured takes reasonable care to maintain heat in the building or shuts off the water supply and drains the system and appliances of water. When an ice storm cuts off electricity, an insured must take reasonable steps to prevent freezing of pipes and other appliances if freezing losses to plumbing systems are to be covered.

Find facts and figures on property insurance topics at http://www.nypiua.com.

Many people might expect to see most freezing and loss from weight of ice and snow in the northern part of the United States. However, the opposite is true. Construction in the north is designed for freezing temperatures; in the south, it is not. Although temperatures in the south during the winter are usually milder than in the north, all-time low temperatures are just as cold. For instance, the lowest recorded temperature in January in Atlanta was –8°F; compare this with –7°F in Philadelphia and –3°F in New York City. (Prospect Creek, Alaska, wins first place with –80°F.) When this extremely cold weather strikes in the south, the damage can be tremendous. On December 23, 1983, in Athens, Georgia, the temperature was in the 50s; by Christmas Eve, it was 9°F. Apartments in the community suffered substantial freezing losses because many students and professors turned the heat down or off when they left town for the Christmas holidays. Needless to say, they returned to a watery mess.

Sudden and Accidental Damage from Artificially Generated Electrical Current

An air conditioner damaged by a power surge would be covered by this peril. However, the policy specifically excludes loss to a tube, transistor, or similar electronic component.

Stereos, televisions, and personal computers are the main targets of this exclusion. To help prevent damage to expensive electrical equipment such as personal computers, stereos, and TVs, people should install surge protectors on the equipment.

Volcanic Eruption

Volcanic eruption is a fairly new coverage for the homeowners' program and addresses the problems that arose after the eruption of Mount Saint Helens in Washington. At the time of that explosion, it was not clear whether homeowners' policies covered volcanic explosions. The addition of the peril makes it clear. Loss caused by earthquake, land shock waves, or tremors is not covered.

OPTIONAL PROPERTY ENDORSEMENTS TO HOMEOWNERS' POLICIES

Many property endorsements are available in the homeowner's program. Personal risk managers must decide which, if any, of these endorsements are appropriate for their circumstances. Several of the available endorsements are of particular interest: earthquake, inflation guard, guaranteed replacement cost, personal property replacement cost, unit owner's additions and alterations endorsements, and special personal property coverage.

Earthquake

The peril of earthquake is catastrophic in nature. However, its frequency is so low that few persons purchase the coverage even though they should. This is especially true for those persons living in the western United States, where earthquakes are most likely.

The actual endorsement does not define earthquake; it just states that "any earthquake shocks that occur within a 72-hour period shall constitute a single earthquake." The endorsement usually has a mandatory deductible of 5 percent of the appropriate limit of insurance, and it applies separately to Coverages A, B, and C. The minimum deductible is $250.

In the area of exclusions, the endorsement eliminates loss from flood or tidal wave caused by an earthquake and loss to exterior masonry veneer. For an additional premium, the latter item can be covered, and such coverage is recommended for people living in brick houses. Two earthquake deductible endorsements actually are available, the difference between the two being the amount of the deductible. The first has a 5 percent deductible; the second has a 10 percent deductible and is found most often in the western states. Perhaps this 10 percent deductible is why some people do not purchase earthquake insurance. On a dwelling with a replacement cost of $150,000, the deductible would be $15,000.

Inflation Guard

When inflation occurs at a rapid rate, the problem of maintaining adequate property limits has to be addressed. It has not been uncommon for construction costs to rise 10 percent per year. The reader should remember that it is the construction cost inflation rate in one's community that is important. When replacement cost protection is desired, an 80 percent coinsurance clause must be maintained, and policy limits need to be adjusted periodically. However, if one adjusts only once a year, problems can arise because the loss may occur right before it is time to increase the policyholder's limit. The inflation guard endorsement is a partial solution to the problem; under it, a person's limit is raised a set percentage every three months. The standard percentages are 1.5 and 2 percent. Higher percentages can be used. However, persons still need to review their policy limits annually, because the inflation guard adjustments might have been inadequate.

PROFESSIONAL PERSPECTIVES

Playing for High Shakes

In January 1994, the most severe earthquake since 1906 hit California. Losses ran into the billions of dollars, but, unlike other earthquakes, the impact on the insurance industry was severe. Insured losses amounted to more than $12.5 billion. After the earlier quakes, people had bought more earthquake insurance. Usually, people are reluctant to purchase earthquake insurance for two reasons: (1) the earthquake exposure has a low frequency, and (2) because of its high severity, insurance companies tend to charge fairly high premiums for the coverage. For instance, on a $200,000 brick home in Georgia, the HO-3 premium with replacement cost coverage on contents might be $600; the cost of adding earthquake as an additional peril would be more than $250. Furthermore, the coverage would have a $10,000 deductible, as opposed to a $250 deductible for all of the other perils insured against. Of course, in California the rates are even higher, and a 10 percent deductible ($20,000 in this example) is required.

Related to the earthquake peril is loss from *sinkhole collapse*. This peril is defined as property damage caused by the sudden settlement or collapse of the earth supporting a structure. The settlement or collapse must result from subterranean voids created by the action of water on limestone or similar rock formations. The peril occurs in Florida, southern Georgia, Alabama, and other southern coastal states. This endorsement was developed specifically to meet the needs of insureds living there.

Guaranteed Replacement Cost

The **guaranteed replacement cost** endorsement applies to the dwelling and provides the policyholder with full replacement cost at the time of the loss. A policy limit is not set in the traditional sense for Coverage A. The policyholder is required to insure 100 percent to value when the policy is purchased and increase the stated value as requested by the insurer. The stated value is used to determine the premium. Most versions of this endorsement limit the policy to 125 to 150 percent of the stated value and may or may not increase the limits for Coverages B, C, and D. The guaranteed replacement cost endorsement is an attractive endorsement and a good way to eliminate the potential coinsurance problem that can occur when a hurricane or tornado strikes a city and building costs explode during the rebuilding period.

Personal Property Replacement Cost

For many years, homeowners have been able to purchase replacement cost coverage on the dwelling and other structures. However, before 1980 an individual could not purchase replacement cost coverage on an unscheduled basis on personal property in the homeowners' program. In 1980, a new endorsement was introduced; it stated that the insured could collect the lesser of four amounts for personal property:

1. Replacement cost at the time of loss
2. Full repair cost at the time of loss
3. Any special limits of liability pertaining to Coverage C
4. The limit of liability for unscheduled personal property in Coverage C, which is usually 50 percent of the dwelling coverage

Certain types of property are excluded from the replacement cost recovery. They include (1) fine arts, paintings, and antiques; (2) memorabilia and collector's items; (3) property that is not kept in working condition; and (4) obsolete property.

Usually no payment is made until the item is actually repaired or replaced, unless the loss is less than $500. Thus, for losses less than $500, one does not have to replace the item to obtain the replacement cost coverage.

Unit Owners, Building Additions, and Alterations

This endorsement is designed to meet the special needs of condominium unit owners, who in many states hold an indivisible interest in the condominium complex and sole ownership of the air space inside their units. This is called the **bare wall doctrine**. The unit owner owns everything inside the bare walls, except for some electrical and structural items. Consequently, unit owners need to insure all their personal property, as well as additions and alterations to the bare walls. The $1,000 limit for improvements in the basic HO-6 is inadequate. By endorsement, limits may be increased and coverage can be placed on an open-perils basis. Examples of items the unit owner will be insuring are paneling, wall-to-wall carpeting or hardwood floors, wallpaper, wall and ceiling fixtures, and, when carried to an extreme, non-load-bearing interior walls.

The insurance protection on the condominium itself and swimming pools, tennis courts, and other buildings associated with the condominium complex is carried by the condominium association. Thus, if one building of the complex is destroyed by fire, the association's insurance pays to rebuild it. The unit owner's insurance pays (on an ACV basis) to furnish the unit and replace personal property contained in the unit at the time of the loss.

Unit owners in a condominium may be assessed for losses paid by the condominium association. To protect against this potential loss, the HO-6 policy may be endorsed to cover an assessment due to a loss caused by a peril insured under the building additions and alterations coverage, except earthquake. By another endorsement, the peril of earthquake may be added. A second area of coverage involves losses that the liability section of the policy would pay. The endorsement has a minimum $250 deductible and a limit separate from the rest of the policy.

Special Personal Property

The special personal property endorsement (HO-15) provides *open-perils* coverage for personal property. The combination of this endorsement and the HO-3 form gives the insured open-perils coverage on both the dwelling and personal property.

Like the open-perils coverage on the dwelling for the HO-3 form, the special personal property endorsement has numerous exclusions, such as enforcement of building laws or ordinances, earthquake, flood, war, and intentional loss. In addition, several exclusions are unique to the special property form, such as breakage of eyeglasses, glassware, statuary marble, and porcelain (these items are insured for certain specified perils, such as fire and theft); collision; repair or refinishing of personal property; and dampness of atmosphere or extreme change in temperature.

Inboard Watercraft

Inboard watercraft and sailboats are generally classified as yachts for insurance purposes. Consequently, they are insured on an ocean marine package policy, appropriately called a *yacht policy*, that gives coverage on the hull (the boat) and on liability arising from collision with other vessels. By endorsement, one can add general watercraft liability (called *protection and indemnity coverage*), medical payments, and Longshoremen's and Harbor Workers' Compensation. Insured perils with respect to the hull include, but are not limited to, collision, windstorm, fire, and theft. However, for most people it is the outboard motor and boat policy that is of interest, and that is the policy we now examine.

Outboard Watercraft

The **outboard watercraft** policy is not uniform, so the description provided here will summarize what one generally finds in such a policy. Typically, the policy covers outboard motors and outboard motor boats used for personal pleasure. The insured must warrant that the watercraft is not held for hire or charter. Coverage applies while on the water and on shore. Insured perils may be on an open-perils or a broad named-perils basis. The open-perils approach is the most popular, and under this form the boat, its motor or motors, its equipment, and its trailer are covered. Recovery is on an ACV basis, but often market value is used in place of ACV. However, depreciation charts do exist, and depreciation rates of 10 to 15 percent per year are common. No replacement cost protection is available. The premium rate for open-perils protection can be expensive, but high deductibles may be used to help lower the cost to the insured.

FLOOD INSURANCE

Flood insurance for residential properties is generally administered by the Federal Emergency Management Association (FEMA). In this program, FEMA underwrites losses and works through private vendors and insurance agents to market and service the policies. To be eligible for the program, a community must apply to FEMA and conduct extensive floodplain studies, make floodplain maps, and develop a floodplain management program. The FEMA program is attractive to insureds because the federal government subsidizes the rates.

The peril of **flood** is defined in the policy as including the following:

1. Overflow of inland or tidal waters
2. Unusual and rapid accumulation of runoff of surface waters from any source
3. Mudflow
4. Collapse or subsidence of land along the shore of a lake or similar body of water as a result of erosion or undermining caused by waves or currents of water exceeding anticipated cyclical levels that results in a flood as previously defined.

This definition covers water damage from hurricanes along the Atlantic and Gulf coasts, flash floods in desert areas, mudslides in California, and unusual erosion around the Great Lakes and the Great Salt Lake.

In Table 15-4, the limits of the federal insurance program are given. The limits of the regular program are high enough to meet the needs of most individuals.

PERSONAL ARTICLES FLOATER (PAF)

The **personal articles floater (PAF)** is an open-perils contract designed to give broad coverage to valuable personal possessions. Included in this category are such items as personal jewelry, furs, fine arts, cameras, golfer's equipment, musical instruments, silverware, and stamp and coin collections. Typically, it is added to the homeowners' form when an insured has property in these categories that needs protection. For instance, a person may keep a $5,000 diamond ring at home. The HO-3 policy only provides $1,500 theft insurance on the ring, and loss of the stone from its setting is not covered.

TABLE 15-4   **Federal Flood Insurance**

Category	Emergency Limit ($)	Regular Limit ($)
Building		
Single family	35,000	250,000
Small business	100,000	500,000
Contents		
Residential	10,000	100,000
Nonresidential and small business	100,000	500,000

Source: Federal Emergency Management Agency, http://fema.gov.nfip/, Jan. 30, 2004.

The PAF provides coverage for a stone lost from its setting and has limits on jewelry on a scheduled basis. If the insured schedules the stone for $5,000, then $5,000 worth of protection is available. Except for fine arts, coverage is on a worldwide basis.

MOBILE HOME ENDORSEMENT TO HOMEOWNERS' POLICY

Because millions of year-round mobile home units exist in the United States, a special endorsement has been developed to serve this market. Not only has the number of mobile homes increased significantly, but the quality of their construction also has improved. Construction codes are more demanding, units are often permanently attached to a foundation, and mobile home parks have been upgraded.

Mobile Home Eligibility

The **mobile home endorsement** is designed for a mobile home that is a portable unit, built to be towed on its own chassis, comprised of frame and wheels, at least 10 feet wide and 40 feet long, and designed for year-round living (but seasonal occupancies are allowed). The unit is supposed to be used for private residential purposes and may be occupied by the owner or a tenant.

Mobile Home Coverage

As used in the endorsement, the term *mobile home* includes the unit itself, equipment originally built into it, steps, and oil or gas tanks connected to it for the purpose of furnishing heating or cooking.

In prior years, a mobile home program was in place similar to the homeowners' policy. Today, mobile home coverage has been made a part of the homeowners' approach. By endorsement (MH-0401), mobile homes are insured under an HO-2 or HO-3 policy. This endorsement changes the definition of the insured residence to fit a mobile home. The coverage parts are similar to the homeowners' policy, but it costs 20 to 30 percent more.

Coverage A is for the mobile home unit and must be for at least $10,000. Recovery is on a replacement cost basis, and carpeting and appliances are considered part of the coverage.

Coverage B is for separate structures and is 10 percent of Coverage A, subject to a minimum of $2,000. A toolshed is an example of a separate structure.

Coverage C is unscheduled personal property and is 40 percent of A, subject to a $4,000 minimum. The percentage may be raised or lowered.

Coverage D is for additional living expenses and is 20 percent of Coverage A.

Several additional endorsements may be used with the MH-0401 endorsement. For example, the transportation endorsement (MH-0403) provides coverage for up to 30 days during which the mobile home is transported. The perils insured against include collision, upset, stranding, and sinking. The territorial limits are the continental United States and Canada.

If the insured does not want replacement cost on the mobile home (because it is too expensive), or if the insurer does not want to offer it (because loss exposure is too high), the basis of recovery may be changed from replacement cost to actual cash value. Endorsement MH-0401 is used to make this change.

SHOPPING TIPS FOR HOMEOWNERS

Like most types of insurance, it pays to shop around for a homeowners' policy. Following are some tips for covering property with a homeowners' policy:

1. Buy adequate limits. At a minimum, purchase a limit of 80 percent of the replacement cost of the home. A guaranteed replacement cost policy is recommended.

2. Determine if the property is in a floodplain or earthquake zone. If so, endorse the policy for coverage, because these two perils are excluded. If it is an earthquake insurance purchase, increase the limits to cover the cost of foundations.

3. Make a complete written inventory of personal property on a room-by-room basis. Also videotape the rooms. Place the inventory list and tapes in a safety deposit box.

4. Determine the value of personal property and, if needed, increase the limit of Coverage C.

5. Purchase replacement cost coverage on personal property. Again, check the adequacy of your limits on a replacement cost basis versus the actual cash value.

6. Identify and insure valuable jewelry (value greater than $1,500) with a personal article floater. Guns, stamp and coin collections, and fur coats would also fall into this category.

7. Be sure to have adequate limits for business property. The base policy's limit is $2,500, and computers and other business equipment can easily exceed this limit.

8. It is best to insure outboard and/or inboard motorboats under a separate policy.

9. Choose a deductible that matches your situation. No one rule is generally best. Remember, when you move from a $250 to $1,000 deductible, you eliminate almost all coverage for a single item like a television set, a dress suit, a mountain bicycle, an evening dress, an overcoat, or a stereo system. Many of these items represent property that college students take to college and place in their dorm rooms or apartments. However, a higher deductible can substantially reduce the policy's premium.

PERSONAL LIABILITY AND MEDICAL PAYMENTS INSURANCE

Section II of the homeowners' policy is liability coverage. Coverage E provides **comprehensive personal liability (CPL)** protection, and Coverage F provides medical payments to others. The basic amount of coverage is $100,000 for personal liability and $1,000 for medical payments. If additional protection is needed, the limits may be raised. If catastrophic loss limits are desired, a personal umbrella policy should be purchased. The personal umbrella liability policy has a limit of at least $1 million, and will be discussed later in this chapter.

HO-3 Coverage E—Personal Liability

Coverage E provides liability coverage for bodily injury and property damage claims against an insured. It also provides standard supplementary benefits including:

1. Defense costs. The defense cost protection in the CPL is in addition to the policy limits, and the insurer's obligation to pay it ceases when the policy limits have been exhausted. Under this provision, the insurer agrees to defend the insured, even if the lawsuit is groundless, false, or fraudulent. The insurance company has the right to defend the suit or to settle it without the consent of the insured. That is, as long as the insurance company is paying for the defense, it makes the decision whether to settle or defend.

2. Premiums on appeal bonds, not to exceed the limit of Coverage E.

3. Reasonable expenses incurred by the insured at the request of the insurer to aid in the investigation or defense of a suit. Up to $250 per day for actual loss of earnings will be paid by the insurer to the insured for assisting the insurer in the suit.

Damage to the Property of Others

In addition to standard liability insurance supplementary benefits, the CPL has an additional benefit: coverage for damage to the property of others. Under this provision, the insurer promises to pay up to $500 per occurrence for damage to the property of others caused by any insured. It is not necessary to prove liability due to negligence. For example, if you borrowed your neighbor's power mower and hit a hidden steel stake that breaks the mower, coverage would exist, even if you were not negligent. However, this clause is constrained by several exclusions. The insurer will not pay for the following:

1. Property damage covered under Section I of this policy
2. Property damage caused intentionally by any insured who is 13 years of age or older
3. Damage to property owned by any insured, or owned by or rented to any tenant of any insured, or owned by or rented to a resident of the insured's household
4. Property damage arising out of (a) business pursuits; (b) any act or omission in connection with premises owned, rented, or controlled by any insured, other than the insured location; or (c) the ownership, maintenance, or use of a motor vehicle, aircraft, or watercraft

Section I property is property that is insured for such perils as fire, explosion, theft, and the like in the HO-2 policy or on an open-perils basis in the HO-3 policy. The major significance of this exclusion is to make the property insurance primary and to make such a loss subject to the deductible on Section I losses. The damage-to-property-of-others clause has no deductible. For instance, if you had started a fire while refueling the mower, Section I would apply, so damage to property of others would not cover the loss.

The damage-to-property-of-others provision covers intentional acts of children under 13 years of age. For example, if the insured's 12-year-old child intentionally threw a rock through a neighbor's window, the damage would be covered. If the insured's 14-year-old child did exactly the same thing, it would not be covered.

Persons Insured

In the homeowners' program, the terms *you* and *your* refer to the named insured. The insurance company is identified as *we*, *us*, and *our*. The term *insured* in the policy means the following members of your household: (1) you, (2) your resident relatives, and (3) any other person under the age of 21 who is in the care of any person previously named. Resident relatives include sons or daughters under the age of 24 who are away at college and enrolled full time. For liability coverage, *insured* also means (4) with respect to animals or watercraft to which this policy applies, any person legally responsible for these animals or watercraft that are owned by you, or any person included in categories 1, 2, or 3. A person or organization using or having custody of these animals or watercraft in the course of any business, or without permission of the owner, is not an insured. So a person who keeps an insured's pet while the insured is away on vacation is covered, but a veterinarian who has custody of the animal in the course of business is not. And (5) with respect to any vehicle to which this policy applies, any person while engaged in your employment or the employment of any person included in categories 1, 2, or 3 is an insured. For example, a person employed to maintain the yard would be covered while operating a riding mower or a small garden tractor.

Exclusions

Like all liability contracts, the CPL has exclusions. The following list identifies several of the most important ones.

1. Intentional losses expected or intended by one of the insureds are excluded.
2. Loss arising out of business activities or the rental of an insured location is not insured. The definition of business does not include activities for which the insured receives less than $2,000 per year in compensation, volunteer activities, or providing home day care services either for no charge or for a relative of the insured. The business exclusion also does not include activities of an insured under age 21 involved in a part-time self-employed business with no employees, or the rental or holding for rental of a residence of yours (a) on an occasional basis for the exclusive use as a residence; (b) in part, unless intended for use as a residence by more than two roomers or boarders; or (c) in part, as an office, school, studio, or private garage.

Examples of activities that would generally not be excluded are occasional babysitting in your home and hobbies that may produce a little outside income. Commonly insured schools include those giving ballet or music lessons.

3. Loss arising out of rendering or failing to render professional services is excluded. Physicians, attorneys, insurance agents, and others must purchase professional liability insurance elsewhere. The CPL gives no such coverage.

4. Liability loss arising out of any premises owned or rented to any insured that are not insured premises under the CPL policy is not covered. This exclusion prevents any unspecified premises from being covered.

5. The policy contains exclusions regarding motor vehicle liability, watercraft liability, aircraft liability, and hovercraft liability. The exclusions related to aircraft and hovercraft are clear and absolute. The watercraft and motor vehicle exclusions deserve more attention.

   Watercraft liability is not absolutely excluded. While larger watercraft are not covered, the insured still receives protection on smaller ones, such as sailboats under 26 feet, inboard-outdrivens with 50 or less horsepower not owned by the insured, and outboards with 25 horsepower or less. Rental outboards are insured without any motor power restrictions. So if the insured rents a ski boat on a vacation, coverage is provided. If the insured owns an outboard watercraft that exceeds the 25 horsepower limit, it can be covered as long as the insured declares it at policy inception. Outboard watercraft that are acquired during the policy period are automatically covered until the policy is renewed.

   The policy excludes liability coverage for motor vehicles that are required to be registered for use on public roads or property. The definition of *motor vehicle* as used in the homeowners' policy is different from that of *private passenger automobile* used in automobile insurance policies. The homeowners' (CPL) policy defines a *motor vehicle* as (1) a self-propelled land or amphibious vehicle; or (2) a trailer or semitrailer that is being towed by or carried on a vehicle described in (1). Coverage is provided for vehicles in dead storage on an insured location, vehicles used solely to service an insured's residence, and vehicles used to assist the handicapped. In addition, vehicles designed for recreational use off public roads are covered if they are not owned by the insured, or if the occurrence takes place on an insured location. Golf carts are covered while used for golfing purposes.

6. Liability losses due to war are excluded.

7. Loss resulting from liability assumed under unwritten contracts is excluded, as are all types of liability losses resulting from business contracts. Coverage does exist for certain written contracts.

8. Damage to property owned by or rented to the insured or in the insured's care is not covered. With respect to nonowned property, the perils of fire, smoke, and explosions are covered. Also, the additional coverage section provides $500 of protection that has been previously discussed.

9. Bodily injury to any person eligible to receive workers' compensation benefits is excluded.

10. Lawsuits between insureds covered by the CPL are excluded. The CPL will not cover a mother sued by her son who is a resident of her household.

11. Losses arising out of the transmission of communicable disease by an insured are not covered. If an insured transmits AIDS to another person, the CPL policy will not defend or pay losses arising out of such transmission.

12. Losses arising out of sexual molestation, corporal punishment, or physical or mental abuse are excluded.

13. Losses arising out of the use, sale, manufacture, delivery, transfer, or possession by any person of a controlled substance are not covered. Included under this exclusion are such items as cocaine, LSD, and marijuana. Alcohol is not considered a controlled substance.

HO-3 Coverage F—Medical Payments to Others

In addition to the bodily injury and property damage liability protection provided in the CPL, coverage also exists for **medical payments to others**. As stated in the policy, the coverage applies to bodily injury:

1. To a person on the insured location with the permission of the insured; or

2. To a person off the insured location if the bodily injury:

    a. Arises out of a condition on the insured location or the ways immediately adjoining;

    b. Is caused by the activities of the insured;

    c. Is caused by a residence employee in the course of the residence employee's employment by an insured; or

    d. Is caused by an animal owned by or in the care of an insured.

The insurer agrees to pay the necessary medical expenses incurred or medically ascertained within three years from the date of the accident. Note that this is coverage for medical payments to *others*; the named insured and regular residents of the insured household are not covered for medical expenses. Also, coverage is on a no-fault basis. This protection is not like liability insurance, where legal liability must exist. Because the subrogation clause does not apply to medical benefits, an injured party may collect medical payments and still sue a negligent third party. Such a party could be the insured.

The description of Coverage E refers to the *insured location*. The policy defines the *insured location* to include the residence premises, as well as the following:

1. The part of any other premises, other structures, and grounds used by you as a residence and that is shown in the declarations or that is acquired by you during the policy period for your use as a residence

2. Any premises used by you in connection with the premises included in residence premises or in item 1 of this list

3. Any part of premises not owned by any insured but where any insured is temporarily residing

4. Vacant land owned or rented to any insured, other than farmland

5. Land owned by or rented to any insured on which a one- or two-family dwelling is being constructed as a residence for any insured

6. Individual or family cemetery plots or burial vaults of any insured

7. Any part of premises occasionally rented to any insured for other-than-business purposes

Examples of the previous locations where coverage for medical payments to others would apply are newly acquired residence premises and secondary premises, such as a mountain cabin. (The cabin would have to be specified on the declarations page.) Additional locations include a motel room, an oceanfront apartment rented for two weeks, and even a dormitory room used by a son or daughter. The last category would include a rented lodge or hall used to give a dance or wedding reception.

Examples of situations in which medical payments would cover injuries are: a person falls down the insured's stairs, an insured cuts down a tree that hits a neighbor, an insured's elbow accidentally hits another player's eye while playing basketball, a resident employee (not covered by workers' compensation) falls and is injured while taking the insured's daughter for a walk around the block, and an insured's cat scratches a friend's child.

Like liability, coverage for medical payments to others has a number of exclusions. All the relevant exclusions discussed under personal liability also apply to medical payments coverage. Also, injury to a resident employee is excluded if it occurs off the premises and is not in the course of employment. Workers' compensation-related losses are not insured, and losses resulting from radiation or radioactive contamination are not covered.

Optional Liability Endorsements to the Homeowners' Policy

Although the basic CPL gives broad coverage, certain endorsements can be used to meet specific needs. Endorsements can be added to cover watercraft liability, personal injury, business pursuits, and personal umbrella liability.

Watercraft Liability

When an insured owns a watercraft that is larger than those covered by the CPL, the policy may be endorsed to cover such boats. However, because physical damage to the vessel cannot be covered in the homeowners' policy, most people insure their watercraft exposure in a separate policy.

Personal Injury

The basic CPL only covers bodily injury and property damage. It does not insure loss resulting from slander, false arrest, malicious prosecution, defamation of character, and the like. The CPL can be endorsed to cover these exposures through the use of the personal injury endorsement.

Business Pursuits

The CPL can be endorsed to give limited business pursuits coverage. Protection is only available for the business specified on the endorsement, and the insured cannot be the owner or have financial control of the business. Teachers are likely persons to purchase this coverage, and the endorsement can be modified to cover liability resulting from corporal punishment.

Business Insurance Coverage

As U.S. society changes from an industrial base to an informational one, homeowners' policies are also changing. Many new technology companies have their start in the home of the company's founder. In the past, homeowners' policies provided no liability coverage for a business owned and operated in the home of the named insured. However, through the use of the *home business insurance coverage endorsement*, this exposure can be insured. The business must be solely owned by the named insured and resident relatives. Bodily injury, personal, and advertising liability may be insured, as well as products. No professional liability coverage is provided.

Personal Umbrella

In today's litigation-conscious society, certain persons, such as physicians, corporate executives, and successful business owners, need broad coverage and high limits to protect their assets. The **personal umbrella** is designed to accomplish this task. Its minimum limit is $1 million, and it broadens the protection of the CPL. The umbrella is designed to give protection against catastrophic losses, and it assumes that an underlying CPL exists as well as certain other coverages. The umbrella will not contribute on a loss until the limit of these policies has been exceeded. If one of these policies were allowed to lapse, the insured would have to assume any loss covered by the lapsed primary policy up to the limits of that policy. The umbrella will only pay after the required primary limits are exhausted.

The umbrella policy is a liability policy designed to give greater breadth of coverage than the comprehensive personal liability policy. It is purchased in addition to the CPL, and its limits are in addition to the limits of the CPL. Desirable contract provisions are examined, as well as eligible persons.

Personal umbrellas are not standard contracts, and significant variations occur between the policies of the various companies that offer them. For this reason, it is important that prospective insureds examine the specific contract they intend to purchase.

Not everyone should purchase an umbrella. Such policies are purchased by people who need to protect large accumulations of assets and/or high incomes. However, insurers will not sell the policy to all such people. From time to time, certain categories of persons have been deemed unattractive for the purpose of selling personal umbrellas, and these people may have had difficulty in obtaining coverage. Among such group of people are assigned-risk drivers; professional politicians; professional entertainers; newspaper reporters, editors, and publishers; labor leaders; and athletes.

Limits of Liability and Self-Retained Limits. The minimum limit for an umbrella is $1 million above the **self-retained limit** (deductible) or the required primary coverage. Policies may be purchased with limits as high as $10 million. A $1 million policy can cost as little as a couple of hundred dollars or less. The premium is a function of the location and operation of the insured, as well as the insurance company's desire to write the business.

With respect to self-retained limits, $250 is most frequently chosen. This deductible is applied when no underlying primary coverage exists. If the primary coverage applies, then the deductible is not employed. Certain states and insurers require a deductible greater than $250. This situation is undesirable to the insured because usually little rate credit is given for higher deductibles. Under most circumstances a deductible greater than $250 is not a wise decision because the premium savings are only minimal.

Underlying Limits. Umbrellas require certain types and amounts of underlying insurance. Table 15-5 shows some typical **underlying limit** requirements. Obviously, if the insured does not have certain exposures (like watercraft) some of the underlying policies in the table would not be required.

Umbrella Contract Provisions. The umbrella contract has many provisions that should be examined before purchasing the policy. The following paragraphs review several of the more important clauses and describe some coverage that is desirable from the viewpoint of the consumer. Insureds need to determine which provisions are important to them and purchase their umbrella policies accordingly. It should be remembered that umbrella policies are not standardized and their content has significant variation.

Personal Injury. The definition of personal injury used in umbrellas has a much broader meaning than that used in primary coverages. As used in the umbrella, personal injury includes bodily injury, property damage, libel, slander, defamation of character, invasion of privacy, humiliation, wrongful eviction, wrongful entry, malicious persecution, false imprisonment, wrongful detention, and false arrest.

Property in the Insured's Care, Custody, or Control. Property owned by or rented to he insured is excluded. Also, when the insured agrees to assume liability for property

TABLE 15-5   **Typical Underlying Policy Limits Required for Umbrella Policies**

Policy	Limit ($)
Automobile	500,000
Business	100,000–500,000
Comprehensive personal liability	100,000–300,000
Recreational vehicle	500,000
Watercraft	300,000–500,000

damage under a contract, such losses are excluded. However, with respect to other nonowned property, the umbrella is designed to provide some protection. For example, if you borrow your neighbor's expensive digital recorder and break it, the umbrella will cover the loss.

Incidental Business Pursuits. Typically, insureds' umbrellas will provide coverage for incidental business pursuits, but often it is no broader than the underlying primary coverage. This limitation is important in automobile coverage. Somewhat related to the business pursuits coverage is that of board-of-directors' liability. If an insured is on the board of directors of a religious, charitable, or civic nonprofit corporation, coverage is often given. No coverage exists if the board of directors is for business purposes.

Automobiles. Some umbrellas give broader coverage than underlying auto policies; however, many do not. Therefore, it is important to have as broad a primary policy as feasible. The one area in which some umbrellas give broader coverage than the primary insurance is the business auto section. In these broader policies, some bodily injury liability coverage exists for the operation of trucks in a business situation.

Figure 15-1 shows that the primary insurance pays first, and then the umbrella. Where the umbrella provides broader coverage than the primary, a $250 deductible applies to the loss. Then the umbrella will cover up to its limit ($1 million).

DWELLING PROGRAM (NOT HOMEOWNERS')

The **dwelling policy** program is a monoline (property only) program designed to provide coverage for properties that cannot be insured under the homeowners' program or where the insured does not want to purchase a homeowners' policy.

Underwriting Eligibility

As a general rule, to meet the criteria used to determine eligibility for a dwelling policy, the property must be one of the following:

1. A dwelling used exclusively for dwelling purposes; not excluded are incidental occupancies, such as offices; private schools; music or photography studios; and small service

FIGURE 15-1   Integration of Umbrella and Primary Insurance

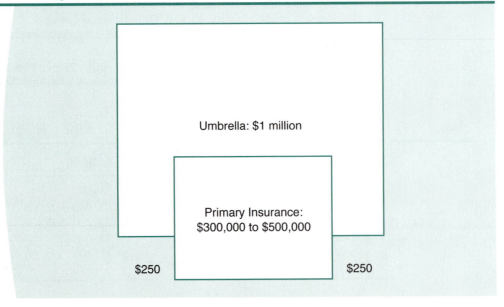

Umbrella: $1 million

Primary Insurance:
$300,000 to $500,000

$250 $250

occupancies, such as barber shops, beauty salons, and shoe repair shops with not more than two persons at work at any one time. The dwelling should not have more than five rooms for boarders in total. Included are trailer homes or mobile homes used exclusively for dwelling purposes at a fixed location and floating unpowered houseboats located at a specified location.

2. A one- to four-family dwelling in a townhouse or rowhouse structure.
3. Household and personal property in an apartment or private living quarters of the insured.
4. A dwelling used as a temporary residence while in the course of constructing a permanent residence.

As you can see, more kinds of structures are eligible for the dwelling program than for the homeowners' program. The structure need no longer be owner-occupied; and it may be a trailer, a mobile home, or even a houseboat.

Property Insured

The dwelling program and homeowners' program are similar in that the dwelling program contains many of the same property coverages: A = dwelling, B = other structure, and C = unscheduled personal property. In the broad and special form, two additional coverages apply: fair rental value and additional living expense. **Fair rental value** includes the rent the building could have earned if a covered loss had not made it unfit for use. Additional living expense may be added by endorsement to the basic dwelling form. The three forms available in the dwelling program are summarized in Table 15-6.

Insured Perils of Dwelling Forms

The basic form is quite limited in its perils coverage. Unendorsed, this form insures against fire, lightning, removal, and internal explosion. However, coverage may be modified to include windstorms, hail, explosion, riot, civil commotion, aircraft, vehicles, and smoke. This collection of perils is often written together and is called **extended coverage (EC)**. It represents one of the very first multiple-peril endorsements developed in the insurance industry. In addition to extended coverage, vandalism and malicious mischief (V&MM) also can be added. Actually, all these perils are included in the forms, but an additional premium must be paid to make each (EC and V & MM) active.

The basic form is rather limited in its coverage, and for mobile home, trailer, and houseboat dwellers, knowledge of these restrictions is important, because this basic form is the only dwelling form they can use. The broad and special forms are not used with these three types of dwellings.

With respect to insured perils, the broad form and the special form are much like their homeowners' counterparts, HO-2 and HO-3. Also, a personal liability supplement is available with this program.

TABLE 15-6 Dwelling Program Covered Perils

Dwelling Form	Building	Personal Property
Basic	Limited named perils	Limited named perils
Broad	Broad named perils	Broad named perils
Special	Open perils	Broad named perils

FARMOWNERS'-RANCHOWNERS' POLICY

The **farmowners'-ranchowners' policy** is designed to cover (1) the dwelling and commercial structures on the farm and (2) the personal and commercial liability that might arise from living and working on the farm.

To be eligible for the farmowners'-ranchowners' program, the main farm dwelling must be a one- or two-family dwelling used exclusively for residential purposes. The standard incidental office, professional and private schools, and studio activities are excepted. The farm dwelling does not have to be owner-occupied, but it must not be vacant. The farmowner may occupy the dwelling and not operate the farm.

When the farm is incorporated, the insured (the farmer), as well as the interest of the corporation, is covered. A major function of the farmowners'-ranchowners' policy is to cover personal and business interest in the same policy.

Numerous forms exist for the farmowners'-ranchowners' program. These forms are designed to insure the dwelling and its contents as well as farm structures and equipment. One can insure property on a basic named-perils, a broad named-perils, or an open-perils basis. The personal and commercial liability of the farmer may be covered, and by endorsement, the liability of a corporate farm.

RISK MANAGEMENT—PERSONAL LINES

A reason commonly given by a business for not self-insuring is this: "The firm may not have a sufficient number of homogenous exposure units so situated that aggregate losses to which they are subject can be predicted within sufficiently narrow limits." For this same reason, little self-insurance takes place in personal lines. However, the risk management principles of loss control and loss retention can and should be practiced.

In the remainder of this section, loss control, loss retention, and claims-settling procedures are examined. Also, the open-perils versus named-perils approach to insuring property is reviewed, as is the question of adequate limits.

Loss Control

In the area of loss control, the purchase of smoke detectors is a very wise investment. The detectors should operate on their own batteries, or be hard wired with a battery backup. They should have a signal to alert the insured when the batteries are weak. They should be placed close enough to the household's sleeping areas so that adequate warning time will be given. In a two-story home, at least one detector should be placed on each floor. Modern detectors are quite efficient, and in several cases detectors that had been activated but not yet even installed have detected fires, saving lives and property.

A house alarm system is another loss control option. Such a system generally produces a loud sound locally and also should be connected to a central alarm switchboard so that the police are notified quickly. Systems can be arranged to sound an alarm when any window or door is opened, as well as when glass is broken and even when motion is detected inside the house. Insurers will sometimes give a discount on insurance if an alarm system is installed. In the case of fine art insurance, the insurer may even require the alarm system.

Aside from an alarm system, several other loss control steps may be taken to deal with the theft peril. All doors should have dead bolt locks. Storm windows not only conserve energy but also make it difficult for intruders to enter your home. Most police departments have marking tools so that residents can inscribe identification numbers on valuable belongings. In many communities, the police will periodically check homes of residents who are on vacation or away for a while. Generally, notifying the police of departure and return dates is all that is necessary. (In the case of an early return, it would be wise to inform the police that you are back home.) In addition, the insureds, when going on vacation, should leave with a friend or neighbor a set of house keys, a travel itinerary, and telephone numbers where they can be reached. If a loss does occur, it is important that the insured can be notified.

Besides these loss control activities, people should use common sense in their daily routines. Valuable stamp and coin collections should be kept in safe deposit boxes. Minimal amounts of cash should be kept in the dwelling. Good lighting should be provided around the home. While all of these procedures will not stop a determined burglar, they will make an insured's dwelling an unattractive place to rob and encourage burglars to go elsewhere.

The following are loss prevention steps college students should use to protect personal property:

1. Keep your doors locked.

2. Engrave valuable electronic equipment and bikes with an identification number.

3. Leave very expensive items at home.

4. Protect your notebook computer at all times. Desktop computers can be secured to furniture. Back up all important data.

5. If you have to leave your book bag unattended, don't put anything in it that you can't afford to lose. It only takes a second to steal a book bag.

 ## Loss Retention

In the personal lines area, about the only reasonable loss retention step a homeowner can take is the use of deductibles. A deductible of $250 or more deserves consideration. The problem with higher deductibles in homeowners' insurance is that sometimes the insured receives little premium savings. As always, the insured should balance the risk being retained with the premium dollars saved to make the deductible decision. The correct choice will vary by person.

Claims-Settling Procedure

An important precaution that should be taken by homeowners to reduce losses is to identify their possessions before a loss occurs. If one cannot remember what was lost, it is quite difficult to recover losses from the insurer. One should take several pictures or videos of the items in each room in the home and put the pictures in a safe deposit box (not in the home). An inventory should be made of clothing, furniture, silverware, appliances, and jewelry, and the inventory list should also be placed in the safe deposit box. If these precautions are taken, an insured has a much stronger case in making a claim.

A fact to remember in making a homeowners' claim is that the insurance company pays the insured on a replacement cost basis only after the insured replaces or repairs the damaged dwelling. The only exception to this rule is when the loss is less than $2,500 and less than 5 percent of the amount of insurance on the building. However, the contract does state that the policyholder may collect immediately on an ACV basis and later make replacement cost recovery.

By filing the ACV claim first, insureds receive their cash sooner so that they can pay the contractor or invest the money in some interest-bearing security while the house is being rebuilt. It seems logical to most people to exercise this option.

Open-Perils versus Broad Named-Perils Coverage

The question of whether to purchase an HO-2 or HO-3 policy (Table 15-2) has been discussed at length. The difference is that HO-3 gives open-perils coverage on the dwelling and other structures, whereas HO-2 covers only broad named perils.

The following discussion gives some reasons for the use of the HO-3 policy. Keep in mind that HO-3 costs more, and consequently it should provide better coverage or it would be a poor buy.

One of the advantages of an open-perils form is the fact that the burden of proof is placed on the insurance company. It has to prove the loss was excluded; the insured must only prove an accidental loss occurred. Besides this conceptual advantage, numerous cases have occurred where HO-3 gave coverage and the HO-2 did not. The following is a list of several such instances:[2]

1. Battery acid leaked onto a hardwood floor. A large section of the floor had to be replaced.

2. A bucket containing ammonia was tipped over and ruined wall-to-wall carpeting.

3. A deer jumped through a picture window and went wild, denting walls and spilling blood all over the house. The HO-3 policy paid for the damage to the dwelling, but the broad named-perils coverage on contents paid nothing.

4. While working in an unfloored attic, an insured was walking on the ceiling joists and fell through the living room ceiling.

5. While mowing the lawn with a power lawn mower, an insured cut some coil wires and piping to an air conditioner. Repair and replacement costs were paid by the HO-3 policy.

6. One insured converted from oil to gas heat but left the oil input pipe in place. The fuel-oil truck pumped 500 gallons of oil into the disconnected input pipe, flooding the insured's basement.

7. An insured, while driving up his driveway, hit a patch of ice and skidded into a fence.

8. A lawn sprinkler sprayed water through an open window, damaging wall-to-wall carpeting.

Most of the preceding cases are situations in which falling objects (acid, blood, a person) damaged the dwelling without causing exterior damage. In named-perils coverage, exterior damage must occur before damage by a falling object to an interior portion of the dwelling is covered. In open-perils coverage, no exterior damage has to occur; consequently, if paint is spilled on wall-to-wall carpeting, the loss is covered. However, if paint is spilled on a sofa, no coverage exists, because coverage on contents is on a named-perils basis and no exterior damage to the dwelling has occurred.

PERSONAL RISK MANAGEMENT

In this section, we will examine risk management from the perspective of an individual as well as how small business exposures interact with personal loss exposures. This analysis will involve examining the personal risk management exposures of an upper-income family.

Ellen and Clark Porat live in a midwestern city and have two college-age children, Martha and Catherine. Clark, age 47, works for a manufacturing company and earns $150,000 per year. Ellen, age 51, is a vice-president of an insurance firm and earns $225,000 per year. The family's health insurance is a PPO plan provided by Ellen's employer, and it has an unlimited lifetime benefit, a $200 per-person in-network deductible, and a $400 per-person out-of-network deductible. Above the deductible, the plan pays for 90 percent of costs for in-network care and 60 percent for out-of-network care. The plan includes coverage for dental and eye care. The plan has a $2,000 per-person, $5,000 per-family annual maximum out-of-pocket provision (these are doubled for out-of-network care); that is, when an employee's deductible and coinsurance payments equal $2,000 in a given year, the employee does not have to pay any more coinsurance for the year. Both Ellen and Clark have $50,000 in term life insurance provided by their employers and long-term disability plans that pay 50 percent of the employee's salary after one year of disability. Clark's retirement plan is a 401(k) plan, in

---

2 All of these examples and more may be found in *PF&M Property Coverages* (Indianapolis: Rough Notes Company, 1999): 190.20.5.

which the employer matches Clark's contributions up to 6 percent of salary. Ellen's plan is a defined benefit plan in which the employer agrees to pay 1.5 percent times the number of years with the firm times the average of the employee's five highest consecutive years' salaries. Clark's pension account value is $300,000, and Ellen has 21 years with the firm and an average salary for retirement purposes of $150,000. She will be eligible for retirement at age 62.

Ellen and Clark live in a $500,000 home with a $300,000 mortgage, and their daughters attend private universities. Catherine is in her junior year, and Martha is a second-year medical student. Both daughters live in apartments and have an automobile with them at school. The family owns a total of four automobiles: a 2004 Mercedes SL600 convertible, a 2002 Ford Mustang GT, a 2000 GMC Jimmy SLT, and a 1999 Toyota Camry XLE. Outstanding car loans total $80,000. The Porats also own a houseboat that is located in Florida, where they own a cabin on the Gulf of Mexico worth $300,000. The houseboat is paid for; the cabin has a $100,000 mortgage.

Ellen's hobby is collecting antiques; she has more than $150,000 worth of them in the home. Clark likes to restore old automobiles and is presently working on a 1953 BMW in the garage. They are both active in civic affairs. Ellen is the president of the local chamber of commerce, and Clark is treasurer of the Lions Club. The entire family likes to travel, and they have taken family vacations to Europe, South America, and Japan. Ellen has several valuable pieces of jewelry: a pearl necklace valued at $20,000, a diamond ring valued at $60,000, and a diamond tennis bracelet valued at $30,000.

The first step in the risk management process is to identify the loss exposures, and the second step is to measure their size and frequency. From what we've read, we know that both Ellen and Clark work outside the home and that they have a combined income of $375,000 per year. This figure represents a very, very comfortable income, and one would expect them to have more savings than indicated, as well as more life insurance. To obtain additional information, an on-site inspection and interview were conducted. When the Porats were asked about their life insurance, they indicated that Clark has $150,000 of term life insurance on his life and Ellen has $100,000 on hers. They are both in good health and, as far as they know, they are insurable. Neither has a will. With respect to investments, they jointly own $300,000 in a balanced mutual fund (50 percent bonds and 50 percent stocks). They also have $20,000 in a 5-year certificate of deposit with their bank and $15,000 in a joint checking account. Each daughter has her own checking account with an average balance of $1,500; both receive all their money from their parents. The annual cost to send Martha and Catherine to college is $90,000, or about 33 percent of their after-tax income. Clark and Ellen expect to continue to support Martha in her residency and to send Catherine to graduate school.

In discussing their outside interests, Clark mentioned that he has been recently elected to the local school board, and Ellen has started a flower shop in a nearby shopping center. The flower shop is not making a profit, but they hope it will in the near future.

Once the interview was complete, it was determined that the Porats should begin to organize their finances and their risk management program. To treat the loss exposures, noninsurance steps were first.

1. The first item that needed to be addressed was the lack of wills. The family attorney was contacted, and wills were drawn up for both Ellen and Clark.

2. An inventory was taken of personal belongings in their regular home and in the oceanside vacation home. Videos were taken at both locations, so that in case a loss occurs, the insurance company can see what property existed before the loss and that the property actually was in the home. A copy of the video was placed in a safe deposit box along with the inventory list. While taking inventory, it was determined that the Porats have 36 place settings of sterling silver tableware, as well as numerous silver trays and 3 sterling silver tea sets. Ellen wants to give each daughter a tea set and 12 place settings of sterling silver tableware when they get married.

3. All nonsolid outside doors in their homes were replaced with solid wood doors. Dead bolt locks were placed on all outside doors. Both homes were equipped with fire and smoke alarms connected to a central station so that the fire department will automatically be called if the alarms go off. Their primary home also was equipped with a burglar alarm connected to a central station. Additional lighting was installed and connected to a photoelectric cell, so that it would automatically turn on at night and off at daybreak. New fire extinguishers were purchased for both homes and placed in the kitchens. Besides providing increased safety, these steps made them eligible for a discount on their homeowners' policy.

4. The house in Florida is subject to flood damage, especially the first floor. The furniture was rearranged so that the furniture least susceptible to flood damage was on the first floor. Also, the roof of the Florida home was inspected, and correct roof tiedowns were installed. All the windows were equipped with proper locks, and the Porats were advised to disconnect all electrical appliances when they return home to the midwest. This last step was taken in order to avoid lightning damage to any electrical appliance; the same procedure is followed at their midwestern home when they are away in Florida. In addition, they purchased surge protectors for their more valuable electrical appliances.

5. A home safe was purchased so that Ellen's jewelry can be more safely stored. The safe is secured to the floor. Although storing the jewelry in a safe deposit box would be safer, Ellen wants to keep the jewelry at home so she can wear it more often.

6. Clark's workshop was cleaned up, and all flammable chemicals were placed in proper containers. An exhaust fan was installed to vent any harmful and/or foul-smelling fumes. His more expensive tools were engraved with his identification numbers so that they can be identified if stolen.

7. Clark had the habit of keeping several thousand dollars in the house. Upon review, he decided to make more frequent visits to the ATM and reduce the amount of cash kept at home. Because of potential robbery problems, the family decided to make only limited use of ATM machines during evening hours.

8. Both Ellen and Clark have company personal computers they use at home on evenings and weekends. They have arranged for their employers' insurance to cover the PCs if they are stolen or damaged while in their care, custody, or control. They are allowed to use the PCs for personal matters.

9. Because Clark is treasurer of the Lions Club, he often has club money at home. He has had the club's insurance policies endorsed to cover the money while in his possession, extend general liability coverage to his home, and to bond him. Ellen and Clark are covered by the chamber of commerce's and the Lions Club's Director and Officers (D&O) liability insurance, as well as by their automobile insurance. Likewise, the board of education provides Clark with D&O coverage. Clark has great faith in his insurance agent, Jack Slipper, and Jack assures him that the flower shop is properly covered.

10. All family members have signed up to take a defensive driver course. This action may reduce their auto insurance premiums, depending on their accident record, and it should help them improve their driving. All of the cars are equipped with airbags. They and their children almost always use their lap and shoulder belts when driving or riding in an auto. They do not purchase collision insurance on their autos that are more than five years old (the Mercedes will be an exception to this rule).

11. When they leave the home for more than a few days, the Porats notify the local police department. The police check on the house at least twice a day. They leave a house key and the code to the alarm system with a trusted neighbor who can let the police in, if the need arises.

The preceding actions represent several different ways to treat risks other than purchasing insurance. Numerous examples of loss prevention and protection are given. For example, airbags reduce the severity of the accident once it occurs. Noninsurance transfers were accomplished by making the Porats' employers responsible for business computers used at home. Also, they have made sure that the chamber of commerce's and Lions Club's insurance provides adequate protection for them.

However, in the final analysis, individuals almost always have to use personal insurance to cover their major loss exposures, such as their home(s) and auto and personal liability. The following insurance recommendations have been made to the Porats:

1. They have a good health insurance program. The deductibles and retention levels of their group program are well within their ability to absorb the loss. Depending on the cost and the details of the group plan, they might consider using Ellen's plan to cover the family and Clark's to cover only him. This approach would give them extra flexibility and may not cost as much or any more than the current arrangement.

2. They need to consider some type of short-term disability policy. Presently, their disability coverage has a one-year waiting period. Given their financial commitments to their children, the level of their savings, and their lifestyle, a disability program with a three- to six-month waiting period is recommended. Both Ellen and Clark need disability insurance.

3. Clearly, they do not have enough life insurance. At least an additional $800,000 to $1 million is needed on each of their lives. They are dependent on two high salaries, have $480,000 in mortgages and car loans, and are spending $90,000 per year on their children's education. Probably they should buy some combination of one-year renewable term and cash-value life insurance.

4. Assuming that Ellen can work until she is 65 and Clark's pension account continues to grow, they will receive a fairly high level of retirement income. Ellen will receive 52.5 percent of the average of her five highest years' salary. Clark's fund should be in excess of $600,000. Once the children are finished with their education, they should concentrate on reducing the amount of their debts and creating greater savings. A balanced or indexed mutual fund would be a good vehicle for their saving plan. Roth IRA accounts would be a very good idea to further enhance their retirement savings.

5. Although Mr. Slipper may be a good insurance agent, he has not reviewed the flower shop's lease. Ellen needs to study her lease on the flower shop to determine her liability if the shop is damaged. She clearly needs commercial general liability insurance with personal injury coverage, commercial property insurance on her business personal property, workers' compensation and employers' liability insurance, commercial automobile insurance for her delivery van, and a commercial umbrella with a $10,000 self-retention limit. Depending on the amount of inventory (fresh flowers) on hand, she may want to purchase spoilage insurance. As an alternative, she could purchase a small, gasoline-operated generator to provide electric power in case it is interrupted. Because the store must be operated by someone other than Ellen, she needs to establish operating procedures that reduce the probability of employee theft. She also may consider purchasing fidelity insurance. In terms of the most coverage for her dollar, she should purchase a broad-form business owners policy endorsed for fidelity and mechanical breakdown. Of course, the auto, workers' compensation, and umbrella policies would represent additional purchases.

6. With respect to their own automobiles, the Porats should self-insure the Camry for collision. Collision insurance with $1,000 deductibles should be purchased for the other three cars. All cars should have loss-other-than-collision coverage with $250 to $500 deductibles. Liability limits of $500,000 should be purchased, with at least $100,000 of uninsured motorist insurance coverage. A personal umbrella policy with limits of at least $2,000,000 should be purchased. The umbrella will pay after the $500,000 of automobile liability limit is exhausted.

7. The Porats probably do not want to purchase towing and labor coverage because of the low limits of coverage. Also, such coverage requires that a claim be made with the insurance company, and often it is better not to make claims with the insurance company. If this type of coverage is desired, it can be purchased from the American Automobile Association and not affect their insurance rates.

8. Given the high quality of their group health insurance plan, little or no auto medical insurance is needed. If their state requires auto no-fault coverage, it will have to be purchased.

9. The houseboat in Florida should be insured with a watercraft policy on an ACV basis. Primary watercraft liability insurance of $500,000 should be purchased. The umbrella policy will pick up after the primary limit is exhausted.

10. The Porats' homeowners' policies should have a comprehensive personal liability limit of $500,000 and be endorsed to give personal injury protection as well as business insurance coverage. Five thousand dollars of medical payments to others should be purchased in the homeowners' policies.

11. The major property insurance contract to be purchased by the Porats will be their homeowners' policy. The coverages necessary in Florida will be examined first, and then those for the home in the midwest. The cabin will probably have to be insured by the Florida Fair Plan, because it is beachfront property, and after hurricanes Andrew and Opal, insurers are not anxious to insure such property, particularly when it is unoccupied most of the year. They need to insure on a replacement cost basis (dwelling and, if possible, contents) for as broad a set of perils as they can buy. Also, they need to buy a flood policy from the National Flood Program to cover the cabin and its contents. Because the Porats' cabin is a vacation home, they do not have any sterling silverware, antiques, or other expensive items at that location and thus do not need additional endorsements.

12. For their midwestern home, an HO-3 policy with a limit of $450,000 should be purchased. Although the home is worth $500,000, at least $50,000 of the value is for land and foundation costs, which are not covered by HO-3. If available, a guaranteed replacement cost policy should be considered, because it will protect against higher-than-expected replacement costs. Their policy should be endorsed to cover personal property on a replacement basis. Because the Porats live within 250 miles of the New Madrid, Missouri fault, they should consider the purchase of earthquake insurance. If they decide to buy it, they will need to increase the amount of coverage to cover the cost of foundations, which are insured under the earthquake endorsement. Their home is situated on a hill, no water is nearby, and mudslides do not occur in their area, so they do not need flood insurance.

13. With respect to personal property, the Porats need to consider several endorsements to their policy. They may want to consider adding an HO-15 endorsement, the open-perils endorsement for personal property. This endorsement will expand the perils insured against from what would be covered under broad named perils. The blanket theft limit on jewelry, watches, furs, and semiprecious stones should be raised to $5,000 and the cash limit to $500. Theft coverage on silverware should be raised to $20,000. The antiques and expensive pieces of jewelry should be scheduled on a personal articles floater. They will have to be appraised by an approved appraiser when the floater is purchased. The 1953 BMW should be insured under an antique car policy to eliminate disagreements concerning whether it is covered by the homeowners' or auto policy. The problem is not so much with liability but the value of the car for replacement or repair purposes and at what point in the restoration process it is considered an auto.

14. Given the value of the Porats' house and their wealth, a $500 or $1,000 deductible should be chosen. They also are eligible for a 10 percent safety device credit because of the fire and burglary prevention steps they have taken.

15. The daughters' personal property at college is covered by the family's homeowners' policy. However, with a $1,000 deductible, it will take a fairly large loss (with respect to the daughters' belongings) before the policy will pay. An alternative to this approach is for the daughters to purchase an HO-4 policy for property at college.

   Because the family's homeowners' insurance covers the daughters' liability while they are away at college, personal property and liability would be covered by the family homeowners' policy. Consequently, they may want to consider a $250 deductible in the homeowners' policy versus the cost of an HO-4 policy for the daughters' apartments.

SUMMARY

1. The homeowners' policy is designed to give both property and liability coverage to insureds. It covers the insured's dwelling, its contents, additional living expenses resulting from an insured loss occurring to the dwelling, and personal liability claims against the insured.

2. Several different homeowners' forms exist. These forms are designed to meet the needs of homeowners, renters, and owners of condominiums. Coverage is available on a named-perils or open-perils basis.

3. The homeowners' policy is flexible and may be endorsed to cover earthquakes, improvements made by the unit owner of a condominium dwelling, and the problem of inflating construction costs.

4. The homeowners' policy covers direct as well as indirect losses. The indirect losses insured are additional living expenses and rental value.

5. Individuals need to be aware of claims-settling procedures of insurers. Records of major purchases should be maintained and pictures taken of personal property contained in one's home.

6. One of the biggest advantages of open-perils coverage versus named-perils coverage is that the burden of proof is on the insurance company. It must prove that the peril causing the loss was excluded.

7. In the homeowner's program, liability insurance is provided by comprehensive personal liability coverage (Coverage E).

8. Comprehensive personal liability (CPL) is designed to meet the needs of the typical householder for premises liability as well as for other liability arising from ordinary nonbusiness pursuits, such as sports, hobbies, and the ownership of animals.

9. In conducting personal risk management, individuals should examine all types of loss exposures: life, health, property, and liability.

10. Loss prevention and protection activities—such as burglar and smoke alarms, dead bolt locks, and solid doors—are appropriate for a personal risk management program. Taking defensive driving courses helps improve driving skills and may reduce accidents as well as insurance premiums.

11. It is important to conduct a survey of an individual's entire house in order to determine loss exposures and to film the contents of the house so that their existence and original condition can be verified if they are damaged or destroyed in an accident.

12. In the final analysis, individuals will need to purchase auto, homeowners', and personal umbrella policies to protect their assets and liability.

internetexercises

1. Set your Web browser to http://www. disasterhelp.gov and explore the advice and resources available to homeowners following a disaster. Which of these would be most important if a tornado destroyed your home? What about loss from a flood or hurricane? Describe how you can use this information to help you in preparing to deal with possible future disasters.

2. Set your Web browser to http://www. rateyourrisk.org.secure.moses.com/burglary.html and take the "Rate Your Risk" test to assess the chances your home will be burglarized. What changes can you make to decrease the likelihood of this type of crime?

QUESTIONS FOR REVIEW AND DISCUSSION

1. Ms. Marshall owns a house with a $200,000 replacement cost. She purchases a $100,000 homeowners' policy with an 80 percent coinsurance clause. A $30,000 loss occurs. How much should she receive on her loss settlement?

2. How does the HO-2 form differ from the HO-3 and HO-6?

3. B owns a residence and insures it for $135,000 on an HO-3 policy. Show the extent to which the following losses would be covered, and give your reasons in each case:
   a. Smoke damage from a fireplace necessitates a $250 repainting job in the living room.
   b. A valuable wooden table worth $1,000 is accidentally damaged by heat when it is placed too near a hot air register.
   c. A grass fire threatens B's house. For safety, B removes all the contents and places them in three warehouses, as follows: warehouse X, $7,000 worth; warehouse Y, $4,000; and warehouse Z, $4,000. Water damages the goods at warehouse Z and causes a $2,000 loss two days after the goods had been stored there. Also, $500 worth of goods is stolen from warehouse Y.
   d. A neighbor's house burns. Firefighters' trucks gouge deep holes in B's yard.
   e. Three teenage boys "have it in" for B and cause $250 worth of damage to the house by spray painting on it.

4. Ms. Vancura owns an $180,000 house insured under an HO-3 policy with a face value of $170,000. From the following data, determine how much she could recover under the HO-3 policy for additional living expenses and rental value after a fire: She rents an apartment for $450 a month, which includes utilities; her normal utilities bill is $100 a month. It now costs her $300 a month for food; her normal cost is $200 a month. Cleaning and transportation costs are $150 a month where normally she would pay $50 a month for these. Restoration takes five months.

5. Mr. Vera's 12-year-old son intentionally throws several rocks through the local middle school's windows and causes $1,000 worth of damage. How will Mr. Vera's CPL respond? If his son were 15 years old, would your answer be different?

6. C, on a business trip, rents an outboard motorboat for some pleasure fishing. Due to careless handling, the boat runs into a swimmer, causing severe injuries. Will the CPL pay the claim? Why or why not?

7. Which of the following claims, if any, would be defended under the CPL (give your reasons in each case):
   a. A child riding a bicycle struck and injured a pedestrian. The child's parents were sued.
   b. A child, Connie, struck another child, Bob, and threw him down an embankment, breaking his leg. The court found Connie's parents liable because of their knowledge of her vicious propensities.
   c. Two hunters, firing at the same time at a quail, injured a third hunter, who obtained a $10,000 judgment from each.
   d. The insured was sued when a guest tripped on steep stairs leading to the beach from an oceanfront cabin that the insured maintained as a second residence.
   e. The insured's dog bit a "trespasser" who turned out to be the meter reader.
   f. The insured's dog, an attack-trained rottweiler, killed a smaller dog in a fight.

8. How should individuals create their own risk management plans?

9. What endorsements to the homeowners' policy are often needed to provide the proper coverage?

10. Describe a risk management plan you might advise an individual to create for his or her automobile loss exposures.

11. Explain why individuals need to purchase a personal umbrella policy and how such a policy operates.

12. What advantages and disadvantages are there for the average homeowner under the homeowners' program that covers multiple-peril risks?

13. Mr. Marquez leases a building from Ms. Valdez, and he causes a $10,000 fire loss. Ms. Valdez tells him not to worry, because she has homeowners' insurance and the insurance company will pay the loss. Should Mr. Marquez worry?

14. In California, a series of losses has occurred due to the slow movement of earth that becomes loosened when water used for lawns seeps down and causes the shale to slip. When a large crack in the foundation of his house appeared, Underman submitted a claim. The insurer paid the loss and immediately cancelled the policy. A month later, Underman's house fell into the bay when the entire cliff gave way. Underman made a claim for

loss, but the insurer rejected the claim, arguing that the loss occurred after the policy was cancelled. Discuss the rights of the parties.

15. Tom, a married college student, visited his mother-in-law's house. A fire in the house destroyed his personal belongings. He filed a claim under his mother's homeowners' policy. At the time of the loss, Tom was going to college and was entirely supported by his mother, whose address was on all his legal documents. Tom had never held a job. Under what circumstances can he collect under his mother's homeowners' policy?

16. Under what circumstances should an insured raise the deductible on a homeowners' policy?

17. If you have no assets and little income, explain why you might or might not purchase liability insurance.

18. Refer to the Porats' situation and discuss additional (or lesser) insurance coverages you would recommend.

Risk Management Applications: Life, Health, and Income Exposures

PART 4

chapter 16

Loss of Life

Bill and Debbie Grom have been married for three years. Bill, age 28, is the development manager for a computer software designer. Although he has worked for this firm for only three years, he is regarded as a valuable member of the management team and has received generous salary increases each year. Bill currently earns $65,000, and he believes his prospects for future advancement are excellent. Debbie, age 27, earns $35,000 a year teaching U.S. history at a high school close to the condominium she and Bill purchased a year ago. Their outstanding mortgage on the condo is currently $150,000, with the unit's market value estimated at about $170,000.

Bill and Debbie have a two-year child, Sarah. In the next three years, they hope to have another child. Bill's mother, Ann, age 70, lives near the Groms and has been Sarah's regular babysitter for the past year. But as Sarah gets older, Bill and Debbie worry that she'll be too much for Ann to handle, so they are now investigating day care alternatives. In the long run, the Groms expect Sarah and any additional children they may have to attend college and perhaps graduate school. Although retirement seems far away at this point, Bill and Debbie sometimes dream of it, hoping to travel and have plenty of money to do as they please.

Last week during dinner Bill received a phone call from Steve, an old friend. Steve is now selling life insurance and wanted to speak with the Groms about the family's financial needs should Bill and/or Debbie die during the next few years. Both Bill and Debbie were a bit reluctant to discuss this topic, but they eventually agreed to meet with Steve the following week. For the time being, the Groms are giving considerable thought to the subject of their deaths. How will they choose the best method for dealing with this loss exposure? What are the different types of life insurance coverage? How much life insurance (if any) do they need? Will they be able to understand the real implications of the policy wording? Can life insurance help them save for college and retirement, as well as provide death protection? These and similar questions are addressed in this chapter.

CHAPTER OBJECTIVES

After studying this chapter, you should be able to

1. Distinguish among the insurer, the beneficiary, the insured, and the policyowner of a life insurance policy.

2. Describe the major characteristics of term life, whole life, universal life, variable life, and other forms of life insurance and give examples of appropriate uses for each.

3. List three general premium payment arrangements for whole life insurance and discuss the effects of each arrangement on the buildup of the policy's cash value.

4. Explain how life insurance premiums, death benefits, and cash values are treated for federal income tax purposes.

5. Explain the intent of the following contract provisions: incontestability clause, suicide clause, misstatement-of-age clause, misstatement-of-sex clause, entire contract clause, provisions related to policy assignment, war hazard exclusion, aviation hazard exclusion, spendthrift trust clause, and grace period and reinstatement provisions.

6. Explain the nature of policyowner dividends, nonforfeiture options, and settlement options and describe the choices available for each of these items.

7. Give examples of important considerations in wording the beneficiary designation in a life insurance policy.

8. Explain the intent of the waiver of premium benefit, the accidental death benefit, and living benefit options.

For many people, the risk management tool most appropriate for dealing with the exposure of premature death is **life insurance**. There are many different types of life insurance, but the standard arrangement is a contract specifying that upon the death of the person whose life is insured, a stated sum of money (the policy's **face amount**) is paid to the person or organization designated in the policy as the **beneficiary**.

Many life insurance contracts also have benefits that may be payable due to circumstances other than death. One example is the savings element that accumulates under some policies. When it exists, this savings element (called the **cash value**) can be refunded to the owner of the policy if the contract is terminated prior to death. Thus, a life insurance policy with a cash value can be used to save for other concerns, such as retirement, as well as to protect against the financial consequences of premature death.

The basic concepts associated with the many different types of life insurance available to individuals are discussed in this chapter. Another form of life insurance, known as group life, can be sold only to groups of individuals and is discussed in Chapter 19.

TYPES OF LIFE INSURANCE

In 2002, the face amount of new life insurance sold in the U.S. was $2.9 trillion, and total life insurance in force by the end of that year was $16.3 trillion.[1] On the basis of the percentages of life insurance policies sold in the United States in recent years, there are three major types of life insurance: term, whole life, and universal life. Other types of life insurance also exist; some were more prevalent in past years but decreased in popularity as newer forms of life insurance were developed and marketed. Many of these additional varieties of life insurance are discussed to a limited extent in this section. The emphasis, however, is on the three most popular forms being sold today.

Term Insurance

Term insurance, which is designed to provide protection if the insured person dies during a specified period of time, accounts for a substantial portion of the face amount of all life insurance purchased by individuals in the United States each year. In most cases, term insurance has no cash value and thus cannot be used to meet savings needs. Its exclusive focus on death protection means that, for a given amount of premium dollars, a person can usually buy a larger face amount of term insurance

For a brief description of some of the most common types of life insurance policies and other topics of interest, visit http://www.prudential.com/insurance/.

coverage than what can be purchased with any other type of life insurance. Another way of stating this fact is that of all forms of life insurance, term insurance provides the most death protection per premium dollar spent.

Term policies differ according to many factors, including the length of time for which protection is provided, the guarantees regarding coverage options, and the changes (if any) in the amount of protection during the time the policy is in force.

---

1   Unless otherwise noted, statistics cited in this chapter are all obtained from the *2003 Life Insurers Fact Book* (Washington, D.C.: American Council of Life Insurers, 2003).

Duration of Term Coverage

Term insurance contracts are issued for a specific period of time, such as 1 year, 5 years, or 20 years. At the end of the period, the insurance protection ceases unless the coverage is renewed. Some term insurance is sold with the expectation that the coverage will be renewed several times, as discussed in the next section. Other forms of protection, known as **straight term**, generally are not renewable. An example of straight term insurance written for a very short period of time is the flight insurance sold at airports. Such coverage usually is in effect only during one particular flight and expires without value or right of renewal at the end of that flight.

Instead of specifying an exact number of years, another way of stating a policy's duration of coverage is to have the contract remain in effect up to a particular age, such as 65 or 75 years. When the length of the protection period is specified in this way, the policy is less likely to have renewal guarantees.

Coverage Options and Guarantees

A legitimate concern regarding the purchase of term insurance would arise if there were no guarantees allowing insureds to renew their term insurance protection. A person's health might deteriorate while the coverage was in effect, and the individual could be considered uninsurable in the future. In that case, when the term period ended, the insurance protection would expire, and the former insured would not be able to obtain new coverage. If future insurance protection is not needed, this possibility is not a problem. However, because many insureds want to protect their right to buy coverage in the future regardless of their health, most insurers issue what is known as **renewable term** insurance.

Renewable term policies are written for a specified number of years and are renewable for similar periods of time, regardless of the insured's health. Each time the policy is renewed, the premium increases to reflect the insured's current age. But changes in health status that may have taken place since the policy was issued are not reflected in future premiums. For example, consider 25-year-old Michael Kroger, who has applied for $100,000 worth of 10-year renewable term insurance. Term insurance rates vary among insurers, but if Michael is in good health, he could probably obtain this coverage for about $120 a year, payable during each of the first 10 years. If he chose to renew the coverage at age 35, his premium would increase to about $150 a year, regardless of his health at that time. At age 45, the premium might jump to $200 a year, with the rate of future premium increases becoming greater each time the policy was renewed.

Term insurance renewal rights usually are not completely unlimited, due to insurers' concerns about adverse selection.[2] For example, the high premiums associated with renewals at very advanced ages cause many healthy people to decide against exercising a renewal option. On the other hand, people in very poor health are often more inclined to keep their life insurance in effect, regardless of the cost. Without some limitation on the right to renew, overall mortality rates among insureds would be higher due to these types of behaviors, and term insurance premiums would have to be greater. In the past, this concern about adverse selection caused many insurers to offer the renewability option only until about age 60 or 65. With greater experience and in response to competitive pressures, however, it is now common for insurers to issue policies that can be renewed until more advanced ages, such as 85, 90, or even 100.

In addition to being renewable, most term policies are **convertible** into a different form of life insurance. The standard conversion provision gives the insured the option to change the

---

2   The concept of adverse selection was discussed in Chapter 6.

term policy into some form of permanent coverage to remain in effect for the person's entire lifetime, rather than expiring on a specified date. When term insurance is convertible, the right to change to permanent coverage is provided regardless of the insured's health at the time of conversion.

Some policies can be converted at any time before they expire. However, term insurance contracts that can be renewed up to very advanced ages often are more restrictive regarding conversion rights. For example, it is not unusual for conversion rights to end after age 65 or 70, even though the right to renew the policy as term insurance exists to age 90 or beyond. Insurers limit conversion rights because of a concern about adverse selection.

Because the premiums for permanent forms of life insurance are greater than for term coverage, the conversion option makes it possible for individuals with limited premium dollars to afford large amounts of protection through term insurance, while at the same time preserving the right to convert to permanent forms of coverage at a later time. Thus, convertible term insurance may be appealing to families with young children, where the need for death protection often is great but the available premium dollars may be less plentiful.

Face Amount Variability

The majority of term insurance policies have a face amount that does not change over time; hence, these policies are referred to as **level term** contracts. Term insurance can also be arranged so that the face amount either decreases or increases over time. When the face amount gradually declines each year, the policy is described as **decreasing term** insurance. This type of coverage is usually purchased for a specific purpose, such as providing cash to pay off a mortgage or other debt if the insured dies with some of the loan still outstanding. For example, suppose Julie Kang buys a $200,000 home using $30,000 in cash as a down payment. She obtains a 30-year mortgage for the remaining $170,000 and begins making monthly mortgage payments. With each payment that she makes, her outstanding loan balance declines. So if Julie wanted to obtain a life insurance policy to pay off her mortgage in the event of her death, a 30-year decreasing term policy would be an appropriate product choice. Because decreasing term insurance is often used to provide mortgage protection, life insurers have designed policies so that the face amount can decline exactly in correspondence with a person's outstanding mortgage balance.

Sometimes the need for death protection increases rather than decreases over time. Because of concerns about adverse selection, however, insurers must be especially careful when writing **increasing term** insurance, under which the face amount increases periodically on a predetermined basis. A more common approach for meeting an increasing need is through either a cost-of-living rider or a guaranteed insurability rider. Both of these items are attachments (endorsements) to a basic level term or permanent insurance policy.

The **cost-of-living rider** automatically increases the amount of protection by the same percentage that the Consumer Price Index has increased since the basic policy was issued. As long as the insured accepts (and pays for) the additional amount of coverage each time it is offered, no evidence of insurability is required. Due to concerns about adverse selection, however, if the insured ever refuses to accept the additional coverage under the cost-of-living rider, then no further cost-of-living adjustments will be made to the basic policy unless the insured proves that he or she is still in good health.

The **guaranteed insurability rider** provides that the insured will be able to purchase additional amounts of insurance protection in the future, regardless of health, subject to stated maximums. The right to make future purchases may be associated with specific future dates, the attainment of particular ages, or the occurrence of family events, such as the birth of a child.

Whole Life Insurance

In contrast to term insurance, which expires at the end of a specified period of time, **whole life insurance** may be kept in force for the insured's entire lifetime, and thus is one of the forms of permanent insurance.[3] In recent years, whole life insurance has accounted for more than half of all life insurance policies sold in the United States, although it lags behind term insurance with respect to the total face amount of coverage issued.

Whole life insurance contracts contain the previously mentioned savings elements called cash values. If the owner of a whole life policy decides to terminate it before the insured's death, then the cash value can be refunded. This is in contrast to term insurance, where discontinued policies simply cease to provide coverage without any type of refund for the policyowner. Whole life cash values arise as a by-product of the method selected for paying the premiums. Several premium payment methods exist. A **straight life** contract is arranged so that the premiums are payable as long as the insured lives. In a **limited-pay life** policy, premiums are paid only for a specified period of time, such as 20 years (called **twenty-pay life**) or until age 65. After that time, no further premiums are necessary, but the coverage remains in effect until the insured's death. Rather than paying premiums in installments, it is also possible to pay for a whole life policy with only one premium; when this arrangement is used, the contract is known as **single-premium life**.

Consider 25-year-old Don Poole, who wants to purchase a $100,000 whole life policy. Don is told by his agent that he has the following options regarding how to pay for this coverage:

1. Pay $12,432 now and then never pay any more premiums
2. Pay $965 for each of the next 20 years and then pay nothing
3. Pay $676 each year for the rest of his life

Under which of these options could Don receive the largest cash value refund? Intuitively, it seems obvious that if Don chooses option 1, the single-premium life policy, and then cancels his coverage after only a few years, he should receive a larger cash value refund than if he had selected option 2 or 3, which would allow him to pay lower premiums before terminating the policy. This intuitive observation is indeed true, as explained in the following discussion of how premiums are calculated and used by the insurer.

When a premium for whole life insurance is paid to the insurer, part of the premium is used to help pay the policy's fair share of death benefits for insureds who die that year. This fact is in accordance with the law of large numbers. Part of the premium not needed to pay that year's death benefits is used to pay current expenses of the insurer, and any remaining amounts are invested to earn interest. Life insurance premiums are calculated such that, when they are combined over time with the premiums and investment earnings from other similar policies, all mortality and expense costs can be paid as incurred until all insureds are dead.

If insureds terminate their whole life contracts before death, however, they are entitled to refunds of the excess premiums that have accumulated for their policies to date. That sum is the policy's cash value. It should be clear that the more premium dollars that are paid earlier in the life of the contract, the greater the cash value available on policy termination.

In computing premiums, life insurers make various assumptions about mortality costs, interest earnings, and expenses. On the basis of these assumptions, it is possible to guarantee

---

3 Technically, insurers must choose an age at which to assume all insureds will be dead. For some contracts this age is 100, but sometimes an age greater than 100 is used. If an insured is still alive at this assumed age, then the whole life policy matures and a "claim" is paid, just as if the insured had died.

within the contract the cash values that will be generated by policy termination at various times. For example, consider the sample $100,000 whole life policy included in Appendix D issued to a male age 37, with premiums scheduled to be paid for the remainder of the insured's life. This policy guarantees a cash value of $41,700 at age 65. That means that if the contract is terminated at age 65, the insured would be entitled to a refund of $41,700. This refund can be paid in cash or through other means.

Universal Life Insurance

A new form of life insurance, known as **universal life**, was first introduced in the United States in 1979, and quickly grew in popularity. Given its growth and acceptance, universal life contracts should now be considered as one of the major, standard arrangements available for providing life insurance protection.

Universal life contracts offer more flexible premium payment options than do most other forms of life insurance. The minimum initial premium required to activate the policy is specified by the insurer, but the policyowner usually decides the timing and size of subsequent premiums. (Tax considerations may constrain the possible choices in this regard, as discussed later in this chapter.) Policyowners can also periodically adjust the size of the death benefit in most universal life contracts, although insurers may require proof of insurability if a request is made to increase the death benefit. In addition, the cash value of a universal life policy, unlike the cash value of whole life insurance, is not merely a by-product of the premium payment method used. Rather, the cash value is established deliberately and varies regularly, depending on such factors as the insurer's investment earnings, mortality experience, and expenses, as well as the amount and timing of premiums paid by the insured.

There are two basic versions of universal life contracts, which differ only with respect to how the death benefit is designated. In **Type A universal life**, the death benefit is an amount that remains the same while the policy is in force. This death benefit is the cash value plus whatever additional amount is necessary to bring the total to the specified amount. Suppose Betty Bartling, age 25, insures her life for $100,000, using a Type A universal life policy. If her cash value after one year equals $1,000, then the mortality charge that year must be sufficient to purchase an additional $99,000 of death protection, making the total death benefit $100,000. As the cash value in a Type A policy grows over time, the additional death protection that must be purchased decreases. Thus, if Betty's cash value reaches $5,000 in a few years, only an additional $95,000 in death protection must be purchased. In contrast, **Type B universal life** policies have fluctuating death benefits that are made up of a specified amount of death protection plus the policy's cash value. Table 16-1 provides an illustration of the structure of a Type B universal life policy. As the cash value grows over time, so does the death benefit.

Each month, the universal life cash value is credited with interest and charged for mortality and expenses, according to terms specified in the policy. The insurer usually guarantees that interest will be credited to the cash value at a minimum rate of at least 4 or 4.5 percent throughout the policy duration. The actual rates credited correspond closely to the interest paid on high-grade short-term obligations issued by the government or by corporations — so-called money market rates. Similarly, insurers often guarantee maximum amounts to be charged for mortality and expenses, but they may actually assess lower charges during most of the contract duration. The mortality charge in Table 16-1 is 75 percent of what would be indicated by the 2001 CSO Mortality Table for males. Many variations for assessing expense charges exist; the expense charges in Table 16-1 are higher in early years of the contract and eventually disappear after the policy has been in force for 10 years. Finally, premiums paid by the insured also affect the cash value amount. If at any time the required mortality and expense charges exceed the cash value amount, the policy will lapse unless the policyholder

TABLE 16-1   Illustration of Type B Universal Life Insurance Policy Structure (Issued to a Male, Age 25)

Age	Annual Premium ($)	Mortality Charge ($)	Expense Charge ($)	5 Percent Interest ($)	Year-end Cash Value ($)	Death Benefit ($)
25	2,000	80	500	71	1,491	101,491
26	0	84	200	60	1,267	101,267
27	0	88	100	54	1,133	101,133
28	0	88	50	50	1,045	101,045
29	0	86	50	45	955	100,955
30	2,000	86	50	141	2,960	102,960
31	0	85	50	141	2,966	102,966
32	0	85	50	142	2,973	102,973
33	0	86	50	142	2,979	102,979
34	0	89	50	142	2,982	102,982
35	2,000	91	0	245	5,136	105,136
36	0	96	0	252	5,292	105,292
37	0	101	0	260	5,451	105,451
38	0	108	0	267	5,611	105,611
39	0	116	0	275	5,770	105,770
40	2,000	124	0	382	8,028	108,028
41	0	134	0	395	8,289	108,289
42	0	147	0	407	8,549	108,549
43	0	161	0	419	8,807	108,807
44	0	179	0	431	9,059	109,059
45	2,000	199	0	543	11,403	111,403
46	0	218	0	559	11,745	111,745
47	0	238	0	575	12,083	112,083
48	0	250	0	592	12,425	112,425
49	0	264	0	608	12,769	112,769
50	2,000	282	0	724	15,211	115,211
51	0	305	0	745	15,652	115,652
52	0	335	0	766	16,083	116,083
53	0	370	0	786	16,498	116,498
54	0	413	0	804	16,890	116,890
55	2,000	463	0	921	19,349	119,349
56	0	516	0	942	19,775	119,775
57	0	573	0	960	20,162	120,162
58	0	620	0	977	20,518	120,518
59	0	674	0	992	20,836	120,836
60	2,000	740	0	1,105	23,202	123,202
61	0	821	0	1,119	23,500	123,500
62	0	919	0	1,129	23,711	123,711
63	0	1,028	0	1,134	23,816	123,816
64	0	1,143	0	1,134	23,807	123,807
65	2,000	1,264	0	1,227	25,771	125,771

either pays the deficiency or acts to lower the size of the death benefit, thereby decreasing the mortality charge.

When considering the purchase of a universal life policy, potential insureds should be aware that many variations exist regarding interest rates, mortality charges, and the timing of expense charges. The interest rate that is credited is an especially crucial item in determining the size of the cash value (and also the death benefit for Type B contracts). Life insurance agents usually provide prospective insureds with computer printouts similar to Table 16-1, illustrating the universal life death benefits and cash values under various circumstances. In using such illustrations to project actual results, however, insureds should be careful that a realistic interest rate has been assumed.

In the first several years following their introduction, universal life cash values were credited with interest that substantially exceeded the minimum guarantees. Illustrations for selling policies were often based on the assumption that interest rates of 10 or 11 percent (or even more) would continue throughout the life of the policy. In the early 1990s, however, interest rates dipped to their lowest levels in decades. In response, some insurers tried to continue crediting universal life policies with the high interest that had been previously illustrated. But as economic conditions persisted, by the mid-1990s insurers were forced to credit universal life cash values with much lower interest, leading to dissatisfaction among many policyowners. Many insurers who had been crediting in excess of 11 percent gradually reduced their rates. That development decreased the inherent attractiveness of universal life as an investment product, while at the same time allowing agents to focus on the insurance elements of what they were selling. For the policy illustrated in Table 16-1, a wide range of potential cash values may result at various ages, depending on the interest rate assumption. Some of the possible results are shown in Table 16-2.

Other Types of Life Insurance

In addition to term, whole life, and universal life, many other types of life insurance policies are sold. Many of these forms are either variations or combinations of the three major types already discussed.

Variable Life

In a form of whole life insurance known as **variable life insurance**, the death benefit and cash value fluctuate with the investment performance of one or more portfolios of securities. From

TABLE 16-2   **Interest Rate Sensitivity of Type B Universal Life Policy Cash Values (Issued to a Male, Age 25, for Initial Death Benefit of $100,000)**

| Interest Rate (%) | Year-end Cash Value | | | | |
	Age 25 ($)	Age 35 ($)	Age 45 ($)	Age 55 ($)	Age 65 ($)
4	1,477	4,850	10,132	15,795	17,960
5	1,491	5,136	11,403	19,349	25,771
7	1,519	5,779	14,583	29,400	51,373
9	1,548	6,529	18,860	45,283	99,933
11	1,576	7,406	24,628	70,463	191,896
13	1,604	8,429	32,419	110,458	365,752

PROFESSIONAL PERSPECTIVES

The Agent's Role

It is sometimes said that life insurance is a product that is "sold" rather than "purchased." Reasons for this statement include the complexity of policies and the fact that life insurance deals with an issue many people prefer not to think about: death. For these reasons, the role of the life insurance agent can be particularly crucial in assuring that needs are met in ways appropriate to particular situations.

Scott Foster is a State Farm agent in Conyers, Georgia. Having focused his efforts in the life insurance area for many years, Scott finds the current business climate to be a challenging one. With interest rates at relatively low levels, Scott is careful to provide realistic policy illustrations when discussing the potential use of universal life insurance. Further, clients who purchased universal life policies several years ago are periodically notified in writing about the potential consequences of lower interest rates. New policy illustrations are also generated and sent to policyowners whenever they make partial withdrawals of cash values.

Scott's experience with other life insurance agents is that they are predominantly hard-working professionals. One sad exception came to light when Scott was asked to review the universal life policy sold by another agent to a 74-year-old man. The insured did not need additional death protection but was told that he could convert his existing $150,000 whole life policy to a $200,000 universal life policy without increasing his premium payments. What was not disclosed was the fact that more than $7,000 of the whole life policy's cash value would be used as a lump-sum premium payment for the universal life policy. This maneuver not only depleted cash from the policy but also provided the agent with more commission dollars from the "extra" premium. After determining what had happened, Scott advised the client to explore remedial action by writing directly to the president of the insurer that had issued the policy.

Source: Scott Foster, CLU, State Farm Insurance, Conyers, Georgia.

among these choices provided by insurers, policyholders can designate the types of investments that they want supporting their policies. If the selected investments increase in value, both the face amount and the cash value of the variable life contract also will increase. Poor investment performance will result in decreasing coverage and cash values, although a minimum face amount is usually guaranteed regardless of the performance of the underlying investments. Variable life policies were originally designed to provide an inflation hedge for both the death protection and savings elements of the policy. The structure of the contract makes such a hedge possible, but there is no guarantee that investment performance will mirror changes in the cost of living. Insureds who are concerned about maintaining the purchasing power of their policies might better achieve their goal by attaching a cost-of-living rider to one of the other standard forms of coverage.

As an example of the basic structure of a variable life policy, consider a contract offered by Insurer XYZ. Policyowners are given the following four investment portfolio choices: growth stocks, income-oriented common stocks, high-quality corporate bonds, and short-term money market securities. Melissa Martin purchases a $100,000 variable life policy and designates that half of the investments support

netlink

Many resources are available on the Web to help people determine how much life insurance they need. For one example, see http://info.insure.com/life/lifeneedsestimator/.

ing it are to be in growth stocks and the other half are to be in corporate bonds. Insurer XYZ will allow Melissa to change this allocation decision up to four times a year. Thus, if Melissa anticipates a strong increase in short-term interest rates, she may want to decrease the proportion designated for growth stocks and allocate some of the investments to the money market portfolio. The insurer limits the number of times a year that Melissa can change her investment allocation decision so that the insurer's administration and investment expenses can be kept at a reasonable level.

Variable Universal Life

As its name implies, a **variable universal life** policy combines some of the features of both universal life and variable life insurance. This combination is sometimes referred to as *flexible premium variable life*. The policy structure varies among insurers, but the contract usually is designed similarly to a universal life policy with respect to death benefits and flexible premium arrangements. A primary difference is that policyowners are given a choice of investments to be used to support the contract, rather than using only high-grade, short-term money market instruments as in the standard universal life policy. In contrast to variable life contracts, usually only the cash value (not the death benefit) of a variable universal policy varies with the performance of the underlying securities.

Modified Life

The term **modified life** can describe many different policy structures, although usually the contract is a form of whole life insurance with premiums that are lower than usual for an initial period of time, such as 5 or 10 years. After that time, the premiums are somewhat higher than they otherwise would be. Only a small percentage of policies are currently sold on this basis, although the contract does meet the needs of a particular market segment of individuals. Modified life can be especially appropriate for insureds with limited incomes who want to own permanent life insurance but cannot currently afford it. Of course, convertible term insurance can meet the same need, but many persons who plan to convert their term insurance do not actually do so because of the substantial premium increase. In this regard, an advantage of modified life is that the policyowner does not have to initiate any type of positive action to obtain the permanent insurance.

Endowment

Once a very popular form of life insurance, the amount of **endowment insurance** sold in the United States is now negligible. Endowment contracts provide death benefits for a specified period of time, just as term insurance does. However, unlike term insurance, endowment insurance has a cash value, and the policyowner is paid the contract's face amount at the end of the protection period if the insured is still alive. Thus, while the policy does provide death protection, on a relative basis it emphasizes savings to a much greater degree than any policy discussed thus far. In the past, endowment policies sometimes were used to accumulate savings for specific purposes, such as a child's college education or an individual's retirement. Even though the structure of an endowment policy might seem appropriate for some needs, most insureds now seek other alternatives because of the adverse tax treatment now accorded to endowment policies.

Industrial Life

A special form of coverage, known variously as **industrial life**, **home service life**, or **debit insurance**,[4] refers to a type of cash value life insurance that is sold in very small amounts,

---

4   The term *debit insurance* derives its name from the fact that a debit originally meant the premium to be collected in a particular geographical area.

primarily to meet burial needs of low-income insureds. The face amount is only a few thousand dollars, and some older policies have a death benefit that is less than $1,000. The contract is set up so that premiums are only a few dollars a week, and agents usually collect these premiums personally at insureds' homes. Over time, many insureds are sold multiple policies of this sort.

Industrial life is more expensive on a relative basis than other forms of life insurance because of the high cost of its premium collection method and because mortality rates tend to be higher for persons who purchase this form of coverage. However, because the face amount is so small, underwriting standards often are fairly liberal, and medical exams are rarely required. It can easily be argued that insureds who purchase industrial life would be better served by regular term or whole life insurance. However, the low-income status of most of these insureds makes it unlikely that they will be approached by traditional life agents. Thus, such persons may not be aware that alternatives to industrial life insurance exist. Even so, this form of coverage now accounts for only a minute fraction of the new purchases of life insurance in the United States.

Credit Life

Credit life insurance is protection offered in connection with installment sales of consumer durables, such as automobiles. It is decreasing term insurance issued without a medical examination and arranged to expire when the installment sales contract is paid off. The cost of protection is incorporated into the regular payment made by the purchaser. If the insured dies before the loan is repaid, sufficient coverage exists to repay the balance of the debt, thus protecting the insured's dependents as well as the lender.

INCOME TAX TREATMENT OF LIFE INSURANCE

So far in this chapter, very little has been mentioned regarding life insurance and income taxes. However, no discussion of life insurance is complete without some discussion of income tax ramifications. These considerations can be especially important in implementing an individual risk management plan, such as that illustrated in Chapter 21.

Premiums

In most cases, individuals cannot deduct the premiums they pay for individual life insurance when they compute their taxable incomes. The primary exception is for someone who is paying premiums on a life insurance policy owned by a charitable organization. For example, suppose John Chang is an avid alumnus of the University of Illinois. In response to a university fund-raising drive, John applies for a $100,000 life insurance policy and names the university as both beneficiary and policyowner. John plans to pay the premium on this policy on an annual basis. Because the university owns the policy, he is able to take an income tax deduction for the amount of the premium each year. When John dies, the university will receive the $100,000 face amount.

Death Benefits

As a general rule, when an insured dies and a death benefit is paid by an individual life insurance policy, the beneficiary does not have to report the death benefit as taxable income if the proceeds are paid in a lump sum. The income taxation rules are more complex if the policy proceeds are paid in any other manner. (Several payment options in this regard are discussed later in this chapter.) When settlement is made through a series of periodic payments from the insurer, the beneficiary generally can exclude only part of each payment from taxable income.

Specifically, the amount of each payment that represents a distribution of the original death benefit is not taxed, while the portion that is due to interest earnings is subject to taxation.[5]

Cash Values

If a life insurance policy with a cash value is terminated before death and the contract is surrendered for cash, it is likely that there will be taxable income that must be reported in the year of the surrender. The amount of taxable income in this case is the difference between the cash received at termination and the premiums that were paid during the life of the contract. While a cash value policy is in force, the annual increments to the cash value (sometimes called the **inside buildup**) often escape immediate taxation. In many policies, these increments are not taxed at all until the policy is surrendered for its cash value. Thus, if the cash value of Alice's whole life policy increases from $15,000 to $16,000 in one year, Alice would not report the $1,000 increment as taxable income.

In some policies, however, taxation of part of the inside buildup occurs every year. The determining factor regarding the manner in which the cash value accumulation is taxed depends on whether the policy meets the statutory definition of life insurance as specified in the Internal Revenue Code. Policies that meet this definition are not subject to immediate taxation of their inside buildup; cash values of policies that cannot meet the requirements of this definition will be partially taxed each year.[6]

According to the Internal Revenue Code, a policy is considered to be life insurance for tax purposes only if it meets at least one of two tests. These alternative tests are quite technical, and the details are beyond the scope of this text.[7] It is important to note, however, that the intent of both tests is to assure that the cash value in a particular policy is not excessive in relationship to the policy's death benefit. Contracts that are primarily savings vehicles and have only a nominal death benefit will be unable to pass these tests, and therefore such contracts will not be granted an income tax advantage for the inside buildup of their cash values. This possibility is especially relevant for universal life policies and for endowment contracts.

LIFE INSURANCE CONTRACT PROVISIONS

The contractual provisions of a life insurance policy are of special significance to the insured because it is through a wise use of these rights that some of the most valuable benefits of protection can be obtained. Many of the basic policy provisions and options are discussed in this section.

Incontestability Clause

The **incontestability clause** states that if the policy has been in force for a given period, usually two years, and if the insured has not died during that time, the insurer may not afterward refuse to pay the proceeds, nor may it cancel or contest the contract, even due to fraud. Thus, if an insured is found to have lied about his or her physical condition at the time the application was made for life insurance, but this misrepresentation is not discovered until after the

---

5 See Section 101 of the Internal Revenue Code for a complete description of the rules in this regard.
6 For policies that do not meet the statutory definition of life insurance, the amount of the inside buildup that is taxable each year is determined based on a theoretical separation of the policy into two separate elements: death protection and savings. The interest on the savings component is considered to be taxable income each year.
7 For additional details see *2003 Tax Facts* 1 (Cincinnati, OH: National Underwriter Company, 2003), 121.

expiration of the incontestability clause, the insurer may neither cancel the policy nor refuse to pay the face amount if the insured has died from a cause not excluded under the basic terms of the policy. Thus, the incontestability clause serves as a time limit within which the insurer must discover any fraud or misrepresentation in the application or be barred thereafter from asserting what would otherwise be its legal right—namely, the right to cancel the agreement.

Such a statute of limitations is not typical of most other types of insurance contracts. The legal justification for this clause in life insurance is protection of beneficiaries from doubtful claims by an insurer that the deceased had made misrepresentations after it becomes impossible for the deceased to defend against or to deny the allegation.

Suicide Clause

The **suicide clause** partially protects the beneficiary from the financial consequences of suicide. The clause states that if the insured does not commit suicide for at least a stated period, usually two years, after issuance of the contract, the insurer may not deny liability under the policy for subsequent suicide. If suicide occurs within two years of the issuance of the policy, the insurer's only obligation is to return without interest the premiums that have been paid. A one- or two-year period is justified on the grounds that if the applicant's plans to commit suicide have motivated the purchase of life insurance, it is likely that these plans will abate after as long as one or two years.

Misstatement of Age or Sex

Misrepresenting one's age in life insurance is material to accepting the risk and normally would become a defense against payment of the proceeds if it were not for the incontestability clause. Without some control over this possibility, it would become possible for people to understate their ages for the purpose of obtaining lower life insurance premiums. Proof of age is therefore required before proceeds are paid. Under the **misstatement-of-age clause**, if it is determined that the policyholder's age has been misrepresented, the insurer adjusts the amount of proceeds payable rather than canceling the agreement altogether. The actual amount payable is the amount of insurance that would have been purchased for the premium paid had the policyholder's true age been stated.

In situations in which a person's sex has been misstated, the policy may also provide that the proceeds will be adjusted in a similar manner through the **misstatement-of-sex clause**. This provision is not required and is relevant only when premiums differ on the basis of sex. When such sex-based rates are used in life insurance, which is very common, females pay lower premiums than do males of the same age. Suppose Chris Thomas is a 30-year-old male who misstates his sex on his application for a $50,000 life insurance policy. On the basis of the application, the insurer believes Chris is a female and therefore charges a lower premium than would be required if the truth were known. If the policy contains the misstatement-of-sex clause, when Chris dies his beneficiary will receive less than the $50,000 face amount because the premiums will have been insufficient to fund a $50,000 policy for a male Chris's age.

Entire Contract Clause

The life insurance contract generally contains an **entire contract clause** that provides that the policy, together with the application, constitutes the entire contract between the parties. This clause is desirable for the protection of the insured and the beneficiary because without the clause it might be possible to affect the rights of the respective parties through changes in the bylaws or in the charter of the insurer.

Assignments

An insured may wish to **assign** the benefits of a life insurance policy, often as collateral for a loan. Permission of the insurer is not necessary for the insured to assign the contract, but the

ETHICAL PERSPECTIVES

The Incontestability Clause

The incontestability clause in life insurance policies can present some interesting legal and ethical dilemmas for insurers and the courts. In one such case, an individual who was HIV positive applied for a life insurance policy but sent another person to take his physical examination. The insurance company issued a policy with a $180,000 death benefit. When the insured died of AIDS more than two years after the policy had been issued, the insurer tried to deny the claim on the basis of fraud. But the incontestability clause prevailed, and the insurer was required to pay the death benefit.

Another case involved a Kansas City man who lost several million dollars in the 1987 stock market crash. Despondent over his losses, he entered the local branch of

the brokerage house where he traded regularly and shot the office manager, his broker, and then himself. Upon investigation, it was shown that the man had a history of substantial criminal activity, including insurance fraud. Because he had revealed nothing about his past history when applying for several life insurance policies, the insurers denied his widow's death claims. The insurers alleged that there had not been a "meeting of the minds," which is necessary to form a valid contract. That is, they argued that they would not have insured this individual had they known about his history. In spite of the probable truth of this argument, the district court once again upheld the incontestability clause and ordered the insurance companies to pay the life insurance benefits.

Sources: Diane West, "Despite Fraud, Co. Must Pay AIDS Claim," *National Underwriter, Life and Health*, March 3, 1997, 3; and *Bankers Security Life Ins. Soc. v Kane* 689 F. Supp. 1164 (S.D.Fla. 1988).

insurer must be properly notified in writing of an assignment or else is not bound by it. If the insured dies, the insurer pays the holder of the assignment that part of the proceeds equal to the outstanding debt and then pays the remainder to the named Beneficiaries.

Dividend Options

Some life insurance policies are **participating**, which means that they pay the policyowner dividends. In contrast to dividends payable to stockholders of a corporation, a policyowner dividend is not a distribution of profit; rather, it is a partial return of the premium payment and reflects the insurer's experience with respect to mortality, investment income, and expenses. Because dividends are considered to be a return of premium, they are not taxable to the recipient. Insurers are not required to pay dividends, even if an insurance contract is participating. Many insurers provide their insureds with illustrations of projected future dividends; these estimates are simply that—estimates—and as such they are not legally binding for the insurer. However, dividends may be substantial, and there are several options available for the use of dividends paid on participating contracts.

Cash or Payment of Premium

A policyowner may specify that all dividends are either to be paid to the policyowner in cash or applied toward the payment of the next premium due. Thus, the prospect of substantial dividends may make it possible for some people to afford higher face amounts of coverage than would otherwise be the case.

Accumulation at Interest

Another option is for the insurer to retain the dividends and pay interest on the accumulated amount. A minimum guaranteed interest rate is stated in the policy for policyowners who select this option, although insurers often pay more than the guaranteed minimum. The dividends themselves are not taxable, but interest paid on them through this option is taxable to the policyowner in the year in which it is credited. When dividends are paid under this option and are not withdrawn prior to the insured's death, the accumulated dividends are added to the policy face amount and are paid to the beneficiary as part of the death benefit. Just as a lump-sum distribution of the policy face amount is not taxable as income to the beneficiary, accumulated dividends distributed to a beneficiary as part of the death benefit are not considered taxable income.

Paid-Up Additions

Policyowners of whole life policies usually are offered the **paid-up additions option**, in which each dividend is used to purchase as much single-premium whole life insurance as possible. This approach is an economical way to buy additional life insurance, because no commission or other acquisition expenses must be paid. Further, no medical examination or other evidence of insurability is required, so this option may enable the purchase of insurance when it is impossible to obtain additional coverage in any other way. Another advantage of the paid-up additions option is that the insurance purchased under this option not only provides additional death protection but also has a cash value. As discussed previously, cash value growth is treated favorably for income tax purposes. Thus, there are many reasons to consider the paid-up additions option if it is offered. However, if an insured needs the maximum additional death protection possible, then the policyowner should consider the one-year term option.

One-Year Term Option

Sometimes called the fifth dividend option, the **one-year term option** uses each year's dividend to purchase as much one-year term insurance as possible. In this way, insureds can increase their death protection to the maximum extent without additional premium payment. Sometimes the amount of term insurance may be limited to the size of the policy's accumulated cash value or its face amount. When such a limit exists, any remaining dividend can be taken under another dividend option. Because of concerns about adverse selection, insurers usually require that the one-year term option be selected when the policy is first issued. The insured may be required to prove insurability to obtain the option at a later time.

Nonforfeiture Options

The **nonforfeiture options** in a life insurance policy guarantee that the savings element in a policy will not be forfeited to the insurer under any circumstances but will always accrue to the benefit of the insured. Before the advent of nonforfeiture options, which are required by law in all states, there were cases in which aged persons agreed to sell their policies to speculators when they could no longer afford to pay the premiums. Speculators' offers depended on the physical condition of the person, and a public sale often took place with the insured person present so that he or she could be examined. Needless to say, the insured seldom fared well in these transactions, and such practices were eventually outlawed. There are now three ways in which the policyowner may receive a policy's cash value: a lump sum paid in cash, paid-up insurance of a reduced amount, or extended-term insurance.

Cash Value Option

Under the **cash value option**, the policy may be surrendered for cash. A schedule of guaranteed minimum cash values is included in the policy, although the actual cash value in policies such as universal life may vary considerably from the minimums guaranteed. Before payment is made, any outstanding indebtedness is subtracted. When a policyowner exercises the cash value option, the cash is usually paid immediately, although the insurer has the right to delay payment for as long as six months. After 30 days, the insured is entitled to interest on the amount due.

Paid-Up Insurance Option

When the **paid-up insurance option** is exercised, the insurer uses the cash value to buy as much single-premium insurance as possible on the life of the insured, given the size of the cash value. The same type of insurance is purchased as existed for the original policy. Thus, if the original policy was whole life insurance, the new paid-up coverage also will be whole life. The only difference is that the new death benefit will be for a lower amount than before, and no more premiums will be required after the option is exercised. This option may be appropriate when the insured's need for death protection has declined but is expected to continue at a reduced level until death. The contract guarantees the amount of paid-up insurance that can be purchased at various times. For example, the $100,000 sample whole life policy in Appendix D guarantees that the coverage can be converted into $77,300 worth of paid-up whole life insurance at age 65. At age 60, the cash value is lower and can only purchase $69,400 worth of paid-up coverage. (Refer to the "Table of Guaranteed Values" section of the sample policy in Appendix D for these particular numbers.)

Extended-Term Option

If the insured does not select a nonforfeiture option and has not implemented the automatic premium loan provision, most insurers automatically place a cash value policy on the **extended-term option** if premiums remain unpaid after expiration of the grace period (assuming the policy is not one of the flexible premium types). Under this option, the policy's cash value is used to purchase term insurance for as many years and months as are allowed by the rates in effect for the insured's age when the lapse occurs. As is true for the paid-up insurance option, minimum guarantees regarding this option are included in the policy itself.

Refer once more to the $100,000 sample whole life policy in Appendix D. Suppose the insured, John Doe, quits paying premiums at the end of the tenth policy year. According to the minimum guarantees included in the policy, John could elect to have $8,000 paid to him in cash (the cash value option), or he could convert the coverage into $34,300 of paid-up whole life insurance. If he does neither of these, the extended-term option will take effect, and John will continue to have $100,000 worth of death protection for 11 years and 50 days. The death benefit will remain the same, but the coverage will be term insurance rather than whole life. Thus, at the end of the specified term, the coverage will expire without further value.

Policy Loans

Sometimes the policyowner may need access to funds that are only available through the cash value of his or her life insurance policy, and it may not be desirable to terminate the policy. In such a situation, the cash value may be borrowed from the insurer, with the insurance coverage remaining intact. If the insured dies with an outstanding policy loan, the amount of the loan is subtracted from the policy proceeds before payment is made to the beneficiary. Otherwise, there is no obligation to repay policy loans. However, because the insurer calculates premiums on the assumption that interest will be earned on the funds supporting the policy, interest is charged to anyone—including the policyowner—who borrows some of those funds. Unpaid interest accumulates and is added to the total loan outstanding. If the entire cash value has been borrowed, or if the loan plus the unpaid interest equals the cash value, then it becomes necessary for the insured to pay subsequent interest assessments to avoid having the contract lapse.

If the policyowner takes a policy loan but still wants to maintain the full amount of death protection, the one-year term dividend option can be helpful, assuming that the contract is participating. For example, suppose Mike Bernelli has a $100,000 participating whole life policy with a $20,000 cash value. Mike wants to borrow the entire $20,000 but realizes that if he does so, his beneficiary will receive only $80,000 (the policy face minus the indebtedness) if he dies. To avoid this situation, Mike borrows the $20,000 and then exercises his option to purchase one-year term insurance of $20,000, using dividends from the basic policy to pay the necessary premium.

Because policies without flexible premium arrangements will lapse after expiration of the grace period if premiums are not paid when due, many insurers encourage use of an **automatic premium loan provision**. This provision automatically authorizes the insurer to use cash values to pay unpaid premiums that are due. Under this provision, a loan is established against the policy just as though the insured had borrowed the amount for another purpose. In this way, the policy continues without interruption, with the only change being that there is a loan outstanding.

Policy loans from cash value life insurance contracts generally are not taxable as income. The only exception is for some contracts that meet the statutory definition of life insurance and were issued on or after June 21, 1988. To the extent that the cash values exceed the premiums paid (less policyowner dividends), loans from such policies are taxed as ordinary income, unless the policy passes what is known as the **seven-pay test**. This test is intended to reduce the use of policy loans, particularly with respect to single-premium life insurance contracts.

In general terms, the seven-pay test compares the actual premiums paid during the first seven years (A) with the premiums that would have been payable if the policy had been set up on a level annual premium basis (B). If A is greater than B, the policy fails the test. The consequences of failing the seven-pay test are less severe than those applied when a policy does not meet the statutory definition of life insurance. The penalty is not the loss of tax deferral on the inside buildup, but merely the loss of the tax advantage otherwise associated with policy loans. Policies that meet the statutory definition of life insurance, fail the seven-pay test, and were issued on or after June 21, 1988, are classified in the tax code as **modified endowment contracts**.

Beneficiary Designation

As discussed in Chapter 6, the beneficiary of a life insurance policy generally must have an insurable interest in the insured's life at the time the policy is issued. Although technically the insured can specify anyone as the beneficiary regardless of insurable interest considerations, insurers, out of concern for moral hazard, generally reject applications for coverage if an insurable interest does not exist.

Attention should be given to the way the beneficiary designation is worded so that the death benefit will be paid to the intended person. If children are listed by name, then any subsequent children born to the insured will be excluded. Thus, it is better to say "children of the insured" if the policy is intended to benefit all children at the time of the insured's death. On the other hand, it is usually best to be specific regarding the identity of a spouse named as a beneficiary. For example, suppose John Allgood is married to Leslie at the time he purchases a $500,000 term policy. John specifies that the beneficiary is "my wife." Three years later John and Leslie are divorced, and John later marries Patricia. When John dies, there is a possibility that both Leslie and Patricia may claim to be the rightful beneficiary. After all, Leslie was the wife when John obtained the coverage, even though Patricia was the wife when John died. In such a situation, the courts will award the proceeds to the person who is the wife at the time of the insured's death. But such disputes can be avoided in the first place by very clear wording of beneficiary designations, with appropriate updates made to reflect changed circumstances.

Policyowners have the right to change beneficiaries without notice to those affected, provided that a beneficiary was not named irrevocably. A **revocable beneficiary** has no control over the policy, but an **irrevocable beneficiary** can be changed only if the beneficiary gives written consent. Irrevocable designations usually are made after an event such as a divorce to give additional security to the beneficiary.

It is common to name **contingent beneficiaries** who will receive the policy proceeds if the primary beneficiary is not alive at the time of the insured's death. If both the insured and the primary beneficiary die under circumstances such that it cannot be determined who died first, the general rule is that the policy proceeds will be paid to the contingent beneficiaries. However, if the primary beneficiary clearly survives the insured (even briefly) and then dies, the death benefit is payable to the primary beneficiary's estate. For example, suppose Bob and Karen Potter each have children by a previous marriage. Karen has a $200,000 whole life policy, in which Bob is the primary beneficiary and her children are the contingent beneficiaries. If Karen and Bob are both killed instantly in the same auto accident, the $200,000 will be paid to Karen's children, consistent with her wishes. But if Bob lives a short while at the scene of the accident and perhaps speaks to the ambulance driver before dying on the way to the hospital, then the $200,000 from Karen's policy will be paid to Bob's children because they are his heirs and he lived long enough to legally inherit the proceeds of Karen's insurance.

To avoid possibilities such as the one just described, a **common disaster clause** may be used in the beneficiary designation. Such a clause specifies that upon the insured's death, the insurance proceeds are to be held by the insurer (with interest) for a period of time, such as 30 or 60 days. After that period, if the primary beneficiary is alive, the proceeds are distributed to that person. Otherwise, the death benefit is paid to the contingent beneficiaries. In situations where no primary or contingent beneficiaries are alive when the insured dies, the death benefit is paid to the insured's estate.

Excluded Causes of Death

It is uncommon for life insurers to exclude coverage for death arising out of specific causes. One exclusion that is occasionally used, however, is the **war hazard exclusion**. During periods when there is a serious threat of war or other hostilities involving the military forces of at least two countries, insurers may insert a war hazard exclusion in policies issued to insureds who are either in the military or who are of an age that may cause them to become subject to military duty. When used, this exclusion eliminates insurance coverage for death that is a direct result of war or other hostile actions between countries.

Another exclusion, the **aviation hazard exclusion**, eliminates coverage for death from aviation activities other than as a fare-paying passenger on a commercial aircraft. Although it is rarely found in policies currently being issued, some older policies may contain this exclusion.

Settlement Options

Settlement options are the different ways in which the policyowner or beneficiary may elect to have the benefits of a policy paid. The vast majority of life insurance benefits are paid in one lump sum to the designated beneficiary. However, as described in this section, other payment options are available.

Lump-Sum Option

Under the **lump-sum option**, proceeds of the life insurance are paid in a lump sum, and the insurer's obligations are thus ended. The insurer exercises no further control over the money, and the various services offered in connection with other options are lost. Most policies are settled in this way.

Fixed-Period Option

Under the **fixed-period option**, the insurer pays the proceeds in equal installments over a specified time period. The size of each installment varies with the desired frequency of payment (often monthly), the length of the total time period during which payments are to be made, and the interest rate paid by the insurer on proceeds not yet distributed. Once payments

INTERNATIONAL PERSPECTIVES

Paying Holocaust Victims

Life insurance policies covering persons who perished in concentration camps during the Holocaust of World War II have been the source of controversy for many years. Many policies issued to Jewish persons in Germany during the 1920s and 1930s were cancelled due to nonpayment of premium when insureds were sent to concentration camps. Further, death certificates were never issued for those who were killed, thus eliminating the proof of death necessary for beneficiaries to collect. In other cases, no survivors remained to collect the death benefits. Numerous allegations have been made of insurer complicity with Nazi Germany to avoid payment on these policies.

During the 1990s, numerous lawsuits were filed against European life insurers in an attempt to force payment to the heirs of Holocaust victims. In 1998, following negotiations among European insurers, the U.S. National Association of Insurance Commissioners, Israel, and international Jewish organizations, the International Commission on Holocaust Era Insurance Claims (ICHEIC) was formed with the goal of resolving claims disputes outside of court. The Commission is funded by insurers. It researches records and attempts to identify life insurance policies for which a benefit has never been paid. Efforts are also made to identify heirs of the insureds under such policies and notify them of their rights. In many cases, insurers have also agreed to contribute to humanitarian programs seeking to aid Holocaust victims who are in need financially. As of the end of 2003, member companies had paid over 2,000 claims totaling more than $32 million through the ICHEIC process. For additional information, see http://www.icheic.org.

begin to be made under this option, it usually is still possible for the beneficiary to withdraw the present value of unpaid future installments; however, partial withdrawals may not be allowed.

Insurance policies contain guarantees regarding the minimum payments that will be possible under this and other settlement options. The sample whole life policy in Appendix D bases its guarantees (see Option 2A Table, in "Payment of Policy Proceeds" section) on a 3.5 percent interest rate assumption. If the insurer earns more than 3.5 percent, the excess interest will be used to increase the amount of each payment without affecting the length of the payout period. To illustrate this option, consider the insured John Doe, referred to in the sample policy in Appendix D. The beneficiary is currently John's estate, but can be changed in the future. Suppose that when John dies, the beneficiary at that time (assumed to be someone other than John's estate) elects to receive the policy proceeds under the fixed-period option for a period of 10 years. As shown in the Option 2A Table of Appendix D, the policy guarantees that for each $1,000 of face amount, a monthly payment of at least $9.83 will be made for 10 years. Because the policy has a $100,000 face amount, the guaranteed monthly payment for 10 years is $100 \times \$9.83 = \$98.30$. The payments will be more than this amount if interest greater than 3.5 percent is earned and paid by the insurer.

Fixed-Amount Option

In contrast to the fixed-period option, the **fixed-amount option** is used when a specified amount of income is desired. The length of time that payments are made is a function of the size and frequency of each payment, as well as the interest rate paid by the insurer on the proceeds. Whereas under the fixed-period option, interest earned in excess of the guaranteed level increases the size of payments, under the fixed-amount option, excess interest increases the length of time during which payments are made.

Consider again the example involving John Doe and the sample whole life policy in Appendix D. When John dies, suppose that the beneficiary decides that an income of $250 a month is needed for as long as possible. At 3.5 percent interest on a $100,000 policy, the Option 2A Table indicates that a monthly income of $291.90 can be paid for exactly 3 years. An income of $222.70 per month can be paid for exactly 4 years. Through interpolation, it can be estimated that the beneficiary is guaranteed to receive $250 a month for about 3 years and 7 months. This period will increase if the insurer pays interest greater than the guaranteed 3.5 percent.

Interest Option

Under the **interest option**, the insurer holds the proceeds of the policy and pays the beneficiary an income consisting of interest only. A guaranteed minimum rate is stated in the policy, with excess interest often used to increase the amount of each payment. When this option is in effect, the beneficiary usually has the right to withdraw some or all of the principal amount. Such rights can be restricted, however, if desired.

Life Income Options

Several variations of settlement options guarantee a beneficiary an income for his or her remaining lifetime. In addition to the life income, additional guarantees may be made concerning the minimum number of payments that will be made or the guaranteed total dollars to be paid, regardless of how long the beneficiary lives. The many variations of life income options and the rationale for their structure are the same as that for annuities, which form the subject matter of Chapter 18. Therefore, at this point it is sufficient merely to provide an example illustrating how two of the life income options work.

Once again, consider the $100,000 whole life policy in Appendix D. Suppose John has changed the beneficiary designation to be his wife Helen. When John dies, Helen is age 60. The policy could be settled by a monthly payment to Helen of about $475 (not specifically stated in the sample policy), to continue for as long as Helen lives. As soon as Helen dies, payments will cease. But suppose Helen wants to make sure that either she or her children receive payments for at least some minimum period of time. In this case, she might decide to select the life income option with a **10-year certain period**. According to the Option 3A Table in the sample policy, the monthly payment with this additional guarantee would be 100 × $4.65 = $465. If Helen dies within the first 10 years after payments begin, the $465 monthly amount would continue to be paid to her heirs until a total of 10 years of payments were made. Then all payments would cease. However, if Helen is still living after the first 10 years, she will continue to receive the $465 until she dies.

Coverage Extension Options

Two options for increasing the amount of coverage in a life insurance policy, the cost-of-living rider and the guaranteed insurability rider, were discussed previously. In this section, three additional options affecting either the amount or the nature of the coverage are briefly noted.

Waiver of Premium Benefit

For a low additional premium, a **waiver of premium benefit** can be added to life insurance policies. This extension of coverage provides that insureds who become disabled before a specified age (often 60 or 65) will be excused from paying premiums for as long as the disability continues. The life insurance policy will have the same cash values, death benefits, and dividends as it would have had if all premiums had been paid. Policies vary as to how they define disability for this purpose, and many contracts also require a six-month waiting period after the onset of the disability before premiums are waived. The use of the waiver of premium benefit is not expensive and is generally recommended as a way of assuring that the life insurance policy will remain intact regardless of the insured's health.

Accidental Death Benefit

Another relatively inexpensive benefit that can be added to most life policies is the **accidental death benefit**. This option makes it possible for the beneficiary to receive an additional death benefit if the insured dies from an accident. The size of the accidental death benefit is often equal to the face amount of the underlying policy. Numerous restrictions exist on this benefit, however, in contrast to the lack of exclusions for basic life insurance policies. Common exclusions that apply to accidental death benefit provisions include death from suicide, death that occurs more than 120 days following an accident, death from illness, and deaths due to war or aviation (other than as a fare-paying passenger on a commercial aircraft). Although the charge for the accidental death benefit often is only about $1.25 per $1,000 of face amount, this type of coverage may lead naive insureds to believe that their total death protection has doubled for only a small extra premium. However, accidents are far from being the leading cause of death, and accidents that satisfy the definitions of the accidental death benefit are even less common. Thus, insureds who need life insurance to provide beneficiaries with necessary death benefits should be careful to arrange adequate coverage regardless of the cause of death.

Accelerated Death Benefit

In the early 1990s, a new option for life insurance policies was developed, known either as a **living benefit option** or an **accelerated death benefit**. The basic idea is that under specified circumstances, a percentage of the policy's face amount, discounted for interest, can be paid to the insured before death. Some insurers consider such payments to terminate all future contractual rights to benefits. Others allow some or all of any remaining face amount to be paid to the beneficiary when the insured dies. Accelerated death benefits can be an important income source for persons with terminal illnesses. Some insurers also offer this option to help pay for an insured's long-term care needs. In this case, an additional agreement known as a **long-term care rider** may be attached to a permanent form of coverage, with an extra premium charged for the option.

Variations exist among insurers regarding (1) the percentage of the death benefit that can be paid on an accelerated basis, (2) whether an additional premium is charged, (3) the types of policies for which living benefit options are available, (4) whether the accelerated death benefit can be payable in a lump sum or only via installments, and (5) whether complete surrender of all future policyowner rights accompanies the payment of accelerated benefits. One of the factors impeding the growth of living benefit options is a concern that their payment erodes the death protection provided for beneficiaries—often one of the major reasons for purchasing a life insurance policy in the first place. Another problem until recently had been the unclear tax status. That is, should living benefits be exempt from income taxes in the same way that death benefits are? The Health Insurance Portability and Accountability Act of 1996 clarified the tax treatment of living benefits paid after December 31, 1996. From that point forward, accelerated death benefits are excludable from taxable income if a physician certifies that the insured has a terminal illness that is expected to result in death within 24 months or less.

Spendthrift Trust Clause

One of the legal rights granted to the life insurance owner in most states is the exemption of death proceeds and cash values from the claims of creditors. Creditors of the insured cannot attach the cash value of life insurance for the payment of the insured's debts unless the

ETHICAL PERSPECTIVES

Viatical Settlements

A recently developed innovation in life insurance is the **viatical settlement**, which involves the purchase of a life insurance policy from a terminally ill individual by an unrelated third party. The amount paid for the policy depends on the insured's expected remaining lifetime. For example, suppose Joe owns a $100,000 policy and has an illness from which he expects to die within six months. On the basis of this life expectancy, Joe might be able to receive about $70,000 for his life insurance policy from an interested "investor." When Joe dies, the person who purchased his policy will then receive the full face amount as a death benefit. A large percentage of the insureds who originally initiated viatical settlements in the United States had AIDS. Because they often had high medical costs and no dependants, a viatical settlement on a life insurance policy could be particularly attractive.

Ironically, when insureds sold their policies through viatical settlements, they were often able to afford better medical care that actually extended their lives. The use of expensive new drug treatments in the fight against AIDS is a prime example in this regard. For investors interested in buying life insurance policies through viatical settlements, this development presented an interesting dilemma. The response was that investors decreased the dollar amounts they were willing to pay for policies, due to the increased uncertainty about expected remaining lifetimes of the insureds. Thus, fewer funds from this source became available for persons with AIDS.

insured has wrongfully bought or paid up a life insurance policy with money rightfully subject to creditors' claims. Neither may the insured's creditors attach the death proceeds of life insurance. This is an important right because the beneficiary is thus protected from the claims of the insured's creditors, and indiscretions of the insured are not allowed to wreck the income security of the beneficiaries.

A question arises, however, concerning the beneficiary's creditors: May the beneficiary incur large debts, using as security the right to receive income from life insurance proceeds? This is technically possible unless the state law has a provision to the contrary or unless the law has permitted the attachment of what is called the **spendthrift trust clause**. If this clause is attached to a life insurance policy, the beneficiary's rights to the promised income cannot be attached by creditors in any court in the state of residence. Such a clause is a valuable security measure, for without it there might be a temptation for an unscrupulous creditor to persuade a beneficiary to purchase goods beyond the ability to pay, secure in the knowledge that the life insurance could be attached. Once the proceeds have been paid to the beneficiary, the protection is lost since the money loses its identity as life insurance proceeds.

Grace Period and Reinstatement Clauses

Policies with nonflexible premiums lapse for nonpayment of premium, but the **grace period clause** always gives the insured an extra 30 days in which to pay any premium that is due before lapse takes place. Further, as discussed previously, the automatic premium loan provision can forestall policy lapses as long as sufficient cash values exist to cover the premium due. Once the policy actually does lapse, however, special application must be made under the reinstatement clause to restore coverage. Under the **reinstatement clause**, contracts may be reinstated within a certain period after lapse, usually three or five years, with evidence of insurability. Sometimes a new medical examination must be taken, but in most cases the insured is required only to make a statement of personal good health at the time of reinstatement. All premiums in arrears plus interest must be paid. Reinstatement reopens the incontestability clause for another two years, but generally the suicide clause is held not to be reopened.

It is sometimes desirable to reinstate an old policy rather than to take out a new one because the old policy may have certain provisions, such as more favorable settlement options, immediate eligibility for dividends, or higher interest assumptions, which are not available in the new policy. Furthermore, no new acquisition costs have to be paid on the reinstated policy, as they would on a new contract. Because acquisition costs can be substantial, often amounting to about one year's annual premium on ordinary life policies, this factor can be a great saving.

SUMMARY

1. The standard life insurance arrangement provides that upon the insured's death, the policy face amount will be paid to the beneficiary. When terminated prior to death, some policies have cash values that can be refunded to the policyowner.

2. The three major types of life insurance are term, whole life, and universal life. Term policies usually do not have cash values. The contracts differ according to the length of time for which protection is provided, the guarantees regarding coverage options, and the possible changes in the amount of death protection while the policy is in force. Whole life insurance may be kept in force for the insured's entire lifetime. Many different premium payment arrangements are possible; the method selected influences the size of the policy's cash value at any given time. Universal life policies usually provide for flexible premiums and possible changes in the size of the death benefit. Cash values vary over time, depending on the timing and amount of premiums paid and the insurer's investment earnings, mortality experience, and expenses.

3. Variable life insurance death benefits and cash values vary with the performance of one or more investment portfolios selected by the policyowner; changes in portfolio selection usually can be made periodically each year. A form of insurance that combines many of the features of both variable and universal life is known as flexible premium variable life, or variable universal life insurance.

4. There are many other special forms of life insurance sold. Some of these include modified life contracts, endowment insurance, industrial life, and credit life insurance.

5. Individuals usually cannot deduct life insurance premiums from their federal taxable income. At death, however, policy proceeds paid to the beneficiary are not reportable as taxable income. If a cash value policy is surrendered for cash before death, taxable income usually must be reported. Taxation of a policy's cash value buildup before surrender of the contract occurs only when the cash value is excessive relative to the death benefit, as judged by specified Internal Revenue Service tests.

6. Contractual provisions in life insurance are important, because it is only through a wise use of a policyowner's rights that many of the valuable benefits of protection are obtained. Policyowners should be especially careful in wording the beneficiary designations in their contracts.

7. Participating life insurance policies pay dividends to policyowners. These dividends are a return of premiums based on the insurer's investment, mortality, and expense experience. Dividends can be paid to the policyowner in cash, can be used to reduce future premiums, can be accumulated with interest by the insurer, or can be used to buy additional amounts of either paid-up cash value coverage or one-year term insurance.

8. Policyowners of cash value contracts can borrow the cash values without terminating the policies. Such loans accrue interest but do not need to be repaid. However, at the insured's death, outstanding indebtedness is subtracted from the policy proceeds before payment is made to the beneficiary.

9. Policyowners wishing to terminate their cash value policies before the insured's death can elect to receive the savings element in cash, use it to buy paid-up insurance for a reduced amount, or use it to buy term insurance for the same face amount for as long as allowed by the rates in

effect for the insured's age when the policy is terminated.

10. Most life insurance policies are settled by payment of the face amount in a lump sum to the beneficiary upon proof of the insured's death. Alternative settlement options include payment of the proceeds over a fixed period or in fixed amounts, payment of only the interest on the face amount while the proceeds are held and invested

by the insurer, and several arrangements that guarantee payment as long as one or more beneficiaries remain alive.

11. For a relatively small additional charge, waiver of premium benefits, accidental death benefits, and accelerated death benefit options often can be added to life insurance policies to increase the contracts' usefulness to insureds.

internet*exercises*

1. Suppose that you are 30 years old and the proud parent of a newborn set of twins. You are interested in buying a substantial amount of term insurance at a low cost. Consult the following Web site and select an amount of insurance and an insurer that you believe will best meet your needs: http://www. insure.com. What will be the annual premium for

your selected policy? Why did you choose the particular policy you chose?

2. Visit the following Web site to see the underwriting guidelines some life insurers use for various rate classifications: http://www.3dquotes.com/ guide.html. Do any of the requirements surprise you? Why is it necessary for the insurer to gather such extensive information?

QUESTIONS FOR REVIEW AND DISCUSSION

1. List and briefly describe the distinguishing features of the three major types of life insurance sold in the United States.

2. Define renewable term insurance and explain the features of this form of insurance that would make it desirable for an individual who needs a large amount of coverage over a specific period of several years.

3. Explain convertible term insurance and describe a situation in which this would be a desirable option for a potential insured.

4. What is a level term contract?

5. Explain the nature of cash values in the context of a whole life contract. Include in your explanation the source of the cash value accumulation and the ways that insureds can access these funds.

6. Why might adverse selection become a problem for insurance companies in (a) a renewable term policy, (b) a universal life policy that allows the insured to periodically increase the amount of coverage, and (c) a term policy with a cost-of-living rider?

7. Differentiate between the two basic versions of universal life contracts.

8. Explain the following terms as they relate to beneficiary designations:
   a. Revocable beneficiary
   b. Irrevocable beneficiary
   c. Contingent beneficiary
   d. Common disaster clause

9. Briefly describe each of the following five settlement options:
   a. Lump-sum option
   b. Fixed-period option
   c. Fixed-amount option
   d. Interest option
   e. Life income options

10. Explain the difference between a reinstatement clause and a grace period clause. Why might an insured prefer to use a reinstatement clause following the lapse of a policy instead of simply purchasing a new policy? When would an insured be precluded from doing so?

11. Explain the typical terms of a policy loan on the cash value of a permanent form of life insurance.

12. Explain the federal income tax treatment of life insurance premiums and death benefits.

13. Distinguish between situations in which a life policy's inside buildup is and is not subject to federal income taxation. What is the rationale for this differential treatment?

14. What word of caution might you express to those who are considering the purchase of a whole life insurance policy and who anticipate using the savings features of the policy to fund their retirement and the insurance portion to ensure that their heirs receive a benefit regardless of whether they die before or after retirement?

15. What typically included clause would prevent a person's purchase of life insurance on the day before an intended suicide? Why do you feel that this clause typically has a time limitation instead of simply excluding this peril altogether? In your opinion, should this clause apply to terminally ill patients who refuse artificial life support?

16. A 30-year-old male who knowingly suffers from a congenital heart defect states on his life insurance application that he is a 27-year-old female in perfect health. How do you think the insurance company will treat a death claim made 3 years later if the contract includes a 2-year incontestability clause and a misstatement-of-age or misstatement-of-sex clause? Do you feel that this is fair to the insurance company? Why?

17. Mrs. Brown dies with a valid life insurance policy in force, in which her husband is named as the primary beneficiary. Which settlement option would you recommend that Mr. Brown exercise if he is a shrewd investor? Might your answer change if you knew that Mr. Brown had been diagnosed with Alzheimer's disease?

chapter 17

Loss of Health

Jim Carson, age 22, is a recent college graduate who is looking for employment. Jim majored in agricultural engineering and hopes to be able to put his specialized knowledge to work. One problem that Jim is encountering in his job search is that he has had asthma since childhood and sometimes suffers severe problems in this regard. Thus, he must be especially careful about the type of job he takes and the environment in which he will work. Jim also fears that when he does accept a job, his new employer's health insurance plan might exclude him (either temporarily or perhaps permanently) from coverage for any problems related to his asthma. While he was in college, Jim's parents' health insurance provided protection for him, but that coverage will soon end now that he has graduated.

Jim's parents are urging him to buy an individual health insurance policy as soon as possible. But Jim is afraid that it will be difficult to find an insurer that is willing to sell him coverage, given his health history. If he does find such an insurer, Jim is not confident that he will be able to choose the appropriate set of coverage options for his circumstances. Plus, he is worried about not being able to go to the doctors with whom he feels most comfortable. Finally, given the publicity in recent years about health care reforms, Jim wonders about the potential implications for his own situation. These and related issues are discussed in this chapter.

CHAPTER OBJECTIVES

After studying this chapter, you should be able to

1. Describe the similarities and differences among commercial insurers, traditional Blue Cross and Blue Shield associations, and the new for-profit Blues organizations.

2. Explain the major characteristics of health maintenance organizations and explain how point-of-service plans and preferred provider organizations differ from them.

3. Compute the amount of a covered loss that would be reimbursable from an insurer, given the amount of the loss and applicable deductibles, coinsurance provisions, and limits.

4. Distinguish among forms of basic health insurance policies and describe three forms of major medical insurance.

5. List several characteristics to consider when purchasing a long-term care and disability income insurance contracts.

6. Explain the nature and structure of Medicare benefits and the approach used to standardize Medigap policies.

7. Explain the mandatory and allowable provisions in individual health insurance with respect to grace periods, reinstatement, claim procedures, occupational issues, the misstatement of age when applying for coverage, and the existence of more than one policy covering the same loss.

8. Describe health care reforms recently enacted or currently under consideration in the United States.

As a tool in personal risk management plans, the importance of health insurance cannot be overemphasized. However, the high cost of health care, combined with concerns about the lack of availability of health insurance for some persons, has led to a rapidly changing environment in which health care is delivered in the United States. This chapter focuses on methods to manage the two primary losses arising out of an individual's loss of health, as discussed in Chapter 4, with particular emphasis on recent changes. The losses that are discussed include (1) expenses for medical services and (2) income losses when the person is unable to work due to an accident or illness.

HEALTH INSURANCE PROVIDERS

Health insurance is provided by several types of organizations: commercial insurers, Blue Cross and Blue Shield associations, health maintenance organizations (HMOs), point-of-service (POS) plans, and preferred provider organizations (PPOs). When payment for health expenses is provided as an employee benefit (see Chapter 19), many employers set up self-insurance arrangements to either replace or supplement coverage obtained from one or more of these types of providers. In addition, some health insurance is provided by the Medicare and Medicaid systems, the social insurance arrangements set up through the federal and state governments.

Insurers and the Blues

Until recently, commercial insurers and **Blue Cross and Blue Shield associations** (the *Blues*) were legally very different in terms of structure, though from the perspective of an individual insured they appeared to be very similar. The Blues were originally designed to be nonprofit organizations allowing their subscribers (insureds) to prepay some types of health care expenses. Blue Cross associations focused on the prepayment of hospital expenses, whereas Blue Shield groups covered physicians' services. When combined, the medical expense coverage offered by the Blues could be virtually identical to that available from commercial insurers. Beginning in the mid-1990s, however, even the structural differences between the Blues and insurers began eroding. In an effort to become more competitive, Blues in several states began forming or acquiring for-profit subsidiaries, and a number of the Blues organizations converted to a for-profit status in their entirety.

It must be emphasized that there never was one national plan called "Blue Cross–Blue Shield." Rather, the Blues were independent groups organized by doctors, hospitals, and other medical service providers in a particular geographic region. The groups agreed to meet certain common standards in exchange for authorization to use the Blues' name. Many states granted the Blues preferential tax treatment because of their nonprofit status, thus lowering one source of operational expenses for them in comparison with for-profit insurers. But as changes in the health care delivery system evolved, many of the Blues found themselves insuring a large percentage of individuals who had difficulty obtaining health insurance elsewhere. In turn, this situation caused the Blues to experience substantial financial losses. In addition, traditional not-for-profit Blues have more limited access to capital than for-profit stock companies. Thus, most of the Blues are now transforming themselves in part or in whole, and it is quite possible that within a few years Blue Cross–Blue Shield associations as they once existed will be a thing of the past.

Health Maintenance Organizations

By the beginning of the 21st century, over 80 million persons in the United States were enrolled in **health maintenance organizations (HMOs)**.[1] HMOs can be structured in several

---

1 Unless otherwise noted, all health care statistics cited in this chapter are obtained from *Source Book of Health Insurance Data* (Washington, D.C.: Health Insurance Association of America, 2002).

ETHICAL PERSPECTIVES

What Do the Blues Owe the States?

As Blue Cross–Blue Shield organizations convert themselves into regular insurance companies, often with for-profit objectives, an interesting question arises: Who really owns the funds that have built up over the years within a particular Blues association? Is it the Blues entity itself? Or because of its past nonprofit status, is it the subscribers (insureds)? What about the substantial tax advantages granted by many of the states over many years? These subsidies allowed the Blues to compete more effectively than would otherwise have been possible, so perhaps some of the accumulated funds belong to the states. Or are the Blues charitable organizations whose assets should be used for health-related charitable purposes?

As the Blues convert some or all of their operations to a for-profit orientation, a variety of answers are emerging to these questions. For example, the conversion of Blue Cross of California resulted in a contribution of more than $3 billion to endow two foundations whose purposes are to improve state residents' access to health care—a goal previously espoused by Blue Cross. In contrast, the conversion of the Blues association in Virginia yielded a contribution of about $175 million in cash and stock to the state treasury, with additional shares of stock in the new insurer given to existing policyholders. But the conversion in Georgia was accompanied only by the offering of stock rights to policyholders, without any additional contribution to either the state or to charity. A subsequent lawsuit resulted in an out-of-court settlement in which the company agreed to transfer over $70 million to a charitable foundation. With such significant money at stake and no generally accepted principles regarding the appropriate outcome, conversions are often highly contentious. Blue Cross and Blue Shield of North Carolina simply dropped its plan to convert to a for-profit company after spending nearly two years trying unsuccessfully to get approval from the state. As additional Blues associations convert in the future, the issue of who is entitled to accumulated funds is certain to be a recurring concern.

Sources: Ruth Simon, "How the New Blue Cross May Bite You," *Money*, January 1997, 98–102; Kristi W. Swartz and Danielle Deaver, "Blue Cross of North Carolina Drops Bid to Become For-Profit Company," *Knight Ridder Tribune Business News*, July 9, 2003, 1.

ways, but all are designed to provide their members with comprehensive health services within a well-defined geographical area. The HMO is paid a set fee per month by its members, and it provides all necessary medical services. Coverage is usually broader than that provided by insurers, and both cost control and prevention of health problems tend to be emphasized. By stressing regular health care, early diagnosis and treatment, and disease prevention, HMOs can be effective in helping their members identify and correct small health problems before they become major ones.

Persons belonging to an HMO generally must receive all medical care from physicians associated with that HMO. Each person chooses a **primary care physician** within the HMO; this doctor is responsible for coordinating all medical care for the patient, including access to medical specialists. The role of the primary care physician is very important in controlling costs by limiting care to only that deemed to be medically necessary. For this reason, primary care physicians are sometimes referred to as **gatekeepers**. Most medical specialties are represented within the HMO, but if highly specialized treatment is required, patients can be referred to other doctors at no additional cost to the patient. Arrangements also exist with hospitals in the area for the provision of hospital services when needed.

One type of HMO is the **group practice HMO**, in which a large group of physicians share facilities and support personnel and work out of one or a few main locations. A group practice HMO in a city with a population of 100,000 likely would have only one location; a group practice HMO in a city of several million people might have several locations. The doctors within a group practice HMO are not employees of the HMO; rather, as a group they have a contractual agreement with the HMO to provide the medical services needed. Compensation arrangements for the doctors vary, but most are paid based either on the amount of services provided (called a **fee-per-service basis**) or on a **capitation basis**. The latter arrangement involves payment of a specified, periodic amount based on the number of patients for which a physician is responsible, regardless of the amount of medical services provided to each one.

Another HMO that operates out of only a few main locations is the **staff model HMO**. The primary difference between staff model and group practice HMOs is that doctors working for staff model HMOs are indeed HMO employees and are paid salaries. From the perspective of the patient, however, both types of HMOs may appear identical. In contrast is the **individual practice HMO**, which has no centralized location. Physicians work out of their individual offices and usually are paid on a fee-per-service basis, although capitation payments are used by some HMOs of this type.

Many people prefer individual practice HMOs because of the greater choice of physicians that is usually provided and the number of different locations in which medical treatment can be sought. However, others feel this flexibility can be a disadvantage. They appreciate the group practice and staff model HMOs because interacting medical personnel can provide treatment in a single environment; that is, the services of medical specialists, mental health providers, nurses, pharmacists, and others are all present within a single system.

Point-of-Service Plans

One modification of the HMO concept is the **point-of-service (POS) plan**, which is sometimes referred to as an **open-ended HMO**. A POS plan can be organized in all of the same ways as an HMO, and the philosophies of comprehensive care, prevention, and cost control are present in both types of plans. Just as in an HMO, patients select their own primary care physicians who are responsible for coordinating necessary medical services. The primary difference between a POS plan and an HMO is that individuals in POS plans have more freedom of choice in selecting doctors and other medical care providers. Whereas an HMO member must use only HMO doctors, POS members have the option of using either the POS providers or doctors unaffiliated with the POS plan. Furthermore, this choice exists each time medical services are needed.

Because of the emphasis on prevention and cost control, care can usually be provided in a more cost-effective manner if members use POS doctors than if they go outside the plan for care. To encourage patients to select POS providers, patients must pay a significantly larger share of their medical bills whenever they use non-POS doctors. In this way, the element of choice is preserved, but the higher cost associated with it is borne primarily by the individuals exercising that right to choose. The flexibility of POS plans has made them quite popular. Between 1997 and 2001, the market share of POS plans grew from 17 to 22 percent, while the market share of HMOs dropped from 31 to 23 percent.

Preferred Provider Organizations

Preferred provider organizations (PPOs) represent another variation within the network of health care delivery systems, and currently hold a significantly larger share of the health care market than either HMOs or POS plans. In 2001, about half of people receiving their health insurance through their employers were members of PPOs. Specific arrangements vary, but most PPOs offer a reduction in the price of health care services in return for certain concessions by the sponsoring organization. For example, doctors in a particular PPO might agree to lower their fees by 15 percent for PPO participants, many of whom are employees receiving health insurance through their employers. In exchange for the lower fees, the employers agree to (1) provide the PPO with a minimum number of patients each month, (2) pay their premiums promptly, and (3) encourage their employees to take advantage of health education programs that are designed to lessen health problems and hence lower costs. Health services provided through PPO arrangements may be extensive, as is the case with HMOs and POS plans. In other instances, services provided by PPOs are extremely narrow and may be focused only on a particular form of treatment, such as vision care or prescription drugs. Sponsors of PPOs may include insurers, HMOs, POS plans, employers, or some combination of these groups.

From an individual's perspective, a PPO may seem very similar to a POS plan, in that cost sharing is greater when unaffiliated health care providers are used. However, a major difference between PPOs and POS plans is that PPOs generally do not use primary care physicians to coordinate individuals' medical care. As noted, this feature is an important cost control element in POS plans.

Medicaid and Medicare

Both federal and state governments also are involved in the provision of health benefits. **Medicaid** is the generic name for the variety of state-administered programs that provide medical care to low-income persons who can show sufficient financial need to qualify them for assistance. Such programs are financed by both state and federal tax revenues; benefits vary somewhat among the states. Overall, care provided through Medicaid has been growing at double-digit rates for several years. In 2002, about 51 million persons received Medicaid benefits worth approximately $257 billion.[2]

In 1965, the U.S. Congress created **Medicare**, designed to meet the growing need for health insurance for persons age 65 or older, as well as those under age 65 who have been receiving Social Security disability benefits for at least two years.[3] Traditionally, Medicare has had two basic parts: a compulsory hospital plan and a voluntary medical plan, called supplemental medical insurance. Beginning in 2006, a third part of Medicare will take effect, offering optional prescription drug benefits to Medicare beneficiaries for the first time. The details of these plans are discussed later in this chapter.

MECHANICS OF COST SHARING

Many health plans contain cost-sharing provisions that apply at the time of a loss. They can be effective ways to help control the use of medical services because insureds are more aware of the cost of treatment. Descriptions of the major types of cost-sharing provisions used with health insurance are included in this section, together with examples illustrating how these provisions work together in various situations.

Deductibles

Just as with property-liability insurance, deductibles are used in health insurance to combine the risk management tools of risk retention and transfer. The most common deductible arrangement in health insurance is the calendar-year deductible, in which covered losses are accumulated throughout the calendar year until they exceed the stated deductible. Only after that point does the insured receive any reimbursement from the policy. For example, Bob has a health care policy with a $300 calendar-year deductible. On February 1, Bob falls and bruises his leg, resulting in a $250 bill from his doctor. None of this loss is payable by Bob's insurance because the $250 loss is less than the $300 deductible. However, if Bob falls again

---

2   John Holahan and Brian Bruen, "Medicaid Spending: What Factors Contributed to the Growth Between 2000 and 2002? " Kaiser Commission on Medicaid and the Uninsured Issue Paper, September 2003.

3   Social Security disability benefits are discussed in Chapter 19.

in April of the same year and incurs another $250 in medical expenses, he will then be entitled to some reimbursement from his health insurance. Taken together, the two $250 losses total $500, which is $200 more than the $300 deductible applicable for that year. Bob is eligible to collect some or all of this $200, with the actual amount of the reimbursement dependent on the other cost-sharing provisions that may be present within the policy. With a calendar-year deductible, the accumulation period starts over each January 1. Thus, if Bob falls a third time but waits until the following January to do so, he will once again have to absorb the $300 deductible before being able to collect from his insurance.

Other forms of deductibles are possible in health insurance policies. One variation is the **per-cause deductible**, in which each new sickness or accidental injury results in the assessment of a deductible. Sometimes deductibles are applied on a family basis rather than on an individual basis. Another variation is to waive individual deductibles after two or three members of the same family have had claims exceeding their applicable calendar-year deductibles.

Copays

HMOs and POS plans sometimes charge patients a small dollar amount for some types of treatment. This amount is actually a deductible applied on a per-service basis and is generally referred to as a **copay**. For example, an HMO may require a copay of $15 for each visit to a member physician's office. Other than this small dollar amount, all covered services associated with the visit are paid in full by the HMO.

Coinsurance

In addition to deductibles and copays, many plans use a coinsurance provision that is stated as a percentage. The policy specifies that the insurer will pay a percentage (often 80 percent) of the covered loss after the applicable deductible has been satisfied. Consider Eva, who is insured by a health insurance policy with an 80 percent coinsurance provision and a $500 calendar-year deductible. If Eva is hospitalized and incurs $3,000 of expenses covered by her policy, her total insurance reimbursement will be 80% × ($3,000 − $500) = $2,000. Eva will have to pay the remaining $1,000 of the loss.

Coinsurance is a particularly important element of POS and PPO plans, where it often provides the primary financial incentive for encouraging insureds to seek medical care from a particular network of doctors. For example, one arrangement is to pay 90 percent of expenses after a small deductible, if the patient receives care from a provider within the network. But if the patient receives care from a doctor who is outside of the network, the reimbursement rate may be only 60 percent.

Caps

If a policy has both a deductible and a coinsurance provision, the cost sharing associated with a major health problem can be substantial. For example, suppose Wayne Kannaday's health policy has a $200 calendar-year deductible and an 80 percent coinsurance provision. If Wayne has a heart attack, spends several days in intensive care, and then has open-heart surgery followed by more days in intensive care, his hospital bill could easily exceed $200,000. Even though his insurance pays 80 percent, Wayne will still have medical bills of $40,000 or more. To prevent such situations, policies with coinsurance provisions may include an upper limit on the amount of cost sharing required. For example, if Wayne's policy had a $2,000 **coinsurance cap**, then the most he would have to pay would be the $200 deductible plus $2,000 in coinsurance payments, or a total of $2,200. Sometimes coinsurance caps are implied rather than stated explicitly. For example, Wayne's policy might specify that its coinsurance provision is 80 percent for the first $10,000 of covered losses exceeding the $200 deductible, with a 100 percent coinsurance provision thereafter. For losses in excess of $10,200, the most Wayne will have to pay is the $200 deductible plus 20 percent of the first $10,000 in losses above the deductible. This amount is exactly the same ($2,200) as computed previously, even though no explicit reference to a $2,000 coinsurance cap is made.

Yet another variety of cap is known as the **out-of-pocket cap**, which applies the limit to amounts that the insured pays for both coinsurance and applicable deductibles. In the previous example, if Wayne's policy had a $2,000 out-of-pocket cap, then he would have to pay no more than $2,000 total, counting both his deductible and his cost sharing through coinsurance.

Maximum Limits

A few health insurance plans have no limit on the amount of benefits that can be paid for covered expenses, whereas others have a **lifetime maximum** that applies to the sum of all benefits payable under the plan. This term is somewhat misleading, however, because lifetime maximums may be able to be restored, thus potentially allowing an individual to collect more than the overall lifetime maximum stated in the policy. Automatic restoration of a maximum may occur gradually over time. For example, suppose Insurance Company KDG issues a health insurance policy with a lifetime maximum of $1 million. As losses occur, this limit is automatically restored at the rate of $5,000 per year, with the increase taking effect each January 1. Suppose Ramón Santos is an insured under this policy issued by KDG. On June 20 he is involved in an automobile accident resulting in $400,000 of insurance benefits (after Ramón absorbs the applicable deductible and coinsurance). If he has any other losses that same year, the insurance will pay no more than the $600,000 remaining in the lifetime maximum. However, on January 1 of the next year, $5,000 of the maximum will be restored, thus giving Ramón up to $605,000 of protection for future losses. The following year, another $5,000 in benefits will be restored, and so on, until the maximum once again reaches $1 million.

As an alternative to this gradual restoration process, some health policies allow insureds to provide evidence of insurability that is then used to justify restoration of the entire lifetime maximum all at once. Such evidence usually consists of a medical examination showing that the individual meets the same health standards required for new applicants for health insurance. In the absence of such a provision, insureds who have recovered fully from major health problems might be persuaded to change insurers in order to once again have the full amount of protection desired.

In addition to a lifetime maximum, a health insurance policy may have various **internal maximums** that apply to particular health problems. Treatment for alcohol and drug abuse, for example, often is insured for much less than the coverage provided for other types of health problems. For example, a policy with a $1 million lifetime maximum might have only a $25,000 lifetime limit for alcohol or drug abuse treatment. Internal maximums of this magnitude serve to protect the insurer from potentially excessive claims. If such internal limits were not included, premiums for health insurance would need to be higher to cover the increased cost of paying for the resultant losses.

Other types of limits also are found in health insurance policies. For example, payment for some types of expenses may be limited each time they are incurred. A $500 limit on the amount payable for an ambulance trip illustrates this concept. Similarly, there may be annual limits on benefits payable due to specified causes.

HEALTH EXPENSE INSURANCE

A diagram of the groupings used to classify health insurance policies is shown in Figure 17-1. With respect to health expense insurance, no sharp distinction among policies exists as to the type of medical expense for which indemnity is provided. Several general forms of coverage are discussed in this section, but it should be noted that more than one of these forms

FIGURE 17-1   Health Insurance Classifications

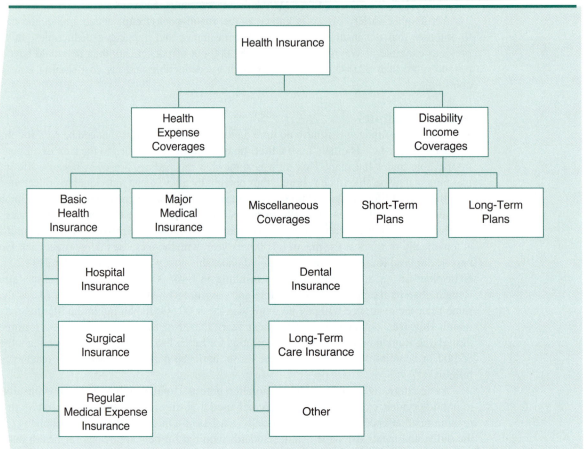

of insurance may cover medical expenses incurred in a particular situation. Insureds should familiarize themselves with their specific coverages because there is much less standardization among health expense coverage than for many other types of insurance.

Hospital Insurance

A **hospital insurance** contract is one of the basic health insurance policies. Traditionally, **basic health insurance policies** have had fewer cost-sharing provisions than policies that are not considered to be basic health contracts. A hospital insurance policy provides indemnification for necessary hospitalization expenses, such as room and board while hospitalized, laboratory fees, nursing care, use of the operating room, and certain medicines and supplies. Specific dollar limits for hospital room and board may be stated in the contract. However, because such costs increase regularly over time, a more useful arrangement is for the insurer to pay the cost of semiprivate accommodations and then to periodically adjust the premium charged in order to cover the increasing costs. Some contracts limit coverage by specifying a maximum time period, such as 365 days, for which costs will be reimbursed for any one illness or injury. Covered expenses other than room and board are often referred to as **ancillary charges**. Ancillary charges may have a limit of a specified multiple of the daily room and board limit, or they may be covered in full while the patient is hospitalized, up to the overall limit of the policy.

ETHICAL PERSPECTIVES

Mental Health Parity

Health insurers often use internal maximum limits for the treatment of mental health problems. This practice is sometimes criticized as unfairly discriminatory against those afflicted with mental and emotional problems. While the use of such limits holds down the cost of health insurance for everyone, many persons are calling for the elimination of such limits, in what is called a quest for mental health parity in health insurance.

In 1996, the Mental Health Parity Act was enacted to partially address this issue. This law applies only to health plans offered by employers with 50 or more employees. (Group health benefits are discussed in greater detail in Chapter 19.) The law provides that employer plans must not impose different overall dollar limits for mental health benefits than for other medical and surgical expenses. However, limits on the number of annual mental health care visits are still possible, and higher coinsurance and copayment requirements also can be imposed for mental health expenditures than for other types of expenses. Such exceptions lessen the impact of the legislation, and are viewed by mental health advocates as major "loopholes" that weaken the law. Bills have been introduced in Congress in recent years to expand the law by closing these perceived loopholes, but none has yet been enacted.

Source: Steve Bates, "Mental Health Parity Legislation Re-Introduced in Congress," *HRMagazine*, April 2003, 25–26.

As with all insurance contracts, certain exclusions are contained in hospital insurance policies. No standard set of exclusions exists, but some general statements can be made. Many policies exclude convalescent, custodial, or rest care; voluntary hospital stays for some types of cosmetic surgeries; private-duty nursing; and physical examinations that are unrelated to the treatment of an injury or a sickness.

Surgical Insurance

Another type of basic health insurance is the **surgical insurance** contract, which covers physicians' fees associated with covered surgeries. Both inpatient and outpatient surgical procedures are usually covered in order to prevent unnecessary hospitalizations when a procedure can be performed without an overnight stay in a hospital. Some surgical policies pay only the fees charged by the doctor who actually performs the surgery, whereas other policies also provide coverage for charges associated with assistant surgeons and anesthesiologists. In the past, many surgical policies were written on a **scheduled basis**, in which several surgical procedures were listed in the policy together with the specified maximums payable for each one. It is better for the insured, however, if the policy is written on a **nonscheduled basis**, in which covered procedures are insured up to the full amount of what is **reasonable and customary** (or usual, customary, and reasonable, as stated in some policies). In judging whether a particular expense exceeds what is reasonable and customary, insurers analyze the range of fees prevailing in the relevant geographical area at the time the surgery is performed. If the fee is more than what would be charged by most other surgeons in that general area, then some of the charges will be disallowed and will not be eligible for reimbursement under the surgical policy.

Regular Medical Expense Insurance

The third type of basic health coverage is **regular medical expense insurance**, which usually is written in conjunction with other basic coverages rather than as a stand-alone contract. Most policies primarily cover physicians' services other than for surgical procedures. Some policies require that the individual be hospitalized, whereas others do not have this restriction. As with surgical policies, this coverage may be written to pay reasonable and customary fees, or there may be specific limits associated with each covered service. Exclusions vary among policies, but typical exclusions usually relate to routine physical examinations, dental care, and vision care.

Major Medical Insurance

Major medical insurance policies usually have higher limits and fewer exclusions than do hospital, surgical, and regular medical expense contracts. Some major medical policies are designed to be coordinated with underlying basic health insurance. Other major medical contracts, known as **comprehensive** forms, are designed to replace basic health coverages and insure all medical expenses within one policy. Although basic health insurance may have only limited cost-sharing provisions, major medical policies usually have substantial deductibles and coinsurance provisions and are nearly always written on a reasonable-and-customary-fee basis.

Major medical insurance covers all of the same types of expenses insured by hospital, surgical, and regular medical expense contracts. In addition, after satisfaction of applicable cost-sharing provisions, major medical policies may cover expenses not addressed by basic health contracts. Just a few of the possible examples of additional coverage are prescription drugs, ambulance services, physical therapy, crutches, and wheelchairs. Again, insureds must carefully check the provisions of their individual policies to be sure of both covered expenses and relevant exclusions.

A special type of major medical insurance is **excess major medical**, which usually pays only after another major medical policy has exhausted its limits. For example, suppose Harold Skillrud's employer provides him with major medical insurance that has only a $250,000 limit. Because this limit may not be high enough to provide complete protection for expenses arising out of a serious illness or injury, Harold may want to purchase excess major medical coverage to supplement his employer-provided insurance. Typically, an excess major medical policy has both a high limit and a very large deductible, such as $25,000 or even $50,000. The size of the deductible effectively eliminates coverage for all but very serious situations, thus making the policy much more affordable than would otherwise be the case.

Dental Insurance

Dental insurance is a newer form of health expense coverage than those discussed so far in this chapter. Covered services typically include fillings, crowns, extractions, bridgework, dentures, root canal therapy, inlays, treatment of gums, and orthodontics. In addition, preventive care, such as oral examinations, X rays, and semiannual cleanings are nearly always covered because a primary component of dental insurance plans is an emphasis on loss prevention. Most policies have relatively low annual limits, such as $2,500, and some further limit coverage by applying fee schedules for various dental procedures. Deductibles and coinsurance provisions normally are used for nonpreventive types of care. However, so that insureds will not be discouraged from obtaining appropriate periodic preventive care, cost sharing is usually waived for routine examinations, cleanings, and X rays.

Long-Term Care Insurance

With increased life expectancies and an aging population, there is an increasing risk of loss associated with the eventual need of many persons for nursing home care or other assistance with daily living. As a result, the market for **long-term care (LTC) insurance** is growing rapidly. In 1987, fewer than 1 million total LTC policies had been sold; by the end of 2001, more than 8 million policies had been sold.[4] All states have adopted legislation regulating LTC

---

4 *Long-Term Care Insurance in 2001*, New York: Health Insurance Association of America, 2003.

insurance to some extent. In most states, the law is similar to the Long-Term Care Insurance Model Act issued by the National Association of Insurance Commissioners (NAIC).[5] Through this act, the model regulations accompanying it, and the long-term care provisions included in federal legislation enacted in 1996, some standardization is achieved for a product that is still evolving.

When contemplating the purchase of LTC insurance, it is important to consider the following points in comparing different policies:

1. Some policies cover only the named insured, whereas others cover the insured's spouse as well.

2. Policies must specify the conditions that trigger benefit payments. To qualify for the favorable tax treatment made available by the Health Insurance Portability and Accountability Act of 1996, LTC policies issued in 1997 or later must make benefits available when insureds cannot perform two or more of the following **activities of daily living (ADLs)**: eating, bathing, toileting, transferring, dressing, and continence. Policies issued before 1997 may be more restrictive or may list ADLs other than these and yet still qualify for favorable tax treatment, according to a grandfathering provision in the law.

3. Most policies specify a maximum daily benefit and an overall maximum limit on the number of days for which the benefit will be paid. Some policies do not contain an overall limit, and others may provide that the maximum daily benefit will increase with inflation over time. Although an inflation option makes a policy more expensive than one that does not include such an option, it is also more useful to the insured. Further, just as major medical policies may provide for the restoration of maximum limits, some LTC policies specify that the overall maximum can be restored under various conditions. For example, the policy may state that, following a loss, if the insured recovers and does not require LTC assistance for at least six months, then the full maximum once again will be available for subsequent losses.

4. When selecting a policy, insureds usually must select an **elimination period**, which is a form of deductible. For example, a policy with a 20-day elimination period would not pay benefits during the first 20 days of a covered stay in a nursing home or other eligible facility. The longer the elimination period, the lower will be the premium, assuming all other factors are comparable.

5. Some early LTC policies excluded losses related to Alzheimer's disease or paid only for skilled and intermediate nursing home care and not for custodial care. Plans that make no provision for custodial care are less expensive but leave the insured without protection against an important cause of loss. Further, under the NAIC Model Act, insurers must offer substantially the same level of benefits for skilled, intermediate, and custodial care.[6] The 1996 federal legislation also requires that cognitive impairment (which includes Alzheimer's disease) must be a condition that would trigger benefits in tax-favored plans, regardless of whether the ADL requirement noted in point 2 is met.

6. Many policies have options that make benefits available for adult day care, home health care, and other miscellaneous forms of assistance that might be needed by people at an advanced age. Home health care is a particularly popular option, since most people can envision needing some assistance while still living at home, while they have a harder time seeing themselves living in a nursing home.

In general, LTC insurance can be expected to continue to change as insurers attempt to respond to the increasing demand exhibited for this type of protection.

---

5   The NAIC and the concept of model acts are discussed in Chapter 24.
6   See Chapter 4 for a discussion of the differences among these levels of care.

Medicare

As noted previously in this chapter, Medicare currently includes both a compulsory hospital insurance plan and a voluntary medical insurance plan. The hospital insurance, often referred to as Part A, provides coverage in the following main areas:

1. *Inpatient hospital care.* A maximum of 90 days' care for any individual period of illness is provided. The patient must bear a deductible of $876 (as of 2004) for the first 60 days and $219 a day for each day between 60 and 90 days. In addition, care is offered for an extra 60 days, known as *reserve days* and available only once, subject to the patient's obligation to pay $438 a day.

2. *Skilled nursing home care.* A maximum of 100 days' care in a skilled nursing facility is provided, with the first 20 days free. After 20 days, the patient must pay a deductible equal to one-eighth of the inpatient hospital deductible.

3. *Home health services.* Expenses for home health services are paid in full as long as services are prescribed by a doctor. No prior hospital stay is required. Services include part-time skilled nursing, physical therapy, social services, medical supplies, and rehabilitation equipment.

4. *Hospice care.* Terminally ill patients can receive up to 210 days of care in a certified hospice, with additional days possible if a doctor verifies that the patient is terminally ill. A **hospice** is designed to give humane, nonaggressive, dignified care for dying patients. The emphasis is on improving the quality of the person's remaining days. A separate set of deductibles and coinsurance payments is applicable for hospice benefits.

Medicare's **supplementary medical insurance** (referred to as Part B) covers doctor bills and related expenses that are medically necessary. Persons covered under Part A of Medicare are automatically covered under Part B, unless they reject the coverage. A monthly premium is also charged for Part B, which has its own set of deductibles and coinsurance provisions. Currently, all Part B beneficiaries pay the same flat monthly premium.[7] However, beginning in 2007, under the Medicare reform law passed in 2003, beneficiaries with incomes exceeding $80,000 ($160,000 for couples) will pay higher Part B premiums. Expenses covered under Part B are bills for physicians' services, physical and occupational therapy, speech pathology, diagnostic X-ray and laboratory tests, blood transfusions, radioactive isotope therapy, medical equipment and supplies, ambulance services, organ replacements, and artificial limbs and eyes. In general, neither Part A nor Part B of Medicare will pay for the following: (1) services that are not medically necessary; (2) payments covered by workers' compensation benefits; (3) services performed by a relative; (4) services rendered outside the United States; (5) routine physicals, eye exams, hearing aids, dental care, foot care, and cosmetic surgery; (6) prescription drugs taken at home; (7) most immunizations; and (8) private nurses.

One of the largest gaps left by Medicare Part A and B is the lack of coverage for prescription drugs. Under Medicare reform legislation passed in 2003, optional prescription drug coverage for Medicare beneficiaries will be available beginning in 2006. The monthly premium for the prescription drug coverage will initially be about $35. The plan will have a $250 deductible. After that, the beneficiary will pay 25 percent of the cost for drug costs up to $2,250. The beneficiary is then responsible for all drug costs between $2,250 and $3,600. For drug costs exceeding $3,600, the beneficiary will pay 5 percent of costs or a modest copayment.

Because of the existence of deductibles, coinsurance, and coverage limitations in the Medicare program, many persons purchase private insurance to "fill in the gaps." Sometimes referred to as **Medigap insurance**, these policies were the subject of past controversies alleging deceptive sales practices and coverages. Currently, standardization of Medigap policies is

---

7   The monthly premium for Part B of Medicare is $66.60 as of 2004.

achieved through a system devised by the NAIC. To assist consumers in comparing policy provisions, policies are labeled with a letter from A to J, with each letter denoting a standardized set of provisions. For example, policies labeled A include only a minimum, core set of benefits. Policies labeled B include the same core benefits, plus payment of the Medicare Part A deductible. In general, both the premiums and the coverages increase as the label letters move toward J, the most comprehensive (and most expensive) plan.

Other Health Expense Insurance

Many other specialized forms of health insurance are available. Examples include prescription drug coverage that is separate from both major medical and basic health insurance coverages; vision care insurance, which covers the cost of eyeglasses, contact lenses, and periodic routine eye examinations; dread disease coverage, designed to pay expenses associated only with particular diseases (primarily cancer); and accident insurance, which pays specified amounts only when the medical expenses are due to an accident.

DISABILITY INCOME INSURANCE

Disability income insurance is a different type of health insurance than has been discussed thus far. Rather than covering specified medical or other health expenses, disability income insurance provides periodic income payments to the insured while he or she is unable to work as a result of sickness or injury. For reference, a sample disability income insurance policy is included in Appendix E.

Benefit Duration

Under all disability income policies, benefits terminate at the earlier of two occurrences: (1) as soon as the disability ends or (2) when benefits have been paid for the maximum benefit duration period. **Short-term disability (STD) insurance** usually pays benefits for up to six months, although some STD policies have benefit periods of one or two years. **Long-term disability (LTD) insurance** arrangements pay for a longer period of time, such as 5 or 10 years. Some LTD policies pay until age 65 or 70, and still others pay lifetime benefits.

Definition of Disability

Both STD and LTD policies must specify exactly what is meant by the term *disability*. Contracts with very strict definitions tend to be both less expensive and less useful to insureds. For example, if an insured is not considered disabled unless confined to his or her home except for trips to see a doctor, few people would qualify for benefits even though their health conditions may prevent them from earning a living. Fortunately, most policies link their definitions of disability to one's ability to work. In some policies, the insured must be unable to engage in any type of paid work in order to collect benefits. A more useful definition is one that provides that the insured is disabled if unable to perform the major duties of any occupation for which he or she is reasonably suited through education, training, or experience.

The most liberal definition, which also results in the highest premiums, is the **own occupation** definition. Policies that use this definition specify that the insured is considered disabled if unable to perform the major duties of his or her own occupation. To illustrate this concept, consider James, who is a dentist. If James develops arthritic hands and can no longer perform dentistry, then he is disabled according to an "own occupation" definition of disability. But since James may still be able to earn an income by selling dental supplies or by engaging in research activities, then he would not be considered disabled under the **any occupation for which reasonably suited** definition. Most LTD policies that use the "own occupation" definition do so only for an initial period of time, such as two years. After that, the definition changes to the less liberal "any occupation for which reasonably suited."

Many LTD policies also provide some coverage for partial disability, but such protection may be restricted only to those periods of partial disability that follow a period of total disability. The definition of partial disability often is similar to the definition of total disability used in the policy. For example, if a contract uses the "own occupation" definition for total disability, then partial disability might be defined as the ability to perform some but not all of the major functions of one's own occupation. Such descriptions are not always clear in their application to particular situations, however, and disputes may arise.

As an alternative, partial disability may be defined solely in terms of a person's earnings. For example, suppose Karen earns $3,000 a month before falling down a flight of steps and breaking several bones. After being completely unable to work for three months, she recovers sufficiently to return to her former work for a few hours a day. Karen's new monthly income is $1,000. Without assessing the major duties of her job and how many of them she can still perform, the mere fact that Karen is now earning only one-third of what she was formerly making would be sufficient evidence to allow her to collect partial disability benefits under some policies. Contracts that use this type of income-related definition usually specify that an insured is considered to have some **residual disability** that qualifies him or her for partial disability payments as long as earnings are less than some percentage (such as 80 percent) of the former level.

Elimination Period

The concept of an elimination period was discussed previously in connection with LTC insurance. Both STD and LTD policies use elimination periods. When a disability occurs, no benefits are payable during the elimination period. Thus, elimination periods are really deductibles that reduce premiums by eliminating coverage for small losses (in other words, short-term disabilities). Lower premiums are associated with longer elimination periods, but premium savings tend to decrease at a diminishing rate as the elimination period becomes longer.

Sometimes STD policies have different elimination periods that depend on the cause of the disability. When such a difference exists, disabilities due to sickness are subject to a longer elimination period than those resulting from an accident. For example, an STD policy might have a seven-day elimination period for sickness, but no elimination period if the disability is due to an accident. The reason for such differential treatment is the greater moral hazard present for losses due to illness. In other words, sickness is easier to fake than is accidental injury.

Benefit Level

Disability insurance policies are designed to replace only a percentage of earnings so that the insured has a financial incentive to recover and return to work. Benefit levels of 50 to 75 percent of prior earnings are common, subject to overall maximum limits, with 67 percent being a common benefit level. In addition, some policies provide for cost-of-living adjustments in benefits, up to a maximum adjustment of about 5 or 6 percent a year.

When purchasing disability income insurance, insureds should be aware that if they are completely unable to engage in any type of gainful employment due to accident or illness, Social Security may provide some disability income benefits for covered persons after a five-month elimination period. (See Chapter 19.) However, if the definition of disability in the insurance policy is more liberal than the Social Security definition, then an insured may be eligible for insurance benefits but not for Social Security payments. To assist insureds in their personal risk management planning dealing with such possibilities, insurers offer Social Security income options that can be added to basic disability income policies. When such an option is in effect, the basic monthly payment is increased by a stated amount if the insured is receiving insurance benefits but does not qualify for disability payments under Social Security.

HEALTH INSURANCE
POLICY PROVISIONS

An understanding of the contractual provisions of health insurance policies is very important, especially because health policies are not nearly as standardized as are many other types of personal insurance contracts. Health insurance policy provisions can be classified in three ways: continuation provisions, mandatory provisions, and optional provisions.

Continuation Provisions

The term **continuation provisions** is used to describe the contractual rights regarding the renewal of a health insurance policy. As might be expected, policies with more guarantees for renewal will have higher premiums, all else being the same. The importance of these provisions for medical expense policies has diminished somewhat with the passage in 1996 of the Health Insurance Portability and Accountability Act, which requires insurers to continue to renew their health expense insurance policies regardless of the health of the insureds. This act does not affect the continuation rights in other types of health policies, though, including disability income insurance, stand-alone dental and/or vision care policies, accident-only policies, long-term care insurance, and Medigap contracts. For these policies, the continuation provisions are still an important feature of the contract.

A **term contract** expires at the end of a specified period of time and cannot be renewed. Such policies are generally used in connection with special events or trips for which a particular form of health insurance is desired. For example, the White Water Expedition Company might encourage those who go on their weekend rafting trips to buy special accident insurance designed to cover medical expenses arising out of accidents on the trip. When the weekend is over, the coverage ceases. Because of the limited nature of the coverage, term insurance is relatively inexpensive.

If an insurer retains the right to cancel a policy at any time for any reason, then the contract is said to be **cancellable**, although states generally require that at least five days' notice of the cancellation be provided. Because of widespread discontent with such policies, however, it is more common for a policy to be either **optionally renewable** or **conditionally renewable**. Insurers can decline to renew either kind of policy (or can significantly raise their premiums) on any policy anniversary date, but coverage and premiums between anniversary dates cannot be changed. The difference between these two continuation provisions involves the allowable reasons for premium increases or nonrenewal. Optionally renewable policies generally place no restrictions on the rights of insurers in this regard; increases in premiums and termination of coverage are solely at the discretion of the insurer. Conditionally renewable policies specify the allowable reasons for nonrenewal but prohibit termination due to deterioration of the insured's health. Clearly, if an insurer is able to terminate coverage whenever an insured person's health has declined, that individual may be left without protection at precisely the time that it is needed.

The most valuable (and hence, the most expensive) continuation provisions are those associated with **guaranteed renewable** policies and **noncancellable** contracts. In both cases, termination of coverage is prohibited before a specified age (such as 65) as long as the insured pays all premiums when due. The difference between these two provisions involves possible increases in premiums. A guaranteed renewable policy can have its premium increased only if premiums are raised for an entire class of insureds; rate increases applicable only to particular individuals are not allowed. In contrast, the premiums for noncancellable contracts are fixed in advance and cannot be increased during the life of the contract. Premiums do not have to be level during the entire period, but they cannot deviate from the schedule specified when the policy is issued. Noncancellable health policies once were popular in the disability income insurance market. Because of adverse claims experience, though, many insurers lost considerable money during the early 1990s and subsequently switched to writing guaranteed renewable disability contracts rather than noncancellable ones.

Mandatory Provisions

Several contractual provisions are required by law to be included in individual health insurance policies. Group health policies, such as those used in employee benefit plans (see Chapter 19), are exempt from these requirements. A brief description of the mandatory provisions follows.

Grace Period and Reinstatement

As in life insurance, insurers must provide a grace period for the payment of premiums not received by the due date. The length of the period is often 31 days, although a period as short as 10 days is allowable for premiums payable on a monthly basis. Coverage remains in effect for claims arising during the grace period, but the policy lapses following expiration of the period. A lapsed policy can be reinstated under conditions stated in the contract, but the insurer is not required to reinstate a lapsed policy. In some cases, an insurer may agree to a reinstatement but may add restrictive conditions limiting the coverage to less than was previously provided.

Claims

When an illness or accidental injury occurs, the insured generally is required to provide written notice to the insurer within 20 days or as soon as practical. The insurer is then required to provide appropriate claim forms within 15 days after being notified of the claim. Generally, within 90 days of the loss, the insured must submit details proving the incurred expenses being submitted for payment by the insurer. (The 90-day period can be extended if circumstances make it reasonable to do so.)

After the insurer receives all of the information supporting a particular claim, it is allowed a reasonable period to check the claim's validity. If the insurer deems it necessary, it has the right to require the insured to submit to a physical examination (or autopsy, if the person is deceased). Statements originally made in the application for the insurance also may be checked to see if they were true at that time. With few exceptions, after three years have passed since the insurance was issued, misstatements in the application generally cannot be used as grounds for denying a claim, unless fraud was involved. For some guaranteed renewable and noncancellable policies, even fraudulent misstatements may not constitute grounds for denying a claim after three years have passed.

Following the claim investigation phase, legitimate medical expenses covered by the policy must be paid immediately, with disability income claims payable at monthly (or shorter) intervals. Generally, benefits are paid directly to the insured, although they can also be paid to physicians, hospitals, or other medical providers if the insured requests it and the insurer agrees. When an insurer denies a claim, an insured may file a lawsuit disputing the decision. Individual health insurance policies specify that such suits are not valid if filed sooner than 60 days or later than three years following the submission of all relevant facts concerning the loss. The 60-day minimum period provides the insurer with a reasonable time to process claims. But by placing a three-year limit on possible suits, the insurer is better able to predict the ultimate claims that may have to be paid from particular health insurance policies.

Miscellaneous

Individual health insurance policies must contain clauses stating that the policy and attached endorsements constitute the entire contract between the insured and the insurer. Only changes that are endorsed on the policy by officers of the insurer are valid. Finally, if a health policy contains a death benefit, the insured must be allowed to change the designated beneficiary by providing written notification to the insurer.

Optional Provisions

In addition to the mandatory provisions, many individual health insurance policies contain contractual statements addressing a number of issues. If a policy includes any of these optional provisions in its policy language, the provision must be at least as favorable to the insured as what is described in the following paragraphs.

Occupation

Insurers can specify that no coverage will be provided for losses incurred while committing a felony or while working in an illegal occupation, if such actions contributed to the resultant injury or illness. Another occupational issue arises when insureds change to more hazardous occupations following the issuance of a health insurance policy. In this case, the insurer is allowed to reduce the benefits to whatever the paid premium would have purchased for a person engaged in the more hazardous occupation.

Misstatement of Age

If age is misstated in a health insurance application, the benefits can be adjusted to equal what could have been purchased had the true age been known. Thus, the effect of misstating one's age is exactly the same in individual health insurance as it is in individual life insurance.

Other Insurance

Many health insurance policies contain clauses stating how much the contract will pay when there are other policies that also cover the loss. The intent is to protect against the moral hazard that results from potential indemnification exceeding a particular loss. Insurers are allowed to reduce their benefits when there is other health insurance covering a loss, particularly if the insurer has not been notified about the existence of such coverage before the loss. In such cases, a premium refund for the excess coverage must be paid to the insured. Generally, this provision would not apply to group insurance provided by an employer, to medical payments from automobile insurance, or to workers' compensation benefits.

A special situation may arise in disability income cases where the total benefits payable under all policies is greater than what the insured was earning before becoming disabled. In such situations, benefits can be reduced, and premiums paid for excess coverage are refunded to the insured. As with medical expense plans, such provisions generally do not apply to coverage provided as an employee benefit or from the workers' compensation system in a particular state.

Miscellaneous

It is common for health insurance policies to state that contractual provisions that conflict with state statutes are automatically amended to meet minimum requirements specified by the state in which the insured resides at the time the policy is issued. In this way, special policy forms for states with unusual requirements are not necessary. Another possible policy provision is to allow the insurer to deduct unpaid premiums from claim payments. This situation might arise for claims that occur during a premium grace period. Finally, some insurers provide that losses resulting from the use of drugs or other intoxicants are not payable unless the drugs were taken on the advice of a physician.

HEALTH CARE REFORM

In 1993, President Bill Clinton proposed the most comprehensive overhaul of the health care delivery system ever officially and seriously contemplated within the United States. The emphasis placed on the proposal by the president led to substantial debate about the way in which Americans receive and pay for their health care. Within less than two years, however, the entire Clinton proposal was dead with no hope of being enacted. Beginning in the late

INTERNATIONAL PERSPECTIVES

Canada's National Health Plan

As the United States struggles with issues of health care reform, reference is sometimes made to the pros and cons of adopting the Canadian system to provide universal health insurance for all its citizens. Canada has what is called a single payer plan, because all care is provided through programs administered through the government—rather than through private plans that compete against each other.

The Canadian health plan provides comprehensive care for medically necessary services for all citizens. The cost is paid from several revenue sources, including both gasoline and income taxes. Physicians are not government employees, and hospitals are not owned by the government. However, hospitals do receive some government funding, and doctors are paid via fee schedules that are annually negotiated between the provinces and health care providers.

While the universal care provided by Canada's system is attractive, it does not come without cost. Perhaps the most commonly heard criticism of the Canadian system is that citizens sometimes must endure lengthy waits for elective care and other services not deemed to be urgent. For example, the waiting time for some nonemergency surgeries can be up to two years. A second criticism is the lack of cutting-edge technological equipment, such as CAT scanners and magnetic resonance imagers, as well as fewer medical specialists. Although such equipment has proliferated throughout the United States, it is in much shorter supply in Canada. Nevertheless, Canadian officials usually contend that their equipment is adequate to meet the demand, while not being excessive and thereby causing an exorbitant increase in costs.

Source: Elena Cherney, "Universal Care Has a Big Price: Patients Wait," *The Wall Street Journal*, November 12, 2003, 1.

1990s, numerous proposals were made to enact into federal law a "Patient's Bill of Rights," which would protect patients in a variety of ways from alleged abusive practices by insurers, HMOs, and other health insurance providers. Philosophical disagreements and other pressures have prevented enactment of such proposals. However, with health care costs rising rapidly and the number of uninsured increasing, heath care reform is once again taking center stage politically. In this section, some recently enacted reforms are discussed, together with other issues that may lead to additional future actions.

Guaranteed Access to Health Care

One concern repeatedly voiced in the national debate on health care is the plight of those who have no health insurance, particularly those who are unable to obtain coverage due to existing health problems. A major step in addressing this problem was the passage of the Health Insurance Portability and Accountability Act of 1996. This legislation guarantees that many individuals and small businesses (those with no more than 50 employees) will be able to obtain health insurance, regardless of the health of the individuals involved. As already noted in this chapter, once an insurer sells a medical expense insurance policy, that insurer is also required to renew the contract, even if the insured's health deteriorates. Finally, as will be discussed in Chapter 19, limitations now are placed on the right of an employer to deny health benefits to new employees who have ongoing health problems when hired.

The protection provided under this new law is not universal for individuals, because the guarantees generally apply only to individuals who have previously had health insurance protection (often from an employer). Thus, no provision exists for unemployed persons or those who have not yet been able to obtain insurance. However, the law represents a first step toward dealing with the problem of access to health insurance. As a consensus emerges in dealing with the problem of the uninsured, it is possible that additional protections may be added.

Health Savings Accounts

In 2003 Congress passed legislation, signed by President George W. Bush, authorizing the creation of **Health Savings Accounts (HSAs)**. The basic idea behind HSAs is that people will be more careful consumers of health care if they are paying for much of their care with their own money, rather than relying on insurance to pay for most health care costs. To be eligible for an HSA, a person must be covered under a high deductible health plan, defined as a plan with a deductible of at least $1,000 for individual coverage or at least $2,000 for family coverage. The individual or his or her employer then has the ability to make an annual contribution to an HSA up to the amount of the deductible. All contributions to the HSA are tax-deductible (or not included in income if paid by the employer), and distributions from the HSA are tax-free as long as they are used to pay for qualified medical expenses. Unused HSA balances can roll over from year to year and invested, potentially accumulating a substantial "health care nest egg" over time.

Proponents of Health Savings Accounts argue that HSAs will introduce a new element of consumerism into the health care market. With traditional health insurance, insureds pay so little of the actual cost of care that they have little incentive to control their use of care, to negotiate with health care providers, or to otherwise worry about the cost of health care in the way they consider cost when purchasing a home, a car, food, or anything else. HSA supporters feel that HSAs will introduce stronger market forces into the health care arena that will result in reduced health care cost increases. Opponents of HSAs argue that these plans are only beneficial to the healthy and wealthy, and will result in adverse selection as healthy people opt for HSAs, leaving only unhealthy people in traditional health plans. HSA opponents also argue that people with HSAs may consume too little health care, leading to poor health and ultimately higher health care costs. Because HSAs are so new, it is impossible at the moment to predict their full consequences.

Minimum Required Benefits

The zeal of some HMOs and POS plans in pursuing the goal of cost control has led some of these plans to deny inpatient hospital stays in perhaps questionable circumstances. Situations that have attracted publicity in this regard include childbirth and mastectomies. Federal legislation enacted in 1996 (the Newborns' and Mothers' Health Protection Act) addressed one of these situations by mandating that plans that cover childbirth provide a minimum of 48 hours of inpatient hospital care following a regular delivery, with at least 96 hours of inpatient care following a cesarean section delivery. It is likely that additional mandates of this nature will be enacted in the future if practices by HMOs and similar organizations offend the sensibilities of significant sectors of the U.S. population.

The states also have been very active in this area, by enacting **state mandated coverages** that insurers, HMOs, and others must include in plans offered to employers. Areas often addressed in state mandates include mental health care, mammography and other screening tests for cancer, alcohol and drug abuse treatment, and well-child care. While such mandates can certainly be beneficial to insureds needing certain types of care, it should be remembered that such mandates are not without negative consequences. Mandated coverages increase the cost

netlink

The National Association of Health Underwriters closely monitors pending health care legislation. Set your Web browser to http://www.nahu.org/government/issues/index.htm for a good view of current legislation, together with the health insurance industry's perspective on it.

of health insurance, and this in turn may lead some employers to cease offering health insurance to their employees at all, increasing the number of uninsured.

Patient's Bill of Rights

Several of the practices of HMOs, POS plans, and PPOs have irritated many insureds and, consequently, their legislators. Many of the provisions in the various versions of the Patient's Bill of Rights that have been debated in Congress for the past several years are attempts to deal with these irritations. Some of the issues and proposed solutions are discussed in this section. It should be noted that although no federal Patient's Bill of Rights has been enacted, many managed care companies have voluntarily changed their policies in recent years to address many of these concerns.

Direct Access to Specialists

As discussed previously in this chapter, HMOs and POS plans utilize primary care physicians to manage the overall health care provided to participants. Such management usually includes controlling the accessibility of their patients to specialists. Many patients find this particular feature of HMOs and POS plans to be particularly annoying and, as a consequence, proposals abound to allow patients to bypass their primary care physicians when they need to see certain types of specialists. Obstetrics, gynecology, and pediatrics are specialties for which direct access is especially desired. While the federal legislation was debated, many states enacted their own provisions allowing these types of direct access. Lobbying in individual states has sometimes also resulted in specialties such as dermatology and physical therapy being allowed direct access in addition to the previously mentioned ones.

Definition of an Emergency

HMOs require that their physicians be used in all cases except for emergency situations, and POS plans have similar requirements for patients hoping to minimize their share of cost-sharing payments. However, when individuals are confronted by actual situations, they often have found themselves in disagreement with their health providers about the definition of an emergency. Suppose Charles resides in Pennsylvania but is in California on business. One night he is awakened in his hotel room by severe stomach cramps and goes to a nearby hospital emergency room for relief. Charles may be shocked to learn that his HMO may refuse to pay for this treatment because it does not consider Charles's situation to have been a true "emergency." These types of disputes are causing many of the federal proposals to include a provision requiring HMOs and POS plans to define emergencies in a standard manner, consistent with a prudent nonmedical person's definition. Many states have already passed similar legislation.

Liability Provisions

The area most disputed among the various federal proposals in recent years revolved around whether an HMO or other such entity should be legally liable for coverage decisions. For example, if an HMO improperly refuses to pay for a heart transplant and the patient dies, should the family be able to sue the HMO for damages? This has been a highly contentious issue both in Congress and in the courts, and the outcome is uncertain.

Other Proposed Restrictions
Any Willing Provider Laws

The essence of the cost savings potential of HMOs, PPOs, and POS plans is the ability of these organizations to construct networks of select physicians and other health care providers who agree to adhere to the networks' cost-saving philosophy and goals, as well as their

PROFESSIONAL PERSPECTIVES

Defining an Emergency

Traditional insurance programs, in addition to state and federally funded medical programs such as Medicaid and Medicare, have usually provided incentives for patients to seek care from the hospital emergency room. This practice has created a very large and expensive market in which many emergency room (ER) admissions are not truly considered emergencies. In excess of half of the 90.5 million annual ER visits are for treatment of minor ailments, such as colds, sore throats, and muscle aches, and the cost associated with an ER visit is 2 to 3 times that of comparable care provided at traditional physicians' offices. Estimates of the unnecessary excess resultant costs run as high as $7 billion a year.

To help control the escalating cost of health insurance, HMOs and insurers have been seeking ways in which they can control access to costly emergency care without eliminating coverage for needed care. This goal has been accomplished through various benefit changes, such as increasing the cost of accessing the treatment. For example, in some plans the patient copay has been changed from the traditional $10 physician visit fee to a $100 ER fee.

The definition of what constitutes an emergency is also a way in which health plans have influenced patients. Although limited by many state insurance laws, most health plans have begun to define an emergency as care that requires immediate or surgical intervention. If care sought at an ER does not meet a company's definition of this type of emergency, and could otherwise have been provided later in a physician's office, most plans will not pay for the cost of this care. Many states have found this definition to be too restrictive and have mandated that health plans add "prudent layperson" language into the definition. Although the prudent layperson language has weakened plans' ability to control their costs, the concept of controlling access to care in an emergency room is still undeniably effective in reducing medical costs.

Source: Thomas L. Mangan, CMCE, BlueCross BlueShield of Georgia.

---

mechanisms for reviewing the quality of care provided. However, some providers who are not included in the networks being formed believe they will suffer financially as a result of their exclusion. Consequently, they have convinced legislatures in many states to pass **any willing provider (AWP) laws**. These laws force HMOs and other networks to accept all physicians and other health care providers who agree to the networks' terms and fee structures. In essence, AWP laws eliminate the ability of HMOs to select only certain doctors, and many observers believe that HMOs' ability to control costs is thereby lessened.

Anti-Gag Provisions

Because of the emphasis on cost control, some early HMOs and POS plans discouraged their physicians from discussing alternative forms of treatment with their patients. These "gag clauses" in providers' network contracts prohibited doctors from acting as advocates for their patients. In response, several states passed legislation prohibiting these types of gag provisions, thereby allowing physicians more freedom to act in the best interests of their patients, rather than being concerned only about the lowest cost treatment plan. As doctors also reacted negatively to gag provisions in their contracts, many HMOs and POS plans dropped the concept entirely.

SUMMARY

1. The main providers of health insurance protection are commercial insurers, Blue Cross and Blue Shield associations, health maintenance organizations, point-of-service plans, and preferred provider organizations. Health maintenance organizations are designed to provide their members with comprehensive health services within a well-defined geographical area. Members pay a specified monthly fee and receive all necessary medical services in return. Group practice HMOs and staff model HMOs usually have one or two main locations, whereas individual practice HMOs have no central location and operate out of individual physicians' offices. Point-of-service plans are similar to HMOs, while preserving the ability of individuals to choose their doctors each time medical services are needed. Some preferred provider organizations offer a broad range of medical services, while others offer a narrowly focused set of services.

2. Deductibles, copays, coinsurance provisions, and maximum limits are forms of cost-sharing provisions used in medical expense policies. The most common form of deductible is established on a calendar-year basis. When both deductibles and coinsurance are used, policies may specify a cap that limits the amount of cost sharing required in any one year. Health expense policies specify maximum limits in a variety of ways. Some policies provide for the restoration of some of those maximums over time.

3. Basic health insurance usually means hospital insurance, surgical coverage, and regular medical expense insurance. Some forms of major medical insurance are designed to coordinate with underlying basic coverage; other forms of major medical coverage both replace and expand the coverage offered under basic health policies.

4. Long-term care insurance is growing in popularity, and the coverage provisions and options are achieving some degree of standardization through federal legislation and actions of the National Association of Insurance Commissioners.

5. Medicare includes both a compulsory hospital insurance plan and a voluntary medical insurance plan. The hospital insurance provides coverage for inpatient hospital care, skilled nursing care, home health services, and hospice care for the terminally ill. Medicare's supplemental medical insurance covers doctor bills and related expenses that are medically necessary. Beginning in 2006, Medicare will also provide a voluntary prescription drug coverage plan.

6. When purchasing either a short-term disability or a long-term disability income policy, an insured should carefully check the definition of disability included in the contract, the provisions for partial disability benefits, the length of the elimination period, the time period during which benefits will be payable, and the overall benefit level.

7. The circumstances in which individual health insurance policies can be renewed and/or be assessed increased premiums vary. Potential insureds should carefully check a policy's continuation provision regarding these concerns.

8. Several contractual provisions are required by law to be included in individual health insurance policies. Several other provisions are optional, but if a policy includes any of the optional provisions, the provision must be at least as favorable to the insured as that specified in the law.

9. Health care reform is being enacted gradually, through focused actions at both the federal and state levels. Recent federal actions include the establishment of health savings accounts and minimum hospital stays following childbirth. State actions and additional federal proposals are focusing on HMO practices that insureds often find objectionable.

internet*exercises*

1. Set your Web browser to http://www.ehealthinsurance.com. Enter information related to your Zip code and your birthdate. Pick two of the health policies that are available for your situation and compare the benefits provided with the monthly premium quoted. Which of the options offered seems to be the most desirable for you at this time? Explain why.

2. Medicare and Medicaid policies change regularly. Set your browser to the Health Care Financing Administration's Web site at http://cms.hhs.gov/ and browse the site to find recent updates to these programs. For example, what are the current premiums for Medicare Parts A and B? What other major changes have taken place recently?

QUESTIONS FOR REVIEW AND DISCUSSION

1. Identify and briefly describe the different types of health insurance providers.

2. What are the distinguishing characteristics of (a) group practice HMOs, (b) staff model HMOs, and (c) individual practice HMOs? How do these differ from POS plans?

3. List some examples of concessions that an organization sponsoring a PPO might make in favor of a health care provider in return for a reduction in the fee.

4. John Smith owns a health insurance policy with a $1,000 calendar-year deductible, an 80 percent coinsurance provision, and a $5,000 coinsurance cap. Assuming that all charges are covered and are reasonable and customary, find the amount that the insurance company would pay for each of the following expenses that occurred in the same calendar year.

   a. On January 15, John broke an arm and incurred medical expenses of $750.

   b. On April 17, John consulted a cardiologist in reference to chest pain he had experienced and was billed $375.

   c. On June 1, John was admitted to the hospital for diagnostic testing in relation to the chest

   pain that he had experienced. His expenses totaled $2,750.

   d. On July 30, John suffered a heart attack and was hospitalized for several days with bills of $3,100.

   e. On November 2, John underwent open-heart surgery, spent two weeks in the hospital, and incurred medical charges of $42,500.

5. In question 4, how much of John's expenses would the insurer have paid for each of the incidents listed if the policy had a $250 per-cause deductible, an 80-percent coinsurance provision, and a $5,000 out-of-pocket cap?

6. How do insurers determine whether surgical expenses are "reasonable and customary"?

7. Explain the difference between surgical policies written on a scheduled basis and those written on a nonscheduled basis. Which are generally more advantageous to the insured?

8. What types of expenses are generally covered under a comprehensive form of a major medical policy?

9. What are the important points that should be considered before the purchase of a long-term care insurance policy?

10. What is the difference between Parts A and B of Medicare? What is the purpose of Medigap insurance? How are prescription drugs covered under Medicare?

11. How can disability income insurance be distinguished from the other forms of health insurance discussed in this chapter?

12. Distinguish between the "own occupation" and "any occupation for which reasonably suited" definitions of disability.

13. Explain the terms of each of the following continuation provisions that may be found in a health insurance policy: (a) term contract, (b) cancellable, (c) optionally renewable, (d) guaranteed renewable, and (e) noncancellable.

14. Briefly explain the terms of each of the following provisions that may be found in an individual health insurance contract: (a) grace period and reinstatement, (b) claims, (c) occupation, (d) misstatement of age, and (e) other insurance.

15. What are health savings accounts? What are their pros and cons?

16. What is the insurer's major motive in not allowing a potential insured to purchase a disability policy that covers 100 percent of lost income? Why might insureds also not want to pay for coverage of 100 percent of their income? Discuss some expenses that a disabled worker may not incur while disabled.

17. Elizabeth is a 37-year-old unmarried attorney with an annual income of about $200,000. She currently has no health insurance coverage and is now considering purchasing some to protect her from various health-related exposures. List some health-related loss exposures that she can probably afford to retain. In your opinion, what health-related exposures should she strongly consider transferring to an insurance company? Discuss the reasoning behind your answers.

18. Edward, a Harvard MBA, gave up a very lucrative position as an investment banker five years ago in order to become a ski instructor in Vail, Colorado—a career that he finds much less stressful and more personally rewarding. Recognizing the danger of his present occupation, Edward has decided to purchase a disability policy to protect his reduced income. What cautions would you express to Edward about the definition of disability that he should select? Discuss your answer.

19. Carl has called several insurance agents to request quotes for a long-term total disability income policy and has been unable to find a quote in the price range that is affordable to him. For the sake of comparability, Carl has limited his request to policies with a lifetime payment period, an "own occupation" definition of disability, a 30-day elimination period, and a benefit level equal to 75 percent of prior earnings, plus cost-of-living adjustments. Discuss at least four ways in which Carl can adjust his request to make the cost of the insurance more affordable.

20. Of the current subjects that states and the federal government are debating in the area of health care reform, which ones do you think have the most merit? Which ones have the least merit? Why?

chapter 18

Retirement Planning and Annuities

G lenndy Sculley is an energetic 25-year-old computer genius who designs software packages for small businesses. As a self-employed entrepreneur in a volatile market, Glenndy's income is highly erratic. Two years ago she earned $450,000, but last year she earned only $25,000. Glenndy lives by herself, in the same Philadelphia suburb as Mary, her recently widowed, 58-year-old mother. Mary owns her own home and lives primarily on the interest payable on a $400,000 life insurance settlement.

Although Glenndy's computer skills exceed those of nearly everyone, her financial prowess is less developed. In fact, her tendency to lose money through bad investments is so great that she has almost decided that the best thing to do is simply put her money in a bank and stick to computers. Glenndy's mother is not much better regarding investment matters.

Glenndy suspects that her "100 percent banking" strategy is probably less than optimal, especially given her potentially high income taxes in good earning years. The fact that she works for herself and therefore must eventually provide for her own retirement income complicates matters. And she worries that her mother's $400,000 nest egg may not be sufficient to last another 30 or more years.

A trusted friend, Lowell, has suggested that both Glenndy and her mother consider some serious retirement planning. In particular, he recommends that they place some of their money in annuities. Lowell claims that annuities have some tax advantages that may be helpful in both Glenndy's and Mary's situations. Furthermore, he says that Glenndy can put money into an annuity over a long period of time, on a schedule as erratic as her income flow, while Mary can make a one-time deposit and immediately begin collecting monthly payments. One of Lowell's most appealing contentions is his statement that an annuity can actually protect Mary against the possibility of outliving her income. These and other characteristics of annuities are discussed in this chapter.

CHAPTER OBJECTIVES

After studying this chapter, you should be able to

1. Give examples of situations in which an annuity might be an appropriate personal risk management tool.
2. Explain the two elements of an annuity certain and the three elements of an annuity based on one or more persons' lives.
3. Distinguish among three different ways of paying for annuity contracts.
4. Explain the difference between immediate and deferred annuities.
5. Identify and discuss the relevant factors determining the size of benefits payable under a joint and survivor annuity.
6. List and explain three minimum guarantees that can be added to life annuities.
7. Discuss the concept and structure of a variable annuity.
8. Describe the process for calculating the federal income tax payable on a benefit paid out under a life annuity.

Different degrees of uncertainty usually exist regarding how long individuals will need the income that is to be provided by their savings, particularly if the income will be needed throughout the retirement years. Retirement income for most individuals consists of funds from three different sources: Social Security, one or more employer-sponsored retirement plans, and personal savings. Financial planners sometimes refer to a "three-legged stool" approach to retirement planning to emphasize the critical importance of all three income sources (see Figure 18-1). This chapter emphasizes how a particular savings product (annuities) can be used as part of the personal savings "leg" of the stool. The other two legs (Social Security benefits and employer plans) are discussed in Chapter 20.

If investment earnings alone will not provide a sufficient retirement income, then periodic withdrawals from the principal will be required. Under such circumstances, individuals living to advanced ages may outlive their income sources. This possibility results in the need for a systematic means for liquidating resources, together with a means for protecting against the risk of living beyond one's financial resources. A product that can be arranged to meet such needs is known as an **annuity**.

An annuity is a contract that provides for the liquidation of a sum of money through a series of payments during a specified period of time. Often, the period coincides with the lifetime of one or more persons. In this way, the **annuitant** (the person receiving the payments) is protected against the risk of outliving his or her financial resources. As discussed in this chapter, other ways of specifying the period for receiving payments exist, as do many other variations in annuity contracts.

STRUCTURE OF ANNUITIES

Annuities differ with respect to several factors, but they are all structured so that annuitants' payments are composed of both interest earnings and a partial liquidation of principal. For

FIGURE 18-1   **Three-Legged Stool Approach to Retirement Planning**

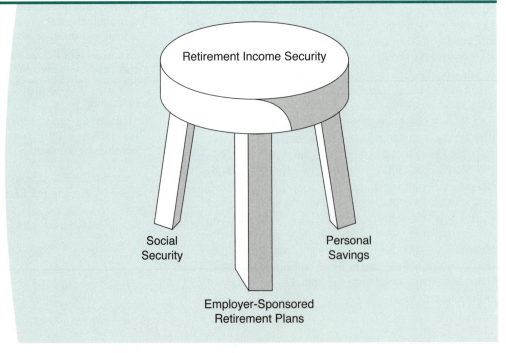

contracts guaranteeing payments for as long as an annuitant is alive, each payment consists not only of interest and principal but also of a third element called the **survivorship benefit**.

To illustrate the role of the survivorship benefit for annuities, suppose 10,000 employees are retiring from ABC Company. Each person is exactly 65 years old, and each has just been given a $500,000 lump-sum settlement from ABC's retirement plan. From an individual perspective, no one knows exactly how long he or she will live. Consequently, none of the retirees know how much of the $500,000 principal can safely be withdrawn each month without depleting the funds before death. But if all of the employees join together to allow the law of large numbers to reduce the risk inherent in this situation, the problem can be resolved. As discussed in Chapter 4, it can be predicted how many members of a sufficiently large group of persons will die at various ages. It is not necessary (or possible) to specify the identity of the particular individuals who will die at given times; only the ability to predict aggregate deaths is necessary for an annuity arrangement to be feasible. If predictions regarding aggregate deaths are reasonably accurate, then the unused principal of those persons who die at younger ages can be used to help finance the monthly payments for those who live to very advanced ages. The increase in each annuitant's monthly payment that is attributable to the release of funds from those who have already died is the survivorship benefit that is part of all life annuity arrangements.

Continuing with the example of the 10,000 new retirees from ABC, suppose each person uses his or her $500,000 to purchase an annuity guaranteeing a monthly payment until death, regardless of whether death occurs at age 66, age 96, or even later. At recent annuity rates offered by many insurers, $500,000 would be enough to guarantee a 65-year-old annuitant at least $2,000 a month for life, with actual monthly payments being $3,500 or more when interest rates sufficiently exceed the minimums used by insurers in computing the guarantees. These amounts exceed what many individuals would be able to earn over the long run by investing the $500,000 distributions on their own. At the same time, the annuity provides a built-in guarantee that the payments will continue, regardless of how long the annuitant may live. These features make the annuity contract a practical tool to be used in many personal risk management plans.

ANNUITY CHARACTERISTICS

As noted, some annuities are payable for the life of the annuitant, whereas others are payable for periods of time that do not depend on any one person's life or death. In selecting the appropriate personal risk management tools, individuals must understand the many distinguishing features of annuities, which are discussed in this section.

How Are Annuity Premiums Paid?

An annuity can be purchased with one lump-sum payment, or it can be purchased in installments over a period of years. If the annuity is paid for with one payment, it is called a **single-premium annuity**. If it is paid for in regular annual installments, it is known as an **annual-premium annuity**. If considerable latitude is allowed regarding the timing and amount of premiums, the installment arrangement is a **flexible-premium annuity**; in this case, the size of the eventual annuity benefit is a function of the accumulated premium dollars at the time the annuitant decides to begin collecting benefits.

Many of the life insurance settlement options discussed in Chapter 16 are in essence single-premium annuities; the life insurance proceeds are used as the single premium to purchase a particular income stream described in the policy. Single-premium annuities are used in many employee retirement plans, as well as on an individual basis in connection with retirement planning. Annual-premium and flexible-premium annuities also are used with retirement arrangements, as discussed in more detail in Chapter 20.

When Do Benefits Begin?

Benefits can begin as soon as the annuity is purchased and continue at specified intervals (usually monthly) thereafter. In this case, the contract is called an **immediate annuity**. Life insurance settlement options paid under annuity arrangements usually are set up on an immediate annuity basis, although this is not required. Another example might involve savings that have been accumulating in many different investments during a person's working career. At retirement, some or all of the various investments can be consolidated and used to purchase an annuity that will begin to pay a retirement income immediately.

The alternative to an immediate annuity is a **deferred annuity**, in which benefits are deferred until some future time. The particular time when benefits are to begin may or may not be specified ahead of time. If such a time is designated, changes usually can be made if desired.

How Long Are Benefits Payable?

The annuity characteristic that has the most variations is the specification of how long benefits are payable. Several different possibilities are discussed in this section.

Annuity Certain

An annuity that is payable for a specified period of time, without regard to the life or death of the annuitant, is called an **annuity certain**. For example, benefits might be payable for exactly 10 years. If the annuitant dies before all payments have been made, the remaining benefits continue to be paid to either the annuitant's heirs or a secondary person named in the annuity contract. An annuity certain has no survivorship benefit; payments consist entirely of interest earnings and liquidation of principal.

The fixed-period settlement option in a life insurance policy is an example of an annuity certain, purchased on a single-premium basis with the proceeds payable at the death of the insured. Beneficiaries selecting the fixed-amount option in a life policy are in essence purchasing an annuity certain with the policy proceeds. For example, suppose Lisa Smith dies, leaving $100,000 in life insurance benefits to her husband and beneficiary, Sam. Instead of taking the money in a lump sum, Sam decides that he wants a monthly income of $2,000 for as long as the money lasts. At the low guaranteed interest rate of 3 percent found in many life insurance policies, a $100,000 single premium will purchase a $2,000 monthly annuity certain for a period of about 4.5 years. (As explained in Chapter 16, if the insurer earns more than the interest rate guaranteed, the $2,000 monthly payments may continue for longer than the 4.5 years.)

Straight Life Annuity

A **straight life annuity** pays benefits only during the lifetime of the annuitant. If the annuitant dies the day after purchasing the annuity, there is no obligation for the insurer to return any of the purchase price. Rather, the money is used to provide the survivorship element of the payments made to those persons still living and collecting benefits. The older an annuitant is when benefits begin under a straight life annuity, the greater is the size of each periodic payment (assuming all other factors are the same). The reason is that, on average, older persons can be expected to die before collecting as many annuity payments as their younger counterparts. Thus, if the purchase price for two contracts is the same, the size of each payment made to a younger annuitant must be less than that paid to an older person.

As an example, consider 85-year-old Bob and 65-year-old Michael, each of whom has accumulated $500,000 in savings. Each is considering using that amount to buy a straight life annuity with benefits beginning immediately. The insurer checks its annuity rates and indicates that for a $500,000 single premium, the annuity benefit payable to Michael would be a minimum of $3,000 per month, while the monthly benefit for Bob would be at least $8,400.

(Greater amounts might be possible for both persons if actual interest earnings exceed the guaranteed minimum in the contract.) Bob would receive a considerably greater monthly benefit because he is 20 years older than Michael and is therefore expected to die sooner. The difference in income is especially significant in this example because of the high probability of death at Bob's advanced age of 85. Because he probably will receive considerably fewer payments under the annuity contract than will Michael, Bob's $500,000 will purchase a much greater amount per month than will Michael's $500,000.

netlink

To learn more about topics related to individual and corporate retirement planning, visit http://www.retirement-planning.com.

Joint and Survivor Annuity

An annuity may be issued on more than one life. A very common arrangement, known as a **joint and survivor annuity**, provides that annuity payments will continue as long as either annuitant is alive. The periodic payment may be constant during the entire period, or it may be arranged so that the amount of each payment is reduced upon the death of the first annuitant. The size of the survivor's benefit (payable when only one of the two persons is still alive) is often stated as a percentage of the joint benefit (payable while both annuitants are living), using the terminology **joint and _x_ percent survivor annuity**. Thus, a joint and 100 percent survivor annuity would pay the same benefit regardless of whether one or two annuitants were still alive. But a joint and 50 percent survivor annuity would pay the survivor only one-half of the joint benefit.

Assuming all other factors are the same, the greater the reduction in benefits when the first person dies, the larger will be the joint benefit while both persons live. For example, suppose 65-year-old John Jaeger and his 65-year-old wife, Hazel, are considering buying a joint and survivor annuity. One of their decisions involves the trade-off between the size of their annuity income while they both are alive versus the survivor's income after the first of them dies. One insurer indicates that for the same premium, the Jaegers can buy either (1) a joint and 100 percent survivor annuity providing an income of $5,000 a month that ends only when both John and Hazel are dead or (2) a joint and 50 percent survivor annuity paying $5,570 per month while both persons are alive and $2,785 for the life of the survivor. (For the same premium, they could also buy a straight life annuity of $6,329 per month for John; however, after John dies, nothing would be payable to Hazel.)

Another important determinant of benefit size for joint and survivor annuities is age. As with straight life annuities, joint and survivor annuity benefits are more expensive at younger ages. In the previous example, both individuals were 65 years old. Now consider the situation of Tom and Jill Robertson. Tom is age 65, whereas Jill is only 35. Because Jill is so much younger than Tom, it is very probable that she will eventually find herself in the role of the survivor if they purchase a joint and survivor annuity. Furthermore, Jill is likely to collect her survivor annuity for many more years than if she were older. Because of such probabilities, it will cost the Robertsons more for any particular annuity compared with the Jaegers in the previous example. Or, stated differently, for the same amount of premium dollars, the Robertsons will be able to purchase relatively lower annuity benefits on a joint and survivor basis. For example, the premium for a $6,329 straight life annuity on Tom's life would be sufficient to buy only a $3,575 joint and 100 percent survivor annuity or a $4,731 joint and 50 percent survivor annuity. By comparing these joint income figures with the corresponding numbers in the previous example, the substantial impact of age on the cost of annuities becomes immediately apparent.

Period-Certain Guarantees

Annuities based on the lives of one or more persons can be arranged so that, regardless of the life or death of the annuitant(s), at least a minimum number of annuity payments is made. For example, a **10-year period-certain life annuity** issued to annuitant Amanda Carson would pay benefits as long as Amanda lives. However, if Amanda were to die within the first 10 years, the annuity would continue payments until a total of 10 years of payments are made. In general, a period-certain life annuity ceases payments when the later of the following events occurs: (1) death of the annuitant or (2) expiration of the minimum guarantee period.

If an annuitant is relatively young, the addition of a period-certain guarantee to a life annuity will not have a large effect on the size of each annuity payment. For example, suppose 55-year-old Mike Smith has accumulated $500,000 in retirement savings. Used as a single premium, this sum will be sufficient to buy a straight life annuity of $4,260 per month from one low-cost insurer. If Mike is concerned about the possibility of "losing" his savings should he die before collecting many annuity payments, he may want to consider adding a period-certain guarantee to his annuity contract. Because his probability of death is not very high at age 55, Mike can add a 10-year period-certain guarantee to his annuity and still receive at least $4,175 per month (a decrease of only $85). If Mike had been considerably older, however, the relative difference between benefits under the straight life annuity and the period-certain life annuity would have been much greater. For example, for the same premium, the same insurer would sell an 80-year-old man a straight life annuity of $7,184 per month or a 10-year period-certain life annuity of only $5,525 per month, a decrease of $1,659 per month. The reason for the much greater effect on benefits at older ages is the increased likelihood that the period-certain guarantee will be the factor governing the length of the payout period. That is, the probability of dying within 10 years is much greater for an 80-year-old person than for someone age 55. It is therefore more expensive at older ages to add a guarantee providing at least a minimum number of payments regardless of the annuitant's life or death. The increased price for the guarantee is reflected in relatively lower benefits.

Refund Guarantees

Other arrangements to ensure at least a minimum return from an annuity are the refund guarantees that can be added to straight life and joint and survivor annuities. When a straight life annuity has an **installment refund guarantee**, benefits continue after the death of the annuitant until the combined benefits paid before and after death equal the original purchase price. For example, suppose 60-year-old Debbie Jones uses $500,000 to buy a monthly annuity of $4,170 with an installment refund guarantee. If Debbie dies after one year, she will have collected a total of $12 \times \$4,170 = \$50,040$. Payments will continue to a designated beneficiary until a total of $500,000 has been paid. On the other hand, if Debbie had added the **cash refund guarantee** to her annuity contract, then the difference between the total payments received and the original premium would be paid immediately in cash to her beneficiary. The cash refund guarantee is more expensive than the installment refund option because the insurer forfeits the right to earn interest on the money immediately refunded.

Temporary Life Annuity

The **temporary life annuity**, which is rarely used, pays benefits until the expiration of a specified period of years or until the annuitant dies, whichever event occurs first. Thus, a temporary life annuity can be considered the opposite of a period-certain life annuity. An example in which such a contract might be used is illustrated by the situation of 50-year-old Wayne White, who is childless and unskilled at working and who was financially dependent on his recently deceased wife, Linda. When Wayne reaches age 60, he will be eligible to collect Social Security benefits as Linda's widower. To fill his income gap until then, Wayne may consider using the proceeds of some of Linda's life insurance to purchase a 10-year temporary life annuity. If Wayne survives for 10 years, he will begin receiving his Social Security wid-ower's benefits and will no longer need the annuity payments. If he dies within the next 10 years, there also will be no further need for the annuity. By choosing a temporary life annu-ity rather than a 10-year annuity certain, Wayne's monthly payment can be maximized. At rel-atively young ages, however, this increase in benefits is slight.

Is the Contract Fixed or Variable?

An annuity that has a benefit expressed in terms of a stated dollar amount based on a guaran-teed rate of return is known as a **fixed annuity**. In practice, the actual benefit paid under a fixed annuity may vary over time if interest earnings, expenses, and/or mortality experience are better than what was assumed in computing the annuity premium. Thus, a relatively low interest rate, such as 4 percent, might be assumed in computing the minimum guaranteed ben-efit under a fixed, straight life annuity. If actual investment earnings exceed 4 percent, annu-ity payments likely will be higher than the minimum amount guaranteed in the contract.

A variation of the fixed annuity is the **market value–adjusted (MVA) annuity**, some-times referred to as the **modified guaranteed annuity**. The MVA option can be used with fixed deferred annuities to provide relatively higher minimum interest rate guarantees during the first several years after a contract is issued but before benefits begin. For example, the 4 percent guaranteed interest on a fixed annuity might be increased to 6 percent for the first 10 years under an MVA contract. This 6 percent minimum would be payable only on funds that are not withdrawn during the initial 10-year period, with lower rates possible on with-drawals during the first 10 years. Deferred annuity owners who are truly using the contracts as long-term investments may find the higher minimum guarantees of MVA annuities espe-cially attractive.

In contrast to fixed and MVA annuities, the benefit associated with a **variable annuity** is expressed in terms of **annuity units**. The value of each annuity unit fluctuates with the per-formance of a specified portfolio of investments, thus causing the annuity income to fluctu-ate as well. The general objective of a variable annuity is to provide the annuitant with an in-come that fluctuates in dollar value but remains reasonably constant in terms of purchasing power. To be successful in this goal, the investment portfolio underlying the variable annuity must increase in value when general price levels increase. In past years, variable annuities were invested almost exclusively in common stocks; today, many different investment choices are available. A problem with relying entirely on stocks is that although there is a long-term correlation between price indices and common stock returns, exactly the opposite may be true in the short term. Thus, a retiree whose major source of income comes from a variable annu-ity invested exclusively in common stocks may have a serious problem when prices increase and stock returns decline significantly.

To illustrate the mechanics of the variable annuity, consider 65-year-old John Jackson, who wants to use $300,000 of his retirement savings to purchase a single-premium variable annuity with benefits to begin immediately. On a straight life basis, one insurer agrees to sell John a variable annuity paying 100 annuity units per month. If the current value of each unit is $25, then John will begin receiving a monthly income of $2,500. If the underlying invest-ment portfolio increases in value so that each annuity unit is subsequently valued at $30, then John's monthly income will increase to $3,000.

Due to their favorable tax status, as discussed in the next section, many persons purchase variable annuities over time, making the mechanics of the contract slightly more complex. Suppose 25-year-old Ted Kimura decides to contribute $100 per month toward the purchase of a variable annuity that will begin paying benefits at age 65. Each $100 premium is used to purchase **accumulation units** that vary in price according to the performance of the invest-ment portfolio. For example, if the current value of an accumulation unit is $50, then a $100 premium will buy 2 units. The next month the value of an accumulation unit may have

ETHICAL PERSPECTIVES

Investment Choices

The oldest variable annuity plan in operation was started in 1952 by the College Retirement Equities Fund (CREF). CREF is a subsidiary of the Teachers Insurance and Annuity Association, a life insurer offering insurance and annuities primarily to college personnel. Originally, investments supporting CREF annuities were composed entirely of common stocks. An annuitant who invested in the stock fund when it began would have seen his or her account grow at an average annual rate of about 10.5 percent as of the end of 2003. Beginning in 1988, annuity owners were offered additional choices other than just the stock fund. First, a money market fund option was introduced. Gradually, additional choices were added: a bond market fund, a global equities fund, a growth stock fund, an equity index fund, an inflation-linked bond fund, and a "Social Choice Account," set up to avoid investments in firms that do not meet specified social criteria. At the end of 2003, this fund attempted to avoid investing in securities of companies that derive any revenue from the manufacture of alcohol or tobacco products; that derive any revenue from gambling; that derive significant revenue from the production of military weapons; and that are electric utilities involved in nuclear energy. The fund also considers things such as the safety of companies' products, their environmental record, their involvement in philanthropic activities, and their diversity. In addition to CREF, a number of other companies also offer mutual funds that use social criteria in making investment decisions. One fund exists, called the Vice Fund, that invests primarily in those firms often considered socially irresponsible, such as those in the alcohol, tobacco, weapons, or gambling industries.

increased to $55, so a $100 premium will purchase only 1.82 accumulation units. At age 65, Ted's total accumulation units will be converted by formula into annuity units. His monthly annuity income will then fluctuate with the value of the annuity units.

ANNUITY TAXATION

It is important for personal risk managers to be aware of how annuities are taxed, especially because the contracts play such an important role in retirement planning. In this section, the basic principles of federal income taxation of individual annuities are discussed. Additional tax issues associated with annuities in employee benefit plans are discussed in Chapter 20.

Taxation of Annuity Benefits

In determining the income tax payable on annuity benefits, it would be unfair to tax the entire amount of benefits paid, because each payment consists partly of a return of an individual's principal. Thus, if Michelle Lewis uses $400,000 of her savings to purchase a single-premium straight life annuity, she should not have to pay taxes on the part of each monthly benefit that represents a partial return of her original $400,000. One way of handling this problem might be for Michelle to collect all annuity benefits tax-free until she has received a total of $400,000. After that, her benefits would be fully taxable. Although this method would be attractive for annuitants, it should not be surprising that a different method is required by law. The general approach currently required is to exclude a portion of each annuity payment from federal income taxes until the sum of all the

Set your Web browser to
http://info.insure.com/annuity/
for answers to many common
questions about annuities.

excluded amounts exactly equals the original purchase price of the annuity. After that time, the entire amount of each annuity payment becomes fully taxable. The amount of each benefit that can be excluded from taxes is computed according to rules specified by the Internal Revenue Service (IRS). The general principles involved are explained in the next paragraph.

Suppose Michelle is age 60 and her $400,000 single premium is sufficient to purchase a monthly lifetime income of $3,400 per month, or $40,800 per year. The IRS publishes tables, such as that illustrated in Table 18-1, for use in computing the probable number of years that a person can be expected to live and thus continue to receive annuity benefits. For a straight life annuity with payments commencing at age 60, Table 18-1 indicates that payments can be expected for 24.2 years. According to this table, Michelle can expect to receive annuity benefits of $40,800 × 24.2 = $987,360. Because $400,000 is merely a return of her original money, 40.5 percent ($400,000 ÷ $987,360 = 40.5 percent) of the total dollars Michelle expects to receive from the annuity are paid through a return of her principal. This percentage,

TABLE 18-1   Expected Years to Receive Straight Life Annuity, Unisex Basis

Age When Benefits Begin	Expected Number of Annual Payments	Age When Benefits Begin	Expected Number of Annual Payments	Age When Benefits Begin	Expected Number of Annual Payments
40	42.5	66	19.2	91	4.7
41	41.5	67	18.4	92	4.4
42	40.6	68	17.6	93	4.1
43	39.6	69	16.8	94	3.9
44	38.7	70	16.0	95	3.7
45	37.7	71	15.3	96	3.4
46	36.8	72	14.6	97	3.2
47	35.9	73	13.9	98	3.0
48	34.9	74	13.2	99	2.8
49	34.0	75	12.5	100	2.7
50	33.1	76	11.9	101	2.5
51	32.2	77	11.2	102	2.3
52	31.3	78	10.6	103	2.1
53	30.4	79	10.0	104	1.9
54	29.5	80	9.5	105	1.8
55	28.6	81	8.9	106	1.6
56	27.7	82	8.4	107	1.4
57	26.8	83	7.9	108	1.3
58	25.9	84	7.4	109	1.1
59	25.0	85	6.9	110	1.0
60	24.2	86	6.5	111	0.9
61	23.3	87	6.1	112	0.8
62	22.5	88	5.7	113	0.7
63	21.6	89	5.3	114	0.6
64	20.8	90	5.0	115	0.5
65	20.0				

Source: *2003 Tax Facts* 1 (Cincinnati, OH: National Underwriter Co.), 944.

PROFESSIONAL PERSPECTIVES

Tips for Buying Variable Deferred Annuities

When fears of rising income taxes take hold, variable deferred annuity sales increase as well. Many sellers tout the attractiveness of the contracts' tax deferral characteristics while glossing over some of the pitfalls. In the increasingly competitive variable annuity market, buyers should be sure to check the following:

- *Annual expense charges.* The expenses associated with most variable annuities are in the 1.25 to 2.25 percent range, although it is possible to find a few contracts with fees below 1 percent.
- *Surrender charges.* For full or partial withdrawals, most insurers charge 7 to 10 percent of the amount withdrawn during the first few contract years. This surrender charge usually declines on a graded basis, reaching 0 percent by the seventh or eighth year. A few contracts continue the surrender charge through the tenth year, but a minority of contracts have no such charges at all.
- *Front-end load.* Some contracts subtract a percentage (for example, 5 percent) from the amount initially invested, although the more common approach now is to have no charge in this regard.

- *Maintenance fees.* For small accumulations, some insurers charge a flat dollar maintenance fee, such as $25, but others do not charge this fee at all. A few insurers charge an annual contract fee regardless of the amount accumulated.
- *Number and quality of investment choices.* Investment choices should include a selection of different types of stock funds, as well as a bond fund, a money market fund, and perhaps a global or international fund. The relative past performance of such funds can be compared by consulting publications such as Morningstar Inc.'s Variable Annuity Performance Report, available in many public libraries.
- *Annuity income level.* The mortality and interest assumptions inherent in a particular annuity affect the minimum income promised during the distribution phase of the contract. Thus, one annuity may promise to pay a lifetime monthly income of $7 per $1,000 accumulation at age 65, while another contract may promise only $6.50. This is obviously a critical factor in evaluating and comparing annuities.

known as the **exclusion ratio**, is the fraction of each payment that can be excluded from income taxation. It is the ratio of Michelle's total investment in the annuity to the total return she expects to receive from the contract. The other 59.5 percent of Michelle's expected benefits, derived from investment earnings and survivorship benefits, are fully taxable.

To summarize the tax situation illustrated by this example, Michelle will be able to exclude 40.5 percent of each annuity payment from income taxes for the first 24.2 years that she receives benefits. So instead of paying taxes each year on the entire $40,800 payment, she will be taxed on only $(1 - 0.405) \times \$40,800 = \$24,276$. After 24.2 years, Michelle will have excluded a total of $400,000 from taxes. She will then be required to pay taxes on the full amount of each subsequent annuity payment.

Tax Issues before Benefits Begin

In recognition of their role as long-term savings vehicles, annuities usually do not produce taxable income for their owners until income benefits begin. Thus, if Tom Brown purchases a flexible-premium deferred annuity at age 30, he can generally defer paying taxes on accrued investment earnings and survivorship benefits until he begins to collect the annuity benefits. At that time, Tom will be taxed according to the rules described in the previous section.

Just like life insurance policies, some annuities are participating and may pay dividends to their owners. If the owner of a deferred annuity receives a dividend before benefits begin, the dividend is considered to be a return of premium and is not subject to income taxation. After annuity benefits begin, however, dividends serve to increase the size of the periodic benefit and are taxed accordingly.

One situation that may result in taxable income for an annuitant before benefits become payable is if the owner of a deferred annuity makes a partial withdrawal of funds. The withdrawal is treated as taxable income to the extent that the annuity value exceeds the total premiums paid. For example, suppose Beth Kroger owns a deferred annuity for which she has paid a total of $5,000 in premiums by the time she is age 40. Due to interest and survivorship benefits, the annuity is currently valued at $7,000, which is $2,000 more than what Beth has paid in premiums. If Beth withdraws $3,000 from the contract, the first $2,000 will be taxed as ordinary income. The other $1,000 will be considered a withdrawal of premiums and will not be taxable. (If Beth had withdrawn $2,000 or less, the entire amount of the withdrawal would have been taxable.)

The previous rule regarding the taxation of withdrawals was enacted to lessen the possibility that annuities might be used as short-term, temporary tax shelters. In this way, it is more likely that the income tax advantages of annuities will be used to facilitate the long-term purposes for which such contracts are intended. To ensure this result to an even greater extent, the tax law adds yet another consideration: for withdrawals that occur before age 59.5, a penalty tax of 10 percent may be added to the regular income tax payable on the withdrawal. So, in the previous example, Beth Kroger would have to pay a penalty tax of $200 (10 percent of the $2,000) in addition to the ordinary income tax owed on the $2,000. Withdrawals associated with some circumstances (such as death, disability, and a few others) are exempt from the additional penalty tax.[1] But the exemptions are few enough to cause many potential buyers of deferred annuities to think twice before committing their funds to such contracts at young ages. Unless an individual seriously intends to use the funds accumulating in a deferred annuity to help provide income during retirement, alternative savings vehicles may be the better choice.

SUMMARY

1. An annuity is a contract that provides for the liquidation of a sum of money through a series of payments during a specified period of time. The person who receives the payments is called the annuitant. Each annuity payment consists partly of investment earnings and partly of a partial liquidation of principal. For contracts guaranteeing payments for as long as an annuitant is alive, each payment also contains an element known as the survivorship benefit.

2. Annuities that are paid for in one lump sum are called single-premium annuities. Alternatives include not only annual-premium annuities but also flexible-premium annuities, in which the timing and amount of premiums are at the discretion of the annuity owner.

3. Annuity benefits can begin as soon as the annuity is purchased, or they can be deferred until a later date.

4. How long annuity benefits are payable depends on the type of annuity. An annuity certain pays benefits for a specified period of time, without regard to the life or death of the annuitants. Such contracts do not have a survivorship element. A straight life annuity pays benefits only during the lifetime of the annuitant. Annuities also can be

---

1   Additional situations in which withdrawals are exempt from the penalty tax are those in which the withdrawal is paid as a life annuity; those involving the withdrawal of premiums invested before August 14, 1982; and those involving a distribution from a qualified pension plan.

issued on more than one life. A common arrangement is the joint and survivor annuity, which provides that payments will continue as long as either annuitant is alive. For both straight life annuities and joint and survivor annuities, guarantees can be added to ensure that at least a minimum number of payments is made, regardless of the life or death of the annuitant(s). Period-certain guarantees are common, as are installment refund contracts. A slightly different type of guarantee is the cash refund option. A temporary life annuity pays benefits until the expiration of a specified period of years or until the annuitant dies, whichever event occurs first.

5. Fixed annuities express their benefits in terms of a stated dollar amount, based on a minimum guaranteed interest rate. The market value–adjusted annuity is a variation of the fixed annuity that allows a higher minimum guarantee to apply during an initial period after the contract is purchased.

Variable annuities express their benefits in units that fluctuate in value with the investment performance of an underlying portfolio of securities.

6. An annuitant can exclude a portion of each annuity benefit received until the sum of all the excluded amounts exactly equals the original purchase price. Subsequently, each benefit is fully taxable. The excluded portion is determined by the exclusion ratio, which is the original purchase price divided by the total return expected from the contract, taking into consideration life expectancies published by the IRS.

7. Before benefits begin, annuities usually do not produce taxable income for their owners. An exception occurs if an early withdrawal is made. In this case, the withdrawal is taxable, to the extent that the annuity value exceeds the total premiums paid in. Further, many withdrawals before age 59.5 will result in an additional 10 percent penalty tax.

internet*exercises*

1. Set your browser to http://www.annuityfyi. com/. Then select two different companies that issue variable annuities. Use the links to investigate the features of their annuities. In what way are the product features similar? Different?

2. Different annuity types are most appropriate for various situations. Go to http://www.annuitysite. com and check out the section on selecting annuities. Try to predict what type of annuity will be recommended for each situation described, then look at the recommendations. Can you explain the reasoning behind the recommendations?

QUESTIONS FOR REVIEW AND DISCUSSION

1. What is an annuity? Briefly describe three situations in which an annuity might represent an appropriate personal risk management tool.
2. Identify the three elements that may combine to make up an annuity payment to an annuitant.
3. Explain what is meant by "the risk of living beyond one's financial resources," as used in this chapter.
4. Define the concept of a survivorship benefit as it relates to annuity contracts that guarantee payments for as long as a person is alive.
5. List the distinguishing characteristics of each of the following types of annuity:
   a. Single-premium annuity
   b. Flexible-premium annuity

   c. Annuity certain
   d. Straight life annuity
   e. Joint and survivor annuity
   f. Market value–adjusted annuity
   g. Variable annuity
6. Explain the meaning of each of the following annuity payment guarantees:
   a. Period-certain guarantee
   b. Installment refund guarantee
   c. Cash refund guarantee
7. Generally, what is the objective behind the purchase of a variable annuity?
8. Describe the process by which the amount of monthly annuity distributions are computed when a variable annuity has been purchased over time.

9. Ben Nolen, currently age 65, purchased an annuity several years ago for a single premium of $100,000. Ben has just received his first annual distribution of $15,000. Using Table 18-1, calculate Ben's exclusion ratio and the amount of the distribution that will be taxable.

10. Describe the tax treatment of dividends paid to the owner of a participating annuity.

11. In each of the following situations, list the types of annuity that might be particularly appropriate for the situation and discuss the reasons for your selections:

   a. Donna, a 50-year-old widow with no children, is considering the purchase of an annuity to fund her retirement. She works as a securities broker and is paid a commission that varies greatly from year to year. She anticipates retiring in 15 years and currently has very little savings.

   b. George, a 55-year-old married school teacher with three grown children, is considering the purchase of an annuity with $200,000 he recently inherited from his father. He intends to use the funds to help fund his retirement in five years. George's wife does not work outside of the home.

   c. Mary, a 59.5-year-old single woman with no children, recently received a $300,000 distribution from her company-sponsored profit-sharing plan. She intends to use a portion of these funds to purchase an annuity to fund her intended travels during the next 10 years. Each year, she intends to use $10,000 to take a month-long trip to some exotic destination.

12. An annuity salesperson recently stated, "Annuities are the ultimate risk management tool. You identify a risk, and I can sell you an annuity that will allow you to avoid it."

   a. Do you believe this statement?

   b. Identify as many risks as you can think of that can be avoided through the purchase of an annuity.

   c. Can you think of some risks that cannot be avoided through the purchase of an annuity?

   d. Could an annuity be developed to avoid any of the risks you listed in part c of this question? Why?

13. Considering the main tax advantage of an annuity, state a tax-related reason indicating that the purchase of an annuity might be preferable to a savings bond with an equivalent annual return if the annuity payments will begin before the owner's age reaches 59.5 and will be subject to the 10 percent penalty tax. Discuss the factors to be considered before purchasing an annuity with distributions that will be subject to the penalty tax.

14. Stock dividends are taxed in the year paid, with increases in the value of the stock taxed in the year that the stocks are sold. If a stock were found that retains all of its earnings without paying a single dividend but experiences fairly steady growth in value, would the tax treatment of an investment in this stock vary significantly from an investment in an annuity? Explain.

15. In your opinion, are annuities more like insurance or investments? Discuss the arguments that could be used to support each choice.

16. Annuities are most often thought of as an investment vehicle used to help fund retirement. Identify and discuss several reasons why annuities are well suited for this use.

17. Should purchasers of single-premium immediate annuities receive the same annuity income regardless of their health? If an insurer decided to differentiate payments on the basis of health status, would healthier individuals receive more or less monthly income than unhealthy persons? Why? Do you think there would be a market for this type of annuity product? Why or why not?

chapter 19

T he Get 'Em While They're Hot (GWTH) Company is a bakery firm with retail locations throughout the United States. GWTH is particularly known for its specialty breads and pastries. It employs 2,000 workers as bakers, managers, and sales personnel. As GWTH has grown, its owners have gradually added to the list of benefits given to their workers. Initially, only legally required items such as Social Security, workers' compensation, and unemployment insurance were provided. Later, a small death benefit was added for a few key individuals, and medical expense insurance was implemented soon after.

At this time, GWTH owners believe that a complete revision of the benefit package may be in order. They are concerned that there was never an overall plan for the benefits or the manner in which they were designed. Over time, the GWTH benefits package simply evolved in whatever ways various insurance sales personnel recommended when money seemed to be available. As GWTH now takes a more systematic approach to its benefits package, one of the key issues it faces is whether the benefits provided are appropriate to the particular needs of its employees. Is the death benefit adequate? Are the "correct" eligibility requirements in place to accomplish GWTH's goals? Is the focus of the medical expense insurance appropriate, and have reasonable measures been implemented to control the costs? What about the peril of disability? Should GWTH provide benefits that address that need, or should premium dollars be spent elsewhere? Such issues form the basis of this chapter.

Employee Benefits: Life and Health Benefits

CHAPTER OBJECTIVES

After studying this chapter, you should be able to

1. List three features that distinguish group insurance from individual insurance and describe the characteristics of a group that would be desirable from a group insurance underwriting perspective.
2. Explain the overall approach used to provide Social Security survivor and disability benefits.
3. Explain the typical eligibility requirements associated with premature death benefit programs and health expense benefit plans offered by employers.
4. Distinguish among the different types of group life insurance used in premature death benefit plans.
5. Explain the important considerations in choosing among health benefit providers.
6. List several approaches used to contain health expense benefit costs and give examples of each approach listed.
7. Determine the amount and order of payment among several different health plans covering the same loss to the same individual.
8. Compare sick leave plans with both short-term and long-term disability income plans.

Each year, billions of dollars are spent on employer-sponsored programs designed to provide security and other services for employees. These **employee benefits** have become an important aspect of total compensation in the United States, with average employer costs for employee benefits equal to about 39 percent of payroll in 2001.[1]

Some benefits are provided by employers primarily to enhance the overall compensation package offered to their employees. Paid holidays, paid vacations, discounts on products sold by the employer, subsidized meals, and free parking spaces are examples of the wide range of possibilities in this regard. Due to their nature, further discussion of these types of benefits is beyond the scope of this text. Instead, this chapter focuses on identifying and explaining the employee benefits that can be used as risk management tools in dealing with life, health, and loss of income exposures.

REASONS FOR EMPLOYEE BENEFITS

To understand how employee benefits may be included in personal risk management plans, it is important to know the two major reasons why employers offer benefits to their workers. Usually, employers make benefits available to their employees in order to (1) improve employee relations and (2) take advantage of the special income tax status granted to many benefit programs.

Employee Relations

In earlier years, employee benefits frequently were referred to as *fringe benefits*, in light of many employers' opinions that they were forms of extra compensation that were not required in the sense that salaries are thought of as "required." Some employers' attitudes suggested that they viewed employee benefits essentially as freely given gifts. As such, employers expected employees to be grateful for their benefits and to respond with increased loyalty, improved productivity, and better morale in the workplace.

Over time, however, attitudes of both employers and employees evolved. Benefits that address basic security issues, such as health care expenses, survivor needs due to premature death, and retirement income, are no longer viewed by employees as frills that command special gratitude. Rather, they have become an expected part of most compensation packages. When such benefits are provided, employees' attitudes are often unaffected because the employer is doing only what is expected. If such benefits are not provided, however, the impact on employee relations is generally negative. Employee turnover may increase, and the employer may experience difficulty in recruiting workers, especially in highly competitive labor markets. In essence, some employee benefits now function primarily as potential dissatisfiers if they are not provided or are not as generous as employees believe they should be. Employers hoping to significantly improve employee relations through their benefit packages must go beyond merely providing what is expected. In addition, employers are becoming increasingly flexible in allowing employees to select the benefits that best meet their individual needs. As single-parent and/or childless families and double-income couples have proliferated, it has become harder for a standard benefit package to efficiently meet the varying needs of all workers. Now and in the future, firms that emphasize flexibility in benefit structure may gain the most employee-relations value associated with their benefit packages.

Tax Advantages

Many employee benefits are treated more favorably for tax purposes than are wages and salaries. When such tax advantages exist, it usually is to an employee's advantage to receive the benefit rather than to receive a higher salary and then purchase the product separately. For

---

1   Stephen Taub, "Benefits Nearly 40% of Payroll, Study Finds," *CFO.com*, February 5, 2003.

example, suppose Jason Burke's employer gives Jason the choice of receiving either (1) a $40,000 salary plus health insurance estimated to cost the employer $4,000 a year or (2) a $44,000 salary and no health insurance. Because employers can provide health insurance for their workers and deduct its cost from the employer's taxable income in the same way that they take a tax deduction for wages and salaries, Jason's employer will have a $44,000 tax deduction regardless of Jason's choice. But although employees must report salaries as income on their tax returns, they do not have to report the cost of health insurance or the benefits received from the insurance. Assuming that Jason needs health insurance and will attempt to purchase comparable coverage on an individual basis if he does not receive it from his employer, Jason would be better off if he chooses the first alternative. Under this option, he will report only $40,000 of income for tax purposes rather than the $44,000 under the second alternative. (In many cases Jason would not be able to buy comparable health insurance at as low a price as his employer can, so the first alternative is even more attractive.)

In general, four tax advantages may be associated with employee benefits if specified requirements, known as **qualification rules**, are met. Sometimes a benefit provides some but not all four advantages. Throughout this and the next chapter, tax advantages available for particular benefits are noted.

The first potential advantage, which is nearly universally granted, is the ability of the employer to deduct the cost of the benefit from current taxable income. Unless this right exists, most employers will not provide the benefit.

A second potential advantage is the ability of employees to avoid reporting benefit costs paid by their employers as taxable income. It was noted in the previous example that Jason Burke would not have to pay taxes on the $4,000 in health insurance premiums paid by his employer. But what about the actual benefit payments that would be made by the insurer if Jason were to be sick or injured? The answer to this question leads to the third potential tax advantage that applies to health insurance and many other benefits: such benefit payments may be partially or totally exempt from income taxes. If employees cannot avoid taxes entirely in this regard, they may at least be given the right to defer the tax for many years. The fourth and final tax advantage is the employer's ability to fund some benefit costs in advance, with taxes on associated investment earnings either deferred or avoided completely.

 Although favorable tax status is a major factor affecting an employer's willingness to grant employee benefits, the continuation of current tax advantages is not assured. Frequent changes in the U.S. tax laws affecting employee benefits are common, especially when Congress seeks ways to fund new programs. Periodic proposals are made to restrict the tax advantages associated with one or more benefits, and qualification rules are changed regularly—sometimes in minor ways and sometimes as part of sweeping new tax laws. For example, The Economic Growth and Tax Relief Reconciliation Act of 2001 made a whole host of changes in benefits-related tax provisions that were very favorable to both employers and employees. However, all of these changes are scheduled to expire after 2010. Many observers expect that most of the provisions will eventually be extended beyond 2010, but it is impossible to know for certain. Perhaps the most reliable assertion concerning the taxation of employee benefits is that specific tax rules rarely stay the same for long. Employers attempting to design and administer meaningful benefit packages for their employees must find ways to deal with this increasingly uncertain environment. Similarly, employees who include benefits in their personal risk management plans must be prepared for the inevitable modifications that will be necessary over time due to changes in the tax laws.

PREMATURE DEATH BENEFITS

Recall that death before a planned retirement age is often classified as premature death. From an individual employee's perspective, the financial needs likely to be associated with prema-

INTERNATIONAL PERSPECTIVES

Benefits Networks

Companies with operations in many different countries face unique problems in providing benefits to their employees. To assist in meeting the needs of such employers, multinational benefits networks are gaining in popularity. These networks are arrangements for providing a variety of benefits in multiple countries through one master contract. Advantages include increased standardization and cost savings through economies of scale. Some benefits networks are set up by large insurance companies that operate throughout the world. Others are the result of coop-

erative arrangements between U.S. insurers and overseas partners. Still other networks are sponsored entirely by foreign insurers.

The most common benefits provided through such networks include death, medical expense, and disability income benefits. As benefit costs continue to escalate throughout the world, it can be expected that benefits networks will continue to evolve to meet the ever-changing needs of multinational employers.

---

ture death include the cost of funeral, burial, and other executor fund expenses, as well as the possible provision of income for surviving dependents. Death benefits provided by employers are often designed to address all of these needs, at least to some extent. Employers usually provide death benefits through group life insurance, as described in this section. However, both employers and employees should recognize that some death benefits also may be available to employees through Social Security or workers' compensation. Both of these forms of social insurance are funded either partially or fully by employers and should be recognized as forms of employee benefits. Social Security death benefits are discussed in this section, whereas workers' compensation benefits were discussed in Chapter 10.

Social Security Benefits

The Old Age, Survivors', Disability and Health Insurance Program (OASDHI), better known as **Social Security**, was established in 1935. The four major categories of Social Security benefits are retirement (see Chapter 20), disability income, survivors' income, and Medicare (see Chapter 17). Social Security benefits are financed through a tax on employees and employers. Originally, an employee paid a 1 percent tax on the first $3,000 of annual income earned in covered employment, but this base has increased gradually. By 2004, workers and their employers each paid 6.2 percent on the first $87,900 of earned income. Because this tax pays for all but the Medicare (health) element of Social Security, the $87,900 level is referred to as the **OASDI wage base** (where the *H* for "health" is excluded from the acronym OASDHI). The wage base increases automatically each year as earnings levels rise. To finance Medicare, an additional 1.45 percent tax is payable on all earned income. No Medicare taxable wage base exists, so this tax applies to all earned income with no limit.

Social Security benefits are payable only if the worker meets certain tests based on the length of service in a job for which OASDHI taxes have been paid. A person becomes **fully insured** after meeting either of two tests: (1) having worked in covered employment for 40 quarters (10 years) or (2) subject to a minimum of six calendar quarters, having worked in covered employment at least one-fourth of the number of calendar quarters elapsing from the starting date (1951, or the year during which the person attained age 22, if later), until age 62 is attained, or disability or death occurs, whichever happens first. Workers are **currently insured** if they have worked in covered employment at least 6 of the last 13 quarters, including the quarter in which death occurs or in which they become entitled to benefits.

Dependents of covered workers who die are entitled to Social Security survivors' benefits, payable as a monthly income for as long as the survivors meet specified eligibility criteria. For example, widows and widowers may receive survivor income benefits as long as they have dependent children under 16, and again, upon reaching age 60. Benefits may be reduced, however, if the surviving spouse earns more than a specified amount ($11,640 in 2004, for those below the normal retirement age). Children of deceased workers also receive survivors' benefits until they are age 18 (22 if disabled). The specific amount of monthly income depends on the earnings of the deceased worker, subject to specified minimum and maximum levels.[2]

Distinguishing Features of Group Insurance

Before employee group life insurance programs are discussed, it is useful to consider the nature of group insurance in general. The characteristics of group insurance that tend to distinguish it from individual insurance arrangements are described in the following paragraphs.

Underwriting Unit Is a Group

By their nature, group insurance plans cover more than one person. **Underwriting**, the selection by the insurer of which risks to insure, is based on group characteristics rather than on evidence of insurability for individuals within the group. Membership in a group that has been formed for purposes other than obtaining insurance is often sufficient evidence of insurability for an insurer. For example, if an employee is well enough to go to work, he or she likely will be judged well enough to be insured without passing a medical examination. Insurers often adopt the philosophy that if a group is properly selected, its losses should be roughly similar to those for a group of individually underwritten lives. Thus, emphasis is placed on appropriate selection of groups for coverage by insurers.

As noted, one of the underwriting considerations for group insurance is the purpose for which the group exists. If members have been assembled for the sole purpose of obtaining group coverage, the prospective insurer will be very concerned about the presence of adverse selection (discussed in Chapter 6). For employee groups, however, this possibility is not a problem. Other factors that may be important in underwriting employee group insurance include the group's size, age composition, and expected losses. Insurers prefer larger groups to smaller ones in order to minimize the likelihood of severe adverse selection. It also is considered best from an underwriting perspective if there is a flow of persons through the group so that the younger members replace the older members over time. In this way, the average age of persons in the group is fairly constant, and loss experience tends to be more stable. Finally, insurers are often interested in specific design features of a group insurance program because such features may have an impact on the losses experienced by the group members. The design characteristics of group insurance programs are discussed in more detail later in this chapter.

Lower Expenses

Although no reason should exist to expect actual losses in group insurance to be less than for individual coverage, three factors tend to lower some other expenses when insurance is purchased on a group basis. The first factor is that insurers usually pay lower commissions to their group sales force than to those selling individual insurance. Second, because individual selection is not required, group underwriting expenses tend to be lower than would be the case if a similar number of persons were to be insured on an individual basis. Third, employers may handle some administrative tasks for employee groups, such as recordkeeping and the

---

2   See the Social Security Web site, http://www.ssa.gov, for additional details regarding eligibility and benefit levels.

collection of employee-paid premiums. Thus, the administrative expense component of group insurance may be less than for individual coverage.

Experience Rating

A third distinguishing feature of group insurance is the way in which rates are determined. With group insurance, the losses experienced by the group influence the rates charged. Known as *experience rating*, this feature means that the group will have greater or smaller premiums in the year ahead if its losses are larger or smaller, respectively, during the preceding year. Experience rating provides employers with an incentive to try to lessen group losses through various types of loss control activities.

Group Life Insurance

Most medium- and large-sized firms in the United States provide group life insurance benefits for some or all of their employees. Sometimes employers seek only to provide assistance with funeral, burial, and other final expenses associated with an employee's death. In other cases, the intent is to provide death benefits sufficient to replace income for some period of time for a deceased employee's survivors. By 2002, group life insurance accounted for over 40 percent of all life insurance in force in the United States, with most of that group life coverage attributable to employee groups.[3]

Eligibility for Benefits

The first step in integrating an employer's death benefits into an individual's personal risk management plan is to determine whether the person is eligible to participate in the employer's plan. Eligibility requirements often specify that a person be employed on a full-time basis, although some employers do provide death benefits for permanent part-time workers and many employers continue death protection after an employee retires. Eligibility may be further restricted to those working in particular job classifications. Some employers limit eligibility to those persons who have worked for the firm for some minimum period of time, such as 30 days or six months. In establishing eligibility criteria for death benefits, employers must adhere to various state laws regarding employment discrimination as well as federal laws that discourage employers from favoring very highly paid workers.[4] Employees themselves generally have little or no control over their eligibility for death benefits. Either they qualify under the rules established by the employer or they do not.

In addition, many death benefit plans have two other eligibility requirements. First, employers usually specify that employees who want to participate in the plan must elect to do so soon after meeting the eligibility requirements. Employees are usually not required to participate in a plan even if they are eligible. However, if they do not elect to participate within a specified time (such as 30 days) after becoming eligible, they will not be allowed to enter the plan at a later date unless they prove at that time that they are insurable. Thus, it is important that individuals exercise care when deciding whether to participate in an employer's benefit program, because participation without proving insurability may be offered only once.[5] The reason for this restriction is to guard against excessive losses caused by adverse selection. As

---

3   *2003 Life Insurers Fact Book* (Washington, D.C.: American Council of Life Insurers, 2003, 92.

4   For a more complete discussion of eligibility restrictions imposed at the state and federal levels, see Burton T. Beam, Jr., and John J. McFadden, *Employee Benefits*, 6th ed. (Chicago: Dearborn Financial Publishing, Inc., 2001).

5   An exception occurs when employers establish open enrollment periods, during which employees who are not currently participating in a benefit program can begin to participate regardless of their insurability. Open enrollment periods are offered to enhance employee relations. But to minimize adverse selection, they are usually offered infrequently and irregularly, with the length of the open enrollment period generally being only one or two weeks.

an illustration, suppose Bill Foege accepts a job with BNM Corporation, which has a death benefit plan in which employees who participate must pay some of the cost. Bill believes he is quite healthy and has better alternatives for his money, so he decides not to participate in the plan. Two years later, Bill discovers that he has cancer and wishes that he was covered by the BNM plan. If the plan had no restrictions governing Bill's ability to enter it under these circumstances, it is easy to envision how losses might become excessive over time.

The other eligibility consideration is that the death benefit usually does not become effective for a particular employee unless that person is actively at work on the day the coverage is scheduled to go into force. As an example, consider the situation of Ann, who is a new employee with RTY Company. RTY has a death benefit plan that provides $50,000 in group life insurance for all employees who have worked for RTY for at least one month. Suppose Ann's coverage is due to begin on May 15, but she becomes ill on May 13 and remains at home sick for several days before dying on May 20. Because she was not actively at work on May 15, her group life insurance never went into effect, and no death benefit is payable from RTY's plan when Ann dies. It should be emphasized that this provision only relates to initial eligibility. Had Ann become ill on May 16 or later, her coverage would have gone into effect May 15 as scheduled and a death benefit would have been payable upon her death.

Contributory versus Noncontributory Plans

As previously noted, some death benefit programs require employees to pay part of the cost. These plans are said to be **contributory**. When the employer pays the full cost of the death benefits, the plan is **noncontributory**. It is generally assumed that all eligible employees in noncontributory plans will in fact participate, whereas less than 100 percent participation usually occurs with contributory plans.

If a contributory plan is established, the primary decision for eligible employees is whether to participate. In making this decision, employees should compare the required contribution to the benefits to be received, both currently and in future years. Group life insurance is usually less expensive than individual insurance, but exceptions exist. It is wise to consider the costs in relationship to the benefits rather than to assume that the group coverage offered in a particular situation is more economical than all alternative risk management tools.

The tax consequences should also be considered when deciding whether to participate in a contributory employee benefit program. Just as individual life insurance premiums are not tax deductible, neither is the part of the premium paid by the employee in group life insurance. However, the part of the premium paid by an employer for group life insurance is usually not fully taxable as income for the employee. Other tax effects to consider include the fact that death benefits paid from group life insurance proceeds are not taxable to the beneficiary for income tax purposes.

Structure and Level of Death Benefit

The amount of group life insurance provided for a particular worker is usually a function of either salary or job classification. If the employer's goal is merely to provide for funeral and burial costs, all participating employees may be given a flat amount of coverage, such as $10,000 or $15,000. More often, however, the amount of the death benefit depends on other factors. For example, suppose DSA Company structures its group life insurance program using the **salary bracket approach**, in which workers whose earnings are within various ranges are eligible for a specified amount of death protection. DSA workers earning less than $30,000 receive $20,000 in group life benefits, those who earn between $30,000 and $50,000 are eligible for $30,000 of coverage, and employees whose salaries exceed $50,000 have a $40,000 death benefit. Similar schedules can be devised for various job classifications for an employer that structures its group life program using the **job classification approach**. Thus, secretaries might receive $20,000 of coverage; factory workers, $25,000; sales personnel, $30,000; and managers, $35,000.

For employers interested in tying the size of the death benefit more closely to individual situations, an **earnings multiple approach** often is used. With this method, the death benefit for a particular employee is a specified multiple of that person's salary for the year. Multiples of one or two are commonly used by employers. Thus, if VBN Company uses a multiple of two in its group life program and Sam earns $40,000 this year, then Sam will be eligible for $80,000 in group life benefits under the VBN program.

Type of Insurance

The overwhelming majority of group life insurance plans provided by employers use **group term insurance** rather than some form of cash value coverage. One reason for this is related to the cost of coverage, while another is based on tax issues. As discussed in Chapter 16, for a given amount of premium dollars, more death protection can be purchased on a term insurance basis than with any other form of life insurance. Thus, if an employer is primarily interested in providing employees with death protection, term insurance is a logical choice. Income tax laws also tend to reinforce this decision. A portion of all premiums paid by the employer for cash value life insurance is usually treated as currently taxable income for employees. However, employer-paid premiums for the first $50,000 of term insurance for each worker are not taxable for employees. Term insurance can also be provided to cover the death of an employee's dependent. This form of group term protection is known as **dependent life**.

A variation of group term insurance is **survivor income benefit insurance (SIBI)**, which differs from regular group term insurance in that the benefit is expressed as income to specified survivors rather than as a flat amount. If no eligible survivors (such as a spouse or young children) exist at the time the employee dies, then no SIBI benefits are payable. As an example of the benefit structure in an SIBI plan, consider the program provided to employees of ABC Company. The death benefit under ABC's plan is 25 percent of the deceased employee's salary for a surviving spouse and 10 percent of salary for each surviving child under the age of 22. An overall maximum family benefit of $2,500 per month is used, with benefits payable for up to five years.

Many employers supplement their group term plans with **group accidental death and dismemberment (AD&D)** coverage. The AD&D benefit is payable only for deaths due to accidents, and the death usually must occur within 90 days of the accident's occurrence. Commonly excluded causes of death are suicide, disease, mental infirmity, infection, war, and flight in an aircraft other than a regularly scheduled commercial flight. Due to these limitations, the premium is much less than for regular group term coverage, and employees often pay most or all of the cost. As the name implies, AD&D policies also pay in the event of dismemberment. Loss of one hand, one foot, or sight in one eye results in a fractional payment of the face amount. For example, an AD&D policy that pays $100,000 for accidental death typically would pay $50,000 if the insured's right hand were to be severed at or above the wrist. If both feet, both hands, or sight in both eyes were lost, the full $100,000 likely would be payable.

In addition to providing current death benefits, some employers are interested in helping employees provide for financial needs because of death after retirement. One way to accomplish this goal is to continue term insurance coverage for retirees, although this option may be too costly for many firms. An alternative is for the employer to facilitate their employees' purchase of permanent insurance protection. Two forms of group coverage for retiring employees are **group ordinary** insurance and **group universal life**. The tax rules governing group ordinary insurance, which is usually a whole life coverage, are complicated. Thus, it is not a popular benefit. On the other hand, group universal life is growing in usage. To avoid tax complications, employees who participate in group universal programs must often pay the entire premium for such insurance. But because the coverage is written on a group basis, it may be less expensive than comparable protection purchased individually. In this way, the employer is providing a service to the employee by offering a group universal plan, even though the employer may not pay any of the premiums. As with other employee benefits, employees who have the opportunity to participate should carefully consider the costs and benefits in relation to their overall personal risk management programs.

Contractual Provisions

Group life insurance policies have many of the same contractual provisions found in individual policies. Examples include the right to assign benefits to others, a 30-day grace period, a waiver of premium option, and an incontestability clause. The misstatement-of-age clause differs, however, in that the amount of death benefit payable is not affected due to a misstatement of age. Instead, the employer is subject to an adjustment in the premium payable. As in individual coverage, the insured has the right to name a beneficiary to receive the policy proceeds. Most group plans also offer the same settlement options as in individual policies.

One provision in group life contracts that is not found in individual policies is the **conversion clause**. This clause, which is required in all states, provides that when an employee is no longer eligible for group coverage (usually due to termination of employment), he or she has the right to convert the coverage to an individual policy without having to prove insurability. To take advantage of the conversion privilege, an individual generally must apply within 31 days after termination from the group and must pay the premium applicable at the person's current age. In many cases, group coverage can be converted only into an individual cash value policy, although conversion of term coverage to an individual term policy may be allowed.

HEALTH EXPENSE BENEFITS

In addition to losses due to premature death, exposures associated with an individual's loss of health were introduced in Chapter 4. In this section, employee benefits designed to help employees pay for health care expenses are discussed.

Eligibility

As with death benefits, the first step in integrating employer-provided health expense benefits into an individual's personal risk management plan is to determine the extent to which a person and his or her dependent family members are eligible for the employer's plan. Most of the same considerations that were important for premature death benefits also are relevant for health expense benefits; that is, the employer may have a minimum service requirement before benefits are available. Furthermore, benefits may be limited to those employees who work at least a stated minimum number of hours each week and/or those persons employed in particular job classifications.

For a person to be eligible for benefits as a dependent of an employee, the first requirement is that the employee must be participating in the employer's plan. Dependent benefits are further restricted to those persons who meet other specified requirements. For example, if dependent coverage is offered, the spouse of an employee is nearly always eligible for the benefits. For an employee's children to be eligible, they usually must be unmarried and under a certain age, such as 19. If they are enrolled as full-time students, this age often is extended to age 22, or perhaps 25. Some plans provide dependent coverage regardless of age for mentally or physically handicapped children who are completely dependent on the employee for financial support. Natural and legally adopted children are treated the same for benefit eligibility purposes; stepchildren may or may not be eligible for benefits, depending on the circumstances and the plan provisions. If an employee has dependent coverage in effect, a

ETHICAL PERSPECTIVES

Duty to Inform

The importance of the group life conversion clause, and the employer's obligation to provide adequate benefits information to their terminating employees, is illustrated in a case involving a woman named Brown who was covered by a group life insurance policy. The policy provided that it could be converted to an individual policy without evidence of insurability within 31 days of termination of the group coverage. Brown was terminated by her employer, and her termination letter stated that she would receive information describing the impact of termination on her benefits. She did not receive the information for over three months, after at least two phone calls from Brown and two letters from her attorney requesting benefits information. Once Brown received her life insurance conversion form, she turned it in and was denied coverage because the 31-day conversion clause had expired. Brown sued her employer and was awarded $11,550 in penalties. In addition, the employer was required to provide her with life insurance coverage for the amount she was unable to convert minus the costs she would have incurred from the conversion.

Source: *Brown v Aventis Pharmaceuticals, Inc.* (2003 U.S. Court of Appeals 8th Circuit).

newborn is covered from birth in many plans. In less generous plans, coverage for the newborn may not become effective until the child reaches a specified age, such as 14 days.

Another eligibility consideration is whether retirees are included in the health benefit program. This issue has received intense scrutiny in recent years, as health care costs continue to mount and as regulatory bodies look more closely at promises made by employers in this regard. When benefits are granted to retirees, it is usually either through a Medigap policy that pays for items not covered by Medicare or through a **Medicare carve-out** arrangement, in which applicable Medicare payments are deducted before paying promised benefits.

Due to regulatory changes during the 1990s and the continuing sharp increases in the cost of health care, coverage for retirees of many employers is not as generous as was the case many years ago. In 1993, the Financial Accounting Standards Board (FASB) began requiring firms to report retiree health benefits as a liability that is accrued over employees' working lives. This requirement contrasts sharply with the prior practice of reporting such expenses on a pay-as-you-go basis, in which only the actual expenses paid for health benefits and/or insurance during the year were charged against income. Now, each year that employees work and earn the right to future health benefits during retirement, the employer must recognize these future costs on its balance sheet. All else remaining the same, this change results in reduced corporate earnings. In response to this change and in reaction to the continuing cost increases, many employers have made substantial cuts in their retiree health benefits. Some companies have eliminated the benefits entirely, while other firms have made changes in their retiree medical plans. Examples include increasing retiree contribution requirements, increasing the level of cost-sharing through deductibles and coinsurance, and tightening eligibility requirements. To preserve the right to make such changes, it is important that employers specifically state the right to reduce or eliminate retiree medical benefits in their medical plan documents.

Contributory versus Noncontributory Plans

Many employers provide noncontributory death benefits, but it is quite common to require employee contributions for participation in an employer's health expense benefit program. As health care costs continue to increase, it can be expected that the level of contributions required of employees will also increase as employers become less able to pay the full cost of meaningful health care benefits for their workers.

When an employee pays part of the cost for health expense benefits, employers are allowed to offer their employees a **premium conversion** option. In a premium conversion plan, premiums for health benefits are paid with pre-tax dollars rather than after-tax dollars, reducing the employee's taxable income. If premium conversion is not used, and therefore premiums are paid with after-tax dollars, the amount paid may or may not be tax deductible, depending on the employee's situation. According to the tax law, medical expenses (including medical insurance premiums) are deductible only from an individual's current taxable income to the extent that total medical expenses exceed a threshold level equal to 7.5 percent of adjusted gross income for the year. Thus, for practical purposes, many persons are unable to benefit from the tax deductibility of contributions for health expense benefits. For example, consider the Loshuertos family. Bob earns $50,000 a year; his wife, Shirley, earns $35,000. This year, they contributed $2,000 for their health coverage at work, and they had $3,000 worth of unreimbursed medical expenses. Assuming that their adjusted gross incomes for tax purposes exactly equal the sum of their salaries, then the 7.5 percent threshold this year is $0.075 \times (\$50,000 + \$35,000)$, which equals $6,375. Because the total of their medical expenses ($3,000) and contributions for health benefits ($2,000) is less than this $6,375 threshold, the actual tax deduction associated with these expenses will be $0. This computation is summarized in Table 19-1. Now consider the case in which the total of the Loshuertos' medical expenses and contributions for health benefits is $7,000 instead of $5,000. As illustrated in Table 19-1, their medical deduction would be $625, which is the excess of their expenses ($7,000) above the threshold level ($6,375). Had Bob's and Shirley's employers both offered premium conversion plans, both of them could have avoided taxation on the full amount of their health insurance premiums.

Whether the employee premiums are paid with pre-tax dollars or after-tax dollars, the opportunity to participate in an employer's health expense benefit plan will prove cost-effective for most people. However, in some instances it makes sense to reject coverage under a contributory plan. In the most common situation, a husband and wife are covered under different employee health plans. If coverage for their dependents is an option under each plan, then they must decide whether to cover their children under one or possibly both of their employee

TABLE 19-1   Deductibility of Medical Expenses: The Loshuertos Family

	Case 1	Case 2
Bob's earnings	$50,000	$50,000
Shirley's earnings	35,000	35,000
Adjusted gross income	$85,000	$85,000
	× 0.075	× 0.075
Medical threshold (A)	$ 6,375	$ 6,375
Health insurance premiums paid	$ 2,000	$ 2,000
Unreimbursed medical expenses	3,000	5,000
Total health expenses (B)	$ 5,000	$ 7,000
Tax deduction (B − A or $0 if A is greater than B)	$ 0	$ 625

health plans. In making this decision, they will need to compare benefits, exclusions, and limitations, in addition to the relative costs associated with each plan.

Providers of Coverage

As discussed in Chapter 17, the major providers of health expense coverage are insurance companies, Blue Cross–Blue Shield organizations, health maintenance organizations (HMOs), point-of-service (POS) plans, and preferred provider organizations (PPOs). Within their health expense benefit programs, employers often use more than one of these providers. Some employers also set up self-funded benefit programs that do not involve any of these providers. In so doing, such an employer may contract for the services of a third-party administrator to handle claims and other administrative functions associated with their plans, but the employer remains responsible for paying all promised benefits from their own funds.

In this section, the emphasis is on the characteristics of health benefit providers that should be considered by employees when analyzing their health expense benefits. Such analysis is especially important when employees must select their health benefits from among several alternatives presented by the employer.

Choice of Physician

When an insurer, the Blues, or a self-funding arrangement is used to provide health expense benefits, the employee will typically have freedom of choice regarding the physicians, hospitals, and other settings in which to seek medical care. In contrast, employees covered by an HMO must obtain medical services from doctors and others who belong to the HMO, except in emergency situations arising while the employee is out of town. When a PPO or POS plan is used in an employee benefit plan, the employee can make a choice regarding physicians each time medical services are needed, but higher cost-sharing will be required if an out-of-network provider is chosen.

When an employee is new in town and has not yet established any relationships with doctors, the restrictions that some benefit arrangements place on the selection of physicians may be inconsequential. But when long-standing relationships exist, many employees prefer to maintain those relationships through participation in a benefit program that grants freedom of choice among medical care providers.

Coverage and Exclusions

No standard set of medical needs is always covered or always excluded in employee health expense benefit programs. Thus, employees must analyze all of the programs available to them to ascertain which ones are likely to meet their needs. Health care expenses often are categorized as to whether they involve hospitalization, physicians' and surgeons' services, dental care, mental health care, long-term care, prescription drugs, or other types of medical expenses. Not all benefit programs cover all of these needs to the same extent. However, several characteristics that are often associated with plans offered by various kinds of providers can be noted.

First, traditional insurance plans may exclude routine types of medical expenses on the grounds that insurance benefits should be reserved for unexpected medical problems. An annual physical exam, for example, may not be covered under a benefit program provided through an insurer, whereas it usually is covered within an HMO or a POS plan. These latter plans usually place more emphasis on preventing small problems from becoming larger ones. Due to the demonstrated success in this regard, though, traditional insurance plans are now beginning to pay for more routine, preventive types of medical expenditures than was the case several years ago. Another difference may involve benefits that various states require to be offered. In some jurisdictions, these state-mandated benefits apply only to plans offered through insurers and the Blues. Examples include coverage of at least a specified amount for alcohol

and drug abuse treatment. Regardless of the benefit provider, federal law requires all employers with at least 15 employees to provide coverage for pregnancy-related expenses on the
same basis that they cover other health problems.[6]

Cost to the Employee

In analyzing health benefit plans, an important point of comparison is the relative cost of each
plan. Two cost aspects should be considered. The first is the amount of monthly contribution
(if any) that is required of the participating employee. This amount depends more on the employer's plan design than on the type of benefit provider. The second consideration is the
amount of cost-sharing that will be incurred by the employee at the time medical services are
sought. Plans offered by insurers and by the Blues usually have both coinsurance and deductibles, as described in Chapter 17. If coverage is provided for dependents, the coinsurance
and deductible provisions may be established on a family basis, with an overall limit on the
amount of cost-sharing to be borne by the employee's family in any one year. Most plans offered by insurers also have stated lifetime limits. In contrast to this type of plan design, cost-
sharing for participants in HMOs usually is minimal, and maximum benefit limits may not
exist. Between these two extremes are the POS and PPO arrangements. When employees
choose to receive care from nonnetwork doctors, the cost-sharing provisions are greater than
when treatment is provided by specified providers.

Other Provisions

Employers must make a number of decisions about their health expense benefit plans in addition to who is eligible, who will pay the cost of benefits, and who will provide the service.
Several of these decisions that have particular importance for employees are discussed in this
section.

Cost Containment

As noted throughout this and many previous chapters, health care costs have increased rapidly in recent years. In response to this, employers now include a number of cost-containment
provisions in their health benefit programs. The generic name used for many such provisions
is **managed care**. The challenge of managed care is to control costs in a manner such that
quality medical care is available at an affordable price. One general approach in this regard is
to try to reduce the unnecessary use of health services by employees and their families. The
various forms of cost-sharing that have already been discussed are examples of one way to reduce use. The required use of primary care physicians rather than allowing direct access to
specialists would be another example. Another way to reduce unnecessary use of health services is **precertification** of benefits, which requires that certain nonemergency medical services be authorized before the delivery of treatment. Although once used primarily with dental care benefits, precertification is now used for many types of medical procedures. If the
required precertification is not obtained, then the benefits provided by the employer's plan are
usually reduced. Precertification is a special case of the more general **utilization review** programs that are not limited to the time before treatment. Utilization review can be ongoing,
with the degree of review often dependent on the benefit dollars involved. Many businesses
specializing in utilization review have opened in recent years to take advantage of the increased demand for these types of services.

Another general approach for containing health care costs is to try to have treatment provided at the least costly locations. For example, some surgeries may be performed in a doctor's office or in a hospital on an outpatient basis, thus saving the cost of hospital room and

---

6   More details of state mandates in health insurance are discussed in Chapter 17.

PROFESSIONAL PERSPECTIVES

A Bitter Pill to Swallow

The rising cost of prescription drugs has become a hot issue in recent years. Adjusted for inflation, the cost of prescription drugs to private health insurance plans has more than tripled between 1993 and 2000, skyrocketing from $17.4 billion to $56.3 billion. Possibly more concerning to plan sponsors is the fact that private insurance has gone from paying 28 percent of the prescription drug bill to 46 percent over that same period.

One of the factors behind this rise in prescription drug spending is the explosive growth of direct-to-consumer (DTC) advertising, which promotes specific brand name drugs through the popular media. As a result of these marketing techniques, consumers may feel as if prescription drugs can be a simple solution to problems that previously required behavioral modification (Lipotor®—cholesterol reducer), therapy (Prozac®—antidepressant), or simply acceptance (Propecia®—hair loss treatment). According to a study by the Kaiser Family Foundation, every dollar of the $2.5 billion spent on DTC drug advertising in 2000 generated over $4 in new sales.

How can plan sponsors combat these increasing costs to their plans? Many are taking a harder look at their plan's provisions for covering prescription drugs. The implementation of a drug *formulary* can help. A formulary is a publication by the plan sponsor listing brand name prescription drugs for which the plan sponsor can negotiate the best price. Combining the formulary with the enticement of a lower copayment to use formulary-listed drugs should yield a reduction in drug costs. Further, "lifestyle drugs" may be omitted from coverage or have their coverage rationed. Lifestyle drugs are those that are primarily used for cosmetic purposes, have questionable medical value or treat poor lifesytle choices like smoking. Finally, employers can analyze their utilization data to find a "heavy hitter" drugs that are primary drivers of total drug costs. Armed with this information, plan sponsors can further fine-tune their cost containment strategies.

Source: Joseph Ruhland, University of Georgia, with statistics from *Source Book of Health Insurance Data 2002* (Washington, D.C., 2002): 104 and Kaiser Family Foundation, *Impact of Direct-to-Consumer Advertising on Prescription Drug Spending* (June 2003), 4, 6.

---

board charges. Some employers design their benefit programs to encourage these forms of treatment by applying lower coinsurance and/or deductibles when the employee chooses the less costly alternative. Even when a person must be admitted for an overnight hospital stay, some tests may be performed on an outpatient basis, thus reducing the number of days for which room and board expenses will be incurred. Another example involves the authorization of hospice use by terminally ill employees or dependents. A hospice can be located in a special wing of a hospital or in a freestanding location, or it can be an organization that provides care at terminally ill patients' homes. Regardless of its structure, the intent of a hospice is to provide for the humane, dignified care of dying persons. No aggressive, expensive treatment is given merely for the purpose of prolonging life for a few extra days or hours. Rather, persons are allowed to "die with dignity," often at home in the presence of their families. By including hospices within their definitions of allowable facilities for the receipt of medical services, employers can reduce the expenses that might otherwise be incurred by terminally ill employees.

A third general approach to containing health care costs involves trying to avoid payments for charges never incurred. In addition to increased efforts to detect fraud by employees and/or physicians and hospitals, this approach also includes efforts to eliminate overpayments resulting from billing errors by hospitals. Because many hospitals are understaffed and overworked, it is not uncommon for charges to appear on hospital bills by mistake. For example, a particular test may be ordered and later cancelled, with the charge for the test still being made. Or supplies such as bandages and tissues may be charged to the wrong patient. If the overall hospital bill is more than $15,000, then the employer, insurer, or other provider may request an audit to verify all of the charges. However, such audits cost money themselves, and they are rarely cost-effective when the original bill is not large. For cases involving smaller amounts, employers sometimes structure financial incentives for the employees themselves to monitor their hospital expenses. When an employee detects an unwarranted charge on a bill not scheduled for audit, some employers will share the expense savings with the employee. For example, if Jim is hospitalized and discovers a $200 charge on his bill for drugs that he never received, his employer may share the savings by giving Jim half—in this case, $100. By this practice, the employer pays less than it would in the absence of the employee's discovery, and other employees may be encouraged to monitor their bills in the future.

In another approach to containing health care costs, many employers are increasing their efforts to try to prevent medical problems in the first place. For most employers, a small portion of their employees use a disproportionate share of the health care dollars. These high-cost users are not only treated for the same conditions over and over again but also have a high probability of being heavy smokers and drinkers and have a tendency toward obesity. Development of aggressive fitness and **wellness programs** for employee groups, as an effort to modify the behavior of this "high-health dollar consumption" group, can have a major impact on the frequency and severity of medical claims. Benefit plan design that encourages early detection of small problems before they become larger and more expensive is receiving more widespread acceptance. Thus, the payment for routine health care that has traditionally been part of HMOs can be included in programs offered by other types of benefit providers as a way to contain long-term costs.

Finally, many employers are trying to contain health care costs by moving toward something called **consumer-driven health care**. The idea behind consumer-driven health care is to try to make employees better consumers of health care by giving them financial incentives to control costs, as well as providing them the information they need to make sound health care decisions. The financial incentives generally take the form of high deductibles. The employer generally partially funds the high deductible with a health reimbursement account. Unused amounts in the health reimbursement account can carry over from year to year, providing the employee with an incentive to control health care consumption. Along with the high deductibles and health reimbursement accounts, consumer-driven health plans usually try to provide extensive information to employees, most often via the Internet, to support employees in making the best health care decisions, considering both quality and cost. The movement toward consumer-driven health care received a major boost in 2004, when the federal government authorized the use of health savings accounts, as described in Chapter 17. These health savings accounts can be used in place of the health reimbursement accounts described previously, and are in many ways more flexible and attractive than health reimbursement accounts. It remains to be seen whether consumer-driven health care plans are the wave of the future, but many are predicting that they will revolutionize the health care system. Others argue they will be harmful, because they will penalize those who consume the most health care.

Coordination of Benefits

Sometimes an employee or a dependent is covered not only by the employer's health expense benefit plan but also by another benefit program or insurance arrangement. For example, Kathleen McCullough is covered as an employee under her own employer's plan and also as a dependent under her husband's plan. It is possible that her children might be covered as dependents under the plans of both of their parents' employers. Furthermore, Kathleen might have a small personal health insurance plan that covers some of the same expenses payable by her employer's plan. When a loss is incurred in such situations, the amounts payable by the various plans are governed by their **coordination of benefits (COB) provisions**. If a particular benefit plan does not have a COB provision, then it pays its promised amount, regardless of the amounts paid from other sources.

Because uniformity among employers is helpful in this regard, individual states generally specify the COB provisions to be included in plans offered by employers. Many states adhere to the COB provisions suggested by the National Association of Insurance Commissioners. Four basic principles are involved:

1. When a person owns personal insurance, the amount payable from the insurance does not lessen or otherwise affect the amount payable from benefit programs provided by employers. (Note, however, that the existence of benefits from an employer may very well affect the availability of benefits from personal insurance.)

2. The maximum reimbursement from all employer-sponsored plans is 100 percent of necessary and reasonable medical expenses incurred and covered by at least one of the employers' plans. (Note that, as a cost-saving measure, some employers provide that the combined reimbursement should actually be less than 100 percent. One approach is to specify that the total reimbursement will be at a level that is no greater than what the most generous plan would have paid if it had been the only one providing coverage.)

3. Dependent coverage is provided in excess of coverage as an employee. So if David is covered as an employee under Plan A and as a dependent under Plan B, then Plan A will pay all of its promised benefits first. Plan B will pay only if there are unreimbursed, covered expenses remaining after Plan A's benefits have been fully paid.

4. Children are covered first by the plan of the parent whose birthday is earlier in the year, unless the parents are separated or divorced. In such cases, the plan of the parent who has custody of the child pays first.

An example will clarify the application of these principles. Consider the Morales family. Victor is employed by BVC Corporation, which provides noncontributory health expense benefits for Victor; his wife, Angela; and their young son, Tony. The BVC plan has a $200 per-person deductible and an 80 percent coinsurance provision. Angela is employed by AGL Company, which covers Angela and her family on a noncontributory basis. The AGL plan has a $500 per-person deductible, but all other provisions are identical to the BVC plan. (See Table 19-2 for a summary of this example.) Suppose Victor and Tony are injured in an automobile accident. Victor incurs $1,000 in medical expenses, and Tony has $2,000 in expenses. Because Victor is a BVC employee, the BVC plan will pay first on his behalf. It will pay $640, which is 80 percent of the loss that exceeds the deductible [$0.80 \times (\$1,000 - \$200) = \$640$]. The remaining $360 of Victor's expenses are payable by the AGL plan. In Tony's case, the order of payment depends on when in the year Victor's and Angela's birthdays fall.

TABLE 19-2   Coordination of Benefits: The Morales Family

	BVC Plan	AGL Plan
Covered employee	Victor	Angela
Covered dependents	Angela, Tony	Victor, Tony
Deductible	$200	$500
Coinsurance	80%	80%
Payment for Victor's $1,000 loss	$0.8 \times (\$1,000 - \$200) = \$640$	$\$1,000 - \$640 = \$360$
Payment for Tony's $2,000 loss	$\$2,000 - \$1,200 = \$800$	$0.8 \times (\$2,000 - \$500) = \$1,200$

Suppose Victor was born on July 8, 1970, and Angela was born on March 8, 1974. Even though Victor is older than Angela, her birthday comes before his each year. Therefore, her employer's plan must pay first with respect to their son Tony's medical expenses. The AGL plan pays $1,200 [0.80 × ($2,000 − $500)], and the BVC plan pays the remaining $800. Note that in each situation the second plan pays the remaining expenses, so that the total reimbursement is 100 percent, or as specified by the second principle described previously.

Pre-Existing Conditions

In health benefit terminology, a **pre-existing condition** is a health problem that exists before health expense coverage becomes effective. Suppose a newly hired employee is six months pregnant at the time she begins work for WTO Company. The question arises as to whether the WTO health plan must pay for her maternity expenses, because the pregnancy was established before the employee was hired. In some senses, the provision of health benefits in such a case might be viewed in the same way as buying fire insurance on a building that is known to be burning. Before the 1996 passage of the Health Insurance Portability and Accountability Act (HIPAA), employees often were provided no coverage under employers' health plans for a period of time (such as one or two years) for problems arising out of pre-existing conditions. Thus, in the WTO example, the employer's plan would not have paid for the employee's maternity expenses if WTO used this provision. Any health problems that were not related to the pregnancy, however, would have been covered under the WTO health plan's usual provisions.

HIPAA changed things in this regard, however. Employers can now impose pre-existing conditions limitations in their health plans for a maximum period of one year. Furthermore, in satisfying this one-year period, employees must receive credit for the time that they were covered under previous employers' plans, individual health insurance policies, Medicare, and/or Medicaid if it has not been more than 63 days since this previous coverage was in effect. In this way, once an individual satisfies one 12-month pre-existing condition period, he or she will not be subjected to another for as long as continuity of coverage is maintained. For example, suppose George Anderson recently developed a kidney problem. He works for the Alliance Corporation and has been covered by Alliance's health benefits program for several years. George is contemplating resigning from Alliance to work for Bandstag, Inc. In earlier years, George might have hesitated to make this change, fearing that medical care for his kidney problem would not be covered under Bandstag's health plan. Now, though, since George was covered for more than a year under Alliance's plan, Bandstag must cover George under its plan and cannot limit his coverage due to his pre-existing condition.

Termination Rights

What happens to an employee's health expense benefits when he or she terminates employment with the sponsoring employer? If the termination is due to retirement, the employee may be eligible for coverage in a special retiree health plan. If the reason for the termination is disability, some employers will continue to cover the disabled employee in the group plan. When neither of these alternatives exists or is relevant for the situation, conversion to an individual health plan may be desirable. Many states require that an individual health insurance policy be offered in place of a group policy when an employee ceases to be an eligible group member. HIPAA provides additional protection. Under this legislation, individuals are assured of the availability of individual coverage, as discussed in Chapter 17. But this individual protection does not necessarily have to be as broad as the group insurance. Furthermore, the cost is nearly always more than before, because individual health insurance is more expensive than group coverage.

In an effort to deal with these types of problems, Congress passed the Consolidated Omnibus Budget Reconciliation Act (COBRA) in 1985, which applies to firms employing 20 or more employees. In general, COBRA grants former employees and previously covered dependents the right to continue participation in their group health plans for a specified period, even after they are no longer eligible under the plan's eligibility rules. Such persons can be required to pay the full cost of coverage plus an additional amount to cover expenses, but the total paid often is less than would be required if they converted to individual health insurance (often with less generous benefits). The maximum length of time for continued participation in the group program generally is 18 months for former employees and 36 months for formerly covered dependents, although the periods may be more or less, depending on the circumstances. After group participation ends, COBRA requires that individual conversion rights again be available to the extent that such rights exist. Because of the complexity of the rules and the need for extensive recordkeeping, COBRA often results in extra administrative costs for the employer. For terminating employees or dependents with no alternative health benefits, though, COBRA provides valuable rights that should not be overlooked.

netlink

For more details concerning your rights under COBRA, as well as information regarding COBRA-like statutes that many states have passed covering small firms, peruse the following site: http://www.insure.com/health/cobra.html.

DISABILITY INCOME BENEFITS

As noted in Chapter 4, the loss of health can result not only in substantial medical expenses but also in a reduction or cessation of income due to the inability to work. Some disabilities are only temporary, whereas others are permanent. Employee benefit programs vary considerably in the extent to which they address workers' potential loss of income due to injury or illness. When offered, benefits are usually restricted primarily to full-time workers and are designed as one or more of the following types: sick leave plans, short-term disability income plans, and long-term disability income plans. Many of the basic characteristics of disability income insurance, which can be used in connection with these employee benefits, were discussed in Chapter 17. The emphasis in this section is on the employee benefit-related issues involving the risk of loss due to disability.

Social Security Disability Income Benefits

Social Security provides for the payment of disability benefits, with the amount of the benefit dependent on the disabled person's previous earnings history. Benefits are increased if the worker has dependents, with each dependent receiving one-half of the benefit payable to the disabled worker, subject to a family maximum.

To be eligible for disability benefits, workers must have a specified minimum work record. Specific work requirements depend on the age at which disability occurs, but in general, one must have worked half of the 10 years before the time one applies for disability benefits. To prove disability, medical evidence must be provided, proving that the insured is unable to engage in substantial gainful activity. A 5-month waiting period is required, and the impairment must be such that it is expected to continue at least 12 months. Thus, an illness that is expected to be disabling for a period longer than 5 months but less than 12 months is not compensable under the law.

Sick Leave Plans

Sick leave plans, often called *salary continuation plans*, are usually designed to pay the full amount of an employee's salary during periods of temporary disability. Sick leave plans usually do not involve either disability income insurance or any other formal mechanism for funding the promised benefits. They are merely commitments made by the employer to continue paying an employee's regular salary for a specified time under stated conditions. If the period of illness or other health problem is only a few days, verification of the problem by a physician usually is not required. But if the inability to work extends beyond about a week, many employers require medical certification of the illness or injury.

Employees who are entitled to sick leave benefits should be aware of the rules regarding the accrual of benefit rights. For example, many firms specify that their workers accrue one day of sick leave for each month worked. Maximum limits on the number of days that can be accrued and/or carried forward to the next year may also be part of the plan design. For example, employees at EYO Company accrue one day of sick leave per month up to a maximum accrual of 30 days, and unused sick leave can be carried over from one year to the next. Karen has worked for EYO for three years (36 months) and has never taken a day of sick leave. When she falls and breaks her leg, she has the maximum limit of 30 working days of accumulated sick leave to draw on. If Karen is unable to work that entire time, her salary will continue without interruption. When those days are exhausted, further continuation of income benefits will depend on whether EYO has a disability income plan to supplement its sick leave arrangements.

Disability Income Plans

Short-term disability (STD) income plans and **long-term disability (LTD) income plans** are distinguished in the same way as STD and LTD insurance: STD plans have maximum benefit periods of about two years; any arrangement that might pay for longer than two years is usually classified as an LTD plan. From an employee's perspective, the most valuable LTD plan would be one that would pay, if necessary, until the age at which the employee would have retired had he or she not become disabled. But such plans can be quite expensive, and their availability varies. Other characteristics of disability income plans that are of importance to individual employees as they assess their personal risk management plans are discussed in the following sections.

Definition of Disability

As discussed in Chapter 17, *disability* may be defined in many possible ways. When an employer has an STD plan, the usual definition is the one requiring that the employee be unable to perform the major duties of his or her own occupation. For LTD plans, the definition is usually expressed in two parts. For the first one or two years, the own occupation definition usually applies. After that, an individual is classified as disabled only if unable to perform the major duties of any occupation for which he or she is qualified through education, training, or experience. As a further inducement to encourage disabled workers to try to return to gainful employment, many LTD plans also include partial disability benefits that are payable following periods of total disability. The definition of *partial disability* may be based on the applicable definition of total disability, or it may be based solely on the wages earned by the partially disabled employee in comparison to what he or she earned before the illness or injury.

Elimination Periods

Just as disability income insurance nearly always has an elimination (waiting) period before the payment of benefits, so do most STD and LTD employee plans. In analyzing their disability income benefits, employees should note the relative lengths of elimination periods and maximum benefit periods for STD, LTD, and sick leave plans. When more than one form of these benefits is provided, gaps and overlaps in payment periods sometimes result. For example, consider RFM Company, which has both an STD plan and an LTD plan but no special sick leave plan. The STD plan has a two-week elimination period and a maximum benefit period of six months. Although its LTD plan will pay benefits to age 65 if necessary, the LTD elimination period is a full year. Thus, a disabled RFM worker can start receiving STD benefits after two weeks but will have a six-month gap in benefits between the time the STD benefits end and the LTD benefits begin. Employees who are confronted with such potential gaps in their disability income benefits may want to make individual arrangements to fill those gaps with either individual disability income insurance or personal savings dollars.

Benefit Levels

Whereas most sick leave plans are designed to provide full income replacement, disability income plans usually provide only partial income benefits. In STD plans, the benefit may be as much as 75 percent of the salary before the disability, while in LTD plans the percentage is more often between 60 and 70 percent of salary. In both cases, dollar maximums also may apply. Suppose an STD plan has a benefit of 75 percent of salary but is subject to a $700 weekly maximum. If Jack is earning $1,200 a week at the time he is disabled in a freak accident at home, his weekly STD benefit will be $700. That amount, which is the maximum benefit payable, is less than 75 percent of what Jack was earning before his accident (0.75 × $1,200 = $900).

In contrast to individual disability income insurance, the benefits payable under most employer-sponsored STD and LTD plans are reduced to reflect any disability payments the employee receives from Social Security, workers' compensation, the employer's pension or other retirement plan, and the employer's sick leave plan. Thus, when the STD or LTD benefit is stated as a percentage of salary, that percentage is generally intended to be the total disability income payable to the worker from all sources other than private insurance benefits purchased individually. (An exception would be sick leave pay that fully replaces lost income.) As an example of the benefit reduction that takes place, consider Linda, who earns $1,000 a week before being injured at work. Her employer has an STD plan that will replace 70 percent of her earnings, but that benefit will be reduced to recognize the $200 weekly benefit Linda is scheduled to receive from workers' compensation. Thus, Linda will receive only $500 from the STD plan. Together with the $200 workers' compensation payment, she will have $700 a week, which is 70 percent of what she was making before her injury. Without reductions of these types, it is thought that employees would not have sufficient financial motivation to recover from their disabilities in a timely manner.

Contributory versus Noncontributory Plans

Because sick leave plans generally have no formal funding arrangements, in most cases they are noncontributory. STD plans also are often established on a noncontributory basis, although some employers require their employees to pay part of the cost. In contrast, most LTD plans are contributory and some are financed entirely by employee contributions. As with most employee benefit plans, employers receive a tax deduction equal to the contributions they make to fund disability income plans. Such employer contributions are not considered as taxable income for employees. When employees help fund the disability income plan, however, their contributions are not tax deductible.

The extent to which disability income benefits paid to an employee are taxable as income depends on how much the employee has contributed during a specified period (often the previous three years) toward the cost of the employer's plan. For noncontributory plans, all disability income benefits are fully taxable.[7] Benefits paid from employee-pay-all plans are completely exempt from income taxes. The reason for the distinction is that if employees do not

---

7 A small tax credit is available for persons who are permanently and totally disabled. See Section 22 of the Internal Revenue Code.

receive a tax deduction for their contributions, it is deemed unfair to tax them on benefits received from the plan. A similar rationale explains the taxation of benefits from contributory plans in which the employer and the employee share the cost of the plan. Suppose that during the three years preceding Carl's disability, he paid 40 percent of the cost of his coverage under his employer's LTD income plan. If Carl becomes disabled and collects LTD benefits from this plan, then 40 percent of those benefits will not be taxable because they are attributable to Carl's nondeductible contributions to the plan. But the remaining 60 percent of each benefit is attributable to the employer's contribution and is therefore considered to be taxable income for Carl when it is received.

SUMMARY

1. Employers make benefits available to their employees to improve employee relations and to take advantage of the special income tax status granted to many benefit programs.

2. In group insurance underwriting, the following criteria are especially important: purpose for which the group exists, group size, age composition, expected losses, and plan design features related to the possibility of adverse selection.

3. In specifying eligibility for their benefits, employers often use minimum age requirements, minimum service requirements, and restrictions regarding full-time service or work in particular job classifications.

4. If employees pay part of the cost for a benefit, the plan is contributory. When the employer pays the full cost, the benefit is noncontributory. Employee contributions for various benefits are treated in many different ways for income tax purposes.

5. There are several different forms of group life insurance, including group term, dependent life, survivor income benefit insurance, group accidental death and dismemberment, group ordinary, and group universal. Employees should carefully consider the costs and benefits of the available group plans in relation to their overall personal risk management program.

6. If an employee is given the right to choose among health expense benefits from many different providers, relevant factors to consider include whether a freedom of choice is given regarding doctors and hospitals, the monthly cost and the cost-sharing at the time medical services are rendered, and the coverage and exclusions associated with each plan.

7. Employers often include cost-containment measures in their health benefit plans. General approaches include designs to reduce unnecessary use of health services, attempts to shift treatment to the least costly locations, efforts to avoid payments for charges never incurred, and efforts to prevent medical problems from occurring.

8. In analyzing their health expense benefits, employees should consider the provisions related to the coordination of benefits, the coverage for preexisting conditions, and the rights given to employees who terminate employment.

9. Sick leave plans, short-term disability income plans, and long-term disability income plans are used to various extents by employers to help employees deal with the possible loss of income due to injury or illness.

internet*exercises*

1. Set your Web browser to the following site: http://www.insure.com/ and consider that you are a small local company looking for group medical insurance. Use the links to obtain quotes from at least three different insurers, using hypothetical ages for five different employees. What is the range of premiums you are quoted for the same set of plan provisions? What might explain this range of results?

2. Although many online sites are available for comparing insurance policies designed for individuals, it is harder for employers to do so yet. One such Web site designed for employers is at http://www.benefitmall.com. Explore this site from the perspective of a medium-sized employer with 75 employees. What features would be helpful in establishing a program that includes group life, health, and disability benefits? What additional features would you recommend for future online sites of this type?

QUESTIONS FOR REVIEW AND DISCUSSION

1. What are the main reasons that employers provide employee benefits?

2. List and briefly describe the four tax advantages that may apply to an employee benefit.

3. List three ways in which group insurance can be distinguished from individual insurance arrangements.

4. If a friend was considering participation in a contributory death benefit program and asked your advice about whether you felt participation was advisable, what factors would you urge your friend to consider?

5. ABC Corporation provides a choice of health benefit plans from which employees may choose. If an employee is deciding whether to choose a plan provided by an insurer, an HMO, a POS plan, or a PPO, what distinguishing characteristics would be important to consider?

6. What are consumer-driven health care plans? Would you be interested in having such a plan? Why or why not?

7. Define the term *pre-existing condition*. Explain how the Health Insurance Portability and Accountability Act of 1996 has affected employers' ability to impose pre-existing condition limitations in their health plans.

8. Define each of the following types of disability income benefit plans:
   a. Sick leave plans
   b. Salary continuation plans
   c. Short-term disability income plans
   d. Long-term disability income plans

9. What is the role of the OASDI wage base in financing the Social Security system?

10. A person recently complained, "My employer spends too much on employee benefits that I don't even need. I wish that employers would just give the money that they spend on benefits to the employees and let us decide what benefits we want to purchase." Do you agree with this statement? Why or why not?

11. A nursing administrator at a large hospital is considering discontinuing a long-standing hospital policy of paying nurses their full regular salaries for days that they are sick, up to a maximum of two days per month. The administrator has noticed that the nurses claim to be sick more often than hospital employees who are not eligible for full sick pay compensation. Discuss the factors that you believe the administrator should consider before making this decision.

12. As a general rule, individuals may purchase a given amount of insurance coverage at a lower price from a contributory employee group insurance plan than they can purchase on their own. State several reasons that explain this general rule. Discuss situations in which this general rule might not be true.

13. Jim and Peg Carmichael are married and have two young children. Jim's employer provides a contributory health expense plan for both Jim and his dependents. Peg is currently looking for a new job. One firm that has offered her a job has a noncontributory group health plan for employees, but dependents are added on a contributory basis. If Peg accepts this job offer, which employer plan(s) should the Carmichaels select for coverage of their family? What are the relevant factors they should consider in making this decision? Explain.

chapter 20

Los Amigos Mexican Restaurants, Inc., is beginning its fifth year of operation in the Chicago metropolitan area. The company, owned by José and Maria Garcia, opened its first restaurant two blocks from Wrigley Field and enjoyed immediate success with both local residents and Cubs baseball fans. After only a year, Los Amigos opened its second restaurant in a western suburb; it currently operates in seven different locations throughout the area. Thus far, Los Amigos' fast growth has prevented the Garcias from spending much time considering things like retirement and employee benefits, but that situation is about to change.

As the number of Los Amigos locations has expanded, José and Maria have been forced to rely on the management skills of others to actually run the restaurants. They are very careful in choosing managers, but when they find the right people, they hope to keep them on the job for many years. Thus, it is clear that Los Amigos must analyze and improve the employee benefits it offers to its workers, especially its managers.

The Garcias know that employees will differ in their appreciation of various benefits. At the same time, they realize that all workers should be concerned with whether they will have sufficient income after they are no longer able or willing to be fully employed. In investigating ways they might provide some retirement benefits for their employees and at the same time improve morale and employee retention, José and Maria were surprised at the many different possibilities and the complexity involved with each one. For example, should they set up a pension plan, a deferred profit-sharing plan, or both? How can they restrict eligibility to avoid spending too much on short-term employees? Can the plan be designed to provide the most generous benefits to restaurant managers? How do the Social Security taxes paid by the Garcias affect their employees' retirement income? Are there arrangements Los Amigos can make at little cost that would facilitate additional retirement savings by the employees? These and similar questions are addressed in this chapter.

Employee Benefits: Retirement Plans

CHAPTER OBJECTIVES

After studying this chapter, you should be able to

1. Describe the factors important in determining Social Security retirement benefits and explain the implications of the Social Security retirement test for retirees.

2. Differentiate between defined benefit and defined contribution pension plans, and describe the cash balance version of the defined benefit pension.

3. Explain the basic pension qualification rules regarding eligibility, retirement ages, form of payment, maximum benefits, maximum contributions, and vesting.

4. Explain the importance of actuarial cost assumptions.

5. Describe the nature and purpose of deferred profit-sharing plans.

6. Distinguish between thrift plans and 401(k) plans and explain the tax advantages associated with each of them.

7. Describe the special purposes for which SIMPLE, Keogh, and 403(b) plans were designed.

As noted in Chapter 18, the traditional ("three-legged stool") approach to retirement planning involves three pieces: Social Security, personal savings, and one or more employer-sponsored retirement plans. Employer-sponsored retirement programs can be an especially crucial element in individuals' plans for dealing with their loss of income upon leaving the workforce. Numerous types of retirement income benefits can be provided to employees, and many employers offer more than one type of benefit. Some retirement benefits can be given to all employees, whereas others may be provided as options to supplement a basic retirement plan. When combined with Social Security and supplemented with personal savings, many retirement plans make it possible for individuals to maintain their standard of living after their exit from the workforce. The most commonly available retirement income benefits are described in the following sections.

SOCIAL SECURITY RETIREMENT BENEFITS

Risk managers must consider alternative tools available for managing the retirement risk. Government programs such as Social Security are important in this regard. The level of retirement income that can be expected from Social Security depends on many factors, including the age an individual elects to begin receiving benefits, the number of years he or she worked in employment subject to Social Security taxes, and the wages earned in such employment. The age at which retirees can begin collecting their full benefit amounts, sometimes called the **Social Security normal retirement age**, has historically been 65. However, as detailed in Table 20-1, this age is gradually increasing and is scheduled to reach 67 for those born in 1960 or later.

Workers retiring at the Social Security normal retirement age after a lifetime of full-time employment at salaries equal to the OASDI wage base (see Chapter 19) can now expect to receive a benefit of approximately 25 percent of what they earned just before retirement. Workers with a lower earnings history can expect a benefit that is relatively higher in relationship to prior earnings. For example, if John Barker earns (in 2002 dollars) $25,000 per year during his career he can expect a Social Security retirement benefit of about 45 percent of his

TABLE 20-1	**Future Social Security Normal Retirement Ages**

Year of Birth	Retirement Age
1937 and before	65
1938	65 and 2 months
1939	65 and 4 months
1940	65 and 6 months
1941	65 and 8 months
1942	65 and 10 months
1943–1954	66
1955	66 and 2 months
1956	66 and 4 months
1957	66 and 6 months
1958	66 and 8 months
1959	66 and 10 months
1960 and after	67

preretirement wages.[1] As explained in this chapter, workers can retire earlier than their Social Security normal retirement age, but their benefits will be relatively lower than would otherwise be the case. A worker also may be entitled to additional benefits on behalf of a spouse or dependent children; such benefits will increase the overall Social Security benefits in comparison with preretirement wages.

Relationship of Work History to Benefit Amount

Social Security retirement benefits are based on average earnings in employment subject to Social Security taxes. The actual calculations necessary to derive a particular individual's benefit can be quite complex. Thus, the intent of this section is to provide you with sufficient details to understand the basic principles underlying the relationship between benefits and earnings history, without describing every detail of the calculations.[2]

The period for computing average earnings begins with the year 1950 (or the year in which an individual reaches age 22, if later) and ends in the year before the individual's attaining age 62. The actual earnings during this period are adjusted for changes in average wage levels. The resulting figure is called the **average indexed monthly earnings (AIME)**. From this number is calculated the **primary insurance amount (PIA)**, on which all retirement benefits are based.

The formula for transforming the AIME into the PIA is intentionally designed to weight lower earnings more than higher earnings. For example, Holly Liersch and Steve Cooper each became eligible for Social Security benefits in 2004. Holly's AIME was $500, whereas Steve's was $3,000. Given these inputs, Holly's PIA is calculated to be $450, which is 90 percent of her AIME. Steve's PIA is $1,314.96, which is greater than Holly's on an absolute dollar basis. But on a relative basis, Steve's PIA is only 43.8 percent of his AIME.[3] The actual retirement benefits that will be paid to Holly and Steve will be based on their PIAs, in conjunction with other relevant factors.

Benefits Payable to Retired Workers

The initial monthly Social Security benefit for a retired worker equals that person's PIA if he or she begins receiving benefits at the Social Security normal retirement age. Many retirees elect to begin collecting benefits before that age, however, with 62 being the earliest age at which benefits may begin. An actuarial reduction of 5/9 of 1 percent occurs for each of the first 36 months that a worker retires "early" (in other words, before the Social Security normal retirement age), plus an additional 5/12 of 1 percent for each additional month early. This reduced benefit will continue to be payable even after an early retiree reaches the normal retirement age.

Benefits for workers who delay benefits until *after* the normal retirement age also are adjusted actuarially, through increases for each month "late" (again, after the Social Security normal retirement age). The specific amount of the increase is 7.5 percent per year for those reaching age 62 in 2004; this percentage figure is scheduled to increase to 8 percent for those reaching age 62 in 2005 or later.

---

1   The 25 and 45 percent numbers are estimated average replacement ratios (initial Social Security benefit divided by prior year's earnings) that are applicable in 2003 for the earnings levels noted. See *2003 Social Security Summary* (Philadelphia: Hay Group, Inc., 2003), 24.

2   For a more detailed explanation in this regard, see *2003 Social Security Summary* (Philadelphia: Hay Group, Inc., 2003), 12–19.

3   For 2004, the PIA equals 90 percent of the first $612 of the AIME, plus 32 percent of AIME between $612 and $3,689, plus 15 percent of the amount by which the AIME exceeds $3,689. The dollar amounts in this formula are adjusted annually to reflect changes in average wage levels.

To illustrate the impact of the actuarial adjustments due to retirement age, consider the situation of Joe Walker, who was born in 1942 and thus turns 62 in 2004. Joe's AIME yields a PIA of exactly $1,000. Given Joe's Social Security normal retirement age of 65 and 10 months (see Table 20-1), if he were to begin collecting Social Security benefits immediately upon turning 62, he would be considered to be beginning his benefits 46 months "early." Therefore, Joe's monthly benefit would equal $[1 - (5/9)(0.01)(36 \text{ months}) - (5/12)(0.01)(10 \text{ months})] \times \$1,000 = \$758$. On the other hand, if Joe waits until he's 65 and 10 months, he can receive the full $1,000 as a monthly benefit. Suppose, however, Joe discovers that he is not ready to retire at 65 and 10 months. If he were to delay retirement until age 67 in the year 2009, the annual actuarial increase will be 7.5 percent for each year after normal retirement age, and his benefit would be $[1 + (0.075)(1.167 \text{ years late})] \times \$1,000 = \$1,088$ per month.

It is also possible to receive Social Security retirement benefits without totally exiting from the workforce. But limits are placed on how much younger retirees, those under the Social Security normal retirement age, may earn before a reduction in Social Security benefits is triggered. Once retirees reach their Social Security normal retirement age, they may earn an unlimited amount of income and still collect the full Social Security benefits to which they are entitled. Retirees who are younger than the Social Security normal retirement age can earn up to $11,640 per year (as of 2004) without penalty. This dollar limit for this **retirement test** is adjusted annually with changes in average wages. For earnings exceeding this limit, the worker's Social Security benefit is reduced by $1 for every $2 in wages. A variation of this rule applies during the year in which a worker reaches Social Security normal retirement age. For that calendar year in those months prior to the worker reaching normal retirement age, the limit is $2,590 per month (as of 2004) and benefits are reduced by $1 for every $3 in wages above the limit. In considering the effects of these limitations, it should be noted that only earned income is counted. Funds received from investments, pensions, annuities, and interest are not considered in applying the retirement test.

The application of the retirement test is illustrated by the case of 63-year-old Darleen Krautwurst, who earned $21,640 in 2004, when the applicable limit was $11,640. When Darleen exceeded the yearly limit of $11,640, her monthly benefits decreased by one-half of the excess. Thus, because Darleen earned $10,000 above the limit, she lost $5,000 (which is one-half of the excess) in Social Security benefits for the year. No penalty will apply after Darleen attains Social Security normal retirement age.

After an individual begins receiving retirement benefits, those benefits are automatically increased annually for changes in the cost of living. For this purpose, the cost of living is measured by the Consumer Price Index for All Urban Wage Earners and Clerical Workers, as published by the U.S. Department of Labor. The purpose of these annual cost of living adjustments is to help assure that Social Security retirement benefits maintain their purchasing power throughout a person's retirement.

Benefits Payable to Spouses and Children

As previously noted, a retired worker's spouse and dependent children may be entitled to Social Security benefits based on the worker's earnings. The benefit amount for a spouse who has attained the normal retirement age is 50 percent of the worker's PIA. However, spouses can elect to collect as early as age 62 at an actuarially reduced level or at any age if they are caring for children under age 16. The spouse is not required to be financially dependent on the retired worker in order to collect the benefit, but spouses who have earned income are impacted by the retirement test in the same manner as for retirees, as previously described.

An increasingly common situation is for both husband and wife to be entitled to Social Security retirement benefits on the basis of their own earnings history. The question arises as to whether such people are still entitled to receive spouses' benefits from Social Security. The basic rule governing these cases is that an individual is entitled to receive only the one Social Security benefit that will pay the greatest monthly income. Consider Wayne and Linda Linke, who are both about to retire at age 65. Wayne's PIA is $1,000, and Linda's is $800. The monthly benefit that Wayne would be entitled to as Linda's husband ($400) is less

Visit the U.S. government's Social Security Web site (http://www.ssa.gov/) for current news updates, index of topics, and an online request form regarding your earnings history.

than the $1,000 he could collect based on his own earnings. Similarly, Linda can collect more due to her own earnings ($800) than what she would receive as Wayne's wife ($500). Thus, they should each elect to collect their Social Security benefits based on their own earnings.

In some cases, children of retired workers are young enough to be entitled to Social Security benefits. The child's benefit amount is 50 percent of the worker's PIA, and eligibility is generally limited to unmarried children under the age of 18. This age limit is extended through age 19 if a child is a full-time student in elementary or high school, and the age limit is removed entirely for unmarried children who became severely disabled before age 22 and who continue in that condition.

Taxation of Benefits

Social Security retirement benefits are not subject to federal income tax unless one's adjusted gross income, including nontaxable interest income and one-half of the Social Security benefit itself, exceeds certain limits. For example, if half of an individual's Social Security benefit plus investment income exceeds $25,000 (or $32,000 if married and filing jointly), then one-half of the Social Security benefit is taxable. But if this same amount exceeds $34,000 (or $44,000 for married persons filing a joint return), then 85 percent of the Social Security benefit is taxable.

For example, widower David Ludvigson is age 68. His income this year consists of $60,000 from investments and $10,000 from Social Security. Because $60,000 + (0.5 × $10,000) is $65,000, which exceeds the $34,000 limit, David must pay federal income taxes on 85 percent (0.85 × $10,000 = $8,500) of his Social Security benefit.

PENSION PLANS

Another important retirement tool available to risk managers is the **pension plan** which is an employer-sponsored arrangement established with the primary goal of systematically providing retirement income for employees. Pension plans can be structured in different ways. Three of the most common structures are explained in the following sections.

Traditional Defined Benefit Pension

A traditional **defined benefit plan** has a formula for determining the monthly pension payments during retirement. Often, an employee's salary history and number of years of service are inputs for the formula. It is up to the employer to make sure that enough money has been set aside to fund the promised pension at the level indicated by the benefit formula. For example, consider JKL Company's benefit formula, which specifies that retirees will receive a pension equal to 2 percent of their final salary for every year of service with JKL. Ginny White is retiring after working for JKL for 30 years. Her final annual salary is $80,000. Based on her salary and years of service, Ginny is entitled to a pension of $48,000 a year (0.02 ×

$80,000 \times 30$), or $4,000 a month. While Ginny was still working, it was JKL's responsibility to contribute enough to the pension plan to fund this promised benefit.

Defined Contribution Pension

In contrast to the traditional defined benefit approach is the **defined contribution pension**. With this type of plan, the employer's annual contribution to the pension is specified, and the exact amount of the eventual retirement benefit is left undetermined until each person retires. For example, the employer may decide to contribute 7 percent of each participant's salary annually to the pension plan. These contributions will be invested during the employee's working career. The pension amount will depend not only on the level of the yearly contributions but also on the investment return earned on the contributions.

Many employers favor defined contribution plans because it is easier to budget the definite costs involved. Many employees also prefer knowing the value of their accounts throughout their working years, as is possible with defined contribution plans. Such plans also tend to be appealing to employees who anticipate changing jobs several times in their careers, because accumulated amounts usually are easily cashed out or rolled over to a new employer's plan when a worker terminates employment.

Cash Balance Pension

Starting in the late 1990s, many large employers with traditional defined benefit pension plans began converting them into **cash balance pension plans**. Although still technically considered to be defined benefit plans for Internal Revenue Code purposes, the converted plans look like defined contribution pensions in many ways. In particular, employees with cash balance pension plans have individual accounts that grow annually through both employer contributions and investment earnings. For example, consider the cash balance plan established by the RTY Company. Each participating RTY employee has an individual account balance that grows annually through: (1) a contribution by RTY equal to 5 percent of the employee's salary and (2) guaranteed interest equal to the current yield on 30-year U.S. Treasury bonds. Actually, both of these credits are merely bookkeeping entries and do not exactly correspond to what RTY actually contributes to fund the plan. Since RTY likely will invest plan assets in a variety of investment vehicles, the investment return often will be better than the guaranteed minimum. While RTY may occasionally elect to share some of these excess investment earnings with its employee participants, it is not required to do so and may instead use the favorable investment results to reduce its contribution below the 5 percent of salary credited to employee accounts. However, RTY will have to make up any investment losses that occur, since all employee accounts are credited each year with at least the guaranteed investment return. The fact that RTY retains the investment risk in a cash balance plan is the primary factor that makes such plans defined benefit plans from a technical perspective.

The cash balance plan is utilized to address perceived problems with the other pension structures. For example, many employees find defined benefit pensions difficult to understand. Because employees cannot see the dollar value of their accounts in a traditional defined benefit arrangement, they may not fully appreciate this retirement benefit. Further, traditional defined benefit plans are most valuable to employees who work for 30 or 35 years for the same employer. The traditional defined benefit pension is less useful to employees who work for several employers over the course of their careers. Of course, exactly this latter situation is becoming most prevalent in today's work environment. The cash balance plan effectively addresses this problem with the traditional defined benefit plan, while also meeting a concern with defined contribution pensions. That is, participants in a defined contribution plan may be uncertain as to whether they will have sufficient funds to provide themselves with an adequate pension. Investment earnings influence the ultimate size of the defined contribution pension fund, and no guarantees can be made about how large this fund will be at retirement

ETHICAL PERSPECTIVES

Cash Balance Plan Conversions

During the spring of 1999, in what soon would become a wave of such conversions, International Business Machines, Inc. (IBM), announced that it would convert its traditional defined benefit pension plan into a cash balance plan. IBM's announcement was met with outrage from many long-time employees, who alleged that the change would hurt them by reducing their retirement benefits far below what they had expected.

Although cash balance plans have many attractive features for young, mobile employees, transition problems often result when a company converts an existing defined benefit pension into a new cash balance plan. Employees who are close to retirement at the time of conversion will almost always fare better under the former defined benefit (DB) plan. Because traditional DB plans base benefits on employees' salaries at the end of their careers, workers' benefits tend to grow slowly in the early years of their careers, then rapidly in the final years. In cash balance plans, by contrast, benefits tend to grow steadily throughout employees' careers. Thus, older workers are often worse off after a cash balance conversion, since they will not experience the rapid growth in their benefit that they were an-

ticipating during their final years of work. Therefore, when a firm decides to convert an existing defined benefit pension plan, older workers are typically exempt from the conversion and are allowed to remain in the old plan. Midcareer workers also may be hurt by such a conversion; some companies allow such employees to remain in the old plan, some employers require them to move to the new plan, and some provide special transition benefits to help offset the perceived loss.

In the fall of 1999, IBM yielded to the pressure and announced that more of its midcareer workers could remain in the old defined benefit pension plan. However, many employees were still unhappy and eventually a lawsuit was filed against IBM alleging that the conversion constituted age discrimination. In the summer of 2003, a federal court ruled against IBM. That decision is under appeal, but the future of cash balance plans remains in doubt. Many analysts believe that under the reasoning applied in the IBM ruling, all cash balance plans would be illegal. This issue is being watched with great interest, considering about one-third of the largest 100 U.S. corporations have implemented cash balance plans.

Sources: "IBM to Increase Number of Workers Allowed to Choose Pension Plan," *Business Insurance*, September 20, 1999, 1–2; and Mary Williams Marsh, "Judge Says IBM Pension Shift Illegally Harmed Older Workers," *The New York Times*, August 1, 2003, A1, C9.

due to uncertainty about the performance of the securities markets over many years. This uncertainty is considerably lessened with cash balance plans, due to their guaranteed minimum return.

PLAN QUALIFICATION

Pension plans can be set up so that they are **qualified plans**, meaning that they meet the qualification rules in the Internal Revenue Code for favorable tax status. Employers sponsoring qualified pension plans can deduct their contributions from current taxable income, and taxation of investment earnings is deferred until the pension benefits are paid to retirees. Employees do not have to report employer contributions to qualified pension funds as taxable income before receiving benefits. At retirement, however, as pension income is received, it is considered taxable to the extent that the income was funded by the employer. If a pension plan is contributory, employees are not allowed to deduct their contributions from taxable income. But when benefits are received, rules similar to those governing the taxation of annuities (discussed in Chapter 18) are applied. That is, a portion of each pension benefit payment escapes taxation until the total amount of the employee's contribution has been recovered tax-free.

The amount that is not taxed is calculated by dividing the employee's total contribution to the plan by the number of expected benefit payments to be received, as specified in the following table:

Age When Distribution Begins	Number of Expected Payments
Less than age 55	360
Ages 55 to 60	310
Ages 61 to 65	260
Ages 66 to 70	210
More than age 70	160

For example, suppose Howard Mettee, age 65, contributed $390,000 during his working years to his employer's pension plan. If Howard is now scheduled to begin collecting a pension of $2,000 per month for life, he will have to pay taxes on only $500 of each $2,000 payment [$2,000 − ($390,000 ÷ 260) = $500].

The qualification rules for pension plans were established in 1974 by the landmark **Employee Retirement Income Security Act (ERISA)**. Many changes have occurred since the original passage of ERISA, with each new tax law generally making several adjustments in the qualification rules. In general, the rules for pension plans are more extensive than for other benefits, due to the sizable dollar sums involved, the magnitude of the tax advantages granted, and the overall importance of pensions to individual risk management plans. Some of the pension qualification rules are noted in the following sections, although a full and complete listing is beyond the scope of this book.[4]

Eligibility

As with other benefit programs, employers must establish eligibility standards for participation in pension plans. Employers do not have to use the same eligibility rules as used for other benefit programs, and many employers have stricter eligibility requirements for pension plan participation than for benefits such as group life and health insurance. It is not unusual to exclude part-time personnel and those working in specified job classifications from pension plans. Many employers also use both minimum age and minimum service requirements to establish an employee's eligibility for a pension.

Although employers are relatively free with other benefits to establish whatever logical eligibility requirements may be desired, their choices with respect to pensions are more limited. For example, the qualification rules prohibit use of a minimum age requirement exceeding age 21 or a minimum service requirement of more than one year. Consider CXZ Company, which has a defined benefit pension plan with the most restrictive minimum age and service requirements allowed by law. If Jim Liang, age 19, has just accepted a full-time job with CXZ, he does not have to be included in the pension plan until he satisfies both the age and the service requirements. After one year, Jim will meet the minimum service requirement, but he will still be only 20 years old. He will need to wait another year, until he is 21, to participate in the CXZ plan.

In establishing pension eligibility rules, employers also are particularly constrained by qualification rules designed to eliminate the favoring of very highly paid employees. These rules are quite complicated, but in general they establish two categories of workers: highly

---

4   See Burton T. Beam, Jr., and John J. McFadden, *Employee Benefits*, 6th ed. (Chicago: Dearborn Financial Publishing, Inc., 2001), Part Five, for a detailed discussion of retirement plan qualification rules.

compensated and nonhighly compensated. The tax code specifies tests for comparing the eligibility and participation of these two groups for the pension plan. If participation is not sufficient among persons in the nonhighly compensated group, then the pension plan may lose its qualified status.

Retirement Ages

All qualified pension plans specify a **normal retirement age**, which is the earliest age at which employees can retire and receive full pension benefits. Often, the normal retirement age is specified to be a particular age, such as 65 or 62. In other cases, the normal retirement age is whatever age an employee is when he or she completes a specified number of years of service. For example, consider TUI Company and WRE Corporation. Employees of TUI can retire with full pension benefits whenever they complete 30 years of service with TUI. WRE's pension plan uses a combination of age and years of service to specify its normal retirement age. A WRE employee can retire with full benefits at age 65 or after completing 25 years of service, whichever comes first.

Many pension plans provide special **early retirement** options for workers who want to retire before the plan's normal retirement age. Various age and service requirements usually exist before early retirement benefits are payable. Furthermore, the early pension benefit is usually at a reduced level to reflect the increased cost to the plan of early retirement. An example will clarify why the benefit is at a lower level. Consider SDF Company, whose defined benefit pension plan provides for a $2,000 monthly pension for all employees who retire at the normal retirement age of 65. However, retirement is allowed as early as age 55 for employees who have at least 20 years of service. SDF is putting aside money now to fund the promised lifetime pensions of $2,000 a month for employees retiring at age 65. Suppose Brett, who has worked for SDF for 20 years and is now 55 years old, selects SDF's early retirement option. How will Brett's early retirement affect SDF's planned funding? First, Brett will receive 10 additional years of payments by retiring at age 55 rather than waiting until age 65. Second, SDF will have 10 fewer years in which to set aside money for Brett's pension if he begins collecting benefits at age 55. Finally, contributions to the plan before Brett turns 55 will not earn as much interest as they would have if they had had an additional 10 years in which to accumulate before the start of benefit payments. For all of these reasons, it is unrealistic to expect the same $2,000 monthly benefit that would be payable at age 65 to be available at age 55. Unless the early retirement benefit is reduced to what is called its **full actuarial equivalent**, then SDF will have to pay additional money into the plan to pay for the increased cost associated with early retirement. By making appropriate assumptions about interest and mortality rates, actuaries can compute the reduced early retirement benefit that is mathematically equivalent to the benefit payable at the plan's normal retirement age. Using one set of interest and mortality assumptions, Brett's $2,000 pension starting at age 65 would be equivalent to about $845 a month starting at age 55. Employers are free to pay an early retirement benefit in excess of this amount. If they do so, however, additional funding obligations must be paid into the pension fund.

Retirement after the normal retirement age is classified as **late retirement**. Although early retirement benefits are not required, it is necessary for a plan to specify how it will treat workers who continue working beyond the normal retirement age. Before 1986, many employers were able to specify a **mandatory retirement age** of 70 years (or higher), at which all workers could be forced to retire if they had not already done so. A mandatory retirement age is now prohibited for most jobs. As a consequence, many pension plans experience instances in which workers do not retire at the normal age specified for the plan. What happens to the pension benefit in these cases? The same rationale that explained why early retirement benefits are reduced can be used to justify actuarial increases for late retirement benefits. Such increases are not required by law, however, and hence are rarely granted by employers.

ETHICAL PERSPECTIVES

Early Retirement Offers

In recent years, several of the largest U.S. employers have made special offers designed to encourage some of their employees to retire earlier than the ages specified in their retirement plans. A typical pattern is to first announce a large target number of jobs to be eliminated. Then employees meeting specified eligibility criteria are offered the opportunity to retire. If enough employees do not volunteer to leave, layoffs may be enacted to meet the targeted reduction.

A complicating feature of early retirement offers involves the provision of health insurance following retirement. If retiree health benefits are not included in the early retirement offer, the probability that significant numbers of employees will choose to retire early is much lower. Thus, the question arises as to whether an employer should be allowed to promise to provide health benefits and then renege on the promise at a future date. Several companies have done so, and many of them have had to argue their cases in court after affected employees filed lawsuits.

Employees typically assert that they relied on employer promises when deciding to give up well-paying jobs, future earnings increases, and additional years of service—all of which would have eventually translated into higher pensions and Social Security retirement benefits. They argue that they would have remained on the job, had they known their employers would not continue to provide retiree health benefits as promised. Thus, employees claim that the withdrawal of such benefits should not be allowed. The issue is particularly problematic when employers themselves are often struggling for survival in a fiercely competitive market environment.

Benefit increases associated with late retirement are primarily found in plans sponsored by employers seeking to provide additional incentives to encourage employees to continue working past the normal retirement age.

Form of Payment

Pensions are usually paid in some form of annuity (see Chapter 18). If an employee is married when the pension benefits begin, then the qualification rules specify that the benefit will be a joint and survivor annuity in which the survivor's portion is at least 50 percent of the joint portion. However, employees can select a different form of payment under various circumstances. For example, if the employee's spouse agrees in writing, then the joint and survivor pension can be waived in favor of a single life annuity paying a greater monthly benefit. In this case, when the employee dies, payments cease. Also, the plan design may allow employees to add a period-certain option to either the single life or the joint and survivor annuity. All of these options are the same in principle as those described for annuity contracts in general.

Sometimes employers offer an additional option, under which an employee reaching retirement age can elect to receive some or all of the promised pension immediately. Known as a **lump-sum distribution option**, this choice is most commonly provided in defined contribution pensions because the dollar value of an employee's pension account is easily determinable at the time of retirement. Employees who are offered this option should carefully analyze several factors before accepting it. Consider Jim, age 65, who is trying to decide whether to receive his pension as a single life annuity paying $5,000 a month for life or as one lump sum of $800,000. Jim may believe that he can invest the $800,000 to yield a more favorable rate of return than would be inherent in converting the $800,000 to a $5,000 monthly annuity. Jim's assumption about his investment prowess may or may not be true over the long run, but by taking the lump-sum distribution option, he gives up the lifetime income guarantee associated with the annuity option. Thus, regardless of his investing expertise, the

ETHICAL PERSPECTIVES

Pension Max

For married employees approaching retirement, financial advisors sometimes recommend an arrangement referred to as *pension max*. It involves the rejection of the joint and survivor pension option in favor of the higher single life benefit payable under the employer's retirement plan. To replace the protection that would otherwise be available to the retiree's spouse, a life insurance policy on the retiree is purchased, with the premiums paid from the higher monthly income received from the retirement plan. If the retiree's spouse dies first, then the insurance policy can be cancelled, and the retiree will have a higher pension benefit than would otherwise have been payable. To illustrate these concepts, suppose Joe Berry is about to retire and is given the choice of receiving either $5,000 a month for as long as he lives or $4,000 for as long as either he or his wife, Mary, is alive. Under the pension max approach, Joe would select the $5,000 option and then buy life insurance on his life, paying the premiums with some (or all) of his additional $1,000 monthly income.

This idea has its advocates and its skeptics. Some financial advisors have expressed doubt as to whether policies are readily available that are priced low enough to pay the same benefit to the worker's spouse. Furthermore, if the retirement plan makes provisions for periodic benefit increases due to changes in the cost of living, the pension max alternative will be less attractive. Other factors—such as interest rates, tax brackets, and the health of the retiree and spouse—can affect the desirability of pension max in a particular case. In many cases, the idea is more likely to be feasible for female retirees than for males. On average, women live longer than men, so the life insurance used to replace the joint and survivor option will be less expensive for a woman than for a man.

No universally true guideline regarding the desirability of pension max is possible. Perhaps the most that can be said is that each individual situation should be carefully examined before the guarantees associated with a joint and survivor option are rejected in favor of this type of alternative.

---

possibility exists that Jim may outlive his income if he takes the lump sum. On the other hand, if Jim has adequate retirement income from other sources, then the $800,000 may enhance the flexibility in Jim's personal financial plan without endangering his future income. A final consideration for Jim in making this decision is the role of income taxes. Assuming that the pension plan is a noncontributory one, both the $800,000 lump-sum payment and the $5,000 monthly payments would generally be taxable as ordinary income for Jim immediately on receipt. Although a few possible maneuvers are open to Jim to reduce his taxes on the $800,000 if he selects the lump-sum distribution option, the effectiveness of many of these possibilities has been reduced by tax law changes in recent years.

Other Plan Design Factors

Because the topic of pension plans is so complex, only the briefest of introductions is possible in this chapter. However, a number of factors not yet discussed warrant some consideration because they may be encountered by employees in analyzing the retirement income sources available to them.

Benefit and Contribution Limits

By law, the annual defined benefit pension for newly retiring individuals is limited to a specified dollar amount that is adjusted each year as average wages increase. For 2004, this limit was $165,000. For defined contribution plans, the yearly contribution to the plan is limited, not the annual pension. Currently, annual contributions to any one participant's account are limited to the lesser of 100 percent of that person's salary or $41,000. In addition to these limits, only the first $205,000 of earnings can be considered in either the benefit or contribution formula. The significance of all of these limits is primarily important for highly paid employees.

Suppose, for example, that LKJ Company contributes 10 percent of each person's salary into its defined contribution pension plan, subject to the legal limits. If Craig is the president of LKJ and earns $500,000, LKJ will be allowed to contribute only $0.10 \times \$205,000 = \$20,500$ to the plan on his behalf, instead of the $50,000 that would otherwise be required according to the LKJ contribution formula. To achieve its retirement income objectives for Craig and other highly paid workers, LKJ may decide to establish a nonqualified plan to supplement its qualified pension plan. Alternatively, Craig may need to save additional money on his own to maintain his desired standard of living following retirement.

Inflation Protection

When pension benefits or contributions are a function of salary, some inflation protection before retirement is automatically built into the plan. But the situation often is different once the worker retires. As noted previously in this chapter, the Social Security part of a worker's retirement income is subject to annual adjustments for inflation. But most plans provided by employers are not protected at all from inflation once the pension payments have begun, resulting in severe erosion of the retiree's purchasing power over time. As shown in Table 20-2, if a pension starts out at $100,000 a year and inflation is 4 percent, the purchasing power of this pension will be reduced to $82,190 after 5 years, to $67,560 after 10 years, and to only $45,640 after 20 years. If the inflation rate is greater than 4 percent, the erosion is even more severe. To counteract these results, some employers make periodic adjustments in pensions paid so that retirees receive the same or similar increases as are awarded to active workers. Other employers make annual adjustments to correspond to changes in the cost of living, usually with some annual limit. However, employees should be aware that inflation adjustments by employers are unlikely to completely offset the effects of inflation. This is one more reason why personal savings to supplement what is provided by employers and by Social Security are important components of a retirement plan.

Permitted Disparity

The benefit or the contribution in a pension plan may be affected by Social Security. Once called *Social Security integration* but now known in federal tax law as **permitted disparity**, this concept can be incorporated into a pension plan to allow the employer to "take credit" for the Social Security taxes paid on behalf of employees. As discussed in Chapter 19,

TABLE 20-2   **Effect of Inflation on Retirement Income—Real Dollar Value of a $100,000 Pension**

Years	Annual Inflation Rate (%)		
	4	6	10
5	82,190	74,730	62,090
10	67,560	55,840	38,550
15	55,520	41,730	23,940
20	45,640	31,180	14,860

Source: Calculated by the authors. See present value tables in Appendix A for other assumed rates of inflation.

employers pay half of the total Social Security tax for their employees, and employees pay the other half. However, no taxes are paid for earnings above an established level, which is adjusted each year to reflect changes in average wages in the country. Furthermore, at retirement, Social Security benefits restore a larger proportion of the wages of lower-paid workers than of higher-paid workers. All of these factors form the basis for the rationale of allowing pension plans to be more generous to higher-income employees than to lower-income employees. In this way, the combined retirement benefit from Social Security and the private pension replaces approximately the same percentage of preretirement income for everyone. For lower-paid workers, a proportionately greater share of the total will be from the Social Security system. Higher-paid workers will receive a greater proportion of their total from the pension plan. To keep employers from discriminating in favor of higher-paid workers to an unwarranted degree, complex rules govern the amount of the permitted disparity that is allowable.

Vesting

The degree to which a plan participant's pension rights are nonforfeitable, regardless of whether the employee continues working for a particular employer, is called **vesting**. The vesting provisions in a pension plan are relevant only for the contributions or benefits associated with the employer's contributions. An employee in a contributory pension plan always is entitled to a full refund (with interest) of his or her own contributions when terminating employment. The most common vesting provision in pension plans is to have full vesting take effect after five years. Before that time, workers who terminate employment are not vested at all and thus have no pension rights under the plan. This approach is sometimes referred to as **five-year cliff vesting**. A less common approach is for vesting rights to be phased in gradually. Various schedules are possible in this regard. For example, a worker might be 60 percent vested after three years of service and 100 percent vested after six years. Employers seeking to use a gradual method must vest at least as quickly as defined by the **graded seven-year vesting** method. According to this method, employees become 20 percent vested after three years of service, 40 percent after four years, 60 percent after five years, 80 percent after six years, and 100 percent after seven years.

Suppose 30-year-old Steve works for GHJ Company, which uses graded seven-year vesting in its noncontributory defined contribution pension plan. If Steve quits his job after five years when the value of his pension account equals $12,000, then the 60 percent vesting factor would be applied to the $12,000, resulting in a vested account value of $7,200. This $7,200 would remain in the GHJ pension fund unless GHJ offered to pay it immediately to Steve and he agreed to accept it. If left in the GHJ fund, it would continue to earn interest and would eventually be used to pay Steve a pension when he reached the plan's normal retirement age. Over time, the laws governing vesting have been modified several times, making it possible for more employees to achieve full vested pension rights much more quickly than was often the case in the past.[5] This fact, and the probability that many employees will change jobs several times during their working careers, make it likely that many future retirees will collect retirement income from many employers' plans.

Disability Provisions

Pension plans may provide special benefits if an employee dies or becomes disabled before retirement. Employees who have achieved at least some degree of vesting will have a death

---

5 In fact, as discussed later in the chapter, vesting requirements for some qualified plans, such as 401(k) plans, were recently made more generous to employees than those described here for pension plans.

benefit available to a surviving spouse either as a lump sum or as a survivor's pension. If the pension is funded using life insurance, then an extra benefit may be available.

With respect to disability, some pension plans make no special provisions and thus treat employment termination due to disability in the same way as any other termination; that is, a future pension is payable only if the participant achieved vested pension rights before the termination. In other plans, the accrued pension may become payable immediately if the employee becomes disabled. In this case, the pension may take the place of a separate disability income benefit program.

For those employers electing to provide disability benefits apart from their pension plans, a decision must be made regarding the continued accrual of pension rights during disability. For example, suppose Barbara becomes disabled at age 40, after working for TRE Company for 10 years. TRE has a long-term disability income insurance plan that will pay Barbara benefits until she reaches age 65, at which time her vested pension rights will become payable. If TRE's benefit formula provides for a pension of $50 per month for every year of service, Barbara will receive a monthly pension of $500 at age 65. However, if TRE gives full credit for the years she is disabled, instead of only $500 a month starting at age 65, Barbara will receive $1,750 a month [$50 × (10 years worked + 25 years disabled)]. Clearly, the presence or lack of such disability provisions in a pension plan will have a strong effect on an individual's personal risk management planning.

Pension Funding

As previously noted, an employer cannot wait until an employee retires before contributing funds to pay his or her pension. Rather, the funds must be set aside in advance, because the employee is earning the rights to those future benefits. Each qualified pension plan has a funding agency that handles plan contributions. Approximately two-thirds of all pension assets are in **trust fund plans**. In these plans, the employer places monies to pay plan benefits with a trustee (usually a bank), which in turn manages and invests the pension assets. The trustee pays benefits to retirees or other beneficiaries. Assets are not allocated to particular employees but rather are held and managed for the benefit of all employees as a group. If the employer becomes dissatisfied with the performance of a trustee, it is relatively simple for the employer to switch pension assets to another trustee. The main advantage of a trust fund plan is flexibility. The trustee has a wide range of investments in which pension assets may be placed and can be given instructions regarding how the investments will be made, how the benefits are to be paid, and how eligibility and other provisions of the plan should be administered. However, the trustee does not guarantee investment results, safety of principal of the assets invested, or mortality rates assumed in making annuity calculations. In contrast, **insured pension plans**, in which the funding agency is an insurance company, frequently guarantee minimum interest rates, safety of principal, and mortality costs.

One way of classifying insured pension plans is on the basis of whether the plan offers benefits to employees identified individually or covers the employee group as a whole. For **allocated plans**, a record is kept of the account of each employee, and each dollar that the employer contributes is associated with a particular worker. With **unallocated plans**, no monies accrue for individually specified employees during their careers. Instead, the fund is kept in trust for the employees as a group, and at retirement the pension is paid from the unallocated fund. In some cases, a separate insured annuity may be purchased for employees at the time of their retirement, using monies previously held in the unallocated fund.

Although employees are affected by funding decisions made in connection with their pension plans, they generally have very little control over most of those decisions. The major consideration with defined contribution plans is the manner in which the plan assets are invested, because the rate of return will greatly influence the size of the eventual pensions. With defined benefit plans, additional decisions are important. For example, **actuarial cost**

methods must be selected for computing how much money must be contributed each year to fund the promised pensions. Before the selected cost method can be implemented, though, many **actuarial cost assumptions** must be made about the future. Assumptions are required about (1) the likely rates of investment earnings; (2) the pattern of salary increases if the benefit formula is based on employees' salaries; (3) the expenses likely to be incurred by the plan; (4) the distribution of actual ages at which employees will choose to retire in the future; and (5) the rates of death, disability, and employee turnover. If assumptions are wrong, then underfunding or overfunding of the plan will be the result. Consequently, to ensure continued plan qualification, actuaries are required to periodically examine the plan and its assumptions to certify that the assumptions are reasonable and to make recommendations regarding the fund's adequacy for meeting future pension obligations.

Plan Termination Insurance

In addition to qualification rules designed to ensure adequate funding of pension plans, participants in many pensions receive added security through **plan termination insurance**. The coverage is mandatory for and limited to qualified defined benefit plans. A federal agency called the **Pension Benefit Guarantee Corporation (PBGC)** was established under ERISA in 1974 to oversee this insurance. Premiums for the coverage are based on the number of participants and the degree of funding for particular plans. When a defined benefit plan is terminated, a report must be made to PBGC. If plan funds are insufficient to cover promised benefits to employees, PBGC takes over and pays the benefits, subject to various limitations.

DEFERRED PROFIT-SHARING PLANS

As either an alternative or a supplement to a pension plan, many employers sponsor **deferred profit-sharing plans**, which are formal arrangements for sharing employer profits with employees on a tax-advantaged basis. The word *deferred* is used to distinguish these kinds of plans from bonus arrangements in which profits are distributed to employees and taxed in the same way as employee salaries. Most employers establish deferred profit-sharing plans to enhance employees' financial security in planning for income needs associated with retirement, death, and disability. Some employers design their plans to emphasize retirement benefits, while others have plans with a broader emphasis.

In most deferred profit-sharing plans, the employer expects that the direct link between profits and contributions to the plan will motivate employees to work efficiently. An even stronger motivational device in this regard is possible when employer contributions to qualified plans are made in the form of the employer's common stock. Two versions of this approach are **stock bonus plans** and **employee stock ownership plans (ESOPs)**. A primary difference between the two is that ESOPs usually invest in stock issued by the employer, whereas stock bonus plans have more flexibility regarding plan assets. A complete discussion of these special plans is beyond the scope of this book, but many of the qualification rules governing them are similar to those for deferred profit-sharing plans.

Although some employers tend to contribute the same percentage of profits to their deferred profit-sharing plans each year, no specific contribution formula is mandated by law. An employer is required only to make substantial and recurring contributions to the plan over time, with no minimum contribution required each year.[6] Thus, FGH Company might con-

---

6 Employers desiring to make the maximum possible contribution to a deferred profit-sharing plan generally must limit it to no more than 25 percent of total employee salaries that year. Otherwise, they may not deduct the total contribution for income tax purposes that year.

tribute 10 percent of profits in one year, 5 percent the next year, and nothing the third year. If the amount of FGH's profits fluctuates considerably each year as well, then the actual dollars contributed over time to the plan will vary to an even greater extent. Compared with a pension plan, it is easy to see that deferred profit-sharing plans provide fewer guarantees for employees about the eventual level of retirement income that likely will be paid from the plans.

Although no contribution formula is required, the sponsor of a deferred profit-sharing plan must specify an allocation formula to be used in distributing whatever amounts are contributed to the plan. A popular allocation method is based on employee salaries. For example, an individual whose salary represents 2 percent of total salaries paid in a particular year would have 2 percent of the employer's contribution to the deferred profit-sharing plan allocated to his or her account. The account funds may be invested in many different assets, including stocks, bonds, money market securities, mutual funds, real estate, and annuities. Within limits, employers may allow participants to specify their choice of investments for funds allocated to their deferred profit-sharing accounts.

Several additional qualification rules govern the design of deferred profit-sharing plans. Many of these rules are identical to those for pension plans. Examples include the rules on vesting and minimum age and service requirements for eligibility. Regardless of the legal requirements, however, employers are often more liberal in designing their deferred profit-sharing plans than in designing their pension plans. Because a specified contribution formula is not required and because the number of plan participants will not affect the total amount an employer contributes to a deferred profit-sharing plan, employers can be more generous in designing their plans without increasing their own costs. Further, employers hope to benefit from the link employees perceive between work efficiency and plan contributions, so it is logical for employers to include more workers in deferred profit-sharing plans than in pension plans.

As noted, some deferred profit-sharing plans are designed primarily as retirement income vehicles, whereas others are broader in their intent. Participating employees should be aware of the circumstances in which distribution of some or all of their account balances is allowed. Federal qualification rules specify that distributions from deferred profit-sharing plans can be made for many more reasons than is the case with pensions, although employers may choose not to make distributions under all of the circumstances permitted by law. Situations in which distributions are allowable include retirement, death, disability, layoff, illness, termination of employment, the attainment of a specified age, the passage of at least two years since the contribution was made, and the existence of financial hardship. However, if an employee receives a distribution before age 59.5, he or she may have to pay an extra 10 percent tax on the amount received. The reason for this tax, sometimes called a **premature distribution penalty**, is that Congress wants disbursement of funds from qualified plans to be primarily for retirement income purposes.

EMPLOYEE SAVINGS PLANS

Employees can enjoy the benefits of tax deferral of retirement contributions from more than one type of qualified plan simultaneously. For example, a particular employer might provide a pension plan on a noncontributory basis for full-time workers who meet the plan's eligibility requirements. The same employer might have one or more additional retirement plans in which employees can choose to participate on a contributory basis. The two versions of **employee savings plans** discussed in this section are examples of such additional plans. Thus, an employer may provide one leg of the three-legged retirement income stool through the regular pension plan and also facilitate the individual employee savings required for the third leg. Employees who are eligible to participate in one or more employee savings plans should seriously consider doing so, because the tax advantages, "forced savings" element, and possible employer matching contributions associated with many such plans can help individuals accumulate the savings required to assure an adequate income during retirement.

Thrift Plans

For qualification purposes, a **thrift plan** is designed as a special form of a contributory, deferred profit-sharing plan and is subject to most of the rules governing such plans. But because the notion of a profit-sharing plan in which contributions by employees are required may seem odd, most employers describe their thrift plans using different terminology. In particular, most thrift plans are presented as ways to encourage employees to save their own money. Plans may be designed to emphasize either retirement savings or general purpose savings, as is true for the general class of deferred profit-sharing plans. The encouragement for employee savings comes in the form of matching contributions from the employer. For example, through the thrift plan the employer may agree to contribute 50 cents for each dollar contributed by a participating employee, up to a specified maximum. In this way, employees receive an immediate 50 percent return on their savings. These employer matching contributions, as well as all investment earnings in the plan, are tax deferred until distribution to the employee.

No immediate income tax deduction is provided for employee contributions to thrift plans, but the tax deferral on employer matching contributions and investment income can be quite valuable over time. This tax advantage is particularly attractive to higher-income employees who are subject to the highest rates of income tax. Such persons also may be the ones most able to participate in contributory plans. For example, it likely is easier for someone earning $90,000 a year to set aside savings dollars than it is for an employee earning only $20,000. Consequently, special qualification rules are designed to assure that thrift plans do not favor highly compensated employees relative to their lower-paid colleagues. The general approach used to test for discrimination is to compare the relative extent of participation in the plans by the higher- and lower-paid employee groups.

Section 401(k) Plans

The most popular employee savings plan is similar to a thrift plan but offers the added advantage of an immediate income tax deduction for employee contributions. This plan is known as a **cash or deferred arrangement (CODA)** or, more often, a **401(k) plan**, after the section in the Internal Revenue Code that provides for it. A 401(k) plan can be structured in several ways. Usually, they allow employees to choose the types of assets in which their accounts will be invested, and investment selections can be modified periodically as goals or market conditions change. In many 401(k) plans, employers match employee contributions as in thrift plans. The employee contributions in a 401(k) plan are referred to in the tax code by the term **elective deferrals**. All contributions to 401(k) plans grow tax deferred until distributed to the employee.

Because of the attractiveness of the income tax deduction for elective deferrals, it should not be surprising that extra rules govern 401(k) plans in this regard. Each year the plan must pass special tests designed to guard against favoring highly paid employees. The employer can avoid this annual testing by designing the plan so that it passes at least one of the *safe harbor provisions* specified in the Internal Revenue Code. One example of a safe harbor provision is an employer that fully matches the first 3 percent of employee contributions, with at least a 50 cents on the dollar match of the next 2 percent of monies contributed by employees. A limit also is set for the maximum elective deferral allowable for individual employees. Under the Economic Growth and Tax Relief Reconciliation Act (EGTRRA) of 2001, the elective deferral limit is set at $13,000 for 2004, $14,000 for 2005, and $15,000 for 2006. Employees age 50 and older are allowed to make specified additional pre-tax contributions above the normal elective deferral limit, called **catch-up contributions**. Finally, the rules governing distributions of 401(k) funds before age 59.5 are somewhat restrictive. Some provision for early distribution is made, however, if an employee experiences extreme financial hardship and other resources are not reasonably available.

The concept of vesting was described earlier regarding pension plans. Vesting rules also apply to thrift plans and 401(k) plans. Employer matching contributions in these plans may be subject to either cliff vesting or graded vesting, just as with pension plans. However, for these plans the maximum period for cliff vesting is three years rather than five, and the maximum period for graded vesting is six years rather than seven. With the graded vesting approach, employer matching contributions must become at least 20 percent vested after two years, 40 percent after three years, 60 percent after four years, 80 percent after five years, and 100 percent after six years. Note that these vesting rules only apply to employer matching contributions. Employees are always 100 percent vested in their own contributions.

INDIVIDUAL RETIREMENT ACCOUNTS

An **individual retirement account (IRA)** is an individual retirement plan designed to supplement other sources of retirement income. Sometimes employers facilitate employee savings through IRAs—primarily by offering their employees the opportunity to make IRA contributions through payroll deductions. However, the establishment of an IRA is not dependent on employer sponsorship of any particular plan, as is the case with the other retirement income programs discussed. The only requirements for making IRA contributions in a given year are that the individual must have earned income and, in some cases, must not yet be 70.5 years old. Three types of IRAs are discussed in the following sections.

Traditional IRA

The traditional IRA was created as part of ERISA in 1974. For many years, the maximum that an individual could contribute to this type of IRA was $2,000 annually. If married and filing a joint tax return, a couple could contribute up to $4,000. Under EGTRRA 2001, these limits were raised to $3,000 for individuals ($6,000 for couples), and will rise further to $4,000 ($8,000 for couples) in 2005 and $5,000 ($10,000 for couples) in 2008. IRA funds may be invested in most types of financial securities and will accumulate on a tax-deferred basis until distributed. If an individual is not an active participant in a qualified retirement plan sponsored by an employer, contributions to a traditional IRA are fully tax deductible. However, if an individual is an active participant in a qualified retirement plan, the tax deductibility of contributions is as shown in Table 20-3. To illustrate, consider the situations of Claudia Sewell and Kennon Keane, who are single and each earned $60,000 in 2004. Unfortunately, Claudia's employer does not offer any retirement plans as an employee benefit. If Claudia contributes the maximum allowable $3,000 to her IRA, she will be able to deduct the full amount from her current taxable income because she is not an active participant in a qualified retirement plan. Kennon, however, is covered by her employer's pension plan. Kennon can still contribute $3,000 into a traditional IRA just like Claudia, but none of it will be tax deductible because she earns more than the $55,000 level noted in Table 20-3.

Except in the case of death or disability, funds withdrawn from traditional IRAs before age 59.5 usually result in a 10 percent early distribution penalty tax on the amount withdrawn.[7] This penalty is designed to discourage the use of IRA funds for purposes other than retirement. Amounts withdrawn after age 59.5 are taxed as ordinary income, except to the

---

7   Withdrawals taken as part of a series of periodic payments based on the life or life expectancy of the individual and/or spouse are not subject to the penalty tax.

TABLE 20-3   **Tax Deductibility of IRA Contributions for Active Participants in Qualified Retirement Plans (as of 2004)**

Tax Filing Status	Income Brackets ($) for Which IRAs Are:		
	Fully Deductible	Partially Deductible	Not Deductible
Individual	1 to 45,000	45,001 to 54,999	55,000+
Married couple filing a joint tax return	1 to 65,000	65,001 to 74,999	75,000+
Married couple filing separate tax returns	Not available	1 to 9,999	10,000+

Note: Regardless of income, taxpayers filing as individuals can deduct their IRA contributions if they are not active participants in qualified retirement plans. The dollar amounts are scheduled to increase in future years.

extent that they are attributable to contributions that were not fully tax deductible when made. In this latter case, rules much like those governing the taxation of annuities apply.

Roth IRA

The **Roth IRA** first became available in 1998 as an alternative to the traditional IRA, and has since become very popular. The same annual limitation applies to contributions, but a major difference exists regarding taxation. In contrast to the traditional IRA, contributions to a Roth IRA are never deductible from taxable income, but the entire amount can be withdrawn tax free at retirement. That means that all investment earnings and growth in principal may fully escape income taxation if all relevant rules are met. (One requirement is that the IRA must have been in effect at least 5 years before distribution.) The Roth IRA's tax status is especially attractive for young workers who have many years for their savings to grow before withdrawal. Thus, it may be a very effective personal risk management tool in planning for retirement. Income limitations do exist, however, regarding who is eligible to establish a Roth IRA. As of 2004, the limit was $110,000 for single taxpayers and $160,000 for married persons filing joint tax returns.

Rollover IRA

A **rollover** occurs when the owner takes funds out of one account and places them in another. Two types of rollover IRAs exist: (1) a transfer from one IRA to another and (2) a distribution from an employer-sponsored retirement plan into an IRA set up to receive such proceeds. If certain requirements are met, funds involved in rollovers escape current income taxation and are not subject to the annual contribution limit that applies to other IRA contributions. For example, a saver may move $50,000 of funds from an IRA with ABC Mutual Fund Company to one sponsored by ERT Mutual Fund Company without tax consequences. Rollover IRAs are also an important instrument for avoiding immediate taxation on lump-sum distributions from employer plans.

SIMPLE PLANS

A retirement option intended to be especially attractive to small businesses employing 100 or fewer employees is the **savings incentive match plan for employees (SIMPLE)**. A SIMPLE can be set up either as part of a 401(k) plan or through individual IRAs. For both variations, the rules eliminate much of the administrative work (and expense) that otherwise might prevent small employers from setting up retirement benefits at all. For example, a SIMPLE 401(k) plan is exempt from the rules regarding testing for discrimination in favor of highly paid workers. In exchange for this exemption from testing, the employer sponsoring the SIMPLE 401(k) plan must generally match up to 3 percent of its employees' contributions. The annual dollar limit for employees' elective deferrals is $9,000 for 2004 ($10,000 for 2005), with such contributions granted tax-deductible status and all investment income sheltered from taxation until distribution. Further, all full-time employees must generally be eligible to participate in the SIMPLE, and vesting of employer contributions must be full and immediate. Overall, observers hope that many small employers who have so far elected not to sponsor an employee retirement plan will find SIMPLEs to be feasible arrangements for funding retirement benefits for their employees, as well as for themselves.

KEOGH PLANS

Keogh plans are designed for persons with self-employment income. Frequently, people with "side jobs" shelter part of their earnings in these plans. Consider Jack Smith, who teaches at FGH University; as such, he is an FGH employee and participates in the pension plan sponsored by the university. In addition, Jack earns royalties from a best-selling textbook he authored. He is eligible to establish a Keogh plan for the royalties he makes as an author, in spite of the fact that he is already participating in a qualified pension plan as an employee at FGH. As in fully deductible traditional IRAs, the tax-sheltered contributions and accumulating investment returns in Keogh plans are not subject to current income taxation. Thus, if Jack sets up a Keogh plan, he will be able to contribute some of his book royalties to the plan and deduct those contributions from his current taxable income.

In Keogh plans, the annual amounts that can be contributed and deducted from taxes are based on a person's income from self-employment, with the specific limits dependent on the type of Keogh plan established. For example, a Keogh plan that is set up as a defined contribution pension plan has a contribution limit for 2004 of 25 percent of self-employment income or $41,000, whichever is less. Keogh plans also can be either deferred profit-sharing plans or defined benefit pension plans; in either case, the contribution and benefit limits are the same as for other plans of those types.

SECTION 403(B) PLANS

A **Section 403(b) plan**, also called a *tax-sheltered annuity*, *a tax-deferred annuity*, or a *Section 501(c)(3) annuity*, is another special-purpose retirement plan. The different names refer to the retirement arrangements authorized in Section 403(b) of the Internal Revenue Code. Such plans are specifically designed for certain types of nonprofit institutions that are described in Section 501(c)(3) of the code. In general, employees of public schools, universities, hospitals, and nonprofit organizations operated exclusively for religious, scientific, charitable, literary, educational, cruelty prevention, or public safety testing purposes are eligible to establish Section 403(b) plans. Because such organizations are usually exempt from income taxes and often lack the financial resources necessary to fund adequate retirement incomes for their employees, special rules exist to assist employees of such organizations in saving for retirement on their own.

In setting up a Section 403(b) plan, an employee typically enters into a contract with the employer to reduce his or her contractual salary by the amount the employee wishes to save—similar to the elective deferral agreements discussed for 401(k) plans. Within specified limits,

PROFESSIONAL PERSPECTIVES

Church Pension Plans

Just as private employers are concerned with retirement benefits for their employees, most church bodies in the United States also maintain pension plans to provide retired church workers with continuing income after retirement. The most common form of plan is a defined contribution plan qualified as a tax-sheltered annuity under Internal Revenue Code Section 403(b)(9). The Evangelical Lutheran Church in America (ELCA) plan is an example of one such plan. It has a philosophy of maintaining the pre-retirement standard of living, in combination with Social Security, for workers with approximately 35 years of participation. The following specific features further illustrate this plan:

- A single plan exists for both clergy and other employees. Each congregation determines which, if any, of its employees it will enroll in the plan.
- Congregations and other participating employers contribute 10 to 12 percent of covered compensation. For ordained clergy, covered compensation includes nontaxable housing allowance, as well as taxable salary.

- Pension contributions are credited to the members' individual accounts; the plan offers seven investment funds from which to select.
- The values of the investment funds are subject to fluctuations in the investment market.

At retirement, the pension accumulation is applied to provide a lifetime annuity. The ELCA plan offers four annuity options, including three that provide for continuing income to the surviving spouse. Initial monthly pensions are based on conservative investment return (4.5 percent) and mortality assumptions. The plan then determines the investment policy for the underlying assets and may invest these assets aggressively in order to increase the aggregate payout to retirees. Excess investment earnings are used to increase pensions. This increase provides a "permanent" addition to the pension.

With the growth of corporate defined contribution plans, a trend is emerging among church plans to move away from some of the unique (but rather inflexible) features previously described. Increasingly, church plans are offering a wider range of distribution options.

Source: John Kapanke, president, and David Adams, vice president, Research and Design, Board of Pensions, Evangelical Lutheran Church in America.

the amount contributed in this way can be deducted from the employee's current taxable income, and the investment income on the contributions accumulates tax-free until distribution. The maximum annual contributions are the same as for 401(k) plans. Funds can be invested in annuity contracts issued by life insurers, as well as in shares of mutual funds.

SUMMARY

1. An adequate retirement income for most individuals usually consists of funds from the following sources: Social Security, personal savings, and one or more employer-sponsored retirement plans.
2. The level of Social Security retirement income depends on many factors, including the age at which an individual elects to begin receiving benefits, the number of years he or she worked in employ-

ment subject to Social Security taxes, and the wages earned in such employment. The formula for calculating the benefit is intentionally designed to weight lower earnings to a greater extent than higher earnings. Benefits may also be payable to a retired worker's spouse and children.
3. Retirees may elect to begin collecting Social Security benefits as early as age 62, with an actuarial

reduction for each month that a worker retires before the Social Security normal retirement age. Benefits for workers who delay retirement until after the normal retirement age also are adjusted actuarially, through increases for each month "late" (that is, after the Social Security normal retirement age).

4. Retirees who have not yet reached Social Security normal retirement age can earn up to a specified amount per year without penalty. This limit is adjusted annually with changes in average wages. For earnings exceeding this limit, the worker's Social Security benefit is reduced by $1 for every $2 in wages. A variation of this rule applies during the calendar year that a retiree reaches normal retirement age, when in the months prior to reaching normal retirement age, earnings above a specified limit cause Social Security benefits to be reduced by $1 for every $3 in wages.

5. A pension plan is an employer-sponsored arrangement established with the primary goal of systematically providing retirement income for employees. Traditional defined benefit pension plans have a formula for determining the monthly payment during retirement. Defined contribution plans have a formula for determining the exact amount of the employer's contribution before retirement. Cash balance plans have individual accounts similar to a defined contribution plan, but the employer retains the investment risk associated with these plans.

6. The normal retirement age in a pension plan is the earliest age at which employees can retire and receive full pension benefits. Retirement before the normal retirement age usually results in reduced benefits. Retirement after the normal retirement age may result in increased benefits, but the increase usually is not as much as might be justified purely from an actuarial perspective.

7. Employers must adhere to many rules in designing qualified pension plans, including rules governing eligibility, the form of payment, maximum benefits/contributions, permitted disparity between high- and low-income employees, vesting, and funding.

8. Deferred profit-sharing plans are formal arrangements for sharing employer profits with employees on a tax-advantaged basis. Employers use these plans as either alternatives or supplements to pension plans.

9. Many employers provide employee savings plans to assist their workers in accumulating savings for retirement or other purposes. In a thrift plan, the employer usually matches employee contributions. In a 401(k) plan, the employer also may match employee contributions, but the attractive tax advantages associated with 401(k) plans often make it feasible for them to prosper without employer contributions.

10. Individual retirement accounts are designed to supplement other sources of retirement income. Traditional IRAs may be tax deductible, depending on individual circumstances. The Roth IRA does not provide for tax deductible contributions, but all investment earnings may be withdrawn tax-free at retirement. A special form of IRA that may arise in an employee benefits context is the rollover IRA.

11. SIMPLEs were created in 1996 to provide an easy way for small employers to sponsor retirement benefit plans for their employees. SIMPLEs can be set up either as 401(k) plans or as IRAs.

12. Keogh plans are special versions of either profit-sharing or pension plans and are designed for persons with self-employment income.

13. Section 403(b) plans are special retirement arrangements designed for certain types of non-profit organizations that are exempt from income taxes and often lack the financial resources to fund an adequate retirement income for their employees.

internet*exercises*

1. How much will your Social Security benefits pay when you retire? Set your Web browser to http://www.ssa.gov/OACT/ ANYPIA/download.html and download the Benefit Estimate Program. Estimate your future work experience and enter the corresponding information. Assuming that the U.S. system of Social Security remains unchanged, do you consider this a fair benefit? Explain.

2. On the basis of available retirement plan and earning information regarding either your own or a friend's situation, use the following Web site to estimate the amount of individual savings needed to supplement the amount expected from social security and the employer's plan(s): http://www.quicken.com/retirement/planner/. Are you surprised at your result? Explain.

QUESTIONS FOR REVIEW AND DISCUSSION

1. What factors determine the Social Security retirement income payable to a worker and his or her spouse and children?

2. How does a worker's Social Security benefit change if he or she does not retire at exactly the Social Security normal retirement age?

3. Explain how earnings during retirement may affect an individual's Social Security benefit.

4. Differentiate between a traditional defined benefit pension plan, a defined contribution pension plan, and a cash balance plan.

5. Explain the concept of a qualified retirement plan and discuss the significance of this concept for employees and employers.

6. What is permitted disparity? What is vesting? Why is awareness of these terms important for employees?

7. Describe the difference between an allocated retirement plan and an unallocated plan.

8. What is the maximum amount that an unmarried individual may contribute annually to an IRA? Under what general conditions is this amount deductible from taxable income?

9. What types of employers are eligible to establish Section 403(b) plans?

10. What is the difference between a thrift plan and a 401(k) plan? Which is more favorable for employees? Why?

11. What are the factors an employee should consider before exercising the lump-sum distribution option in a pension plan? Explain.

12. Give an example of the use of a SIMPLE.

13. What is a Keogh plan? Who is eligible to establish such a plan?

14. It has been argued that it is not fair for some workers to receive Social Security benefits and for others who have paid in an equal amount of taxes to be denied benefits because they failed to meet the retirement test. Rather, it is claimed, all workers should be paid as a matter of right. Analyze this argument, and state what results would follow if the situation were "corrected."

15. What factors do you think are important in deciding whether to establish a traditional versus a Roth IRA? Why?

16. If you saw the results of an extensive study that indicated that employees of corporations with stock bonus plans and employee stock ownership plans experienced higher levels of worker productivity, what reasons do you feel would support this finding? Do you believe these plans tend to motivate employees more than an increase in salary? Why?

17. Withdrawals from qualified retirement plans before the age of 59.5 are subject to a penalty tax. Recent studies have indicated that more people are beginning to retire at relatively young ages. In light of the recent trend, do you think that Congress should lower the age that benefits can be withdrawn from qualified plans without penalty? What disadvantages might result from lowering this age?

18. Do you agree with the assertion that employees generally prefer defined benefit plans over defined contribution plans? Why or why not? Between a defined contribution plan, a traditional defined benefit plan, and a cash balance plan, which would you prefer? Why?

chapter 21

Financial and Estate Planning

Lee Colquitt is a 55-year-old founding partner and chief executive of High Tech Systems, which has experienced rapid growth since its inception in the late 1990s. Lee estimates that if he wanted to sell the business today, the sales price would be at least $10 million. The two other partners in the firm are Randy Dumm, age 35, and Cassandra Cole, age 34, but Lee is the prime mover behind the success achieved to date.

Lee is married, has two children, and is tiring of the 80-hour weeks he has been working since the business began. He realizes that he needs to make plans concerning his future and that of his family. Because it is his major asset, High Tech Systems' continuation is of major concern, regardless of whether Lee is actively working, retired, dead, or disabled. Some of the questions he is currently thinking about include the following: If he were to die suddenly in the near future, would High Tech Systems provide the income necessary for his family? What if he were to become severely disabled? Can he make some provision now to sell his share in the business to his surviving partners at his death? Will estate and inheritance taxes be a major problem? If so, how can he minimize such payments? These and other related issues are discussed in this chapter.

CHAPTER OBJECTIVES

After studying this chapter, you should be able to

1. Explain the differences between the goals of financial planning and estate planning.
2. List three factors that may result in estate shrinkage.
3. Describe the nature of death taxes and explain the basic approach for computing federal estate taxes.
4. Explain why a will is an important estate planning tool.
5. Provide an example illustrating how gifts can be used to achieve estate planning goals.
6. List the basic elements of a trust and explain how trusts can be used in estate planning.
7. Analyze a family situation and make recommendations to deal with the risks of premature death and loss of health.
8. Explain the important factors in selecting an insurer, an insurance policy, and appropriate ways to compare the costs of different policies.

In Chapter 4, many different risks related to life, health, and loss of income exposures were identified and discussed. Subsequent chapters provided detailed explanations of various insurance products available for dealing with these risks. This final chapter of Part 4 explains how insurance, annuities, and employee benefits can be combined and used together within individuals' comprehensive financial plans. As part of this chapter, a detailed case study is included to illustrate the application of the concepts discussed.

FINANCIAL PLANNING

The term *financial planning* achieved widespread usage during the 1970s and 1980s, as individuals sought ways to deal with the effects of high interest, inflation, and taxation. While many people talked about financial planning and many businesspersons began calling themselves financial planners during these years, little apparent agreement existed as to what these terms really meant. To some people, financial planning primarily involved schemes to shelter income from taxation. To others, financial planning was synonymous with investment activities. To still others, financial planning was merely another term for insurance sales.

 Different ideas concerning financial planning still persist. But agreement has emerged about some aspects of the concept and about those who call themselves financial planners. In this book, **financial planning** is defined as a process involving the establishment of financial goals, the development and implementation of a plan for achieving those goals, and the periodic review and revision of the overall plan. Many similarities exist between the financial planning process and the risk management process. But when viewed from a broad perspective, personal risk management is properly classified as a subset of financial planning. In developing a comprehensive financial plan, the personal risk management topics discussed thus far in Part 4 are vital components. Consideration of property and liability loss exposures are important as well. But a complete financial plan also involves analysis of elements not associated with pure risk. Examples include cash flow management, income taxes, investments, and estate transfer plans.

Although it is important to recognize the broad nature of financial planning, a detailed description of the overall process is beyond the scope of this book.[1] Instead, the emphasis in this text is on illustrating those aspects of the financial planning process that relate to the life, health, and loss of income exposures discussed in Chapters 4 and 16 through 20. Recognition of the overall financial planning context should lead to a better understanding of the ways in which life and health insurance, annuities, and employee benefits can best be used to solve personal risk management problems.

ESTATE PLANNING

As noted in Chapter 4, an executor fund is one of the financial needs often associated with death. Some of the major components of the executor fund are related to settling the deceased person's estate and transferring the assets to his or her heirs. Advance arrangements designed to ensure that assets are preserved and distributed in the manner the owner intends constitute **estate planning**. More specifically, the four objectives of estate planning are (1) minimizing the cost of transferring property to heirs, (2) providing liquid funds to pay transfer costs in the most economical way possible, (3) assuring that estate assets will be transferred to the desired

---

1   Numerous texts devoted to the subject of financial planning exist. See, for example, Lawrence J. Gitman and Michael D. Joehnk, *Personal Financial Planning*, 9th ed. (Mason, OH: South-Western, 2001).

beneficiaries, and (4) planning for the most efficient use of estate assets. Life and health insurance contracts often play an important role in effective estate planning. However, before discussing specific ways to use insurance in estate planning, a more detailed description of the costs associated with estate transfer is necessary.

Estate Transfer Costs

Several factors may cause a reduction in the size of the estate distributed to the heirs after an individual dies. Sometimes known as **estate shrinkage**, this reduction is caused by one or more of the following factors: debts, costs incurred by the person administering the estate, and taxes.

Debts

Individuals use credit to varying degrees. At death, existing debts must be paid before remaining assets can be distributed to any heirs. Typical debts include mortgages, charge accounts, income taxes due, and installment obligations. As a percentage of estate size, debts average from 4 to 8 percent of total assets, with higher percentages often associated with smaller estates.

Administrative Costs

The executor of an estate is the person appointed to carry out the terms of the deceased person's will. If a person dies without a will, he or she is said to have died **intestate**, and the courts will appoint an **administrator** to handle the duties that otherwise would have been performed by the estate executor. Depending on the types of property owned and the complexity of the plan for distributing the estate assets, sizable administrative costs may be incurred by the estate executor or administrator that usually must be paid in cash. Examples of administrative costs include appraisal fees, brokerage fees, court costs, legal fees, accounting charges, premiums for property and liability insurance on estate assets, and fees to compensate the executor or administrator for services rendered.

 If a person dies intestate, the administrative costs may be more substantial because some fees that can be waived within a will cannot be avoided. An example is the cost of a bond to guarantee the performance of the person administering the estate. Most states allow such a bond to be waived through a provision in the will.

Death Taxes

A major reason for estate shrinkage is taxes. Federal law provides for an **estate tax** on the right of a **decedent** (the deceased estate owner) to transfer property at death. States also may levy estate taxes, although the primary estate tax burden generally is at the federal level. Because estate taxes usually must be paid from estate assets before distribution to the heirs, effective estate plans consider both the size of the estate tax burden and the availability of liquid assets for paying the taxes. If the estate is not sufficiently liquid, assets may have to be sold in order to pay estate taxes. In addition to estate taxes, some states levy an **inheritance tax** on those who inherit property. Although inheritance taxes are collected from the heirs rather than the estate itself, it is wise to note applicable inheritance taxes when formulating an overall estate plan.

 The first step in computing the federal estate tax is to calculate the value of all property owned by the decedent at the time of death. If property was jointly owned with others, only the decedent's interest in the property is counted. From this total, the costs associated with the decedent's funeral and burial, debts, and estate administration are subtracted. Two major categories of deductions are then considered. First, if the decedent was married at the time of death, all estate assets left to the surviving spouse are deductible. It may be possible to use this **marital deduction** to effectively eliminate all estate taxes payable upon the death of the first spouse who dies. A **charitable deduction** also is allowed if estate assets are left to charitable organizations.

After subtracting the marital and charitable deductions, one more step is necessary before computing the estate tax. If the decedent made any gifts after 1976 that exceeded allowable gift tax exclusions, the total of those gifts must be added back to the estate and considered in computing the estate tax payable. The rationale for this requirement is a principle included in the Internal Revenue Code since 1976. This principle states that for tax purposes, all property transfers by an individual are linked together in a cumulative manner, regardless of whether the transfers are made at death or while the individual is still alive. Thus, whenever a transfer is made, it is necessary to consider all prior transfers in order to compute the current gift or estate taxes payable.

The Economic Growth and Tax Relief Reconciliation Act (EGTRRA) of 2001 made massive changes in federal estate tax rules. Before the passage of EGTRRA, the maximum estate tax rate was 55 percent, as shown in Table 21-1. Under EGTRRA, as shown in Table 21-2 on page 432, the maximum rate is scheduled to gradually fall to 45 percent by 2009, then to zero percent in 2010, when all estate taxes will be repealed. In addition is the **unified transfer tax credit**, which effectively eliminates all estate taxes for taxable estates up to a certain dollar amount. Before EGTRRA, this exemption amount was $675,000. As shown in Table 21-2, this exemption is scheduled to gradually rise through 2009, then become irrelevant in 2010 when estate taxes are repealed. It is extremely important to note that like all provisions of EGTRRA, the estate tax provisions will expire at the end of 2010. Thus, the law only actually "repeals" the estate tax for one year. In 2011, if Congress does not act before then to extend the law, the maximum estate tax rate will once again jump back to 55 percent. So unless you plan to make sure you die in 2010, estate planning is still very important!

Aside from the estate tax exemption previously discussed, two other credits are available to reduce the actual estate tax that must be paid. First, if any gift taxes have been paid in the past, they are subtracted from the estate tax payable. Second, the amount of state death taxes payable (subject to specified maximums) is credited against the federal tax due. An illustration of the estate tax computation is provided as part of the case study included later in this chapter.

Estate Planning Tools

Various tools are available for estate planning. Some focus on reducing estate transfer costs, whereas others address several of the estate planning goals previously noted. A brief description of some of the major tools is included in this section, with an emphasis on those tools that involve life and health insurance.

netlink

Use the following Web site to quickly estimate federal estate taxes for routine situations: http://personal.fidelity.com/ planning/estate/index_calc.shtml.

Wills

A **will** is one way to transfer ownership of property at death. To be valid, a will must usually be in writing and be witnessed by two or more persons. Because each state has specific laws regarding wills, each time an individual moves from one state to another, his or her will should be reviewed for changes that may be necessary or desirable. When a person with a will dies, the will's validity is established through a process called **probate**, which usually occurs in a special court called a **probate court**. In addition to validating the authenticity of a will, the probate court oversees the work of the estate executor throughout the estate settlement process.

TABLE 21-1   Unified Rate Schedule for Estate and Gift Taxes, Pre-EGTRRA

If the Amount With Respect to Which the Tax to Be Computed Is	The Tax Before Credits Is
Not over $10,000	18% of such amount
Over $10,000 but not over $20,000	$1,800 plus 20% of the excess of such amount over $10,000
Over $20,000 but not over $40,000	$3,800 plus 22% of the excess of such amount over $20,000
Over $40,000 but not over $60,000	$8,200 plus 24% of the excess of such amount over $40,000
Over $60,000 but not over $80,000	$13,000 plus 26% of the excess of such amount over $60,000
Over $80,000 but not over $100,000	$18,200 plus 28% of the excess of such amount over $80,000
Over $100,000 but not over $150,000	$23,800 plus 30% of the excess of such amount over $100,000
Over $150,000 but not over $250,000	$38,800 plus 32% of the excess of such amount over $150,000
Over $250,000 but not over $500,000	$70,800 plus 34% of the excess of such amount over $250,000
Over $500,000 but not over $750,000	$155,800 plus 37% of the excess of such amount over $500,000
Over $750,000 but not over $1,000,000	$248,300 plus 39% of the excess of such amount over $750,000
Over $1,000,000 but not over $1,250,000	$345,800 plus 41% of the excess of such amount over $1,000,000
Over $1,250,000 but not over $1,500,000	$448,300 plus 43% of the excess of such amount over $1,250,000
Over $1,500,000 but not over $2,000,000	$555,800 plus 45% of the excess of such amount over $1,500,000
Over $2,000,000 but not over $2,500,000	$780,800 plus 49% of the excess of such amount over $2,000,000
Over $2,500,000 but not over $3,000,000	$1,025,800 plus 53% of the excess of such amount over $2,500,000
Over $3,000,000 but not over $10,000,000	$1,290,800 plus 55% of the excess of such amount over $3,000,000

The existence of a valid will is important for ensuring that a decedent's property is distributed in the way desired rather than in the arbitrary manner that might otherwise be dictated by state **intestacy laws**. However, not all property owned at the time of death necessarily is governed by the terms of a person's will. For example, when property is owned jointly with the **right of survivorship**, ownership automatically transfers to the surviving owners when one of the owners dies. The decedent's interest in such jointly owned property is subject to estate taxation, but administrative cost savings associated with bypassing the decedent's probate estate are likely. Life insurance provides another important illustration of the

TABLE 21-2   **Estate Tax Rates and Exemption Amount Under EGTRRA**

Year	Size of Exemption from Estate Taxes ($)	Associated Unified Transfer Tax Credit	Maximum Estate Tax Rate
2002	1 million	345,800	50%
2003	1 million	345,800	49%
2004	1.5 million	555,800	48%
2005	1.5 million	555,800	47%
2006	2 million	780,800	46%
2007	2 million	780,800	45%
2008	2 million	780,800	45%
2009	3.5 million	1,455,800	45%
2010	Not applicable (Estate tax repealed)		

ability to transfer property outside of the probate process. Policy proceeds that are payable to a named beneficiary are not part of the decedent's probate estate. Thus, the simple act of naming a beneficiary (other than the insured's estate) in a life insurance policy may result in administrative savings during the estate settlement process.

Although some estate planning tools do involve the transfer of some property in ways other than through a will, it must be emphasized that a valid will is considered to be an essential part of most effective estate plans. In addition to providing security about the distribution of estate assets, wills also facilitate some cost-reducing estate planning tools. For example, without a will, part of the marital deduction for federal estate taxes may be lost if the surviving spouse receives less under state law than the marital deduction provision allows.

Life Insurance

Estate liquidity can be enhanced through the use of life insurance. Unless sufficient liquidity exists within an estate, other assets will need to be sold to pay estate taxes and other transfer costs. If those other assets are not readily convertible into cash, forced sales may result in unnecessary losses for the heirs. However, if life insurance proceeds are payable in an amount approximately equal to the transfer costs, then the estate will have liquid resources available precisely at the time that they are needed, making forced sales unnecessary.

In this regard, the unlimited marital deduction for federal estate tax purposes is helpful to most couples' financial and estate plans, but it may lead to a very large estate tax liability after the second spouse dies. Sometimes the payment of estate taxes at that point will require the liquidation of family businesses or other assets that the couple would have preferred to keep in the family. To help overcome this problem, insurers offer **survivorship life insurance**, sometimes referred to as **second-to-die life insurance**. Second-to-die policies insure two lives but pay only after both insureds have died. Coverage is generally less expensive than either an equivalent amount of insurance on one spouse's life or half of the amount on both spouses. For example, the premium for a $1 million second-to-die policy would be less than for a $1 million policy on one spouse's life or two $500,000 policies, one on the life of each person. The price difference results from the fact that the insurer expects to pay out benefits later than on individual policies.

 Life insurance also can be used as a risk management tool to safeguard the continuation of a business. Small businesses in particular face loss exposures arising out of the death of a sole proprietor, partner, or major stockholder. One method of addressing this problem is for owners to enter into **buy-sell agreements** while all of them are still alive and well. Such

PROFESSIONAL PERSPECTIVES

Bonus Funded Buy-Sell Agreement

Many times, as financial planners, we find ourselves working with successful business owners who own 100 percent of the stock in their corporation, but have no one in their family interested in continuing the business. As we look at the four primary areas of planning (estate planning, retirement planning, investment planning, and business continuation planning) we have to become creative to make sure that the family receives the full value when transferring a service sector corporation.

This situation was the case with our client, a 46-year-old female owner of a very successful advertising and public relations firm. After working with the client's accountant to establish a business valuation, the next step was to find an interested buyer, and to create the funding needed to purchase the company from our client's family in the event of her premature death.

One employee had been with the company since day one, and was the right hand of our owner. The employee wanted to buy the business some day, so why not create

the market and the funding with life insurance? We applied for $4 million of 15-year term life insurance to create the funding and paid for it with compensation bonuses. Specifically, the owner-employer simply wrote the checks to the insurance carrier, and then included them as income to the employee.

A written "Buy and Sell" agreement also was drawn by the owner-employee's attorney, stating the terms of the purchase that would be funded by the $4 million death benefit. This arrangement resulted in a win-win-win situation for our owner-employer:

1. She created a market for the sale of her business at a set price of $4 million for her family.
2. She created the funding with premium dollars that were tax-deductible to her company.
3. She created loyalty in her long-time employee by agreeing to sell her the business in the event of her premature death.

Source: David L. Burch, CLU, ChFC, president and regional CEO, Lincoln Financial Group, Atlanta, Georgia.

agreements state that a deceased owner's share in a firm is to be purchased by one or more specified individuals during the estate settlement process. Through a buy-sell agreement, the buyer agrees to buy and the seller agrees to sell, with the sale price or the method for determining the price specified in the agreement. Even with a buy-sell agreement in place, however, a remaining element needed to ensure business continuation is a way to fund the sale. This need often is met through the purchase of life insurance. For example, two business partners may each own life insurance on the life of the other person, thereby making certain that the necessary funds to buy the deceased partner's share will be available when needed. Buy-sell agreements also can be funded through life insurance purchased by the business itself.

Gifts

Reducing an estate through gifts while the owner is still alive is another way to reduce estate transfer costs. As noted, federal gift taxes may apply to living transfers. However, individuals can give up to $11,000 per donee per year without incurring any gift taxes. Married couples can give up to $22,000 per donee per year if each spouse consents to the gift.[2] Further, gifts from one spouse to another and to charitable organizations are fully excludable from gift taxes.

2   These amounts will be adjusted periodically for inflation.

Gifts of life insurance policies can be especially effective for estate planning purposes because such gifts are valued at their pre-death values. In most cases, that amount approximately equals the policy's cash value at the time the gift is made and is considerably less than the face amount that might otherwise be included in the decedent's estate for tax purposes. One technical consideration in making a gift of a life insurance policy has to do with timing. If the donor dies within three years of making a gift of life insurance, the face amount of the policy is added back to his or her estate for estate tax purposes. Because of this rule, gifts of life insurance must be made far in advance of death in order to achieve estate tax savings.

Trusts

Another estate planning device is the **trust**. It involves the transfer of property from a **donor** to a **trustee** for the benefit of one or more beneficiaries. Trustees have legal ownership of the trust property, but they are required by law to manage and distribute it in accordance with the instructions specified in the trust agreement. If a trust is set up while the donor is still alive, it is called an *inter vivos* or **living trust**. If it is created at the donor's death through a will, the trust is known as a **testamentary trust**. Trusts can be used in numerous ways as estate planning tools. Depending on the purpose for which the trust is created, the arrangements may be very simple or extremely complex. Although a detailed description of all the many types of trusts is not possible in this chapter, some of the ways that trusts can be used for estate planning purposes are provided in the following two examples.

Carol Murphy is a 35-year-old single parent of three children, all of whom are under 10 years of age. In addition to being the sole provider for her children, Carol provides substantial financial assistance to her 90-year-old widowed aunt, who is mentally unstable. After analyzing the consequences associated with her premature death, Carol has decided to purchase $900,000 in term life insurance. She is having a problem deciding how to make the appropriate beneficiary designation, however. She wants the insurance to provide protection for her children and her aunt, but none of these four individuals would be capable of managing the $900,000 proceeds if Carol were to die in the near future. One solution is for her to select a policy settlement option in which the insurance proceeds would be payable in installments to the appropriate people at her death.[3] A more flexible solution is the establishment of a **life insurance trust**, which will collect, invest, and distribute the policy proceeds when Carol dies. An individual, a bank, or another financial institution is specified as the trustee. The trustee is the beneficiary of the life insurance policy, and the trust agreement specifies how the proceeds should be used to benefit Carol's children and her aunt. In a situation such as Carol's, the flexibility of the life insurance trust may be especially attractive, in comparison with the relative inflexibility of some insurance settlement options. In a trust agreement, the trustee can be granted considerable discretion in distributing the proceeds to the trust beneficiaries.

Further, the donor can specify how the proceeds are to be invested by the trustee. Some donors desire a very restrictive investment policy, whereas others want the trustee to have a broad range of options. The ability to make such specifications generally is not possible when life insurance proceeds are payable under settlement options stated in the policy.

Another example of the use of trusts is illustrated by the Warren family. Ron Warren, age 45, is a successful stockbroker. His wife, Neva, age 43, is an equally successful real estate agent. Together they have accumulated investments valued at more than $4 million, of which each person is a one-half owner. Ron wants all of his assets to go to Neva if he dies before she does. Similarly, Neva wants all of her estate to go to Ron if she is the one to die first. They each want their remaining estates to go to their two children when the second spouse dies. Such goals are very common among married couples, but estate plans that implement these

---

3   See Chapter 16 for a discussion of settlement options in life insurance policies.

PROFESSIONAL PERSPECTIVES

Estate Equalization

A unique application of life insurance for the small business owner involves estate equalization. For example, a business owner with three children, only one of whom works in the business, has a total estate of $3 million. The business makes up one-third of that figure, or $1 million. Typically, the estate taxes will be paid with assets that do not include the business, unless necessary. After payment of approximately $1 million in estate taxes, only $2 million is left for the three children to split.

An owner usually will follow one of two courses in designing his or her estate distribution. The business could be left to the daughter who is active in the business and everything else could be given to the other two children. Alternatively, the business owner could split the business and other assets equally among all three children. With the

first choice, the children who are not involved in the business receive a disproportionately small share of the estate. In the second scenario, the business is faced with the sticky situation of owners who are unfamiliar with the day-to-day operations now involved with major business decisions. Bickering and sibling rivalry often compound the problem.

Life insurance is an excellent solution for this business owner. A $1 million life insurance policy could be obtained, with the beneficiaries (typically through an irrevocable trust) being the two children who are not involved in the business. Now the business owner can leave the business to the child who works in it and $1 million worth of assets and/or death benefit to the other two children.

Source: Howard Katz, CFP, Lincoln Financial Advisors, Atlanta, Georgia.

goals exactly as stated may cause the federal estate tax burden to be higher than necessary. For example, suppose Ron dies today and Neva dies six months later. No estate tax is payable at Ron's death because of the unlimited marital deduction. However, when Neva dies, the full value of her estate will be subject to estate taxes before being distributed to their children.

Assuming a $4 million estate at Neva's death in 2004, $10,000 in funeral and burial expenses, $20,000 in estate administration costs, and state death taxes equal to the maximum credit allowed on the federal estate tax, the total state and federal estate taxes due at Neva's death will be $1,170,600. This amount is computed by first applying the uniform rate schedule for estate and gift taxes to $3,970,000 (which is $4 million less funeral, burial, and administration costs) and then subtracting the $555,800 unified transfer tax credit. In applying the uniform rate schedule from Table 21-1, note that in 2004 the top two marginal rates will have been eliminated and the 49 percent rate will have been lowered to 48 percent. Thus, the tax is calculated as $780,800 + [0.48 × ($3,970,000 − $2,000,000)] − $555,800. Part of the $1,170,600 would be for state death taxes and part for the federal estate tax. No additional state tax is necessary because of the assumption that state death taxes equal the maximum credit allowed in computing the federal tax.

By using a special kind of trust known as a **credit shelter trust**, it is possible to decrease this tax amount while still retaining most of the same advantages for the surviving spouse. To implement this arrangement in a particular situation, both spouses can insert provisions into their wills that would establish a credit shelter trust when the first of them dies. Instead of transferring ownership of all assets directly to the surviving spouse, some of the assets owned by the first of them to die would be placed into the trust, with the remaining assets given to the survivor. The amount placed in trust should equal the amount exempted from estate taxes (see Table 21-2). The marital deduction eliminates all taxes on the assets transferred immediately to the surviving spouse, and the unified transfer tax credit exactly offsets the estate tax that would otherwise be due on the amount placed in the trust. Thus, no estate taxes are payable when the first person dies, and the eventual estate that will be taxed when the second spouse dies has been reduced by at least $1,500,000.[4] If desired, the trust agreement can specify that all income from the trust assets be used to benefit the surviving spouse but that the principal will be payable to the children when the second spouse dies.

The results associated with a credit shelter trust for the Warren family example are summarized in Table 21-3. Suppose Ron predeceases Neva in 2004. If a credit shelter trust is established at Ron's death, the taxes payable when Neva dies are reduced from $1,170,600 to $450,600. This savings results in an additional $720,000 that can be transferred to the Warren children to better accomplish the specified estate planning goals.

A CASE STUDY: THE JOHNSON FAMILY

To further illustrate the concepts discussed thus far, a case involving the Johnson family is presented and analyzed in this section. Because of the ages of the persons in the case, the emphasis is on losses associated with premature death and loss of health.

TABLE 21-3	**Illustration of Estate Transfer With and Without Credit Shelter Trust**		
		Without Credit Shelter Trust ($)	With Credit Shelter Trust ($)
Assets owned jointly		4,030,000	4,030,000
Funeral and burial #1		(10,000)	(10,000)
Estate administration #1		(20,000)	(20,000)
Assets placed in trust when first spouse dies in 2004		0	(1,500,000)
Estate tax payable when first spouse dies in 2004		0	0
Assets owned by surviving spouse		4,000,000	2,500,000
Funeral and burial #2		(10,000)	(10,000)
Estate administration #2		(20,000)	(20,000)
Taxable estate		3,970,000	2,470,000
Estate tax payable when second spouse dies in 2004*		(1,170,600)	(450,600)
Spouse's assets transferred to children		2,799,400	2,019,400
Trust assets transferred to children		0	1,500,000
Total transfer to children		2,799,400	3,519,400

*Estate tax shown is sum of federal and state taxes, assuming state tax equals maximum credit allowed in computing federal tax, and is based on the top marginal rate and unified credit shown in Table 21-2 for 2004.

---

4   The second spouse also has his or her own credit available at death, which effectively doubles the amount of assets sheltered from the estate tax.

The Facts of the Case

Tim and Gwen Johnson are both 33 years old. They have two sons: Daniel, age 6, and Phil, age 3. The family lives in Atlanta, where Tim owns and manages his own construction firm (AAA Builders) and Gwen works 30 hours a week as a registered nurse at a hospital. Tim works about 60 hours a week and draws a $50,000 annual salary from AAA Builders, while Gwen earns $25,000 a year. She could increase this salary to at least $35,000 by working more hours on less desirable shifts, but she believes her current work schedule is best until Daniel and Phil are a little older. Both Tim and Gwen expect their salaries and living expenses to increase at an average annual rate of 4 percent. Their take-home pay is approximately 60 percent of their gross salaries.

As the sole stockholder and manager of AAA Builders, Tim has not established any employee benefits for his firm. However, he and his employees are covered by all programs required by the government, including Social Security. Gwen is covered by Social Security through her employment at the hospital. In addition, she has $25,000 of noncontributory group term insurance protection from her employer, and she participates in a contributory group medical insurance plan covering her entire family. The hospital does not sponsor any retirement benefits for its employees.

A summary of the Johnsons' assets is given in Table 21-4. Both Tim and Gwen have Individual Retirement Accounts (IRAs; see Chapter 20). Tim's IRA is invested in common stocks, while Gwen's consists of bank certificates of deposit. The $3 million in undeveloped land that Gwen owns was inherited from an uncle. The property is in the northwest part of the United States and is not currently producing any income. However, it is expected to increase considerably in value over the next 25 to 30 years. The value for AAA Builders shown in

TABLE 21-4	Assets Owned by Tim and Gwen Johnson		
Asset	Owned by Tim ($)	Owned by Gwen ($)	Owned Jointly in Equal Shares ($)
Very liquid:			
Money market account	—	—	5,000
Checking account	—	—	1,000
Life insurance	—	25,000*	—
	—	25,000	6,000
Less liquid:			
IRAs	10,000	6,000	—
Undeveloped land	—	3,000,000	—
	10,000	3,006,000	—
Not liquid:			
AAA Builders	20,000	—	—
Equity in home	—	—	10,000
Personal effects	3,000	3,000	4,000
	23,000	3,000	14,000
Total	33,000	3,034,000	20,000

*Valued according to the policy's face amount, payable at death.

Table 21-4 is based on Tim's estimate that he could sell the firm at a price roughly equal to its net worth of $20,000. Tim expects the value of his company to increase in the future, although the cyclical nature of the construction industry will cause much variation in the growth rate from year to year.

Tim and Gwen have never prepared a personal risk management analysis. They know that they would like to retire at about age 65 and have talked about selling Gwen's land at that time to help finance their retirement. In addition, if either Daniel or Phil is interested in taking over operation of AAA Builders when Tim retires, Tim would be pleased. If neither son is interested in the business, however, then at retirement Tim will sell the firm to the highest bidder. With respect to the risks of premature death and disability, neither Tim nor Gwen has given the issues much thought. Consequently, neither of them has made a will, and they have no plans for dealing with such losses. When asked, Tim and Gwen indicate that they want each other to receive all of their assets when the first of them dies. They want Daniel and Phil to inherit all remaining assets, in equal shares, after the second of them dies.

Risk of Premature Death

Once the Johnsons realize that the risk of premature death can cause a significant exposure to loss, the next step in their personal risk management planning should be to evaluate the likely frequency and severity of losses due to premature death in their particular situation. In this regard, Tim and Gwen estimate that funeral and burial expenses will be approximately $5,000 per person if death occurs in 2004. Estate administration costs at that time are estimated to be $10,000 if Tim dies, but they will be $20,000 if Gwen is the one who dies, because the land she owns in another state likely will require the involvement of courts beyond the State of Georgia. To meet the family's income needs after the death of either Tim or Gwen, the Johnsons predict that 80 percent of their current combined take-home pay would be necessary to prevent a decrease in the survivors' standard of living. They also expect income needs to decrease by 10 percent as each son reaches age 23. Of course, as prices increase over time, survivors' income needs also are expected to increase.

The estimates in the previous paragraph are based on a desire to maintain the current standard of living after the death of either Tim or Gwen. However, the Johnsons' current living standard includes child care services now being provided partly by Gwen and partly through paid child care workers. If either parent dies in the near future, child care expenses will increase. If Tim dies, Gwen anticipates that she would increase her use of professional child care services to allow her to work more hours, thereby increasing her salary to $35,000. Expressed in 2004 dollars, she estimates her child care costs would increase by about $3,000 a year. On the other hand, if it is Gwen who dies, Tim may incur even greater expenses for child care because he works so many hours a week. The Johnsons estimate the extra annual expense in this case to be $6,000 in 2004. The cost for child care will increase over time but will not continue forever. The Johnsons have decided that in their situation, extra child care expenses can be eliminated after both Daniel and Phil are 10 years old.

Problems Resulting from Gwen's Premature Death

In evaluating the risk of Gwen's premature death, her lack of a will causes many unnecessary problems. Without a will, she is subject to the intestacy laws of Georgia, which specify that Tim, Daniel, and Phil would inherit Gwen's property in equal amounts. This result would not only conflict with Gwen's stated desires but would also unduly complicate the ownership of Gwen's land, because a guardian for Daniel and Phil might have to be appointed before their property could be sold or leased. Furthermore, estate taxes that otherwise might have been avoided would become payable. As detailed in Table 21-5, if Gwen owns the assets listed in Table 21-4 and dies intestate, her estate taxes will total $275,095. Because she does not have a will, the marital deduction used in computing her estate taxes is limited to the property

TABLE 21-5   **Estate Tax Payable At Gwen's Death In 2004**

Assets		Gwen's Ownership Interest ($)
Money market account		2,500
Checking account		500
Group life insurance		25,000
IRA		6,000
Undeveloped land		3,000,000
Equity in home		5,000
Personal effects		5,000
		3,044,000
Less:		
Funeral/burial		(5,000)
Estate administration		(20,000)
Marital deduction*		(914,635)
Net result to which to apply estate tax rate		2,104,365
Estate tax before credits**	830,895	
Less unified credit	(555,800)	
Estate tax payable		275,095

*Marital deduction is one-third of (assets – funeral and burial – estate administration – estate tax payable), because Georgia intestacy laws provide that a surviving spouse and children will inherit the estate in equal shares.

**Estate taxes are calculated based on the top marginal rate and unified credit shown in Table 21-2 for 2004.

transferred to Tim under Georgia's intestacy laws. Thus, the Johnsons will not be able to take full advantage of the marital deduction and other estate planning tools that could have been used to eliminate all estate taxes in this situation. Further, because the land she owns is located in another state, Gwen's estate will incur settlement expenses that might be avoided or decreased through advance planning.

Considering estate taxes plus $5,000 in funeral and burial costs and $20,000 of administration expenses, a total of $300,095 in executor fund obligations must be paid soon after Gwen's death. Comparing this amount to the much smaller total of Gwen's most liquid assets (see Table 21-4), it is clear that Gwen's estate does not have nearly sufficient liquidity to pay all anticipated expenses. This fact most likely means that some of her land would need to be sold, regardless of her survivors' wishes. However, forced sales rarely result in optimum prices for sellers, and a partial land sale may not be as lucrative as a sale of the entire property. Further, by selling even part of the land before its expected increase in value, Gwen's survivors would forfeit a potentially valuable asset.

Another problem resulting from Gwen's death in the near future arises out of the continuing income needs of Tim, Daniel, and Phil. Using the goals and assumptions discussed so far in this case study, an estimate of their income situation for selected years after Gwen's death is provided in Table 21-6. The Johnsons' income needs and sources are predicted to increase at a 4 percent annual rate, and Social Security benefits for Daniel and Phil are

TABLE 21-6   **Income Needs for Johnsons—Gwen's Death in 2004 or Later (in Dollars)**

	2003	2004	2005	...	2009	2010	2011	...	2021	2022	2023
Daniel's age (years)	6	7	8		12	13	14		24	25	26
Phil's age (years)	3	4	5		9	10	11		21	22	23
Income sources:											
Tim's take-home	30,000	31,200	32,448		37,960	39,478	41,057		60,774	63,205	65,734
Gwen's take-home	15,000	0	0		0	0	0		0	0	0
Social Security— Daniel	0	3,600	3,744		4,380	4,555	4,737		0	0	0
Social Security— Phil	0	3,600	3,744		4,380	4,555	4,737		0	0	0
	45,000	38,400	39,936		46,720	48,588	50,531		60,774	63,205	65,734
Income needs:											
Regular income	45,000	36,000	37,440		43,800	45,551	47,374		63,112	65,636	61,436
Extra child care	0	6,000	6,240		7,300	0	0		0	0	0
	45,000	42,000	43,680		51,100	45,551	47,374		63,112	65,636	61,436
Income deficit:	0	3,600	3,744		4,380	0	0		2,338	2,431	0
Present value of current & future income deficits:											
At 6% interest		29,629	27,590	...	16,454	12,798	13,566	...	4,631	2,431	0
At 8% interest		26,522	24,756	...	14,410	10,833	11,699	...	4,588	2,431	0

estimated to be $300 per child per month until age 18.[5] Thus, if Gwen dies in 2004, the difference between the income needed versus that available for Tim, Daniel, and Phil is $3,600 in 2004, $3,744 in 2005, and so on. For years in which the income sources exceed the estimated income needs, an income deficit of $0 is shown in Table 21-6. Although Tim makes a good income, it is not sufficient to maintain the family's current standard of living if extra child care expenses must be paid. Similarly, after Social Security benefits end for Daniel and Phil but before the children are completely self-supporting, Tim's income will not be sufficient to meet projected income needs.

Before deciding how to deal with projected income deficits, it is helpful to compute the present value of those deficits. (The concept of present value is discussed in Chapter 8.) Two such present value computations are included in Table 21-6 for each year—one based on a 6 percent after-tax interest rate and one based on an 8 percent rate of return. To interpret the numbers shown, suppose that Gwen dies at the beginning of 2004 and that her survivors have exactly $29,629, which is invested to earn a 6 percent return, after taxes. That investment will be exactly sufficient to allow Tim, Daniel, and Phil to withdraw $3,600 in 2004, $3,744 in 2005, and so on, to meet their projected income deficits. As shown, the present value of the deficits declines in the future if Gwen dies in 2005 or later. After Daniel and Phil are both age 23 or older, Gwen's death would not produce any income deficit for Tim.

---

5   See Chapters 19 and 20 for a detailed discussion of Social Security benefits. No Social Security benefits are assumed for the surviving spouse in this case study due to the high level of the spouse's earnings.

Now consider both the $300,095 of expenses that must be paid shortly after Gwen's death in 2004 and the present value of the projected income deficits for her surviving family members ($29,629). These amounts total $329,724. Gwen's current estate would provide only $34,000 in reasonably liquid assets, consisting of Gwen's group term insurance, her IRA, and half the value of the money market and checking accounts. If the remaining need ($295,724) is not reduced or provided through another source, then it will be necessary to sell some or all of Gwen's land when she dies. As already noted, this solution may not be optimal. Furthermore, if Tim predeceases Gwen or if the couple divorces, the estate taxes at Gwen's death will be even greater. Using only the information from Table 21-5, the elimination of the marital deduction would cause Gwen's estate tax to increase from $275,095 to $714,120 plus possible additional taxes associated with Gwen's inheritance of some or all of Tim's assets. Because Gwen and Tim are relatively young, they may be tempted to disregard the possibility that they both could die soon. However, incidents such as automobile accidents can instantly take the lives of an entire family. There are no guarantees in this regard.

Problems Resulting from Tim's Premature Death

If Tim dies in the near future while Gwen is still living, no estate taxes will need to be paid because of the small size of Tim's estate. However, the intestacy laws will still cause problems because Gwen, Daniel, and Phil will inherit Tim's estate in equal shares. Selling AAA Builders in those circumstances will be more complicated because two of the owners will be minor children and a guardian would need to be appointed in order to sell their interest.

But the major problem resulting from Tim's premature death would be the lost income for his family. The estimated income deficits and present value of those deficits at selected years in the future are shown in Table 21-7.[6] The present value figures are based on income deficits between the time of Tim's death and Gwen's age 65. Because Gwen's future income is never projected to be enough to maintain her current standard of living without additional resources, the size of the future income deficits is substantial. Further, the pattern of the present value calculations is different than it was for the analysis of Gwen's situation. Rather than always decreasing over time, as in Table 21-6, the present values increase for several years, with the maximum ($244,622 at 6 percent) projected to occur if Tim dies at age 49.

Possible Solutions

The following suggestions address several of the problems identified in the previous sections. First, Gwen should consider ways to reduce probate expenses associated with the undeveloped land she owns in a distant state. If she is confident that her marriage to Tim is strong, she might want to give him half ownership in her land, with the right of survivorship. Such a gift would not cause any gift taxes to be payable, and it would allow Tim to inherit the land without it passing through any state's probate courts. Thus, Gwen's estate administration expenses will be reduced. If Gwen is not comfortable giving half her land to Tim, she could transfer ownership to a living trust with herself as the beneficiary. The trust agreement could be written so that Tim (or others) would become the owner at Gwen's death. In this way, too, ownership of the land could be transferred without involving any probate courts, thus saving estate administration expenses.

A second suggestion is for both Tim and Gwen to write wills naming guardians for their children and specifying their desires with respect to the transfer of their property. Although each of them has indicated that they want their surviving spouse to inherit all of their property, that arrangement may not be optimal. Suppose Gwen decides to give Tim half of her

---

6 Because Tim's earnings exceed Gwen's, larger Social Security benefits for Daniel and Phil are assumed than was the case for Gwen's premature death.

TABLE 21-7   Income Needs for Johnsons—
Tim's Death in 2004 or Later (in Dollars)

	2003	2004	2005	...	2009	2010	2011	...	2019	2020	2021
Gwen's age (years)	33	34	35		39	40	41		49	50	51
Daniel's age (years)	6	7	8		12	13	14		22	23	24
Phil's age (years)	3	4	5		9	10	11		19	20	21
Income sources:											
Tim's take-home	30,000	0	0		0	0	0		0	0	0
Gwen's take-home	15,000	21,000	21,840		25,550	26,572	27,635		37,820	39,333	40,906
Social Security— Daniel	0	7,200	7,488		8,760	9,110	9,475		0	0	0
Social Security— Phil	0	7,200	7,488		8,760	9,110	9,475		0	0	0
	45,000	35,400	36,816		43,070	44,792	46,585		37,820	39,333	40,906
Income needs:											
Regular income	45,000	36,000	37,440		43,800	45,551	47,374		64,834	60,685	63,112
Extra child care	0	3,000	3,120		3,650	0	0		0	0	0
	45,000	39,000	40,560		47,450	45,551	47,374		64,834	60,685	63,112
Income deficit:	0	3,600	3,744		4,380	759	789		27,014	21,352	22,206
Present value of current & future income deficits:											
At 6% interest		144,012	148,836	...	169,524	175,053	184,751	...	244,622	230,665	221,871
At 8% interest		104,882	109,384	...	129,546	135,179	145,174	...	216,453	204,594	197,901

land. Both she and Tim could then include provisions in their wills so that the decedent's ownership rights in the land would be placed into a credit shelter trust at the death of the first of them. This tactic would reduce the estate tax bill for the second member of the couple to die, thus assuring a larger eventual inheritance for Daniel and Phil. Property not placed into the credit shelter trust could be willed to the surviving spouse, thus taking full advantage of the marital deduction to eliminate all estate taxes when the first person dies.

Finally, the Johnsons must plan how to deal with estate liquidity and survivor income needs. If the previous suggestions are implemented, then Gwen's estate taxes will be eliminated if she is the first to die and her estate administration costs will be reduced. The total need for liquid resources at her death is estimated to be about $45,000 (consisting of funeral and burial expenses, reduced estate administration costs, and the present value of her survivors' future income deficits). To reach this total, only a small life insurance policy would be needed to supplement Gwen's $34,000 of liquid assets, assuming Gwen dies before Tim.

If Tim dies first, however, then Gwen's estate taxes might once again become an issue, depending on the value of the land and other assets at the time of her death. As noted, Tim's survivors would have a substantial need for continuing income after his death. All things considered, if Tim wants to include Gwen's future income needs in his plans, then he will need a sizable life insurance policy. A face amount of about $146,000 may be adequate for the immediate future, especially if some guaranteed purchase options exist for the future. This estimate is obtained by adding funeral and burial expenses ($5,000), administration expenses ($10,000), and the present value of the income deficits due to death in 2004 ($144,012), and then subtracting the value of Tim's IRA ($10,000) and half the money market and checking accounts ($3,000). If budgetary constraints are not a major problem, a larger initial face amount could be purchased. For both Gwen and Tim, a universal life policy might be appropriate for their needs at this time because it provides for flexibility in premium payments. Additional factors to consider in selecting a particular insurer and policy are discussed later in this chapter.

Loss of Health

As noted previously in this case study, Gwen participates in her employer's contributory group medical insurance plan, which also covers Tim, Daniel, and Phil. If Gwen changes employers in the future, she will need to be careful that no gaps in her family's insurance protection result. If a new employer's plan will not go into effect immediately, then the Johnsons probably should continue their current coverage by using their COBRA rights (see Chapter 19). The alternative of converting to an individual policy generally would not be preferable unless no other options were available for obtaining coverage. The other factor to be considered currently is whether required deductibles, coinsurance, and health care expenses excluded by Gwen's plan can readily be paid when incurred. Such items are not currently causing the Johnsons financial difficulty. In the future, if such expenses exceed the Johnsons' regular monthly budget, the $6,000 in liquid assets shown in Table 21-4 is available.

With respect to possible loss of income due to disability, analyses should be performed for both Tim and Gwen. Most of the same assumptions used in the premature death analysis also apply in this case. One difference is that the regular income needs during disability are assumed to continue at the 100 percent level rather than the 80 percent figure used for premature death. Second, Social Security benefits for Daniel and Phil, as well as the overall maximum Social Security payable to the family, will be lower when the loss is due to disability rather than death. (See Chapter 19.) The results of the disability analyses for selected years are illustrated in Tables 21-8 and 21-9. In these tables, the annual income deficits are not converted to present value figures because disabilities may last for varying periods of time and disability income insurance is rarely paid in a lump sum. In accordance with the analyses in these tables, suppose that either Tim or Gwen becomes disabled in 2004 and that the condition is permanent. The initial income deficits are $17,400 for Gwen's disability and $20,400 for Tim's. The deficits fluctuate in future years before reaching a maximum level in the year 2019 in both situations. At that point, the Johnsons still need to contribute to the support of both Daniel and Phil, but neither child will be eligible for Social Security benefits. The maximum annual deficit is $19,450 if it is Gwen who is disabled and $29,175 if Tim is the disabled one.

Disability income insurance is recommended for both Tim and Gwen, although they probably will not be able to purchase as much as they might like to, based on the previous analysis. Insurers limit the amount of protection they will sell to a particular person, based on the current level of the individual's earnings. Many insurers limit the amount of coverage that can be issued to 80 percent (or less) of an individual's current after-tax income. Such limits would translate to only $12,000 for Gwen and $24,000 for Tim. Premiums may be quite expensive, but could be lowered by the selection of an elimination period of more than 30 days if the Johnsons decide to assume the risk of losses for shorter periods of disability. (Elimination periods are discussed in Chapter 17.) For example, at Tim's and Gwen's current age of 33, one insurer offers a 39 percent premium reduction for extending the elimination period on a long-term disability policy from 30 to 90 days. A 20 percent reduction is available for a 60-day elimination period. Riders can be attached to most policies to provide for cost-of-living adjustments in benefits as well as the ability to purchase additional coverage in the future as the Johnsons' income increases. Finally, as noted in Chapter 17, a Social Security option is recommended in case a disability does not meet the definition of disability established for Social Security benefits.

TABLE 21-8   Income Needs for Johnsons—Gwen's Disability in 2004 (in Dollars)

	2003	2004	2005	...	2009	2010	2011	...	2019	2020	2021
Tim's age (years)	33	34	35		39	40	41		49	50	51
Gwen's age (years)	33	34	35		39	40	41		49	50	51
Daniel's age (years)	6	7	8		12	13	14		22	23	24
Phil's age (years)	3	4	5		9	10	11		19	20	21
Income sources:											
Tim's take-home	30,000	31,200	32,448		37,960	39,478	41,057		56,189	58,437	60,774
Gwen's take-home	15,000	0	0		0	0	0		0	0	0
Social Security— Gwen	0	2,800	4,992		5,840	6,074	6,316		8,645	8,990	9,350
Social Security— Daniel	0	700	1,248		1,460	1,518	1,579		0	0	0
Social Security— Phil	0	700	1,248		1,460	1,518	1,579		0	0	0
	45,000	35,400	39,936		46,720	48,588	50,531		64,834	67,427	70,124
Income needs:											
Regular income	45,000	46,800	48,672		56,939	59,217	61,586		84,284	78,890	82,046
Extra child care	0	6,000	6,240		7,300	0	0		0	0	0
	45,000	52,800	54,912		64,239	59,217	61,586		84,284	78,890	82,046
Annual income deficit:	0	17,400	14,976		17,519	10,629	11,055		19,450	11,463	11,922

CONSIDERATIONS IN BUYING LIFE AND HEALTH INSURANCE

As part of their financial planning, estate planning, and personal risk management processes, many individuals conclude that insurance is an appropriate risk management tool for their particular situations. That conclusion must then be implemented through the selection of a particular insurance company and a specific insurance contract. Such decisions are important ones that should be made only after an informed comparison of alternatives. Assumptions that all insurance companies and policies are the same may lead to inefficient purchases and unnecessary future problems.

Selecting an Insurer

In choosing among potential life insurers, prospective policyowners should make sure that a particular insurer offers the type of coverage needed. A thorough analysis of an insurer's financial strength and ability to provide the desired level of service also should be performed before making a final selection.

Coverage Needed

Some people mistakenly assume that all insurers offer the same coverages. In fact, some insurers write only very basic forms of insurance, such as term and whole life contracts. Other insurers offer many innovative variations of the basic policy forms. Similarly, some insurers write very little health insurance, while others concentrate their efforts on the health expense and/or disability income insurance markets. Finally, some insurers have developed expertise in specialized niches. An example is insurers who write large amounts of life insurance

TABLE 21-9   Income Needs for Johnsons— Tim's Disability in 2004 (in Dollars)

	2003	2004	2005	...	2009	2010	2011	...	2019	2020	2021
Tim's age (years)	33	34	35		39	40	41		49	50	51
Gwen's age (years)	33	34	35		39	40	41		49	50	51
Daniel's age (years)	6	7	8		12	13	14		22	23	24
Phil's age (years)	3	4	5		9	10	11		19	20	21
Income sources:											
Tim's take-home	30,000	0	0		0	0	0		0	0	0
Gwen's take-home	15,000	21,000	21,840		25,550	26,572	27,635		37,820	39,333	40,906
Social Security— Tim	0	5,600	9,984		11,680	12,147	12,633		17,289	17,981	18,700
Social Security— Daniel	0	1,400	2,496		2,920	3,037	3,158		0	0	0
Social Security— Phil	0	1,400	2,496		2,920	3,037	3,158		0	0	0
	45,000	29,400	36,816		43,070	44,793	46,584		55,109	57,314	59,606
Income needs:											
Regular income	45,000	46,800	48,672		56,939	59,217	61,586		84,284	78,890	82,046
Extra child care	0	3,000	3,120		3,650	0	0		0	0	0
	45,000	49,800	51,792		60,589	59,217	61,586		84,284	78,890	82,046
Annual income deficit	0	20,400	14,976	...	17,519	14,424	15,002	...	29,175	21,576	22,440

on persons who regularly engage in extremely hazardous activities (for example, race car driving).

Evaluating Financial Strength

An insurance policy is of little use if the insurer selling it does not have the financial strength to pay losses when they occur. Two important factors in assessing an insurer's financial condition are the quality of its investments and the relative size of its surplus (the excess of assets over liabilities). All states regulate both of these factors, but concern does exist about the ability of states to adequately regulate the solvency of large insurers operating in numerous states, particularly if the insurers are part of large conglomerates. The losses in the early 1990s that some insurers suffered due to investments in speculative real estate and junk bonds (high-yield bonds issued by firms with significant default risks) exacerbated this concern and caused many people to become more interested in the financial condition of current and prospective insurers.

Most insurance purchasers are ill-equipped to analyze the financial strength of insurers directly. To assist them in this task, several secondary sources of information are available. The publication *Best's Insurance Reports*, issued annually by A.M. Best Company, can be found in numerous public libraries. It reports financial and operating information about many insurers, together with a rating of the financial strength for most insurers that have been in business at least five years and have annual net premiums of at least $1.5 million. In addition, Best's Insurance Reports classifies insurers into categories based on the size of policyowners' surplus. Other groups also rate life insurers, although the number of insurers rated is generally less than the number rated by A.M. Best. These other groups include Standard and Poor's Corporation; Moody's Investors Service, Inc.; and Duff and Phelps, Inc. As a general rule, potential policyowners are advised to exercise caution before committing substantial premium dollars either to insurers with low ratings or to new, small insurers about which little information is available. At the same time, seemingly high ratings by one or more rating services are no guarantee that an insurer will not experience financial difficulties in the future.

Evaluating Service

The element of service in the selection of an insurer may have two aspects: the service provided by the agent and the service provided by the insurer's home office. Sometimes agents act merely as order takers. At the other extreme, they may develop and maintain comprehensive plans of insurance designed to meet changing client needs for a lifetime. An agent can write letters on behalf of a customer, take care of details such as beneficiary changes, and handle premium collections as a convenience to the client. Or an agent can ignore requests for aid and refer customers to the home office for answers and assistance. Finally, agents may sell policies that come closest to meeting the real needs of their insureds, or they may sell policies that provide themselves with the highest commissions regardless of whether the policies are appropriate.

Prospective insureds should ask questions about the degree of service that can be expected of an agent. Variations in service can mean the difference between a satisfactory insurance arrangement and one that fails to accomplish many of the insured's goals. In judging the quality of service that may be received from an agent, some factors to consider are:

1. The methods employed in selling the coverage.
2. The length of time the agent has been in business.
3. References from impartial sources.
4. Evidence of professional accomplishments, such as possession of CLU or ChFC designations.[7]

Service from an insurer's home office is also important. Life and health insurance policies often are long-term contracts involving 30 or 40 years of premium payments to the insurer and 20 or 30 years of benefit payments to the insured or to beneficiaries. The speed and reliability with which these payments are handled are vital to the success of an insurance plan. Because agents come and go, the continuing service provided by the insurer over the years is of greater importance than it would be if the insured could deal with only one agent indefinitely.

Selecting a Contract

Two important considerations in buying life and health insurance are a good understanding of the goals and purposes the buyer wants to achieve and a general idea as to how much can be spent on premiums. For example, if the goal is to increase an estate's liquidity for the payment of estate taxes, some form of permanent life insurance might be an appropriate choice, if budget constraints permit. If, however, premium dollars are scarce and the primary goal is to provide additional income for survivors until children are old enough to support themselves, then decreasing term insurance would probably be the best decision. Careless selection of the insurance contract may result in an inappropriate policy that will not accomplish the desired goals. It also may mean that the contract will be dropped after a year or so, causing the high first-year commissions paid when the policy was purchased to be repeated when a replacement contract is obtained. In the remainder of this section, two other factors important in selecting a contract are considered: contractual provisions and policy costs.

---

7   CLU stands for Chartered Life Underwriter, and ChFC stands for Chartered Financial Consultant. Both these designations are given by the American College of Life Underwriters, Bryn Mawr, Pennsylvania, after an individual has passed a series of comprehensive examinations in life insurance and related fields.

Contractual Provisions

Although relatively few basic types of life and health insurance exist, literally hundreds of different arrangements of these basic types are sold. Often, it is not an easy task to verify that two policies being considered are indeed directly comparable, with equivalent contractual provisions. For example, before Sue Gamelin compares the costs of two whole life insurance policies, she should make sure that each has the same waiver of premium provision, settlement options, policy loan clause, and nonforfeiture and dividend options. If Steve Cooper is comparing prices for disability income policies, factors he should consider include the elimination period, definition of disability, and maximum period for the payment of benefits. The health expense area can be even more complicated. Suppose Bill Alderfer is interested in a major medical insurance policy. He must pay attention not only to coinsurance, deductibles, copays, and policy limits but also must carefully compare exclusions and special limitations for various health expenses or conditions. Contracts vary most in the health expense area. Fortunately, a certain degree of policy standardization is mandated by state laws, thus simplifying the task of policy comparison to some extent.

Cost Factors

If two health insurance contracts are sufficiently alike to warrant a comparison of costs, the next step is to compare their premiums. As noted in earlier chapters, some policies may be participating, meaning that policyowner dividends are payable periodically if experience warrants. Such policies usually have higher gross premiums than comparable nonparticipating contracts, but may be less expensive after dividends.

Comparisons of life insurance costs are more complex. One cost comparison method that has achieved some acceptance within the industry is the **net payment index**. This method computes the level annual payment that, if invested at a stated interest rate for a specified time period, will accumulate to the same total as would the policy's net premiums if invested in the same way. For example, suppose Susan Turner is considering buying a $100,000 participating whole life policy. In comparing the costs of several such policies, Susan wants to know what her relative cost would be in each case if she were to keep the policy in force for 20 years and then die at the end of that time. For each contract under consideration, Susan should obtain not only premium information but also projected dividends so that she can more accurately compare costs. Suppose Susan is considering a $100,000 policy from ABC Company, with an annual gross premium of $1,500 payable at the beginning of each year. At 6 percent interest, those premiums would accumulate to $58,489 by the end of 20 years (see Appendix A). Suppose ABC's illustrated dividends are estimated to accumulate to $20,000 at the end of the same 20 years. The net payment index is the difference between these two numbers divided by the accumulated value of an annuity of $1 per year invested for the same time period at the same interest rate. In this example, the net payment index for the ABC policy being considered would be ($58,489 – $20,000) ÷ 38.99273 = $987.08 per year. To obtain the cost per $1,000, this amount ($987.08) is divided by 100, yielding a net payment index of $9.87 per $1,000 of coverage for this policy.

An alternative cost comparison method that is often used is the **surrender cost index**. It is similar to the net payment index, but it incorporates consideration of a policy's cash value as of a particular point in time. A formula for computing the N-year surrender cost index is

$$\frac{P - D - CV}{A}$$

where P = accumulated premiums for N years

D = accumulated dividends for N years

CV = cash value at the end of N years

A = accumulated value of an annuity of $1 for N years

Continuing with the previous example, if the $100,000 ABC policy will have a $25,000 cash value after 20 years, then its 20-year surrender cost index, computed at 6 percent interest, is

$$\frac{\$58,489 - \$20,000 - \$25,000}{38.99273} = \$349.94$$

or $3.46 per $1,000 of coverage.

Note that the surrender cost index is most appropriately used to compare policy costs when an individual plans to keep a policy in force until a specified time, after which it will be surrendered for its cash value. One of the drawbacks of this method is that it can be manipulated by insurers through the judicious specification of their cash values at intervals most likely to be selected by buyers for surrender cost index comparisons. In spite of this possibility, the method remains in use because of its relative simplicity. Note, however, that for insureds who intend to keep their coverage in force until death, the net payment index is a more appropriate method to use. It has the added advantage of being less subject to insurer manipulation.

SUMMARY

1. Financial planning is the process through which financial goals are established, a plan for achieving those goals is developed and implemented, and a periodic review of the plan takes place.
2. The objectives of estate planning are minimizing estate transfer costs, assuring estate liquidity, planning for the efficient use of estate assets, and ensuring that assets will be transferred to the desired beneficiaries.
3. Estate shrinkage can be caused by debts, estate administration expenses, and taxes. Death taxes include federal estate, state estate, and inheritance taxes.
4. When a person with a will dies, the will's validity is established through the process of probate. If a person dies without a valid will, his or her property is distributed according to the applicable state intestacy laws.
5. Life insurance has many potential purposes in estate planning, including the enhancement of estate liquidity and the provision for the income needs of the decedent's survivors. Second-to-die policies can be especially helpful to married couples in providing estate liquidity.

6. A trust involves the transfer of property from a donor to a trustee for the benefit of one or more beneficiaries. Living trusts are established while the donor is still alive. Testamentary trusts are created at the donor's death through his or her will. A credit shelter trust can be used by married couples to decrease the estate tax liability that must be paid at the death of the second spouse.
7. In selecting an insurer, consideration should be given to the type of coverage needed, the insurer's financial strength, and the service expected from both the agent and the home office. In selecting a particular insurance policy, the contractual provisions should be carefully compared.
8. The surrender cost index can be used to compare life insurance policy costs if an insured intends to surrender a policy for its cash value after a specified period of time. If a policy is to be kept in force until the insured's death, then the net payment index is a better measure of the relative cost between two policies.

internet*exercises*

1. Set your Web browser to http://www. choosetosave.org/tools/fincalcs.htm and click on "What will it take to become a millionaire?" Using reasonable assumptions, how much will you need to save each year to become a millionaire by age 65? If you increase your assumed rate of return by five percentage points, how much does your previous answer change?

2. Go to http://www.insweb.com/learningcenter/
default.htm and locate the Life Insurance Needs
Analyzer. Use this term life insurance estimator
tool to estimate the amount of life insurance
needed by the Johnson family in this chapter's

case study. How does the answer in the chapter
compare with that from this Web estimator? What
factors account for the difference? What amount
of insurance do you think is the "true" amount
needed?

QUESTIONS FOR REVIEW AND DISCUSSION

1. Define *financial planning* as the term is used in
this chapter.
2. How is the personal risk management process related to the personal financial planning process?
3. List some of the major components of the executor fund.
4. What are four specific objectives of estate
planning?
5. Briefly describe each of the three major sources
of estate shrinkage.
6. Distinguish between the terms in each of the following pairs of terms.
   a. Executor and administrator
   b. Estate tax and inheritance tax
   c. Testamentary trust and *inter vivos* trust
7. Why must the value of prior gifts be added
back to the estate when computing the estate
tax liability?
8. Define and briefly explain the following terms related to estate taxes.
   a. Marital deduction
   b. Charitable deduction
   c. Unified transfer tax credit
   d. Decedent
9. Describe the function of a probate court.
10. A trust involves a donor, a trustee, and at least
one beneficiary. Briefly explain the role each of
these parties plays in relation to the trust.
11. Describe the features and purpose of a credit shelter trust.
12. Compute the estate tax liability in each of the following situations for a death in 2004. Assume that
each estate includes no debt, incurs $6,000 in fu-
neral and burial expenses, and has $4,000 in es-
tate administration expenses.
    a. Dick Gantt, a widower whose wife died sev-
    eral years ago, dies with an estate of
    $2,010,000 that he leaves to the American
    Lung Association.
    b. Barbara Jolley dies with an estate of
    $2,010,000 that she leaves entirely to her
    favorite son-in-law.

c. John Weber dies with an estate of $2,010,000.
His will gives $600,000 to his grandmother
and the remainder to his wife.
d. Holly Liersch dies with an estate composed
entirely of cash in the amount of exactly
$1,500,001 that she bequeaths to her three
children equally.
13. List and describe three important considerations
when choosing an insurer.
14. What is the surrender cost index, and how is it
computed?
15. Financial planning is considered a relatively new
profession, even though it involves a collection of
services that have long been available from attorneys, accountants, insurance agents, bank trust officers, investment brokers, tax advisors, and several other professionals. Why do you feel that
financial planning emerged as a profession when
most of the services were already being offered to
consumers? Discuss any advantages that you believe a consumer could obtain by using the services of a financial planner in addition to some or
all of the other financial advisors mentioned.
16. Under current law it is generally permissible to
convey property to a trust with the same person
serving as donor, trustee, and beneficiary, as long
as a legitimate and legal purpose for the creation
of the trust exists. Suppose Allen conveys all of
his property to a trust that contains the following
terms:
a. Allen is the sole beneficiary of the trust until
his death, at which time the trust is to terminate and pay all benefits to his wife.
b. Allen is the trustee of the trust unless he becomes disabled, at which time his wife becomes trustee.
c. Allen retains complete power to amend or re-
voke the trust at any time.
   Identify and briefly discuss two legitimate
purposes of the trust. Do you believe that the
assets held in this trust should be subject to estate tax? Why? Do you feel that these assets

should be safe from legitimate claims of creditors? Why?

17. Refer to the Johnson family case study discussed in this chapter. If you were Tim, list at least three specific estate planning changes that you would make. Discuss your rationale. Now list three specific changes in your estate plan that you would make if you were Gwen. Discuss your rationale.

18. How might Tim and/or Gwen use a testamentary trust to avoid the possibility of problems associated with transferring real or business property to a minor? Discuss some of the terms that might be included in this trust.

19. Joe Tombs' financial planner, whom you know to be very competent, has recommended the purchase of at least $50,000 in life insurance after performing a very involved analysis to determine how much insurance Joe needs. If you are Joe's insurance agent and he approaches you to purchase a $50,000 policy, what factors would you consider before recommending a specific life insurance policy? Why?

The Risk Management Environment

PART 5

chapter 22

Risk Management and the Insurance Industry

The insurance industry faces many new challenges in the 21st century. A number of major hurricanes since 1990, including $20 billion Hurricane Andrew, have caused many insurers to realize that they had insured too much property along coastal areas. As these insurers reduce their writings in coastal areas, who will insure the nonrenewed policyholders? Will state or federal government become the major insurer? And even if it does, how will it be able to treat the concentration of property values it must insure? It is estimated that more than 9 million people live along the coastline in Florida.

Insured losses arising from the terrorist attacks of September 11, 2001, are estimated at over $40 billion. Not surprisingly given the magnitude of these losses, insurers have sought to limit their exposure to future losses of this type. Can private insurers ever cover losses from terrorist attacks? How might the global nature of the insurance industry affect the ability of private insurers to address these exposures? This chapter should help you to reflect on these problems and how they might be solved.

When buying tangible goods, such as a car or a house, the buyer seldom inquires into the nature of the social or economic institutions that were responsible for making those products available, nor is there any compelling reason to do so. However, when purchasing intangibles, such as the services of a lawyer or a doctor, the qualifications of the professional providing the services are of as much importance as the services themselves—and rightly so, for the two factors cannot be separated. So should the insurance buyer have a knowledge of the social institutions that provide the service? The position taken in this and the next chapter is affirmative: the buyer should have that knowledge. The nature of the insurer and the type of distribution system employed greatly influence both the cost and the quality of the insurance service received. If the security of income and property are to be entrusted to an insurer, the buyer should certainly study that insurer's basic characteristics.

CHAPTER OBJECTIVES

After studying this chapter, you should be able to

1. Indicate the size of the insurance industry.
2. Describe how the insurance business is divided between the private and public sectors.
3. Explain why personal insurance has a larger premium volume than property insurance.
4. Identify and explain the differences between stock companies, mutual companies, Lloyd's associations, and reciprocal insurers.
5. Indicate which types of insurance have the largest volume.
6. Explain how insurance guaranty funds operate.
7. Describe how insurance is distributed from insurers to consumers and list the differences between types of agents and brokers in insurance.
8. Describe the global nature of risk management and the insurance industry.

INTERNATIONAL PERSPECTIVES

The New Lloyd's of London

Lloyd's of London's involvement in the Unites States began in the 1880s when Cuthbert Heath, a prominent Lloyd's underwriter, wrote the first Lloyd's reinsurance policy on American risks for a British company doing business in the Unites States. Two decades later Lloyd's underwriters met policyholders' claims for losses following the 1906 San Francisco earthquake, thus establishing the Lloyd's market's credibility and strength. Since then Lloyd's syndicates have insured and reinsured some of the most well-known risks in the Unites States—from space shuttles to skyscrapers, and from Bruce Springsteen's voice to Jennifer Lopez's bottom. In addition to the specialized risks for which the Lloyd's market is most famous, syndicates at Lloyd's write a substantial amount of U.S. surplus lines and reinsurance business. In fact, the United States is Lloyd's largest overseas market—accounting for approximately one-third of Lloyd's worldwide premiums. In 2002 Lloyd's U.S. premium income reached $8.2 billion. With about half of its 2002 U.S. income coming from surplus lines insurance, Lloyd's accounted for approximately one-fifth of the U.S. surplus lines market. The other half of Lloyd's U.S. income is mostly attributable to reinsurance.

Lloyd's relationship with the Unites States proved to be near fatal as claims related to asbestos and pollution liability contributed significantly to the huge losses suffered by the Lloyd's market in the late 1980s and early 1990s. In the span of a few years the Lloyd's market incurred losses that exceeded its cumulative profits from three centuries of underwriting. As a result of these losses Lloyd's was forced to restructure itself by reinsuring pre-1993 U.S. liabilities out of the Lloyd's market and by finding a way to recapitalize the market. The pre-1993 U.S. liabilities were reinsured into "Equitas," a special-purpose vehicle established in 1996 to pay for claims on U.S. policies covering liabilities. Equitas is simply a "run-off" company, i.e., it does not issue new policies but serves only as a vehicle for paying claims on policies issued prior to 1993. Prior to the 1990s Lloyd's syndicates were capitalized entirely by individual investors, known as "Names," who were subject to unlimited liability for underwriting losses. The unprecedented losses of the late 80s and early 90s led to a depletion of Lloyd's capital base as many individual Names lost their personal fortunes, and several even committed suicide as losses mounted. In 1994, for the first time in Lloyd's 300-year history, corporate capital was introduced into the Lloyd's market. Today, the old adage of Names being "liable down to their last cufflink" is almost defunct as over 80 percent of total capital at Lloyd's is provided by corporate members operating under limited liability.

Source: André Liebenberg, University of Georgia.

THE FIELD OF INSURANCE

Insurance coverages can be divided into various opposing categories: personal (life and health) versus property (buildings, homes, autos), government (flood insurance) versus private (product liability), or involuntary (Social Security) versus voluntary (fire insurance). The categories are not mutually exclusive, and they overlap. Figure 22-1 depicts the major classifications of insurance and what they have in common with each other.

Personal Coverages

Personal coverages are those related directly to the individual; the risk they cover is the possibility that some peril may interrupt the individual's income. Four such perils exist: death, accidents and sickness, unemployment, and old age. Insurance is written on each. Private insurers are active in providing insurance for death, accidents and sickness, and old age, whereas governmental units are active in all four categories.

FIGURE 22-1   Major Classifications of Insurance

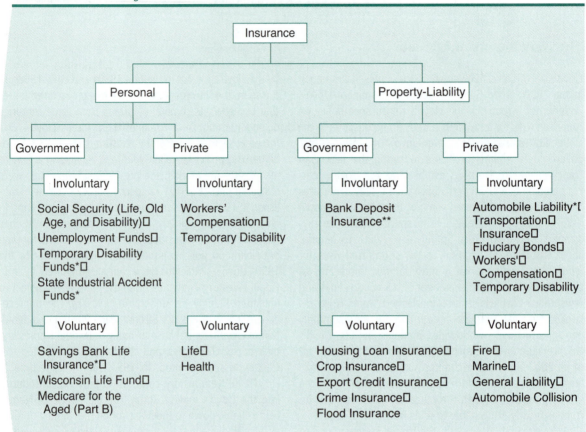

*Applicable only in some states.

**Bank deposit insurance is required only in certain types of banks.

Note: In interpreting this figure, observe that the types of coverage under each heading are meant to be suggestive of each type and not a comprehensive listing. In addition, government insurance includes coverage offered by both state and federal agencies, and includes areas in which some government body merely sponsors or guarantees the coverage that is actually offered by a private agency (such as savings bank life insurance). Involuntary private insurance includes those offerings required to be purchased under certain conditions in some states.

Property Coverages

Property coverages are directed against perils that may destroy property. Property insurance is distinguished from personal insurance in that personal insurance covers perils that may prevent one from earning money with which to acquire property in the future, whereas property insurance covers property that is already acquired. Property insurance as used here includes fire, marine, liability, casualty, and surety insurance. Sometimes property insurance is referred to as **general insurance**, property/liability insurance, or property and casualty insurance.

Private and Public Insurance

Insurance institutions in this country have taken two basic forms of ownership: private and public. (The latter is also called *government* or *social insurance.*)

Private insurance consists of all types of coverage written by privately organized groups, whether they consist of associations of individuals, stockholders, policyholders, or some combination of these. **Public insurance** includes all types of coverage written by government bodies—federal, state, and local—or operated by private agencies under government supervision.

Voluntary and Involuntary Coverages

Private and public insurance may be further classified into two subgroups: voluntary and involuntary coverages. Most private insurance comes under the rubric of **voluntary coverage**, although the purchase of some types is required by law. Examples of required insurance include automobile liability insurance and workers' compensation insurance. A major part of government insurance is **involuntary coverage**; that is, it is required by law that insurance be purchased by certain groups and under certain conditions.

The importance of private passenger auto insurance is shown in Table 22-1 (37.0 percent of all premiums). When commercial auto insurance is added, auto insurance represents 42.5

TABLE 22-1	Net Premium Written (NPW) by Line of Property Liability Insurance—2002		
		NPW ($, millions)	Percentage of 2002 NPW
Private passenger auto:			
Liability		$ 81,995	
Physical damage		57,547	
Total private passenger auto		$139,542	37.0
Homeowners' multiple peril		40,014	10.6
Total homeowners and private passenger auto		$179,556	47.6%
Workers' compensation		$ 36,519	9.7%
Commercial multiple peril		25,384	6.7
Commercial auto		24,537	6.5
General liability		30,886	8.2
Fire and allied lines		15,403	4.1
Inland marine		7,037	1.9
Medical malpractice		7,043	1.9
Total larger commercial lines		$146,809	39.0%
Surety and fidelity		$ 4,302	1.1%
Ocean marine		2,411	0.6
Farmowners' multiple peril		1,785	0.5
Aircraft		1,470	0.4
Boiler and machinery		1,410	0.4
Burglary and theft		112	0.0
Total smaller commercial lines		$ 11,490	3.0%
Accident and health		14,119	3.7
Reinsurance		15,739	4.2
Other lines		9,447	2.5
Total property liability premiums		$377,160	100.0%

Source: Property/Casualty Insurance Facts, in *The Fact Book 2004* (New York: Insurance Information Institute, 2004), 15.

percent of all lines. While much of this text is directed toward commercial risk management, it should be noted that personal lines account for over 47 percent of all premiums written (personal auto plus homeowners').

Table 22-2 shows that PPA made up 33.1 percent of total premiums in 1980, 34.3 percent in 1985, 36.0 percent in 1990, 39.3 percent in 1995, 39.9 percent in 2000, and 37.0 percent in 2002. Part of this relative decline since 2000 is due to the dramatic increases in commercial lines insurance premiums during the hard insurance market.

TYPES OF INSURERS

Insurers generally are classified according to ownership arrangements. Four distinct types are stock companies, mutual companies, reciprocals, and Lloyd's associations.

Stock Companies

A **stock company** is a corporation organized as a profit-making venture in the field of insurance. For companies organized in the United States, a minimum amount of capital and surplus is prescribed by state law to serve as a fund for the payment of losses and for the protection of policyholders' funds paid in advance as premiums. Stock companies, like all insurers, are organized with authority to conduct certain types of insurance business; under the so-called multiple-line laws of most states, stock companies can be authorized to deal in all types of insurance.

Stock companies in property insurance normally conduct their operations through the independent agency system. They usually, but not always, operate by setting a fixed rate with the approval of the insurance commissioner of any state in which they are admitted to do business. Some stock companies pay dividends to policyholders on certain types of insurance. Stock companies never issue what is called an **assessable policy**, wherein the insured can be assessed an additional premium if the company's loss experience is excessive. The stockholders are expected to bear any losses, and they also reap any profits from the enterprise.

Mutual Companies

A **mutual company** is organized under the insurance code of each state as a nonprofit corporation owned by the policyholders. This type of insurer has no stockholders. Also, no profits are made, because any excess income is returned to the policyholder-owners as dividends, or used to reduce premiums, or retained to finance future growth. The company is managed by a board of directors elected by policyholders. The bylaws of a mutual may provide for additional assessments to policyholders in the event that funds are insufficient to meet losses and expenses. In most mutuals, however, assessments are not permitted once the company reaches a certain size. Only in very small mutuals are assessments stipulated, and even then the assessment is usually limited to one additional annual premium.

TABLE 22-2	Private Passenger Auto as a Percentage of Total P-L Premium
1980	33.1
1985	34.3
1990	36.0
1995	39.3
2000	39.9
2002	37.0

Many types of mutual organizations exist and operate under different laws and with different types of businesses. In any state, it is necessary to examine the insurance code in order to determine the precise nature of the mutual.

Class Mutuals

Some organizations, known as **class mutuals**, operate in only a particular class of insurance, such as farm property, lumber mills, factories, or hardware risks.

Farm Mutuals. A class mutual specializing in farm property insurance is known as a **farm mutual** and may be organized under a separate section in the insurance code. Such mutuals insure a large portion of the farm property in some states, primarily because of the specialized nature of the risks. Many farm mutuals operate on the assessment plan, and in some cases the assessments are unlimited; each policyholder is bound to a pro-rata share of all losses and expenses of the company.

Factory Mutuals. A class mutual specializing in insuring factories is known as a **factory mutual**. These organizations have been noted for the emphasis that they place on loss control activities. Each potential policyholder must meet high standards of safety before being accepted into the group. Factory mutuals generally do not solicit small risks due to the relatively high cost of inspections, engineering services, surveys, and consultations that are provided by the organization in an attempt to prevent losses before they occur. FM Global, one of the largest insurer's of commercial property risks, is a factory mutual.

General Writing Mutuals

Perhaps the most commonly known mutual in property insurance, the **general writing mutual** is one that accepts many types of insureds; it is not a specialist writing in a certain class. General writing mutuals require an advance premium calculated on roughly the same basis as that of a stock insurer. In contrast to specialized mutuals, general writing mutuals operate in several states or even internationally. They may or may not pay a refund of a portion of the premium as a dividend if experience warrants it. Many mutuals insist on relatively high underwriting standards, taking only the best risks so that a dividend will more likely be paid. Some general writing mutuals reduce the initial rate below the stock company level, however, and do not plan to pay dividends. Some mutuals are both *participating* and *deviating*; that is, they plan both to cut the initial rate somewhat below stock company levels and to pay a dividend, if warranted. State Farm Insurance Company is a general writing mutual.

Fraternal Carriers

A **fraternal carrier** is defined as a nonprofit corporation, society, order, or voluntary association, without capital stock, organized and carried on solely for the benefit of its members and their beneficiaries. Fraternal benefit societies, which offer only life and health insurance contracts, are authorized to do business under a special section of the insurance code, provided that certain requirements are met. Fraternals have a lodge system with a ritualistic form of operation and a representative form of government that provides for the payment of benefits in accordance with definite provisions in the law. As charitable, benevolent associations, they usually are exempt from taxation.

Consolidation and increased competition in the financial services industry has increased the need for capital by life and health insurers. Stock companies are able to raise large amounts of capital in equity markets. However, mutual companies find it difficult to raise capital since they cannot issue equity. Thus, many mutual insurer executives have either demutualized or created mutual holding companies. With a mutual holding company, the mutual firm forms a stock insurance company. That firm issues stock and operates as a typical stock company. The mutual, the holding company, and the stock company may well have a common board of directors, and several people may serve as executives in all three firms. The number of mutual life and health insurers in the United States has dropped from 135 in 1980 to 83 in 2002. More significantly, some of the largest mutual insurers have converted to stock firms including Metropolitan, Prudential, and John Hancock.

Reciprocals

A **reciprocal**, or an **interinsurance exchange** as they are sometimes called, is like a mutual in that both are formed for the purpose of making the insurance contract available to policyholders "at cost"; that is, no profits are made, as such, and no stockholders are compensated. In both cases, the policyholders own the company.

However, basic differences exist between the legal control and capital requirements of reciprocals and mutuals. In a reciprocal, the owner-policyholders appoint an individual or a corporation known as an **attorney-in-fact** to operate the company, as opposed to a board of directors. A mutual is incorporated with a stated amount of capital and surplus, whereas a reciprocal is unincorporated with no capital as such. Some state laws require that a reciprocal furnish a contingent fund in the form of a deposit with the insurance commissioner for the benefit of the subscribers. Otherwise, the reciprocal organization has no capital other than the advance premiums deposited by the owners.

Reciprocals operate mainly in the field of automobile insurance. Most reciprocals, however, tend to be small, local associations with records of uncertain financial stability.

Lloyd's Associations

A **Lloyd's association** is an organization of individuals joined together to underwrite risks on a cooperative basis. The most important distinguishing characteristic of a Lloyd's association is that each member assumes risks personally and does not bind the organization for these obligations. Each **name** (investor) is individually liable for losses on the risks assumed to the fullest extent of personal assets, unless the liability is intentionally limited.

Lloyd's associations are similar to reciprocals in that each underwriter is an insurer. However, a reciprocal is composed of individuals who are both insurers *and* insureds at the same time in an attempt to obtain insurance at cost, whereas a Lloyd's association is a proprietary organization operated for profit.

London Lloyd's

Lloyd's of London is the best known insurer in the world and was, in fact, one of the earliest known types of insuring operations. Lloyd's started in 1688 in London as an informal group of merchants taking marine risks. They first met at Lloyd's Coffee House. Their operations are now worldwide, and they operate extensively in the United States, largely in what is known as the **surplus line market**. This market consists of risks that domestic insurers have rejected for one reason or another. Lloyd's business is sold through registered brokers who are given the authority to represent them in this country.

In 2004 nearly 66 underwriting syndicates of Lloyd's existed. *Syndicates* are groups of names that combine their resources and employ a manager, who determines which risks to insure. The underwriting capacity of Lloyd's can only be accessed through a Lloyd's broker of which there were 166 firms in 2004. Due to the adverse operating results of these syndicates, corporate capital was

netlink

For insurance information at Lloyd's of London, visit their site at http://www.lloyds.com. Some short video interviews about Lloyd's also are available on this site.

PROFESSIONAL PERSPECTIVES

The Big Boys

A relatively few property-liability insurers account for a significant share of total premiums written. The five top-ranking insurers by 2002 premium volume were State Farm, Zurich/Farmers, Allstate, AIG, and Travelers Property Casualty Group. These five groups wrote more than 30 percent of total premiums in 2002.

Source: *The Fact Book 2004* (New York: Insurance Information Institute, 2004), 8.

introduced at Lloyd's in 1994. The number of individual investors has fallen from a high of more than 32,000 to 2,198 in 2003. Corporate capital now makes up close to 90 percent of the capacity at Lloyd's.

Relative Importance of Private Insurers

Thousands of insurance companies operate in the United States. Most of the business, however, is done by relatively few insurers. It is estimated that only about 15 percent of property-liability insurers operate in all or most states.

The leading states for property-liability insurers are Vermont (464), Texas (239), New York (215), and Pennsylvania (202).

Leading states for life insurers are Arizona (286), Texas (175), and New York (103).[1]

Stock companies tend to dominate as underwriters of various lines of property-liability insurance. Stock companies write more than 80 percent of commercial multiple peril premium volume, and about two-thirds of the fire and commercial automobile/bodily injury premiums. Mutuals enjoy their greatest markets in the fields of personal automobile and workers' compensation insurance. Lloyd's and reciprocals account for only a small share of the total property-liability insurance market.

In the field of life and health insurance, there are more than 12 times the number of stock companies than mutuals. With the demutualization of many larger insurers in the 1990s, mutuals account for a declining portion of the market. In 2002 mutuals wrote about 12 percent of the life and health insurance business.

In property-liability insurance, mutual companies have grown more rapidly than stock insurers, primarily because the mutuals have tended to specialize in the types of insurance (particularly automobile coverages) for which the markets have been growing most rapidly. Furthermore, mutuals have used cost-cutting methods that generally have made the product available at lower rates than those offered by stock insurers.

In summary, the data show that in the field of property-liability insurance, stock insurers underwrite more than half of all insurance volume. Mutuals have been losing market share in the life and health lines but are gaining in property-liability lines.

Insolvency of Insurers

The continuing financial solvency of the insurer with whom you deal is of obvious importance to risk managers. Unless your insurer has the ability to respond to claims, the whole purpose of insurance is defeated. Insurance institutions are not backed by a federal agency in

---

1   *The Fact Book 2004* (New York: Insurance Information Institute, 2004), 12.

ETHICAL PERSPECTIVES

The Harder They Fall

A report released in 1990 by the U.S. House Committee on Energy criticized state regulation of insurance company solvency. Called the Dingell Report, the study found no evidence that would threaten the existence of the insurance industry but stated that if the industry did not address certain weaknesses, it could face a solvency crisis rivaling the 1990 savings and loan crisis. Among the weaknesses cited were:

- Delegation of too much responsibility to managing general agents who are seeking only a fast profit.
- Use of holding companies and affiliates to hide weaknesses of their subsidiaries.
- Lack of regulation of the reinsurance business.

- Lack of reliable information and failure to verify independently the information provided by insurers.
- Infrequent examination and communication; lack of resources to make thorough audits.
- Inadequate investigation of the causes of insolvencies and inadequate punishment of those who are responsible.

In response to this report, the NAIC developed an accreditation program that requires state insurance departments to meet certain prescribed standards. It also established minimum capital requirements for insurers, based on the riskiness of their business.

Sources: Howard Greene, "RM Spectrum," *Risk Management*, April 1990, 7–8; Insurance Information Institute, "Insolvencies/Guaranty Funds," January 2004.

the same way bank deposits are protected. Instead, the danger of loss from insolvent property-liability insurers has been recognized by the establishment in all states of *guaranty funds*. Under the terms of most insurance laws, these funds must reimburse the policyholders for any losses caused by bankrupt insurers, subject to stated deductibles and maximum loss limits that vary from state to state. Each state has a separate guaranty fund. The amounts a given fund will pay per loss vary by state. The funds are supported by assessments against other insurers operating in the same state. From the introduction of guaranty funds in 1969 through 2002, more than $8.8 billion has been assessed against solvent companies to pay losses of insolvent insurers.[2] These data do not include assessments made under New York's law. New York State operates a pre-loss assessment fund and pays losses from that fund. Although almost all states have guaranty funds for failed life insurers, detailed data on their operation are not published. During the past several years, a number of life insurance companies have merged or ceased business.

Various reasons exist for property-liability insolvencies. Principal among these is inadequate pricing, which is usually discovered when loss reserves are insufficient to pay claims. Other leading causes are rapid growth (really too rapid), fraud, and overstatement of the value of certain assets. The effects of catastrophic natural disasters also can be a cause of insolvency.

Employment in Insurance

The insurance industry employed approximately 2,222,000 persons in 2002, divided roughly as shown on the following page:

2 *Ibid.*, 31.

Employed by property-liability insurers	586,000
Employed by life and health insurance companies	785,000
Employed as agents, brokers, and service personnel	821,000
Employed by reinsurers	30,000
Total	2,222,000

Most of the jobs in insurance are salaried positions, and fewer than one-third are in marketing or distribution. This information contradicts the frequently held opinion that most jobs in insurance are in sales.[3]

Ownership of Insurance

Data from the Insurance Information Institute reveals that the property-liability insurance industry has been able to reach most U.S. citizens who own homes or autos. Roughly 95 percent of the homeowners indicated that they had purchased property or liability insurance on their homes and possessions. Some type of life insurance is owned by approximately 75 percent of all Americans.

CHANNELS OF DISTRIBUTION IN INSURANCE

Many kinds of arrangements may be made to distribute the insurance contract. These arrangements are comparable to the channels taken by physical goods. For example, life insurance generally takes a short, direct channel, whereas property insurance normally uses a long, indirect channel with one or more independent intermediaries involved. In some fields of property insurance in recent years (notably automobile coverage), increasing emphasis has been placed on the use of more direct channels. Some of the reasons for these developments will be explained here.

Direct Distribution in Life Insurance

Life insurance is distributed in two main ways: through salaried group insurance representatives and through individual insurance agents, who usually work on commission. Life insurance also is sold by direct contact with the consumer through advertising, mail order, or the Internet—sometimes called *direct response*. Under each of these methods, the contact between the insurer and the customer is a direct one in which the insurer maintains a one-on-one relationship with the insured and in which independent intermediaries usually are not involved.

Group Insurance

Life insurers offer many of their products on a group basis, that is, under contracts covering groups of persons rather than individuals. Examples include group life insurance, group health insurance, and group pensions.

The customers for group coverage are generally business firms. Persons employed to sell and service this business usually receive a salary and bonus. The group representative often works closely with commissioned agents, who may first locate a potential customer for group insurance and who receive a commission if the group representative succeeds in making the sale.

Individual Agents

Policies sold to individuals are usually handled by persons known as agents, underwriters, or financial planners. The agent or underwriter contacts the ultimate consumer and reports

---

3 *Ibid.*, 10.

directly to the insurer or to an intermediary, commonly called a general agent, who in turn reports to the insurer. The authority of the underwriter or agent is limited; the agent cannot be called an independent intermediary because he or she is actually working under contract with the insurer or the insurer's representative.

A **general agent** in life insurance is an individual employed (usually at a state or county level) to hire, train, and supervise agents at lower levels. The general agent sometimes collects premiums and remits them to the insurer's home office. Today, a general agent may have one primary company, but the firm will represent several different companies in order to gain special markets for disability insurance, annuities, and retirement plans. The general agent is not an independent intermediary in the sense that a typical wholesaler is, for the general agent does not exercise final control over the issuance and the terms of the contract. The company normally is not bound by the general agent in putting a contract in force. The general agent exercises no control over the amount of the premium, has no investment in inventory, does not own any business written, and has no legal right to exercise any control over policyholders once he or she leaves the employment of the company.

Reasons for Direct Distribution in Life Insurance

The system of direct, or short channel, distribution has grown up in life insurance because of several basic factors:

1. The insurer's need to maintain close control over the policy "product"
2. The insurer's need to exercise control over sales promotion and competition
3. The infrequent purchase of life insurance
4. The agent's ability to make a better living through specialization

Need for Close Control over Product

The insurer needs to maintain close control over the policy product because of its complicated nature, its long duration, and the fiduciary relationship required between the insurer and the insured. A short channel is appropriate where such close control is desired.

Need for Control over Sales Promotion and Competition

Life insurance is very competitive. The policies of the many companies vying for business are similar in nature. Hence, extra promotion and competition on the basis of superior sales techniques of agents often represent the difference between rapid and mediocre rates of growth for a life insurer. The insurer can exercise much greater control over these factors by employing a short channel of distribution.

Infrequent Purchase of Life Insurance

No compelling reasons exist for life insurance to be offered as one of the many contracts available from a given agent, as is true in property insurance. A buyer usually purchases life insurance infrequently, has infrequent need for claims service, and has little day-to-day contact with the agent regarding endorsements on policies, requests for information, and the like.

This is not to imply that the life insurance agent renders no service once the contract has been put in force. The agent stands ready as the local representative to the insured, answers questions, and writes letters to the insurer on behalf of the insured. But this service is not so demanding of the agent's time that a large business operation would be required to provide it. An agent's time is best spent in securing new sales.

Better Living through Specialization

An agent generally can make a higher income if he or she specializes. Because of its technical nature, the most successful life insurance agent specializes in life, health, and disability insurance, as well as pension planning. Fitting life insurance to an individual's particular needs requires the professional service supplied by the agent. Advanced knowledge of the subject is needed to render the quality of sales service usually expected. An agent generally does not become an expert in all lines of insurance but rather concentrates in one area. With the frequent changes in tax laws during the past several years, this statement is truer than ever.

The latest development in marketing insurance is e-commerce. Insurers are selling insurance over the Internet. Potential buyers can surf the net and seek the insurance they desire. Actually, one completes an application and submits it to the insurance company. The company underwrites the policy, and if everything is correct and acceptable to the insurer, the policy is issued through the mail. California enacted legislation that allows the entire transaction to occur over the Internet. This approach has great potential to reduce administrative and marketing costs. Only time will tell if it will be a valid distribution method. Most people believe it will be easier for a new company to use this approach versus existing ones because of relationships with agents and existing employees.

The Changing Environment in the Life Insurance Company

From the 1950s to 1987, individual life insurance new premiums maintained respectable growth greater than, or equal to, the rate of inflation. Real growth in new premiums was occurring. However, beginning in 1987, that pattern ceased. The growth rate began to slow to less than 2 percent in 1985, and, in 1988, new premiums actually declined. By 2002, premiums for all life insurance policies totaled $134 billion, but over 65 percent of the premiums for individual policies represented renewals rather than new policies being sold.[4]

Changes in U.S. demographics have contributed to the shift in business volume away from individual life insurance. As the overall population aged (from 8.1 percent above age 65 in 1950 to 12.5 percent in 1996), people became more interested in financial products that were accumulation centered, rather than protection and accumulation. Annuity sales increased from $24 billion in 1985 to $269 billion in 2002. Of course, if mutual fund and individual stock investments are added, the accumulated segment of the market is much greater. These changes in business mix have meant that life insurers increasingly find themselves competing with banks and mutual fund companies for consumers' investment dollars.

Direct Writing in Property-Liability Insurance

In some lines of property and liability insurance, independent intermediaries have been eliminated, and the contract is marketed directly from the insurer to the insured through either exclusive agents or employees who work on salary and commission. The exclusive agent (or salaried employee) solicits prospects, takes care of paperwork, and in general serves as the insurer's direct contact with the insured. Insurers who employ this type of distribution are called **direct writers**. They include some of the largest insurers in the business.[5]

An **exclusive agent** of a direct writer (sometimes called a *captive agent*) represents only one insurer. The exclusive agent does not own the business written and generally does not handle loss claims or collect premiums; these are sent directly to the insured from the home office of the insurer. The exclusive agent receives a commission, but it is a lower percentage than the commissions allowed independent agents. The main tasks of the exclusive agent are to sell new business, keep in contact with customers, and serve as a communications link between the insurer and the insured.

Direct writers have their greatest volume in the field of automobile insurance, but they are expanding into other lines such as homeowners' and commercial property insurance. In

---

4 *Life Insurance Fact Book 2003* (Washington, D.C.: American Council of Life Insurance, 2003), 53.
5 Examples are State Farm, Allstate, Nationwide, and Liberty Mutual.

general, direct writers have been able to sell insurance at a lower cost to the final consumer, and this, plus a vigorous advertising campaign, has contributed greatly to their success. The lower cost has been achieved by the insurer largely through stricter underwriting and smaller allowances to the agent for the production and servicing of business.

An explanation of the growth of property-liability companies employing direct channels of distribution may be found in some observations about the nature of consumer buying habits in insurance and other fields. Channels of distribution tend to be fixed in a free-enterprise system according to whether they are as efficient as alternative methods. In the tangible goods field, the post-World War II years have seen the growth of discount houses that generally concentrate on the sale of shopping goods, which are relatively high-priced items, subject to infrequent purchase, and substantially standardized in nature. These stores take a considerably lower markup on such goods than is traditional and still make enough profit to justify their existence. They generally offer few of the frills associated with the traditional department store.

In the sale of automobile insurance, a situation similar to that of the discount house exists. The product consists of a fairly standardized policy issued once or twice a year, costing a substantial sum of money, and requiring little service, except when a claim arises. The traditional allowance to the independent agent is about 15 percent of the premium dollar. This allowance is granted year after year, even though the agent may do little to earn it after the business is first procured. With the tremendous growth in the number of autos in the United States, a mass market in this field became possible, and some insurers saw an opportunity to capture a large amount of it by devising more efficient methods of business development. Accordingly, innovations such as continuous policies, lower agents' commissions, direct billing from the insurer to the consumer, and specialized adjusting offices to handle claims were instituted.

The gains made by direct writers were accomplished at the expense of insurers using the American Agency System, described next.

Indirect Distribution (American Agency System)

The channel of distribution for a majority of property and liability insurance lines is indirect. The insurance is not sold directly by the insurer to the policyholder but rather is sold through a system of intermediaries, comparable to the wholesaler-retailer system in tangible goods marketing. This indirect system has been termed the **American Agency System**.

The **independent agent** is an autonomous, local intermediary in the property insurance business. As the "retailer," the independent, or local, agent deals with the final consumer of insurance. The independent agent usually represents 10 to 30 or more separate insurers and has authority to bind these insurers on most of the contracts that are written. In most cases, the independent agent is supplied with forms and has the authority to write a policy and deliver it to the insured.

The **local agent** "owns" the business he or she writes; that is, the local agent has the legal right of access to customer files and to solicit renewal of policies. The insurer does not have the right to give this renewal information to another agent. The local agent works on a commission basis and may or may not have the responsibility of collecting premiums.

Brokers versus Agents

Brokers operate in a manner similar to local agents, although legally they represent the consumer, not the insurer. Thus, if the consumer asks a broker to obtain insurance, the broker must make contact with the insurer before coverage is binding. Agents may bind coverage immediately, because they are the legal representatives of the insurer. Of course, many brokers also hold agency contracts with insurers and may bind coverage immediately because of this status.

Is the American Agency System Doomed?

Naturally, those insurers and their agents committed to the traditional long channel of distribution have become concerned over the future of their business, since direct writers have been growing in market share until recently. As shown in Table 22-3, while the direct writers have taken a significant portion of the personal lines market, insurers using independent agents have maintained their dominance in commercial insurance lines. Interestingly, from 2000 to 2002 direct writers actually lost market share in both personal and commercial lines.

Although the volume of business undertaken by local independent agents is usually relatively small, such is not the case for national brokers. Table 22-4 gives the name and size of the five largest brokers, each of which has gross revenues in excess of $600 million.

Outlook for the Agency System and Direct Writing. Direct writing has grown fastest in lines for which there is a mass market for a standardized product that requires little continuous service. As these conditions do not exist in all areas of insurance, particularly in the commercial market, it is extremely doubtful that direct writers will capture that market. It is perhaps true that the basic nature of a typical agency contract will be amended to reflect the changed conditions that have been brought on by direct writing. For example, insurers might take over some of the services now performed by agents and brokers and reduce commissions accordingly or keep commissions level and ask the agents to do more of the underwriting, policy issuing, and claims adjusting. It seems unlikely, however, that the independent agency

TABLE 22-3

Market Share (%) by Distribution System, 1998, 2000, 2002

System	1998	2000	2002
In Personal Lines			
Agency companies	32.8	31.7	34.3
Direct writers	67.2	68.3	65.7
In Commercial Lines			
Agency companies	67.3	65.3	70.6
Direct writers	32.7	34.7	29.4

Source: *The Fact Book 2004*, "Property/Casualty Insurance Facts" (New York: Insurance Information Institute, 2004), 34.

TABLE 22-4

Five Largest Brokers in the World, 2002

	2002 Brokerage Revenue, billions ($)
Marsh and McLennan Companies, Inc.	8.3
AON Corp.	6.0
Willis Group Holdings, Ltd.	1.7
Arthur J. Gallagher & Co.	1.1
Jardine Lloyd Thompson Group P.L.C.	0.6

Source: *The Fact Book 2004*, "Property/Casualty Insurance Facts" (New York: Insurance Information Institute, 2004), 4.

system will be replaced by direct writing unless the property insurance business becomes much more concentrated than it is now.

While direct writers continue to gain market share in the property-liability field, the life insurance industry is going in the opposite direction. Agents are representing several different companies and are selling annuities, life, and health insurance.

Direct Response

Some insurance is sold without agents or other intermediaries through the **direct response** technique.[6] Under direct response, which is used in both the personal and property fields of insurance, customers are found through advertising on television, radio, newspapers, magazines, direct mail, or other methods. This area is where the Internet appears to have the greatest potential. No sales agents are employed. The policies sold in this manner tend to be fairly standardized and more specialized and less costly than other policies. Examples are accident insurance, hospital indemnity, term life, automobile, homeowners', and short-term disability income contracts. By 2001 direct response channels represented about 8 percent of the personal lines market.

Mass Merchandising

Mass merchandising, as it has come to be known, is a method of distributing property-liability insurance directly to customers through employer payroll deduction. Underwriting is done on an individual basis. Although premiums are usually cheaper because of various economies in mass merchandising (reduced marketing costs and accounting economies), employers do not normally contribute to the premium on behalf of employees, as is common in the field of group life insurance plans. A major reason for this is the fact that such contributions are not tax-deductible to the employer, and payments so made are taxable income to the employee.

In spite of their advantages, mass merchandising plans have not become extremely popular. Independent agents have generally opposed the adoption of such plans because many agents depend on individually issued personal-lines business for their livelihood. Mass merchandising plans threaten the growth of their markets.

Another limiting factor in mass merchandising is the element of adverse selection, which has often produced poor underwriting experiences. Enrollment in plans is voluntary. For example, employees who have had poor driving records and are paying high rates on their car insurance may be attracted to a mass merchandising plan in which rates may be lower.

GLOBALIZATION OF RISK MANAGEMENT AND THE INSURANCE INDUSTRY

Advances in technology and improvements in transportation, coupled with reduced trade barriers in many countries, have steadily led to a globalization of business. Globalization affects risk management and insurance in two important ways. First, firms and organizations that do business internationally face differences in their loss exposure and in the risk-handling methods they use. Second, globalization and difference in future growth potential have led many insurers to reevaluate the focus of their business and to consider expansion overseas.

Global Risk Management

A broad spectrum of firms and organizations face international exposure. Almost all firms and organizations have some employees who travel overseas. Additionally, in the increasingly

---

6   Examples of insurers using this method are AMICA, USAA, Progressive, and GEICO Direct.

global marketplace, firms export goods and services overseas, manufacture or import products from overseas, and hire part-time or permanent employees overseas. Each of these activities can give rise to unique exposures that are not faced if the firm operates exclusively within its own home country. Also, some of the loss exposure that a firm already faces within its home country can be either more likely to occur or can be more severe once the firm becomes involved overseas.

Global Risk Exposure

Some kinds of risk exposure faced by international firms are the same as those faced by firms that do business only in their home country. For example, most firms face loss potential from fire, natural disasters, or damage to goods in transit. However, many of these similar exposures can be altered in both frequency and severity potential by differences in various parts of the world. While natural disasters occur in all parts of the world, most of the deaths from natural disasters are in developing countries, while most of the property damage resulting from natural disasters occurs in industrial nations. Fire loss potential is much greater in countries with poor infrastructure and lower-quality building standards. Transit losses are much more likely to seriously affect the business continuity of a firm that depends on shipments from overseas, especially from countries with a poorly developed transportation infrastructure.

Global firms also face a number of unique kinds of loss exposure that arise as a result of conducting business in multiple countries. These can include risk such as terrorism, kidnapping, political instability, uncertain legal environment, currency risk, import/export restrictions, technology and communication problems, financial markets' weaknesses, and substandard infrastructure. The inability to assess risk accurately due to an absence of information in some underdeveloped countries can be one of the biggest challenges that a risk manager of a global firm faces. Also, the lack of a well-developed insurance industry in some countries can lead to an absence of high-quality risk management services, such as claims handling, loss assessment, and loss control.

netlink

Companies retain security consultants to assess risks in foreign lands. Visit Corporate Risk International at http://www.corprisk.com.

In addition to exposure differences internationally, the rate of insurance in business and the use of insurance by individuals can differ dramatically around the globe. Tax treatment of insurance differs from country to country. Local laws in some countries require the purchase of certain types of insurance and either require that insurance be purchased from a locally admitted insurer or disallow tax-favored treatment if the insurance is purchased from a nonadmitted insurer. For example, in China and Argentina, nonadmitted insurance is prohibited, while in the United Kingdom, nonadmitted insurance is permitted except for the compulsory lines of employers liability and automobile liability. The attitude toward risk management also can differ. In some areas, businesses are not accustomed to retaining part of the risk through the use of deductibles. Customary limits of coverage can vary significantly from country to country. Further, in some societies, religious beliefs discourage arrangements involving the payment of interest and often limit the purchase of insurance. Finally, in a number of countries, the significant reliance of government social insurance programs reduces the demand for private life and health insurance and annuity products.

Global Insurance Programs

Global firms basically have three options with respect to how they structure their international insurance program. First, they can primarily rely on nonadmitted insurance on a worldwide basis. That is, they buy insurance in their home country and arrange for coverage wherever they do business. This approach has the advantage of being easy to administer and leaves the decision making in the home country. However, the disadvantages are that it might be illegal in some countries that require admitted insurance, favored tax treatment of insurance premiums and loss payments may be lost, and the insured does not have a local insurer to provide claims and other services overseas.

In the second approach, insurance program design and the purchase of insurance can be left to the firms' management in each of the countries in which it does business. This structure has the advantage of meeting any local laws regarding admitted insurance and compulsory coverage requirements, and this can preserve favorable tax treatment for premium and loss payments. However, a disadvantage is that this approach tends to lead to a very inefficient program structure if the firm is doing business in a number of countries. The inefficiency stems from the costs associated with negotiating a large number of individual policies in the various countries where the firm operates. Also, coverage limits and terms often differ significantly across countries and can lead to important gaps in protection.

The third, and perhaps most popular, approach for many global firms today is a so-called global controlled master program. In this structure, a global insurer works through its own subsidiaries or partner insurers in each of the countries in which the insured corporation does business to provide uniform coverage globally. The involvement when necessary by the locally admitted subsidiaries or partners assures that the program meets the laws and requirements related to compulsory and admitted insurance. Additionally, these subsidiaries or partners provide local expertise in managing claims and assessing risk. Coordination of the overall insurance program through a global insurer is more cost-effective and assures consistent coverage for the firm, regardless of where the losses arise.

Globalization of the Insurance Business

Table 22-5 provides market share data for the six largest insurance markets in the world. Perhaps the biggest driver of the increasing international focus of the insurance business is the globalization of the firms that buy insurance and purchase risk management services from insurers. Additionally, multinational firms are becoming increasingly sophisticated regarding risk management practices, and they demand the ability to combine and integrate their risk management programs on a global basis. Finally, these sophisticated global customers increasingly demand high-quality risk management services, such as claims management and loss control, wherever they do business. These changes in the needs and demands of the risk management customer have caused many insurers to further develop their international capabilities.

TABLE 22-5	Percentage Share of World Insurance Market, 2002		
Country	Total Business (%)	Life Business (%)	Nonlife Business (%)
United States	38.08	31.28	47.66
Japan	16.96	23.08	8.36
United Kingdom	9.01	10.39	7.03
Germany	5.17	3.96	6.87
France	4.76	5.23	4.09
Italy	3.20	3.41	2.90

Source: Swiss Reinsurance, SIGMA No. 8/2003.

An additional important factor in the expansion of U.S. and European insurers overseas has been the recognition that insurance markets in the industrial countries do not offer the same opportunities for growth in the next 10 years. The emerging economies in the countries of Eastern Europe and the Pacific Rim offer double-digit growth potential in insurance demand, while even with the recent hard insurance market projected growth in industrial countries is relatively modest. According to Swiss Re Group, real premium growth in 2002 was 8.9 percent in the U.S. and 3.5 percent in the United Kingdom, but 50.3 percent in Vietnam, 45.8 percent in China, 45.5 percent in Ukraine, and 66.8 percent in Lithuania. The tremendous potential for future growth of the insurance markets in some emerging economies can be seen by comparing the percentage of gross domestic product (GDP) spent on insurance. In North America and Western Europe, insurance premiums as a share of GDP were 9.39 and 8.58 percent, respectively. However, by comparison, insurance premiums were 2.76 percent of GDP in Eastern Europe and in the People's Republic of China, with more than a billion citizens, insurance expenditures represent only 2.98 percent of GDP.

SUMMARY

1. Insurance may be classified by type of coverage (personal or property), by ownership (private or public), and by type of demand (voluntary or involuntary).

2. Two predominant legal forms are taken by insurers: stock companies and mutual companies. While mutuals are important providers of insurance in all lines, increased emphasis on access to capital has led a number of insurers to convert to the stock form, especially in life insurance. Lloyd's and reciprocals, as types of insurers, do a negligible portion of the total insurance business in the United States.

3. As measured by premiums collected, the field of personal insurance (coverages involving the risk of loss of a person's income) is more than four times as large as that of property insurance (coverages involving the risk of loss of a person's property).

4. In general, two basic methods exist for distributing the insurance service. The first method, direct distribution, is found in life insurance and direct writing and uses semi-independent representatives whose authority is limited. The second method, indirect distribution or the American Agency System, follows the pattern of distributing tangible consumer goods and uses intermediaries that operate independent businesses.

5. Although the direct writing method of distribution is gaining in prominence in lines where standardized contracts and large-scale sales are possible, the traditional American Agency System continues to dominate the insurance distribution scene because it enjoys certain basic advantages. Undoubtedly the two systems will exist side by side for the foreseeable future.

6. Although some kinds of risk exposures faced by international firms are the same as those faced by firms that do business only in one country, many of these similar exposures are altered in both frequency and severity potential by differences in various parts of the world. Global firms also face a number of unique kinds of loss exposure. The globalization of business generally is also contributing to the increasing international focus of the insurance business. Insurers are expanding into new markets attracted by the prospect of relatively untapped demand for insurance in some emerging economies.

internetexercises

1. Virtually all major insurers now maintain extensive Web sites. Go to the list at http://www.barryklein.com/ and select one company that you've heard of and one that is new to you. Compare their Web sites. Which features would particular buyers find especially helpful? Are there aspects of the sites that would be useful for insurance agents?

2. Several organizations rate the financial strength of insurers. Go to http://www.moodys.com/insurance/ and use the links to identify one U.S. life insurer rated "Aa" or better, and one rated "Ba" or worse. You will need to register to use this site. How important would these ratings be if you were purchasing life insurance? Short-term disability coverage? Long-term health insurance? Explain.

QUESTIONS FOR REVIEW AND DISCUSSION

1. a. What are two major types of insurance? Explain the basic logic behind the classification of insurance used in this chapter.
   b. Which type of insurance is most important from the standpoint of premium income? What reasons would you suggest for the relationship observed?

2. a. Do mutual insurers provide for assessments?
   b. What advantages and disadvantages are there to the policyholder in being subject to assessments?

3. Suggest possible reasons why stock insurers dominate in such lines as commercial multiple-perils policies but have a smaller share of the auto collision insurance market.

4. In both reciprocals and Lloyd's associations, individuals are the underwriters. What significant differences exist between individuals in the two forms of organization?

5. What trends characterize the respective market shares of stocks and mutuals in property and life insurance? Can you suggest any reasons for these trends?

6. Does the American Agency System involve a long channel or a short channel of distribution? Is this system doomed because of the action by direct writers? Discuss.

7. The text states that survey data expose opportunities for further market penetration by the insurance industry. In what areas could additional sales efforts logically be made in insurance? Why?

8. What is the difference between direct distribution and indirect distribution in the insurance industry? Give examples of each.

9. What is meant by the term *mass merchandising* as applied to the insurance industry?

10. What is the direct response method of distribution? What do you see as the main limitation of this method from the standpoint of the insurer?

11. Mutual insurers have been called "communistic" in concept because they have no stockholders. Mutual advocates counter this charge with the statement that gain is the motive of the organizers of both stock and mutual companies. Evaluate both of these arguments.

12. Three items relating to insurer failures are as follows:
    a. In 1973 it was disclosed that one of the largest life insurers in the United States, the Equity Funding Life Insurance Co., had claimed assets that did not exist and had sold large amounts of fictitious insurance policies to reinsurers. A court-appointed attorney handling the reorganization under Chapter 10 of the bankruptcy statutes found no top executives on hand to help because they had all been fired. About 80 percent of the assets were found to be nonexistent, as were two-thirds of the claimed policyholders. Yet in three years the company was reorganized under a new name, the Orion Capital Corp., and it continues in business today. Most of the $380 million in claims against Equity Funding were settled with notes and stock in Orion.
    b. A news report stated, "Allied Reciprocal Insurers, formerly Peoples Inter-Insurance Exchange . . . is broke. Attorney says the company can't meet judgments and calls in Idaho department. . . . The underwriting exhibit of the company showed total income of $636,777, disbursements of $677,046, incurred losses of $4,274,627, underwriting expenses of $365,482, and total net underwriting losses of $106,326 . . . the only out to pay off outstanding claims will be for the insurance department to assess the policyholders unless some other reciprocal should decide to angle its deficits."
    c. Another news report stated, "The New York Insurance Department took over control of Professional Insurance Co. The department said that Professional's capacity was impaired by about $1.6 million. Professional writes primarily professional malpractice insurance. New

York has . . . fund that would protect most New York policyholders."

What are the major reasons for insurer insolvencies, and which would appear to be important in the previous cases?

13. Lloyd's of London issued contracts guaranteeing against cancellation of computer leases and lost as much as $1 billion when the introduction of a new, improved, less costly computer that gave incentive for leasing companies to replace computers and to cancel old leases triggered an avalanche of computer lease cancellations. If a lease were cancelled, the insurer was to pay the leasing company any revenues that it lost, after taking into account the proceeds from placing the computer with a new user. In your opinion, does the leasing policy meet the requirements of insurable perils? Why or why not?

chapter 23

Functions and Organization of Insurers

Most of this chapter deals with insurance company operations. While reading this material, you should reflect on how changes in the world at large will affect insurance operations. For instance, interest rates were at a 30-year low in early 2004. How should this fact have influenced the pricing of life insurance and long-tail liability lines (those loss exposures that take an extended period of time from when the policy is sold to when claims are made and paid out)? Or consider these developments: The cost of handling information is rapidly declining, the paperless office may exist by the year 2015, and insurance is becoming more internationalized. How will these factors affect insurer operating costs and the spread of risk? And what is the role of government in offering insurance?

Risk managers play a big role in the insurance process, but in that process they stand opposite to insurers. What is revenue to insurers is expense to risk managers, who are very sophisticated in their use of insurance. Risk managers usually retain losses that are predictable, manage those that are less predictable, and insure those that are catastrophic. This strategy leaves insurers with only the most difficult-to-predict commercial exposures to insure: product liability, pollution, and property losses in excess of $10 million. These types of loss exposures are catastrophic in nature (in other words, cause hundreds of millions of dollars in claims), and the possible product and pollution liability may be unknown at the time the policy is written, because case law is constantly changing and what is not compensable in 2004 may be in 2014. If this behavior is carried to an extreme, can insurers, as we have known them in the 20th century, survive? If you look at the experience of Lloyd's of London in the 1990s for insight to this question, you may say no!

CHAPTER OBJECTIVES

After studying this chapter, you should be able to

1. Explain why "production" in insurance is called "selling" elsewhere.
2. Explain the meaning of underwriting.
3. Show how insurance premiums are calculated and adjusted.
4. Understand the concept of credibility as it relates to rate making.
5. Differentiate between experience and retrospective rating.
6. Know what fair claim settlement laws are.
7. Understand the advantages and limitations of reinsurance.

Basic to understanding insurance is knowledge of what insurance companies do and how they are organized. The manner in which insurers determine rates, how they use reinsurance to spread their risks, and how they handle claims are examples of important functions that affect the insurance consumer and the risk manager. This chapter also discusses some of the problems facing risk managers in handling commercial insurance programs.

FUNCTIONS OF INSURERS

The functions performed by any insurer necessarily depend on the type of business it writes, the degree to which it has shifted certain duties to others, the financial resources available, the size of the insurer, the type of organization used, and other factors. Nevertheless, it is possible to describe the usual activities that are carried out, although it should be remembered that the specific nature and extent of each varies somewhat from insurer to insurer. These functions, which are normally the responsibility of definite departments or divisions within the firm, are:

1. Production (selling).
2. Underwriting (selection of risks).
3. Rate making.
4. Managing claims and losses.
5. Investing and financing.
6. Accounting and other record keeping.
7. Providing miscellaneous other services, such as legal advice, marketing research, engineering, and personnel management.

Production (Sales)

One of the most vital needs of an insurance firm is securing a sufficient number of applicants for insurance to enable the company to operate. This function is often called **production** in the context of the insurance industry; it corresponds to the sales or marketing function in an industrial firm. The term is a proper one for insurance because the act of selling is production in its true sense. Insurance is an intangible item and thus does not exist until a policy is sold. The production sales management team of any insurer supervises the relationships with agents in the field. In firms such as exclusive agents, where a high degree of control over field activities is maintained, it recruits, trains, and supervises the agents or salespersons. However, many insurers support marketing research departments whose job is to assist the production department in planning marketing activities, such as determining market potentials, designing and supervising advertising, conducting surveys to ascertain consumer attitudes toward the company's services, and forecasting sales volume.

Underwriting

Underwriting includes all the activities necessary to select risks offered to the insurer in such a manner that general company objectives are fulfilled. In life insurance, underwriting is performed by home or regional office personnel, who scrutinize applications for coverage and make decisions as to whether they will be accepted, and by agents, who produce the applications initially in the field. In the property-liability insurance area, agents can make binding decisions in the field, but these decisions may be subject to postunderwriting at a higher level because the contracts are cancellable on due notice to the insured. In life insurance, agents seldom have authority to make binding underwriting decisions. In all fields of insurance, however, agency personnel usually do considerable screening of risks before submitting them to home office underwriters.

The Objective of Underwriting

The main objective of underwriting is to see that the applicant accepted will not have a loss experience that is very different from that assumed when the rates were formulated. To this end, certain standards of selection relating to physical and moral hazards are set up when rates are calculated, and the underwriter must see that these standards are observed when a risk is accepted. For example, a company may decide that it will accept no fire exposures situated in areas where no fire department protection exists or will accept no one for life insurance who has had cancer within the previous five years.

When reviewing an application for property insurance for a piece of property, such as a farm, that is located where no fire department protection exists or when reviewing an application for life insurance in which the individual had cancer four and one-half years ago, the underwriter asks the question, "Can I make an exception for this application, or must I reject it because it does not come within the technical limitations of my instructions?" In answering this question, the underwriter visualizes what would happen to the company's loss experience if a very large number of identical risks were accepted. If the aggregate experience would be very unfavorable, the underwriter will probably reject the application. Alternatively, the underwriter may be willing to accept the risk for an additional premium charge.

netlink

Many opportunities are available for employment in the insurance industry. Review the featured jobs of the day at http://greatinsurancejobs.com, or search for "hot jobs" in insurance at http://hotjobs.yahoo.com. Students also can view short video clips on selected insurance careers such as actuary, insurance underwriter, insurance adjuster, and insurance salesperson by visiting http://www.acinet.org and browsing the career resources library.

Services That Aid the Underwriter

In life insurance, the underwriter is assisted by medical reports from the physician who examined the applicant, by information from the agent, by an independent report (called an *inspection report*) on the applicant prepared by an outside agency created for that purpose, and by advice from the company's own medical advisor. In property-liability insurance (as well as life insurance), the underwriter has the services of reinsurance facilities and credit departments to report on the financial standing of applicants and also can review loss histories of applicants. Underwriters increasingly have been making use of the applicant's credit history as an additional rating factor. Although statistical analysis suggests that the "insurance score" is a valid rating factor, its use has been somewhat controversial. For a discussion regarding the use of credit as a rating factor go to http://www.iii.org/media/hottopics/insurance/creditscoring/.

Policy Writing

Part of the work of the underwriting department may be most concisely described as **policy writing**. In property-liability insurance, the agent frequently issues the policy to the customer, filling out forms provided by the company. Or the form may be printed in the agent's office on a printer controlled by the insurer's computer. A check on the work of the agent to determine the accuracy of the rates charged, whether a prohibited risk has been taken, and other matters is done by the examining section in the home office of the insurer. In life insurance, the policy usually is written in a special department whose main task is to issue written contracts in accordance with instructions from the underwriting department and, because most policies are long term in nature, to keep a register of them for future reference.

Conflict between Production and Underwriting

Because the underwriting department may have turned down business that previously has been sold by an agent, an apparent conflict of interest arises between these two areas. The problem is similar to that which exists between credit and sales in other firms, with a good sale ruined because credit is not approved. Neither the agent nor the underwriter will profit long by underwriting that is too strict or too loose. The former will choke off acceptable business and may create unnecessary expenses in cancelling business already bound by the agent, whereas the latter invites such substantial losses that the company may be forced to withdraw entirely from a given line, to the detriment of the agent.

Underwriting Associations

Many independent associations have been formed by insurers to assist in underwriting. These associations, often called *pools* or *syndicates*, normally specialize in certain areas, such as nuclear energy, foreign coverages, aviation risks, marine risks, windstorms, and the like. Through such cooperation, the risk in these areas is spread among a large number of insurers,

Search the Web for a multitude of insurance links, including underwriting, in the "Business and Economy" section of http://www.yahoo.com.

and specialized personnel can be hired economically to supervise loss control procedures and handle other underwriting decisions. In this way, the underwriting function can be carried out more efficiently and with less risk to individual insurers. Nuclear reactors are insured by an underwriting pool.

Rate Making

Closely allied to the function of underwriting is that of **rate making**, which is extremely technical in most lines of insurance. In general, rate making involves the selection of classes of exposure units on which to collect statistics regarding the probability and severity of loss. In life insurance, this particular task is relatively uncomplicated because the major task is to estimate mortality rates according to age and other factors such as sex, smoking and/or drinking habits, and occupation. In other fields, such as liability and workers' compensation, elaborate classifications are necessary. In the latter field, for example, several hundred classes of employment are distinguished, and a rate is promulgated for each. Rate making is usually supervised by specialists known as *actuaries*. (See Figure 23-1.)

Once the appropriate classes have been set up, the problem becomes one of developing reliable loss data for each class over a sufficiently long period of time. Converting that data into a useful form for the purpose of developing a final premium is the next step. This requires incorporating estimates of the cost of doing business into the premium structure on an equitable basis. Rate making involves an estimation of the cost of including certain policy benefits or of changing policy provisions or underwriting rules, as well as the cost of writing business for which no data whatsoever have been accumulated.

Makeup of the Premium

The **insurance rate** is the amount charged per unit of exposure. The premium is the product of the insurance rate and the number of units of exposure. Thus, in term life insurance, if the annual rate is $1.50 per $1,000 of face amount of insurance, the premium for a $1 million policy is $1,500.

The premium is designed to cover two major costs: the expected loss and the cost of doing business. These are known as the **pure premium** and the **loading**, respectively. The pure premium is determined by dividing the total expected loss by the number of exposures. In automobile insurance, for example, if an insurer expects to pay $750,000 of collision loss

FIGURE 23-1   Organization Chart of a Large Stock
                Insurance Group That Handles All Lines

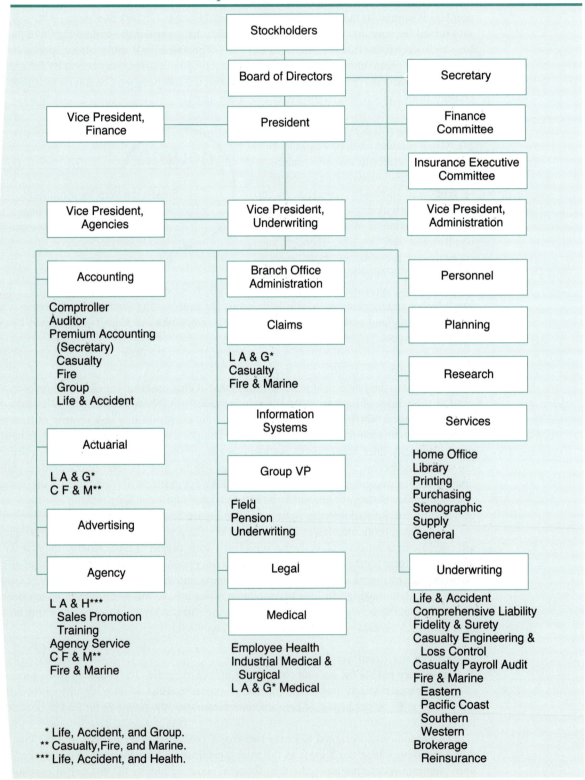

claims in a given territory and 1,000 autos are in the insured group, the pure premium for collision will be $750,000 ÷ 1,000, or $750 per car. The loading is made up of such items as agents' commissions, general company expenses, premiums, taxes and fees, and allowance for profit. The sum of the pure premium and loading is termed the **gross premium**. Usually the loading is expressed as a percentage of the expected gross premium; in property-liability insurance, for example, a typical loading might be 25 percent. This relationship is expressed in the following equation:

$$GP = PP + LP(GP)$$

where GP = gross premium
PP = pure premium
LP = loading percentage

It is common to rearrange the terms of the previous formula as follows:

$$GP - LP(GP) = PP$$

$$GP(1 - LP) = PP$$

$$GP = \frac{PP}{(1 - LP)} = \frac{750}{1 - 0.25} = \$1,000$$

The pure premium is the estimate of loss cost, and the ratio of the loss cost to the gross premium is called the *loss ratio*, which is represented by the term $(1 - LP)$ in the previous formula. As you can see, the loss ratio in that example is 75 percent. Thus, the gross premium of $1,000 may be found directly by dividing the loss cost by the loss ratio ($750 ÷ 0.75 = $1,000).

Modifying the previous example so that the pure premium is again assumed to be $750 per car but the loading is 30 percent means that the gross premium would be calculated as follows:

$$GP = \frac{750}{(1 - 0.30)}$$

$$GP = \$1,071$$

Another way to explain rate making in insurance is by analogy with retail store pricing. If a grocer buys a loaf of bread for $1 and sells it at retail for $1.50, the grocer's gross margin (or markup) is $0.50 and is expressed as a percentage of the selling price of $1.50, namely 33.33 percent ($0.50 ÷ $1.50). The grocer's cost of bread corresponds to the pure premium in insurance ($1 in the preceding case), the expected cost of loss. The grocer's gross margin, or markup, corresponds to the loading in insurance, that is, 33.33 percent for the case in question.

A basic difference between pricing bread and pricing insurance is that in the case of bread, the grocer knows the cost of merchandise in advance, whereas in insurance the expected cost of loss, or pure premium, must be estimated. The loss, if it occurs, happens at some future time after the policy is in force. Two factors must be estimated and are subject to errors in forecasting: *frequency* of occurrence and *severity* of loss. The insurer does not know in advance exactly how often a loss will occur or what its size will be. The expected cost of loss is a function of both frequency and severity of loss. For example, the insurer cannot know who an insured will hit in an auto accident. It could be an 80-year-old retired person or a successful 45-year-old brain surgeon.

Insurers handle forecasting errors in rate making by calculating estimates of both objective and subjective risk (discussed in Chapter 1). For example, the underwriters may use a probability distribution of loss frequency and severity. They also may add extra margins of safety in the estimate to compensate for a large perceived subjective risk.

Investment Earnings

The basic rate-making method used in property-liability insurance does not make a direct allowance for investment income to be earned on policyholders' funds held by the insurer until they must be paid out as losses. In life insurance, an allowance is made for a minimum assumed rate of return on policyholders' funds. From the 1950s through the early 1980s, a steady rise occurred in interest rates in the United States. Even the declines at the end of the 1980s still left long-term interest rates at near record levels (see Table 23-1). Given this increase in interest rates, policyholders and regulators demanded that some recognition be given to the investment income factor in rate making, especially in those lines of insurance that had a long payout period (medical malpractice, workers' compensation, and general liability). Today, insurers rarely make an **underwriting profit** (combined ratios less than 100) in these lines, because they rely on investment income for part of their profit. (Underwriting + investment revenue – expenses = profit.)

In Table 23-2, one can see that insurers almost always have a **combined ratio** greater than 100 for the selected liability lines. Clearly, they are relying on investment income to retain their profitability. In 2002, for the entire industry, underwriting losses were $31.9 billion, and investment income was $40.1 billion. Thus, operating income before taxes was $7.7 billion for that period.

Rate-Making Guidelines

All states establish certain criteria that insurers are expected to observe in calculating rates. These include the following specifications:

1. The rate should be adequate to meet loss burdens, yet not be excessive.
2. The rate should allocate cost burden among insureds on a fair basis.
3. The rate should encourage loss control efforts among insureds, if possible.

TABLE 23-1   **Aaa and Baa Corporate Bond Rates (in Percent), 1950–2002**

	Aaa	Baa
1950	2.62	3.24
1955	3.06	3.53
1960	4.41	5.19
1965	4.49	4.87
1970	8.04	9.11
1975	8.83	10.61
1980	11.94	13.67
1985	11.37	12.72
1990	9.32	10.36
1995	7.59	8.20
2000	7.62	8.36
2002	6.49	7.80

Source: *Economic Report of the President, 2003* (Washington, D.C.: U.S. Government Printing Office, 2003).

TABLE 23-2	Combined Ratios* for Selected Insurance Lines, 1994–2002			
	Private Passenger Auto Liability	Medical Malpractice	Workers' Compensation	Other General Liability
1994	105.7	96.4	101.6	123.6
1996	100.3	106.6	102.4	117.6
1998	102.0	115.7	111.2	112.3
2000	113.7	133.8	120.8	110.3
2002	110.1	140.8	112.2	124.2

*The combined ratio is the loss ratio plus the expense ratio.
Source: *The Fact Book 2004* (New York: Insurance Information Institute, 2004), 35, 72, 73, and 75.

Although these criteria seem simple enough on casual review, applying them raises many difficult problems. Some of these problems, many of which probably never will be solved completely either by insurers or by regulatory authorities, are described in the following paragraphs.

Adequacy of the Rate

If a rate is to be adequate but not excessive, how wide a margin should these limits impose? From one standpoint, an underwriter may reason that to have an adequate premium, it is necessary to collect an amount sufficient for all possible contingencies, whereas another underwriter may have a much different view of the size of these possible contingencies. This problem arises from the fact previously noted that the insurance rate must be set before all the costs are known. In many lines of business, the entrepreneur may ascertain all or nearly all costs before setting a price. If costs cannot be determined, the entrepreneur usually will insist that the contract of sale be subject to later adjustment to reflect the actual costs or will insist on a cost-plus type of contract. In insurance, however, a definite estimate must often be made in advance, with no possibility of later negotiation if the estimation of loss was incorrect. Frequently, these estimates are inaccurate because they are derived from past experience; the insurance contract may involve a substantial future period during which conditions change drastically. It is easy to see that opinions as to the future of insurance costs can vary widely.

The problem of preventing rates from becoming excessive has been the subject of much legislation, yet unrestricted competition often leads to rates that are too low for the long-term solvency of insurance companies. Having rates that are too low is just as bad as, if not worse than, having ones that are too high. Above all, the insured is seeking assurance that personal losses will be paid if and when they occur.

Fair Allocation of Cost Burden

Just how far should the underwriter go in developing a rate that completely reflects the true quality of the individual hazard, thus making the rate fair? The issue is of particular concern to risk managers of businesses as they select appropriate risk management tools for various situations. Theoretically, for life insurance purposes an attempt should be made to set individual premiums on the basis of occupation, income, marital status, drug or alcohol consumption, smoking record, and longevity of parents. In practice, none of these factors affects the premium individually because age, sex, and smoking habits are almost the sole determinants. If the criterion of fairness is carried to an extreme, it might be said that each person should receive a slightly different rate to reflect that person's particular situation. This, of course, would be impossible to administer and would make the rate-making task hopelessly complex. However, a decision must be made concerning where to draw the line and what criteria of fairness to use.

Another class of problems arising out of the criterion of fairness deals with the determination of the exposure unit to which the rate is applied. Automobile rates, for example, apply to the individual car; workers' compensation rates, to each $100 of payroll; property insurance rates, to each $100 of building value; and life insurance rates, to each $1,000 of policy amount on an insured life. Consider workers' compensation insurance. Two employers are in the same rating class, one paying 200 workers an average of $9 per hour and the other paying 300 workers an average of $6 per hour. Assuming that each has an hourly payroll of $1,800, each would pay the same workers' compensation premiums. But the first employer has an exposure of 200 workers, while the second has 300 workers. Should each employer pay the same premium?

Rate-Making Methods

One of the most difficult problems in insurance is that of developing rate-making methods that meet the criteria under discussion. The methods employed can seldom meet these criteria, and underwriting judgment, unsupported by statistical evidence, often plays a major role in rate making. The calculation of an insurance rate is in no sense absolute or completely scientific in nature. As in most areas of the social sciences, the scientific method in insurance makes its greatest contribution in narrowing the area within which executive judgment must operate. The basic approaches to rate making follow.

Manual or Class Rating (Pure) Method. The **manual**, or **class rating**, **method** sets rates that apply uniformly to each exposure unit falling within some predetermined class or group. These groups usually are set up so that loss data may be collected and organized in some logical fashion. Everyone falling within a given class is charged the same rate. Any differences in hazard attributable to individual risks are considered immeasurable or relatively small.

The major areas of insurance that emphasize use of the manual rate-making method are life, workers' compensation, liability, automobile, health, homeowners', and surety. For example, in life insurance, the central classifications are by age, sex, and smoking habits. In workers' compensation insurance, a national rate-making body collects loss experience data from more than 600 employment groups, and these data are broken down by state. In automobile insurance, the loss data are broken down territorially by type of automobile, age of driver, gender of driver, and major use of automobile. In each case, it is necessary only to find the appropriate page in a manual to determine the insurance rate—hence the term *manual rate making*. The central technique in manual rate making is the pure premium method, as previously illustrated. Today, such manuals are accessible on the computer.

Loss Ratio Method. It may be impractical to employ the manual rating method in developing a rate because of too many classifications and subclassifications in the manual. In other words, so many categories may be involved that losses on only a small number of exposures occur in a given time period. This small number of losses may be deemed insufficient exposure on which to base decisions from a statistical point of view. As a consequence, the new rate is developed by comparing the **actual loss ratio**, A, of combined groups with the **expected loss ratio**, E, and using the formula

$$\frac{A}{E} = \text{percent change indicated}$$

For example, suppose that the actual loss ratio is 0.80, but only 0.70 was expected when the old rate was promulgated. In this example, $A = 0.80$, $E = 0.70$, and the formula yields

$0.80 \div 0.70$. The new rate would be $8/7 = 1.143$ times the old rate, or roughly 14 percent higher. The loss ratio method is actually a rate-revision method rather than a rate-making method.

Individual, or Merit Rating, Method. The **individual**, or **merit rating**, **method** recognizes the individual features of a specific risk and gives a rate that reflects the particular hazard. A variety of merit rating plans are used to give recognition to the fact that some groups of insureds, and some individual insureds, have loss records that are sufficiently credible to warrant reductions (or increases) in their rates from that of the class to which they belong.

One generally used device is for the underwriter to set up **special rating classes** for which discounts from the manual rates are made, either beforehand in the form of a *direct deviation*, as it is called, or as a dividend payable at the end of the period. Presumably only those insureds meeting certain requirements are eligible for the special rate. For example, some direct writing companies, such as factory mutuals, severely restrict the classes of risk they underwrite and, if warranted, pay substantial dividends as a reward for loss control efforts.

In the field of life insurance, mutual insurers pay dividends that differ in amount according to the type of policy. Life insurers also grant rate deviations for special classes of insured groups, known as **preferred risks**, and charge extra premiums on other groups, called **nonstandard risks**. Automobile insurers use this method by distinguishing among applicants on the basis of their type of automobile and their traffic violation records. In workers' compensation, certain groups are entitled to a premium discount that varies according to the size of the annual premium.

Another widely used plan of individual rating is **schedule rating**. The best example of this is in the field of commercial fire insurance, where each individual building is considered separately and a rate is established for it. The physical features of the structure are analyzed for factors (such as the presence of sprinklers, distance from a fire station, and type of construction) that presumably affect the probability and severity of loss, and rate credits are given for good features in the form of a listing, or schedule. In effect, the insured is rewarded in advance for features it is hoped will yield a lower loss cost for all similar structures as a group. Schedule rating also is used in burglary insurance, with the insured being given rate credits for loss control devices such as burglar alarms and burglarproof safes.

A third way in which an individual risk may receive special consideration by the rate maker is through experience rating. Experience rating is permitted in cases where the hazards affecting the insured's operation are sufficiently within the insured's control so that it is reasonable to expect a reduction of losses through special efforts. If such special efforts are made, the insured is permitted a lower insurance rate for the coming period. Unlike schedule rating, which grants a discount for safe features, experience rating requires that the insured prove the ability to keep loss ratios down before being qualified for a loss reduction. Most experience rating formulas also impose a rate increase in case the loss ratios become higher than expected. Experience rating plans are used in workers' compensation, general liability, group health, commercial auto liability, and other lines of insurance.

A final way of recognizing individual differences in risk is through retrospective rating. In contrast to experience rating, under which rate adjustments apply only to the future period, retrospective rating permits an adjustment in rates for the period just ended. The premium is determined, in whole or in part, by the actual record of losses suffered by the insured during the policy year. The final premium is determined after all the facts have been determined. Employers become partial self-insurers, but they use the commercial insurer to limit their losses.

Combination Method. In many lines of insurance, a combination of manual and merit rating is used in different degrees. The rate maker may develop a manual rate and then proceed to set up a system whereby individual members of a group may qualify for reductions from the manual rate if certain requirements are met or may be subjected to increased rates under certain other conditions.

Credibility

A concept of basic importance in insurance rate making is credibility, which is especially important for risk managers of large organizations. In general terms, **credibility** refers to the degree to which the rate maker can rely on the accuracy of loss experience observed in any given area. For example, assume that the rate maker is faced with the task of revising a rate for a certain type of policy issued by the company in a given geographical area. The loss ratio on these policies indicates that losses have been considerably higher than anticipated. Should future rates be based on the experience of these losses, or is there a considerable likelihood that the last year under consideration produced higher-than-average losses only by chance? The rate maker wishes to know how many claims there would have to be before the loss experience observed should be given 100, 90, 80, 50, or 10 percent weight in preparing the rate revisions.

If on the next renewal the rate maker raised the insurance premium of everyone who had suffered a loss, the purpose of loss spreading, which is inherent in the insurance mechanism, would be largely undermined. If each small group were, in effect, required to pay for its own losses, risk transfer would not be achieved. It would not do to raise the fire rates of a small community that had a disastrous fire in only one year because the experience for such a small class for only one year is certainly not credible. Yet the insurer, in the interest of fairness, must make reasonable classifications of insureds and perils and charge an appropriate rate for large groups falling within these classifications. It is not fair for one group to subsidize another group if each group is large enough to develop loss experience that is reasonably credible.

The Credibility Formula

The concept of credibility may be stated succinctly by the formula

$$PP = PPi(Z) + PPp(1 - Z)$$

where PP = pure premium to be developed for a given insured i

PPi = pure premium based on the insured's past loss experience

PPp = pure premium based on the past experience of the largest population to which the insured belongs

Z = the weight (credibility factor) to be applied to the insured's past experience; Z is a number ranging from 0 to 1

Pure premium is developed by collecting all loss data falling into each class to be rated, dividing by the number of exposure units, and arriving at a number representing expected losses.

As Z increases, more weight will be applied to the insured's past experience; if Z equals 1, the pure premium to be charged is based entirely on the insured individual's past experience. This would be the case if the insured has a very large number of homogeneous exposure units at risk and is, in effect, large enough to be self-rated. It should be noted, furthermore, that as Z increases, the term $1 - Z$ decreases, and with it the weight given to the loss experience of the population. This approach is common in workers' compensation insurance experience rating.

For convenience, the values given to Z are expressed as percentages. The rate maker generally develops a scale of credibility for different lines of insurance, running from 0 to 1. As an example, let us assume that an employer's workers' compensation policy is found to produce a loss ratio of 0.70, compared with an expected loss ratio of 0.60 for employers in this occupational group. However, the number of claims on which the 0.70 loss ratio was calculated was of such size and type that only 60 percent credibility can be attached to this ratio. In the formula, $Z = 0.60$, $PPi = 0.70$, and $PPp = 0.60$. The pure premium for the employer in the forthcoming period would be based on a loss ratio of 0.66 rather than 0.70; that is, $PP = 0.70(0.60) + 0.60(1 - 0.60) = 0.42 + 0.24 = 0.66$. Because the employer's experience is not fully credible, the rate would be increased only 10 percent $(0.66 \div 0.60)$ rather than 16.7 percent $(0.70 \div 0.60)$.

Rate-Making Associations

Rate-making associations, or **rating bureaus** as they also are called, are very important. The largest bureau is Insurance Services Organization (ISO). Even though it might appear that rate-making groups would violate antimonopoly laws, most states specifically authorize such groups. This type of cooperation is essential, because many companies do not have a sufficiently large volume of business in certain lines to enable them to develop rates that are statistically sound. When the experience of many companies is pooled, however, as is done by a rate-making organization, a large enough body of data is available to permit a higher degree of credibility.

The influence of rate-making cooperation goes beyond the mere setting of fairly uniform rates. If companies are to charge similar rates, it follows that most of them also must plan fairly similar amounts for losses and expenses. Therefore, policy provisions must be quite uniform; otherwise, the cooperating insurers will not experience uniform loss ratios. Thus, rate-making bodies in general have worked toward uniform policy provisions and standard policies. This has had a far-reaching influence on the insurance business and has enabled an orderly development of coverage.

ISO develops statistical data for use by its member companies in the calculation of rates in various lines of property and liability insurance. It conducts actuarial research, reports loss costs, offers advice to others on rating problems, develops standard policies, files forms to state insurance departments, and offers management advice to its member companies. Other important rating organizations are the National Council on Compensation Insurance, which develops and administers rating plans for workers' compensation coverage, and the Surety Association of America, which makes rates for fidelity and surety bonds.

Because of concerns of regulators and consumers over the degree of price competition in insurance markets, ISO changed its rating philosophy in the 1980s and early 1990s. Rather than filing rates for insurers, it now provides loss costs (pure premiums). Insurers have to add their loading for expense. Because expense factors vary between insurers, this approach facilitates price competition.

Managing Claims and Losses

Settling losses under insurance contracts and adjusting any differences that arise between the company and the policyholder are the functions of **claims management**. In large organizations, risk managers are very involved with this process. Claims management is often accomplished in the field through adjusters who are employed to negotiate certain types of settlements on the spot. Such adjusters may have considerable legal training. The claims department of an insurer will have the responsibility of ascertaining the validity of written proofs of loss, of investigating the scene of the loss, of estimating the amount of the loss, of interpreting and applying the terms of the policy in loss situations, and finally of approving payment of the claim. These functions are more extensive in property-liability insurance than in life insurance because of the higher frequency of losses, the predominance of partial losses, and the uncertainty of the amount of loss in individual cases.

In many cases, the adjuster is a salaried staff employee of the insurer. In territories where an insurer does not have a sufficient volume of business to employ a staff adjuster, the insurer will often make use of an **independent adjuster**. This may be an adjustment bureau such as the General Adjustment Bureau, Cunningham Lindsey, or Crawford and Company, corporations established to handle adjustment for insurers on a fee basis. **Public adjusters** who specialize in adjusting functions are also available to represent policyholders in dealings with insurers. Public adjusters, who are legal agents of the policyholder (not the insurer), usually work on a contingency fee, for example, 10 percent, under which the insured claimant pays the adjuster according to the amount the adjuster is able to collect from the insurer on a given claim.

Careful management of claim settlements is of paramount importance to the success of an insurer. Reluctant claims settlement brings with it public ill will, which may take years to overcome.[1] Often negotiation with the claims department is the only direct contact that the insurance buyer has with the insurer. A bad impression received on that contact may result in loss of business, court action, regulatory censure, or even suspension of the right to carry on business in the jurisdiction involved. On the other hand, an overly liberal claims-settlement policy may ultimately result in higher rate levels and loss of business to competitors charging lower premiums.

Most states have passed **fair claim settlement laws** that are patterned after a model law, the Unfair Claim Settlement Practices Act, adopted by the National Association of Insurance Commissioners in 1971. These laws represent the single most significant legislation affecting the claims-settlement practices of insurers. Their requirements have formed the basis of many lawsuits against insurers by policyholders alleging unfair treatment in handling claims.

Among the practices deemed "unfair" are:

1. Misrepresenting pertinent facts or insurance policy provisions relating to coverages at issue.
2. Failing to investigate claims promptly or to acknowledge communications on claims.
3. Failing to investigate claims promptly.
4. Not attempting to confirm or deny coverage on claims within a reasonable time.
5. Not attempting to settle claims in good faith when liability has become reasonably clear.
6. Attempting to settle a claim for less than that to which a reasonable person would have believed he or she was entitled by reference to advertising material accompanying an application.
7. Delaying payment of claims by requiring an insured to submit a preliminary claim report and then later requiring submission of formal proof-of-loss forms, both of which contain substantially the same information.
8. Failing to provide a reasonable explanation for denial of claims.
9. Failing to maintain complaint-handling procedures.

Some insurers have had to pay punitive damages for bad faith claims for more than $10 million.

Investing and Financing

When an insurance policy is written, the premium is generally paid in advance for periods varying from six months to a year. This advance payment of premiums gives rise to funds held for policyholders by the insurer, funds that must be invested in some manner. Every insurance company has such funds, as well as funds representing paid-in capital, accumulated surplus, and various types of loss reserves. Selecting and supervising the appropriate investment medium for these assets is the function of an **investment department**. Investment income is

---

1 As was stated by one authority: "There is nothing quite so private as public relations. The insurance profession must handle each loss with every person in a satisfactory way. Public relations is the stone stalagmite and personal experience is the drop of water that builds the stone."

a vital factor to the success of any insurer. In life insurance, solvency of the insurer depends on earning a minimum guaranteed return on assets. In property and liability insurance, investment income has accounted for a substantial portion of total profits and has served to offset frequent underwriting losses.

Because the manner in which insurance monies are invested is the subject of somewhat intricate government regulation, the investment manager must be familiar with the laws of the various states in which the company operates. Investments also must be selected with due regard to the financial policies of the insurer. Property insurers typically have a combined capital and surplus ranging between 30 and 50 percent of total assets, and funds equivalent to this may be invested in common and preferred stocks. The extent to which this is done depends on the class of business written and on the need for liquidity. Life insurers have few of their assets invested in common and preferred stocks, primarily because the nature of the life insurance obligation dictates that guaranteed amounts be repaid to policyholders. To accomplish this, bonds and mortgages usually are selected as the major investment mediums. Large insurers have separate departments for major classes of investments, such as real estate loans, policy loans, and mortgages. The separate account divisions of life insurers invest a majority of their assets in common stocks.

As shown in Table 23-3, life insurers in the United States together were responsible for assets of almost $3.4 trillion in 2002, most of it in the form of fixed obligations such as bonds and mortgages. In contrast to property-liability insurers, life insurers had substantial investments in real estate and policy loans. Property-liability insurers as a group had a larger proportion of their assets invested in bonds and stocks than was true of life insurers as a group. In 2002, life insurer investment income was $180.8 billion, and while property-liability insurers earned only $40.1 billion on investments.

Table 23-4 shows the premium revenue of property-liability and life and health insurers. While life insurers have over three times the assets of property-liability insurers, their premium revenue is only 35 percent greater. Life insurers (as a whole) sell products that have larger reserves, and thus greater assets and greater investment income.

Within each group, interesting observations can be made. Within the life side, annuities have become the largest single source of premiums and represent 53.0 percent of premium income. On the property-liability side, private passenger auto and homeowners' lines account for 47.6 percent of premiums, down from 51.9 percent in 1998.

Life insurers manage two sets of portfolios: general account and separate account. The general account represents assets supporting fixed dollar obligations of insurers, such as life insurance policies. Separate accounts are assets supporting the obligations of insurers for such

---

TABLE 23-3   **Distribution of Life Insurer Assets**

| Asset | Distribution of Life Insurer Assets (in Percent), 2002 | |
	General Account	Separate Account
Bonds	72.9	19.8
Stock	3.5	73.7
Mortgages	10.1	0.7
Policy loans	4.3	0.1
Miscellaneous	9.2	5.7
	100.0	100.0

Source: *2003 Life Insurance Fact Book* (New York: American Council on Life Insurance, 2003), 17.

TABLE 23-4   Life and Property-Liability Insurance Premiums, 1985 and 2002

	Property/Liability Insurance			Life/Health Insurance			
	Private Passenger Auto and Homeowners	All Other	Total	Life	Health	Annuity	Total
1985 Premiums ($, billions)	63.5	80.7	144.2	60.1	41.8	53.9	155.8
2002 Premiums ($, billions)	179.6	197.6	377.2	134.5	108.7	269.3	512.5

Sources: For property-liability insurance, *1996 Property/Casualty Fact Book* (New York: Insurance Information Institute, 1996), 21–23; *The Fact Book 2004* (New York: Insurance Information Institute, 2004), 15. For life/health insurance, *2003 Life Insurance Fact Book* (Washington, D.C.: American Council of Life Insurance, 2003), 54.

obligations as pension funds and annuities. It should be noted that the separate account portfolio is much more risk aggressive (73.7 percent stock) than the general account (3.5 percent). The reason for this difference is that the risk bearer for the separate account is the investor, while the risk bearer for the general account is the insurance company.

Financing

Financing refers to the planning and controlling of all activities that are related to supplying funds to the firm. Insurance companies seldom have to raise outside funds, because most of the normal financing requirements are met by reinvested profits. However, problems such as determining dividend policies, meeting state solvency requirements, and handling the occasional negotiations for both long- and short-term capital sources fall within the province of the chief financial officer.

Accounting

The **accounting** function for insurance management has essentially the same purpose as accounting for the operating results of any firm, namely, to record, classify, and interpret financial data in such a way as to guide management in its policy making. However, given the highly regulated and complex financial nature of the insurance business, a special set of accounting rules called Statutory Accounting Principles (SAP) are applied to the financial reporting of insurers. These accounting principles form the basis for the financial filings that insurers must submit to the insurance regulators.

Miscellaneous Functions

Various functions such as legal advice, marketing research, engineering services, and human resource work often are performed for an insurer by individuals or firms outside the company or by a specialized department set up within the company.

Legal Advice

The function of the legal adviser is to assist others in the company in their tasks. Underwriters receive aid in the preparation of policy contracts and endorsements so that the company's intention will be phrased in correct legal terminology. In the administration of claims, partic-

PROFESSIONAL PERSPECTIVES

Trouble with a Claim?

Insure.com offers the following advice to insurance consumers involved in an automobile or homeowners' claim:

1. Know your policy. Ask questions *before* you need to make a claim if you have questions about what is covered.
2. Contact your insurance agent or company quickly. Having your agent involved may help get more timely attention paid to your situation.
3. Avoid using the word *lawyer*. When you hire an attorney, the insurer will only be able to communicate with

the lawyer. If you have difficulty with the claims process, contact your state insurance department.
4. Make temporary repairs to protect your home from further damage. For automobiles, get one or two estimates of the amount of damage.
5. Document everything and keep a copy of any police report that is issued. Photographs and videotapes are useful in documenting losses and the extent of the damage.

Source: http://www.insure.com/gen/claims.html.

---

ularly disputed claims, legal aid is important; if court action is required, the legal staff must represent the company or oversee such representation by outside legal counsel.

Marketing Research

Reference already has been made to the role of marketing research in assisting the production department. As yet, marketing research is not usually performed within the firm, except in the case of very large companies. Marketing research typically involves selected types of research, such as testing and developing effective advertising that can be a vital factor in the long-run success of any insurer. The success that direct writers have had in winning markets away from those insurers using the indirect channel of distribution has increased the interest of the latter in marketing research.

Engineering Services

Engineering services are used as valuable aids to rate making and underwriting. For example, the engineer provides information that will help answer the question, "How long will fireproof glass resist breaking when subjected to the heat of a burning building?" If a building has such glass, the underwriter is in a much better position to assess its importance.

Human Resource Management

Human resource management normally includes selecting and discharging employees, keeping employment records, supervising training and educational programs, administering recreational and fringe benefit programs, and other similar functions. Most large companies and many small ones have separate human resource departments. Regardless of the size of the firm, human resource management is an essential function. Insurance, particularly life insurance, has experienced a somewhat more rapid turnover of employees than other industries. The need for giving increased attention to the problem of turnover and discovering its causes has increased the scope and importance of human resource management among insurance companies.

REINSURANCE

A significant part of an insurance organization is reinsurance, a method created to divide the task of handling risk among several insurers. Often this task is accomplished through cooperative arrangements, called **treaties**, that specify the ways in which risks will be shared by members of the group. Reinsurance also is accomplished by using the services of specific companies and agents organized for that purpose. In turn, reinsurance companies purchase reinsurance from one another on specific kinds of risks. Through reinsurance the entire industrial world is organized to share risks so that a catastrophic loss in one part of the world may affect insurance companies and policyholders everywhere. In Table 23-5, the five largest reinsurers with respect to premiums written are given.

Reinsurance may be defined as the shifting by a primary insurer, called the **ceding company**, of a part of the risk it assumes to another company, called the **reinsurer**. That portion of the risk kept by the ceding company is known as the **line**, or **retention**, and the portion reinsured, the **cession**. The process by which a reinsurer passes on risks to another reinsurer is known as **retrocession**.

Uses and Advantages of Reinsurance

Why would an insurer that has gone to the expense and difficulty of securing business voluntarily transfer some of it to a third party? Four main reasons to do so are:

1. Reinsurance enlarges the ceding insurer's financial capacity to accept risk.
2. Reinsurance stabilizes profits and evens out loss ratios.
3. Reinsurance reduces the ceding insurer's unearned premium reserve requirement.
4. Reinsurance offers a way for an insurer to retire from underwriting a given segment of its insurance business.

Enlarging Financial Capacity

The primary insurer often is asked to assume liability for loss in excess of the amount that its financial capacity permits. Instead of accepting only a portion of the risk and thus causing inconvenience to and even ill will on the part of its customer, the company accepts all the risk, knowing that it can pass on to the reinsurer the part that it does not care to bear. The policyholder thus is spared the necessity of negotiating with many companies and can place insurance with little delay. Using a single policy with a single premium also simplifies insurance management procedures. The policy coverage is not only more uniform and easier to comprehend, but the added guaranty of the reinsurer also makes it that much safer.

TABLE 23-5	Five Largest Reinsurers, 2002		
		Net Premiums Written ($, billions)	Country
1.	Munich Re Group	$24.924	Germany
2.	Swiss Re Group	21.600	Switzerland
3.	Berkshire Hathaway Re Group	13.083	U.S.
4.	Hannover Re Group	8.526	Germany
5.	Employers Re Group	7.892	U.S.

Source: *The Fact Book 2004* (New York: Insurance Information Institute, 2004), 3.

Stabilizing Profits

Stabilized profit and loss ratios are an important advantage in the use of reinsurance. It is true that good business often must be shared with others, but in return some bad business also is shared. In the long run, it is usually considered more desirable to have a somewhat lower but stable level of profits and underwriting losses than it is to have a higher but unstable level.

This is not to imply that reinsurance arrangements necessarily reduce average profit levels, but they do smooth out the fluctuations that normally occur. Furthermore, reinsurance does not always mean the loss of premium volume, for one of the results of reinsurance is the procurement of new business. As a member of a group of ceding companies organized to share mutual risks, one ceding company usually must accept the business of other insurers. Some companies obtain a significant portion of their total premium volume in this manner, and others engage exclusively in the reinsurance business.

Reducing the Unearned Premium Reserve

For new, small companies especially, one of the limiting factors in the rate of growth is the legal requirement that the company set aside premiums received as unearned premium reserves for policyholders. Because no allowance is made in these requirements for expenses incurred, the insurer must pay for producers' commissions and for other expenses out of surplus. As the premiums are earned during the life of the policy, these amounts are restored to surplus.

In the meantime, however, the insurer may not be able to finance some of the business it is offered. Through reinsurance, the firm can accept all the business it can obtain from its agency force and then pass on to the reinsurer part of the liability for loss, and with it the loss and unearned premium reserve requirement.

Retiring from Underwriting

If a firm wishes to liquidate its business, it could conceivably cancel all its policies that are subject to cancellation and return the unearned premiums to the policyholders. However, this would be quite unusual in actual practice because of the necessity of sacrificing the profit that would normally be earned on such business. It would probably be impossible to recover in full the amount of expense that had been incurred in putting the business on the books.

Through reinsurance, however, the liabilities for existing insurance can be transferred, and the policyholders' coverages remain undisturbed. If an insurer desires to retire its life insurance business and to cease underwriting this line, it may do so through reinsurance. Because the life insurance policy is noncancellable, the policyholder has the right to continued protection. If it were not for reinsurance, the insurer would find it difficult, if not impossible, to achieve its objective of relieving itself from the obligation of seeing that the insured's coverage is continued.

Types of Reinsurance Agreements

Organization for reinsurance is found in many forms, from individual contractual arrangements with reinsurers to pools whereby a number of primary insurers agree to accept certain types of insurance on some prearranged basis.

Facultative Reinsurance

The simplest type of reinsurance is an *informal facultative agreement*, or specific reinsurance on an optional basis. Under this arrangement a primary insurer, in considering the acceptance of a certain risk, shops around for reinsurance, attempting to negotiate coverage specifically on this particular contract. A life insurer, for example, may receive an application for $10 million of life insurance on a single life. Not wishing to reject this business but still unwilling to accept the entire risk, the primary insurer communicates full details on this application to another insurer with whom it has done business in the past. The other insurer may agree to assume 40 percent of any loss for a corresponding percentage of the premium. The primary insurer then puts the contract in force.

The reinsurance agreement does not affect the insured in any way. Informal facultative reinsurance is usually satisfactory when reinsurance is of an unusual nature or when it is negotiated only occasionally. Such an arrangement becomes cumbersome and unsatisfactory, however, if reinsurance agreements must be negotiated regularly.

Occasionally, an insurer will have an agreement whereby the reinsurer is bound to take certain types of risks if offered by the ceding company, but the decision of whether to reinsure remains with the ceding company. Such an arrangement is called a *formal facultative contract* or *obligatory facultative treaty*. It is used where the ceding company is bound on certain types of risks by its agents before it has an opportunity to examine the applications. If the exposure is such that reinsurance is not needed or desired, the ceding company may retain the entire liability. In other cases, it will submit the business to the reinsurer, who is bound to take it. Such reinsurance agreements are often unsatisfactory for the reinsurer because of the tendency for the ceding company to keep better business for itself and pass on the more questionable lines to the reinsurer.

Automatic Treaty

To protect all parties concerned from the tendency previously described, to speed up transactions, and to eliminate the expense and uncertainties of individual negotiations, reinsurance may be provided whereby the ceding company is required to cede some certain amounts of business and the reinsurer is required to accept them. Such an agreement is described as an **automatic treaty**.

Two basic types of treaty have been recognized: **pro-rata treaties**, under which premiums and losses are shared in some proportion, and **excess-of-loss treaties**, under which losses are paid by the reinsurer in excess of some predetermined deductible or retention. In excess-of-loss treaties, no directly proportional relationship exists between the original premium and the amount of loss assumed by the reinsurer.

Pro-Rata Treaties. Pro-rata treaties come in many varieties, but perhaps the two most common are the surplus share treaty and the quota share treaty. **Surplus share treaties** cover only specific exposures—policies covering individuals or business firms—whereas **quota share treaties** cover a percentage of an insurer's business, either its entire business or some definite portion thereof.

An example of a surplus share treaty is the *excess line*, or *first surplus*, *treaty*. Here the ceding company decides what its net retention will be for each class of business. The reinsurer does not participate unless the policy amount exceeds this net retention. The larger the net retention, the more the other members of the treaty will be willing to accept. Thus, if the ceding company will retain $100,000 on each homeowner exposure, the agreement may call for cession of up to "five lines," or $500,000, for reinsurance. The primary insurer could then take a homeowners' risk of $600,000 — $100,000 to be retained and $500,000 to be ceded to the reinsurer.

First surplus share treaties call for the sharing of losses and premiums up to a stated limit in proportion to the liabilities assumed. Sometimes a second surplus or even a third surplus share treaty is arranged to take over business that is beyond the limits set by the first surplus share treaty. The surplus share treaty is probably the most common type of reinsurance in use today.

To illustrate how surplus share treaties work, assume that a primary insurer has issued a homeowners' insurance policy in the amount of $1 million subject to a four-line first surplus share treaty, a three-line second surplus share treaty, and a two-line third surplus share treaty. The insurer retains $100,000 of the risk. The risk is divided as follows:

Original policy limits	$1,000,000
Retention by primary insurer	100,000
Surplus	900,000
First surplus retention (4 lines)	400,000
Second surplus retention (3 lines)	300,000
Third surplus retention (2 lines)	200,000
Total cession	$ 900,000

Each reinsurer divides the premium and any losses in proportion to its share of the total limit of coverage. Thus, the primary insurer and the first, second, and third surplus reinsurers would divide premiums and losses on the basis of 1/10, 4/10, 3/10, and 2/10, respectively. If a $100,000 loss occurred, these four parties would pay $10,000, $40,000, $30,000, and $20,000, respectively. Premiums and losses on policies written for less than $1 million would be divided on the basis of the insurers involved. For example, a $500,000 policy would be divided by the primary insurer and the first surplus reinsurer on a 1/5, 4/5 basis. In this case, the capacity of the primary insurer and the first surplus reinsurer is sufficient to cover the $500,000 exposure. The second and third surplus retention policies are not needed. The reinsurer also pays the primary insurer a ceding commission to help pay for the first-year acquisition expense paid by the primary insurer.

Under the quota share treaties, each insurer takes a proportionate share of all losses and premiums of a line of business. An illustration of the quota share treaty is the **reinsurance pool** or **reinsurance exchange**. Pools are usually formed to provide reinsurance in given classes of business, such as cotton, lumber, or oil, for which hazards are of a special nature and for which the mutual use of engineering or inspection facilities provides an economy for participating members. Each member of the pool agrees to place all described business it obtains into the pool, but it shares some agreed proportion, such as 10 percent or 16.67 percent, of the total premiums and losses. Quota share treaties are especially suitable for new, small firms with limited underwriting capacity that would be unable to get started without such an arrangement because of the unearned premium reserve requirements.

Excess-of-Loss Treaties. It is not uncommon for a primary insurer to find that, although it is willing to accept up to $100,000 on each exposure insured in a given class, it is unable to stand an accumulation of losses that exceeds $500,000. To impose a limit on such losses, the excess-of-loss treaty has been developed, whereby the reinsurer agrees to be liable for all losses exceeding a certain amount on a given class of business during a specific period. Such a contract is simple to administer, because the reinsurers are liable only after the ceding company actually has suffered the agreed amount of loss. Because the probability of large losses is small, premiums for this reinsurance are likewise small.

A variation of the excess-of-loss type of reinsurance is the **spread-of-loss treaty**. Under a spread-of-loss treaty, the primary insurer decides what loss ratio it is prepared to stand on a given kind of insurance and agrees with a reinsurer to bear any losses that would raise the loss ratio above the agreed level for a period of years (e.g., five years). Thus, the ceding company has spread its losses over a reasonable time period and, in effect, has guaranteed an underwriting margin through reinsurance. In this way, an unusually high loss ratio in a poor underwriting year is averaged in with other years.

SUMMARY

1. The major functions of an insurer are (a) production (selling), (b) underwriting, (c) rate making, (d) claims management, (e) investing and financing, (f) accounting, and (g) miscellaneous activities, such as legal services, marketing research, engineering services, and personnel management. These functions are performed both by the home office and by the agency staff in the field.

2. Underwriting is the task of selecting subjects for insurance in such a way that the assumptions underlying the rate structure are realized in practice. It is the underwriting, claims-handling, and rate-making tasks that are truly exclusive functions of insurance. The other functions, although they are necessary to carry out these basic tasks, are not exclusively insurance functions, because they are common to most business enterprises.

3. Rate making in insurance is unusual in that the price of the product must be determined before all the costs are known. The rate is composed of two elements: the loss cost, or pure premium, and loading. Various rate-making methods have been devised to cope with the need to keep rates adequate, but not excessive, and fair to different classes of insureds. These methods include manual or class rating, individual or merit rating, and combination rating. Insurers are assisted in the rate-making task through cooperative efforts with rating bureaus or associations.

4. Reinsurance is an important example of one task that is accomplished by an external organization. The virtues of reinsurance include distribution of risk, stabilization of profits, reduction of legal reserve fund requirements, and facilitation of retirement from business. The major types of reinsurance agreements are facultative, pro rata, and excess of loss.

5. Claims-settlement practices in insurance have attracted special legislative attention with passage of fair claim settlement laws in most states. These laws are enforced by state insurance commissioners and represent standards by which insurance consumers can judge the adequacy of claims handling by their own insurers.

internet*exercises*

1. The Health Cost Index Report is an example of information that might be useful to actuaries in rate making for several lines of insurance. Past reports are available for free download at http://www.op.net/~pkreilly/backiss.html. Download and read one of these past reports. For which lines of insurance would this information be useful?

2. The Insurance Services Office (ISO) provides numerous types of information used by property-casualty insurers. Visit ISO's Web site at http://www.iso.com and find two products that you think would be especially helpful for (a) underwriters, (b) claims personnel, and (c) insurance agents. Explain.

QUESTIONS FOR REVIEW AND DISCUSSION

1. What justification is there for using the term *production* in the insurance field to refer to selling?

2. Distinguish between a rate and a premium in insurance.

3. An insurer develops a pure premium of $375 for residential fire insurance in Territory A. The expenses and profit allowance are calculated to be 25 percent of the gross premium. What should the gross premium be? Show your calculations.

4. a. What criteria should a proper insurance rate meet?
   b. Do you believe that an auto insurance rate that depends in part on the age of the driver meets these criteria? Explain why or why not.

5. Distinguish between experience rating and retrospective rating. Is the latter likely to be applied to a large firm or a small firm? Explain.

6. What justification exists for cooperative pricing in insurance when such an activity is often considered illegal "price fixing" in other industries?

7. a. Why does income from investments exceed underwriting income in property-liability insurance but is a smaller percentage of premium income in life insurance?

   b. In which line of insurance, property-liability or life and health, does investment income receive definite recognition in developing the insurance premium?

8. Among the unfair trade practices in insurance that are prohibited by many state laws is misrepresenting pertinent facts or policy provisions relating to coverages at issue. Suggest an example of something an insurer might do that would violate this requirement.

9. A study by the New York Insurance Department found that of 350 insurers that had stopped or suspended doing business in that state, the overwhelming reason for financial difficulty lay in inadequate underwriting. Explain the connection between inadequate underwriting and financial difficulty.

10. a. Explain what is meant by the "conflict between underwriting and production" in insurance.

    b. Do you feel that such a conflict is real, or is it only apparent?

11. Insurer R has written a fire insurance policy in the amount of $2 million on A's factory. R has a net retention of $100,000 on any one fire loss, and it has a pro-rata first surplus share treaty of nine lines, a pro-rata second surplus share treaty of five lines, and facultative reinsurance of $500,000 on A's plant. It now seeks an excess-of-loss treaty that pays any loss in excess of $25,000 on any one risk.

    a. If R has a loss of $1 million from a fire at A's plant, how will the loss be distributed under the existing reinsurance treaties? Explain.

    b. If R is able to obtain the excess-of-loss treaty, how much would it be able to recover from the excess-of-loss reinsurance? Explain.

12. An actuary develops a pure premium of $200 for residential fire, on the basis of a fire-year experience period. The pure premium in Territory A for last year was $400, because a large number of grass fires destroyed several homes. It is believed that the loss experience for Territory A is "25 percent credible."

    a. Using the credibility formula given in the text, show what the new pure premiums for Territory A should be.

    b. Explain why the credibility factor is only 25 percent.

chapter 24

Government Regulation of Risk Management and Insurance

Insurance is one, if not the only, major financial industry that is primarily regulated by the states. Each state has an insurance commissioner who is charged to supervise the insurance industry in that state. Also, there is the National Association of Insurance Commissioners (NAIC), which is much like the United Nations; each state can cast one vote, but the NAIC has little enforcement power. The individual states are left to make and enforce their own laws. An alternative to state regulation is federal regulation, and the federal government is constantly looking over the shoulder of state regulators to see if additional regulation is needed. While reading this chapter, you should examine the facts to determine if federal regulation is needed, and if so, what form it should take.

In addition to the issue of which body should regulate is the question of whom the insurance commissioner represents. The easy answer is that all the citizens and firms operating in the state are represented and that the commissioner is to regulate them in an impartial manner. This statement looks good in a textbook, but the real world is another matter. On one hand, insurance firms have a large number of employees and millions of dollars that can be used legally to influence the decisions that insurance commissioners and state legislatures make. On the other hand, many more votes are in the hands of consumers, and insurance commissioners do not forget that fact. In reading this material, the student should examine how insurance commissioners balance these interests and try to maintain a viable marketplace.

CHAPTER OBJECTIVES

After studying this chapter, you should be able to

1. Explain why insurance needs to be regulated.
2. Identify what aspects of insurance are regulated.
3. State the pros and cons of state versus federal regulation.
4. Indicate how regulation affects insurance rates.
5. Indicate the direction in which insurance regulation is headed.

Government has commonly laid down rules governing the conduct of business; insurance is no exception. In the case of insurance, however, the government has actively and directly engaged itself in the business. Some of the ways in which this has taken place, together with some of the reasons, will be discussed in this chapter.

WHY INSURANCE IS REGULATED

Certain characteristics of insurance set it apart from tangible goods industries and account for the special interest in government regulation. First, insurance is a service that is paid for in advance, but its benefits are reaped in the future (sometimes in the far distant future); often the beneficiary is entirely different from the insured and is not present to protect his or her self-interest when the contract is made. Second, insurance is affected by a complex agreement that few lay people understand and by which the insurer could achieve a great and unfair advantage if disposed to do so. Third, insurance costs are unknown at the time the premium is established, and there exists a temptation for unregulated insurers to charge too little or too much. Charging too little inevitably results in removing the very security the insured thought was being purchased; charging too much results in unwarranted profits to the insurer. Finally, insurance is regulated to control violations of the public trust.

Future Performance

The insurer is, in effect, the manager of policyholders' funds. The management of other people's money, particularly when it has grown to be one of the largest industries in the nation, immediately becomes a candidate for regulation because of the temptation for the unscrupulous to use these funds for their own ends instead of for those to whom the funds belong. One party to the contract (the insurer) receives payment currently, but the ultimate performance is contingent on the occurrence of some event that may not happen for many years. Two questions arise: How can the insured obtain a guarantee that the insurer's performance will be forthcoming? How can justice be obtained in case of failure by the insurer?

Complexity

We know that the insurance contract is not simple. In many instances, even if the layperson understands the implications of every legal clause in a contract, the rights of that person are vitally affected by the operation of certain legal principles or industry customs to which no reference exists in the written contract. The legal battles that have been fought over the interpretation of the contractual wording of a policy bear testimony to the fact that misunderstandings arise over the meaning of provisions even after the best legal minds have attempted to make the intent of the insurer clear. If misunderstandings can arise when they are unintended, it is easy to see that in the absence of any restraint, an insurer would find no difficulty in framing a contract that looked appealing on the surface but under which it would be possible for the insurer to avoid any payment at all.

Unknown Future Costs

The price the insurer must charge for service must be set far in advance of the actual performance of this service. The cost of the service depends on many unknown factors, such as random fluctuations in loss frequency and unexpected changes in the cost of repairing property. To increase business, an insurer may consciously underestimate

netlink

Learn more about the National Association of Insurance Commissioners (NAIC) by perusing its Web site at http://www.naic.org/.

future costs in order to justify a lower premium and thus attract customers. This strategy may ultimately lead to the bankruptcy of the insurer. If the insurer refuses to accept business except at a very high premium, consciously or unconsciously overestimating future costs, those who pay may be overcharged, and those who cannot pay will go without a vital service. Inability to obtain insurance may even prevent potential insureds from engaging in business because of inability to obtain credit or offer surety. Given all these factors, some people argue that at least some outside control over pricing in insurance is desirable for both the insured and the insurer.

Violations of Public Trust

As in any line of business, violations of public trust occur in insurance. These include failure by the insurer to live up to the contract provisions, formulation of contracts that are misleading and that seem to offer benefits they do not cover, refusal to pay legitimate claims, improper investment of policyholders' funds, false advertising, and many others.

Abuses in insurance have been such that major investigations of the insurance business have taken place, many of which resulted in reform legislation that is currently reflected in the regulatory environment. For example, in 1906 the Armstrong investigation in New York uncovered many abuses in life insurance and resulted in the mutualization of many stock insurers. An investigation of health insurance in 1910 in New York resulted in the adoption of uniform standard health insurance provisions. The Meritt Committee Investigation in New York in 1910 resulted in outlawing combinations to fix rates in insurance and also resulted in antirebating laws. In 1939, the Temporary National Economic Committee investigated insurance and uncovered abuses in industrial insurance, but the occurrence of World War II interrupted any significant reform legislation that might have resulted. The Federal Trade Commission investigated false advertising practices in insurance after 1950, resulting in reforms in the field of mail-order health insurance.

The U.S. Senate Committee on the Judiciary has continued to regularly investigate practices in insurance since 1958 and has often been critical of state regulation of the business. Finally, a massive investigation into auto insurance sponsored by the U.S. Department of Transportation in 1970 resulted in pressure on states to pass reforms in the field of automobile insurance, establishing the no-fault principle in about half the states.

The U.S. Department of Housing and Urban Development (HUD) has conducted indepth studies on alleged "redlining" by property insurers. In essence, it is claimed some insurers figuratively draw a red line around impoverished parts of a city and then do not write insurance or have any agents inside these lines. The Supreme Court of the United States has upheld HUD's authority to regulate this behavior.

It should be emphasized that most insurers operate their business in an ethical fashion. However, given the very nature of insurance, the danger of unscrupulous people entering the industry and trying to take advantage of consumers always exists. One of the tasks of insurance regulators is to protect the public from such abuses.

THE LEGAL BACKGROUND OF REGULATION

Insurance has traditionally been regulated by the states. Each state has an insurance department and an insurance commissioner or superintendent who has several specific duties. Before 1850, insurance was operated as a private business, with no more regulation than any other business sector. No financial guarantee was given that losses would be paid when due, and little control was exercised over the investment of funds collected as premiums. In general, the doctrine of *caveat emptor* (let the buyer beware) was the rule.

As a result of the early abuses of insurance, with their resulting ill effects on the consuming public and insurers alike, the need for regulation became apparent. Although many states had passed statutes affecting insurance by 1850, no state established special enforcement agencies until that year, when New Hampshire appointed an insurance commissioner. Massachusetts, California, Connecticut, Indiana, Missouri, New York, and Vermont followed this early example shortly afterward, and by 1871 nearly all states had some type of control or supervision.

In 1868, an important U.S. Supreme Court decision, *Paul v Virginia*, established the right of states to regulate insurance by holding that insurance was not commerce but was in the nature of a personal contract between two local parties.[1] Because insurance was held not to be commerce, the federal government would have no direct regulatory power through its right to govern interstate commerce as given under the commerce clause of the U.S. Constitution. This decision was upheld repeatedly until reversed in 1944 by the famous South-Eastern Underwriters Association case, discussed later.[2]

In 1871 an organization was formed that has had a far-reaching effect on regulation. This organization, later named the National Association of Insurance Commissioners, was composed of a group of state insurance commissioners through whose efforts a considerable measure of uniformity in regulation has been achieved. One of its first tasks was to introduce some uniformity into regulations governing the type of reports that insurance companies were required to make. Another task was to agree on a system of information as to the solvency of insurers so that an insurer did not have to prove solvency to the satisfaction of each state in which it operated. Still another job was to agree on uniform systems for valuation of legal reserves of life insurers.

The **South-Eastern Underwriters Association (SEUA) case** overturned by a vote of four to three the *Paul v Virginia* ruling that insurance was not commerce. The court held that insurance was commerce and that, when conducted across state lines, it was interstate commerce. The impact of this decision was to make insurance subject to federal regulation and, of course, to all federal laws regulating trade practices in interstate commerce. Laws that were to apply included the Sherman Act, the Clayton Act, and the Robinson-Patman Act, dealing with the control of business activities in restraint of fair trade (particularly price fixing), unfair trade practices, false advertising, and the like. The SEUA case overturned many previous Supreme Court decisions that had exempted the insurance industry and thus caused great uncertainty as to the future status of regulation.

THE MCCARRAN-FERGUSON ACT

The SEUA decision made it clear that some insurance associations had influence extending considerably beyond that of cooperative rate making. Certainly it was not the intent of state regulatory laws that boycotts and coercion should be a result of permission to form cooperative rates. Yet the complete abandonment of state regulation of insurance in favor of federal regulation was not desired by either the insurance industry or state insurance commissioners. Accordingly, the National Association of Insurance Commissioners proposed a bill that later became known as the **McCarran-Ferguson Act**. This bill, also known as Public Law 15, became law on March 9, 1945, and made these declarations:

1. It was the intent of Congress that state regulation of insurance should continue and that no state law relating to insurance should be affected by any federal law unless such law is directed specifically at the business of insurance.

2. The Sherman Act, the Clayton Act, the Robinson-Patman Act, and the Federal Trade Commission Act would, after a three-year delay, be fully applicable to insurance but only "to the extent that the individual states do not regulate insurance."

---

1 8 Wall. 168, 183 (1868).
2 322 U.S. 533.

3. That part of the Sherman Act relating to boycotts, coercion, and intimidation would henceforth remain fully applicable to insurance.

Except to the extent indicated by the provisions of the McCarran-Ferguson Act, the insurance business continues to be regulated by the states. However, the law does not exempt the insurance business from federal regulation and in fact provides for a limited applicability of certain federal laws to insurance.

Federal regulation of insurance is carried out by many different agencies. For example, the Federal Insurance Administration (FIA), which administers several government insurance programs, was involved in an extensive investigation of workers' compensation and no-fault automobile insurance. The FIA also is involved in the administration of the Price Anderson Act, which regulates nuclear energy liability insurance. The Export-Import Bank of Washington, D.C., a federal agency, administers the export credit insurance program. The Federal Trade Commission regulates insurance company mergers, mail-order advertising, and other trade practices affecting competition.[3] Regulations of the Security and Exchange Commission govern the issuance of variable annuities and some aspects of insurer accounting practices. The U.S. Department of Labor (DOL) influences coverage of coal miners for black lung disease. It also administers the Occupational Safety and Health Act, which affects the risk management practices of industry. DOL, together with the Internal Revenue Service, administers the Employees' Retirement Income Security Act (ERISA), under which the operations of private pension plans, many of them insured, are carefully regulated. A subsidiary agency, the Pension Benefits Guaranty Corporation, regulates and insures financial operations of private pension plans. It seems clear that federal regulation of insurance activity is a continuing trend.

Following the passage of the McCarran-Ferguson Act, the National Association of Insurance Commissioners formulated a model bill that was designed to accomplish at the state level what the Sherman, Clayton, FTC, and Robinson-Patman Acts accomplish as applied to business generally. This model bill (known as the All-Industry Rating Bill) was adopted in whole or in part by most states and contains many recommendations. In general, the philosophy of the legislation emerging from these recommendations is that rate-making cooperation is *neither required nor prohibited*, except to the extent necessary to meet the general requirement that rates be adequate, not excessive, and nondiscriminatory. Machinery is provided whereby an insurer may file a lower or "deviated" rate on showing that the rate meets these requirements. Membership in a rate-making organization is not required. Currently, rate competition is relatively unrestricted in about half the states.

In recent years, a variety of proposed legislation has been considered by Congress to repeal the McCarran-Ferguson Act or to otherwise increase the federal government's role in insurance regulations. Over the years, bills have been introduced in both the Senate and the House of Representatives to remove, wholly or partially, the immunity from federal antitrust legislation now extended to insurance companies under the McCarran-Ferguson Act. In 2002, bills were introduced in Congress to allow for optional federal chartering of insurers. Under this proposed legislation, insurers would have the option of either remaining under current state-based regulation or obtaining a federal charter and being regulated by the federal government. Proponents argue this approach would make the system more efficient, but others contend that this dual system could create confusion and increase the overall cost of regulation. The insurance industry itself is divided on the issue, and passage of such legislation does not appear imminent.

In summary, both states and the federal government are currently exercising regulatory control over the insurance industry. States still have basic regulatory functions, while the fed-

---

3 Roland W. Johnson, "Section of the Clayton Act as a Tool to Curtail Conglomerate Acquisitions of Insurance Companies," *Washington Law Review* 46, May 1971, 497–539.

eral government exercises regulation in specified areas only. The general trend seems to be for more federal control.

FEDERAL VERSUS STATE REGULATION

For many years, the argument as to whether federal regulation of the insurance industry would be superior to the present system of state regulation has been of considerable concern to parties both inside and outside the insurance business. Federal regulation is a continuing possibility since the SEUA case opened the door, a door that was not entirely closed by the McCarran-Ferguson Act. The chief arguments for federal regulation, many of which amount to criticisms of state control, are:

1. State regulation is not uniform and, in spite of certain accomplishments toward uniformity by the National Association of Insurance Commissioners, is not likely to become so. Insurers are subjected to different requirements in each state.

   For example, if APEX Life wishes to sell a certain policy nationally but State A prohibits the use of a certain policy provision, State B prohibits the use of another, and State C prohibits a third, APEX must amend its policy differently in States A, B, and C. It may decide not to offer the policy at all in these states, thus denying consumers the right to purchase the policy.

   Some insurers have withdrawn from a given state because of its restrictive regulation of rates that can be charged. (This has occurred most commonly with automobile insurance.) When an insurer withdraws from writing a given line of insurance, it may be required to withdraw from selling other lines of coverage in that state as well. The result is that an insurer's operations are greatly complicated; its normal market becomes a patchwork of areas, some in which it can operate freely, some in which it cannot operate at all, and some in which it may operate partially.

2. State regulation is relatively ineffective. It is not a suitable mechanism to regulate or control the activities of an insurer that is nationwide in its operation. If a given state prohibits a certain activity as being dangerous or unlawful, this of course does not affect the operation in another state, and so the objectionable practice continues elsewhere. If the particular practice is really dangerous, its continuation may affect the insurer's operation in the particular state, even though the practice is not carried on in that state.

   This complaint gave rise in the state of New York to a law known as the Appleton Rule, whereby an insurer admitted to do business in New York must adhere to New York's requirements not only in New York but also in all other states where the insurer is doing business.[4] Thus, if New York prohibits an insurer from issuing a certain type of policy in that state, the insurer, as a condition of continued operation there, will have to forgo its right to issue the policy in any other state where it is doing business. The Appleton Rule has had the effect of greatly extending the influence of New York's insurance underwriting requirements in other states because of the great size of the insurance market and the desire of insurers to operate there. However, many insurers either do not operate in New York or they operate a separate subsidiary in New York, in order to avoid subjecting their entire operations to New York's regulation.

3. Federal regulation would be more effective and less costly for insurers than state regulation. Ill-advised statutes have been enacted by various states. These statutes presumably would be avoided under federal control because of the greater political insulation from local pressures enjoyed by national legislators.

Opposing these arguments are those who favor continued state regulation. In general, state insurance commissioners are opposed to federal regulation, as are many (but not all)

---

4 The Appleton Rule has been upheld by the courts. See *Fireman's Insurance Co. of Newark, N.J. v Beha*, 30 F.2d 539 (1928).

PROFESSIONAL PERSPECTIVES

Insuring Terrorism Risk

Prior to September 11, 2001, the risk of terrorism in the United States had not been considered significant. On that date, of course, everything changed. Suddenly, the cost and availability of insurance for terrorism risk became a focus of concern for risk managers, insurers and reinsurers, and the government. It became very difficult for many firms to get any terrorism coverage. Billions of dollars worth of construction projects were reportedly put on hold due to a lack of terrorism coverage, and there was fear that the lack of adequate terrorism coverage had the potential to do serious damage to the U.S. economy. Congress responded to the problem by passing the Terrorism Risk Insurance Act of 2002. Under the law, insurers are required to offer terrorism coverage to their commercial lines consumers. The insurers can set their own premiums for the coverage. In addition, the legislation creates a federal backstop for the insurance industry that would be activated after a terrorism event. Insurers would pay claims for a terrorism event up to a deductible based on each insurer's total premiums written, then the federal government would pay 90 percent of insured losses beyond that, with the government's total losses capped at $100 billion. The backstop program is designed to be temporary and is scheduled to expire at the end of 2005, unless extended by Congress. The appropriate balance between the private sector and the public sector in paying for terrorism losses is an issue that will be debated for years to come.

Source: Mark A. Hoffmann, "Congress OKs Terror Backstop," *Business Insurance*, November 25, 2002, 1–2.

representatives of the insurance industry. The following are the major arguments in favor of state regulation:

1. State supervision and regulation of insurance is reasonably satisfactory, and no overpowering reason exists why federal regulation should be necessary. The burden of proof that a change is necessary should fall on those who seek the change, and such proof has not yet been produced.

2. Most of the arguments of those who favor federal control rest on dubious claims of inefficiency and on unproved claims that federal control would be more efficient. There is reason to believe that federal control would actually be less efficient because of isolation from local conditions and inability to deal with problems from afar. For example, federal regulation led to the well-known savings and loan and bank problems of the recent past.

3. Although lack of uniformity is admitted, the really important needs for uniformity have been achieved or are being achieved through the voluntary cooperation of state insurance commissioners.

4. State regulation is more flexible than federal regulation. State regulation can relate to local needs. It can encourage experimentation and development in insurance procedures and contracts. States can adopt the best practices of other states and avoid other states' mistakes. A mistake in federal regulation would have much greater consequences than a regulatory mistake by a single state.

5. If federal regulation were imposed, the result might be two systems of regulation instead of one. The operations of a very large number of insurance companies are confined entirely within the boundaries of a single state. Presumably, the states would continue to regulate these activities as intrastate commerce. Hence, state insurance departments would have to continue their existence, and the federal system would be superimposed on a state system. This would result in more wasteful overlapping, confusion, and duplication than now exist.

Some form of federal influence and state regulation probably will continue, but outright federal control seems unlikely, at least in the foreseeable future. Increasing federal influence in insurance will likely be felt both in the form of regulation and by means of direct government competition in insurance.

RESPONSIBILITIES OF THE INSURANCE REGULATORS

The responsibilities of the state insurance department can be classified into four primary categories:

1. Licensing and enforcement of minimum standards of financial solvency
2. Regulation of rates and expenses
3. Agents' activities
4. Control over contractual provisions in insurance policies and their effects on the consumer

Licensing and Financial Solvency

It is the primary responsibility of the state insurance department to see that insurers operating within the boundaries of the state are financially responsible. To accomplish this task, the insurance commissioner enforces the state's laws regarding the admission of an insurer to do business, the formation of new insurers, and the liquidation of insurers who become insolvent. The commissioner must see that adequate reserves are maintained for each line of insurance written and that the investments of the insurer are sound and comply with the state requirements.

Minimum Capital

To do business in a state, an insurer must first be licensed. Licenses are granted according to the type of insurance business to be conducted. Different capital standards are applied to each type. Minimum financial standards are set forth in each state, and they vary considerably from state to state and by type of insurer. In many states, no distinction is made in capital requirements according to type of insurance written, but a blanket amount is required for insurers writing any of a long list of contracts. In the 1990s additional capital requirements were added beyond the flat dollar minimums. These are called **risk-based capital (RBC) requirements**. The RBC system was developed by the National Association of Insurance Commissioners. Under this system, the minimum amount of capital an insurer must hold varies according to the insurer's particular asset and liability portfolio. Insurers with investments in riskier assets and those who write riskier lines of insurance are required to hold more capital. The NAIC RBC system has its critics, but most would agree that the basic concept of varying capital requirements according to the specific risks of an insurer makes sense.

Evidence shows that minimum legal capital requirements for some types of insurers have not always been set at adequate levels. The turnover among insurers has been substantial. One of the important reasons for termination of an insurer is financial difficulty that might have been avoided with greater financial resources. For example, one of the principal causes for termination of a newly organized life insurer is lack of adequate capital to meet heavy initial expenses and to write new insurance.

Investments

Insurers do not have complete freedom over how to invest policyholder funds. Excessively risky investments may result in an insurer being unable to meet its obligations to its insureds. Accordingly, all states impose investment limitations on insurers. In general, the philosophy behind these limitations is to require that funds paid in as an advance payment of premiums be invested relatively conservatively. The objective is to maintain safety and to give sufficient liquidity to enable insurers to pay all claims when due, if necessary by selling assets. Often the law will specify that each bond or mortgage invested in meet certain minimum standards of asset protection, interest coverage, and so on. Most states restrict the amount a life insurer may invest in common stocks. A common requirement is to limit stocks to 10 percent of assets but in no case to more than the insurer's surplus. On the other hand, fewer restrictions are placed on how much a property-liability insurer may invest in common stocks. Instead, the laws specify that property-liability insurers must invest funds representing their reserve liabilities in specified ways, such as bonds and mortgages meeting certain requirements.

Furthermore, certain types of assets are not recognized or admitted for purposes of state regulation. Nonadmitted assets typically include office furniture, overdue balances from agents, and other assets not normally subject to liquidation for meeting obligations due to policyholders.

Liquidation

The insurance commissioner is charged with the responsibility of liquidating an insolvent insurer. When this happens, an equitable treatment of policyholders and other creditors is essential. Some types of insurers subject their policyholders to additional assessments in the event of financial inability to pay claims, and the insurance commissioner must see that these obligations are paid.

Security Deposits

Most states require that each insurer licensed to do business within state boundaries make a deposit of securities with the insurance commissioner to guarantee that policyholders will be paid claims due them. These laws have been unpopular for several reasons. The size of the deposit is generally too small in proportion to the volume of business to be of any real protection to the insured. The state should logically depend on the quality of its examinations and other procedures to see that the insurer is solvent. The size of the deposit required generally bears little or no relationship to the size of required amounts of capital and surplus or reserves. It is common for one state to waive the requirements for insurers operating within its boundaries if other states do likewise for insurers chartered in that state. Thus, the security deposits may give little added protection to policyholders while complicating insurance regulation.

Guaranty Funds

All 50 states, Puerto Rico, and the District of Columbia have enacted some type of legislation covering the insolvency of insurance companies. Much of this legislation is patterned after, but not identical to, the model bill proposed by the National Association of Insurance Commissioners (NAIC) in 1969. The purpose of the legislation, as phrased by the NAIC model, is to provide a mechanism for the payment of covered claims under certain insurance policies, to avoid excessive delay in payment, to avoid financial loss to claimants or policyholders because of the insolvency of an insurer, to assist in the detection and prevention of insurer insolvencies, and to provide an association to assess the cost of such protection among insurers.

As part of the system for dealing with insurance company insolvencies, **guaranty funds** have been established by all states. When insurers become insolvent, guaranty funds pay the policyholder claims that the bankrupt insurers are unable to pay. The guaranty funds obtain the money needed to pay these losses through assessments on the remaining insurers. The importance of these guaranty funds can be judged by the fact that from their beginning in 1969 through 2000, assessments of over $7 billion have been made against insurer members. Assessments have occurred in all states, indicating the pervasive nature of the insolvency problem. Table 24-1 lists guaranty fund net assessments during recent years.

TABLE 24-1	**Guaranty Fund Net Assessments, 1993–2002**

Year	Net Assessment ($)*
1993	545,390,211
1994	524,901,618
1995	94,832,290
1996	124,169,554
1997	263,693,050
1998	263,627,912
1999	201,340,339
2000	328,609,659
2001	734,672,749
2002	1,208,952,740

* New York State not included.
Source: *The Fact Book 2004* (New York: Insurance Information Institute, 2004), 31.

The guaranty fund system represents another example of action to forestall the creation of any new federal government control over insurance. The associations are controlled by the private insurance industry under state supervision. They have been critical in maintaining support for state insurance regulation by minimizing losses experienced by policyholders from insurance company insolvencies.

Regulation of Rates and Expenses

The state insurance department is responsible for regulating the rates and expenses of insurance companies. If inadequate rates are charged, insolvency becomes a threat. If excessive or discriminatory rates are allowed, the insurance department must handle public complaints.

Property-Liability Rates

In all states, rates that are used must meet three basic requirements:

1. The rate shall be reasonable.

2. The rate shall be adequate to cover expected losses and expenses.

3. The rate shall not be unfairly discriminatory among different insured groups.

The typical rating law in many states permits insurers to form rating bureaus and to pool statistical information with these bureaus. The Insurance Service Organization (ISO), a prominent rating organization for property-liability insurance, no longer provides "advisory rates" for its members but instead issues "advisory loss costs," which include costs of losses, marketing, underwriting, profit, and contingencies. Insurers are not required to belong to the rating bureau and instead may operate independently.

In about 30 states, **prior approval** laws dictate that a rate must first be filed with the insurance commissioner before it can be used. The commissioner must respond within a period of 10 or 30 days, giving permission to use the rate or not. Insurers are supposed to provide statistical evidence that filed rates meet the requirements of reasonableness, adequacy, and nondiscrimination.

The remaining states have what are called **open competition laws**, under which rating bureaus can publish advisory rates only. In some of these states, insurers are not required to file rates with the commissioner at all, and in others insurers must file rates but are permitted to use them immediately. The latter category makes up what are known as **file-and-use** states. Competition is relied on to see that the rates meet the three requirements discussed earlier.

Prior Approval versus Open Competition Laws

One advantage of open competition laws is their relative flexibility, especially in regard to eliminating the delays in getting approval for rating changes that exist under prior approval laws. Open competition laws also help increase the availability of insurance. Under prior approval laws, if a rate is turned down, the insurer may refuse to issue any coverage, thus restricting the supply of insurance. Under open competition laws, coverage usually is available, even though the rate may be high.

Prior approval laws also are said to discourage innovation. If an insurer develops a new insurance policy, permission must first be obtained to sell it at an approved price. Prior approval laws subject the insurance commissioner to political pressures to refuse to approve rate increases, even though the increases may be justified. Thus, rates are subject to negotiation between the commissioner and the insurers, and are not determined scientifically.

State-Mandated Rates

A few states have passed laws setting rates for given lines of insurance or requiring insurers to reduce automobile insurance rates. Political factors usually have a large role in setting rates in these states. Frequently, private insurers withdraw from states with undue restrictions on rates or on policy coverages.

Another example of state-mandated rates is *unisex rating*. Several states require insurers to pool loss experience for males and females and quote a single rate, rather than specifying separate rates for males and for females. Using sex as a rating factor is not allowed. These laws affect the method used in developing rates rather than the rate itself. The effect of these laws has been to increase the rates women pay for some lines of insurance (such as automobile insurance and individual life insurance) and reduce the rates women pay for other lines (such as individual health insurance), and vice versa for men.

Life Insurance Rates

Life insurance rates are essentially unregulated by states, except indirectly through regulation of expenses and reserves. For example, insurers chartered in New York are subject to a limitation on agents' commissions, which must not exceed 55 percent of the first year's premium of an ordinary life insurance policy. This limitation applies to some of the country's largest life insurers, and it affects their business throughout the United States. Recall that under New York's Appleton Rule, insurers operating in New York must adhere to New York's laws wherever they sell insurance. The commission limitation helps keep life insurance rates lower than they might otherwise be. Many insurers not operating in New York are allowed to pay much larger commissions, sometimes as much as 200 percent or more of the first year's premium of an ordinary life insurance policy.

Life insurance rates also are affected by reserve and mortality assumptions. Life insurance reserves represent an insurer's obligations to the policyholder for the savings element in the life insurance policy. In calculating the reserve, an insurer assumes that it will earn some minimum interest rate and will experience a certain mortality rate. The higher the interest assumption and the lower the mortality rate assumed, the lower the reserve and the associated premium rate will be. States generally regulate the maximum interest assumption and the minimum mortality table in order to be assured that the life insurer will not charge so little that it cannot meet its obligations to the policyholder. Thus, the effect of state regulation of reserves is to set a floor on life insurance rates.

It is assumed that competition among insurers will operate to keep life insurance rates from becoming excessive. However, wide variations exist in life insurance premiums among insurers in the open market. A considerably active movement exists to require life insurers to disclose more information about costs to the policyholder so that a more intelligent buying decision can be made. It may be presumed that as additional cost information is made available, open competition in life insurance will become more efficient and will result in less variation in premium rates than now exists. The Internet also may contribute to reduced variation in rates. A number of Web sites now make it very easy to compare prices of life insurance across a large number of insurers. In the long run, this may contribute substantially to improving the efficiency of the life insurance market. At least for now, however, it certainly pays to shop around for life insurance, as substantial price variation still exists.

Agents' Activities

The agent has been a dominant figure in the insurance industry almost from the beginning, and for most consumers, the agent is the only contact with the insurer. Because insurance is a complex business, it is vital that the agent be well trained and possess a requisite degree of business responsibility. Most states require any insurance representative to be licensed and, as a condition of licensing, to pass an examination covering insurance and the details of the state's insurance law.

Part of the reason for the failure of insurers to insist on higher standards is traceable to the fact that agents generally are paid on a commission basis. The insurer assumes that because nothing is paid out unless the agent produces business, the easiest way to obtain more business is to hire more agents. In such an atmosphere, of course, the insurer is not likely to insist that its agents be exceptionally well trained. However, standards of licensing and training are steadily improving. It is being recognized that a poor agent may cost the insurer dearly in public ill will and lawsuits, not to mention the cost of furnishing the agent with service, training materials, and the like.

Most state laws prohibit such practices as twisting, rebating, and misrepresentation in the sale of insurance. **Twisting** occurs when an agent persuades an insured to drop an existing insurance policy by misrepresenting the facts for the purpose of obtaining an insured's new business. **Rebating** occurs when an agent agrees to return part of the commission to an insured as an inducement to secure business. Some insurers get around antirebate laws by offering identical policies with different premiums to reflect different commission levels to agents. An agent may sell the policy with lower rates to meet competition, accepting a reduced commission in order to make the sale.

An example of **misrepresentation** is making misleading statements about the cost of life insurance. For example, New York has specifically prohibited the use of the traditional net cost method of determining the cost of life insurance by representing that this cost equals the difference between the premiums paid and the sum of dividends and ending cash values.[5] An agent's license can be revoked for these kinds of offenses.

In recent years, the insurance industry has expanded its offerings to include various types of equity products, such as variable life insurance and mutual funds. Because variable annuities are subject to federal as well as state regulation, the Securities Act of 1933, the Securities Exchange Act of 1934, and the Investment Company Act of 1940 affect the insurance business directly. Both the product itself and its distribution are carefully regulated. The 1933 act requires full disclosure to the buyer of all pertinent data regarding an issue of common stock. The 1934 act regulates trading and the operations of the securities markets to prevent fraud and manipulation. The 1940 act gave the Securities and Exchange Commission, which has the responsibility of administering the various securities laws, the power to regulate the type of sales literature, selling behavior, and sales compensation for selling variable annuities and other equity products of insurers.

---

5   Regulation 74, New York Insurance Department, effective January 1, 1975.

As a result of these laws, an insurance sales agent of equity products must pass an examination covering the securities market and variable annuities before selling equity products. These examinations are prepared by such agencies as the National Association of Securities Dealers (NASD), the Securities and Exchange Commission (SEC), and the National Association of Insurance Commissioners (NAIC). In addition, the agent must satisfy any state licensing and education requirements.

Regulation of Contract Provisions

We have seen that the provisions of many insurance contracts are determined by statute. New policy forms must be approved in most states before they are offered to the public. One purpose of such laws is to assure that the rates being used by insurers meet state requirements as to adequacy, nonexcessiveness, and fairness. For example, an insurer could obtain an unauthorized rate increase by reducing its coverage rather than by filing for an increased rate.

Another purpose of such regulation is to protect the public against deceptive, misleading, or unfair provisions. The insurance commissioner's offices in most states have set up departments to handle consumer complaints about insurance policies. Contractual provisions causing the most controversy have been in the fields of automobile and accident and health coverages.

A third purpose of policy provision laws is to approve the language in policies that is intended to make them more readable and understandable by the consuming public. For example, easy-to-read policies will use *you* and *we* when referring to the insured and insurer, respectively. Regulation is needed to assure that such changes do not remove essential coverage given to the public.

A recent trend has been the deregulation in many states of commercial lines contracts and rates. The rationale is that while individuals may need protection from certain unscrupulous insurers, large businesses have the knowledge and resources to be able to take care of themselves. By deregulating commercial lines, not only is the commercial lines insurance market made more efficient, but state regulators can then focus their efforts on personal lines, where consumer protection is likely to be more valuable.

MISCELLANEOUS INSURANCE LAWS

A description of some other government regulations regarding insurance will illustrate the extent of government interest in this field.

Service-of-Process Statutes

When a legal action is brought against an insurer, it is necessary to deliver a court summons to the insurer's representative. For insurers admitted to do business within a given state, the insurance commissioner is generally the individual who is authorized to receive such a summons, under what is called a **service-of-process statute**. Formerly, a problem arose as to how best to serve an insurer that did not operate within a given state. An insured may have obtained a policy by dealing with the insurer by mail, or the insured may have obtained a policy in one state but subsequently moved to another state wherein the insurer was not admitted to do business. Through the National Association of Insurance Commissioners, most states have now passed statutes known as the **unauthorized insurers service-of-process acts**. Under these statutes, it is no longer necessary for an insured to resort to distant courts in order to bring suit on contracts written by such unauthorized insurers. It is only necessary to serve summons on the insurance commissioner or on someone representing the out-of-state insurer.

Retaliatory Laws

Most states have laws requiring that, if an insurer chartered in one state is subjected to some burden, such as an increased tax or license fee on business it does in another state, then the one state will automatically impose a like burden on all of the insurers of the second state that are operating in the first state. Such laws are known as **retaliatory laws**, and about three-fourths of all states have them. The effect of these laws is to discourage each state from passing any unusual taxes on foreign insurers operating within its borders for fear that the same burden will immediately apply to its own insurers operating in other states. Only those states without any domestic companies can ignore retaliatory laws. A tendency does exist, therefore, for states with the most domestic insurers to have the lowest insurance taxes. The constitutionality of these laws has been attacked on the grounds that they cause one state to surrender its taxing authority to another state, but it has been established that the laws are constitutional.[6]

Anticancellation Laws

A majority of states have passed laws restricting the right of insurers of automobiles to cancel policies without good reason. Laws are not uniform as to the type of vehicles covered, but in general only private passenger autos are subject to the restrictions. A few states limit the application of the laws to liability coverages, but in a majority of states the laws apply to all coverages, including both liability and physical damage. Insurers also are required under these laws to give ample advance notice of intent not to renew when the policy is approaching its expiration date.

Most of the laws state that unless an insurer cancels a newly issued policy within 60 days after its effective date, it may cancel after that only for certain specified reasons. These may include nonpayment of premiums, insurance obtained through fraudulent misrepresentation, violation by the insured of any term or condition of the policy, suspension of the driver's operator's license, existence of heart attacks or epilepsy of the insured, existence of an accident or conviction record, and habitual use of alcoholic beverages or narcotics to excess. The list of permissible reasons for cancellation is so long and is phrased so broadly that it appears to give the insurer a great deal of discretion in the matter of cancellation, but it actually gives much protection to an insured whose policy is cancelled capriciously. However, the effect of anticancellation laws is further diluted by the use of six-month auto policies that must be renewed every six months, thus giving the insurer the option not to renew every six months. Because a nonrenewal is not a cancellation, the anticancellation laws do not apply.

Reciprocal Laws

In contrast to retaliatory laws, **reciprocal laws** provide that if one state does something for another, that state shall do the same thing for the first. For example, it is common for state financial responsibility laws to provide that if under the laws of another state an insured motorist would be disqualified from driving, the motorist also shall be prohibited from driving in the first state. Under uniform insurer liquidation acts, it is possible for a claimant of an insolvent insurer in another state to make a claim locally and have it honored, avoiding the necessity of traveling to the other state. In workers' compensation insurance, if an employee is temporarily employed outside a state and if the other state will excuse the employer from complying with that state's compensation law, the first state will do likewise. In this way, state legislation is made to work much more smoothly than it otherwise would.

---

6   *American Indemnity Company v Hobbs*, 328 U.S. 822 (1946).

Anticoercion Laws

Anticoercion statutes are aimed against the former practice of some lending agencies to require, as a condition of granting a loan, the placing of insurance with the agency. Thus, the purchaser of a home might be prevented from placing property insurance with a personally chosen insurer. The borrower had to pay premiums that were not necessarily the lowest obtainable. Such tie-in practices were held to be in restraint of trade and illegal under one or more federal antimonopoly laws.[7] As a result, anticoercion laws were passed in many states.

TORT REFORM

Because of rising liability awards in the nation's courts, public pressure for reform of tort liability rules has existed for years. This topic is one of particular interest to risk managers of many types of organizations. Many states have enacted new laws affecting the liability of a manufacturer for defective products. In the past 20 years, almost all states have enacted bills affecting tort law in some way. Among laws passed by many states to reform the tort system are the following four: those that abolished joint and several liability, those that modified the collateral source rule, those that changed the state-of-the-art defense, and those that limited punitive damages. (See Chapter 3 for an explanation of these areas of liability law.) The purpose of this type of legislation is to reduce the frequency and cost of court awards under liability insurance policies and to make insurance more readily available and more affordable. As liability insurance rates are reduced, more buyers will be able to afford coverage, and more insurers will be willing to offer it.

netlink

Visit http://www.atra.org for information on tort reform legislation in each of the states.

Partly in response to the pressure for tort reform and partly because many kinds of liability insurance were not available at all, the Product Liability Risk Retention Act of 1981, as revised and expanded in 1986, was passed. This federal law permits the formation of private insurance corporations to self-insure commercial liability risks. The intention of Congress was to free these new corporations from many of the restrictions and regulations imposed on commercial insurers by state law.

Two types of companies were authorized under this legislation: risk retention groups and risk purchasing groups. The first enabled a group of buyers to join together and form their own insurance company to insure their own liability risks. The second enabled a group of buyers to join together and purchase liability insurance on a group basis from commercial insurers. However, state insurance regulators brought successful legal actions in some states to limit the operations of risk retention and risk purchasing groups. The extent to which state insurance commissioners will be able to retain their full regulatory powers in the field of liability insurance has not yet been fully determined.

TAXATION OF INSURANCE

Insurance companies represent a relatively substantial source of revenue to states. In 2002, for example, insurance premium taxes amounted to $11.1 billion, about 2.1 percent of total state tax collections.[8] Insurance company taxes are greater than tax collections from public

---

7   *United States v Investors Diversified Services*, Civil No. 3713 DC, Minn. (1954).
8   *The Fact Book 2004* (New York: Insurance Information Institute, 2004).

PROFESSIONAL PERSPECTIVES

The Umpire's New Clothes

Tort reform is not the only way to reduce the cost of resolving disputes. Increasingly, many parties involved in disputes are turning to something called alternative dispute resolution. The most common forms of alternative dispute resolution are mediation and arbitration. Arbitration involves an impartial arbitrator who holds a hearing something like a trial. The arbitrator's decision is generally binding on both parties. Mediation also involves a neutral third party, but the mediator's role is to help facilitate a mutually acceptable resolution among the parties involved. The mediator cannot force an outcome on any of the parties. Mediation and arbitration are in most cases much less expensive than litigation. Rapid growth has occurred in the number of firms specializing in alternative dispute resolution. The American Arbitration Association is a nonprofit group that promotes alternative dispute resolution. Its Web site (http://www.adr.org) offers a vast amount of information on the topic, and was recognized in *Business Insurance* magazine's list of the Best of the Web for 2003.

Sources: Jeffrey Klineman, "Mediation Inflation," *The Boston Business Journal*, June 13, 2003, 32; Paul Winston, "American Arbitration Association," *Business Insurance*, November 3, 2003, 12.

utilities, from death and gift taxes, from corporate licenses, and from taxes on alcoholic beverages.

In each state, these revenues are raised mainly from a tax on gross premiums. Premium taxes vary from 1 to 4 percent, with the most typical amount being 2 percent, plus an additional 0.25 or 0.50 percent for the support of the state fire marshal's office. Many states also have special taxes or assessments in connection with different lines of insurance, such as workers' compensation.

Insurance companies also are subject to federal income taxation. Stock property insurers pay taxes on underwriting and investment income at regular corporate rates. Mutual property insurers are treated differently. If a mutual or a reciprocal insurer has a net income of less than $75,000, it is exempt from taxation.[9] For larger mutuals, the tax is the larger of 1 percent of gross income (net premiums written less policyholder dividends plus net investment income) or the tax that would be collected by applying regular corporate rates to investment income only, as defined.[10]

Life insurers are subject to federal income taxation under the **Deficit Reduction Act of 1984 (DEFRA)**. The law replaced legislation enacted in 1959. In contrast to the 1959 rules, the 1984 law does not distinguish between underwriting and investment income of life insurers but instead subjects all income to the same taxation rules. DEFRA attempted to simplify life insurance taxation and make it more responsive to changing levels of general interest rates.

Under DEFRA, taxable income is defined as gross income less special deductions. These deductions include claims for losses, increases in reserves (as defined), policyholder dividends, and the company's share of tax-exempt interest and dividends.[11] Regular corporate income tax rates apply to the balance. One result of DEFRA was to treat stock and mutual insurers on a more nearly equal basis than before, so that the total tax burden paid by life

9 Section 501(15) Internal Revenue Code (1954).
10 Section 821, 822, 823 Internal Revenue Code (1954).
11 Section 805(a) Internal Revenue Code (1954).

ETHICAL PERSPECTIVES

The High Cost of the U.S. Tort System

Dave Barry, a nationally syndicated newspaper columnist, wrote an article on the results of a lawsuit involving Smith Kline Beecham. It seems the firm manufactured a denture adhesive that contained trace amounts of benzene, a carcinogen. The firm recalled the product after it found the problem. However, an enterprising lawyer got involved and started a class-action suit. The plaintiff, a Mr. Duboff, received a $25,000 award. Six hundred fifty other persons who were parties to the action received $7 each, and the law firm representing the plaintiffs received $954,934.57! What makes this case even more interesting is that, according to Mr. Barry, nobody actually claimed that anyone was hurt.

Source: Dave Barry, "This Is Really Scary: A True Lawyer Joke," *Athens Daily News/Athens Banner-Herald*, November 21, 1993, 5d.

insurers would be in proportion to the share of total assets controlled by each type of insurer. The 1984 law also standardized the reserve computation for tax purposes so that reserve laws of individual states no longer affected federal taxes on life insurers. Excess deductions that existed in some states were not allowed, with the result that amounts that could be deducted for reserves were somewhat lower than before.

Two special deductions for life insurers were incorporated. One deduction applied to small life insurers; that is, those with assets of less than $500 million. Another special deduction was enacted to prevent a dramatic increase in taxes as compared with taxes under the 1959 law. The net effect of these two special deductions was to lower the effective tax rates on taxable income (as defined) of life insurers from 46 percent to about 37 percent.

Future of Insurance Regulation

In 1995, the U.S. Supreme Court ruled in the case of *Nationsbank v Variable Annuity Life Insurance* that annuities were not a form of insurance. Therefore, the restrictions on banks selling insurance did not apply to the sale of annuities. This ruling has allowed banks to greatly expand their annuity business.

In the fall of 1999, Congress passed and the President signed the Gramm-Leach-Bliley Act (GLB). This law is the most comprehensive change in the regulation of financial institutions since the 1930s. It repeals the Glass-Steagall Act, which was passed during the Great Depression to create a firewall between banks, investment companies, and insurers. These firms could not conduct each other's business. You chose one business of the three and stayed with it. You could not mix them. The Glass-Steagall Act was passed to prevent the abuses that occurred in the 1920s and early 1930s.

Today, with the internationalization of financial services, those firewalls are no longer effective. Multinational firms operate all over the world, and U.S. domicile firms must have the freedom to work in such markets.

Under GLB, firms may be in all three businesses at the same time. Insurers can own and operate banks and vice versa. The impact of this law will be felt for many years. During the next several years, more mergers will likely occur between insurers, banks, and investment brokers. With these mergers, an increase in the concentration of economic power will occur. Fewer stand-alone operations will exist. The surviving firms will be financial powerhouses.

Another section of the GLB Act involves the multi-state licensing of insurance agents. Presently, an agent must have a separate license for each state and meet the separate licensing requirement of each state. Over time, the provisions in the GLB Act will likely lead to a national licensing procedure.

Other provisions affect the relationship of state versus federal regulation of insurance companies. The exclusive domain of state regulation will be diminished. Federal regulation will have more influence because of the Treasury Department and the Federal Reserve's need to supervise banks and investment companies. Eventually the insurance activities of these firms also may have more federal regulation, as discussed earlier in this chapter.

SUMMARY

1. Insurance is regulated because of several characteristics that set it apart from tangible goods industries. These include the complexity of insurance, its importance to the financial security of millions of people, the public nature of its many activities, and the necessity for some control over its pricing policies.

2. Insurance is regulated by states, but the federal government, by virtue of both the 1944 decision in the case of the South-Eastern Underwriters Association and the McCarran-Ferguson Act, also has considerable regulatory authority in several areas of insurance.

3. For many years, a debate has existed over the relative merits of federal versus state regulation of insurance. In spite of some possible advantages of federal regulation, it appears unlikely that the present system of state rule will give way com-

pletely unless more convincing proof of the superiority of federal regulation is forthcoming. However, it seems likely that increased federal regulation in specific areas of insurance will occur.

4. The chief areas of state regulation have to do mainly with rate supervision, standards of financial condition, business acquisition methods, and policy provisions. An insurer must be formally admitted to do business in a given state, must give evidence of its financial ability to meet all claims, and must subject almost every phase of its operations to the supervision of the insurance commissioner.

5. In general, regulation of insurance has had a beneficial effect on the institution by maintaining public confidence, securing desirable uniformity, and preventing destructive practices arising from unrestricted competition within the industry.

internetexercises

1. Set your browser to http://www.naic.org/state_contacts/sid_websites.htm and choose the link to your home state's Insurance Commissioner Web site. What assistance is provided to consumers who have complaints about insurance agents and/or companies?

2. New York State has a reputation for strict insurance regulation. Set your browser to http://www.ins.state.ny.us/consindx.htm and study the resources available to insurance consumers in New York. Which ones would you find most useful? Why?

QUESTIONS FOR REVIEW AND DISCUSSION

1. Does the experience to date with state insurer guaranty funds suggest that these funds are needed? In every state? Discuss.

2. What is the difference between prior approval and open competition rating laws? Which type do you prefer? Why?

3. In your opinion, does real competition exist in the field of insurance? If so, give specific examples.

4. You are approached by an insurance agent who promises to return 20 percent of the commission to you if you will give this agent your business. Is

this approach an acceptable business practice? Comment.

5. H buys an insurance policy from a mail-order insurer and, following a loss, is unable to secure payment. In fact, the insurer does not even answer H's letter in which the loss was reported. A local agent informs H that this particular insurer is not "admitted" in H's state and has no representatives there. Is it necessary for H to go to the state in which this insurer is chartered in order to bring legal action? Why?

6. A legislator in your state urges that a good way to raise additional state revenue would be to increase the premium tax on all insurers operating within the state. What point should you investigate first, before recommending that this tax be passed?

7. Differentiate between a retaliatory law and a reciprocal law.

8. What is the main purpose of tort reform legislation?

9. What criteria are usually specified in state laws regarding insurance rates?

10. If states were doing a good job in regulating insurer solvency, would guaranty funds be needed? Why or why not?

11. A representative of an association of insurance agencies stated, "The very nature of our business requires the most rigid adherence to sound methods of operation and therefore there are few who will argue its need for regulation. . . ." Why is it concluded that insurance requires regulation when such an argument would usually be opposed in tangible goods industries as an interference with the right of free enterprise? Comment.

12. The text states that unisex rates have increased the cost of auto and life insurance for women but at the same time have decreased the cost of health insurance for them. Suggest possible reasons for this result, particularly when unisex rates have been endorsed strongly by the National Organization for Women (NOW), a group promoting women's rights.

13. An insurance commissioner of a large state wrote, "The commissioner's position is not a particularly happy one today. He is . . . criticized for increases in rates, for a lack of insurance markets, for the insolvency of some companies, for maintaining too high a degree of uniformity in rates or coverage, or for being much too soft in the regulation of the industry. On the other hand, the commissioner is sometimes criticized by people in the insurance industry for a lack of uniformity and for regulating too severely . . . strangulation of the business instead of . . . regulation." In your opinion, is it the task of the insurance commissioner to deal with each of the questions previously listed? If so, give an example of the type of activity falling under each category.

14. Under federal regulation of insurance, it has been suggested that local conditions could be handled through a system of district offices similar to that which exists in the case of the Federal Reserve System. Each of these offices could be given certain degrees of autonomy to adjust to localized conditions. In this way, all the advantages of national uniformity could be achieved without any of the disadvantages of rigid supervision by distant authorities. Evaluate this plan, pointing out advantages and disadvantages.

15. Many professional insurance agents object strongly to the use of part-time agents and are generally in favor of much stricter licensing requirements than most states presently have. Why would they object to part-time agents more than full-time agents?

Appendixes

Appendix A

Present Value and Annuity Tables

Problems in the use of life insurance and annuities may often be solved more easily by the use of interest tables than by laborious hand calculations or even by use of a computer. Examples of the use of these tables follow.

COMPOUND INTEREST

If $1,000 is left with an insurance company at interest as savings and the insurer pays 3 percent compound interest, what will the value of the savings be in 20 years?

Referring to Table 1, we see that $1 left at 3 percent compound interest for 20 years is $1,806. Therefore, the value of the savings would be $1,806.

PRESENT VALUE

If an uninsured wishes to have the sum of $1,000 in a savings account 20 years from now, how much must be deposited at compound interest if the insured receives interest at the rate of 3 percent? At 6 percent?

Referring to Table 2, we see that at 3 percent interest, the present value of $1 is $0.55367. Therefore, the sum of $553.67 must be deposited at 3 percent in order to accumulate to $1,000 in 20 years. At 6 percent, $311.80 must be deposited.

AMOUNT OF ANNUITY

If an estate planner saves $1,000 a year, to what sum will this savings accumulate if it is earning 6 percent interest? If it is earning 7 percent interest? How much more will this savings be if it earns 7 percent instead of 6 percent after 20 years? After 40 years?

According to Table 3, $1 per year accumulates to $36.785 in 20 years at 6 percent interest. Therefore, the saver would have an account worth $36,785. At 7 percent, the saver would have $40,995. Due to the operation of compound interest, after 20 years the saver has about 11 percent more money in the account at 7 percent than

at 6 percent. After 40 years, the saver would have about 28 percent more in the account at 7 percent than at 6 percent ($199,635 ÷ $154,761 = 1.28).

PRESENT VALUE OF AN ANNUITY

1. If a person wishes to be paid the sum of $1,000 annually over a period of 20 years, how much money must the person pay, assuming the funds earn 6 percent interest? How much must be paid if the person wishes to receive $1,000 a year for 15 years?

   From Table 4 we see that at 6 percent interest the present value of $1 annually for 20 years is $11.469. Therefore, the annuitant must pay $11,469 in order to receive $1,000 a year for 20 years. For 15 years, the annuitant must pay $9,712.

2. If an insured has $25,000 of insurance proceeds available, how much of an annual income will be paid by the insurer in an equal amount over 20 years if the insurer earns 6 percent interest?

   According to Table 4, the present value of $1 a year for 20 years is $11.469. Dividing this amount into $25,000, we obtain an annual equal payment of $2,179.79.

LIFE ANNUITIES

If a male insured, aged 65, has $25,000 of proceeds, how much guaranteed life income per month can he leave his wife, who is the same age, under a 10-year certain, 20-year certain, and joint and last survivorship option?

Referring to Table 5, we see that for each $1,000 of proceeds, the insured wife age 65 may obtain $5.63 monthly under the 10-year certain, $5,02 under the 20-year certain, and $5.23 under the joint and last survivorship option. Multiplying these sums by 25, we obtain $140.75, $125.50, and $130.75, respectively.

TABLE 1   Amount at Compound Interest $(1 + i)^n$

Periods			Rate i		
n	.03 (3%)	.06 (6%)	.07 (7%)	.08 (8%)	.10 (10%)
1	1.0300 0000	1.0600 0000	1.0700 0000	1.0800 0000	1.1000 0000
2	1.0609 0000	1.1236 0000	1.1449 0000	1.1664 0000	1.2100 0000
3	1.0927 2700	1.1910 1600	1.2250 4300	1.2597 1200	1.3310 0000
4	1.1255 0881	1.2624 7696	1.3107 9601	1.3604 8896	1.4641 0000
5	1.1592 7407	1.3382 2558	1.4025 5173	1.4693 2808	1.6105 1000
6	1.1940 5230	1.4185 1911	1.5007 3035	1.5868 7432	1.7715 6100
7	1.2298 7387	1.5036 3026	1.6057 8148	1.7138 2427	1.9487 1710
8	1.2667 7008	1.5938 4807	1.7181 8618	1.8509 3021	2.1435 8881
9	1.3047 7318	1.6894 7896	1.8384 5921	1.9990 0463	2.3579 4769
10	1.3439 1638	1.7908 4770	1.9671 5136	2.1589 2500	2.5937 4246
11	1.3842 3387	1.8982 9856	2.1048 5195	2.3316 3900	2.8531 1671
12	1.4257 6089	2.0121 9647	2.2521 9159	2.5181 7012	3.1384 2838
13	1.4685 3371	2.1329 2826	2.4098 4500	2.7196 2373	3.4522 7121
14	1.5125 8972	2.2609 0396	2.5785 3415	2.9371 9362	3.7974 9834
15	1.5579 6742	2.3965 5819	2.7590 3154	3.1721 6911	4.1772 4817
16	1.6047 0644	2.5403 5168	2.9521 6375	3.4259 4264	4.5949 7299
17	1.6528 4763	2.6927 7279	3.1588 1521	3.7000 1805	5.0544 7029
18	1.7024 3306	2.8543 3915	3.3799 3228	3.9960 1950	5.5599 1731
19	1.7535 0605	3.0255 9950	3.6165 2754	4.3157 0106	6.1159 0904
20	1.8061 1123	3.2071 3547	3.8696 8446	4.6609 5714	6.7274 9995
21	1.8602 9457	3.3995 6360	4.1405 6237	5.0338 3372	7.4002 4994
22	1.9161 0341	3.6035 3742	4.4304 0174	5.4365 4041	8.1402 7494
23	1.9735 8651	3.8197 4966	4.7405 2986	5.8714 6365	8.9543 0243
24	2.0327 9411	4.0489 3464	5.0723 6695	6.3411 8074	9.8497 3268
25	2.0937 7793	4.2918 7072	5.4274 3264	6.8484 7520	10.8347 0594
26	2.1565 9127	4.5493 8296	5.8073 5292	7.3963 5321	11.9181 7654
27	2.2212 8901	4.8223 4594	6.2138 6763	7.9880 6147	13.1099 9419
28	2.2879 2768	5.1116 8670	6.6488 3836	8.6271 0639	14.4209 9361
29	2.3565 6551	5.4183 8790	7.1142 5705	9.3172 7490	15.8630 9297
30	2.4272 6247	5.7434 9117	7.6122 5504	10.0626 5689	17.4494 0227
31	2.5000 8035	6.0881 0064	8.1451 1290	10.8676 6944	19.1943 4250
32	2.5750 8276	6.4533 8668	8.7152 7080	11.7370 8300	21.1137 7675
33	2.6523 3524	6.8405 8988	9.3253 3975	12.6760 4964	23.2251 5442
34	2.7319 0530	7.2510 2528	9.9781 1354	13.6901 3361	25.5476 6986
35	2.8138 6245	7.6860 8679	10.6765 8148	14.7853 4429	28.1024 3685
36	2.8982 7833	8.1472 5200	11.4239 4219	15.9681 7184	30.9126 8053
37	2.9852 2668	8.6360 8712	12.2236 1814	17.2456 2558	34.0039 4859
38	3.0747 8348	9.1542 5235	13.0792 7141	18.6252 7563	37.4043 4344
39	3.1670 2698	9.7035 0749	13.9948 2041	20.1152 9768	41.1447 7779
40	3.2620 3779	10.2857 1794	14.9744 5784	21.7245 2150	45.2592 5557
41	3.3598 9893	10.9028 6101	16.0226 6989	23.4624 8322	49.7851 8113
42	3.4606 9589	11.5570 3267	17.1442 5678	25.3394 8187	54.7636 9924
43	3.5645 1677	12.2504 5463	18.3443 5475	27.3666 4042	60.2400 6916
44	3.6714 5227	12.9854 8191	19.6284 5959	29.5559 7166	66.2640 7608
45	3.7815 9584	13.7646 1083	21.0024 5176	31.9204 4939	72.8904 8369
46	3.8950 4372	14.5904 8748	22.4726 2338	34.4740 8534	80.1795 3205
47	4.0118 9503	15.4659 1673	24.0457 0702	37.2320 1217	88.1974 8526
48	4.1322 5188	16.3938 7173	25.7289 0651	40.2105 7314	97.0172 3378
49	4.2562 1944	17.3775 0403	27.5299 2997	43.4274 1899	106.7189 5716
50	4.3839 0602	18.4201 5428	29.4570 2506	46.9016 1251	117.3908 5288

TABLE 2   Present Value of $1/(1 + i)^n$

Periods	Rate i				
n	.03 (3%)	.06 (6%)	.07 (7%)	.08 (8%)	.10 (10%)
1	0.9708 7379	0.9433 9623	0.9345 7944	0.9259 2593	0.9090 9091
2	0.9425 9591	0.8899 9644	0.8734 3873	0.8573 3882	0.8264 4628
3	0.9151 4166	0.8396 1928	0.8162 9788	0.7938 3224	0.7513 1480
4	0.8884 8705	0.7920 9366	0.7628 9521	0.7350 2985	0.6830 1346
5	0.8626 0878	0.7472 5817	0.7129 8618	0.6805 8320	0.6209 2132
6	0.8374 8426	0.7049 6054	0.6663 4222	0.6301 6963	0.5644 7393
7	0.8130 9151	0.6650 5711	0.6227 4974	0.5834 9040	0.5131 5812
8	0.7894 0923	0.6274 1237	0.5820 0910	0.5402 6888	0.4665 0738
9	0.7664 1673	0.5918 9846	0.5439 3374	0.5002 4897	0.4240 9762
10	0.7440 9391	0.5583 9478	0.5083 4929	0.4631 9349	0.3855 4329
11	0.7224 2128	0.5267 8753	0.4750 9280	0.4288 8286	0.3504 9390
12	0.7013 7988	0.4969 6936	0.4440 1196	0.3971 1376	0.3186 3082
13	0.6809 5134	0.4688 3902	0.4149 6445	0.3676 9792	0.2896 6438
14	0.6611 1781	0.4423 0096	0.3878 1724	0.3404 6104	0.2633 3125
15	0.6418 6195	0.4172 6506	0.3624 4602	0.3152 4170	0.2393 9205
16	0.6231 6694	0.3936 4628	0.3387 3460	0.2918 9047	0.2176 2914
17	0.6050 1645	0.3713 6442	0.3165 7439	0.2702 6895	0.1978 4467
18	0.5873 9461	0.3503 4379	0.2958 6392	0.2502 4903	0.1798 5879
19	0.5702 8603	0.3305 1301	0.2765 0833	0.2317 1206	0.1635 0799
20	0.5536 7575	0.3118 0473	0.2584 1900	0.2145 4821	0.1486 4363
21	0.5375 4928	0.2941 5540	0.2415 1309	0.1986 5575	0.1351 3057
22	0.5218 9250	0.2775 0510	0.2257 1317	0.1839 4051	0.1228 4597
23	0.5066 9175	0.2617 9726	0.2109 4688	0.1703 1528	0.1116 7816
24	0.4919 3374	0.2469 7855	0.1971 4662	0.1576 9934	0.1015 2560
25	0.4776 0557	0.2329 9863	0.1842 4918	0.1460 1790	0.0922 9600
26	0.4636 9473	0.2198 1003	0.1721 9549	0.1352 0176	0.0839 0545
27	0.4501 8906	0.2073 6795	0.1609 3037	0.1251 8682	0.0762 7768
28	0.4370 7675	0.1956 3014	0.1504 0221	0.1159 1372	0.0693 4335
29	0.4243 4636	0.1845 5674	0.1405 6282	0.1073 2752	0.0630 3941
30	0.4119 8676	0.1741 1013	0.1313 6712	0.0993 7733	0.0573 0855
31	0.3999 8715	0.1642 5484	0.1227 7301	0.0920 1605	0.0520 9868
32	0.3883 3703	0.1549 5740	0.1147 4113	0.0852 0005	0.0473 6244
33	0.3770 2625	0.1461 8622	0.1072 3470	0.0788 8893	0.0430 5676
34	0.3660 4490	0.1379 1153	0.1002 1934	0.0730 4531	0.0391 4251
35	0.3553 8340	0.1301 0522	0.0936 6294	0.0676 3454	0.0355 8410
36	0.3450 3243	0.1227 4077	0.0875 3546	0.0626 2458	0.0323 4918
37	0.3349 8294	0.1157 9318	0.0818 0884	0.0579 8572	0.0294 0835
38	0.3252 2615	0.1092 3885	0.0764 5686	0.0536 9048	0.0267 3486
39	0.3157 5355	0.1030 5552	0.0714 5501	0.0497 1341	0.0243 0442
40	0.3065 5684	0.0972 2219	0.0667 8038	0.0460 3093	0.0220 9493
41	0.2976 2800	0.0917 1904	0.0624 1157	0.0426 2123	0.0200 8630
42	0.2889 5922	0.0865 2740	0.0583 2857	0.0394 6411	0.0182 6027
43	0.2805 4294	0.0816 2962	0.0545 1268	0.0365 4084	0.0166 0025
44	0.2723 7178	0.0770 0908	0.0509 4643	0.0338 3411	0.0150 9113
45	0.2644 3862	0.0726 5007	0.0476 1349	0.0313 2788	0.0137 1921
46	0.2567 3653	0.0685 3781	0.0444 9859	0.0290 0730	0.0124 7201
47	0.2492 5876	0.0646 5831	0.0415 8746	0.0268 5861	0.0113 3819
48	0.2419 9880	0.0609 9840	0.0388 6679	0.0248 6908	0.0103 0745
49	0.2349 5029	0.0575 4566	0.0363 2410	0.0230 2693	0.0093 7041
50	0.2281 0708	0.0542 8836	0.0339 4776	0.0213 2123	0.0085 1855

Table 3   Amount of Annuity $[(1 + i)^n - 1]/i$

Periods	Rate i				
n	.03 (3%)	.06 (6%)	.07 (7%)	.08 (8%)	.10 (10%)
1	1.0000 0000	1.0000 0000	1.0000 0000	1.0000 0000	1.0000 0000
2	2.0300 0000	2.0600 0000	2.0700 0000	2.0800 0000	2.1000 0000
3	3.0909 0000	3.1836 0000	3.2149 0000	3.2464 0000	3.3100 0000
4	4.1836 2700	4.3746 1600	4.4399 4300	4.5061 1200	4.6410 0000
5	5.3091 3581	5.6370 9296	5.7507 3901	5.8666 0096	6.1051 0000
6	6.4684 0988	6.9753 1854	7.1532 9074	7.3359 2904	7.7156 1000
7	7.6624 6218	8.3938 3765	8.6540 2109	8.9228 0336	9.4871 7100
8	8.8923 3605	9.8974 6791	10.2598 0257	10.6366 2763	11.4358 8810
9	10.1591 0613	11.4913 1598	11.9779 8875	12.4875 5784	13.5794 7691
10	11.4638 7931	13.1807 9494	13.8164 4796	14.4865 6247	15.9374 2460
11	12.8077 9569	14.9716 4264	15.7835 9932	16.6454 8746	18.5311 6706
12	14.1920 2956	16.8699 4120	17.8884 5127	18.9771 2646	21.3842 8377
13	15.6177 9045	18.8821 3767	20.1406 4286	21.4952 9658	24.5227 1214
14	17.0863 2416	21.0150 6593	22.5504 8786	24.2149 2030	27.9749 8336
15	18.5989 1389	23.2759 6988	25.1290 2201	27.1521 1393	31.7724 8169
16	20.1568 8130	25.6725 2808	27.8880 5355	30.3242 8304	35.9497 2986
17	21.7615 8774	28.2128 7976	30.8402 1730	33.7502 2568	40.5447 0285
18	23.4144 3537	30.9056 5255	33.9990 3251	37.4502 4374	45.5991 7313
19	25.1168 6844	33.7599 9170	37.3789 6479	41.4462 6324	51.1590 9045
20	26.8703 7449	36.7855 9120	40.9954 9232	45.7619 6430	57.2749 9949
21	28.6764 8572	39.9927 2668	44.8651 7678	50.4229 2144	64.0024 9944
22	30.5367 8030	43.3922 9028	49.0057 3916	55.4567 5516	71.4027 4939
23	32.4528 8370	46.9958 2769	53.4361 4090	60.8932 9557	79.5430 2433
24	34.4264 7022	50.8155 7735	58.1766 7076	66.7647 5922	88.4973 2676
25	36.4592 6432	54.8645 1200	63.2490 3772	73.1059 3995	98.3470 5943
26	38.5530 4225	59.1563 8272	68.6764 7036	79.9544 1515	109.1817 6538
27	40.7096 3352	63.7057 6568	74.4838 2328	87.3507 6836	121.0999 4192
28	42.9309 2252	68.5281 1162	80.6976 9091	95.3388 2983	134.2099 3611
29	45.2188 5020	73.6397 9832	87.3465 2927	103.9659 3622	148.6309 2972
30	47.5754 1571	79.0581 8622	94.4607 8632	113.2832 1111	164.4940 2269
31	50.0026 7818	84.8016 7739	102.0730 4137	123.3458 6800	181.9434 2496
32	52.5027 5852	90.8897 7803	110.2181 5426	134.2135 3744	201.1377 6745
33	55.0778 4128	97.3431 6471	118.9334 2506	145.9506 2044	222.2515 4420
34	57.7301 7652	104.1837 5460	128.2587 6481	158.6266 7007	245 4766 9862
35	60.4620 8181	111.4347 7987	138.2368 7835	172.3168 0368	271.0243 6848
36	63.2759 4427	119.1208 6666	148.9134 5984	187.1021 4797	299.1268 0533
37	66.1742 2259	127.2681 1866	160.3374 0202	203.0703 1981	330.0394 8586
38	69.1594 4927	135.9042 0578	172.5610 2017	220.3159 4540	364.0434 3445
39	72.2342 3275	145.0584 5813	185.6402 9158	238.9412 2103	401.4477 7789
40	75.4012 5973	154.7619 6562	199.6351 1199	259.0565 1871	442.5925 5568
41	78.6632 9753	165.0476 8356	214.6095 6983	280.7810 4021	487.8518 1125
42	82.0231 9645	175.9505 4457	230.6322 3972	304.2435 2342	537.6369 9237
43	85.4838 9234	187.5075 7724	247.7764 9650	329.5830 0530	592.4006 9161
44	89.0484 0911	199.7580 3188	266.1208 5125	356.9496 4572	652.6407 6077
45	92.7198 6139	212.7435 1379	285.7493 1084	386.5056 1738	718.9048 3685
46	96.5014 5723	226.5081 2462	306.7517 6260	418.4260 6677	791.7953 2054
47	100.3965 0095	241.0986 1210	329.2243 8598	452.9001 5211	871.9748 5259
48	104.4083 9598	256.5645 2882	353.2700 9300	490.1321 6428	960.1723 3785
49	108.5406 4785	272.9584 0055	378.9989 9951	530.3427 3742	1057.1895 7163
50	112.7968 6729	290.3359 0458	406.5289 2947	573.7701 5642	1163.9085 2880

TABLE 4   Present Value of Annuity $[1 - (1 + i)^{-n}]/i$

Periods		Rate i			
n	.03 (3%)	.06 (6%)	.07 (7%)	.08 (8%)	.10 (10%)
1	0.9708 7379	0.9433 9623	0.9345 7944	0.9259 2593	0.9090 9091
2	1.9134 6970	1.8333 9267	1.8080 1817	1.7832 6475	1.7355 3719
3	2.8286 1135	2.6730 1195	2.6243 1604	2.5770 9699	2.4868 5199
4	3.7170 9840	3.4651 0561	3.3872 1126	3.3121 2684	3.1698 6545
5	4.5797 0719	4.2123 6379	4.1001 9744	3.9927 1004	3.7907 8677
6	5.4171 9144	4.9173 2433	4.7665 3966	4.6228 7966	4.3552 6070
7	6.2302 8296	5.5823 8144	5.3892 8940	5.2063 7006	4.8684 1882
8	7.0196 9219	6.2097 9381	5.9712 9851	5.7466 3894	5.3349 2620
9	7.7861 0892	6.8016 9227	6.5152 3225	6.2468 8791	5.7590 2382
10	8.5302 0284	7.3600 8705	7.0235 8154	6.7100 8140	6.1445 6711
11	9.2526 2411	7.8868 7458	7.4986 7434	7.1389 6426	6.4950 6101
12	9.9540 0399	8.3838 4394	7.9426 8630	7.5360 7802	6.8136 9182
13	10.6349 5533	8.8526 8296	8.3576 5074	7.9037 7594	7.1033 5620
14	11.2960 7314	9.2949 8393	8.7454 6799	8.2442 3698	7.3666 8746
15	11.9379 3509	9.7122 4899	9.1079 1401	8.5594 7869	7.6060 7951
16	12.5611 0203	10.1058 9527	9.4466 4860	8.8513 6916	7.8237 0864
17	13.1661 1847	10.4772 5969	9.7632 2299	9.1216 3811	8.0215 5331
18	13.7535 1308	10.8276 0348	10.0590 8691	9.3718 8714	8.2014 1210
19	14.3237 9911	11.1581 1649	10.3355 9524	9.6035 9920	8.3649 2009
20	14.8774 7486	11.4699 2122	10.5940 1425	9.8181 4741	8.5135 6372
21	15.4150 2414	11.7640 7662	10.8355 2733	10.0168 0316	8.6486 9429
22	15.9369 1664	12.0415 8172	11.0612 4050	10.2007 4366	8.7715 4026
23	16.4436 0839	12.3033 7898	11.2721 8738	10.3710 5895	8.8832 1842
24	16.9355 4212	12.5503 5753	11.4693 3400	10.5287 5828	8.9847 4402
25	17.4131 4769	12.7833 5616	11.6535 8318	10.6747 7619	9.0770 4002
26	17.8768 4242	13.0031 6619	11.8257 7867	10.8099 7795	9.1609 4547
27	18.3270 3147	13.2105 3414	11.9867 0904	10.9351 6477	9.2372 2316
28	18.7641 0823	13.4061 6428	12.1371 1125	11.0510 7849	9.3065 6651
29	19.1884 5459	13.5907 2102	12.2776 7407	11.1584 0601	9.3696 0591
30	19.6004 4135	13.7648 3115	12.4090 4118	11.2577 8334	9.4269 1447
31	20.0004 2849	13.9290 8599	12.5318 1419	11.3497 9939	9.4790 1315
32	20.3887 6553	14.0840 4339	12.6465 5532	11.4349 9944	9.5263 7559
33	20.7657 9178	14.2302 2961	12.7537 9002	11.5138 8837	9.5694 3236
34	21.1318 3668	14.3681 4114	12.8540 0936	11.5869 3367	9.6085 7487
35	21.4872 2007	14.4982 4636	12.9476 7230	11.6545 6822	9.6441 5897
36	21.8322 5250	14.6209 8713	13.0352 0776	11.7171 9279	9.6765 0816
37	22.1672 3544	14.7367 8031	13.1170 1660	11.7751 7851	9.7059 1651
38	22.4924 6159	14.8460 1916	13.1934 7345	11.8288 6899	9.7326 5137
39	22.8082 1513	14.9490 7468	13.2649 2846	11.8785 8240	9.7569 5579
40	23.1147 7197	15.0462 9687	13.3317 0884	11.9246 1333	9.7790 5072
41	23.4123 9998	15.1380 1592	13.3941 2041	11.9672 3457	9.7991 3702
42	23.7013 5920	15.2245 4332	13.4524 4898	12.0066 9867	9.8173 9729
43	23.9819 0213	15.3061 7294	13.5069 6167	12.0432 3951	9.8339 9753
44	24.2542 7392	15.3831 8202	13.5579 0810	12.0770 7362	9.8490 8867
45	24.5187 1254	15.4558 3209	13.6055 2159	12.1084 0150	9.8628 0788
46	24.7754 4907	15.5243 6990	13.6500 2018	12.1374 0880	9.8752 7989
47	25.0247 0783	15.5890 2821	13.6916 0764	12.1642 6741	9.8866 1808
48	25.2667 0664	15.6500 2661	13.7304 7443	12.1891 3649	9.8969 2553
49	25.5016 5693	15.7075 7227	13.7667 9853	12.2121 6341	9.9062 9594
50	25.7297 6401	15.7618 6064	13.8007 4629	12.2334 8464	9.9148 1449

TABLE 5   Monthly Life Income per $1,000 Proceeds (3% Interest Assumption)[1]

Age	10 Years Cert. Men	20 Years Cert. Men	10 Years Cert. Women	20 Years Cert. Women	Joint and Last Survivor[2]
15	2.96	2.96	2.88	2.88	—
20	3.05	3.05	2.96	2.96	—
25	3.17	3.16	3.06	3.05	—
30	3.31	3.30	3.17	3.17	—
35	3.49	3.46	3.32	3.31	3.20
40	3.72	3.67	3.50	3.48	3.35
45	4.00	3.91	3.73	3.69	3.55
46	4.07	3.97	3.78	3.74	3.59
47	4.14	4.02	3.84	3.79	3.64
48	4.21	4.08	3.90	3.85	3.69
49	4.28	4.14	3.96	3.90	3.75
50	4.36	4.20	4.03	3.96	3.80
51	4.44	4.26	4.10	4.02	3.86
52	4.53	4.32	4.17	4.08	3.93
53	4.62	4.39	4.25	4.14	3.99
54	4.71	4.46	4.33	4.21	4.06
55	4.81	4.52	4.42	4.28	4.14
56	4.92	4.59	4.51	4.35	4.22
57	5.03	4.66	4.61	4.42	4.30
58	5.15	4.73	4.71	4.50	4.39
59	5.27	4.80	4.82	4.57	4.49
60	5.40	4.87	4.94	4.65	4.59
61	5.53	4.94	5.06	4.72	4.70
62	5.68	5.00	5.19	4.80	4.82
63	5.83	5.07	5.33	4.88	4.95
64	5.98	5.13	5.47	4.95	5.08
65	6.15	5.18	5.63	5.02	5.23
66	6.32	5.24	5.79	5.09	5.39
67	6.50	5.28	5.96	5.15	5.56
68	6.68	5.33	6.14	5.21	5.74
69	6.88	5.36	6.33	5.27	5.94
70	7.07	5.40	6.53	5.32	6.15
71	7.27	5.42	6.73	5.36	6.38
72	7.48	5.45	6.94	5.40	6.63
73	7.68	5.46	7.16	5.43	6.91
74	7.88	5.48	7.38	5.45	7.21
75	8.08	5.49	7.60	5.47	7.53
80	8.94	5.51	8.64	5.51	—
85	9.42	5.51	9.32	5.51	—

[1]Participating during period certain. Since cost assumptions vary among insurers, these data should be considered as illustrative only.
[2]Man and woman of equal age, life only.

TABLE 6   Monthly Life Income per $1,000 Proceeds (5.75% Interest Assumption) Male Lives*

Age	Without Refund	Ten Years Certain and Life	Installment Refund	Joint Life Income, ⅔ to Survivor 120 Months Certain	
				Female Age	Amount Paid If Male Is Age 65 at Death
45	$ 6.03	$5.81	$ 5.90	—	—
46	6.12	5.87	5.98	—	—
47	6.22	5.94	6.06	—	—
48	6.32	6.01	6.15	—	—
49	6.42	6.08	6.24	—	—
50	6.53	6.15	6.33	50	$4.59
51	6.64	6.23	6.42	51	4.65
52	6.76	6.30	6.52	52	4.71
53	6.88	6.38	6.62	53	4.77
54	7.00	6.45	6.73	54	4.83
55	7.14	6.53	6.84	55	4.90
56	7.27	6.61	6.96	56	4.96
57	7.42	6.69	7.08	57	5.02
58	7.57	6.77	7.21	58	5.08
59	7.73	6.85	7.35	59	5.15
60	7.90	6.93	7.49	60	5.22
61	8.06	6.99	7.61	61	5.29
62	8.22	7.05	7.74	62	5.36
63	8.40	7.10	7.88	63	5.43
64	8.59	7.16	8.03	64	5.51
65	8.79	7.21	8.18	65	5.59
66	8.99	7.25	8.33	66	5.67
67	9.20	7.28	8.48	67	5.75
68	9.42	7.31	8.64	68	5.83
69	9.66	7.34	8.81	69	5.91
70	9.92	7.37	8.99	70	5.99
71	10.20	7.39	9.19	71	6.07
72	10.50	7.41	9.39	72	6.14
73	10.82	7.42	9.61	73	6.22
74	11.16	7.44	9.83	74	6.29
75	11.52	7.45	10.07	75	6.37
76	11.91	7.46	10.33	—	—
77	12.32	7.46	10.60	—	—
78	12.76	7.46	10.89	—	—
79	13.23	7.47	11.19	—	—
80	13.72	7.47	11.51	—	—

*Monthly life income on a female life is approximately equal to that shown for a male life five years younger.

Appendix B

Personal Automobile Policy
(SAMPLE ONLY)

PERSONAL AUTO POLICY
AGREEMENT

In return for payment of the premium and subject to all the terms of this policy, we agree with you as follows:

DEFINITIONS

A. Throughout this policy, "you" and "your" refer to:

1. The "named insured" shown in the Declarations; and

2. The spouse if a resident of the same household.

If the spouse ceases to be a resident of the same household during the policy period or prior to the inception of this policy, the spouse will be considered "you" and "your" under this policy but only until the earlier of:

1. The end of 90 days following the spouse's change of residency;

2. The effective date of another policy listing the spouse as a named insured; or

3. The end of the policy period.

B. "We", "us" and "our" refer to the Company providing this insurance.

C. For purposes of this policy, a private passenger type auto, pickup or van shall be deemed to be owned by a person if leased:

1. Under a written agreement to that person; and

2. For a continuous period of at least 6 months.

Other words and phrases are defined. They are in quotation marks when used.

D. "Bodily injury" means bodily harm, sickness or disease, including death that results.

E. "Business" includes trade, profession or occupation.

F. "Family member" means a person related to you by blood, marriage or adoption who is a resident of your household. This includes a ward or foster child.

G. "Occupying" means in, upon, getting in, on, out or off.

H. "Property damage" means physical injury to, destruction of or loss of use of tangible property.

I. "Trailer" means a vehicle designed to be pulled by a:

1. Private passenger auto; or

2. Pickup or van.

It also means a farm wagon or farm implement while towed by a vehicle listed in **1.** or **2.** above.

J. "Your covered auto" means:

1. Any vehicle shown in the Declarations.

2. A "newly acquired auto".

3. Any "trailer" you own.

4. Any auto or "trailer" you do not own while used as a temporary substitute for any other vehicle described in this definition which is out of normal use because of its:

    a. Breakdown;

    b. Repair;

    c. Servicing;

    d. Loss; or

    e. Destruction.

This Provision (**J.4.**) does not apply to Coverage For Damage To Your Auto.

K. "Newly acquired auto":

1. "Newly acquired auto" means any of the following types of vehicles you become the owner of during the policy period:

    a. A private passenger auto; or

    b. A pickup or van, for which no other insurance policy provides coverage, that:

      (1) Has a Gross Vehicle Weight of less than 10,000 lbs.; and

      (2) Is not used for the delivery or transportation of goods and materials unless such use is:

        (a) Incidental to your "business" of installing, maintaining or repairing furnishings or equipment; or

        (b) For farming or ranching.

2. Coverage for a "newly acquired auto" is provided as described below. If you ask us to insure a "newly acquired auto" after a specified time period described below has elapsed, any coverage we provide for a "newly acquired auto" will begin at the time you request the coverage.

    a. For any coverage provided in this policy except Coverage For Damage To Your Auto, a "newly acquired auto" will have the broadest coverage we now provide for any vehicle shown in the Declarations. Coverage begins on the date you become the owner. However, for this coverage to apply to a "newly acquired auto" which is in addition to any vehicle shown in the Declarations, you must ask us to insure it within 14 days after you become the owner.

(SAMPLE ONLY)

If a "newly acquired auto" replaces a vehicle shown in the Declarations, coverage is provided for this vehicle without your having to ask us to insure it.

b. Collision Coverage for a "newly acquired auto" begins on the date you become the owner. However, for this coverage to apply, you must ask us to insure it within:

(1) 14 days after you become the owner if the Declarations indicate that Collision Coverage applies to at least one auto. In this case, the "newly acquired auto" will have the broadest coverage we now provide for any auto shown in the Declarations.

(2) Four days after you become the owner if the Declarations do not indicate that Collision Coverage applies to at least one auto. If you comply with the 4 day requirement and a loss occurred before you asked us to insure the "newly acquired auto", a Collision deductible of $500 will apply.

c. Other Than Collision Coverage for a "newly acquired auto" begins on the date you become the owner. However, for this coverage to apply, you must ask us to insure it within:

(1) 14 days after you become the owner if the Declarations indicate that Other Than Collision Coverage applies to at least one auto. In this case, the "newly acquired auto" will have the broadest coverage we now provide for any auto shown in the Declarations.

(2) Four days after you become the owner if the Declarations do not indicate that Other Than Collision Coverage applies to at least one auto. If you comply with the 4 day requirement and a loss occurred before you asked us to insure the "newly acquired auto", an Other Than Collision deductible of $500 will apply.

PART 1 – LIABILITY COVERAGE

INSURING AGREEMENT

A. We will pay damages for "bodily injury" or "property damage" for which any "insured" becomes legally responsible because of an auto accident. Damages include prejudgment interest awarded against the "insured". We will settle or defend, as we consider appropriate, any claim or suit asking for these damages. In addition to our limit of liability, we will pay all defense costs we incur. Our duty to settle or defend ends when our limit of liability for this coverage has been exhausted by payment of judgments or settlements. We have no duty to defend any suit or settle any claim for "bodily injury" or "property damage" not covered under this policy.

B. "Insured" as used in this Part means:

1. You or any "family member" for the ownership, maintenance or use of any auto or "trailer".

2. Any person using "your covered auto".

3. For "your covered auto", any person or organization but only with respect to legal responsibility for acts or omissions of a person for whom coverage is afforded under this Part.

4. For any auto or "trailer", other than "your covered auto", any other person or organization but only with respect to legal responsibility for acts or omissions of you or any "family member" for whom coverage is afforded under this Part. This Provision (**B.4.**) applies only if the person or organization does not own or hire the auto or "trailer".

SUPPLEMENTARY PAYMENTS

In addition to our limit of liability, we will pay on behalf of an "insured":

1. Up to $250 for the cost of bail bonds required because of an accident, including related traffic law violations. The accident must result in "bodily injury" or "property damage" covered under this policy.

2. Premiums on appeal bonds and bonds to release attachments in any suit we defend.

3. Interest accruing after a judgment is entered in any suit we defend. Our duty to pay interest ends when we offer to pay that part of the judgment which does not exceed our limit of liability for this coverage.

4. Up to $200 a day for loss of earnings, but not other income, because of attendance at hearings or trials at our request.

5. Other reasonable expenses incurred at our request.

EXCLUSIONS

A. We do not provide Liability Coverage for any "insured":

1. Who intentionally causes "bodily injury" or "property damage".

2. For "property damage" to property owned or being transported by that "insured".

3. For "property damage" to property:

   a. Rented to;

   b. Used by; or

   c. In the care of;

   that "insured".

   This Exclusion (A.3.) does not apply to "property damage" to a residence or private garage.

4. For "bodily injury" to an employee of that "insured" during the course of employment. This Exclusion (A.4.) does not apply to "bodily injury" to a domestic employee unless workers' compensation benefits are required or available for that domestic employee.

5. For that "insured's" liability arising out of the ownership or operation of a vehicle while it is being used as a public or livery conveyance. This Exclusion (A.5.) does not apply to a share-the-expense car pool.

6. While employed or otherwise engaged in the "business" of:

   a. Selling;

   b. Repairing;

   c. Servicing;

   d. Storing; or

   e. Parking;

   vehicles designed for use mainly on public highways. This includes road testing and delivery. This Exclusion (A.6.) does not apply to the ownership, maintenance or use of "your covered auto" by:

   a. You;

   b. Any "family member"; or

   c. Any partner, agent or employee of you or any "family member".

7. Maintaining or using any vehicle while that "insured" is employed or otherwise engaged in any "business" (other than farming or ranching) not described in Exclusion A.6.

   This Exclusion (A.7.) does not apply to the maintenance or use of a:

   a. Private passenger auto;

   b. Pickup or van; or

   c. "Trailer" used with a vehicle described in a. or b. above.

8. Using a vehicle without a reasonable belief that that "insured" is entitled to do so. This Exclusion (A.8.) does not apply to a "family member" using "your covered auto" which is owned by you.

9. For "bodily injury" or "property damage" for which that "insured":

   a. Is an insured under a nuclear energy liability policy; or

   b. Would be an insured under a nuclear energy liability policy but for its termination upon exhaustion of its limit of liability.

   A nuclear energy liability policy is a policy issued by any of the following or their successors:

   a. Nuclear Energy Liability Insurance Association;

   b. Mutual Atomic Energy Liability Underwriters; or

   c. Nuclear Insurance Association of Canada.

B. We do not provide Liability Coverage for the ownership, maintenance or use of:

1. Any vehicle which:

   a. Has fewer than four wheels; or

   b. Is designed mainly for use off public roads.

   This Exclusion (B.1.) does not apply:

   a. While such vehicle is being used by an "insured" in a medical emergency;

   b. To any "trailer"; or

   c. To any non-owned golf cart.

2. Any vehicle, other than "your covered auto", which is:

   a. Owned by you; or

   b. Furnished or available for your regular use.

3. Any vehicle, other than "your covered auto", which is:

   a. Owned by any "family member"; or

   b. Furnished or available for the regular use of any "family member".

   However, this Exclusion (B.3.) does not apply to you while you are maintaining or "occupying" any vehicle which is:

   a. Owned by a "family member"; or

   b. Furnished or available for the regular use of a "family member".

4. Any vehicle, located inside a facility designed for racing, for the purpose of:

   a. Competing in; or

   b. Practicing or preparing for;

   any prearranged or organized racing or speed contest.

(SAMPLE ONLY)

LIMIT OF LIABILITY

A. The limit of liability shown in the Declarations for each person for Bodily Injury Liability is our maximum limit of liability for all damages, including damages for care, loss of services or death, arising out of "bodily injury" sustained by any one person in any one auto accident. Subject to this limit for each person, the limit of liability shown in the Declarations for each accident for Bodily Injury Liability is our maximum limit of liability for all damages for "bodily injury" resulting from any one auto accident.

The limit of liability shown in the Declarations for each accident for Property Damage Liability is our maximum limit of liability for all "property damage" resulting from any one auto accident.

This is the most we will pay regardless of the number of:

1. "Insureds";

2. Claims made;

3. Vehicles or premiums shown in the Declarations; or

4. Vehicles involved in the auto accident.

B. No one will be entitled to receive duplicate payments for the same elements of loss under this coverage and:

1. Part **B** or Part **C** of this policy; or

2. Any Underinsured Motorists Coverage provided by this policy.

OUT OF STATE COVERAGE

If an auto accident to which this policy applies occurs in any state or province other than the one in which "your covered auto" is principally garaged, we will interpret your policy for that accident as follows:

A. If the state or province has:

1. A financial responsibility or similar law specifying limits of liability for "bodily injury" or "property damage" higher than the limit shown in the Declarations, your policy will provide the higher specified limit.

2. A compulsory insurance or similar law requiring a nonresident to maintain insurance whenever the nonresident uses a vehicle in that state or province, your policy will provide at least the required minimum amounts and types of coverage.

B. No one will be entitled to duplicate payments for the same elements of loss.

FINANCIAL RESPONSIBILITY

When this policy is certified as future proof of financial responsibility, this policy shall comply with the law to the extent required.

OTHER INSURANCE

If there is other applicable liability insurance we will pay only our share of the loss. Our share is the proportion that our limit of liability bears to the total of all applicable limits. However, any insurance we provide for a vehicle you do not own shall be excess over any other collectible insurance.

PART B – MEDICAL PAYMENTS COVERAGE

INSURING AGREEMENT

A. We will pay reasonable expenses incurred for necessary medical and funeral services because of "bodily injury":

1. Caused by accident; and

2. Sustained by an "insured".

We will pay only those expenses incurred for services rendered within 3 years from the date of the accident.

B. "Insured" as used in this Part means:

1. You or any "family member":

a. While "occupying"; or

b. As a pedestrian when struck by;

a motor vehicle designed for use mainly on public roads or a trailer of any type.

2. Any other person while "occupying" "your covered auto".

EXCLUSIONS

We do not provide Medical Payments Coverage for any "insured" for "bodily injury":

1. Sustained while "occupying" any motorized vehicle having fewer than four wheels.

2. Sustained while "occupying" "your covered auto" when it is being used as a public or livery conveyance. This Exclusion (**2.**) does not apply to a share-the-expense car pool.

3. Sustained while "occupying" any vehicle located for use as a residence or premises.

4. Occurring during the course of employment if workers' compensation benefits are required or available for the "bodily injury".

5. Sustained while "occupying", or when struck by, any vehicle (other than "your covered auto") which is:

a. Owned by you; or

b. Furnished or available for your regular use.

6. Sustained while "occupying", or when struck by, any vehicle (other than "your covered auto") which is:

a. Owned by any "family member"; or

b. Furnished or available for the regular use of any "family member".

However, this Exclusion (**6.**) does not apply to you.

7. Sustained while "occupying" a vehicle without a reasonable belief that that "insured" is entitled to do so. This Exclusion **(7.)** does not apply to a "family member" using "your covered auto" which is owned by you.

8. Sustained while "occupying" a vehicle when it is being used in the "business" of an "insured". This Exclusion **(8.)** does not apply to "bodily injury" sustained while "occupying" a:

    a. Private passenger auto;

    b. Pickup or van that you own; or

    c. "Trailer" used with a vehicle described in **a.** or **b.** above.

9. Caused by or as a consequence of:

    a. Discharge of a nuclear weapon (even if accidental);

    b. War (declared or undeclared);

    c. Civil war;

    d. Insurrection; or

    e. Rebellion or revolution.

10. From or as a consequence of the following, whether controlled or uncontrolled or however caused:

    a. Nuclear reaction;

    b. Radiation; or

    c. Radioactive contamination.

11. Sustained while "occupying" any vehicle located inside a facility designed for racing, for the purpose of:

    a. Competing in; or

    b. Practicing or preparing for;

    any prearranged or organized racing or speed contest.

LIMIT OF LIABILITY

A. The limit of liability shown in the Declarations for this coverage is our maximum limit of liability for each person injured in any one accident. This is the most we will pay regardless of the number of:

1. "Insureds";

2. Claims made;

3. Vehicles or premiums shown in the Declarations; or

4. Vehicles involved in the accident.

B. No one will be entitled to receive duplicate payments for the same elements of loss under this coverage and:

1. Part **A** or Part **C** of this policy; or

2. Any Underinsured Motorists Coverage provided by this policy.

OTHER INSURANCE

If there is other applicable auto medical payments insurance we will pay only our share of the loss. Our share is the proportion that our limit of liability bears to the total of all applicable limits. However, any insurance we provide with respect to a vehicle you do not own shall be excess over any other collectible auto insurance providing payments for medical or funeral expenses.

PART C – UNINSURED MOTORISTS COVERAGE

INSURING AGREEMENT

A. We will pay compensatory damages which an "insured" is legally entitled to recover from the owner or operator of an "uninsured motor vehicle" because of "bodily injury":

1. Sustained by an "insured"; and

2. Caused by an accident.

The owner's or operator's liability for these damages must arise out of the ownership, maintenance or use of the "uninsured motor vehicle".

Any judgment for damages arising out of a suit brought without our written consent is not binding on us.

B. "Insured" as used in this Part means:

1. You or any "family member".

2. Any other person "occupying" "your covered auto".

3. Any person for damages that person is entitled to recover because of "bodily injury" to which this coverage applies sustained by a person described in **1.** or **2.** above.

C. "Uninsured motor vehicle" means a land motor vehicle or trailer of any type:

1. To which no bodily injury liability bond or policy applies at the time of the accident.

2. To which a bodily injury liability bond or policy applies at the time of the accident. In this case its limit for bodily injury liability must be less than the minimum limit for bodily injury liability specified by the financial responsibility law of the state in which "your covered auto" is principally garaged.

3. Which is a hit-and-run vehicle whose operator or owner cannot be identified and which hits:

   a. You or any "family member";

   b. A vehicle which you or any "family member" are "occupying"; or

   c. "Your covered auto".

4. To which a bodily injury liability bond or policy applies at the time of the accident but the bonding or insuring company:

   a. Denies coverage; or

   b. Is or becomes insolvent.

However, "uninsured motor vehicle" does not include any vehicle or equipment:

1. Owned by or furnished or available for the regular use of you or any "family member".

2. Owned or operated by a self-insurer under any applicable motor vehicle law, except a self-insurer which is or becomes insolvent.

3. Owned by any governmental unit or agency.

4. Operated on rails or crawler treads.

5. Designed mainly for use off public roads while not on public roads.

6. While located for use as a residence or premises.

EXCLUSIONS

A. We do not provide Uninsured Motorists Coverage for "bodily injury" sustained:

1. By an "insured" while "occupying", or when struck by, any motor vehicle owned by that "insured" which is not insured for this coverage under this policy. This includes a trailer of any type used with that vehicle.

2. By any "family member" while "occupying", or when struck by, any motor vehicle you own which is insured for this coverage on a primary basis under any other policy.

B. We do not provide Uninsured Motorists Coverage for "bodily injury" sustained by any "insured":

1. If that "insured" or the legal representative settles the "bodily injury" claim without our consent.

2. While "occupying" "your covered auto" when it is being used as a public or livery conveyance. This Exclusion (B.2.) does not apply to a share-the-expense car pool.

3. Using a vehicle without a reasonable belief that that "insured" is entitled to do so. This Exclusion (B.3.) does not apply to a "family member" using "your covered auto" which is owned by you.

C. This coverage shall not apply directly or indirectly to benefit any insurer or self-insurer under any of the following or similar law:

1. Workers' compensation law; or

2. Disability benefits law.

D. We do not provide Uninsured Motorists Coverage for punitive or exemplary damages.

LIMIT OF LIABILITY

A. The limit of liability shown in the Declarations for each person for Uninsured Motorists Coverage is our maximum limit of liability for all damages, including damages for care, loss of services or death, arising out of "bodily injury" sustained by any one person in any one accident. Subject to this limit for each person, the limit of liability shown in the Declarations for each accident for Uninsured Motorists Coverage is our maximum limit of liability for all damages for "bodily injury" resulting from any one accident.

This is the most we will pay regardless of the number of:

1. "Insureds";

2. Claims made;

3. Vehicles or premiums shown in the Declarations; or

4. Vehicles involved in the accident.

B. No one will be entitled to receive duplicate payments for the same elements of loss under this coverage and:

1. Part A. or Part B. of this policy; or

2. Any Underinsured Motorists Coverage provided by this policy.

C. We will not make a duplicate payment under this coverage for any element of loss for which payment has been made by or on behalf of persons or organizations who may be legally responsible.

D. We will not pay for any element of loss if a person is entitled to receive payment for the same element of loss under any of the following or similar law:

1. Workers' compensation law; or

2. Disability benefits law.

OTHER INSURANCE

If there is other applicable insurance available under one or more policies or provisions of coverage that is similar to the insurance provided under this Part of the policy:

1. Any recovery for damages under all such policies or provisions of coverage may equal but not exceed the highest applicable limit for any one vehicle under any insurance providing coverage on either a primary or excess basis.

2. Any insurance we provide with respect to a vehicle you do not own shall be excess over any collectible insurance providing such coverage on a primary basis.

(SAMPLE ONLY)

3. If the coverage under this policy is provided:

   a. On a primary basis, we will pay only our share of the loss that must be paid under insurance providing coverage on a primary basis. Our share is the proportion that our limit of liability bears to the total of all applicable limits of liability for coverage provided on a primary basis.

   b. On an excess basis, we will pay only our share of the loss that must be paid under insurance providing coverage on an excess basis. Our share is the proportion that our limit of liability bears to the total of all applicable limits of liability for coverage provided on an excess basis.

ARBITRATION

A. If we and an "insured" do not agree:

   1. Whether that "insured" is legally entitled to recover damages; or

   2. As to the amount of damages which are recoverable by that "insured";

   from the owner or operator of an "uninsured motor vehicle", then the matter may be arbitrated. However, disputes concerning coverage under this Part may not be arbitrated.

Both parties must agree to arbitration. If so agreed, each party will select an arbitrator. The two arbitrators will select a third. If they cannot agree within 30 days, either may request that selection be made by a judge of a court having jurisdiction.

B. Each party will:

   1. Pay the expenses it incurs; and

   2. Bear the expenses of the third arbitrator equally.

C. Unless both parties agree otherwise, arbitration will take place in the county in which the "insured" lives. Local rules of law as to procedure and evidence will apply. A decision agreed to by two of the arbitrators will be binding as to:

   1. Whether the "insured" is legally entitled to recover damages; and

   2. The amount of damages. This applies only if the amount does not exceed the minimum limit for bodily injury liability specified by the financial responsibility law of the state in which "your covered auto" is principally garaged. If the amount exceeds that limit, either party may demand the right to a trial. This demand must be made within 60 days of the arbitrators' decision. If this demand is not made, the amount of damages agreed to by the arbitrators will be binding.

PART D – COVERAGE FOR DAMAGE TO YOUR AUTO

INSURING AGREEMENT

A. We will pay for direct and accidental loss to "your covered auto" or any "non-owned auto", including their equipment, minus any applicable deductible shown in the Declarations. If loss to more than one "your covered auto" or "non-owned auto" results from the same "collision", only the highest applicable deductible will apply. We will pay for loss to "your covered auto" caused by:

   1. Other than "collision" only if the Declarations indicate that Other Than Collision Coverage is provided for that auto.

   2. "Collision" only if the Declarations indicate that Collision Coverage is provided for that auto.

   If there is a loss to a "non-owned auto", we will provide the broadest coverage applicable to any "your covered auto" shown in the Declarations.

B. "Collision" means the upset of "your covered auto" or a "non-owned auto" or their impact with another vehicle or object.

   Loss caused by the following is considered other than "collision":

   1. Missiles or falling objects;

   2. Fire;

   3. Theft or larceny;

   4. Explosion or earthquake;

   5. Windstorm;

   6. Hail, water or flood;

   7. Malicious mischief or vandalism;

   8. Riot or civil commotion;

   9. Contact with bird or animal; or

   10. Breakage of glass.

   If breakage of glass is caused by a "collision", you may elect to have it considered a loss caused by "collision".

C. "Non-owned auto" means:

   1. Any private passenger auto, pickup, van or "trailer" not owned by or furnished or available for the regular use of you or any "family member" while in the custody of or being operated by you or any "family member"; or

   2. Any auto or "trailer" you do not own while used as a temporary substitute for "your covered auto" which is out of normal use because of its:

      a. Breakdown;

      b. Repair;

      c. Servicing;

      d. Loss; or

      e. Destruction.

(SAMPLE ONLY)

TRANSPORTATION EXPENSES

A. In addition, we will pay, without application of a deductible, up to a maximum of $600 for:

1. Temporary transportation expenses not exceeding $20 per day incurred by you in the event of a loss to "your covered auto". We will pay for such expenses if the loss is caused by:

a. Other than "collision" only if the Declarations indicate that Other Than Collision Coverage is provided for that auto.

b. "Collision" only if the Declarations indicate that Collision Coverage is provided for that auto.

2. Expenses for which you become legally responsible in the event of loss to a "non-owned auto". We will pay for such expenses if the loss is caused by:

a. Other than "collision" only if the Declarations indicate that Other Than Collision Coverage is provided for any "your covered auto".

b. "Collision" only if the Declarations indicate that Collision Coverage is provided for any "your covered auto".

However, the most we will pay for any expenses for loss of use is $20 per day.

B. If the loss is caused by:

1. A total theft of "your covered auto" or a "non-owned auto", we will pay only expenses incurred during the period:

a. Beginning 48 hours after the theft; and

b. Ending when "your covered auto" or the "non-owned auto" is returned to use or we pay for its loss.

2. Other than theft of a "your covered auto" or a "non-owned auto", we will pay only expenses beginning when the auto is withdrawn from use for more than 24 hours.

C. Our payment will be limited to that period of time reasonably required to repair or replace the "your covered auto" or the "non-owned auto".

EXCLUSIONS

We will not pay for:

1. Loss to "your covered auto" or any "non-owned auto" which occurs while it is being used as a public or livery conveyance. This Exclusion **(1.)** does not apply to a share-the-expense car pool.

2. Damage due and confined to:

a. Wear and tear;

b. Freezing;

c. Mechanical or electrical breakdown or failure; or

d. Road damage to tires.

This Exclusion **(2.)** does not apply if the damage results from the total theft of "your covered auto" or any "non-owned auto".

3. Loss due to or as a consequence of:

a. Radioactive contamination;

b. Discharge of any nuclear weapon (even if accidental);

c. War (declared or undeclared);

d. Civil war;

e. Insurrection; or

f. Rebellion or revolution.

4. Loss to any electronic equipment designed for the reproduction of sound and any accessories used with such equipment. This includes but is not limited to:

a. Radios and stereos;

b. Tape decks; or

c. Compact disc players.

This Exclusion **(4.)** does not apply to equipment designed solely for the reproduction of sound and accessories used with such equipment, provided:

a. The equipment is permanently installed in "your covered auto" or any "non-owned auto"; or

b. The equipment is:

(1) Removable from a housing unit which is permanently installed in the auto;

(2) Designed to be solely operated by use of the power from the auto's electrical system; and

(3) In or upon "your covered auto" or any "non-owned auto" at the time of loss.

5. Loss to any electronic equipment that receives or transmits audio, visual or data signals and any accessories used with such equipment. This includes but is not limited to:

a. Citizens band radios;

b. Telephones;

c. Two-way mobile radios;

d. Scanning monitor receivers;

e. Television monitor receivers;

f. Video cassette recorders;

g. Audio cassette recorders; or

h. Personal computers.

This Exclusion **(5.)** does not apply to:

a. Any electronic equipment that is necessary for the normal operation of the auto or the monitoring of the auto's operating systems; or

b. A permanently installed telephone designed to be operated by use of the power from the auto's electrical system and any accessories used with the telephone.

6. Loss to tapes, records, discs or other media used with equipment described in Exclusions **4.** and **5.**

7. A total loss to "your covered auto" or any "non-owned auto" due to destruction or confiscation by governmental or civil authorities.

This Exclusion **(7.)** does not apply to the interests of Loss Payees in "your covered auto".

8. Loss to:

a. A "trailer", camper body, or motor home, which is not shown in the Declarations; or

b. Facilities or equipment used with such "trailer", camper body or motor home. Facilities or equipment include but are not limited to:

(1) Cooking, dining, plumbing or refrigeration facilities;

(2) Awnings or cabanas; or

(3) Any other facilities or equipment used with a "trailer", camper body, or motor home.

This Exclusion **(8.)** does not apply to a:

a. "Trailer", and its facilities or equipment, which you do not own; or

b. "Trailer", camper body, or the facilities or equipment in or attached to the "trailer" or camper body, which you:

(1) Acquire during the policy period; and

(2) Ask us to insure within 14 days after you become the owner.

9. Loss to any "non-owned auto" when used by you or any "family member" without a reasonable belief that you or that "family member" are entitled to do so.

10. Loss to equipment designed or used for the detection or location of radar or laser.

11. Loss to any custom furnishings or equipment in or upon any pickup or van. Custom furnishings or equipment include but are not limited to:

a. Special carpeting or insulation;

b. Furniture or bars;

c. Height-extending roofs; or

d. Custom murals, paintings or other decals or graphics.

This Exclusion **(11.)** does not apply to a cap, cover or bedliner in or upon any "your covered auto" which is a pickup.

12. Loss to any "non-owned auto" being maintained or used by any person while employed or otherwise engaged in the "business" of:

a. Selling;

b. Repairing;

c. Servicing;

d. Storing; or

e. Parking;

vehicles designed for use on public highways. This includes road testing and delivery.

13. Loss to "your covered auto" or any "non-owned auto", located inside a facility designed for racing, for the purpose of:

a. Competing in; or

b. Practicing or preparing for;

any prearranged or organized racing or speed contest.

14. Loss to, or loss of use of, a "non-owned auto" rented by:

a. You; or

b. Any "family member";

if a rental vehicle company is precluded from recovering such loss or loss of use, from you or that "family member", pursuant to the provisions of any applicable rental agreement or state law.

LIMIT OF LIABILITY

A. Our limit of liability for loss will be the lesser of the:

1. Actual cash value of the stolen or damaged property; or

2. Amount necessary to repair or replace the property with other property of like kind and quality.

However, the most we will pay for loss to:

1. Any "non-owned auto" which is a trailer is $500.

2. Equipment designed solely for the reproduction of sound, including any accessories used with such equipment, which is installed in locations not used by the auto manufacturer for installation of such equipment or accessories, is $1,000.

B. An adjustment for depreciation and physical condition will be made in determining actual cash value in the event of a total loss.

C. If a repair or replacement results in better than like kind or quality, we will not pay for the amount of the betterment.

PAYMENT OF LOSS

We may pay for loss in money or repair or replace the damaged or stolen property. We may, at our expense, return any stolen property to:

1. You; or
2. The address shown in this policy.

If we return stolen property we will pay for any damage resulting from the theft. We may keep all or part of the property at an agreed or appraised value.

If we pay for loss in money, our payment will include the applicable sales tax for the damaged or stolen property.

NO BENEFIT TO BAILEE

This insurance shall not directly or indirectly benefit any carrier or other bailee for hire.

OTHER SOURCES OF RECOVERY

If other sources of recovery also cover the loss, we will pay only our share of the loss. Our share is the proportion that our limit of liability bears to the total of all applicable limits. However, any insurance we provide with respect to a "non-owned auto" shall be excess over any other collectible source of recovery including, but not limited to:

1. Any coverage provided by the owner of the "non-owned auto";
2. Any other applicable physical damage insurance;
3. Any other source of recovery applicable to the loss.

APPRAISAL

A. If we and you do not agree on the amount of loss, either may demand an appraisal of the loss. In this event, each party will select a competent appraiser. The two appraisers will select an umpire. The appraisers will state separately the actual cash value and the amount of loss. If they fail to agree, they will submit their differences to the umpire. A decision agreed to by any two will be binding. Each party will:

1. Pay its chosen appraiser; and
2. Bear the expenses of the appraisal and umpire equally.

B. We do not waive any of our rights under this policy by agreeing to an appraisal.

PART E – DUTIES AFTER AN ACCIDENT OR LOSS

We have no duty to provide coverage under this policy unless there has been full compliance with the following duties:

A. We must be notified promptly of how, when and where the accident or loss happened. Notice should also include the names and addresses of any injured persons and of any witnesses.

B. A person seeking any coverage must:

1. Cooperate with us in the investigation, settlement or defense of any claim or suit.
2. Promptly send us copies of any notices or legal papers received in connection with the accident or loss.
3. Submit, as often as we reasonably require:
   a. To physical exams by physicians we select. We will pay for these exams.
   b. To examination under oath and subscribe the same.
4. Authorize us to obtain:
   a. Medical reports; and
   b. Other pertinent records.
5. Submit a proof of loss when required by us.

C. A person seeking Uninsured Motorists Coverage must also:

1. Promptly notify the police if a hit-and-run driver is involved.
2. Promptly send us copies of the legal papers if a suit is brought.

D. A person seeking Coverage For Damage To Your Auto must also:

1. Take reasonable steps after loss to protect "your covered auto" or any "non-owned auto" and their equipment from further loss. We will pay reasonable expenses incurred to do this.
2. Promptly notify the police if "your covered auto" or any "non-owned auto" is stolen.
3. Permit us to inspect and appraise the damaged property before its repair or disposal.

PART F – GENERAL PROVISIONS

BANKRUPTCY

Bankruptcy or insolvency of the "insured" shall not relieve us of any obligations under this policy.

CHANGES

A. This policy contains all the agreements between you and us. Its terms may not be changed or waived except by endorsement issued by us.

B. If there is a change to the information used to develop the policy premium, we may adjust your premium. Changes during the policy term that may result in a premium increase or decrease include, but are not limited to, changes in:

1. The number, type or use classification of insured vehicles;

2. Operators using insured vehicles;

3. The place of principal garaging of insured vehicles;

4. Coverage, deductible or limits.

If a change resulting from **A.** or **B.** requires a premium adjustment, we will make the premium adjustment in accordance with our manual rules.

C. If we make a change which broadens coverage under this edition of your policy without additional premium charge, that change will automatically apply to your policy as of the date we implement the change in your state. This Paragraph **(C.)** does not apply to changes implemented with a general program revision that includes both broadenings and restrictions in coverage, whether that general program revision is implemented through introduction of:

1. A subsequent edition of your policy; or

2. An Amendatory Endorsement.

FRAUD

We do not provide coverage for any "insured" who has made fraudulent statements or engaged in fraudulent conduct in connection with any accident or loss for which coverage is sought under this policy.

LEGAL ACTION AGAINST US

A. No legal action may be brought against us until there has been full compliance with all the terms of this policy. In addition, under Part **A,** no legal action may be brought against us until:

1. We agree in writing that the "insured" has an obligation to pay; or

2. The amount of that obligation has been finally determined by judgment after trial.

B. No person or organization has any right under this policy to bring us into any action to determine the liability of an "insured".

OUR RIGHT TO RECOVER PAYMENT

A. If we make a payment under this policy and the person to or for whom payment was made has a right to recover damages from another we shall be subrogated to that right. That person shall do:

1. Whatever is necessary to enable us to exercise our rights; and

2. Nothing after loss to prejudice them.

However, our rights in this Paragraph **(A.)** do not apply under Part **D,** against any person using "your covered auto" with a reasonable belief that that person is entitled to do so.

B. If we make a payment under this policy and the person to or for whom payment is made recovers damages from another, that person shall:

1. Hold in trust for us the proceeds of the recovery; and

2. Reimburse us to the extent of our payment.

POLICY PERIOD AND TERRITORY

A. This policy applies only to accidents and losses which occur:

1. During the policy period as shown in the Declarations; and

2. Within the policy territory.

B. The policy territory is:

1. The United States of America, its territories or possessions;

2. Puerto Rico; or

3. Canada.

This policy also applies to loss to, or accidents involving, "your covered auto" while being transported between their ports.

TERMINATION

A. Cancellation

This policy may be cancelled during the policy period as follows:

1. The named insured shown in the Declarations may cancel by:

a. Returning this policy to us; or

b. Giving us advance written notice of the date cancellation is to take effect.

2. We may cancel by mailing to the named insured shown in the Declarations at the address shown in this policy:

a. At least 10 days notice:

(1) If cancellation is for nonpayment of premium; or

(2) If notice is mailed during the first 60 days this policy is in effect and this is not a renewal or continuation policy; or

b. At least 20 days notice in all other cases.

3. After this policy is in effect for 60 days, or if this is a renewal or continuation policy, we will cancel only:

a. For nonpayment of premium; or

b. If your driver's license or that of:

(1) Any driver who lives with you; or

(2) Any driver who customarily uses "your covered auto";

has been suspended or revoked. This must have occurred:

(1) During the policy period; or

(2) Since the last anniversary of the original effective date if the policy period is other than 1 year; or

c. If the policy was obtained through material misrepresentation.

B. Nonrenewal

If we decide not to renew or continue this policy, we will mail notice to the named insured shown in the Declarations at the address shown in this policy. Notice will be mailed at least 20 days before the end of the policy period. Subject to this notice requirement, if the policy period is:

1. Less than 6 months, we will have the right not to renew or continue this policy every 6 months, beginning 6 months after its original effective date.

2. 6 months or longer, but less than one year, we will have the right not to renew or continue this policy at the end of the policy period.

3. 1 year or longer, we will have the right not to renew or continue this policy at each anniversary of its original effective date.

C. Automatic Termination

If we offer to renew or continue and you or your representative do not accept, this policy will automatically terminate at the end of the current policy period. Failure to pay the required renewal or continuation premium when due shall mean that you have not accepted our offer.

If you obtain other insurance on "your covered auto", any similar insurance provided by this policy will terminate as to that auto on the effective date of the other insurance.

D. Other Termination Provisions

1. We may deliver any notice instead of mailing it. Proof of mailing of any notice shall be sufficient proof of notice.

2. If this policy is cancelled, you may be entitled to a premium refund. If so, we will send you the refund. The premium refund, if any, will be computed according to our manuals. However, making or offering to make the refund is not a condition of cancellation.

3. The effective date of cancellation stated in the notice shall become the end of the policy period.

TRANSFER OF YOUR INTEREST IN THIS POLICY

A. Your rights and duties under this policy may not be assigned without our written consent. However, if a named insured shown in the Declarations dies, coverage will be provided for:

1. The surviving spouse if resident in the same household at the time of death. Coverage applies to the spouse as if a named insured shown in the Declarations; and

2. The legal representative of the deceased person as if a named insured shown in the Declarations. This applies only with respect to the representative's legal responsibility to maintain or use "your covered auto".

B. Coverage will only be provided until the end of the policy period.

TWO OR MORE AUTO POLICIES

If this policy and any other auto insurance policy issued to you by us apply to the same accident, the maximum limit of our liability under all the policies shall not exceed the highest applicable limit of liability under any one policy.

Appendix C

Homeowners 3—Special Form
(SAMPLE ONLY)

HOMEOWNERS 3 – SPECIAL FORM

AGREEMENT

We will provide the insurance described in this policy in return for the premium and compliance with all applicable provisions of this policy.

DEFINITIONS

A. In this policy, "you" and "your" refer to the "named insured" shown in the Declarations and the spouse if a resident of the same household. "We", "us" and "our" refer to the Company providing this insurance.

B. In addition, certain words and phrases are defined as follows:

1. "Aircraft Liability", "Hovercraft Liability", "Motor Vehicle Liability" and "Watercraft Liability", subject to the provisions in **b.** below, mean the following:

   a. Liability for "bodily injury" or "property damage" arising out of the:

   (1) Ownership of such vehicle or craft by an "insured";

   (2) Maintenance, occupancy, operation, use, loading or unloading of such vehicle or craft by any person;

   (3) Entrustment of such vehicle or craft by an "insured" to any person;

   (4) Failure to supervise or negligent supervision of any person involving such vehicle or craft by an "insured"; or

   (5) Vicarious liability, whether or not imposed by law, for the actions of a child or minor involving such vehicle or craft.

   b. For the purpose of this definition:

   (1) Aircraft means any contrivance used or designed for flight except model or hobby aircraft not used or designed to carry people or cargo;

   (2) Hovercraft means a self-propelled motorized ground effect vehicle and includes, but is not limited to, flarecraft and air cushion vehicles;

   (3) Watercraft means a craft principally designed to be propelled on or in water by wind, engine power or electric motor; and

   (4) Motor vehicle means a "motor vehicle" as defined in **7.** below.

2. "Bodily injury" means bodily harm, sickness or disease, including required care, loss of services and death that results.

3. "Business" means:

   a. A trade, profession or occupation engaged in on a full-time, part-time or occasional basis; or

   b. Any other activity engaged in for money or other compensation, except the following:

   (1) One or more activities, not described in (2) through (4) below, for which no "insured" receives more than $2,000 in total compensation for the 12 months before the beginning of the policy period;

   (2) Volunteer activities for which no money is received other than payment for expenses incurred to perform the activity;

   (3) Providing home day care services for which no compensation is received, other than the mutual exchange of such services; or

   (4) The rendering of home day care services to a relative of an "insured".

4. "Employee" means an employee of an "insured", or an employee leased to an "insured" by a labor leasing firm under an agreement between an "insured" and the labor leasing firm, whose duties are other than those performed by a "residence employee".

5. "Insured" means:

   a. You and residents of your household who are:

   (1) Your relatives; or

   (2) Other persons under the age of 21 and in the care of any person named above;

   b. A student enrolled in school full time, as defined by the school, who was a resident of your household before moving out to attend school, provided the student is under the age of:

   (1) 24 and your relative; or

   (2) 21 and in your care or the care of a person described in **a.(1)** above; or

c. Under Section **II**:

  (1) With respect to animals or watercraft to which this policy applies, any person or organization legally responsible for these animals or watercraft which are owned by you or any person included in **a.** or **b.** above. "Insured" does not mean a person or organization using or having custody of these animals or watercraft in the course of any "business" or without consent of the owner; or

  (2) With respect to a "motor vehicle" to which this policy applies:

    (a) Persons while engaged in your employ or that of any person included in **a.** or **b.** above; or

    (b) Other persons using the vehicle on an "insured location" with your consent.

Under both Sections **I** and **II,** when the word an immediately precedes the word "insured", the words an "insured" together mean one or more "insureds".

6. "Insured location" means:

  a. The "residence premises";

  b. The part of other premises, other structures and grounds used by you as a residence; and

    (1) Which is shown in the Declarations; or

    (2) Which is acquired by you during the policy period for your use as a residence;

  c. Any premises used by you in connection with a premises described in **a.** and **b.** above;

  d. Any part of a premises:

    (1) Not owned by an "insured"; and

    (2) Where an "insured" is temporarily residing;

  e. Vacant land, other than farm land, owned by or rented to an "insured";

  f. Land owned by or rented to an "insured" on which a one, two, three or four family dwelling is being built as a residence for an "insured";

  g. Individual or family cemetery plots or burial vaults of an "insured"; or

  h. Any part of a premises occasionally rented to an "insured" for other than "business" use.

7. "Motor vehicle" means:

  a. A self-propelled land or amphibious vehicle; or

  b. Any trailer or semitrailer which is being carried on, towed by or hitched for towing by a vehicle described in **a.** above.

8. "Occurrence" means an accident, including continuous or repeated exposure to substantially the same general harmful conditions, which results, during the policy period, in:

  a. "Bodily injury"; or

  b. "Property damage".

9. "Property damage" means physical injury to, destruction of, or loss of use of tangible property.

10. "Residence employee" means:

  a. An employee of an "insured", or an employee leased to an "insured" by a labor leasing firm, under an agreement between an "insured" and the labor leasing firm, whose duties are related to the maintenance or use of the "residence premises", including household or domestic services; or

  b. One who performs similar duties elsewhere not related to the "business" of an "insured".

A "residence employee" does not include a temporary employee who is furnished to an "insured" to substitute for a permanent "residence employee" on leave or to meet seasonal or short-term workload conditions.

11. "Residence premises" means:

  a. The one family dwelling where you reside;

  b. The two, three or four family dwelling where you reside in at least one of the family units; or

  c. That part of any other building where you reside;

and which is shown as the "residence premises" in the Declarations.

"Residence premises" also includes other structures and grounds at that location.

DEDUCTIBLE

Unless otherwise noted in this policy, the following deductible provision applies:

Subject to the policy limits that apply, we will pay only that part of the total of all loss payable under Section **I** that exceeds the deductible amount shown in the Declarations.

SECTION I – PROPERTY COVERAGES

A. Coverage A – Dwelling

1. We cover:

   a. The dwelling on the "residence premises" shown in the Declarations, including structures attached to the dwelling; and

   b. Materials and supplies located on or next to the "residence premises" used to construct, alter or repair the dwelling or other structures on the "residence premises".

2. We do not cover land, including land on which the dwelling is located.

B. Coverage B – Other Structures

1. We cover other structures on the "residence premises" set apart from the dwelling by clear space. This includes structures connected to the dwelling by only a fence, utility line, or similar connection.

2. We do not cover:

   a. Land, including land on which the other structures are located;

   b. Other structures rented or held for rental to any person not a tenant of the dwelling, unless used solely as a private garage;

   c. Other structures from which any "business" is conducted; or

   d. Other structures used to store "business" property. However, we do cover a structure that contains "business" property solely owned by an "insured" or a tenant of the dwelling provided that "business" property does not include gaseous or liquid fuel, other than fuel in a permanently installed fuel tank of a vehicle or craft parked or stored in the structure.

3. The limit of liability for this coverage will not be more than 10% of the limit of liability that applies to Coverage **A.** Use of this coverage does not reduce the Coverage **A** limit of liability.

C. Coverage C – Personal Property

1. **Covered Property**

   We cover personal property owned or used by an "insured" while it is anywhere in the world. After a loss and at your request, we will cover personal property owned by:

   a. Others while the property is on the part of the "residence premises" occupied by an "insured"; or

   b. A guest or a "residence employee", while the property is in any residence occupied by an "insured".

2. **Limit For Property At Other Residences**

   Our limit of liability for personal property usually located at an "insured's" residence, other than the "residence premises", is 10% of the limit of liability for Coverage **C,** or $1,000, whichever is greater. However, this limitation does not apply to personal property:

   a. Moved from the "residence premises" because it is being repaired, renovated or rebuilt and is not fit to live in or store property in; or

   b. In a newly acquired principal residence for 30 days from the time you begin to move the property there.

3. **Special Limits Of Liability**

   The special limit for each category shown below is the total limit for each loss for all property in that category. These special limits do not increase the Coverage **C** limit of liability.

   a. $200 on money, bank notes, bullion, gold other than goldware, silver other than silverware, platinum other than platinumware, coins, medals, scrip, stored value cards and smart cards.

   b. $1,500 on securities, accounts, deeds, evidences of debt, letters of credit, notes other than bank notes, manuscripts, personal records, passports, tickets and stamps. This dollar limit applies to these categories regardless of the medium (such as paper or computer software) on which the material exists.

   This limit includes the cost to research, replace or restore the information from the lost or damaged material.

c. $1,500 on watercraft of all types, including their trailers, furnishings, equipment and outboard engines or motors.

d. $1,500 on trailers or semitrailers not used with watercraft of all types.

e. $1,500 for loss by theft of jewelry, watches, furs, precious and semiprecious stones.

f. $2,500 for loss by theft of firearms and related equipment.

g. $2,500 for loss by theft of silverware, silver-plated ware, goldware, gold-plated ware, platinumware, platinum-plated ware and pewterware. This includes flatware, hollow-ware, tea sets, trays and trophies made of or including silver, gold or pewter.

h. $2,500 on property, on the "residence premises", used primarily for "business" purposes.

i. $500 on property, away from the "residence premises", used primarily for "business" purposes. However, this limit does not apply to loss to electronic apparatus and other property described in Categories **j.** and **k.** below.

j. $1,500 on electronic apparatus and accessories, while in or upon a "motor vehicle", but only if the apparatus is equipped to be operated by power from the "motor vehicle's" electrical system while still capable of being operated by other power sources.

Accessories include antennas, tapes, wires, records, discs or other media that can be used with any apparatus described in this Category **j.**

k. $1,500 on electronic apparatus and accessories used primarily for "business" while away from the "residence premises" and not in or upon a "motor vehicle". The apparatus must be equipped to be operated by power from the "motor vehicle's" electrical system while still capable of being operated by other power sources.

Accessories include antennas, tapes, wires, records, discs or other media that can be used with any apparatus described in this Category **k.**

4. **Property Not Covered**

We do not cover:

a. Articles separately described and specifically insured, regardless of the limit for which they are insured, in this or other insurance;

b. Animals, birds or fish;

c. "Motor vehicles".

(1) This includes:

(a) Their accessories, equipment and parts; or

(b) Electronic apparatus and accessories designed to be operated solely by power from the electrical system of the "motor vehicle". Accessories include antennas, tapes, wires, records, discs or other media that can be used with any apparatus described above.

The exclusion of property described in **(a)** and **(b)** above applies only while such property is in or upon the "motor vehicle".

(2) We do cover "motor vehicles" not required to be registered for use on public roads or property which are:

(a) Used solely to service an "insured's" residence; or

(b) Designed to assist the handicapped;

d. Aircraft meaning any contrivance used or designed for flight including any parts whether or not attached to the aircraft.

We do cover model or hobby aircraft not used or designed to carry people or cargo;

e. Hovercraft and parts. Hovercraft means a self-propelled motorized ground effect vehicle and includes, but is not limited to, flare-craft and air cushion vehicles;

f. Property of roomers, boarders and other tenants, except property of roomers and boarders related to an "insured";

g. Property in an apartment regularly rented or held for rental to others by an "insured", except as provided in **E.10.** Landlord's Furnishings under Section I – Property Coverages;

h. Property rented or held for rental to others off the "residence premises";

i. "Business" data, including such data stored in:

(1) Books of account, drawings or other paper records; or

(2) Computers and related equipment.

We do cover the cost of blank recording or storage media, and of prerecorded computer programs available on the retail market;

j. Credit cards, electronic fund transfer cards or access devices used solely for deposit, withdrawal or transfer of funds except as provided in **E.6.** Credit Card, Electronic Fund Transfer Card Or Access Device, Forgery And Counterfeit Money under Section **I** – Property Coverages; or

k. Water or steam.

D. Coverage D – Loss Of Use

The limit of liability for Coverage **D** is the total limit for the coverages in **1.** Additional Living Expense, **2.** Fair Rental Value and **3.** Civil Authority Prohibits Use below.

1. Additional Living Expense

If a loss covered under Section **I** makes that part of the "residence premises" where you reside not fit to live in, we cover any necessary increase in living expenses incurred by you so that your household can maintain its normal standard of living.

Payment will be for the shortest time required to repair or replace the damage or, if you permanently relocate, the shortest time required for your household to settle elsewhere.

2. Fair Rental Value

If a loss covered under Section **I** makes that part of the "residence premises" rented to others or held for rental by you not fit to live in, we cover the fair rental value of such premises less any expenses that do not continue while it is not fit to live in.

Payment will be for the shortest time required to repair or replace such premises.

3. Civil Authority Prohibits Use

If a civil authority prohibits you from use of the "residence premises" as a result of direct damage to neighboring premises by a Peril Insured Against, we cover the loss as provided in **1.** Additional Living Expense and **2.** Fair Rental Value above for no more than two weeks.

4. Loss Or Expense Not Covered

We do not cover loss or expense due to cancellation of a lease or agreement.

The periods of time under **1.** Additional Living Expense, **2.** Fair Rental Value and **3.** Civil Authority Prohibits Use above are not limited by expiration of this policy.

E. Additional Coverages

1. Debris Removal

a. We will pay your reasonable expense for the removal of:

(1) Debris of covered property if a Peril Insured Against that applies to the damaged property causes the loss; or

(2) Ash, dust or particles from a volcanic eruption that has caused direct loss to a building or property contained in a building.

This expense is included in the limit of liability that applies to the damaged property. If the amount to be paid for the actual damage to the property plus the debris removal expense is more than the limit of liability for the damaged property, an additional 5% of that limit of liability is available for debris removal expense.

b. Fallen Trees

(1) If circumstances of a loss meet those specified in **(2)** below, we will pay your reasonable expense, up to $1000, for the removal from the "residence premises" of:

(a) Your tree(s) felled by the peril of Windstorm Or Hail or Weight Of Ice, Snow Or Sleet; or

(b) A neighbor's tree(s) felled by a Peril Insured Against under Coverage **C.**

The $1000 limit is the most we will pay in any one loss regardless of the number of fallen trees. No more than $500 of this limit will be paid for the removal of any one tree.

This coverage is additional insurance.

(2) Tree removal coverage as described in **b.(1)** above applies only if:

(a) The tree damages a structure covered under this policy;

(b) Windstorm or Hail or Weight of Ice, Snow or Sleet causes damage to a structure covered under this policy and the Pennsylvania Governor declares the area in which the "residence premises" is located to be a disaster area as a result of such weather conditions; or

(c) The tree does not damage a structure covered under the policy, but:

(i) Blocks a driveway on the "residence premises" which prevents a "motor vehicle", that is registered for use on public roads or property, from entering or leaving the "residence premises"; or

(ii) Blocks a ramp or other fixture designed to assist a handicapped person to enter or leave the dwelling building

2. Reasonable Repairs

a. We will pay the reasonable cost incurred by you for the necessary measures taken solely to protect covered property that is damaged by a Peril Insured Against from further damage.

b. If the measures taken involve repair to other damaged property, we will only pay if that property is covered under this policy and the damage is caused by a Peril Insured Against. This coverage does not:

(1) Increase the limit of liability that applies to the covered property; or

(2) Relieve you of your duties, in case of a loss to covered property, described in **B.4.** under Section I – Conditions.

3. Trees, Shrubs And Other Plants

We cover trees, shrubs, plants or lawns, on the "residence premises", for loss caused by the following Perils Insured Against:

a. Fire or Lightning;

b. Explosion;

c. Riot or Civil Commotion;

d. Aircraft;

e. Vehicles not owned or operated by a resident of the "residence premises";

f. Vandalism or Malicious Mischief; or

g. Theft.

We will pay up to 5% of the limit of liability that applies to the dwelling for all trees, shrubs, plants or lawns. No more than $500 of this limit will be paid for any one tree, shrub or plant. We do not cover property grown for "business" purposes.

This coverage is additional insurance.

4. Fire Department Service Charge

We will pay up to $500 for your liability assumed by contract or agreement for fire department charges incurred when the fire department is called to save or protect covered property from a Peril Insured Against. We do not cover fire department service charges if the property is located within the limits of the city, municipality or protection district furnishing the fire department response.

This coverage is additional insurance. No deductible applies to this coverage.

5. Property Removed

We insure covered property against direct loss from any cause while being removed from a premises endangered by a Peril Insured Against and for no more than 30 days while removed.

This coverage does not change the limit of liability that applies to the property being removed.

6. Credit Card, Electronic Fund Transfer Card Or Access Device, Forgery And Counterfeit Money

a. We will pay up to $500 for:

(1) The legal obligation of an "insured" to pay because of the theft or unauthorized use of credit cards issued to or registered in an "insured's" name;

(2) Loss resulting from theft or unauthorized use of an electronic fund transfer card or access device used for deposit, withdrawal or transfer of funds, issued to or registered in an "insured's" name;

(3) Loss to an "insured" caused by forgery or alteration of any check or negotiable instrument; and

(4) Loss to an "insured" through acceptance in good faith of counterfeit United States or Canadian paper currency.

All loss resulting from a series of acts committed by any one person or in which any one person is concerned or implicated is considered to be one loss.

This coverage is additional insurance. No deductible applies to this coverage.

b. We do not cover:

(1) Use of a credit card, electronic fund transfer card or access device:

(a) By a resident of your household;

    (b) By a person who has been entrusted with either type of card or access device; or

    (c) If an "insured" has not complied with all terms and conditions under which the cards are issued or the devices accessed; or

  (2) Loss arising out of "business" use or dishonesty of an "insured".

 c. If the coverage in **a.** above applies, the following defense provisions also apply:

  (1) We may investigate and settle any claim or suit that we decide is appropriate. Our duty to defend a claim or suit ends when the amount we pay for the loss equals our limit of liability.

  (2) If a suit is brought against an "insured" for liability under **a.(1)** or **(2)** above, we will provide a defense at our expense by counsel of our choice.

  (3) We have the option to defend at our expense an "insured" or an "insured's" bank against any suit for the enforcement of payment under **a.(3)** above.

7. Loss Assessment

 a. We will pay up to $1,000 for your share of loss assessment charged during the policy period against you, as owner or tenant of the "residence premises", by a corporation or association of property owners. The assessment must be made as a result of direct loss to property, owned by all members collectively, of the type that would be covered by this policy if owned by you, caused by a Peril Insured Against under Coverage **A**, other than:

  (1) Earthquake; or

  (2) Land shock waves or tremors before, during or after a volcanic eruption.

The limit of $1,000 is the most we will pay with respect to any one loss, regardless of the number of assessments. We will only apply one deductible, per unit, to the total amount of any one loss to the property described above, regardless of the number of assessments.

 b. We do not cover assessments charged against you or a corporation or association of property owners by any governmental body.

 c. Paragraph **P.** Policy Period under Section **I** – Conditions does not apply to this coverage.

This coverage is additional insurance.

8. Collapse

 a. With respect to this Additional Coverage:

  (1) Collapse means an abrupt falling down or caving in of a building or any part of a building with the result that the building or part of the building cannot be occupied for its current intended purpose.

  (2) A building or any part of a building that is in danger of falling down or caving in is not considered to be in a state of collapse.

  (3) A part of a building that is standing is not considered to be in a state of collapse even if it has separated from another part of the building.

  (4) A building or any part of a building that is standing is not considered to be in a state of collapse even if it shows evidence of cracking, bulging, sagging, bending, leaning, settling, shrinkage or expansion.

 b. We insure for direct physical loss to covered property involving collapse of a building or any part of a building if the collapse was caused by one or more of the following:

  (1) The Perils Insured Against named under Coverage **C**;

  (2) Decay that is hidden from view, unless the presence of such decay is known to an "insured" prior to collapse;

  (3) Insect or vermin damage that is hidden from view, unless the presence of such damage is known to an "insured" prior to collapse;

  (4) Weight of contents, equipment, animals or people;

  (5) Weight of rain which collects on a roof; or

  (6) Use of defective material or methods in construction, remodeling or renovation if the collapse occurs during the course of the construction, remodeling or renovation.

c. Loss to an awning, fence, patio, deck, pavement, swimming pool, underground pipe, flue, drain, cesspool, septic tank, foundation, retaining wall, bulkhead, pier, wharf or dock is not included under **b.(2)** through **(6)** above, unless the loss is a direct result of the collapse of a building or any part of a building.

d. This coverage does not increase the limit of liability that applies to the damaged covered property.

9. **Glass Or Safety Glazing Material**

   a. We cover:

   (1) The breakage of glass or safety glazing material which is part of a covered building, storm door or storm window;

   (2) The breakage of glass or safety glazing material which is part of a covered building, storm door or storm window when caused directly by earth movement; and

   (3) The direct physical loss to covered property caused solely by the pieces, fragments or splinters of broken glass or safety glazing material which is part of a building, storm door or storm window.

   b. This coverage does not include loss:

   (1) To covered property which results because the glass or safety glazing material has been broken, except as provided in **a.(3)** above; or

   (2) On the "residence premises" if the dwelling has been vacant for more than 60 consecutive days immediately before the loss, except when the breakage results directly from earth movement as provided in **a.(2)** above. A dwelling being constructed is not considered vacant.

   c. This coverage does not increase the limit of liability that applies to the damaged property.

10. **Landlord's Furnishings**

   We will pay up to $2,500 for your appliances, carpeting and other household furnishings, in each apartment on the "residence premises" regularly rented or held for rental to others by an "insured", for loss caused by a Peril Insured Against in Coverage **C,** other than Theft.

This limit is the most we will pay in any one loss regardless of the number of appliances, carpeting or other household furnishings involved in the loss.

This coverage does not increase the limit of liability applying to the damaged property.

11. **Ordinance Or Law**

   a. You may use up to 10% of the limit of liability that applies to Coverage **A** for the increased costs you incur due to the enforcement of any ordinance or law which requires or regulates:

   (1) The construction, demolition, remodeling, renovation or repair of that part of a covered building or other structure damaged by a Peril Insured Against;

   (2) The demolition and reconstruction of the undamaged part of a covered building or other structure, when that building or other structure must be totally demolished because of damage by a Peril Insured Against to another part of that covered building or other structure; or

   (3) The remodeling, removal or replacement of the portion of the undamaged part of a covered building or other structure necessary to complete the remodeling, repair or replacement of that part of the covered building or other structure damaged by a Peril Insured Against.

   b. You may use all or part of this ordinance or law coverage to pay for the increased costs you incur to remove debris resulting from the construction, demolition, remodeling, renovation, repair or replacement of property as stated in **a.** above.

   c. We do not cover:

   (1) The loss in value to any covered building or other structure due to the requirements of any ordinance or law; or

   (2) The costs to comply with any ordinance or law which requires any "insured" or others to test for, monitor, clean up, remove, contain, treat, detoxify or neutralize, or in any way respond to, or assess the effects of, pollutants in or on any covered building or other structure.

Pollutants means any solid, liquid, gaseous or thermal irritant or contaminant, including smoke, vapor, soot, fumes, acids, alkalis, chemicals and waste. Waste includes materials to be recycled, reconditioned or reclaimed.

This coverage is additional insurance.

12. Grave Markers

We will pay up to $5,000 for grave markers, including mausoleums, on or away from the "residence premises" for loss caused by a Peril Insured Against under Coverage **C**.

This coverage does not increase the limits of liability that apply to the damaged covered property.

SECTION I – PERILS INSURED AGAINST

A. Coverage A – Dwelling And Coverage B – Other Structures

1. We insure against risk of direct physical loss to property described in Coverages **A** and **B**.

2. We do not insure, however, for loss:

   a. Excluded under Section I – Exclusions;

   b. Involving collapse, except as provided in **E.8.** Collapse under Section I – Property Coverages; or

   c. Caused by:

      (1) Freezing of a plumbing, heating, air conditioning or automatic fire protective sprinkler system or of a household appliance, or by discharge, leakage or overflow from within the system or appliance caused by freezing. This provision does not apply if you have used reasonable care to:

         (a) Maintain heat in the building; or

         (b) Shut off the water supply and drain all systems and appliances of water.

      However, if the building is protected by an automatic fire protective sprinkler system, you must use reasonable care to continue the water supply and maintain heat in the building for coverage to apply.

      For purposes of this provision a plumbing system or household appliance does not include a sump, sump pump or related equipment or a roof drain, gutter, downspout or similar fixtures or equipment;

      (2) Freezing, thawing, pressure or weight of water or ice, whether driven by wind or not, to a:

         (a) Fence, pavement, patio or swimming pool;

         (b) Footing, foundation, bulkhead, wall, or any other structure or device that supports all or part of a building, or other structure;

         (c) Retaining wall or bulkhead that does not support all or part of a building or other structure; or

         (d) Pier, wharf or dock;

      (3) Theft in or to a dwelling under construction, or of materials and supplies for use in the construction until the dwelling is finished and occupied;

      (4) Vandalism and malicious mischief, and any ensuing loss caused by any intentional and wrongful act committed in the course of the vandalism or malicious mischief, if the dwelling has been vacant for more than 60 consecutive days immediately before the loss. A dwelling being constructed is not considered vacant;

      (5) Mold, fungus or wet rot. However, we do insure for loss caused by mold, fungus or wet rot that is hidden within the walls or ceilings or beneath the floors or above the ceilings of a structure if such loss results from the accidental discharge or overflow of water or steam from within:

         (a) A plumbing, heating, air conditioning or automatic fire protective sprinkler system, or a household appliance, on the "residence premises"; or

         (b) A storm drain, or water, steam or sewer pipes, off the "residence premises".

      For purposes of this provision, a plumbing system or household appliance does not include a sump, sump pump or related equipment or a roof drain, gutter, downspout or similar fixtures or equipment; or

      (6) Any of the following:

         (a) Wear and tear, marring, deterioration;

(b) Mechanical breakdown, latent defect, inherent vice, or any quality in property that causes it to damage or destroy itself;

(c) Smog, rust or other corrosion, or dry rot;

(d) Smoke from agricultural smudging or industrial operations;

(e) Discharge, dispersal, seepage, migration, release or escape of pollutants unless the discharge, dispersal, seepage, migration, release or escape is itself caused by a Peril Insured Against named under Coverage **C**.

Pollutants means any solid, liquid, gaseous or thermal irritant or contaminant, including smoke, vapor, soot, fumes, acids, alkalis, chemicals and waste. Waste includes materials to be recycled, reconditioned or reclaimed;

(f) Settling, shrinking, bulging or expansion, including resultant cracking, of bulkheads, pavements, patios, footings, foundations, walls, floors, roofs or ceilings;

(g) Birds, vermin, rodents, or insects; or

(h) Animals owned or kept by an "insured".

Exception To c.(6)

Unless the loss is otherwise excluded, we cover loss to property covered under Coverage **A** or **B** resulting from an accidental discharge or overflow of water or steam from within a:

(i) Storm drain, or water, steam or sewer pipe, off the "residence premises"; or

(ii) Plumbing, heating, air conditioning or automatic fire protective sprinkler system or household appliance on the "residence premises". This includes the cost to tear out and replace any part of a building, or other structure, on the "residence premises", but only when necessary to repair the system or appliance. However, such tear out and replacement coverage only applies to other structures if the water or steam causes actual damage to a building on the "residence premises".

We do not cover loss to the system or appliance from which this water or steam escaped.

For purposes of this provision, a plumbing system or household appliance does not include a sump, sump pump or related equipment or a roof drain, gutter, down spout or similar fixtures or equipment.

Section I – Exclusion **A.3.** Water Damage, Paragraphs **a.** and **c.** that apply to surface water and water below the surface of the ground do not apply to loss by water covered under **c.(5)** and **(6)** above.

Under **2.b.** and **c.** above, any ensuing loss to property described in Coverages **A** and **B** not precluded by any other provision in this policy is covered.

B. Coverage C – Personal Property

We insure for direct physical loss to the property described in Coverage **C** caused by any of the following perils unless the loss is excluded in Section I – Exclusions.

1. Fire Or Lightning

2. Windstorm Or Hail

This peril includes loss to watercraft of all types and their trailers, furnishings, equipment, and outboard engines or motors, only while inside a fully enclosed building.

This peril does not include loss to the property contained in a building caused by rain, snow, sleet, sand or dust unless the direct force of wind or hail damages the building causing an opening in a roof or wall and the rain, snow, sleet, sand or dust enters through this opening.

3. Explosion

4. Riot Or Civil Commotion

5. Aircraft

This peril includes self-propelled missiles and spacecraft.

6. Vehicles

7. Smoke

This peril means sudden and accidental damage from smoke, including the emission or puffback of smoke, soot, fumes or vapors from a boiler, furnace or related equipment.

This peril does not include loss caused by smoke from agricultural smudging or industrial operations.

8. **Vandalism Or Malicious Mischief**

9. **Theft**

   a. This peril includes attempted theft and loss of property from a known place when it is likely that the property has been stolen.

   b. This peril does not include loss caused by theft:

      (1) Committed by an "insured";

      (2) In or to a dwelling under construction, or of materials and supplies for use in the construction until the dwelling is finished and occupied;

      (3) From that part of a "residence premises" rented by an "insured" to someone other than another "insured"; or

      (4) That occurs off the "residence premises" of:

         (a) Trailers, semitrailers and campers;

         (b) Watercraft of all types, and their furnishings, equipment and outboard engines or motors; or

         (c) Property while at any other residence owned by, rented to, or occupied by an "insured", except while an "insured" is temporarily living there. Property of an "insured" who is a student is covered while at the residence the student occupies to attend school as long as the student has been there at any time during the 60 days immediately before the loss.

10. **Falling Objects**

    This peril does not include loss to property contained in a building unless the roof or an outside wall of the building is first damaged by a falling object. Damage to the falling object itself is not included.

11. **Weight Of Ice, Snow Or Sleet**

    This peril means weight of ice, snow or sleet which causes damage to property contained in a building.

12. **Accidental Discharge Or Overflow Of Water Or Steam**

    a. This peril means accidental discharge or overflow of water or steam from within a plumbing, heating, air conditioning or automatic fire protective sprinkler system or from within a household appliance.

    b. This peril does not include loss:

       (1) To the system or appliance from which the water or steam escaped;

       (2) Caused by or resulting from freezing except as provided in Peril Insured Against **14.** Freezing;

       (3) On the "residence premises" caused by accidental discharge or overflow which occurs off the "residence premises"; or

       (4) Caused by mold, fungus or wet rot unless hidden within the walls or ceilings or beneath the floors or above the ceilings of a structure.

    c. In this peril, a plumbing system or household appliance does not include a sump, sump pump or related equipment or a roof drain, gutter, downspout or similar fixtures or equipment.

    d. Section I – Exclusion **A.3.** Water Damage, Paragraphs **a.** and **c.** that apply to surface water and water below the surface of the ground do not apply to loss by water covered under this peril.

13. **Sudden And Accidental Tearing Apart, Cracking, Burning Or Bulging**

    This peril means sudden and accidental tearing apart, cracking, burning or bulging of a steam or hot water heating system, an air conditioning or automatic fire protective sprinkler system, or an appliance for heating water.

    We do not cover loss caused by or resulting from freezing under this peril.

14. **Freezing**

    a. This peril means freezing of a plumbing, heating, air conditioning or automatic fire protective sprinkler system or of a household appliance but only if you have used reasonable care to:

       (1) Maintain heat in the building; or

       (2) Shut off the water supply and drain all systems and appliances of water.

       However, if the building is protected by an automatic fire protective sprinkler system, you must use reasonable care to continue the water supply and maintain heat in the building for coverage to apply.

    b. In this peril, a plumbing system or household appliance does not include a sump, sump pump or related equipment or a roof drain, gutter, downspout or similar fixtures or equipment.

15. Sudden And Accidental Damage From Artificially Generated Electrical Current

This peril does not include loss to tubes, transistors, electronic components or circuitry that are a part of appliances, fixtures, computers, home entertainment units or other types of electronic apparatus.

16. Volcanic Eruption

This peril does not include loss caused by earthquake, land shock waves or tremors.

SECTION I – EXCLUSIONS

A. We do not insure for loss caused directly or indirectly by any of the following. Such loss is excluded regardless of any other cause or event contributing concurrently or in any sequence to the loss. These exclusions apply whether or not the loss event results in widespread damage or affects a substantial area.

1. Ordinance Or Law

Ordinance Or Law means any ordinance or law:

a. Requiring or regulating the construction, demolition, remodeling, renovation or repair of property, including removal of any resulting debris. This Exclusion **A.1.a.** does not apply to the amount of coverage that may be provided for in **E.11.** Ordinance Or Law under Section I – Property Coverages;

b. The requirements of which result in a loss in value to property; or

c. Requiring any "insured" or others to test for, monitor, clean up, remove, contain, treat, detoxify or neutralize, or in any way respond to, or assess the effects of, pollutants.

Pollutants means any solid, liquid, gaseous or thermal irritant or contaminant, including smoke, vapor, soot, fumes, acids, alkalis, chemicals and waste. Waste includes materials to be recycled, reconditioned or reclaimed.

This Exclusion **A.1.** applies whether or not the property has been physically damaged.

2. Earth Movement

Earth Movement means:

a. Earthquake, including land shock waves or tremors before, during or after a volcanic eruption;

b. Landslide, mudslide or mudflow;

c. Subsidence or sinkhole; or

d. Any other earth movement including earth sinking, rising or shifting;

caused by or resulting from human or animal forces or any act of nature unless direct loss by fire or explosion ensues and then we will pay only for the ensuing loss.

This Exclusion **A.2.** does not apply to loss by theft.

3. Water Damage

Water Damage means:

a. Flood, surface water, waves, tidal water, overflow of a body of water, or spray from any of these, whether or not driven by wind;

b. Water or water-borne material which backs up through sewers or drains or which overflows or is discharged from a sump, sump pump or related equipment; or

c. Water or water-borne material below the surface of the ground, including water which exerts pressure on or seeps or leaks through a building, sidewalk, driveway, foundation, swimming pool or other structure;

caused by or resulting from human or animal forces or any act of nature.

Direct loss by fire, explosion or theft resulting from water damage is covered.

4. Power Failure

Power Failure means the failure of power or other utility service if the failure takes place off the "residence premises". But if the failure results in a loss, from a Peril Insured Against on the "residence premises", we will pay for the loss caused by that peril.

5. Neglect

Neglect means neglect of an "insured" to use all reasonable means to save and preserve property at and after the time of a loss.

6. War

War includes the following and any consequence of any of the following:

a. Undeclared war, civil war, insurrection, rebellion or revolution;

b. Warlike act by a military force or military personnel; or

c. Destruction, seizure or use for a military purpose.

Discharge of a nuclear weapon will be deemed a warlike act even if accidental.

7. Nuclear Hazard

This Exclusion **A.7.** pertains to Nuclear Hazard to the extent set forth in **M.** Nuclear Hazard Clause under Section **I** – Conditions.

8. Intentional Loss

Intentional Loss means any loss arising out of any act an "insured" commits or conspires to commit with the intent to cause a loss.

In the event of such loss, no "insured" is entitled to coverage, even "insureds" who did not commit or conspire to commit the act causing the loss.

9. Governmental Action

Governmental Action means the destruction, confiscation or seizure of property described in Coverage **A, B** or **C** by order of any governmental or public authority.

This exclusion does not apply to such acts ordered by any governmental or public authority that are taken at the time of a fire to prevent its spread, if the loss caused by fire would be covered under this policy.

B. We do not insure for loss to property described in Coverages **A** and **B** caused by any of the following. However, any ensuing loss to property described in Coverages **A** and **B** not precluded by any other provision in this policy is covered.

1. Weather conditions. However, this exclusion only applies if weather conditions contribute in any way with a cause or event excluded in **A.** above to produce the loss.

2. Acts or decisions, including the failure to act or decide, of any person, group, organization or governmental body.

3. Faulty, inadequate or defective:

   a. Planning, zoning, development, surveying, siting;

   b. Design, specifications, workmanship, repair, construction, renovation, remodeling, grading, compaction;

   c. Materials used in repair, construction, renovation or remodeling; or

   d. Maintenance;

   of part or all of any property whether on or off the "residence premises".

SECTION I – CONDITIONS

A. Insurable Interest And Limit Of Liability

Even if more than one person has an insurable interest in the property covered, we will not be liable in any one loss:

1. To an "insured" for more than the amount of such "insured's" interest at the time of loss; or

2. For more than the applicable limit of liability.

B. Duties After Loss

In case of a loss to covered property, we have no duty to provide coverage under this policy if the failure to comply with the following duties is prejudicial to us. These duties must be performed either by you, an "insured" seeking coverage, or a representative of either:

1. Give prompt notice to us or our agent;

2. Notify the police in case of loss by theft;

3. Notify the credit card or electronic fund transfer card or access device company in case of loss as provided for in **E.6.** Credit Card, Electronic Fund Transfer Card Or Access Device, Forgery And Counterfeit Money under Section **I** – Property Coverages;

4. Protect the property from further damage. If repairs to the property are required, you must:

   a. Make reasonable and necessary repairs to protect the property; and

   b. Keep an accurate record of repair expenses;

5. Cooperate with us in the investigation of a claim;

6. Prepare an inventory of damaged personal property showing the quantity, description, actual cash value and amount of loss. Attach all bills, receipts and related documents that justify the figures in the inventory;

7. As often as we reasonably require:

   a. Show the damaged property;

   b. Provide us with records and documents we request and permit us to make copies; and

   c. Submit to examination under oath, while not in the presence of another "insured", and sign the same;

8. Send to us, within 60 days after our request, your signed, sworn proof of loss which sets forth, to the best of your knowledge and belief:

   a. The time and cause of loss;

   b. The interests of all "insureds" and all others in the property involved and all liens on the property;

   c. Other insurance which may cover the loss;

   d. Changes in title or occupancy of the property during the term of the policy;

   e. Specifications of damaged buildings and detailed repair estimates;

   f. The inventory of damaged personal property described in **6.** above;

   g. Receipts for additional living expenses incurred and records that support the fair rental value loss; and

   h. Evidence or affidavit that supports a claim under **E.6.** Credit Card, Electronic Fund Transfer Card Or Access Device, Forgery And Counterfeit Money under Section I – Property Coverages, stating the amount and cause of loss.

C. Loss Settlement

In this Condition **C.**, the terms "cost to repair or replace" and "replacement cost" do not include the increased costs incurred to comply with the enforcement of any ordinance or law, except to the extent that coverage for these increased costs is provided in **E.11.** Ordinance Or Law under Section I – Property Coverages. Covered property losses are settled as follows:

1. Property of the following types:

   a. Personal property;

   b. Awnings, carpeting, household appliances, outdoor antennas and outdoor equipment, whether or not attached to buildings;

   c. Structures that are not buildings; and

   d. Grave markers, including mausoleums;

   at actual cash value at the time of loss but not more than the amount required to repair or replace.

2. Buildings covered under Coverage **A** or **B** at replacement cost without deduction for depreciation, subject to the following:

   a. If, at the time of loss, the amount of insurance in this policy on the damaged building is 80% or more of the full replacement cost of the building immediately before the loss, we will pay the cost to repair or replace, after application of any deductible and without deduction for depreciation, but not more than the least of the following amounts:

      (1) The limit of liability under this policy that applies to the building;

      (2) The replacement cost of that part of the building damaged with material of like kind and quality and for like use; or

      (3) The necessary amount actually spent to repair or replace the damaged building.

      If the building is rebuilt at a new premises, the cost described in **(2)** above is limited to the cost which would have been incurred if the building had been built at the original premises.

   b. If, at the time of loss, the amount of insurance in this policy on the damaged building is less than 80% of the full replacement cost of the building immediately before the loss, we will pay the greater of the following amounts, but not more than the limit of liability under this policy that applies to the building:

      (1) The actual cash value of that part of the building damaged; or

      (2) That proportion of the cost to repair or replace, after application of any deductible and without deduction for depreciation, that part of the building damaged, which the total amount of insurance in this policy on the damaged building bears to 80% of the replacement cost of the building.

   c. To determine the amount of insurance required to equal 80% of the full replacement cost of the building immediately before the loss, do not include the value of:

      (1) Excavations, footings, foundations, piers, or any other structures or devices that support all or part of the building, which are below the undersurface of the lowest basement floor;

(2) Those supports described in **(1)** above which are below the surface of the ground inside the foundation walls, if there is no basement; and

(3) Underground flues, pipes, wiring and drains.

d. We will pay no more than the actual cash value of the damage until actual repair or replacement is complete. Once actual repair or replacement is complete, we will settle the loss as noted in **2.a.** and **b.** above.

However, if the cost to repair or replace the damage is both:

(1) Less than 5% of the amount of insurance in this policy on the building; and

(2) Less than $2,500;

we will settle the loss as noted in **2.a.** and **b.** above whether or not actual repair or replacement is complete.

e. You may disregard the replacement cost loss settlement provisions and make claim under this policy for loss to buildings on an actual cash value basis. You may then make claim for any additional liability according to the provisions of this Condition **C.** Loss Settlement, provided you notify us of your intent to do so within 180 days after the date of loss.

D. Loss To A Pair Or Set

In case of loss to a pair or set we may elect to:

1. Repair or replace any part to restore the pair or set to its value before the loss; or

2. Pay the difference between actual cash value of the property before and after the loss.

E. Appraisal

If you and we fail to agree on the amount of loss, either may demand an appraisal of the loss. In this event, each party will choose a competent and impartial appraiser within 20 days after receiving a written request from the other. The two appraisers will choose an umpire. If they cannot agree upon an umpire within 15 days, you or we may request that the choice be made by a judge of a court of record in the state where the "residence premises" is located. The appraisers will separately set the amount of loss. If the appraisers submit a written report of an agreement to us, the amount agreed upon will be the amount of loss. If they fail to agree, they will submit their differences to the umpire. A decision agreed to by any two will set the amount of loss.

Each party will:

1. Pay its own appraiser; and

2. Bear the other expenses of the appraisal and umpire equally.

F. Other Insurance And Service Agreement

If a loss covered by this policy is also covered by:

1. Other insurance, we will pay only the proportion of the loss that the limit of liability that applies under this policy bears to the total amount of insurance covering the loss; or

2. A service agreement, this insurance is excess over any amounts payable under any such agreement. Service agreement means a service plan, property restoration plan, home warranty or other similar service warranty agreement, even if it is characterized as insurance.

G. Suit Against Us

No action can be brought against us unless there has been full compliance with all of the terms under Section **I** of this policy and the action is started within two years after the date of loss.

H. Our Option

We may repair or replace any part of the damaged property with material or property of like kind and quality if we give you written notice of our intention to do so within 15 working days after we receive your signed, sworn proof of loss.

I. Loss Payment

We will adjust all losses with you. We will pay you unless some other person is named in the policy or is legally entitled to receive payment. Loss will be payable 60 days after we receive your proof of loss and:

1. Reach an agreement with you;

2. There is an entry of a final judgment; or

3. There is a filing of an appraisal award with us.

J. Abandonment Of Property

We need not accept any property abandoned by an "insured".

K. Mortgage Clause

1. If a mortgagee is named in this policy, any loss payable under Coverage **A** or **B** will be paid to the mortgagee and you, as interests appear. If more than one mortgagee is named, the order of payment will be the same as the order of precedence of the mortgages.

2. If we deny your claim, that denial will not apply to a valid claim of the mortgagee, if the mortgagee:

a. Notifies us of any change in ownership, occupancy or substantial change in risk of which the mortgagee is aware;

b. Pays any premium due under this policy on demand if you have neglected to pay the premium; and

c. Submits a signed, sworn statement of loss within 60 days after receiving notice from us of your failure to do so. Paragraphs **E.** Appraisal, **G.** Suit Against Us and **I.** Loss Payment under Section I – Conditions also apply to the mortgagee.

3. If we decide to cancel or not to renew this policy, the mortgagee will be notified at least 10 days before the date cancellation or nonrenewal takes effect.

4. If we pay the mortgagee for any loss and deny payment to you:

a. We are subrogated to all the rights of the mortgagee granted under the mortgage on the property; or

b. At our option, we may pay to the mortgagee the whole principal on the mortgage plus any accrued interest. In this event, we will receive a full assignment and transfer of the mortgage and all securities held as collateral to the mortgage debt.

5. Subrogation will not impair the right of the mortgagee to recover the full amount of the mortgagee's claim.

L. No Benefit To Bailee

We will not recognize any assignment or grant any coverage that benefits a person or organization holding, storing or moving property for a fee regardless of any other provision of this policy.

M. Nuclear Hazard Clause

1. "Nuclear Hazard" means any nuclear reaction, radiation, or radioactive contamination, all whether controlled or uncontrolled or however caused, or any consequence of any of these.

2. Loss caused by the nuclear hazard will not be considered loss caused by fire, explosion, or smoke, whether these perils are specifically named in or otherwise included within the Perils Insured Against.

3. This policy does not apply under Section I to loss caused directly or indirectly by nuclear hazard, except that direct loss by fire resulting from the nuclear hazard is covered.

N. Recovered Property

If you or we recover any property for which we have made payment under this policy, you or we will notify the other of the recovery. At your option, the property will be returned to or retained by you or it will become our property. If the recovered property is returned to or retained by you, the loss payment will be adjusted based on the amount you received for the recovered property.

O. Volcanic Eruption Period

One or more volcanic eruptions that occur within a 72 hour period will be considered as one volcanic eruption.

P. Policy Period

This policy applies only to loss which occurs during the policy period.

Q. Concealment Or Fraud

We provide coverage to no "insureds" under this policy if, whether before or after a loss, an "insured" has:

1. Intentionally concealed or misrepresented any material fact or circumstance;

2. Engaged in fraudulent conduct; or

3. Made false statements;

relating to this insurance.

R. Loss Payable Clause

If the Declarations show a loss payee for certain listed insured personal property, the definition of "insured" is changed to include that loss payee with respect to that property.

If we decide to cancel or not renew this policy, that loss payee will be notified in writing.

SECTION II – LIABILITY COVERAGES

A. Coverage E – Personal Liability

If a claim is made or a suit is brought against an "insured" for damages because of "bodily injury" or "property damage" caused by an "occurrence" to which this coverage applies, we will:

1. Pay up to our limit of liability for the damages for which an "insured" is legally liable; and

2. Provide a defense at our expense by counsel of our choice, even if the suit is groundless, false or fraudulent. We may investigate and settle any claim or suit that we decide is appropriate. Our duty to settle or defend ends when our limit of liability for the "occurrence" has been exhausted by payment of a judgment or settlement.

B. Coverage F – Medical Payments To Others

We will pay the necessary medical expenses that are incurred or medically ascertained within three years from the date of an accident causing "bodily injury". Medical expenses means reasonable charges for medical, surgical, x-ray, dental, ambulance, hospital, professional nursing and prosthetic devices. Medical expenses do not include expenses for funeral services.   This coverage does not apply to you or regular residents of your household except "residence employees". As to others, this coverage applies only:

1. To a person on the "insured location" with the permission of an "insured"; or

2. To a person off the "insured location", if the "bodily injury":

   a. Arises out of a condition on the "insured location" or the ways immediately adjoining;

   b. Is caused by the activities of an "insured";

   c. Is caused by a "residence employee" in the course of the "residence employee's" employment by an "insured"; or

   d. Is caused by an animal owned by or in the care of an "insured".

SECTION II – EXCLUSIONS

A. "Motor Vehicle Liability"

1. Coverages **E** and **F** do not apply to any "motor vehicle liability" if, at the time and place of an "occurrence", the involved "motor vehicle":

   a. Is registered for use on public roads or property;

   b. Is not registered for use on public roads or property, but such registration is required by a law, or regulation issued by a government agency, for it to be used at the place of the "occurrence"; or

   c. Is being:

      (1) Operated in, or practicing for, any prearranged or organized race, speed contest or other competition;

      (2) Rented to others;

      (3) Used to carry persons or cargo for a charge; or

      (4) Used for any "business" purpose except for a motorized golf cart while on a golfing facility.

2. If Exclusion **A.1.** does not apply, there is still no coverage for "motor vehicle liability" unless the "motor vehicle" is:

   a. In dead storage on an "insured location";

   b. Used solely to service an "insured's" residence;

   c. Designed to assist the handicapped and, at the time of an "occurrence", it is:

      (1) Being used to assist a handicapped person; or

      (2) Parked on an "insured location";

   d. Designed for recreational use off public roads and:

      (1) Not owned by an "insured"; or

      (2) Owned by an "insured" provided the "occurrence" takes place on an "insured location" as defined in Definitions **B.6.a., b., d., e.** or **h.;** or

   e. A motorized golf cart that is owned by an "insured", designed to carry up to 4 persons, not built or modified after manufacture to exceed a speed of 25 miles per hour on level ground and, at the time of an "occurrence", is within the legal boundaries of:

      (1) A golfing facility and is parked or stored there, or being used by an "insured" to:

         (a) Play the game of golf or for other recreational or leisure activity allowed by the facility;

         (b) Travel to or from an area where "motor vehicles" or golf carts are parked or stored; or

         (c) Cross public roads at designated points to access other parts of the golfing facility; or

      (2) A private residential community, including its public roads upon which a motorized golf cart can legally travel, which is subject to the authority of a property owners association and contains an "insured's" residence.

B. "Watercraft Liability"

1. Coverages **E** and **F** do not apply to any "watercraft liability" if, at the time of an "occurrence", the involved watercraft is being:

   a. Operated in, or practicing for, any prearranged or organized race, speed contest or other competition. This exclusion does not apply to a sailing vessel or a predicted log cruise;

b. Rented to others;

c. Used to carry persons or cargo for a charge; or

d. Used for any "business" purpose.

2. If Exclusion **B.1.** does not apply, there is still no coverage for "watercraft liability" unless, at the time of the "occurrence", the watercraft:

a. Is stored;

b. Is a sailing vessel, with or without auxiliary power, that is:

(1) Less than 26 feet in overall length; or

(2) 26 feet or more in overall length and not owned by or rented to an "insured"; or

c. Is not a sailing vessel and is powered by:

(1) An inboard or inboard-outdrive engine or motor, including those that power a water jet pump, of:

(a) 50 horsepower or less and not owned by an "insured"; or

(b) More than 50 horsepower and not owned by or rented to an "insured"; or

(2) One or more outboard engines or motors with:

(a) 25 total horsepower or less;

(b) More than 25 horsepower if the outboard engine or motor is not owned by an "insured";

(c) More than 25 horsepower if the outboard engine or motor is owned by an "insured" who acquired it during the policy period; or

(d) More than 25 horsepower if the outboard engine or motor is owned by an "insured" who acquired it before the policy period, but only if:

(i) You declare them at policy inception; or

(ii) Your intent to insure them is reported to us in writing within 45 days after you acquire them.

The coverages in **(c)** and **(d)** above apply for the policy period.

Horsepower means the maximum power rating assigned to the engine or motor by the manufacturer.

C. "Aircraft Liability"

This policy does not cover "aircraft liability".

D. "Hovercraft Liability"

This policy does not cover "hovercraft liability".

E. Coverage E – Personal Liability And Coverage F – Medical Payments To Others

Coverages **E** and **F** do not apply to the following:

1. Expected Or Intended Injury

"Bodily injury" or "property damage" which is expected or intended by an "insured" even if the resulting "bodily injury" or "property damage":

a. Is of a different kind, quality or degree than initially expected or intended; or

b. Is sustained by a different person, entity, real or personal property, than initially expected or intended.

However, this Exclusion **E.1.** does not apply to "bodily injury" resulting from the use of reasonable force by an "insured" to protect persons or property;

2. "Business"

a. "Bodily injury" or "property damage" arising out of or in connection with a "business" conducted from an "insured location" or engaged in by an "insured", whether or not the "business" is owned or operated by an "insured" or employs an "insured".

This Exclusion **E.2.** applies but is not limited to an act or omission, regardless of its nature or circumstance, involving a service or duty rendered, promised, owed, or implied to be provided because of the nature of the "business".

b. This Exclusion **E.2.** does not apply to:

(1) The rental or holding for rental of an "insured location";

(a) On an occasional basis if used only as a residence;

(b) In part for use only as a residence, unless a single family unit is intended for use by the occupying family to lodge more than two roomers or boarders; or

(c) In part, as an office, school, studio or private garage; and

(2) An "insured" under the age of 21 years involved in a part-time or occasional, self-employed "business" with no employees;

3. Professional Services

"Bodily injury" or "property damage" arising out of the rendering of or failure to render professional services;

4. "Insured's" Premises Not An "Insured Location"

"Bodily injury" or "property damage" arising out of a premises:

a. Owned by an "insured";

b. Rented to an "insured"; or

c. Rented to others by an "insured";

that is not an "insured location";

5. War

"Bodily injury" or "property damage" caused directly or indirectly by war, including the following and any consequence of any of the following:

a. Undeclared war, civil war, insurrection, rebellion or revolution;

b. Warlike act by a military force or military personnel; or

c. Destruction, seizure or use for a military purpose.

Discharge of a nuclear weapon will be deemed a warlike act even if accidental;

6. Communicable Disease

"Bodily injury" or "property damage" which arises out of the transmission of a communicable disease by an "insured";

7. Sexual Molestation, Corporal Punishment Or Physical Or Mental Abuse

"Bodily injury" or "property damage" arising out of sexual molestation, corporal punishment or physical or mental abuse; or

8. Controlled Substance

"Bodily injury" or "property damage" arising out of the use, sale, manufacture, delivery, transfer or possession by any person of a Controlled Substance as defined by the Federal Food and Drug Law at 21 U.S.C.A. Sections 811 and 812. Controlled Substances include but are not limited to cocaine, LSD, marijuana and all narcotic drugs. However, this exclusion does not apply to the legitimate use of prescription drugs by a person following the orders of a licensed physician.

Exclusions **A.** "Motor Vehicle Liability", **B.** "Watercraft Liability", **C.** "Aircraft Liability", **D.** "Hovercraft Liability" and **E.4.** "Insured's" Premises Not An "Insured Location" do not apply to "bodily injury" to a "residence employee" arising out of and in the course of the "residence employee's" employment by an "insured".

F. Coverage E – Personal Liability

Coverage **E** does not apply to:

1. Liability:

   a. For any loss assessment charged against you as a member of an association, corporation or community of property owners, except as provided in **D.** Loss Assessment under Section II – Additional Coverages;

   b. Under any contract or agreement entered into by an "insured". However, this exclusion does not apply to written contracts:

      (1) That directly relate to the ownership, maintenance or use of an "insured location"; or

      (2) Where the liability of others is assumed by you prior to an "occurrence";

      unless excluded in **a.** above or elsewhere in this policy;

2. "Property damage" to property owned by an "insured". This includes costs or expenses incurred by an "insured" or others to repair, replace, enhance, restore or maintain such property to prevent injury to a person or damage to property of others, whether on or away from an "insured location";

3. "Property damage" to property rented to, occupied or used by or in the care of an "insured". This exclusion does not apply to "property damage" caused by fire, smoke or explosion;

4. "Bodily injury" to any person eligible to receive any benefits voluntarily provided or required to be provided by an "insured" under any:

   a. Workers' compensation law;

   b. Non-occupational disability law; or

   c. Occupational disease law;

5. "Bodily injury" or "property damage" for which an "insured" under this policy:

   a. Is also an insured under a nuclear energy liability policy issued by the:

      (1) Nuclear Energy Liability Insurance Association;

      (2) Mutual Atomic Energy Liability Underwriters;

(3) Nuclear Insurance Association of Canada;

or any of their successors; or

b. Would be an insured under such a policy but for the exhaustion of its limit of liability; or

6. "Bodily injury" to you or an "insured" as defined under Definitions **5.a.** or **b.**

This exclusion also applies to any claim made or suit brought against you or an "insured":

a. To repay; or

b. Share damages with;

another person who may be obligated to pay damages because of "bodily injury" to an "insured".

G. Coverage F – Medical Payments To Others

Coverage **F** does not apply to "bodily injury":

1. To a "residence employee" if the "bodily injury":

a. Occurs off the "insured location"; and

b. Does not arise out of or in the course of the "residence employee's" employment by an "insured";

2. To any person eligible to receive benefits voluntarily provided or required to be provided under any:

a. Workers' compensation law;

b. Non-occupational disability law; or

c. Occupational disease law;

3. From any:

a. Nuclear reaction;

b. Nuclear radiation; or

c. Radioactive contamination;

all whether controlled or uncontrolled or however caused; or

d. Any consequence of any of these; or

4. To any person, other than a "residence employee" of an "insured", regularly residing on any part of the "insured location".

SECTION II – ADDITIONAL COVERAGES

We cover the following in addition to the limits of liability:

A. Claim Expenses

We pay:

1. Expenses we incur and costs taxed against an "insured" in any suit we defend;

2. Premiums on bonds required in a suit we defend, but not for bond amounts more than the Coverage **E** limit of liability. We need not apply for or furnish any bond;

3. Reasonable expenses incurred by an "insured" at our request, including actual loss of earnings (but not loss of other income) up to $250 per day, for assisting us in the investigation or defense of a claim or suit; and

4. Interest on the entire judgment which accrues after entry of the judgment and before we pay or tender, or deposit in court that part of the judgment which does not exceed the limit of liability that applies.

5. Prejudgment interest awarded against an "insured" on that part of the judgment we pay. Any prejudgment interest awarded against an "insured" is subject to the applicable Pennsylvania Rules of Civil Procedure.

B. First Aid Expenses

We will pay expenses for first aid to others incurred by an "insured" for "bodily injury" covered under this policy. We will not pay for first aid to an "insured".

C. Damage To Property Of Others

1. We will pay, at replacement cost, up to $1,000 per "occurrence" for "property damage" to property of others caused by an "insured".

2. We will not pay for "property damage":

a. To the extent of any amount recoverable under Section **I**;

b. Caused intentionally by an "insured" who is 13 years of age or older;

c. To property owned by an "insured";

d. To property owned by or rented to a tenant of an "insured" or a resident in your household; or

e. Arising out of:

(1) A "business" engaged in by an "insured";

(2) Any act or omission in connection with a premises owned, rented or controlled by an "insured", other than the "insured location"; or

(3) The ownership, maintenance, occupancy, operation, use, loading or unloading of aircraft, hovercraft, watercraft or "motor vehicles".

This exclusion **e.(3)** does not apply to a "motor vehicle" that:

(a) Is designed for recreational use off public roads;

(b) Is not owned by an "insured"; and

(c) At the time of the "occurrence", is not required by law, or regulation issued by a government agency, to have been registered for it to be used on public roads or property.

D. Loss Assessment

1. We will pay up to $1,000 for your share of loss assessment charged against you, as owner or tenant of the "residence premises", during the policy period by a corporation or association of property owners, when the assessment is made as a result of:

a. "Bodily injury" or "property damage" not excluded from coverage under Section II – Exclusions; or

b. Liability for an act of a director, officer or trustee in the capacity as a director, officer or trustee, provided such person:

(1) Is elected by the members of a corporation or association of property owners; and

(2) Serves without deriving any income from the exercise of duties which are solely on behalf of a corporation or association of property owners.

2. Paragraph I. Policy Period under Section II – Conditions does not apply to this Loss Assessment Coverage.

3. Regardless of the number of assessments, the limit of $1,000 is the most we will pay for loss arising out of:

a. One accident, including continuous or repeated exposure to substantially the same general harmful condition; or

b. A covered act of a director, officer or trustee. An act involving more than one director, officer or trustee is considered to be a single act.

4. We do not cover assessments charged against you or a corporation or association of property owners by any governmental body.

SECTION II – CONDITIONS

A. Limit Of Liability

Our total liability under Coverage **E** for all damages resulting from any one "occurrence" will not be more than the Coverage **E** limit of liability shown in the Declarations. This limit is the same regardless of the number of "insureds", claims made or persons injured. All "bodily injury" and "property damage" resulting from any one accident or from continuous or repeated exposure to substantially the same general harmful conditions shall be considered to be the result of one "occurrence".

Our total liability under Coverage **F** for all medical expense payable for "bodily injury" to one person as the result of one accident will not be more than the Coverage **F** limit of liability shown in the Declarations.

B. Severability Of Insurance

This insurance applies separately to each "insured". This condition will not increase our limit of liability for any one "occurrence".

C. Duties After "Occurrence"

In case of an "occurrence", you or another "insured" will perform the following duties that apply. We have no duty to provide coverage under this policy if your failure to comply with the following duties is prejudicial to us. You will help us by seeing that these duties are performed:

1. Give written notice to us or our agent as soon as is practical, which sets forth:

a. The identity of the policy and the "named insured" shown in the Declarations;

b. Reasonably available information on the time, place and circumstances of the "occurrence"; and

c. Names and addresses of any claimants and witnesses;

2. Cooperate with us in the investigation, settlement or defense of any claim or suit;

3. Promptly forward to us every notice, demand, summons or other process relating to the "occurrence";

4. At our request, help us:

   a. To make settlement;

   b. To enforce any right of contribution or indemnity against any person or organization who may be liable to an "insured";

   c. With the conduct of suits and attend hearings and trials; and

   d. To secure and give evidence and obtain the attendance of witnesses;

5. With respect to **C.** Damage To Property Of Others under Section **II** – Additional Coverages, submit to us within 60 days after the loss, a sworn statement of loss and show the damaged property, if in an "insured's" control;

6. No "insured" shall, except at such "insured's" own cost, voluntarily make payment, assume obligation or incur expense other than for first aid to others at the time of the "bodily injury".

D. Duties Of An Injured Person – Coverage F – Medical Payments To Others

1. The injured person or someone acting for the injured person will:

   a. Give us written proof of claim, under oath if required, as soon as is practical; and

   b. Authorize us to obtain copies of medical reports and records.

2. The injured person will submit to a physical exam by a doctor of our choice when and as often as we reasonably require.

E. Payment Of Claim – Coverage F – Medical Payments To Others

Payment under this coverage is not an admission of liability by an "insured" or us.

F. Suit Against Us

1. No action can be brought against us unless there has been full compliance with all of the terms under this Section **II**.

2. No one will have the right to join us as a party to any action against an "insured".

3. Also, no action with respect to Coverage **E** can be brought against us until the obligation of such "insured" has been determined by final judgment or agreement signed by us.

G. Bankruptcy Of An "Insured"

Bankruptcy or insolvency of an "insured" will not relieve us of our obligations under this policy.

H. Other Insurance

This insurance is excess over other valid and collectible insurance except insurance written specifically to cover as excess over the limits of liability that apply in this policy.

I. Policy Period

This policy applies only to "bodily injury" or "property damage" which occurs during the policy period.

J. Concealment Or Fraud

We do not provide coverage to an "insured" who, whether before or after a loss, has:

1. Intentionally concealed or misrepresented any material fact or circumstance;

2. Engaged in fraudulent conduct; or

3. Made false statements;

relating to this insurance.

SECTIONS I AND II – CONDITIONS

A. Liberalization Clause

If we make a change which broadens coverage under this edition of our policy without additional premium charge, that change will automatically apply to your insurance as of the date we implement the change in your state, provided that this implementation date falls within 60 days prior to or during the policy period stated in the Declarations.

This Liberalization Clause does not apply to changes implemented with a general program revision that includes both broadenings and restrictions in coverage, whether that general program revision is implemented through introduction of:

1. A subsequent edition of this policy; or

2. An amendatory endorsement.

B. Waiver Or Change Of Policy Provisions

A waiver or change of a provision of this policy must be in writing by us to be valid. Our request for an appraisal or examination will not waive any of our rights.

C. Cancellation

1. You may cancel this policy at any time by returning it to us or by letting us know in writing of the date cancellation is to take effect.

2. We may cancel this policy only for the reasons stated below by notifying the "insured" named in the Declarations in writing of the date cancellation takes effect. This cancellation notice may be delivered to or mailed to the "insured" named in the Declarations at the mailing address shown in the policy or at a forwarding address. Proof of mailing will be sufficient proof of notice.

   a. When this policy has been in effect for less than 60 days and is not a renewal with us, we may cancel for any reason by notifying the "insured" named in the Declarations at least 30 days before the cancellation takes effect.

   b. When this policy has been in effect for 60 days or more, or at any time if it is a renewal with us, we may cancel only for one or more of the following reasons by notifying the "insured" named in the Declarations at least 30 days prior to the proposed cancellation date:

   (1) This policy was obtained through material misrepresentation, fraudulent statements, omissions or concealment of fact material to the acceptance of the risk or to the hazard assumed by us;

   (2) There has been a substantial change or increase in hazard in the risk assumed by us subsequent to the date the policy was issued;

   (3) There is a substantial increase in hazard insured against by reason of willful or negligent acts or omissions by the "insured";

   (4) The "insured" has failed to pay the premium by the due date, whether payable to us or to our agent or under any finance or credit plan; or

   (5) For any other reason approved by the Pennsylvania Insurance Commissioner.

   This provision shall not apply if the named "insured" has demonstrated by some overt action to us or to our agent that the "insured" wishes the policy to be cancelled.

   Delivery of such written notice by us to the "insured" named in the Declarations at the mailing address shown in the policy or at a forwarding address shall be equivalent to mailing.

3. When this policy is canceled, the premium for the period from the date of cancellation to the expiration date will be refunded pro rata.

4. If the return premium is not refunded with the notice of cancellation or when this policy is returned to us, we will refund it within a reasonable time after the date cancellation takes effect.

D. Nonrenewal

We will not fail to renew this policy except for one of the reasons referred to in **C.** Cancellation above. We may refuse to renew for one of the listed reasons by mailing to the "insured" named in the Declarations at the mailing address shown in the policy or at a forwarding address, written notice at least 30 days prior to the expiration date of this policy.

This provision does not apply if:

1. We have indicated our willingness to renew and the "insured" has failed to pay the premium by the due date; or

2. The named "insured" has indicated to us or our agent that the "insured" does not wish the policy to be renewed.

Delivery of such written notice by us to the "insured" named in the Declarations at the mailing address shown in the policy or at a forwarding address shall be equivalent to mailing.

E. Assignment

Assignment of this policy will not be valid unless we give our written consent.

F. Subrogation

An "insured" may waive in writing before a loss all rights of recovery against any person. If not waived, we may require an assignment of rights of recovery for a loss to the extent that payment is made by us.

If an assignment is sought, an "insured" must sign and deliver all related papers and cooperate with us.

Subrogation does not apply to Coverage **F** or Paragraph **C.** Damage To Property Of Others under Section **II** – Additional Coverages.

G. Death

If any person named in the Declarations or the spouse, if a resident of the same household, dies, the following apply:

1. We insure the legal representative of the deceased but only with respect to the premises and property of the deceased covered under the policy at the time of death; and

2. Insurance under this policy will continue as provided in **a.** or **b.** below, whichever is later:

   a. For 180 days after your death regardless of the policy period shown in the Declarations, unless your premises and property, covered under the policy at the time of your death, is sold prior to that date; or

   b. Until the end of the policy period shown in the Declarations, unless your premises and property, covered under the policy at the time of your death, is sold prior to that date.

   Coverage during the period of time after your death is subject to all the provisions of this policy including payment of any premium due for the policy period shown in the Declarations and any extension of that period;

3. "Insured" includes:

   a. An insured who is a member of your household at the time of your death, but only while a resident of the "residence premises"; and

   b. With respect to your property, the person having proper temporary custody of the property until appointment and qualification of a legal representative.

Appendix D

Sample Whole Life Insurance Policy with Riders

Whole life insurance is a form of permanent insurance that provides lifetime insurance coverage at a level premium rate that does not increase as the insured ages. The following sample whole life insurance policy provides a $100,000 death benefit, and, as noted on the policy face page, is a participating policy that gives the policyowner the right to share in the insurer's divisible surplus by receiving policy dividends.

As you can see by the length of this policy compared to the length of the sample one-year term life insurance policy, a whole life insurance policy is a much more complicated document than is a term life policy. The additional provisions included in a whole life insurance policy are required to specify how the policy's cash value will build-up and the policyowner's rights in that cash value. Page 3, for example, includes a "Table of Guaranteed Values," which lists the minimum guaranteed cash values at the end of specified policy years. Other provisions also describe the policy's cash value features, including the provisions on pages 7 and 8 under the heading "Cash Value and Loans." Additionally, many of the provisions on page 6 concerning "Premiums" are included to describe the options a policyowner has to stop paying policy premiums and to either receive the accumulated cash value or use that cash value to provide continued insurance coverage.

Included along with the sample whole life insurance policy are five sample policy riders that may be attached to such a policy. The sample riders included here are as follows:

◆ An *accidental death benefit (ADB) rider* that provides a benefit if the insured's death is caused by accidental bodily injury while the rider is in effect. (See page 13.) The amount of the accidental death benefit provided is stated as $100,000

(continued on next page)

on the policy data page. (See page 2.) The rider specifies a number of exclusions for which the ADB will not be payable and states that the rider has no cash value or loan value.

◆ A *disability waiver of premium (WP) rider* under which the insurer agrees to waive the payment of renewal premiums if the insured becomes totally disabled. (See pages 15 and 16.) The rider defines the term "total disability" and specifies a number of disabilities that are excluded from coverage.

◆ A *policy purchase option (PPO) rider* that gives the policyowner the right to purchase a new policy on the life of the insured on specified future option dates. (See pages 17 and 18.) The face amount of the new policy must be at least $10,000 and may not be more than the option amount of $50,000 as specified on page 2. The new policy may be any life insurance or endowment insurance plan the insurer is offering for the selected face amount on the specified option date. The premiums payable for the new policy will be based on the insured's age and the insurer's premium rates on the option date.

◆ An *option to purchase paid-up additions (OPP) rider* that gives the policyowner the right to purchase new paid-up life insurance coverage on the insured. (See pages 19-21.) Note that the coverage purchased under this rider is paid-up life insurance that increases the amount of the death benefit payable under the policy. In addition, the paid-up additions purchased have a cash value and a loan value. By contrast, the coverage purchased under the aforementioned PPO rider is provided by a separate policy, and the rider does not have a cash value or a loan value.

◆ An *acceleration of death benefits rider* under which the insurer agrees to pay a specified lump-sum amount, known as the *accelerated death benefit*, if the insured is terminally ill. (See pages 23-26.) In order to receive the accelerated death benefit, the insured must meet a number of requirements, including providing the insurer with evidence that the insured has a life expectancy of 12 months or less as determined by a qualified physician. The rider specifies how the accelerated death benefit is calculated and guarantees that the benefit will never be less than a stated amount based on the amount of the policy cash value. The payment of an accelerated death benefit reduces the amount of the benefit, if any, that will be payable following the insured's death.

INSURED   – JOHN DOE

POLICY NUMBER   – 36 000 000

POLICY DATE   – AUGUST 8, 1999

ABC Life Insurance Company

123 Main Street, Anytown, USA

ABC Life Insurance Company will pay the benefits of this policy in accordance with its provisions. The pages which follow are also a part of this policy.

10 Day Right To Examine Policy. Please examine your policy. Within 10 days after delivery, you can return it to ABC Life Insurance Company or to the agent through whom it was purchased, with a written request for a full refund of premium. Upon such request, the policy will be void from the start, and a full premium refund will be made.

Premiums. The premiums for this policy are shown in the Premium Schedule on the Policy Data page. They are payable in accordance with the Premiums section.

This policy is executed as of the date of issue shown on the Policy Data page.

John Johnson

President

Mary Smith

Secretary

Whole Life Policy.

Life Insurance Proceeds Payable at Insured's Death.

Premiums Payable During Insured's Lifetime, as shown on the Policy Data page.

Policy is Eligible for Dividends.

ABC LIFE

GAT111

```
         INSURED  —  JOHN  DOE              AGE 37          MALE
    POLICY NUMBER  —  36000000              CLASS OF RISK - STANDARD
                                            (NON-SMOKER DISCOUNT)

       POLICY DATE  —  AUGUST 8, 1999       DATE OF ISSUE
                                            AUGUST  15,1999
              OWNER  —  INSURED
```

PLAN   WHOLE LIFE WITH
              OPTION TO PURCHASE PAID-UP ADDITIONS (OPP) AND
              ACCIDENTAL DEATH BENEFIT (ADB) AND
              DISABILITY WAIVER OF PREMIUM (WP) AND
              POLICY PURCHASE OPTION (PPO) - OPTION AMOUNT IS $50,000.00 AND
              ACCELERATION OF DEATH BENEFITS

AMOUNT   FACE AMOUNT $100,000.00
              ACCIDENTAL DEATH BENEFIT $100,000.00
              (ADB, WHEN PAYABLE, IS IN ADDITION TO
              ANY OTHER INSURANCE BENEFIT)

BENEFICIARY
(subject to change) FIRST - ESTATE OF THE INSURED

PREMIUM SCHEDULE
PREMIUMS PAYABLE AT MONTHLY INTERVALS, AS FOLLOWS (SEE ENDORSEMENT HEREON)
        (Premium includes the following amounts for any supplementary benefits)

BEGINNING	AS OF		TOTAL	
MO.	DAY	YR.	PREMIUM	
8-	8-	1999	$144.00	
8-	8-	2008	$134.00	
8-	8-	2027	$130.00	
8-	8-	2032	$123.00	PAYABLE FOR REMAINDER OF INSURED'S LIFE.**

			ADB	WP	PPO
8-	8-	1999	$7.00	$5.50	$8.50
8-	8-	2008	$7.00	$4.00	
8-	8-	2027	$7.00		
8-	8-	2032			

PREMIUM PAYING PERIOD MAY BE SHORTENED BY USING DIVIDEND VALUES TO MAKE POLICY FULLY PAID-UP.

THE EXPENSE CHARGE APPLIED TO ALL PAYMENTS MADE UNDER THE OPTION TO PURCHASE PAID-UP ADDITIONS (OPP) RIDER WILL NOT EXCEED 3%.

THE INTEREST RATES, REFERRED TO IN THE BASIS OF COMPUTATION SECTION, ARE AS FOLLOWS:

    A) 6.25% PER YEAR FOR THE CALCULATION OF CASH VALUES, EXTENDED INSURANCE AND PAID-UP INSURANCE FOR THE FIRST 20 POLICY YEARS.

    B) 5% PER YEAR FOR THE COMPUTATION OF ALL OTHER VALUES.

DIVIDENDS ARE NOT GUARANTEED. WE HAVE THE RIGHT TO CHANGE THE AMOUNT OF DIVIDENDS TO BE CREDITED TO THE POLICY WHICH MAY RESULT IN LOWER DIVIDEND VALUES, OR, IF APPLICABLE, MORE PREMIUMS TO BE PAID, THAN WERE ILLUSTRATED.

GAT111   Page 2

TABLE OF GUARANTEED VALUES*

Alternatives to Cash Value

End of Policy Year	Cash Value	Paid-Up Insurance	or	Extended Insurance		End of Policy Year
				Years	Days	
1	*****	***		**	***	1
2	*****	***		**	***	2
3	$400.00	$2,400		1	18	3
4	1,400.00	7,900		3	114	4
5	2,400.00	12,900		5	62	5
6	3,500.00	17,900		6	328	6
7	4,500.00	22,000		8	55	7
8	5,600.00	26,200		9	109	8
9	6,800.00	30,400		10	121	9
10	8,000.00	34,300		11	50	10
11	9,300.00	38,100		11	321	11
12	11,000.00	43,200		12	325	12
13	12,900.00	48,500		13	323	13
14	14,800.00	53,300		14	239	14
15	16,700.00	57,700		15	91	15
16	18,700.00	61,900		15	287	16
17	20,700.00	65,800		16	73	17
18	22,700.00	69,300		16	187	18
19	24,800.00	72,800		16	291	19
20	26,900.00	75,900		16	358	20
AGE 60	32,300.00	69,400		14	319	AGE 60
AGE 65	41,700.00	77,300		13	198	AGE 65

*This table assumes premiums have been paid to the end of the policy year shown. These values do not include any dividend accumulations, paid-up additions, or policy loans.

POLICY DATA   ABC LIFE INSURANCE COMPANY

WE & YOU

In this policy, the words "we," "our" or "us" refer to ABC Life Insurance Company, and the words "you" or "your" refer to the owner of this policy.

When you write to us, please include the policy number, the Insured's full name, and your current address.

CONTENTS

Note: This policy is a legal contract between the policyowner and the Company.

READ YOUR POLICY CAREFULLY FOR FULL DETAILS.

LIFE INSURANCE PROCEEDS

Life Insurance Proceeds We will pay the life insurance proceeds to the beneficiary promptly when we have proof that the Insured died, if premiums have been paid as called for in the Premiums section. These proceeds will include the face amount and any other benefits from riders or dividends which are payable because of the Insured's death, all as stated in the policy. When we determine these proceeds, there may be an adjustment for the last premium. We will deduct any unpaid loan.

POLICY OWNERSHIP

Owner In this policy, the words "you" and "your" refer to the owner of this policy. As the owner, you have all rights of ownership in this policy while the Insured is living. To exercise these rights, you do not need the consent of any successor owner or beneficiary.

Successor Owner A successor owner can be named in the application, or in a notice you sign which gives us the facts that we need. The successor owner will become the new owner when you die, if you die before the Insured. If no successor owner survives you and you die before the Insured, your estate becomes the new owner.

Change of Ownership You can change the owner of this policy, from yourself to a new owner, in a notice you sign which gives us the facts that we need. When this change takes effect, all rights of ownership in this policy will pass to the new owner.

When we record a change of owner or successor owner, these changes will take effect as of the date you signed the notice, subject to any payment we made or action we took before recording these changes. We may require that these changes be endorsed in the policy. Changing the owner or naming a new successor owner cancels any prior choice of successor owner, but does not change the beneficiary.

BENEFICIARY

Naming of Beneficiary One or more beneficiaries for any life insurance proceeds can be named in the application, or in a notice you sign which gives us the facts that we need. If more than one beneficiary is named, they can be classed as first, second, and so on. If 2 or more are named in a class, their shares in the proceeds can be stated.

The stated shares of the proceeds will be paid to any first beneficiaries who survive the Insured. If no first beneficiaries survive, payment will be made to any beneficiary surviving in the second class, and so on. Beneficiaries who survive in the same class have an equal share in the proceeds, unless the shares are stated otherwise.

Change of Beneficiary While the Insured is living, you can change a beneficiary in a notice you sign which gives us the facts that we need. When we record a change, it will take effect as of the date you signed the notice, subject to any payment we made or action we took before recording the change.

Death of Beneficiary If no beneficiary for the life insurance proceeds, or for a stated share, survives the Insured, the right to these proceeds or this share will pass to you. If you are the Insured, this right will pass to your estate. Unless stated otherwise in the policy or in your signed notice which is in effect at the Insured's death, if any beneficiary dies at the same time as the Insured, or within 15 days after the Insured but before we receive proof of the Insured's death, we will pay the proceeds as though that beneficiary died first.

PREMIUMS

Payment of Premiums Each premium is payable, while the Insured is living, on or before its due date as shown in the Premium Schedule on the Policy Data page. Premiums are payable at our Home Office or at one of our service offices.

The premium for this policy can be paid at intervals of 3 months or 6 months, or once each year. The method we use to determine the premium rate for each of these intervals is the method that was in effect as of the policy date shown on the Policy Data page. The interval can be changed by paying the correct premium for the new interval. Premiums can be paid by any other method we make available.

Grace Period We allow 31 days from the due date for payment of a premium. All insurance coverage continues during this grace period.

Nonpayment of Premium If a premium is not paid by the end of the grace period, this policy will lapse. All insurance will end at the time of lapse, if the policy has no cash value and no dividend values. If the policy has cash value or dividend values, insurance can be continued only as stated in Options 1 or 2 of the Options Upon Lapse provision, but any insurance or benefits from riders or dividends will end at the time of lapse.

Options Upon Lapse If the policy has cash value or dividend values at the time of lapse, it will continue as extended insurance, if available. It may happen that the amount of extended insurance would be less than or equal to the amount of paid-up insurance available, or the Table of Guaranteed Values on the Policy Data page shows that extended insurance is not available. In these cases, the policy will continue under the paid-up insurance option instead.

Instead of extended insurance, paid-up insurance can be elected or you can surrender the policy for cash. The paid-up insurance option can be elected in the application or in your signed notice. We must receive this notice no later than 3 months after the due date of the overdue premium.

1. **Extended Insurance** Extended insurance is level term insurance for which no more premiums are due. It is payable to the beneficiary when we

have proof that the Insured died after the end of the grace period and before the end of the term period. The amount of extended insurance will equal the face amount of this policy, plus the amount of any paid-up additions and dividend accumulations, less any unpaid loan. No insurance or benefits from riders or dividends will be provided after the end of the grace period.

We calculate the term period as of the due date of the overdue premium. We do this by applying the sum of the cash value and dividend values, less any unpaid loan, at the net single premium rate for term insurance for the Insured's age on that date. The term period is measured from that due date.

This insurance can be surrendered at any time for its cash value, but it has no loan value and is not eligible for dividends. All insurance will end when you send us your signed request for the cash value proceeds.

2. **Paid-up Insurance** Paid-up life insurance begins as of the date we record your notice electing it, or begins at the end of the grace period if later. No more premiums are due for this insurance. It is payable to the beneficiary when we have proof that the Insured died while this paid-up insurance option was in effect.

We calculate the amount of paid-up insurance as of the due date of the overdue premium. We do this by applying the sum of the cash value and dividend values, less any unpaid loan, at the net single premium rate for the Insured's age on that date. In most cases, this amount will be less than the face amount of this policy. No insurance or benefits from riders will be provided after this paid-up insurance option goes into effect.

This insurance can be surrendered at any time. It has cash value and loan value, and is eligible for dividends. All insurance will end when you send us your signed request for the cash value proceeds.

3. **Surrender for Cash** Instead of extended insurance or paid-up insurance, you can surrender this policy for its cash value and dividend values, less any unpaid loan, as stated in the Cash Value provision. All insurance will end when you send us your signed request for the cash value proceeds.

PREMIUMS (continued)

Reinstatement Within 5 years after lapse, you may apply to reinstate the policy if you have not surrendered it. We must have evidence of insurability that is acceptable to us. All overdue premiums must be paid, with interest at 6% per year from each of their due dates, unless we declare a policy loan interest rate of less than 6%. In that case, the interest rate for all overdue premiums at the time of reinstatement will be the same as the policy loan interest rate, but not more than 6%. Any unpaid loan, and any loan deducted when we determined the extended or paid-up insurance, must also be repaid. Interest on the loan will be compounded once each year and will be based on the loan interest rate or rates that were in effect since the time of lapse.

All or part of these payments can be charged as a new unpaid loan if there is enough loan value.

We do not need evidence of insurability if we receive the required payment within 31 days after the end of the grace period, but the Insured must be living when we receive it.

Premium Adjustment at Death We will increase the life insurance proceeds by any part of a premium paid for the period after the policy month in which the Insured dies.

If the Insured dies during a grace period, we will reduce the proceeds by an amount equal to the premium for one policy month.

CASH VALUE AND LOANS

Cash Value Cash values for this policy at the end of selected policy years are as shown in the Table of Guaranteed Values on the Policy Data page, if premiums have been paid as called for in the Premiums section. These values do not include dividend values, and they do not reflect any unpaid loan. Cash values at other times depend on the date to which premiums have been paid, and on how much time has passed since the last policy anniversary. When you ask us, we will tell you how much cash value there is.

The cash value on the due date of an unpaid premium will not decrease during the 3 months after that date. Also, the cash value of any extended or paid-up insurance on a policy anniversary will not decrease during the next 31 days after that anniversary.

At any time after the policy has cash value or dividend values, you can surrender it for the sum of these values, less any unpaid loan. All insurance will end when you send us your signed request for these surrender proceeds.

We may defer paying these proceeds for up to 6 months after the date of surrender. Interest will be paid from the date of surrender on any payment deferred more than 10 days. We set the interest rate each year. This rate will be at least 3.5% per year or the rate required by law.

Loan Value You can borrow any amount up to the loan value, using this policy as sole security.

On a policy anniversary, on a premium due date, or during the grace period, the loan value is the cash value, plus any dividend values, less any unpaid loan and accrued interest. At any other time, the loan value is the amount which, with interest, will equal the loan value on the next anniversary or on the next premium due date, if earlier. Extended insurance has no loan value.

We may require that you sign a loan agreement. We may defer a loan, except to pay a premium due us for this policy, for as long as 6 months after we receive your loan request. Interest will be paid on any amount deferred if that amount is not mailed within 10 days after we receive the necessary information to complete the loan transaction. We will set the interest rate to be at least 3.5% per year or the rate required by law.

Loan Interest Loan interest accrues each day. Interest is due on each anniversary, or on the date of death, surrender, a lapse, a loan increase or loan repayment, or on any other date we specify. Interest not paid when due becomes part of the loan and will also bear interest.

Loan Interest Rate The loan interest rate for this policy may go up or down as described in this provision. However, the rate at any given time will apply to the entire amount of an unpaid loan. We will review this rate once every 3 months and, if necessary, adjust it.

CASH VALUE AND LOANS (continued)

The loan interest rate will not be more than the Monthly Average Corporates yield shown in Moody's Corporate Bond Yield Averages published by Moody's Investors Services, Inc., or any successor to that service (the published monthly average), for the second calendar month prior to the date when we set an interest rate for this policy. If the rate, at this time, as determined by the published monthly average, is 0.5% or more above the current loan interest rate, we have the right to increase the loan interest rate to reflect this. However if the rate, at this time, as determined by the published monthly average, is 0.5% or more below the current loan interest rate, we will reduce the loan interest rate to reflect this. The loan interest rate will never be less than the interest rate shown on the Policy Data page plus 1%.

We will tell you the interest rate in effect when a loan, including an Automatic Premium Loan (APL), is made and when we send you notice of loan interest due. If a loan is outstanding 40 days or more before the effective date of an increase in the interest rate, we will notify you of that increase at least 30 days prior to its effective date. We will notify you of any increase in the interest rate when a loan is made during the 40 days before the effective date of the increase.

It may happen that the published monthly average ceases to be published. In this case, we will use a new basis approved by the insurance supervisory official of the state or district in which the policy is delivered.

Automatic Premium Loan (APL) If elected, APL provides an automatic loan which pays an overdue premium at the end of the grace period, subject to 2 conditions. First, the loan value must be enough to pay that premium.

Second, if premiums have been paid by APL for 2 years in a row, the next premium will not be paid by APL. After a premium is paid other than by APL, before the end of the grace period, premiums can again be paid by APL.

APL can be elected in the application. You can also elect APL in your signed notice which we must receive before the end of the grace period. You can cancel this election for future premiums by telling us in your signed notice.

Loan Repayment All or part of an unpaid loan and accrued interest can be repaid before the Insured's death or before you surrender the policy. We will deduct any unpaid loan when policy proceeds are payable.

If the policy is being continued as extended or paid-up insurance, any loan which we deducted in determining that insurance may be repaid only if the policy is reinstated. If that loan is not repaid, we will not deduct it again when policy proceeds are payable.

When Unpaid Loan Exceeds Loan Value In a given policy year it may happen that an unpaid loan and accrued interest will exceed the sum of the cash value and any dividend values. In this case, we will mail a notice to you at your last known address, and a copy to any assignee on our records. All insurance will end 31 days after the date on which we mail that notice, if the excess of the unpaid loan and accrued interest over the sum of the cash value and any dividend values is not paid within that 31 days.

We will not terminate this policy in a given policy year as the sole result of a change in the loan interest rate during that policy year.

DIVIDENDS

Annual Dividend While this policy is in force, except as extended insurance, it is eligible to share in our divisible surplus. Each year we determine the policy's share, if any. This share is payable as a dividend on the policy anniversary, if all premiums due before then have been paid. We do not expect a dividend to be payable before the second anniversary.

Dividend Options Each dividend can be applied under one of the 4 options listed below. An option can be elected in the application. You can also elect or change the option for future dividends if you tell us in your signed notice.

1. Paid-up Addition Applied to provide paid-up life insurance at the net single premium rate for the Insured's age at that time. No more premiums are due for this insurance. It has cash value and is eligible for dividends. Before the Insured's death, you can surrender paid-up additions for their cash value that has not been borrowed against. The amount of this insurance in force at the Insured's death will be part of the life insurance proceeds.

2. Dividend Accumulation Left with us to accumulate at interest. On each policy anniversary, we credit interest at the rate we set each year. This rate will be at least 3.5% per year. Before the Insured's death, you can withdraw accumulations that have not been borrowed against, with interest to the date of withdrawal. Any accumulations which we still have at the Insured's death will be part of the life insurance proceeds.

3. Premium Payment Applied toward payment of a premium, provided any balance of that premium is also paid when due. Any part of the dividend not needed to pay the premium will be used to pay any loan interest due, unless you have asked to have that part paid in cash. Any part of the dividend not used to pay a premium or loan interest will be paid in cash.

4. Cash Paid in cash.

Automatic Dividend Option If no other option is in effect when a dividend becomes payable, we will apply it as a paid-up addition. If we pay a dividend in cash, and the dividend check is not cashed within one year after that dividend became payable, we will apply the dividend as a paid-up addition instead.

Dividend Values Dividend values are any dividend accumulations plus the cash value of any paid-up additions.

Fully Paid-up Policy You may shorten the premium paying period for this policy by having it made fully paid-up with no more premiums due. This may be done on any premium due date, if the sum of the cash value and dividend values equals the total single premium for the policy and any riders, based on the Insured's age on that date. We must receive your signed notice within 31 days of that date.

Dividend at Death The part of any annual dividend earned from the last policy anniversary to the end of the policy month in which the Insured dies will be part of the life insurance proceeds.

PAYMENT OF POLICY PROCEEDS

Payment We will pay the life insurance proceeds in one sum or, if elected, all or part of these proceeds may be placed under one or more of the options described in this section. If we agree, the proceeds may be placed under some other method of payment instead.

Any life insurance proceeds paid in one sum will bear interest compounded each year from the Insured's death to the date of payment. We set the interest rate each year. This rate will be at least 3.5% per year, and will not be less than required by law.

Election of Optional Method of Payment While the Insured is living, you can elect or change an option. You can also name or change one or more beneficiaries for the life insurance proceeds who will be the payee or payees under that option.

After the Insured dies, any person who is to receive proceeds in one sum (other than an assignee) can elect an option and name payees. The person who elects an option can also name one or more successor payees to receive any unpaid amount we have at the death of a payee. Naming these payees cancels any prior choice of successor payee.

PAYMENT OF POLICY PROCEEDS (continued)

A payee who did not elect the option does not have the right to advance or assign payments, take the payments in one sum, or make any other change. However, the payee may be given the right to do one or more of these things if the person who elects the option tells us in writing and we agree.

Change of Option If we agree, a payee who elects Option 1A, 1B, 2A or 2B may later elect to have any unpaid amount we still have, or the present value of any elected payments, placed under some other option described in this section.

Payees Only individuals who are to receive payments in their own behalf may be named as payees or successor payees, unless we agree to some other payee. We may require proof of the age or the survival of a payee.

It may happen that when the last surviving payee dies, we still have an unpaid amount, or there are some payments which remain to be made. If so, we will pay the unpaid amount with interest to the date of payment, or pay the present value of the remaining payments, to that payee's estate in one sum. The present value of any remaining payments is based on the interest rate used to compute them, and is always less than their sum.

Minimum Payment When any payment under an option would be less than $20, we may pay any unpaid amount or present value in one sum.

Options 1A and 1B. Proceeds at Interest

The policy proceeds may be left with us at interest. We set the interest rate each year. This rate will be at least 3.5% per year.

1A. Interest Accumulation

We credit interest each year on the amount we still have. This amount can be withdrawn at any time in sums of $100 or more. We pay interest to the date of withdrawal on sums withdrawn.

1B. Interest Payment

We pay interest once each month, every 3 months or every 6 months, or once each year, as chosen, based on the amount we still have.

Options 2A and 2B. Elected Income

We make equal payments once each month, every 3 months or every 6 months, or once each year, as chosen, for an elected period of years or for an elected amount. We set the interest rate for these options each year. This rate will be at least 3.5% per year. If the rate is more than 3.5%, we will increase each payment to reflect this.

2A. Income for Elected Period

We make the payments for the number of years elected. Monthly payments based on 3.5% interest are shown in the Option 2A Table.

OPTION 2A TABLE
Minimum Monthly Payment per $1,000 of Proceeds

Years		Years		Years		Years	
1	$84.65	5	$18.12	9	$10.75	15	$7.10
2	43.05	6	15.35	10	9.83	20	5.75
3	29.19	7	13.38	11	9.09	25	4.96
4	22.27	8	11.90	12	8.46	30	4.45

When asked, we will state in writing what each payment would be, if made every 3 months or every 6 months, or once each year.

2B. Income of Elected Amount

We make payments of the elected amount until all proceeds and interest have been paid. The total payments made each year must be at least 5% of the proceeds placed under this option. Each year we credit interest of at least 3.5% on the amount we still have.

Options 3A, 3B, and 3C. Life Income

We make equal payments each month during the lifetime of the named payee or payees. We determine the amount of the monthly payment by applying the policy proceeds to purchase a corresponding single premium life annuity policy which is being issued when the first payment is due. Payments are based on the appropriately adjusted annuity premium rate in effect at that time, but will not be less than the corresponding minimum amount based on the tables for Options 3A, 3B, and 3C in this policy. The minimum amounts are based on the "1983 Table **a**" mortality table with projection, and with interest compounded each year at 4%.

PAYMENT OF POLICY PROCEEDS (continued)

When asked, we will state in writing what the minimum amount of each monthly payment would be under these options. It is based on the sex and the adjusted age of the payee or payees in the year the first payment is due. To find the adjusted age, we increase or decrease the payee's age at that time, as follows:

1987–91	1992–98	1999–2006	2007–2013	2014–20	2021–28	2029+
+3	+2	+1	0	−1	−2	−3

3A.   Life Income–Guaranteed Period

We make a payment each month during the lifetime of the payee. Payments do not change, and are guaranteed for 5, 10, 15, or 20 years, as chosen, even if that payee dies sooner.

OPTION 3A TABLE
Minimum Monthly Payment per $1,000 of Proceeds

Payee's Adjusted Age	MALE Guaranteed Period 5 Yrs	10 Yrs	15 Yrs	20 Yrs	FEMALE Guaranteed Period 5 Yrs	10 Yrs	15 Yrs	20 Yrs
60	$5.14	$5.08	$4.98	$4.84	$4.68	$4.85	$4.61	$4.54
61	5.25	5.18	5.07	4.91	4.76	4.73	4.68	4.63
62	5.36	5.28	5.15	4.97	4.84	4.81	4.75	4.67
63	5.48	5.39	5.24	5.04	4.93	4.89	4.83	4.73
64	5.61	5.50	5.33	5.10	5.03	4.99	4.91	4.80
65	5.75	5.62	5.42	5.17	5.13	5.08	5.00	4.87
66	5.89	5.75	5.52	5.23	5.25	5.19	5.09	4.94
67	6.05	5.88	5.62	5.30	5.36	5.30	5.18	5.01
68	6.21	6.02	5.72	5.36	5.49	5.41	5.28	5.08
69	6.39	6.16	5.82	5.42	5.63	5.54	5.38	5.16
70	6.57	6.31	5.92	5.48	5.78	5.67	5.48	5.23
71	6.77	6.46	6.02	5.54	5.94	5.81	5.59	5.30
72	6.97	6.62	6.13	5.60	6.11	5.95	5.70	5.37
73	7.19	6.78	6.23	5.65	6.29	6.11	5.81	5.44
74	7.42	6.95	6.33	5.69	6.49	6.27	5.93	5.50
75	7.66	7.12	6.42	5.74	6.70	6.44	6.04	5.58
76	7.91	7.29	6.52	5.78	6.92	6.61	6.15	5.62
77	8.18	7.46	6.60	5.81	7.16	6.80	6.27	5.67
78	8.47	7.84	6.69	5.84	7.42	6.98	6.37	5.72
79	8.77	7.82	6.77	5.87	7.69	7.18	6.48	5.76
80	9.08	8.00	6.84	5.90	7.98	7.37	6.58	5.80
81	9.41	8.17	6.91	5.92	8.29	7.57	6.67	5.84
82	9.74	8.34	6.97	5.94	8.62	7.77	6.75	5.87
83	10.10	8.51	7.03	5.95	8.96	7.97	6.83	5.89
84	10.46	8.67	7.08	5.96	9.33	8.16	6.91	5.92
85 & over	10.84	8.82	7.13	5.97	9.71	8.34	6.97	5.94

3B. Life Income–Guaranteed Total Amount

We make a payment each month during the lifetime of the payee. Payments do not change, and are guaranteed until the total amount paid equals the amount placed under this option, even if that payee dies sooner.

OPTION 3B TABLE
Minimum Monthly Payment per $1,000 of Proceeds

Payee's Adjusted Age	Male	Female	Payee's Adjusted Age	Male	Female
60	$4.93	$4.57	73	$6.47	$5.87
61	5.02	4.64	74	6.84	6.01
62	5.11	4.71	75	6.81	6.17
63	5.20	4.79	76	7.00	6.34
64	5.30	4.87	77	7.19	6.51
65	5.40	4.96	78	7.40	6.70
66	5.52	5.05	79	7.62	6.90
67	5.63	5.14	80	7.85	7.11
68	5.75	5.25	81	8.09	7.33
69	5.88	5.36	82	8.35	7.57
70	6.02	5.47	83	8.61	7.81
71	6.16	5.60	84	8.89	8.07
72	6.31	5.73	85 & over	9.19	8.35

3C. Life Income–Joint and Survivor

We make a payment each month while both or one of the two payees are living. Payments do not change, and are guaranteed for 10 years, even if both payees die sooner.

OPTION 3C TABLE
10 YEAR GUARANTEED PERIOD
Minimum Monthly Payment per $1,000 of Proceeds

Male Payee's Adjusted Age	Female Payee's Adjusted Age 60	65	70	75	80
60	$4.32	$4.50	$4.67	$4.82	$4.93
65	4.42	4.66	4.91	5.15	5.34
70	4.81	4.81	5.14	5.49	5.80
75	4.57	4.92	5.34	5.81	6.27
80	4.61	4.99	5.49	6.07	6.69

GENERAL PROVISIONS

Entire Contract The entire contract consists of this policy, any attached riders or endorsements and the attached copy of the application. Only our Chairman, President, Secretary, or one of our Vice Presidents can change the contract, and then only in writing. No change will be made in the contract without your consent. No agent is authorized to change this contract.

Application In issuing this policy, we have relied on the statements made in the application. All such statements are deemed to be representations and not warranties. We assume these statements are true and complete to the best of the knowledge and belief of those who made them.

No statement made in connection with the application will be used by us to void the policy or to deny a claim unless that statement is a material misrepresentation and is part of the application.

Incontestability We will not contest this policy after it has been in force during the lifetime of the Insured for 2 years from the date of issue.

Please refer to the Incontestability of Rider provision that may be in any rider or riders attached to this policy.

Suicide Exclusion Suicide of the Insured within one year of the date of issue, is not covered by this policy. In that event, this policy will end and the only amount payable will be the premiums paid to us, less any unpaid loan. **(SEE ENDORSEMENT HEREON)**

Dates Policy years, months, and anniversaries are measured from the policy date.

Age and Sex In this policy when we refer to a person's age on any date, we mean his or her age on the birthday which is nearest that date. If a date on the Policy Data page is based on an age that is not correct, we may change the date to reflect the correct age.

If the age or sex of an insured person is not correct as stated, any amount payable under this policy will be what the premiums paid would have purchased at the correct age and sex.

Policy Changes If we agree, you may have riders added to this policy, or have it changed to another plan or to a smaller amount of insurance.

Assignment While the Insured is living, you can assign this policy or any interest in it. If you do this, your interest, and anyone else's is subject to that of the assignee. As owner, you still have the rights of ownership that have not been assigned.

An assignee may not change the owner or the beneficiary, and may not elect or change an optional method of payment of proceeds. Any policy proceeds payable to the assignee will be paid in one sum.

We must have a copy of any assignment. We will not be responsible for the validity of an assignment. It will be subject to any payment we make or other action we take before we record it.

Protection Against Creditors Except as stated in the Assignment provision, payments we make under this policy are, to the extent the law permits, exempt from the claims, attachments, or levies of any creditors.

Payments to Company Any payment made to us by check or money order must be payable to ABC Life Insurance Company. When asked, we will give a counter-signed receipt, signed by our President or Secretary, for any premium paid to us.

Basis of Computation All cash values and net single premium rates referred to in this policy are based on the 1980 CSO Tables of Mortality. All extended insurance rates and cash values are based on the corresponding 1980 CET Insurance Tables. The interest rate is shown on the Policy Data page. Continuous functions are used.

At the end of each policy year not shown in the Table on the Policy Data page, the cash value is the reserve based on the Commissioner's Reserve Valuation Method. At any time, the cash value of any extended or paid-up insurance or paid-up additions is the reserve on each of these.

We have filed a statement with the insurance official in the state or district in which this policy is delivered. It describes, in detail, the method we used to compute these cash values. Each value is at least as much as the law requires.

Conformity with Law This policy is subject to all laws which apply.

Voting Rights Each year there is an election of persons to our Board of Directors. You have the right to vote in person or by mail if your policy is in force, and has been in force for at least one year after the date of issue. To find out more about this, write to the Secretary at our Home Office, 100 Ordinary Avenue, New York, New York 00000.

RIDER

ACCIDENTAL DEATH BENEFIT (ADB)

Benefit We will pay this benefit to the beneficiary when we have proof that the Insured's death was caused directly, and apart from any other cause, by accidental bodily injury, and that death occurred within one year after that injury and while this rider was in effect.

When Benefit Not Payable We will not pay this benefit if death is caused or is contributed to by any of these items.

1. Disease or infirmity of mind or body.

2. Suicide.

3. Travel in or descent from an aircraft, if the Insured at any time during the aircraft's flight acted in any role other than as a passenger.

4. Any kind of war, declared or not, or by any act incident to a war or to an armed conflict involving the armed forces of one or more countries.

We will not pay this benefit if the Insured dies prior to his or her first birthday, or dies after the anniversary on which he or she is age 70.

Values This rider does not have cash or loan values.

Contract This rider, when paid for, is made a part of the policy, based on the application for the rider.

Incontestability of Rider We will not contest this rider after it has been in force during the lifetime of the Insured for 2 years from its date of issue.

Dates and Amounts When this rider is issued at the same time as the policy, we show the amount of ADB and the rider premium amount on the front page of the policy. The rider and the policy have the same date of issue.

When this rider is added to a policy which is already in force, we also put in an add-on rider. The add-on rider shows the date of issue and the amount of ADB. The rider premium amount is shown in a new Premium Schedule for the policy.

When Rider Ends You can cancel this rider as of the due date of a premium. To do this, you must send the policy and your signed notice to us within 31 days of that date. If this rider is still in effect on the anniversary on which the Insured is age 70, it will end on that date.

This rider ends if the policy ends or is surrendered. Also, this rider will not be in effect if the policy lapses or is in force as extended or paid-up insurance.

When this rider is part of an endowment policy, the rider will end on the day just before the endowment date, and will not be in effect if that date is deferred.

ABC LIFE INSURANCE COMPANY

Mary Smith
Secretary

John Johnson
President

THIS PAGE INTENTIONALLY LEFT BLANK

RIDER

DISABILITY WAIVER OF PREMIUM (WP)

Waiver of Premiums We will start to waive the premiums for this policy when proof is furnished that the Insured's total disability, as defined in this rider, has gone on for at least 6 months in a row.

If a total disability starts on or prior to the anniversary on which the Insured is age 60, we will waive all of the premiums which fall due during that total disability. If it goes on until the anniversary on which the Insured is age 65, we will make the policy fully paid-up as of that date, with no more premiums due.

If a total disability starts after the anniversary on which the Insured is age 60, we will waive only those premiums which fall due during that total disability, and prior to the anniversary on which the Insured is age 65.

Premiums are waived at the interval of payment in effect when the total disability started. While we waive premiums, all insurance goes on as if they had been paid. We will not deduct a waived premium from the policy proceeds.

Definition of Total Disability "Total Disability" means that, because of disease or bodily injury, the Insured can not do any of the essential acts and duties of his or her job, or of any other job for which he or she is suited based on schooling, training, or experience. If the Insured can do some but not all of these acts and duties, disability is not total and premiums will not be waived. If the Insured is a minor and is required by law to go to school, "Total Disability" means that, because of disease or bodily injury, he or she is not able to go to school.

"Total Disability" also means the Insured's total loss, starting while this rider is in effect, of the sight of both eyes or the use of both hands, both feet, or one hand and one foot.

Total Disabilities For Which Premiums Not Waived We will not waive premiums in connection with any of these total disabilities.

1. Those that start prior to the fifth birthday of the Insured, or start at a time when this rider is not in effect.

2. Those that are caused by an injury that is self-inflicted on purpose.

3. Those that are caused by any kind of war, declared or not, or by any act incident to a war or to an armed conflict involving the armed forces of one or more countries while the Insured is a member of those armed forces.

Proof of Total Disability Written notice and proof of this condition must be given to us, while the Insured is living and totally disabled, or as soon as it can reasonably be done. As long as we waive premiums, we may require proof from time to time. After we have waived premiums for 2 years in a row, we will not need to have this proof more than once each year. As part of the proof, we may have the Insured examined by doctors we approve.

Payment of Premiums Premiums must be paid when due, until we approve a claim under this rider. If a total disability starts during a grace period, the overdue premium must be paid before we will approve any claim.

Refund of Premiums If a total disability starts after a premium has been paid, and if it goes on for at least 6 months in a row, we will refund the part of that premium paid for the period after the policy month when that disability started. Any other premium paid and then waived will be refunded in full.

DISABILITY WAIVER OF PREMIUM (WP)

(continued)

Values This rider does not have cash or loan values.

Contract This rider, when paid for, is made a part of the policy, based on the application for the rider.

Incontestability of Rider We have no right to contest this rider after it has been in force during the lifetime of the Insured for 2 years from its date of issue, unless the Insured is totally disabled at some time within 2 years of the date of issue.

Dates and Amounts When this rider is issued at the same time as the policy, we show the rider premium amount on the front page of the policy. The rider and the policy have the same date of issue.

When this rider is added to a policy which is already in force, we also put in an add-on rider. The add-on rider shows the date of issue. The rider premium amount is shown in a new Premium Schedule for the policy.

When Rider Ends You can cancel this rider as of the due date of a premium. To do this, you must send the policy and your signed notice to us within 31 days of that date. If this rider is still in effect on the anniversary on which the Insured is age 65, it will end on that date.

This rider ends if the policy ends or is surrendered. Also, this rider will not be in effect if the policy lapses or is in force as extended or paid-up insurance.

ABC LIFE INSURANCE COMPANY

Mary Smith
Secretary

John Johnson
President

RIDER

POLICY PURCHASE OPTION (PPO)

Benefit The Owner can purchase a new policy on the Insured on each Scheduled Option Date or Special Option Date, without proof of insurability. The new policy will take effect as of the option date, with premiums based on the Insured's age and the Company's premium rates on that date. The face amount of the new policy may not be less than $10,000 or more than the Option Amount of the rider, except when a larger amount can be purchased on a Special Option Date.

During the 3 months prior to a Special Option Date, the Company provides term insurance on the Insured. The amount of this insurance is equal to the largest face amount of the new policy that can be purchased under this rider on that date.

Scheduled Option Dates The Scheduled Option Dates are the anniversaries on which the Insured is age 22, 25, 28, 31, 34, 37, 40, 43, and 46, and on which this rider is in effect. No new policy can be purchased on any Scheduled Option Date which has been cancelled by a prior Special Option Date purchase.

Special Option Dates A Special Option Date is the date 3 months after any of the events listed below.

1. The marriage of the Insured.
2. The birth of a living child to the Insured.
3. The legal adoption of a child by the Insured.

This rider must be in effect on the date the marriage, birth, or adoption takes place. Proof acceptable to the Company, that the event took place, may be required.

Each purchase of a new policy as of a Special Option Date cancels the next available Scheduled Option Date, except where 2 or more children are born or adopted on the same date. In this case, an amount of insurance can be purchased which equals the Option Amount times the number of these children. The number of Scheduled Option Dates cancelled by this amount of purchase is equal to the number of these children.

Savings Allowance The Company provides a savings allowance when a new policy is purchased. The amount of this allowance is on file with the insurance official in the state or district in which the policy is delivered. This allowance is used to reduce premiums that are due during the first policy year of the new policy. At the time of purchase, the Company will tell the Owner how much the total allowance is for the new policy.

Purchase of Policy The Owner's application for the new policy must also be signed by the Insured. The application and the first premium for the new policy, less the savings allowance, may be submitted to the Company during the 60 days before or the 31 days after the option date. However, these must be received by the Company while the Insured is living.

On an option date, if the Owner does not have an insurable interest in the life of the Insured that is acceptable to the Company, the Insured may purchase the new policy instead.

If the Insured dies prior to the option date, any new policy which has been applied for will not take effect, and the Company will refund any premium paid for it.

New Policy The new policy may be on any life, term-life, or endowment plan offered on the option date, for the face amount being purchased.

The new policy may not be on a plan which provides only term insurance or provides an increasing amount of insurance. It will have the same provisions and be subject to the same limitations on the Company's liability as are generally in the series of policies being issued on that date. The Insured's class of risk will be the same as it was for the rider.

POLICY PURCHASE OPTION (PPO)

(continued)

However, if this rider was issued with a policy in a preferred risk class, the new policy will be on a preferred risk basis only if it meets the Company's minimum amount and age limits for that class.

The time periods of the new policy which, relate to a suicide exclusion or to a contest of that policy, will start on the date of issue of this rider. However, in some cases the new policy may be issued with a rider or an additional amount of insurance which the Owner requested, and which required the Company's agreement. If this happens, the time periods for that rider or amount will start instead on the date of issue of the new policy.

Availability of Riders A waiver of premium rider can be made a part of the new policy if one is in effect under this policy on an option date. However, if the Insured has recovered from a total disability that had gone on for at least 6 months in a row, that rider can only be in a new policy for which premiums are payable for the rest of the Insured's life.

An accidental death benefit rider can be made a part of the new policy if one is in effect under this policy on an option date. The amount of that rider may not be more than the face amount of the new policy.

No other riders can be made a part of the new policy, unless the Company agrees.

Waiver of Premiums for New Policy If, on an option date, this policy has a waiver of premium rider in effect, and if the Insured is totally disabled and all conditions for waiver of premiums in that rider have been met, the Company will waive the premiums

for the new policy which fall due during that disability. The new policy must be on a plan with premiums payable for the rest of the Insured's life, and with the same premium interval as this policy.

Values This rider does not have cash or loan values.

Contract This rider, when paid for, is made a part of the policy, based on the application for the rider.

Incontestability of Rider The Company will not contest this rider after it has been in force during the lifetime of the Insured for 2 years from its date of issue.

Dates and Amounts When this rider is issued at the same time as the policy, the Company shows the Option Amount and the rider premium amount on the front page of the policy. The rider and the policy have the same date of issue.

When this rider is added to a policy which is already in force, the Company also puts in an add-on rider. The add-on rider shows the date of issue and the Option Amount. The rider premium amount is shown in a new Premium Schedule for the policy.

When Rider Ends The Owner can cancel this rider as of the due date of a premium. To do this, the policy and the Owner's signed notice must be sent to the Company within 31 days of that date. If this rider is still in effect on the anniversary on which the Insured is age 46, it will end on that date.

This rider ends if the policy ends or is surrendered. Also, this rider will not be in effect if the policy lapses or is in force as extended or reduced paid-up insurance.

ABC LIFE INSURANCE COMPANY

Mary Smith
Secretary

John Johnson
President

RIDER

OPTION TO PURCHASE PAID-UP ADDITIONS (OPP)

Benefit This rider provides you with the right to purchase new paid-up life insurance on the Insured. Any paid-up life insurance purchased under this rider is a paid-up addition, and no more premiums are due for this insurance. The amount of this insurance in force at the Insured's death will be part of the life insurance proceeds of the policy to which this rider is attached.

However, if the policy lapses or is surrendered, the values of any paid-up insurance under this rider will be included in the determination of any proceeds under the Options Upon Lapse provision in the policy.

Scheduled Payments Payments made on a scheduled basis must be received by us while the Insured is living and within 31 days of each of their due dates. Upon receipt of a scheduled payment, the new insurance will take effect as of its due date. If a scheduled payment is not received within 31 days of its due date, payments can no longer be made on a scheduled basis, unless we agree. However, this rider will remain in force, and unscheduled payments can still be made.

It may happen that you make a scheduled payment which is less than the scheduled amount. If this occurs, the amount of any subsequent scheduled payments cannot exceed that reduced payment, unless satisfactory evidence of insurability is furnished. However, we will not require this evidence of insurability if the total of all payments made during the policy year do not exceed the limitations stated in the What Insurance May be Purchased provision.

Unscheduled Payments Unscheduled payments may be made from time to time under this rider, but must be received while the Insured is living. Upon receipt of an unscheduled payment, the new insurance will take effect as of the date we receive the payment.

What Insurance May Be Purchased The amount of the payments made each year to purchase the new insurance is in addition to the premium payable for the policy. The amount of paid-up additions purchased by each payment is based on the net single premium rate for the Insured's age as of the most recent policy anniversary. Prior to the purchase of any insurance, all payments made under this rider are subject to an expense charge shown on the policy data page of the policy. Any payments made more than 31 days after a policy anniversary are subject to a reduction based on the amount of time since the anniversary and an interest rate which we set at the beginning of each calendar year. For the calendar year 1993, the rate is 9.5%. In each subsequent year, the rate will be equal to the Monthly Average Corporates yield shown in the Moody's Investors Services, Inc. or any successor to that service (the published monthly average), for the month of October of the prior calendar year. It may happen that the published monthly average ceases to be published. In this case, we will use a new basis approved by the insurance supervisory official in the state or district in which the policy is delivered. This reduction is in addition to the expense charge.

Unless we agree otherwise, the total of all payments in any given policy year cannot be more than 100% of the annual premium amount for the basic plan of insurance (excluding premiums for any riders and excluding the policy fee), based on a standard class of risk. In addition, unless we agree otherwise, each unscheduled payment or the total of all scheduled payments in a policy year must be at least $100, but in no event can a single scheduled payment be less than $10. Additional payments can be made from time to time, subject to the Excess Purchases provision of this rider. No insurance may be purchased under this rider after it ends, or while it is not in effect.

Waiver of Premium Benefit Not Applicable Scheduled payments for this rider will not be included in any amount being waived under any rider providing waiver of premiums in case of total disability. As long as premiums continue to be waived under any waiver rider, any insurance under this rider will continue, but no scheduled or unscheduled payments will be accepted to purchase new paid-up insurance.

Values The paid-up insurance under this rider has cash value and loan value, and is eligible for dividends. Cash values and net single premiums are based on the 1980 CSO Tables of Mortality (the male

OPTION TO PURCHASE PAID-UP ADDITIONS (OPP)

(continued)

table if the Insured is a male or the female table if the Insured is a female). Continuous functions are used. Interest is compounded at 4%. During the policy year in which a payment is made under this rider, the cash value of paid-up insurance purchased by that payment will be limited to the amount of that payment.

Reinstatement If this rider is reinstated, new paid-up insurance can be purchased only as of a date which is on or after the date of the reinstatement. Evidence of insurability acceptable to us will be required with any such reinstatement.

Contract This rider is made a part of the policy, based on the application for the rider.

Incontestability We will not contest this rider, or any new insurance which does not exceed the limitations specified in this rider, after the rider has been in force during the lifetime of the Insured for 2 years from its date of issue.

We will not contest any excess amount of paid-up insurance purchased in accordance with the Excess Purchases provision of this rider, for which we required evidence of insurability, after such insurance has been in force for 2 years from the date of purchase.

Suicide Exclusion Suicide of the Insured within 2 years of the date of issue of this rider, is not covered by this rider. In that event, this rider will end and the only amount payable will be all payments made under this rider, less any unpaid loan.

Excess Purchases You can make a payment under this rider which exceeds the limits stated in the rider, if we agree. Satisfactory evidence of insurability may be required for the excess amount of insurance. The application used to apply for this excess amount of

insurance will be attached to and made a part of the policy. The excess amount of insurance will be subject to the Incontestability and Suicide Exclusion provisions of this rider beginning as of the date that insurance is purchased.

Dates This rider and the policy have the same date of issue, unless the rider is added to a policy which is already in force. In this case, the date of issue of this rider is shown in an add-on rider which we put in the policy.

When Rider Ends You can cancel this rider as of any date. To do this, a signed notice must be sent to us within 31 days of that date.

This rider ends when no premium for paid-up insurance is paid by the second anniversary or for 3 anniversaries in a row, unless premiums for the policy are being waived on account of total disability. Any paid-up insurance in force when this rider ends will continue, if the policy continues, but no new insurance can be purchased unless this rider is reinstated. It may happen that the policy to which this rider is attached also includes a Dividend Option Term (DO T) rider. In this event, if this rider has ended for any of the reasons mentioned in this paragraph, this rider will automatically be restored after the fifth year the DO T rider has been in effect.

This rider will not be in effect if the policy is in force as paid-up insurance. In this case, the in force paid-up insurance under this rider will continue, except that the amount may be reduced to offset any outstanding policy loan.

Also, this rider will not be in effect if the policy is in force as extended insurance or if the policy lapses, ends or is surrendered.

OPTION TO PURCHASE PAID-UP ADDITIONS (OPP)

(continued)

Table of Cash Values

(per $1,000 of paid-up life insurance in force at attained age indicated)

ATTAINED AGE		ATTAINED AGE		ATTAINED AGE		ATTAINED AGE		ATTAINED AGE		ATTAINED AGE	
M	CASH VALUE	M	CASH VALUE	M	CASH VALUE	F	CASH VALUE	F	CASH VALUE	F	CASH VALUE
1	$ 87	34	$ 244	68	$ 645	1	$ 72	34	$ 209	68	$ 577
2	90	35	252	69	659	2	74	35	216	69	592
3	92	36	261	70	673	3	76	36	223	70	608
4	95	37	269	71	686	4	79	37	230	71	623
5	98	38	278	72	700	5	81	38	238	72	639
6	101	39	288	73	713	6	84	39	246	73	654
7	104	40	297	74	726	7	86	40	254	74	670
8	108	41	307	75	739	8	89	41	262	75	685
9	111	42	317	76	751	9	92	42	271	76	701
10	115	43	327	77	763	10	95	43	280	77	715
11	119	44	337	78	774	11	98	44	289	78	730
12	123	45	348	79	786	12	101	45	298	79	745
13	127	46	359	80	797	13	105	46	307	80	759
14	131	47	370	81	808	14	108	47	317	81	773
15	135	48	381	82	818	15	112	48	326	82	786
16	140	49	393	83	828	16	116	49	337	83	800
17	144	50	405	84	838	17	119	50	347	84	812
18	148	51	417	85	847	18	123	51	357	85	825
19	152	52	429	86	856	19	127	52	368	86	836
20	157	53	442	87	864	20	132	53	379	87	847
21	162	54	455	88	872	21	136	54	391	88	858
22	166	55	468	89	880	22	140	55	402	89	868
23	171	56	481	90	887	23	145	56	414	90	878
24	177	57	494	91	895	24	150	57	426	91	888
25	182	58	507	92	903	25	155	58	438	92	898
26	188	59	521	93	911	26	160	59	451	93	908
27	194	60	534	94	920	27	165	60	464	94	918
28	200	61	548	95	931	28	171	61	477	95	929
29	207	62	562	96	943	29	177	62	491	96	941
30	214	63	576	97	953	30	183	63	505	97	953
31	221	64	590	98	970	31	189	64	519	98	972
32	228	65	604	99	986	32	195	65	533	99	986
33	236	66	617	100	1,000	33	202	66	548	100	1,000
		67	631					67	563		

ABC LIFE INSURANCE COMPANY

By *Mary Smith*
Secretary

John Johnson
President

THIS PAGE INTENTIONALLY LEFT BLANK

ACCELERATION OF DEATH BENEFITS

This rider is attached to and is a part of the entire policy. Please read carefully.

NOTICE: The benefits paid under this rider may effect eligibility for Medicaid or other public assistance programs. The benefits paid may be taxable. If so, you or your beneficiary may incur a tax obligation. As with all tax matters you should consult your personal tax advisor to access the impact of this benefit.

The benefit paid under this rider will reduce the death benefit or amount due upon the death of the insured and other values in your policy.

This rider is non-participating.

DEFINITIONS

"Eligible amount" is the total of the following:

    1.   the Specified Amount, if death benefit Option 1 is in effect; or

    2.   the Specified Amount plus the cash value, if death benefit Option 2 is in effect.

"Accelerated amount" is the portion of the eligible amount you request:

    1.   The accelerated amount may not be more than the lesser of:

        (a) 75% of the eligible amount; or
        (b) $250,000.

    2.   The accelerated amount may never be less than $10,000.

"Accelerated death benefit" is the amount we pay under this rider. This amount is the accelerated amount adjusted for the following:

    1.   An interest discount factor will be applied to the accelerated amount based on the insured's reduced life expectancy not to exceed 12 months. The interest rate will be the rate used by us and will not exceed the rate charged on policy loans.

    2.   Future monthly deductions corresponding to the accelerated amount are based on the insured's life expectancy.

    3.   A portion or any outstanding policy loan balance will be deducted. The portion will be the outstanding policy loan balance multiplied by the ratio of the accelerated amount to the eligible amount.

    4.   The administrative fee in use by us on the date we receive your written request to pay an accelerated benefit.   The administrative fee will not exceed $500.00.

However, the accelerated death benefit will never be less than the cash surrender value of the policy, if any, multiplied by the ratio of the accelerated amount to the eligible amount.

The "effective date" is the Policy Date unless a later date is shown for this rider in the Policy Data.

The "insured" is the primary insured named in the Policy Data.

"Qualified Physician" is a person who is duly qualified, legally licensed in the United States and practicing within the scope of the license who is:

1. a physician or surgeon practicing medicine and surgery, and authorized to and uses the designation MD (Doctor of Medicine); or

2. a physician of osteopathy who uses the designation D.O. (Doctor of Osteopathy).

A qualified physician must be someone other than you or the insured, or a spouse, or step or adoptive or natural brother, sister, parent, grandparent, mother-in-law, father-in-law, or child of yours or the insured's or insured's spouse.

"You, your" is the Owner of this policy.

"We", us" is ABC Life Insurance Company.

"Terminally ill" means having a life expectancy of 12 months or less as determined by a Qualified Physician.

BENEFIT

Subject to the provisions of this rider and the policy, we will pay the accelerated death benefit to you if the insured is terminally ill. The eligible amount is determined as of the date we pay the accelerated death benefit.

EFFECT ON POLICY

If an accelerated death benefit is pard under this rider, the policy will stay in force according to the policy provisions. The following will be reduced in the same proportion as the ratio of the accelerated amount to the eligible amount:

1. the Specified Amount;
2. the policy fund;
3. the table of future surrender charges;
4. the minimum monthly premium.

The outstanding policy loan balance will be reduced by the portion deducted from the accelerated amount as described in the Definitions section of this rider.

A new Policy Data page showing the accelerated benefit payment will be issued and become part of the policy.

GENERAL PROVISIONS AND CONDITIONS

Your right to be paid under this rider is subject to the following:

1. You must submit a written request for the accelerated amount.

2. The accelerated amount is requested while the policy and this rider are in force.

3. The accelerated amount is requested after the incontestability period of the policy.

4. You provide evidence that satisfies us in a written statement signed by a qualified physician that:

   (a) the insured is terminally ill; and
   (b) the insured's life expectancy is not more than 12 months due to the severity and nature of the terminal illness; and
   (c) the diagnosis of the terminal illness was made after the effective date of this rider.

5. We receive consent that the benefit may be paid to you from any irrevocable beneficiary or assignee.

6. The policy must not be assigned except to us as security for a loan.

7. The main purpose of life insurance is to meet your estate planning needs. This rider provides for the accelerated payment of life insurance proceeds. It is not meant to cause you to involuntarily invade proceeds ultimately payable to the named beneficiary. Accelerated death benefits will be made available to you on a voluntary basis only. Therefore, you are not eligible for the benefit provided by this rider if you are required:

   (a) by law to use this option to meet the claims of creditors, whether in bankruptcy or otherwise; or

   (b) by a government agency to use this option in order to apply for, obtain, or keep a government benefit or entitlement.

8. We have the right to have the insured examined at our expense by a physician we choose.

9. This rider does not apply if the insured's illness is the result of an attempt to commit suicide, while any policy suicide exclusion provision is in effect.

10. The payment provided by this rider will be made only once under this policy.

11. The payment will be made in one lump sum to you. The total accelerated amounts under all policies issued by The ABC Life Insurance Company or its subsidiaries or affiliates on the life of the insured will not exceed $250,000.

12. If the death of the insured occurs before approval of the benefit or before the approved benefit is paid, no benefit will be payable under this rider. Our liability will discharged to the extent of any payment made or action taken prior to receipt of proof of the death of the insured.

13. This rider is subject to the terms of the policy incontestability provision.

14. This rider is subject to all the conditions and provisions of the policy, except as otherwise provided in this rider.

15. Only the insured under the base policy is covered by this rider. No coverage is provided for any other person covered by riders attached to the base policy.

16. Any refund of premiums payable as a result of the insured's suicide will not include the premiums for any accelerated amount paid under this rider.

TERMINATION

This rider will terminate if and when any of the following takes place:

1. the policy terminates; or
2. the policy lapses at the end of the Grace Period; or
3. a benefit is paid under this rider; or
4. we receive a written request to cancel this rider.

THE ABC LIFE INSURANCE COMPANY

Mary Smith

Secretary

John Johnson

President

Appendix E

Disability Income Insurance Policy

Insured	John A. Doe
Policy Number	LA R000000
Policy Date	07-01-00
Effective Date	07-01-00

Individual Disability Lifelong Disability ProtectionSM

DISABILITY INCOME POLICY

GUARANTEED RENEWABLE TO AGE 70. WE HAVE A LIMITED RIGHT TO CHANGE PREMIUMS.

This policy provides disability income benefits under stated conditions. Please refer to the policy provisions where we tell you when and how we will pay benefits. You will find an index of these provisions on Page 2.

Your policy cannot be cancelled by us, as long as the premium is paid on time.

TWENTY DAY RIGHT TO EXAMINE POLICY

Within 20 days after this policy is delivered to you or your representative, you may cancel the policy for any reason. To cancel this policy, you or your representative must mail or deliver the policy to our Home Office or to one of our authorized representatives. If this is done, the policy will be cancelled from the beginning and all of the premium paid will be refunded.

Satisfaction guaranteed or full premium refund.

RENEWAL

You may renew this policy on each policy anniversary until the policy anniversary when your age is 70 by paying each premium before the Grace Period ends. We reserve the right to adjust premiums for this policy form on a class basis. Any change in premium will be effective on your policy anniversary. We will send you written notice of any adjustment in premium at least 31 days in advance.

This policy becomes effective on the Effective Date shown on page 3.

This policy is renewable to age 70.

SPECIMEN

(Provisions may vary in certain states)

UNUM.

2211 Congress Street
Portland, Maine 04122

Reprinted with permission.

INDEX OF POLICY PROVISIONS

POLICY SCHEDULE

| Insured | John A. Doe | 07-01-00 | Policy Date |
| Policy Number | LA R000000 | 07-01-00 | Effective Date |

SUMMARY OF PREMIUM

The premium mode at issue is ANNUAL

Premiums are payable as follows:

BEGINNING	ANNUAL	SEMIANNUAL	QUARTERLY
07-01-2000	$536.80	$268.40	$134.20
07-01-2035	Premiums Cease		

SUMMARY OF COVERAGE GROUP 01

Form - INC95

Income Benefit Elimination period - 90 days

Maximum Income Benefit Period -To the later of (A) age 65 policy anniversary or (B) 24 months after disability payments begin.

EFFECTIVE DATE	MAXIMUM INCOME BENEFIT	ANNUAL PREMIUM	PREMIUM CEASE DATE
07-01-2000	$2,000	$498.60	07-01-2035

RIDER FORM	DESCRIPTION	RIDER DATE	BENEFIT AMOUNT	ANNUAL PREMIUM	PREMIUM CEASE DATE

Rider Premiums for the Premium Term are included in the Summary of Premium.

SUMMARY OF COVERAGE GROUP 02

Form - Disability Plus℠ Benefit

Disability Plus℠ Elimination period - 90 days

Disability Plus℠ Benefit Period -To the later of (A) age 65 policy anniversary or (B) 24 months after disability payments begin.

EFFECTIVE DATE	MAXIMUM DISABILITY PLUS BENEFIT	ANNUAL PREMIUM	PREMIUM CEASE DATE
07-01-2000	$2,000	$38.20	07-01-2035

RIDER FORM	DESCRIPTION	RIDER DATE	BENEFIT AMOUNT	ANNUAL PREMIUM	PREMIUM CEASE DATE

Rider Premiums for the Premium Term are included in the Summary of Premium.

Your choice of premium payment schedule.

You can add optional benefits to further customize coverage for your individual needs.

PREMIUMS

All premiums except the first premium are due on or before the due date. They are payable as stated on page 3.

Each premium will keep this policy in effect and continue coverage for the term shown.

The Grace Period is the 31 consecutive days that begin with the day a premium is due. We will keep this policy in effect and continue coverage during that time. If the premium is not paid during those 31 days, this policy and all coverage under this policy will terminate.

If we accept premium after the policy anniversary when your age is 70, we will keep this policy in effect and continue coverage until the end of the period for which we accept it.

If any premium is paid beyond the month in which you die or this policy terminates for some other reason, we will refund the amount of the unearned premium paid.

Premiums must be paid in United States currency.

REINSTATEMENT

Reinstatement is possible for up to six months.

If this policy terminates because a premium is not paid by the end of the Grace Period, you may apply to reinstate this policy at any time until the first unpaid premium is six months overdue.

In order to reinstate this policy, three requirements must be met. They are:

1. you must submit a reinstatement application with evidence of your insurability; and

2. we must approve the reinstatement application; and

3. you must submit the full amount of overdue premium.

If the reinstatement application is prepaid, we will issue a prepayment agreement. The date of the prepayment agreement will be the date the reinstatement application has been completed.

If we approve the reinstatement application, this policy will be reinstated on the approval date. If the overdue premium is paid without submitting a reinstatement application and we keep the premium without requesting a reinstatement application, within a reasonable time, this policy will be reinstated as of the date we received the premium. If we issue a prepayment agreement and do not approve or disapprove your reinstatement application

within 45 days from the date of the prepayment agreement, this policy will be reinstated on that 45th day.

If this policy is reinstated, it will only cover:

1. injury that occurs on or after the date this policy is reinstated; or

2. sickness which first manifests itself more than 10 days after this policy is reinstated.

It WILL NOT cover any injury or sickness which is excluded by name or description.

DEFINITIONS

GENERAL DEFINITIONS

Policy means the contract of insurance between you and us. This form, all applications, and any riders, endorsements, or amendments that are attached to it comprise the entire contract.

Coverage means a type or amount of benefit provided by this policy. Each benefit, each modification of that benefit for which we require evidence of insurability, and each reinstatement of that benefit is a separate coverage.

You and Your refer to the Insured named on page 3. It is the person whom we are insuring. The Insured cannot be changed.

We, our and us refer to UNUM Life Insurance Company of America.

Injury means bodily harm which is the direct result of an accident or trauma that occurs while your policy is in force and is not related to any other cause.

Sickness means an illness or condition which first manifests itself while your policy is in force.

Preexisting Condition means you have an injury or sickness that exists on the effective date of the coverage and, during the past five years:

1) was diagnosed; or

2) caused you to consult a health care provider; or

3) caused symptoms for which an ordinarily prudent person would have consulted a health care provider.

Mental Disorder means any disorder classified in the Diagnostic and Statistical Manual of Mental Disorders (DSM), published by the American Psychiatric Association which is most current on the date of disability, or its replacement. Such disorders include, but are not limited to, psychotic, emotional or behavioral disorders, or disorders related to stress or to substance abuse/dependency.

Medical Care means:

1. you personally visit a doctor as frequently as is medically required, according to standard medical practice; and

2. you are receiving appropriate treatment and care, according to generally accepted medical standards, by a doctor whose specialty is appropriate for your injury or sickness; and

3. such care is intended to return you to your Regular Occupation.

We may waive these requirements depending on the severity of your injury or sickness.

Doctor means:

1. a person performing tasks that are within the limits of his or her medical license; and

2. a person who is licensed to practice medicine and prescribe and administer drugs or to perform surgery; or

3. a person with a doctoral degree in Psychology (Ph.D. or Psy.D.) whose primary practice is treating patients; or

4. a person who is legally qualified medical practitioner according to the laws and regulations of the governing jurisdiction.

We will not recognize you, or anyone related to you by blood or marriage, as a doctor for a claim that you send to us.

INCOME BENEFIT DEFINITIONS

Maximum Income Benefit means the amount shown on page 3.

Maximum Income Benefit Period means the longest period of time we will make payments to you under the Income Benefit for any one period of disability. The Maximum Income Benefit Period is shown on page 3.

For the first 24 months of benefit payments, Regular Occupation means your occupation at the onset of disability. Long Term Own Occupation Protection can be provided in select situations through a policy rider.

Regular Occupation means the occupation you are routinely performing at the time the Income Benefit Elimination Period begins. However, after you have received 24 months of benefits due to the same disability, Regular Occupation then means any gainful occupation for which you are reasonably fitted by training, education or experience. If you are not employed at the beginning of a disability, Regular Occupation means any gainful occupation for which you are reasonably fitted by training, education or experience.

Gainful Occupation means any occupation that provides or can be expected to provide you an income at least equal to 60% of your Prior Monthly Earnings within 12 months of returning to full-time work in your Regular Occupation.

To work full time in your regular occupation means you are able to perform the material and substantial duties of your Regular Occupation and you work, or are able to work, approximately the same average number of hours per week as you were working in the 12 months before the disability began. However, if your average hours worked per week prior to disability exceeds 40, we will consider you to be working full time in your Regular Occupation if you are working, or are capable of working, at least 40 hours per week.

Income Benefit disability and Income Benefit disabled mean that, as a result of injury or sickness:

1. you are unable to perform the material and substantial duties of your regular occupation; or

2. you are able to perform some, but not all, of the material and substantial duties of your regular occupation; or

3. you are able to perform the material and substantial duties of your regular occupation, but you are not able to work full time in your Regular Occupation; and

No loss of income is required to satisfy the elimination period.

4. you are receiving Medical Care.

The suspension, revocation or surrender of a professional or occupational license or certification does not constitute disability.

Material and Substantial Duties means those duties that cannot be reasonably omitted or modified in order to perform your Regular Occupation.

Income Benefit Elimination Period means the number of days, stated on page 3, preceding the date benefits become payable, during which you are Income Benefit disabled. The Elimination Period begins on the first day that you are Income Benefit disabled.

Different elimination periods may apply to different coverages under this policy. The elimination period for each coverage is described on page 3.

There is no new elimination period for related disabilities occurring within 6 months of a previous Income Benefit disability.

If the Income Benefit disability ceases before you satisfy the elimination period and you become disabled again from the same cause within six months, we will combine those periods of disability to determine when benefits begin.

You may choose cash or accrual accounting to calculate Monthly Earnings.

Monthly Earnings means any salary, wages, commissions, bonuses and fees regularly earned for services performed by you.

If you own any part of a business or profession, Monthly Earnings also includes your share of business profits or losses (after deducting the usual and customary business expenses) plus any contributions on your behalf to a deferred compensation, pension or profit sharing plan. Usual and customary business expenses are those expenses which are deductible for federal income tax purposes based on the business fiscal year immediately prior to the start of disability.

Monthly Earnings does not include any forms of unearned income, such as dividends, interest, rent, royalties, annuities, distributions of deferred compensation or pension plans, sick pay, benefits received for disability under a formal wage or salary continuation plan or other disability plans.

Monthly Earnings may be accounted for on a cash or accrual basis. The same method must be used to determine the Prior Monthly Earnings and current Monthly Earnings during a period of disability.

Prior Monthly Earnings means the greater of:

1. your average Monthly Earnings for the 12 months immediately prior to the start of Income Benefit disability; or

2. your average Monthly Earnings for the full calendar year immediately prior to the start of Income Benefit disability.

Loss of Monthly Earnings means your Prior Monthly Earnings minus your Monthly Earnings in the month for which a benefit is claimed. Loss of Monthly Earnings must be caused solely by the injury or sickness which is causing the disability.

DISABILITY PLUS℠ DEFINITIONS

Maximum Disability Plus℠ Benefit means the amount shown on page 3.

Maximum Disability Plus℠ Benefit Period means the longest period of time we will make payments to you under the Disability Plus℠ benefit for any one period of disability. The Maximum Disability Plus℠ Benefit Period is shown on page 3.

Disability Plus℠ disability and Disability Plus℠ disabled mean that as a result of injury or sickness:

1. you are unable to perform two or more Activities of Daily Living without stand-by assistance; or

2. you are cognitively impaired; and

3. you are receiving Medical Care.

Disability Plus℠ Elimination Period means the number of days stated on page 3, preceding the date benefits become payable, during which you are Disability Plus℠ disabled. The Elimination Period begins on the first day that you are Disability Plus℠ disabled.

Different elimination periods may apply to different coverages under this policy. The elimination period for each coverage is described on page 3.

If the Disability Plus℠ disability ceases before you satisfy the elimination period and you become disabled again from the same cause within six months, we will combine those periods of disability to determine when benefits begin.

Activities of Daily Living (ADLs) are:

Bathing: the ability to wash yourself, either in the tub or shower or by sponge bath, with or without equipment or adaptive devices.

Dressing: the ability to put on and take off all garments and medically necessary braces or artificial limbs usually worn, and to fasten or unfasten them.

Toileting: the ability to get to and from and on and off the toilet, to maintain a reasonable level of personal hygiene and to care for clothing.

Transferring: the ability to move in and out of a chair or bed with or without equipment such as canes, quad canes, walkers, crutches or grab bars or other support devices including mechanical or motorized devices.

Continence: the ability to voluntarily control bowel and bladder function, or, in the event of incontinence, the ability to maintain a reasonable level of personal hygiene.

Eating: the ability to get nourishment into the body by any means once it has been prepared and made available to you.

Stand-by Assistance means you require the presence of another human being to ensure that all or part of an ADL may be completed or to ensure your safety.

Additional benefit amounts available to cover catastrophic disabilities under Disability Plus℠.

There is no new elimination period for related disabilities occurring within 6 months of a previous Disability Plus℠ disability.

Ability to perform Activities of Daily Living is the basis used to determine Disability Plus℠ disability.

Cognitive Impairment and Cognitively Impaired mean that you have suffered a deterioration or loss in your intellectual capacity which requires another person's assistance or verbal cueing to protect yourself or others as measured by clinical evidence and standardize tests which reliably measure your impairment. Such loss in intellectual capacity can result from injury, sickness, Alzheimer's Disease or similar form of senility or irreversible dementia.

BENEFITS

INCOME BENEFIT

We will pay an Income Benefit in any month after you have satisfied the Income Benefit Elimination Period that:

1. you are Income Benefit disabled; and
2. your disability is the result of the same injury or sickness which caused you to satisfy the Income Benefit Elimination Period; and
3. you have at least a 20% loss of Monthly Earnings as a result of that same injury or sickness.

The amount payable in any month will be determined by the following formula:

$$\frac{\text{Loss of Monthly Earnings}}{\text{Prior Monthly Earnings}} \times \begin{array}{l}\text{Maximum}\\ \text{Income}\\ \text{Benefit}\end{array}$$

If your loss of Monthly Earnings is greater than 80%, we will pay the Maximum Income Benefit for that month.

Income Benefit payments will cease once you are able to return to work full-time in your Regular Occupation.

Benefits payable in any month shall not exceed the Maximum Income Benefit. The Income Benefit will not be paid beyond the Maximum Income Benefit Period.

Successive Income Benefit Disabilities. A period of Income Benefit disability will be considered a continuation of a prior disability if:

1. it is from the same or related cause; and
2. it occurs within six months of the end of the prior period of Income Benefit disability.

If the new Income Benefit disability is considered a continuation of a prior Income Benefit disability, it will be considered an

extension of the prior disability and you will not need to satisfy a new elimination period.

If the period of Income Benefit disability is from a different or unrelated cause, or if it occurs more than six months after the end of the prior period of Income Benefit disability, it will be considered a new disability, subject to its own elimination period and maximum benefit period.

Waiver of Premium Benefit. After the Income Benefit disability has lasted for 90 days while this policy is in effect, we will waive the premium for this policy. We will refund premium already paid for that period on a pro-rata basis.

Waiver of Premium will cease once:

1. you have returned to work full time in your Regular Occupation; or
2. you are no longer eligible for an Income Benefit payment for that period of disability.

The Waiver of Premium benefit does not apply to any disability caused by a condition excluded from coverage by name or description.

DISABILITY PLUS℠ BENEFIT

We will pay the Maximum Disability Plus℠ Benefit in any month after you have satisfied the Disability Plus℠ Elimination Period that:

1. you are Disability Plus℠ disabled; and
2. your disability is the result of the same injury or sickness which caused you to satisfy the Disability Plus℠ Elimination Period.

Benefits payable in any month shall not exceed the Maximum Disability Plus℠ Benefit. The Disability benefit will not be paid beyond the Maximum Disability Plus℠ Benefit Period.

Successive Disability Plus℠ Benefit Disabilities. A period of Disability Plus℠ disability will be considered a continuation of a prior disability if:

1. it is from the same or related cause; and
2. it occurs within six months of the end of the prior period of Disability Plus℠ disability.

If the new Disability Plus℠ disability is considered a continuation of a prior Disability Plus℠ disability, it will be considered an extension of the prior disability and you will not need to satisfy a new elimination period.

Regardless of whether you are totally or residually disabled, Income Benefit payments are based on your percentage loss of earnings.

The full monthly Income Benefit will be paid if your loss of Monthly Earnings is greater than 80%.

During Income Benefit disability, your premium may be waived. All premiums paid from the date of loss will be refunded. Consecutive days of disability are not required.

The full monthly Disability Plus℠ benefit will be paid in the event of the loss of two or more ADLs (Activities of Daily Living).

If the period of Disability Plus℠ disability is from a different or unrelated cause, or if it occurs more than six months after the end of the prior period of Disability Plus℠ disability, it will be considered a new disability, subject to its own elimination period and maximum benefit period.

OTHER BENEFITS

Rehabilitation. We have a rehabilitation program to assist you to return to work. This program is offered as a service, and is voluntary on your part and on our part.

While you are receiving disability benefits, you may request or we may suggest a review of your medical and vocational documentation to determine if rehabilitation services might help you return to work.

If we determine that such a program is appropriate, we will develop a mutually agreed upon plan of rehabilitation that is beneficial to you and us. This plan may include, but is not limited to:

- Coordination with your employer to assist you to return to work;
- Coordination of medical services;
- Evaluation of adaptive equipment to allow you to work;
- Occupational evaluation;
- Business/financial planning;
- Job development and placement;
- Retraining for a new occupation.

If we determine that such a program is appropriate, we will pay reasonable expenses for such items as tuition, books, training programs, or additional living expenses. The actual expenses covered and the terms of the plan will be subject to mutual agreement. Our agreement will be outlined in a written plan of rehabilitation. Benefits will continue as provided by this policy unless they are modified by the plan of rehabilitation.

Worksite Modification Benefit. A worksite modification might be what is needed to allow you to perform the material and substantial duties of your Regular Occupation. One of our designated professionals will assist you and your employer to identify a modification we mutually agree is likely to help you remain at work or return to work. This mutual agreement will be in writing and must be signed by you, your employer, and us.

When this occurs, we will reimburse your employer for the cost of the modification, up to the lesser of:

- $5,000; or
- Two times your Maximum Income Benefit.

This benefit is payable only once over the lifetime of this policy.

Lifetime Continuation Provision.

This policy may be exchanged for an individual long term care policy issued by us without submitting evidence of medical or financial insurability, at the following times:

1. on or after age 61, if you choose to terminate this disability policy and you are not then Income Benefit disabled or Disability Plus℠ disabled under any of the terms of this policy; or
2. on or after age 65 if you are disabled under the provisions of this disability policy and have received the maximum benefits allowable under this disability policy; or
3. the policy anniversary when your age is 70.

The long term care contract will be issued subject to the following terms:

1. the policy will be the individual long term care policy that we offer when the exchange is made;
2. the policy will meet or exceed all applicable federal and state minimum standards in effect for such contracts on the date the exchange is made;
3. the premium for the long term care policy will be the same as the premium paid for this disability policy in the year immediately prior to the exchange. The monthly benefit for the long term care policy will be the amount that this premium will purchase based on the long term care rates we are then charging for your age on the date the exchange is made.

EXCLUSIONS AND LIMITATIONS

This policy does not pay benefits which are based on injury or sickness caused by, contributed to by or which result from:

1. war or an act of war, whether declared or undeclared; or
2. intentionally self-inflicted injury; or
3. your commission of or your attempt to commit a crime under a state or federal law, or your engagement in an illegal occupation; or
4. the suspension, revocation or surrender of your professional or occupational license or certification.

Flexible rehabilitation program.

Helps employers with worksite modification expenses.

Guaranteed transformation to a UNUM Individual Long Term Care policy.

These are the conditions under which benefits are excluded or limited.

No benefits will be payable for any period of disability in which you are incarcerated in a penal or correctional institution for a period of 30 consecutive days or longer.

Preexisting Condition Limitation.

This policy does not pay benefits for a preexisting condition if:

1. if the preexisting condition is not disclosed or is misrepresented in the application; and

2. during the first two years after the effective date of coverage, the preexisting condition:

a. caused you to consult a health care provider; or

b. caused symptoms for which an ordinarily prudent person would have consulted a health care provider.

Mental Disorder Limitation.

This policy will pay benefits for a maximum of 24 months during the life of the policy for Income Benefit disability or Disability Plus℠ disability, caused by a mental disorder. However, we will pay benefits, subject to the Income Benefit and Disability Plus℠ Maximum Benefit Periods, so long as you are confined as an inpatient in a hospital or institution and under Medical Care.

Hospital or institution means an accredited facility licensed to provide care and treatment for the condition causing the disability. "Hospital or institution" does not include a rest, nursing or convalescent home.

Mental Disorder Limitation does not apply to all conditions.

We will not apply the Mental Disorder Limitation to dementia if it is a result of:

■ stroke;

■ trauma;

■ viral infection;

■ Alzheimer's disease; or

■ other conditions which are not usually treated by a mental health provider or other qualified provider using psychotherapy, psychotropic drugs, or other similar methods of treatment.

CLAIM INFORMATION

How to File a Claim. To make a claim under this policy, the following steps must be taken. You must:

1. Give Notice of Claim (someone must notify us that disability has started as defined in this policy);

2. File Proof of Loss (you, or someone acting on your behalf must fully complete and return the claim form and attached authorization provided by us);

3. Promptly and fully complete and return any other forms or requests for information we require, including personal and/or business federal tax returns, if requested.

Failure to comply with these requirements may impede or delay our ability to process your claim. No benefits will be payable if we are unable, as a result of your failure to comply with these requirements, to evaluate your claim.

We will evaluate the claim and either:

1. Pay the benefits specified in the policy; or

2. Notify you and any loss payee that benefits are not payable and why; or

3. Notify you that additional information is required before a final claim determination can be made.

Conditions and Time Limits. In order for benefits to be considered for payment, there are some conditions and time limits which each of us must meet. They are:

1. We must be given the Notice of Claim within 30 days after the elimination period begins, or as soon as reasonably possible.

2. We will furnish claim forms within 15 days after we receive Notice of Claim. If the forms are not received within 15 days, send us proof of what happened and the extent of the sickness or injury.

3. The claim forms and other information requested by us (Proof of Loss) must be completed and furnished to us within 90 days after each month for which a benefit is payable. However, failure to furnish such proof within 90 days will not reduce or nullify the claim if proof is furnished as soon as reasonably possible within one year after the 90 days. If you are legally unable to notify us, the one year limit does not apply.

4. You must undergo a medical examination, functional capacity examination and/or psychiatric examination, including any related tests as are reasonably necessary to the performance of the examination by a doctor or specialist appropriate for the condition at such time and place and with such frequency as we reasonably require. We reserve the right to select the examiner. We will pay for the examination, including the costs associated with your travel to the examination, if the examination cannot be conducted locally.

5. You must meet with our representative for a personal interview or review of records at such time and with such frequency as we reasonably require.

6. We must be given the information which we need to determine if a benefit is payable and how much that benefit should be. We may require relevant portions of federal income tax returns for you or your business, income statements, vouchers for overhead expenses, and other statements or reports of receipts and payments. We may also require evidence that you were liable for an overhead expense before disability began.

How and When We Pay Benefits. We will pay benefits due under this policy in United States currency. For periods of disability of less than a month, we will pay 1/30th of the monthly benefit for each day of disability.

We will not pay any benefit until we have sufficient Proof of Loss. When we have determined that the claim is payable, we will pay promptly according to the Benefits provision. If any amount is accrued and unpaid when our liability terminates, we will pay it immediately.

Upon acceptance of liability of your claim, the first disability payment will be due one month from the date the appropriate Elimination Period is satisfied. Benefits accumulate and are paid on a monthly basis. No benefits are due or payable for the Elimination Period.

We will pay all benefits to the loss payee if living, otherwise, we will pay you. If you die while you are entitled to receive benefits, we will pay any remaining benefit and any unearned premium to your estate.

GENERAL PROVISIONS

The Contract. This policy represents the entire contract between you and us. Statements by agents or brokers are not part of this contract. Only an executive officer of this Company can approve a change in this policy. The approval must be in writing and be endorsed on or attached to this policy. No one else can change this policy or waive any of its conditions.

Unless we tell you otherwise, years, months and anniversaries that we refer to are calculated from the Policy Date shown on page 3.

Time Limit on Certain Defenses. Except for fraudulent misstatements, we will not contest the policy based on statements made by you in the application for a coverage provided under this policy after that coverage has been in effect for two years.

If disability begins after a coverage has been in effect for two years from the effective date of that coverage, we will not reduce or deny a claim which is based on that disability because of a preexisting condition unless the condition is excluded from coverage by name or description.

"Contest" means that we question the validity of coverage under this policy by letter to you. This contest is effective on the date we mail the letter and refund the premium to you.

Conformity with State Statutes. If any provision of this policy conflicts with the statutes of the state where you reside on the effective date of that provision, it is amended to conform with the minimum requirements of those statutes.

Your state laws prevail.

Legal Actions. No one may start legal action to recover on this policy until 60 days after written Proof of Loss has been given to us. Legal action must be started within three years after the written Proof of Loss is required to be furnished.

Misstatement of Age. If your age has been misstated, any benefit payable will be changed to the amount which the premium paid would have bought for the correct age.

If we accept premium for a coverage which we would not have issued or which would have ceased according to the correct age, our only liability is to refund the premium for the period not covered.

Owner. You own this policy. You have all of the rights and privileges granted by this policy while it is in effect. Some of your ownership rights are:

1. the right to continue or terminate this policy;

2. the right to name someone else (a loss payee) to receive the benefits of this policy;

3. the right to suspend this policy while you are in military service; and

4. the right to assign any or all rights under this policy.

You may reduce the amount of your coverage at any time. Premium will be recomputed for the reduced amount based on your age and premium class on the effective dates of the coverages. The reduction will be effective on the date we receive your written request at our Home Office.

Loss Payee. If you decide to have someone else receive policy benefits, you must notify us in writing on a form satisfactory to us. The notice will be effective when we receive it at our Home Office.

Assignment. You may assign any or all ownership rights to someone else. The assignment must be in writing and must specify the rights which are assigned and for how long. The loss payee is not changed by an assignment unless the assignment specifically names a new loss payee. When an assignment is in effect, *"you"* and *"your"* refer to the assignee in provisions which describe ownership rights.

No assignment is binding on us until the original or an acceptable copy is received at our Home Office. We are not responsible for the validity or effect of any assignment.

SPECIMEN

Glossary

A

abstract: A brief history of title to land.

accelerated death benefit: Under certain circumstances, a percentage of the policy's face amount, discounted for interest, can be paid to the insured prior to death.

accidental death benefit: An endorsement that pays the beneficiary an additional benefit if the insured dies from an accident.

accounting: The function of recording, classifying, and interpreting financial information.

accounts receivable insurance: Indemnifies for losses that are due to an inability to collect from open commercial account debtors because records have been destroyed by an insured peril.

accumulation units: Used with variable annuities purchased over time. The value of a unit fluctuates according to the performance of the investment portfolio, so a premium will buy varying numbers of units each time.

activities of daily living: Activities—such as eating, bathing, toileting, transferring, dressing, and continence—that trigger payment in a long-term care insurance policy, if at least some of them cannot be performed by the insured.

acts of God: Perils that cannot reasonably be guarded against, such as floods and earthquakes.

acts of negligence of the shipper: Causes of loss for which the carrier is not liable, such as improper loading or packing.

actual cash value (ACV): The replacement cost of property less allowance for depreciation.

actual loss ratio: The ratio of losses incurred to premiums earned actually experienced in a given line of insurance in a previous time period.

actual total loss: Loss occurring when property is completely destroyed.

actuarial cost assumptions: Assumptions about rates of investment earnings, mortality, turnover, salary increase patterns, probable expenses, and distribution or actual ages at which employees are likely to retire. These assumptions determine the choice of actuarial cost methods.

actuarial cost methods: Methods for computing how much money must be contributed each year to fund promised pensions.

additional insureds: Persons who have an insurable interest in the property/person covered in a policy and who are covered against the losses outlined in the policy. They may receive less coverage than the primary named insured.

additional living expenses: Consequential property insurance that offers coverage of additional living expenses when insured property is untenantable because of an insured peril.

add-on plan: An automobile insurance system in which injured parties can collect from their own insurers for their injuries just as in no-fault, but with no restrictions on the ability to sue.

administrator: A court-appointed individual who handles the administrative duties of the deceased's estate when the deceased has died without a will.

adverse selection: The tendency of insureds who know that they have a greater than average chance of loss to seek to purchase more than an average amount of insurance.

affirmative warranty: A warranty that must exist only at the time the contract is first put into effect.

agency agreement: An agreement between an insurance company and an agent, granting the agent authority to write insurance from that company. It specifies the duties, rights, and obligations of both parties.

agreed amount clause: Substitutes an agreed amount of coverage in place of coinsurance clause. A very good endorsement to use to manage coinsurance requirements.

aggregate deductible: A type of deductible that applies for an entire year in which the insured absorbs all losses until the deductible level is reached, at which point the insurer pays for all losses over the specified amount.

aggregate dollar limits: Limits that restrict payments to a maximum amount on any one group of items.

aggregate limits: A yearly limit, rather than a "per occurrence" limit. Once an insurance company has paid up to the limit, it will pay no more during that year.

aleatory contract: A legal contract in which the outcome depends on an uncertain event.

allocated plans: A type of pension funding in which specified employees are identified and funding is allocated to them.

American Agency System: A distribution system for insurance in which the agent, called a local agent, is an independent retailer representing several different insurers.

ancillary charges: In hospital insurance, covered charges other than room and board.

annual-premium annuity: An annuity whose purchase price is paid in annual installments.

annuitant: An individual receiving benefits under an annuity.

annuity: A contract that provides for the liquidation of a sum of money through a series of payments over a specified period of time.

annuity certain: An annuity that is payable for a specified period of time, without regard to the life or death of the annuitant.

annuity units: A measure used in valuing a variable annuity during the time it is being paid to the annuitant. Each unit's value fluctuates with the performance of an investment portfolio.

anticoercion statutes: The laws that prohibit lending agencies from requiring the placing of insurance with the agency as a condition of granting a loan.

any occupation for which reasonably suited: A definition of disability in which insureds are considered to be disabled if unable to perform the duties of any occupation suitable to their experience and educational background.

any willing provider (AWP) laws: State laws that force health care networks to include all health care providers who agree to the networks' terms and fee structures.

apportionment clauses: Limitations on the insurer's liability in the event that more than one insurance contract covers the loss.

assessable policy: A policy subject to additional charges, or assessments, on all policyholders in the company.

assign: To use life insurance policy benefits as collateral for a loan.

assignee: The party to whom the rights of the insured under a policy are transferred.

assignment: A clause that allows the transfer of rights under a policy from one person to another, usually by means of a written document.

assignor: The party granting the transfer of the insured's rights to the assignee.

asymmetric information: Knowledge about loss potential that is possessed by one party, usually the insured, and is unavailable to the other party, usually the insurer.

attorney-in-fact: The chief executive officer of a reciprocal insurer, using a power of attorney to bind the members of the group to mutually enforceable contracts of insurance.

attractive nuisance doctrine: A legal doctrine that increases the degree of care owed to a child; greater than ordinary care is required to a child who is a trespasser.

automatic coverage: An insurer agrees to cover accidents from all machinery of the same type as that specifically listed in the endorsement.

automatic premium loan provision: A life insurance clause under which cash values are automatically borrowed to pay premiums if regular premiums are not paid when due.

automatic treaty: An agreement whereby the ceding company is required to cede some certain amounts of business and the reinsurer is required to accept them.

average adjusters: A name applied to claims adjusters in the field of marine insurance.

average indexed monthly earnings (AIME): A figure representing an individual's average earnings, calculated from 1950 or the year in which the individual turned 22 to the year prior to the individual's attaining the age of 62.

aviation hazard exclusion: Eliminates coverage for death from many aviation activities other than as a fare-paying passenger on a commercial aircraft.

B

bailment: A situation in which one has entrusted personal property to another.

bare wall doctrine: A legal doctrine for condominium unit owners. It covers everything inside the bare wall of the unit.

basic health insurance policy: Hospital insurance, surgical insurance, and regular medical expense insurance.

basic premium: Part of retrospective premium that includes administrative and risk transfer loading of insurer.

beneficiary: A person named in a life insurance policy to receive the death proceeds.

bid bond: A surety bond guaranteeing that the bidder will sign the contract and post a construction bond.

bind: In property and liability insurance, the agent customarily is given the authority to accept offers from prospective insureds without consulting the insurer; in such cases, the agent is said to *bind* the insurer.

binder: A temporary insurance contract that becomes effective immediately.

binomial formula: An equation for estimating the likely number of losses, given a stated probability of loss and a number of loss exposures.

blanket bond: A fidelity bond that covers all employees of a given class and may also cover perils other than infidelity.

blanket coverage: Property at several locations or all property at a given location is insured under a single item.

blanket position bond: A blanket bond with a penalty ranging from $2,500 to $100,000 that applies to each employee.

block policy: A type of inland marine insurance usually offering open perils coverage to "floating" property, i.e., property subject to being moved from one location to another.

Blue Cross and Blue Shield associations: Nonprofit organizations set up to allow their subscribers (insureds) to prepay some types of health care expenses. Blue Cross groups cover hospital expenses; Blue Shield groups cover physicians' services.

boiler and machinery insurance: Coverage for explosions caused by steam boilers, compressors, engines, electrical equipment, flywheels, air tanks, and furnaces. Prevention of loss is emphasized even more than indemnification of loss.

bond: A legal instrument whereby one party agrees to reimburse another party should this person suffer loss because of some failure by the person bonded.

bottomry contract: An ancient version of an ocean marine insurance contract in which a ship was considered security for a loan.

broad form: One of three types of hold-harmless agreements, in which the transferee is responsible for all losses arising out of particular situations, regardless of fault.

broad form property damage liability program: A broad property damage policy under which the "care, custody, and control" exclusion is liberalized. It gives specific details on what property is covered and under what terms.

broad named perils: Fire, lightning, explosions, windstorm and hail, smoke, riot or civil commotion, vandalism, sprinkler linkage, sinkhole collapse, volcanic action, falling objects; the weight of ice, sleet, and snow; and accidental discharge of water or steam.

broker: A salesperson who is the legal representative of the client for the purpose of securing insurance or other services.

building and personal property coverage form (BPP): A form providing the definitions of all property insured, as well as any limitations or extensions of coverage.

burglary: The unlawful taking of property from within premises, entry to which has been obtained by force, leaving visible marks of entry.

Business Automobile Policy (BAP): Coverage for the auto liability and property damage needs of corporations and owners of large trucks.

business income insurance: Coverage for the reduction in revenue in the event of an insured peril.

business pursuit: Continued or regular activity for the purpose of earning a livelihood.

buy-sell agreements: Agreements stating that a deceased owner's share in a firm is to be purchased by one or more specified individuals at a given price during the estate settlement process.

C

calendar-year deductible: Covered losses accumulate throughout the calendar year until they exceed the deductible. After that point, the insured receives reimbursement.

cancellable: A health policy that can be cancelled by the insurer at any time for any reason.

capitation basis: Payment of a specified, periodic amount based on the number of patients for which a physician is responsible, regardless of the amount of medical services provided to each one.

captive insurer: A type of insurer that is generally formed and owned by potential insureds to meet their own risk financing needs.

cash balance pension plans: Variation of a defined benefit pension, in which individual accounts are used to make the plan appear more like a defined contribution pension arrangement.

cash loan credit insurance: Government agencies, such as the VA and FHA, sponsor programs to insure cash loans made by banks to individuals and certain businesses that could not obtain credit otherwise.

cash refund guarantee: An annuity guaranteeing to pay in cash to beneficiaries an amount equal to the difference between the original premium and the sum of the payments made at the time of an annuitant's death.

cash value: The savings element that accumulates with some life insurance policies.

cash value option: An option in life insurance policies permitting the insured to take the cash value of the policy on surrender.

ceding company: An insurer, also called a primary insurer, that passes on to other insurers some part of its risk under insurance policies it has accepted.

cession: A reinsurance term meaning that portion of a risk that is passed on to reinsurers by ceding companies.

chance of loss: The long-term chance of occurrence or relative frequency of loss. Expressed by the ratio of the number of losses likely to occur compared to the larger number of possible losses in a given group.

charitable deduction: A deduction from estate taxes allowed if estate assets are left to charitable organizations.

chief risk officer (CRO): New position within some organizations, denoting the responsibility for coordinating an enterprise risk management strategy.

choice no-fault systems: Automobile insurance system in which people can choose to purchase no-fault insurance and give up some rights to sue, or purchase traditional liability insurance and keep full rights to sue.

civil law: Legal proceedings directed toward wrongs against individuals and organizations. Breach of contract is an example of a civil wrong.

claims-made policy: A policy wherein the insurer pays for claims made during the year. The event giving rise to the claim may or may not occur in a prior year.

claims management: The functions performed in handling loss claims.

class mutuals: Mutual insurers specializing in a given line or lines of insurance business.

class rating method: A method of quoting uniform rates for certain categories of exposure by reference to a rate manual.

coefficient of variation: The standard deviation expressed as a percentage of the mean.

coinsurance: A clause that requires the insured to insure to value or share the loss with the insurance company.

coinsurance cap: A health insurance policy provision that limits the maximum annual amount of coinsurance an insured will have to pay.

collateral source rule: When assessing damages, courts may ignore other sources from which a plaintiff may be entitled to receive compensation.

collision: Upset of the covered auto and nonowned auto and/or its impact with another vehicle or object.

combined ratio: The sum of the expense ratio (ratio of expenses incurred to premiums written) and the loss ratio (ratio of losses incurred to premiums earned).

commercial blanket bond: A blanket bond that has a penalty ranging upward from $10,000 that applies to any one loss.

commercial general liability (CGL): A business liability policy designed for a wide variety of business uses, covering bodily injury and property damage liability losses resulting from conditions of the premises, business operations, products, and completed operations; also provides coverage for liability arising out of various intentional torts.

Commercial Package Policy (CPP): A policy offered by the insurance industry; covers most types of property-liability losses.

commercial umbrella: A liability policy designed to cover catastrophic losses.

common disaster clause: A life insurance clause stating what happens to life insurance proceeds if named beneficiaries die in a common accident.

common law: The unwritten law that is based on custom, usage, and court decisions; different from statutory law, which consists of laws passed by legislatures.

comparative negligence: The legal principle that requires parties in a negligence action to share the loss in accordance with the degree of negligence.

completed operations liability: The liability of a contractor for completed work that the owner has accepted or for work abandoned by the contractor.

completion bond: A surety bond guaranteeing that the person who borrows the money for a project will use the money only for the project and will turn over to the lender the completed project.

comprehensive: A major medical contract that replaces basic health coverages and insures all medical expenses within one policy.

comprehensive personal liability (CPL): Liability coverage for individuals that includes bodily injury and property damage.

compulsory insurance laws: Laws that require that auto liability insurance with at least specified minimum limits be purchased before a vehicle can be licensed or registered.

concealment: The failure of an applicant to reveal, before the insurance contract is made, a fact that is material to the risk.

concurrent causation: A legal doctrine that says if two perils (one excluded and one not excluded) occur and cause a loss, coverage applies.

concurrent loss control: Activities that take place at the same time as losses to reduce their severity.

conditional contract: A contract, such as an insurance contract, requiring that certain acts be performed if recovery is to be made.

conditional receipt: A document given to an applicant for life insurance stating that the company's acceptance is contingent upon determination of the applicant's insurability.

conditionally renewable: A policy that can be cancelled or have the premiums raised by the insurer on a specific anniversary date, subject to certain reasons written into the policy.

conditions: Circumstances under which an insurance contract is in force. Breach of the conditions is grounds for refusal to pay the loss.

consequential damage endorsement: Coverage for losses incurred as a result of the failure of an insured object on the insured's premises.

consequential losses: Losses other than property damage that occur as a result of physical loss to a business—for example, the cost of maintaining key employees to help reorganize after a fire.

consideration: In an insurance contract, the specified premium and an agreement to the provisions and stipulations that follow.

constructive total loss: Loss occurring when property is not completely destroyed, but when it would cost more to restore it than it is worth.

consumer-driven health care: An attempt to make people better consumers of health care by giving them financial incentives to control costs, as well as providing them the information they need to make sound health care decisions.

contingent beneficiary: A person named in a life insurance contract to receive the benefits of the policy if other named beneficiaries are not living.

contingent business income insurance: Coverage for losses that result from losses to a supplier or customer on whom the firm depends.

continuance tables: A tool used to help gauge the likely severity of disability for personal risk management purposes.

continuation provisions: Contractual rights regarding the renewal of a health insurance policy.

continuous: Describes variables that can take on any value within a certain interval or range.

contract: An agreement embodying a set of promises that are enforceable by law.

contract construction bond: A surety bond guaranteeing that the principals will complete their work in accordance with the terms of the construction contracts.

contract of adhesion: A contract, such as an insurance contract, in which any ambiguities or uncertainties in the wording will be construed against the drafter (the insurer).

contractors' equipment floater: Insures mobile equipment, such as tractors, steam shovels, drilling equipment, etc., whether it is owned, leased, or borrowed.

contracts without a time element: Insure losses resulting from fire in which the loss cannot be measured either by direct damage by fire or in terms of elapsed time.

contractual liability: Liability arising from contractual agreements in which it is stated that some losses, if they occur, are to be borne by specific parties.

contributory: An employee benefit program that requires the employee to pay part of the cost.

contributory negligence: Partial guilt or negligence in a civil lawsuit where both parties are to blame.

conversion clause: A clause in a group life or health insurance contract allowing the employee leaving a group to convert group coverage to an individual policy regardless of the status of the employee's health.

convertible: A term policy that can be converted to permanent coverage rather than expiring on a specific date.

coordination of benefits (COB) provisions: A clause in a health insurance policy requiring consideration of other sources of benefits in determining the amount of benefits due under an existing contract.

copay: A small fee charged to patients that is actually a deductible applied on a per-service basis.

cost-of-living rider: An endorsement that automatically increases the amount of coverage by the same percentage the Consumer Price Index has risen since policy issue.

cost of risk: The sum of (1) outlays to reduce risks, (2) the opportunity cost of activities forgone due to risk considerations, (3) expenses of strategies to finance potential losses, and (4) the cost of reimbursed losses.

cost shifting: The practice of assigning higher hospital charges to some patients in order to cover the cost of care provided free of charge to indigents.

cost-to-repair basis: The cost to replace property after a loss but perhaps not with like materials and labor.

covered auto: (1) Any vehicle in the declarations; (2) a private passenger auto, pickup truck, or van purchased during the policy period, provided the insured requests coverage within 30 days of ownership; (3) any owned trailer; and (4) any trailer or auto used as a substitute for one of the above while it is temporarily out of commission.

credibility: A measurement that shows the degree to which an insurer may rely on statistical observations in making rates or rate revisions.

credit insurance: The insurance that responds to losses caused by failure of debtors to pay accounts when due; sometimes called bad-debt insurance.

credit life insurance: Life insurance arranged in an amount needed to pay a debt in the event of death of the borrower.

credit shelter trust: A trust wherein part of an estate is placed in trust when the first person dies in order to decrease the amount of estate taxes payable upon the second death.

criminal law: Legal proceedings directed toward wrongs against society,

such as rape, murder, and robbery. Charges are made by a government body, and the guilty party is subject to fine and/or imprisonment.

currently insured: Status under OASDHI in which one may qualify for limited benefits for only short-time coverage under the law.

custodial nursing homes: Institutions that provide personal services, such as assistance with bathing, dressing, and eating, with no medical services provided.

D

debit insurance: *See* industrial life.

decedent: A deceased estate owner.

declarations: The section of an insurance policy, usually the first page, that provides information such as the policy number, the insured's name and address, the agent's name, etc.

decreasing term: Term life insurance in which the amount of coverage declines during the period for which it is issued.

deductible: A definite dollar amount to be borne by the insured before the insurer becomes liable for payment under the terms of the contract.

defensive medicine: The practice of performing extra procedures and tests in addition to those that are probably necessary for a given patient in an attempt to avoid malpractice litigation.

deferred annuity: Benefits that begin at some specified time after the annuity is purchased.

deferred profit-sharing plans: The sharing of employer profits with employees on a tax-advantaged basis.

Deficit Reduction Act of 1984 (DEFRA): A federal law governing how life insurers will pay income tax.

defined benefit plan: A pension plan with a formula that specifies the funds to be contributed to the plan.

defined contribution pension: A retirement plan in which the employer's annual contribution to the person is specified, and the exact amount of the eventual retirement benefit is left undetermined until each person retires.

degree of risk: Relative variation of actual from expected losses.

dental insurance: A health insurance contract providing reimbursement for specified dental expenses.

dependent life: Group term life insurance covering an employee's dependent.

deposit insurance program: A government credit insurance program that insures accounts held in insured institutions.

direct loss: A loss that stems directly from an unbroken chain of events leading from an insured peril to the loss.

direct response: A system to distribute insurance to customers through direct mail, telephone, television, Internet, or other methods without the use of intermediaries.

direct writers: Insurers using a distribution system in which independent agents are bypassed and coverage is offered to the public through salaried or commissioned employees who serve as company-controlled agents, sometimes referred to as exclusive agents or captive agents.

disability income insurance: Health insurance that provides periodic payments if the insured becomes disabled as a result of illness or accident.

disability loss: The inability of a person to work because of an illness or injury.

disappearing deductible: A deductible used in property insurance in which the size of the deductible decreases as the size of the loss increases. At a given level of loss, the deductible completely disappears.

discrete: Describes variables that can take on a finite or countable value (such as 1, 2, 3, . . . etc.).

diversification: Process of spreading risk through a firm's involvement in various businesses or through the location of its operations in different geographic areas.

dollar threshold: The dollar limit above which an insured may bring a tort action in no-fault insurance.

domestic merchandise credit insurance: Protection for sellers against insolvency of domestic debtors on credits arising out of the sale of merchandise on an unsecured basis.

domino theory: A theory originally developed by H. W. Heinrich that lists the chain of factors leading to employee accidents as follows: (1) heredity and environment, (2) personal fault, (3) an unsafe act or existence of a physical hazard, (4) accident, and (5) injury.

donor: In a trust arrangement, the individual transferring property.

dramshop exclusion: An exclusion in liability insurance policies for liability resulting from distribution of alcoholic beverages.

driving while intoxicated (DWI): Generally, drivers are considered intoxicated if their blood alcohol level is 0.10 or higher.

duplication: A form of severity reduction in which spare parts or supplies are maintained to replace damaged equipment and/or inventories immediately.

dwelling: The structure on the residence premises shown in the declarations, used principally as a private residence, including attached structures.

dwelling policy: Covers dwellings that are not owner-occupied, have up to five rooms for boarders, and are ineligible for a homeowner's policy.

dynamic risks: Uncertainties, either pure or speculative, that are produced because of societal changes.

E

Economic Growth and Tax Relief Reconciliation Act (EGTRRA) of 2001: A major tax relief bill that contains numerous provisions related to retirement plans and estate taxation.

early retirement: Retirement that results in a benefit payable prior to the pension plan's normal retirement age.

earnings multiple approach: A group life plan in which an employee receives one or two times salary in life insurance coverage.

elective deferrals: Funds contributed by employees to 401(k) plans.

electronic data processing (EDP) floater: Provides coverage for computer equipment against special perils not ad-dressed in standard property insurance and while used away from the insured premises, as well as providing coverage for data and media and for business income and extra expense associated with loss of use of EDP equipment.

elimination period: The period that must elapse before disability income is payable under a health insurance policy covering disability income loss.

empirical probability distribution: A tool for evaluating the expected frequency and/or severity of losses due to identified risks that involves observing actual events.

employee benefits: A term describing nonsalary compensation to employees, usually on a tax-advantaged basis, including retirement, life and health insurance, and other benefits.

Employee Retirement Income Security Act (ERISA): Legislation enacted in 1974 that established qualification rules for pension and other retirement plans.

employee savings plans: A retirement plan in which employees can participate on a contributory basis.

employee stock ownership plans (ESOPs): Deferred profit-sharing plans in which investment is usually in stock issued by the employer.

endorsement: An addition made to an insurance policy. It usually adds coverage and an additional premium may be charged.

endowment insurance: Life insurance that pays the face amount at the end of a specified time period if the insured is alive; the face amount is payable in the event of death before the end of the period.

enterprise risk management: Approach for managing all forms of risk faced by the firm, regardless of type; another name for integrated risk management.

entire contract clause: A life insurance contract stating that the policy and the application form constitute the entire contract between the parties.

equal shares: A method of apportionment in which insurers covering the same loss share that loss equally, up to their respective limits of liability.

errors-and-omissions policies: Insurance responding to liability of professional persons for malpractice.

estate planning: A process in which plans are made to accumulate and manage property during one's lifetime and to dispose of it at death.

estate shrinkage: The expenses such as debts, taxes, and administrative costs that reduce the value of an estate at the death of the owner.

estate tax: A tax levied on the property and assets of a decedent.

estoppel: A legal doctrine in which a person may be required to do something or be prevented from doing something that is inconsistent with previous behavior; may prevent an insurer from denying liability after a loss.

excess: Describes policies that apply to losses only after the limits of liability of all other applicable insurance contracts have been exhausted.

excess insurance: Either specified or aggregate catastrophic loss coverage that only takes effect after a very high deductible ($25,000 to $100,000) has been met.

excess major medical: A policy that pays only after another major medical policy has exhausted its limits.

excess-of-loss treaties: Reinsurance treaties in which the reinsurer is not obligated to pay until the ceding insurer has first paid a predetermined amount of the loss.

exclusion ratio: The fraction of each annuity payment that can be initially excluded from income taxation.

exclusions: Restrictions for the coverage provided by an insurance policy.

exclusive agent: An individual employed to represent an insurer and who serves only that insurer.

executor: The person appointed to carry out the terms of the deceased's will.

executor fund: The monies required to settle a deceased's estate. May include payment of outstanding debts, estate and inheritance taxes, and expenses to transfer assets to survivors.

expected loss ratio: The ratio of losses incurred to premiums earned; anticipated when rates are first formulated.

expected value: A figure that is a weighted average and reflects the best estimate of long-term average loss for a given loss distribution; also know as the mean.

expediting expenses: The insurer agrees to pay reasonable extra cost for expediting the repair of machinery, including overtime and express transportation.

experience rating: The system of rating or pricing insurance in which the future premium reflects past loss experience of the insured.

exposure doctrine: A liability limit that provides coverage when a person is exposed to a product or dangerous substance.

express warranty: A warranty actually stated in a contract.

extended coverage (EC): An endorsement to a fire insurance policy that adds coverage for losses from windstorm, hail, explosion, riot, riot attending strike, civil commotion, aircraft, vehicles, and smoke.

extended period of indemnity: A provision that allows the insured five years to file a claim for a known event for which claims were not filed during the policy year.

extended-period-of-indemnity endorsement: An endorsement in which the period of loss is defined as the period necessary to return to normal business operations, not just the period to reopen the business physically.

extended reporting period: A provision giving the insured an extra 60 days of coverage for a claim to be filed for an event (unknown to the insured) that occurred before the policy expired.

extended-term option: One of the non-forfeiture options in life insurance; allows the insured to take the cash value in the form of term insurance if premiums remain unpaid after expiration of the grace period.

extra expense insurance: The consequential property insurance that covers the extra expense incurred by the interruption of a business; the policy pays if the business does not close down but continues in alternative facilities, with higher than normal costs.

F

face amount: In a life insurance contract, the stated sum of money to be paid to the beneficiary upon the insured's death.

factory mutual: A mutual insurer specializing in large risks, with special emphasis on loss prevention.

fair claim settlement laws: Laws establishing minimum standards for insurers in handling loss claims.

fair rental value: In a dwelling policy, the rent the building could have earned at the time of the loss whether it was actually rented.

family member: A person defined in the PAP as "related to you by blood, marriage, or adoption, who is a resident of your household, including a ward or foster child."

family-purpose doctrine: A doctrine under which an automobile is considered an instrument to carry out family purposes. Therefore, the owner is responsible when any family member uses the car to carry out a family function.

farm mutual: A mutual insurer organized to insure farm property.

farmowners'-ranchowners' policy: Covers (1) the dwelling and commercial structures on the farm and (2) the personal and commercial liability that might arise from living and working on the farm.

fee-per-service basis: Compensation for doctors based on the amount of services provided.

fidelity bonds: Bonds that protect a principal against loss from dishonesty by employees.

file-and-use: The system under which states allow insurers to file new property-liability rates with state insurance commissioners and use them subject to later approval.

financial planning: A process involving the establishment of financial goals, the development and implementation of a plan for achieving those goals, and the periodic review and revision of the overall plan.

financial responsibility laws: State laws that require automobile drivers to carry stated minimum limits of liability insurance or to meet other conditions to ensure their financial ability to respond to losses for which they may be held liable as a result of driving automobiles.

financial risks: Risk involving credit, foreign exchange, commodity trading, and interest rate; may involve chance for gain as well as loss.

financial statement analysis: A method of risk identification in which each item on a firm's balance sheet and income statement is analyzed regarding potential risks.

financing: The function of planning and controlling the supply of funds.

fire: Combustion in which oxidation takes place so rapidly that a flame or glow is produced.

five-year cliff vesting: The most common vesting provision in pension plans, in which full vesting takes place after five years; prior to that time, workers who terminate employment are not vested at all and thus have no pension rights under the plan.

fixed-amount option: A life insurance option allowing the beneficiary to take the proceeds in the form of a fixed periodic payment.

fixed annuity: An annuity with a benefit expressed in a stated dollar amount.

fixed-period option: Payment of a death benefit in equal installments over a specified time period.

flexible-premium annuity: An annuity that allows considerable latitude regarding the timing and amount of premiums. The ultimate benefit is a function of the accumulated premium dollars.

floater policy: An inland marine insurance policy that covers property subject to movement from one location to another.

flood: (1) An overflow of inland or tidal waves, (2) unusual and rapid accumulation of runoff of surface waters, (3) mudslides, (4) excessive erosion along the shore of a lake or any other body of water, or (5) erosion or undermining caused by a body of water exceeding its anticipated cyclical levels.

floor-of-protection concept: An underlying principle of social insurance specifying that the goal of social insurance is to provide only limited protection, not one's entire need.

flowchart: A risk identification method that helps pinpoint sources of risk in the production process.

forgery: Most commonly involves the issuance of fictitious checks in the context of insurance.

401(k) plan: A tax-deferred retirement plan allowed under federal tax law for employees of profit-making organizations.

franchise deductible: A deductible under which there is no liability on the part of the insurer unless the loss exceeds a certain stated amount and full payment after that amount.

fraternal carrier: A life and health insurer organized by a fraternal benefit society to offer coverage on members.

free-of-capture-and-seizure (FC&S) clause: A clause in ocean marine insurance that excludes war as a covered peril.

free-of-particular-average (FPA) clause: A clause in ocean marine insurance that no partial loss will be paid to a single cargo interest unless the loss is caused by certain perils.

freight: Money paid for the transportation of goods. Freight insurance is a common coverage in marine insurance, purchased by the owners of transporting vessels.

frequency: How often a loss occurs or is likely to occur.

frequency reduction: A method of loss control that lessens the chance that a peril will occur.

friendly fire: A fire confined to the area of a boiler, stove, or other place designed to contain it.

full actuarial equivalent: The retirement benefit that is mathematically equivalent to the benefit payable at normal retirement age; computed using appropriate assumptions regarding interest and mortality rates.

fully insured: Status to be met by those qualifying for most of the benefits of OASDHI.

funded retention: Preloss arrangement to ensure that money is readily available to pay for losses that occur.

G

gatekeepers: A name sometimes given to primary care providers in HMOs, due to their role in limiting care to only that deemed medically necessary.

general agent: A person authorized to conduct all of the principal's business of a given kind in a particular place.

general average clause: A clause in ocean marine insurance that requires ship and freight interests other than the insured to respond to losses suffered by the insured interest when those losses result from voluntary, necessary, and successful sacrifice of the insured's freight because of shipping peril.

general insurance: Another term for property insurance.

general writing mutual: A mutual insurer not specializing in any class of risk.

glass insurance: Covers damage to glass and its lettering or ornamentation, repair or replacement of frame, installation of temporary plates or boarding up of windows, and removal of obstructions necessary when replacing glass.

grace period clause: A clause in life insurance giving the insured an extra 30 days to pay a premium due before lapse takes place.

graded seven-year vesting: A gradual vesting method for pension plans by which employees become 20 percent vested after three years of service, 40 percent after four years, 60 percent after five years, 80 percent after six years, and 100 percent after seven years.

gross premium: The premium charge for insurance that includes anticipated cost of losses, overhead, and profit.

group accidental death and dismemberment (AD&D): A group health insurance plan paying specified sums in case of accidental death or dismemberment of covered workers.

group ordinary: Whole life coverage offered on a group basis to employees after retirement. Not a popular benefit because tax rules governing it are complicated.

group practice HMO: An HMO in which a large group of physicians share facilities and support personnel and work out of one or a few locations. The doctors are not actually HMO employees; they have a contract to provide services as needed.

group term insurance: Term life insurance offered on a group plan basis.

group universal life: Universal life insurance offered on a group basis.

guaranteed insurability rider: A life insurance endorsement permitting the insured to purchase more life insurance without evidence of insurability under given conditions.

guaranteed renewable: A policy that cannot be cancelled by the insurer prior to a specified age. Premiums may be increased only for an entire class of insureds.

guaranteed replacement cost: Insurer agrees to pay for replacing property without policy limit. Used in homeowners' program.

guaranty funds: Funds that have been created by state law to guarantee the payment of bills of insolvent insurers.

guest–host statutes: State laws that reduce the standard of care owed by the driver to a guest riding in a car as a passenger.

H

hard market: An economic condition in insurance that is characterized by high rates, low limits, and restricted coverage.

hazards: Conditions that increase the frequency or severity of loss stemming from the existence of a given peril.

health maintenance organizations (HMOs): Organizations that offer group health care to member families or individuals on a prearranged service basis within a defined geographical area.

health savings accounts (HSAs): Accounts that allow holders of large-deductible health insurance plans to save for out-of-pocket medical expenses on a tax-favorable basis.

hedger: The transferor of a speculative risk via a hedging contract.

hedging: A transfer of risk from one party to another; similar to speculation and may be used to handle risks not subject to insurance, such as price fluctuations.

hold-harmless agreements: Provisions inserted into contracts that transfer responsibility for some types of losses to a party different that the one that would otherwise bear it.

home health care: Health care provided to persons such as the elderly who cannot live completely independently but are unable or unwilling to move to a nursing or personal care home.

home service life: *See* industrial life.

hospice: A health care organization that provides humane, dignified care for dying patients.

hospital insurance: An insurance contract designed to pay hospital room and board, laboratory fees, nursing care, use of the operating room, and medicines and similar expenses.

hostile fire: A fire that occurs outside of its normal confines.

hull insurance: Property insurance policy covering a sea-going vessel.

human life value: The sum of money that when paid in installments of both principal and interest over the individual's remaining working life, will produce the same income the person would have earned, minus taxes and personal expenses.

I

immediate annuity: An annuity in which benefits begin soon after the annuity is purchased.

implied warranties: Warranties not stated in a contract but assumed by the parties to be true.

imputed acts: Acts committed by one person but for which responsibility has been transferred or "imputed" to another.

inboard watercraft: A type of watercraft whose motor is a permanent part of it.

incontestability clause: A life insurance clause that prevents the insurer, after two years, from denying liability under the policy for misrepresentations or concealments by the insured.

increasing term: Term life insurance in which the face amount of the policy in-

creases periodically on a predetermined basis.

indemnify: To restore insureds to the situations that existed prior to a loss.

indemnity agreements: *See* hold-harmless agreements.

independent adjuster: An individual or firm employed by an insurer to settle loss claims.

independent agent: An autonomous, local intermediary in the property insurance business who usually represents 10 to 30 separate insurers and has authority to bind those insurers on most of the contracts that are written.

indirect loss: A loss that occurs indirectly as a consequence of a given peril.

individual bond: A fidelity bond that names a certain person for coverage.

individual method: A rating system in which rates are developed or modified for specific members of the insured group to reflect the degree of risk.

individual practice HMO: An HMO in which many physicians work out of their individual offices and are paid on a fee-per-service basis.

individual retirement account (IRA): An individual retirement plan allowing tax deductibility of some contributions and tax deferral of accumulating interest, under specific conditions and up to specified amounts.

industrial life: Life insurance sold door-to-door, for which premiums are collected or quoted on a weekly or monthly basis.

inherent nature of the goods: A cause of loss that stems from the product itself. A loss due to this cause releases the carrier from liability.

inheritance tax: A tax levied on those who inherit property from an estate.

inland marine insurance: Insurance that covers imports, exports, domestic shipments, instrumentalities of transportation and communication, and various types of floaters.

inland transit policy: A basic contract covering domestic shipments shipped primarily by land transportation systems.

inside buildup: The annual increments to the case value of a life insurance policy.

installment refund guarantee: Benefits continue after the death of an annuitant until the pre- and post-death benefits combined equal the original purchase price.

insurable interest: A legal principle in which an insured must demonstrate a personal loss; prevents the insurance from becoming a gambling contract.

insurable value: In business income coverage, the amount obtained by deducting variable costs and expenses (those that may be discontinued in the event of a shutdown) from the total sales.

insurance: An economic institution that reduces risk by combining under one management a group of objects so situated that the aggregate accidental losses to which the group is subject become predictable within narrow limits; includes certain legal contracts under which the insurer for consideration promises to reimburse the insured or to render services in case of certain described accidental losses.

insurance rate: The price of insurance, expressed as a price per unit of coverage.

insured pension plans: Employee benefit plans managed by an insurance company.

insureds: Those who have combined their own risks in a large group, through the purchase of insurance, to reduce the overall risk to which all are exposed.

insurer: The transferee; the person or agency providing insurance.

insuring agreement: The part of an insurance contract that states what the insurer agrees to do and the conditions under which it so agrees.

integrated risk management: Approach for managing all forms of risk faced by the firm, regardless of type; another name for enterprise risk management.

interest option: A life insurance option allowing the beneficiary to leave the proceeds with the insurer and receive only interest income.

interinsurance exchange: Another name for a reciprocal.

intermediate form: One of three types of hold-harmless agreements, in which the transferee agrees to pay for any losses in which both the transferee and transferor are jointly liable.

intermediate nursing home care: Facilities that offer assistance with all daily activities and some medical services.

internal maximum: A limit that applies to benefits payable on certain types of health problems, e.g., mental and nervous conditions and drug abuse.

inter vivos: A trust set up during the lifetime of the estate owner, usually with the purpose of facilitating the transfer of property at death.

intestacy laws: Laws governing the distribution of an estate not disposed of by a will.

intestate: Without a valid will.

investment department: A division of an insurer set up to manage investments.

invitees: Individuals, such as retail store customers, who are invited onto the insured's premises for their own benefit and that of the insured.

involuntary coverage: Government insurance required to be purchased by certain groups and under certain conditions.

irrevocable beneficiary: A beneficiary designation that may not be changed without the written consent of the named beneficiary.

J

jewelers' block policy: Insures all the stock in the trade of a typical jeweler on an open perils basis.

job classification approach: A method of determining how much coverage is offered an employee under an employee benefit plan. Employees' jobs determine the amount.

joint and several liability: The legal doctrine that allows a plaintiff to collect in full from one negligent party in an accident where there are two or more negligent parties.

joint and survivor annuity: An annuity issued on two lives that guarantees that the annuity in whole or in part will be paid as long as either party shall live.

joint and X percent survivor annuity: A joint and survivor annuity in which the payment after the first annuitant dies equals X percent of the benefit while both were alive.

K

Keogh plans: Retirement plans designed for the self-employed.

key employee: An employee whose services would be difficult to replace if the employee were to die or become disabled.

L

lack of privity: A defense in product liability cases, alleging that no liability exists because no contractual relationship exists between the manufacturer or vendor and the injured party.

larceny: Wrongful or fraudulent taking and carrying away by any person of the personal property of another.

large-loss principle: A rule for buying insurance such that serious loss exposures receive priority over less serious loss exposures.

last clear chance rule: In a case of contributory negligence, the negligent plaintiff may have a cause of action against the defendant if the defendant had a last clear chance to avoid the accident but failed to do so.

late retirement: Retirement after normal retirement age.

law of large numbers: A mathematical principle showing that as the number of exposure units increases, the more certain it becomes that actual loss experience will equal probable loss experience.

leasehold: An interest in real property created by an agreement (a lease) that gives the lessee (the tenant) the right of enjoyment and use of the property for a period of time.

leasehold interest insurance: Consequential property insurance in which the value of a lease is lost because of the occurrence of an insured-peril loss.

legal injury: Wrongful violation of a person's rights.

level term: Term insurance with a constant face amount.

liability risks: Loss exposures arising from the actions of businesses and individuals that cause harm to others.

libel: Written, printed, or pictorial material that damages a person's reputation by defaming or ridiculing the person.

licensees: Individuals who are on the insured's premises for a legitimate purpose and with the permission of the occupier.

life, health, and loss of income risks: Loss exposures associated with the health and well-being of individuals.

life insurance: A personal risk management tool often used in connection with premature death. Upon the insured's death, a certain sum of money is paid to a designated party.

life insurance trust: A trust that collects, invests, and distributes the proceeds of a life insurance policy at the time of the insured's death. An individual, bank, or other financial institution is the trustee.

lifetime maximum: A limit that applies to all benefits payable under an insurance plan. The maximum can often be restored over time, eventually allowing an insured to collect more than the stated maximum.

limited form: One of three types of hold-harmless agreements in which each party is held responsible for liabilities arising from its own actions.

limited named perils: Same perils as broad named perils but with a narrower definition of each.

limited-pay life: A whole life policy where premiums are paid over a specified period of time and coverage remains in effect even after premiums are no longer paid.

line: That portion of a loss to be paid by the ceding insurer, the excess to be passed on to the reinsurer.

liquidating damages: Lump-sum damages paid to a worker for a disability that is permanent but does not totally incapacitate the worker. It is paid in addition to income benefits received during the period of incapacity.

living benefit option: See accelerated death benefit option.

living trust: See inter vivos.

Lloyd's association: An organization of individuals to underwrite insurance on a cooperative basis where individuals are personally liable for losses.

loading: The overhead or administrative expenses of an insurer that is included in the cost of a policy.

local agent: *See* independent agent.

long-term care: Care and service provided to the elderly to assist them with day-to-day living.

long-term care (LTC) insurance: Insurance that covers nursing home care or other assistance with daily living.

long-term care rider: An accelerated death benefit specifically for insureds' long-term care needs.

long-term disability (LTD) income plans: Income replacement that is paid to the disabled employee over a long period of years.

long-term disability (LTD) insurance: Disability insurance that pays over a long period of years, sometimes a lifetime.

loss control: Actions taken to reduce the frequency and/or severity of losses.

loss conversion factor: A multiplying factor used to cover variable costs of the insurer.

loss exposure: A potential loss that may be associated with a specific type of risk.

loss exposure checklist: A risk identification tool used by businesses and individuals that lists many different potential losses. The user can determine which of the potential losses is relevant.

loss payable clause: A clause for the protection of the mortgage stating that the benefits, if any, shall be payable to the person named in the contract.

loss settlement clause: A provision that helps determine if items will be valued at actual cash value or at replacement cost after a loss.

losses other than collision: Losses to an auto caused by missiles, falling objects, windstorm, hail, water, flood, malicious mischief or vandalism, riot or civil commotion, contact with a bird or animal, or breakage of glass.

lump-sum distribution option: A lump-sum payment of some or all of the value of the promised pension.

lump-sum option: A life insurance option in which the beneficiary may elect to take the policy proceeds in a lump sum rather than in installments.

M

major medical insurance: A health insurance contract, usually with a large maximum limit, designed to cover catastrophic expenses that result from sickness or accident.

malpractice policies: Coverage that pays damages occurring as a result of a professional error or accident, as in the legal or medical professions.

managed care: The generic name used for health care cost-containment provisions.

mandatory retirement age: An age at which workers can be forced to retire if they have not already done so. Generally not allowed.

manifestation doctrine: A liability limit that provides coverage when a claimant's disease or injury is discovered.

manual method: *See* class rating method.

manufacturers selling price: Coverage for the loss of the profit element in goods already manufactured but destroyed before they could be sold.

marital deduction: An amount allowed under federal estate tax laws that can be deducted from the gross estate for tax purposes if this amount is given to a spouse.

market value–adjusted (MVA) annuity: A variation of the fixed annuity in which the guaranteed interest rate can be raised during the first several years after a contract is issued but before benefits begin.

mass merchandising: The sale of group property insurance through payroll deduction; most mass merchandising plans specialize in automobile and homeowners' coverage.

material: Describes misrepresentations that, had they been known at the time of a contract's issuance, would have caused it not to be issued at all or issued on different terms.

maximum possible loss: An estimate of the worst loss that might result from a given occurrence.

maximum probable loss: An estimate of the likely severity of loss that might result from a given occurrence.

McCarran-Ferguson Act: A federal law giving states the right to regulate insurance, subject to certain limitations. This act allows insurance companies to work together to collect loss and expense data and gives insurers limited antitrust protection.

mean: The sum of a set of n measurements x_1, x_2, x_3, . . . , x_n divided by n; usually signified by the symbol $\bar{x}$.

measures of central tendency or location: Measures of the midpoint of a probability distribution, such as the mean, the expected value, the median, and the mode.

median: The midpoint in a range of measurements such that half of the items are larger and half are smaller than it.

Medicaid: The generic name for the variety of state-administered programs that provide medical care to low-income persons who can show sufficient financial need to qualify them for assistance.

medical payments: Reasonable and necessary medical expenses caused by an accident and sustained by the insured. Such expenses must occur within three years of the accident.

medical payments to others: Part of the comprehensive personal liability policy that provides payment of medical expenses incurred or ascertained within three years of an accident. It applies only to residence employees and members of the public and is paid without regard to fault.

Medicare: A federal program designed to provide insurance coverage for hospitalization and physician's expense to older workers and to certain other persons.

Medicare carve-out: A health benefit offered to retired employees in which applicable Medicare payments are deducted prior to paying promised benefits.

Medigap insurance: Private insurance policies purchased by persons in the Medicare program for the purpose of "filling in the gaps" caused by Medicare's deductibles, coinsurance, and coverage limitations.

memorandum clause: A deductible clause that lists various types of goods with varying percentages of deductibles that apply on a franchise basis.

merit rating method: *See* individual method.

misrepresentation: A practice, usually prohibited under state law, in which an insurance agent makes a misleading statement in the sale of insurance.

misstatement-of-age clause: A clause in life insurance requiring an adjustment of the amount of insurance payable in the event the age of the insured has been misrepresented.

misstatement-of-sex clause: If a person's sex has been misrepresented, the insurer adjusts the amount of proceeds payable rather than canceling the policy altogether.

mobile home endorsement: Insurance for mobile homes that are not eligible for a dwelling or a standard homeowners' policy.

mode: The value of the variable that occurs most often in a frequency distribution.

modified endowment contracts: Policies that meet the statutory definition of life insurance, fail the seven-pay test, and were issued on or after June 21, 1988.

modified guaranteed annuity: *See* market value–adjusted annuity.

modified life: A whole life policy with low initial premiums and higher ones after 5–10 years.

moral hazard: Intentional acts by an individual that make a loss either more likely or more severe. Insurance fraud would be a special case of moral hazard.

morale hazard: Carelessness or indifference by an individual that make a loss either more likely or more severe.

mortality table: A table that shows the number of deaths per thousand and the expectation of life at various ages; one mortality table in current use in the United States is the 2001 Commissioners Standard Ordinary (CSO) Mortality Table.

mortgagee: A person or organization holding a mortgage.

mortgagee clause: A clause in insurance contracts that gives first right of recovery to the mortgagor of property that is covered.

mutual company: An insurance company owned by policyholders; there are no stockholders.

N

name: A member of a Lloyd's association; essentially an investor and underwriter.

named insured: An individual in whose name the insurance contract is issued and who is specifically identified as the person being covered.

named-perils agreement: An insurance contract that lists perils to be insured; perils not listed are not covered.

negative act: A negligent act that consists of a party's failure to do something he or she should have done.

negligence: The failure to exercise the degree of care required by law.

net payment index: The level annual payment that, if invested at a stated interest rate for a specified period, will accumulate to the same total as the life insurance policy's net premiums if invested in the same way.

net present value: The present value of the cash inflow minus the present value of the cash outflow.

no-fault: An insured does not have to prove another person negligent before compensation can be received. No person is held liable, there is no litigation, and the insurance policy pays without regard to fault.

noncancellable: A policy that cannot be cancelled by the insurer prior to a certain age. Premiums may be increased only by the amounts specified at the time the policy is issued.

noncontributory: An employee benefit plan in which the employer pays the total cost.

nonforfeiture options: Provisions in life insurance that name ways in which the insured may receive the cash value element; there are generally three such options; lump sum, extended-term insurance, or paid-up insurance of a reduced amount.

nonowned auto: Any private passenger auto, pickup truck, van, or trailer not owned by or furnished for the regular use of the insured or any family member

while in the custody of or being operated by the insured or any family member.

nonscheduled basis: A policy in which covered procedures are insured up to the full amount of what is reasonable and customary in a particular geographic location.

nonstandard risks: Groups charged extra premiums by life insurers on the basis of those groups' past history of loss exposures.

normal distribution: A very useful, perfectly bell-shaped probability distribution.

normal retirement age: The earliest age at which employees can retire and receive full pension benefits.

O

OASDI wage base: The first $87,900 (as of 2004) of earned income for which workers and their employers each pay 6.2 percent in tax, which pays for all but the Medicare (health) element of Social Security, or OASDI; the exclusion of *H* from OASDHI reflects this funding exclusion.

objective risk: The probable variation of actual from expected experience.

obligee: In a bond, the party to be reimbursed if he or she suffers a loss because of some failure by the obligor.

obligor: In a bond, the party who is bonded to provide work or services to the obligee (e.g., a contractor).

occupying: Defined in the PAP as "in, upon, getting in, on, out, or off."

occurrence policy: A clause in liability insurance policies under which covered acts must satisfy certain conditions; the results must be accidental and unintended, but the occurrence itself can be a deliberate act of an insured.

one-year term option: A life insurance option allowing the use of dividends to purchase one-year term protection at the owner's attained age.

open competition laws: A system under which states allow insurers in property-liability insurance to charge competitive rates without prior approval.

open contract: A cargo policy wherein all shipments are covered. There is no

termination date, but either party may cancel with 30 days' notice.

open-ended HMO: *See* point-of-service (POS) plan.

open-perils agreement: States that it is the insurer's intention to cover risks of accidental loss to the described property except due to those perils specifically excluded; also called "all risks."

opportunity cost: The cost of keeping monies liquid in a loss reserve fund rather than using them as working capital.

optionally renewable: A policy that can be cancelled by the insurer on the anniversary date. No restrictions, other than the time, are placed on the insurer.

other insurance clauses: Clauses in practically all contracts of indemnity and valued contracts that limit the insurer's liability in case additional insurance contracts also cover the loss.

other structures: Buildings on the residence premises separated from the dwelling by clear space or connected only by a fence or utility line, e.g., a detached garage or greenhouse.

outboard watercraft: A boat whose motor is mounted on the stern and is detachable.

out-of-pocket cap: A limit on the amount an insured must pay due to coinsurance and deductibles in health insurance policies.

own occupation: A definition of disability that allows benefits to be paid if an individual can no longer perform the major duties of his or her own occupation.

owners' protective bond: A contract construction bond that provides that if the principal defaults, the surety must either complete the contract or pay the loss to the owner in cash.

P

paid-up additions option: Each dividend of a whole life policy is used to purchase as much single-premium whole life as possible.

paid-up insurance option: Life insurance on which all of the required premiums have been paid; the policy remains in force until the death of the insured.

pain and suffering damages: Non-economic damages designed to compensate the injured party for the pain endured due to the negligent behavior of the defendant. Often greater than economic losses, such as loss of income and medical expenses.

pair-and-set clause: Used to determine the loss payment when part of a set or one of a pair is lost. The insurance company will pay only the difference in the actual cash value of the item before and after the loss.

partial disability: An illness or injury that decreases an individual's ability to perform some of the major duties of his or her job, but does not cause complete cessation of employment.

participating: A type of life insurance policy in which a dividend (considered a return or a premium overcharge) is payable to the insured.

penalty: The limit of liability on a bond.

Pension Benefit Guarantee Corporation (PBGC): A federal agency that insures pension benefits of defined benefit pension plans.

pension plan: An employer-sponsored plan established with the primary goal of systematically providing retirement income for employees.

per-cause deductible: A deductible that is assessed for each new sickness or accidental injury.

peril: A specific contingency that may cause a loss.

permanent disability: An illness or injury that prevents a person from working for the rest of his or her life.

permitted disparity: The degree to which a benefit or contribution is affected by Social Security. The concept allows an employer to "take credit" for Social Security taxes paid on an employee's behalf.

personal articles floater (PAF): Provides open-perils coverage on scheduled personal property.

Personal Automobile Policy (PAP): A widely used form for personal automobile insurance that generally replaces the older Family Automobile Policy (FAP).

personal care homes: Establishments, usually smaller than regular nursing homes, that provide custodial care for the elderly.

personal coverages: Those lines of insurance designed to cover the risk of perils that may interrupt an individual's income.

personal property: Anything that is subject to ownership other than real property.

personal umbrella: A liability insurance policy that broadens coverage for comprehensive personal liability and personal auto liability. Provides limits of liability of $1 million or more.

physical hazard: A condition stemming from the material characteristics of an object, e.g., icy street (increasing chance of car collision) and earth faults (hazard for earthquakes).

plan termination insurance: Insurance coverage that pays pension benefits in the event that a pension plan is terminated with insufficient funding.

planned retention: A conscious and deliberate assumption of recognized risk.

point-of-service (POS) plan: A modification of the HMO concept that is similar to an HMO in possible organizational structures and philosophy yet differs in that POS plans allow for more freedom of choice in selecting health care providers.

Poisson distribution: A theoretical probability distribution that uses the formula

$$P = \frac{m^r e^{-m}}{r!}$$

where

P = the probability that an event n occurs
r = the number of events for which the probability estimate is needed
m = mean = expected loss frequency
e = a constant, the base of the natural logarithms, equal to 2.71828

Auto accidents, fires, and other losses tend to occur in a way that can be approximated with the Poisson distribution.

policies: Legal contracts in the context of insurance.

policy writing: The function of creating a specific insurance policy for a client, usually by the agent.

policyholder: The insured in an insurance policy.

pooling: Sharing total losses among a group.

positive act: Action often leading to legal injury.

post-loss activities: Severity-reduction measures such as salvaging damaged property rather than discarding it.

power interruption coverage: Available on a boiler and machinery contract to cover two types of losses stemming from power interruption: (1) loss from operations interruptions and (2) loss from spoilage of property.

precertification: A cost-containment measurement requiring that certain non-emergency medical services be authorized prior to delivery of treatment.

pre-existing condition: A health problem that exists prior to the time when health coverage becomes effective.

preferred provider organizations (PPOs): A health care network in which doctors reduce their rates in return for certain concessions by the sponsoring organization, such as a certain number of patients per month, prompt payment, etc.

preferred risks: An insured unit receiving a lower insurance rate to reflect the reduced rate applicable to the group in which the unit is placed.

preloss activities: Loss control methods implemented before any losses occur. All measures with a frequency-reduction focus, as well as some based on severity reduction, are of this type.

premature death: Death that occurs before the stage where it is accepted by society as part of the natural, expected order of life.

premature distribution penalty: A 10 percent tax that is charged employees who receive benefits from qualified retirement plans prior to age 59.5, except for certain specified reasons.

premium: The total cost of insurance, found by multiplying the rate by the number of units covered.

premium conversion: When premiums for health insurance benefits are taken out of an employee's paycheck on a pretax basis.

present value: The amount of money P that must be invested now at interest rate i so that it accumulates to a value of $\$Q$ after N years, or

$$P = \frac{Q}{(1 + i)^N}$$

primary: Describes policies that will pay up to their limits before any other coverage becomes payable.

primary care physician: In an HMO, the doctor responsible for coordinating all medical care for the patient, including access to medical specialists.

primary insurance amount (PIA): A figure, calculated from the average indexed monthly earnings (AIME), on which all Social Security retirement benefits are based.

principal: Another name for the obligor; the person bonded, in a fidelity or security bond.

principle of indemnity: A doctrine that limits the amount that an insured may collect to the actual cash value of the property insured.

prior approval: System under which states must approve property-liability rates before they are used.

private insurance: Insurance coverage written by firms in the private sector of the economy (as opposed to government insurers).

probability: The long-term frequency of an event's occurrence; all events have a probability between 0 (for an event that is certain *not* to occur) and 1 (for an event that is certain to occur).

probability distribution: A mutually exclusive and collectively exhaustive list of all events that can result from a chance process containing the probability associated with each event.

probate: A court process under which property is distributed and the terms of the will are carried out at the owner's death.

probate court: A court that validates the authenticity of a will and oversees the work of the estate executor.

production: The selling function in insurer operations.

professional liability: Liability that arises out of the error of a professional

person in performance of his or her duties.

promissory warranty: An assurance that a certain condition, fact, or circumstance will be true for the entire term of a contract.

property coverages: Insurance lines designed to cover perils that may destroy property.

property risks: Loss exposures affecting buildings, personal property, supplies, or other physical assets owned, rented, or used by businesses or individuals.

pro-rata clause: A clause that requires each insurer covering a risk to share pro rata any losses, in the proportion that its particular coverage bears to the total coverage on the risk.

pro-rata treaties: Reinsurance agreements under which premiums and losses are shared in some stated proportion.

protection and indemnity (P&I) clause: Marine liability insurance covering ocean-going vessels.

proximate cause: The direct cause of loss; exists if there is an unbroken chain of events leading from one act to a resulting injury or loss.

public adjuster: An individual or firm hired by the insured to obtain satisfactory settlement of a loss claim.

public insurance: Insurance coverage written by government bodies or operated by private agencies under government supervision and control.

punitive damages: Assessed when it is deemed that the defendant acted in a grossly negligent manner and deserves to have an example made of his or her behavior so as to discourage others from acting that way. Usually imposed in addition to other damages; may be for very large amounts.

pure premium: The portion of an insurance premium that reflects the basic costs of loss, not including overhead or profit.

pure risk: Uncertainty as to whether a loss will occur.

Q

qualification rules: Requirements that must be met if employer and employee are to benefit from the tax advantages associated with employee benefits.

qualified plans: Retirement plans that meet qualification rules in the Internal Revenue Code for favorable status.

quota share treaties: Reinsurance arrangements in which each insurer accepts a certain percentage of premiums and losses in a given line of insurance.

R

rain insurance: Coverage for the loss of profits and expenses due to rain, hail, snow, or sleet.

rate making: The process of developing pricing structures for insurance.

rate-making associations: Organizations that develop insurance rates on behalf of member insurers. Members may deviate from the rates that are promulgated by the bureau.

ratification: A method by which an agent gains authority to write insurance. The agent writes a policy and, after the fact, presents it to the insurance company. If the insurance company approves the policy, the agent's authority is ratified.

rating bureaus: See rate-making associations.

real property: Land and whatever is growing on it, erected on it, or affixed to it.

reasonable and customary: A test used to judge what expenses an insurance policy will pay. The fee is compared to prevailing fees in the area.

reasonable expectations: An extension of the concept of adhesion, this doctrine makes the proposition that coverage should be interpreted to be what the insured can reasonably expect.

rebating: A practice, usually prohibited under state law, in which a sales agent in insurance returns part of the commission to the purchaser.

reciprocal: A form of insurer owned by policyholders who exchange coverage with each other; commonly found in the field of automobile insurance.

reciprocal laws: State insurance laws that provide equal treatment in one state for similar treatment given by another state on insurance questions.

regular medical expense insurance: Health insurance that covers physicians' services other than surgical procedures, such as doctor calls.

reinstatement clause: A contract in life insurance that allows a policy that has lapsed to be reinstated.

reinsurance: The shifting of risk by a primary insurer (known as the ceding company) to another insurer (known as the reinsurer).

reinsurance exchange: See reinsurance pool.

reinsurance pool: Provides reinsurance for a specific class of business.

reinsurer: An insurer that accepts all or part of the risk that is originally assumed by the primary insurer.

released bill of lading: Limits the dollar liability of the carrier for any loss to the goods.

renewable term: A life insurance policy initially written for a specified number of years and subsequently renewable for similar periods of time.

replacement cost: Property insurance that pays for the current replacement cost of property without deducting for depreciation.

reporting forms: A type of insurance that requires the insured to make periodic reports showing the amount and location of insured property.

representation: A statement made by an applicant for insurance, before the contract is made, which affects the willingness of the insurer to accept the risk.

requisites of insurable risks: From the view of the insurer, there must be a sufficient number of similar objects, the loss must be accidental and measurable, and the objects must not be subject to simultaneous destruction. From the view of the insured, the potential loss must be large enough to cause financial hardship, and the probability of loss must not be too high.

residence premises: A one- to four-family dwelling, other structures, grounds, and that part of any other building where one resides.

residual disability: A condition that prevents a person from performing occupa-

tional duties, resulting in earnings of less than 80 percent of the salary earned prior to the disability.

res ipsa loquitur: "The thing speaks for itself"—a legal doctrine that enables a plaintiff to collect for losses without proving negligence on the part of the defendant.

respondeat superior: A legal doctrine under which a principal is responsible for the acts of his or her agent.

respondentia contracts: Ocean marine contracts in ancient Roman times in which a ship's cargo was considered security for a loan.

retaliatory laws: State laws automatically imposing taxes, license fees, or other burdens on insurers chartered in other states, if those same other states impose such requirements on insurers operating therein but domiciled in the first state.

retention: See line.

retirement test: Set of conditions under OASDHI regulations determining how much, if any, retirement benefits may be paid under OASDHI if the worker is still in covered employment.

retrocession: The process by which a reinsurer passes on risks to another reinsurer.

retrospective rating: A method of pricing insurance in which the premium depends on the actual loss experience of the insured; the premium is adjusted for past periods according to this loss experience.

retrospective rating formula: The basic formula is given by the expression

R = Retrospective premium payable for the year in question

BP = A basic premium (in dollars) designed to cover fixed costs of the insurer in handling the business

L = Losses (in dollars) actually suffered by the employer

LCF = Loss conversion factor, a multiplying factor designed to cover the variable costs of the insurer (such as claim adjustment expenses)

TM = Tax multiplier, a factor designed to reflect the premium tax levied by the state on the insurer's business

revocable beneficiary: A life insurance beneficiary designation that may be changed by the owner.

right of survivorship: Ownership of property automatically transfers to surviving owners when one of the owners dies.

risk: Uncertainty as to economic loss.

risk-adjusted return on capital (RAROC): Assesses how much capital would be required by the organization's various activities (such as products, projects, loans, etc.) to keep the probability of bankruptcy below a specified probability level.

risk avoidance: A conscious decision not to expose oneself or one's firm to a particular risk of loss.

risk management: The process used to systematically manage pure risk exposures.

risk management information system (RMIS): A computer software program that assists in tracking and statistical analysis of past losses.

risk management policy: A plan, procedure, or rule of action followed for the purpose of securing consistent action over a period of time.

risk management process: (1) Identify risks; (2) evaluate risks as to frequency and severity; (3) select risk management techniques; and (4) implement and review decisions.

risk manager: An individual charged with minimizing the adverse impact of losses on the achievement of a company's goals.

risk mapping (risk profiling): Method of risk identification and assessment by arranging all risks in a matrix reflecting frequency, severity, and existing insurance coverage.

risk reduction: A decrease in the total amount of uncertainty present in a particular situation.

risk retention: Handling risk by bearing the results of risk, rather than employing other methods of handling it, such as transfer or avoidance.

risk transfer: A risk management technique whereby one party (transferor) pays another (transferee) to assume a risk that the transferor desires to escape.

robbery: Unlawful taking of property from another person by force, threat of force, or violence.

rollover: A procedure by which one may change the trustee or the type of funding of an IRA or other tax-favored retirement plan without federal income tax consequences.

Roth IRA: An individual retirement plan in which contributions are after-tax, but all qualified withdrawals are tax-free; contribution limits and other regulations apply.

running down clause (RDC): Protection for the hull owner against third-party liability claims that arise from collisions. It also covers damage to the other vessel.

S

salary bracket approach: A group life insurance plan in which the benefit paid depends on the employee's salary.

savings incentive match plan for employees (SIMPLE): A special version of either a 401(k) plan or an IRA, designed to make it easier for small employers to sponsor retirement plans for their employees.

schedule bond: A fidelity bond in which employees are listed by name, with the amounts for which they are bonded.

scheduled basis: A policy written with several procedures listed for payment with a specified maximum for each one.

scheduled property floater: Insures movable business property, such as contractors' equipment, salespersons' samples, etc. The floater describes the specific type of property and the conditions under which it is insured.

schedule rating: Each individual building is considered separately and a rate is established for it.

second-to-die life insurance: Life insurance policy covering two insureds, with proceeds payable only after both persons are dead.

Section 403(b) plans: Tax-deferred retirement plans designed for employees of nonprofit organizations.

security provisions: Motorists without liability insurance must pay for the damages they have caused or give evidence that they were not to blame.

self-insurance: A special form of risk retention in which a firm can establish a fund to pay for losses because it has a group of exposure units large enough to reduce risk and thereby predict losses.

self-retained limit: The deductible on an umbrella liability policy.

separation: A form of severity reduction involving the reduction of the maximum probable loss associated with some kind of risks.

service-of-process statute: A state law enabling a person to bring suit against any insurer doing business in a given state without traveling to the state in which the insurer is incorporated.

settlement options: Provisions in the life insurance policy that offer alternative methods for paying the cash value or the death proceeds.

seven-pay test: A test to determine whether a policy loan can be taxed as ordinary income. Compares actual premiums paid during the first seven years to premiums that would have been paid if the policy had been on a level annual premium basis.

severity: The extent or magnitude of a loss; how serious it is.

severity reduction: A method of loss control that will reduce the seriousness and extent of damage should a loss occur.

short-term disability (STD) income plans: Income replacement paid to the employee for a maximum of from six months to two years.

short-term disability (STD) insurance: Disability insurance that pays for a period of up to two years.

sick leave plans: Plans that pay the full amount of an employee's salary during periods of temporary disability.

single-premium annuity: An annuity whose purchase price is paid in one lump sum.

single-premium life: A whole life policy paid for with one premium.

sistership exclusion: The act of recalling (withdrawing) defective products from the marketplace.

skilled nursing home care: A facility with ongoing medical services where residents are seen regularly by a physician.

slander: Spoken words that are defamatory and/or injurious to a person's reputation.

social insurance: Insurance plans operated by public agencies, usually on a compulsory basis.

Social Security: The more popular name for the Old Age, Survivors', Disability, and Health Insurance Program (OAS-DHI), which was established in 1935. Social Security benefits are financed through a tax on employees and employers.

Social Security normal retirement age: The age at which retirees can begin collecting their full benefit amounts; this age is gradually increasing from 65, and will reach 67 in the year 2027.

soft market: An economic condition in insurance that is characterized by low rates, high limits, and flexible contracts.

South-Eastern Underwriters Association (SEUA) case: A famous 1944 U.S. Supreme Court ruling in which insurers were held to be engaged in interstate commerce and were thus subject to federal regulation.

special agent: A person who is authorized to perform only a specific act or function and who has no general powers within the insurance company.

special rating classes: Rate classes that deviate from standard (manual) rates.

specific coverage: Property insurance coverage that applies at one or more listed locations for the specified amounts.

specific dollar limits: Limits that restrict payments to a maximum on any one definite item of property or from a named peril, as provided in the policy.

speculative risk: The uncertainty of an event that could produce either a profit or a loss, such as a business venture or a gambling transaction.

speculator: A third party to which the risk of price fluctuations is transferred during hedging.

spendthrift trust clause: A clause in life insurance that prevents the beneficiary's creditors from making legal attachment of proceeds of the life insurance.

spread-of-loss treaty: A type of reinsurance wherein losses are spread over a five-year period with little or no risk transfer after the five-year period ends.

staff model HMO: An HMO that operates out of only a few main locations and in which the doctors are actually HMO employees and are paid salaries.

standard deviation: A number that measures how close a group of individual measurements is to its expected value; usually signified by the Greek letter σ.

standard premium: What an employer would pay at manual rates after adjustment for experience rating but before adjustment for retrospective rating.

state mandated coverages: Specific coverages that a state requires be included in every health insurance policy sold in the state.

static risks: Uncertainties, either pure or speculative, that stem from an unchanging society that is in stable equilibrium.

stock bonus plans: Deferred profit-sharing plans in which plan assets may be invested either in company stock or in other stocks.

stock company: A corporation organized as a profit-making venture in the field of insurance.

straight deductible: A deductible that applies to each loss and is subtracted before any loss payment is made.

straight life: A whole life policy in which premiums are payable as long as the insured lives.

straight life annuity: A life annuity in which there is no refund to any beneficiary at the death of the annuitant.

straight term: Term insurance that covers a specific period of time and which cannot be renewed.

subjective risk: The risk based on the mental state of an individual who experiences uncertainty or doubt as to the outcome of a given event.

subrogation: The principle under which one who has indemnified another's loss is entitled to recovery from any liable third parties who are responsible.

sue-and-labor clause: A clause, usually in marine insurance, that requires the insured to attempt to protect the property from further loss, and to recover or attempt to recover from other parties.

suicide clause: A clause in life insurance that requires payment by the insurer, even in the event of suicide, if the suicide occurs after a two-year period from the date the policy was issued.

Superfund legislation: Comprehensive environmental response compensation and liability established by the federal government.

supplemental tail: An endorsement that must be purchased within 60 days of the end of the policy term. It has its own aggregate limit equal to the original policy's limit. The insurer cannot charge more than 200 percent of the original premium.

supplementary medical insurance: Also known as Part B of Medicare; covers doctor bills and other medically necessary nonhospital expenses for Medicare recipients.

surety: In a bond, the party who agrees to reimburse the obligee.

surety bond: A financial guarantee bond that requires one party to respond to another for losses caused by incapacity, inability, or dishonesty, e.g., to guarantee work by a contractor.

surgical insurance: Health insurance that provides coverage for physicians' fees associated with covered surgeries.

surplus line market: Suppliers of insurance coverage in areas rejected by domestic insurers; Lloyd's of London offers most of its coverage in this manner, through special agents or brokers.

surplus share treaties: Pro-rata treaties covering only specific exposures.

surrender cost index: A life insurance cost comparison method, similar to the net payment index, that also incorporates the policy's cash value as of a particular point in time.

survivor income benefit insurance (SIBI): Group term life insurance that is expressed as income to qualified survivors. If no eligible survivors exist at the time of death, no benefits are paid.

survivorship benefit: That amount of money that becomes available for distribution to living annuitants as a result of the death of other annuitants.

survivorship life insurance: *See* second-to-die life insurance.

T

tax multiplier: A factor designed to reflect the premium tax levied by the state on the insurer's business.

temporary disabilities: Illnesses or injuries that prevent a person from working for a limited time.

temporary life annuity: An annuity that pays benefits until the expiration of a specified period of years or until the annuitant dies.

10-year certain period: An income option that guarantees payments to a life insurance beneficiary for at least 10 years.

10-year period-certain life annuity: An annuity that pays benefits until the later of these two events: (1) death of annuitant or (2) expiration of 10 years.

term contract: A health policy that expires at the end of a specified time and that cannot be renewed.

term insurance: A contract of life insurance of which the face value is payable if death of the insured should occur within a stated period.

testamentary trust: A trust created at the donor's death through a will.

theft: Any act of stealing.

theft insurance: Coverage against loss through stealing by individuals not in a position of trust.

theoretical probability distribution: A tool for evaluating the frequency and/or expected severity of losses due to identified risks that involves using mathematical formulas. Three examples used widely in risk management are the bino-mial distribution, the normal distribution, and the Poisson distribution.

third-party administrator (TPA): An administrator hired by an employer to handle claims and other administrative functions associated with employee benefits.

thrift plan: A contributory, deferred profit-sharing plan in which employers match a portion of contributions by employees.

time-element contracts: Measure indirect loss in terms of *x* dollars per unit of time that passes until restoration is completed.

title insurance: Insurance against losses resulting when title to real estate is not marketable because of a title defect.

tort: A legal injury or wrong other than breach of contract.

tort feasor: A wrongdoer; one who commits a tort.

total disability: An illness or injury that renders a person completely incapable of gainful employment during the period of disability.

trailer: A vehicle designed to be pulled by a private passenger-type auto, pickup or panel truck, or van.

transferee: In risk transfer, the party paid by a transferor to assume a risk the transferor wishes to escape; the risk bearer.

transferor: In risk transfer, the party escaping a risk by paying a transferee to assume it.

treaties: Reinsurance contracts.

trespassers: Individuals who enter an insured's premises other than licensees or invitees.

triple-trigger approach: All policies in force during exposure and manifestation periods apply.

trust: An estate-planning device involving the transfer of property from a donor to a trustee for the benefit of one or more beneficiaries.

trustee: The person having legal ownership of the trust property; required by law to manage and distribute it in accordance with the instructions specified in the trust agreement.

trust fund plans: A method of pension funding in which the employer places monies to pay plan benefits with a trustee that invests the funds and pays the benefits.

twenty-pay life: A type of limited-pay life policy in which premiums are paid only for 20 years.

twisting: The acts of a life insurance agent to persuade a client to drop one life policy and accept another, by misrepresenting the terms of either the present policy or the new policy, or both, to the detriment of the insured.

Type A universal life: Death benefit remains constant while the policy is in force.

Type B universal life: Death benefit fluctuates; it is made up of a specified amount of death protection plus the policy's cash value.

U

unallocated plans: A type of pension funding in which benefits are allocated to employees as a group and specific employees are not identified.

unauthorized insurers service-of-process acts: State laws allowing suits to be brought in one's home state against out-of-state insurers.

underinsured motorists endorsement: Coverage that will pay damages when the other party's limits are lower than the insured's and the other party is at fault.

underlying limit: Policy limit of insurance contract that is primary (pays first).

underwriting: All activities carried out to select risks acceptable to insurers in order that general company objectives are met.

underwriting cycle: Prices, coverages, and deductibles exist in an ever-changing marketplace. This cycle is composed of two distinct parts: hard and soft markets.

underwriting profit: A gain equal to 100 minus the sum of the loss and expense ratios.

unfunded retention: Absorbing the expense of losses as they occur, rather than making any special advance arrangements to pay for them.

unified transfer tax credit: A tax credit that offsets the estate and the gift taxes due on the first portion of assets transferred to others.

unilateral contract: A contract, such as an insurance contract, in which only one of the parties makes promises that are legally enforceable.

uninsured motorist insurance: Pays for your bodily injuries that result from an accident with another vehicle if the other driver is negligent and does not have any insurance (or has insurance less than that required by law).

uninsured motor vehicle: A land motor vehicle or trailer to which (1) no bodily injury liability coverage applies at the time of the accident; (2) less insurance than is required by law applies; (3) is a hit-and-run vehicle where the owner or operator cannot be identified; or (4) liability insurance applies at the time of the accident but the insurance company has become insolvent.

universal life: Life insurance contracts that provide more flexible premium payment options than most other forms. The initial premium is specified by the insurer, with the policyholder determining the timing and size of subsequent premiums.

unplanned retention: The implicit assumption of risk by a firm or individual that does not recognize that a risk is acknowledged to exist but the maximum possible loss associated with it is significantly underestimated.

unsatisfied judgment fund (UJF): A fund set up by a state to pay automobile accident awards that cannot be collected by any other means.

unscheduled personal property: Personal property, not a residence, that is owned or used by the insured while anywhere in the world, subject to certain exclusions. Examples include clothes, jewelry, furniture, etc.

use and occupancy: Business income insurance added by endorsement to the boiler and machinery contract.

utilization review: A cost-containment measure in which authorization of treatment is ongoing, not limited only to the time of the treatment.

utmost good faith: A legal doctrine in which a higher standard of honesty is imposed on parties to an insurance agreement than is imposed through ordinary commercial contracts.

V

value at risk (VAR): Estimate of the risk of loss at various probability levels.

valued policy laws: A state law that requires an insurer to pay the entire face amount of the insurance policy in the event of total loss of a covered object from an insured peril.

variable annuity: An annuity whose value may fluctuate according to the value of underlying securities in which the funds are invested.

variable life insurance: Life insurance in which the face amount may fluctuate during the term of the policy in accordance with the value of common stocks or other assets into which the reserve assets are invested.

variable universal life: A policy with death benefits and flexible premiums as in regular universal life. Policyowners may choose investments to support the contract.

variance: The mean of the squared deviations from the mean; the square root of the variance is the standard deviation.

vendor's endorsement: An extension of a manufacturer's or wholesaler's product liability insurance that names the retailer as an additional insured.

verbal threshold: A verbal definition used to determine whether an insured may bring a tort action in no-fault insurance.

vesting: A term describing the conditions under which employer-provided benefits become the property of the employees on an unconditional basis.

viatical settlement: The purchase of a life insurance policy from a terminally ill individual by an unrelated third party.

vicarious liability: Legal responsibility for the wrong committed by another person.

voluntary act: A characteristic of a negligent act—the person committing the act chose to do so and could have chosen not to.

voluntary coverage: Insurance coverage purchased at the discretion of the buyer.

W

waiver: The intentional relinquishing of a known right.

waiver of premium benefit: A clause in life insurance that waives the premium due in the event of disability of the insured.

warehouse-to-warehouse clause: Insurance coverage for goods from the time they leave the warehouse of the shipper until they reach the warehouse of the consignee.

war hazard exclusion: Eliminates insurance coverage for death that is a direct result of war or other hostile action.

warranty: A clause in an insurance contract that requires certain conditions, circumstances, or facts to be true before or after the contract is in force.

wellness programs: Fitness and health awareness programs designed to make "high insurance use" employees modify their behavior, thereby reducing the frequency and severity of medical claims.

whole life insurance: Life insurance offering protection as long as the insured lives.

will: A way to transfer ownership of property at death.

workers' compensation insurance: Insurance that pays medical costs and disability income for persons injured on the job or those who suffer from occupational illness.

Y

youthful driver: A female driver under the age of 25 or a male driver under the age of 30.

Index